Black Education

A Transformative Research and Action Agenda
for the New Century

Black Education

A Transformative Research and Action Agenda for the New Century

Edited by
Joyce E. King

Published for the American Educational Research Association
by Lawrence Erlbaum Associates, Inc.

 AMERICAN EDUCATIONAL RESEARCH ASSOCIATION
Washington, D.C.

 LAWRENCE ERLBAUM ASSOCIATES, PUBLISHERS
2005   Mahwah, New Jersey   London

Lawrence Erlbaum Associates, Inc., Publishers
10 Industrial Avenue
Mahwah, New Jersey 07430
www.erlbaum.com

The American Education Research Association (AERA) publishes books and
journals based on the highest standards of professional review to ensure their
quality, accuracy, and objectivity. Findings and conclusions in publications are
those of the authors and do not reflect the position or policies of the Association, its
Council, or officers.

American Educational Research Association
1230 Seventeenth Street, NW
Washington, DC 20036-3078
www.aera.net

Cover design by Sean Trane Sciarrone, based on a motif for the CORIBE logo
created by Lisa Morrisson, TimberCreek Graphics, Atlanta, GA.
Used by permission.

Library of Congress Cataloging-in-Publication Data

Black education : a transformative research & action
    agenda for the new century / Joyce E. King, editor.
        p.   cm.
    Includes bibliographical references and index.
    ISBN 0-8058-5457-6 (cl : alk. paper)—ISBN 0-8058-5458-4 (pb : alk. paper)
    1. Blacks—Education—Cross-cultural studies.   2. Discrimination in
education—Cross-cultural studies.   3. Action research—Cross-cultural studies.
I. King, Joyce Elaine, 1947–   II. American Educational Research Association.
Commission on Research in Black Education.

    LC2699.B53   2005
    370'.8996—dc22   2004060676

Books published by Lawrence Erlbaum Associates are printed on
acid-free paper, and their bindings are chosen for strength and durability.

Printed in the United States of America
10 9 8 7 6 5 4 3 2 1

99.95

1285495

2/14/07

In a people's rise from oppression to grace, a turning point comes when thinkers determined to stop the downward slide get together to study the causes of common problems, think out solutions and organize ways to apply them.

—Ayi Kwei Armah (1995, p. 9)

The CORIBE logo is the Adinkra symbol, *Hwehwemudua* from the culture of the Akan people of Ghana, West Africa. The symbol represents Excellence, Superior Quality, Perfection, Knowledge, and Critical Examination.

AERA COMMISSION ON RESEARCH IN BLACK EDUCATION

ELDERS COUNCIL

Adelaide L. Sanford   Edmund W. Gordon
Frank Bonilla   Asa G. Hilliard, III
Baba Kwame Ishangi   Thelma L. Spencer (1999)
(Deceased 2004)

COMMISSIONERS

Kathryn Au
Kimberley Edelin Freeman
Henry T. Frierson, Jr.
Antoine Garibaldi
Irving Hamer, Jr.
Irving McPhail
Congressman Major R. Owens

Shirley Brice Heath
Lisa Delpit
Mary Hatwood Futrell
Donna Gollnick
Jonathon Kozol
Susan L. Taylor

AUTHORS, SCHOLARS & THE AERA BLACK INITIATIVE PLANNING GROUP*

Beverly Gordon
Linda C. Tillman
Kassie Freeman
William Franklin
Annette Henry
Ibrahima Seck
James A. Banks*
Cecile Wright
Gloria Ladson-Billings*
Nah Dove
Cirecie West-Olatunji
Shuaib Meacham
Terezinha Juraci Machado da Silva

Etta R. Hollins*
Petronilha B. Gonçalves e Silva
Michèle Foster
Carol D. Lee
Jean Ishibashi
William H. Watkins*
Mwalimu J. Shujaa
A. Wade Boykin
Fannie M. Haughton
Hassimi O. Maiga
Beverly Lindsay
Scott Miller (1999)*

Lorrie A. Shepard, *ex-officio*
Gwendolyn C. Baker, *ex-officio**

* Member, AERA Black Initiative Planning Group

This book is dedicated to the memory of

Baba Kwame Ishangi
Melinda Bartley Martin
Morris F. X. Jeff
Jedi Shemsu Jehewty
(Jacob H. Carruthers)
Beah Richards
Barbara Sizemore
Israel "Ike" Tribble
and
Alma Harrington Young

whose lives and legacies represent the best
of who we are and why we are.

Contents

Foreword   xiii

Acknowledgments   xix

Preface   xxi

Part I   Theorizing Transformative Black Education Research and Practice   1

1   A Transformative Vision of Black Education
    for Human Freedom   3
    Joyce E. King

2   A Declaration of Intellectual Independence
    for Human Freedom   19
    Joyce E. King

Part II   Taking Culture Into Account: Learning Theory and Black Education   43

3   The State of Knowledge About the Education
    of African Americans   45
    Carol D. Lee

4   Intervention Research Based on Current Views of Cognition
    and Learning   73
    Carol D. Lee

ix

Part III   Expanding the Knowledgebase in Black Education and Research Globally   115

5   Colonial Education in Africa: Retrospects and Prospects   117
    William H. Watkins

6   Black Populations Globally: The Costs of the
    Underutilization of Blacks in Education   135
    Kassie Freeman

Part IV   Engaging the Language and Policy Nexus in African Education   157

7   When the Language of Education Is Not the Language
    of Culture: The Epistemology of Systems of Knowledge
    and Pedagogy   159
    Hassimi Oumarou Maiga

8   Initiating Transformations of Realities in African
    and African American Universities   183
    Beverly Lindsay

Part V   Situating Equity Policy and Pedagogy in the Political Economic Context   195

9   New Standards and Old Inequalities: School Reform
    and the Education of African American Students   197
    Linda Darling-Hammond

10 On the Road to Democratic Economic Participation:
    Educating African American Youth in the Postindustrial
    Global Economy   225
    Jessica Gordon Nembhard

Part VI   Humanizing Education: Diverse Voices   241

11 A Detroit Conversation   243
    Joyce E. King and Sharon Parker, Editors

12 Faith and Courage to Educate Our Own: Reflections
    on Islamic Schools in the African American Community   261
    Zakiyyah Muhammad

Part VII   Globalizing the Struggle for Black Education: African and Diaspora Experiences   281

13   **Worldwide Conspiracy Against Black Culture and Education**   285
Ibrahima Seck

14   **Black Educational Experiences in Britain: Reflections on the Global Educational Landscape**   291
Cecile Wright

15   **Black People and Brazilian Education**   297
Terezinha Juraci Machado da Silva

16   **A New Millennium Research Agenda in Black Education: Some Points to Be Considered for Discussion and Decisions**   301
Petronilha Beatriz Gonçalves e Silva

Part VIII   *"Ore Ire"*—Catalyzing Transformation in the Academy: Our Charge to Keep   309

17   **Culturally Sensitive Research and Evaluation: Advancing an Agenda for Black Education**   313
Linda C. Tillman

18   **"Anayme Nti"—As Long As I Am Alive, I Will Never Eat Weeds: The Online Institute As a Catalyst for Research and Action in Black Education**   323
Annette Henry

19   **Incidents in the Lives of Harriet Jacobs's Children—A Readers Theatre: Disseminating the Outcomes of Research on the Black Experience in the Academy**   329
Cirecie A. West-Olatunji

20   **Answering a Call for Transformative Education in the New Millennium—"A Charge to Keep": The CORIBE Documentary Video**   341
Djanna Hill

Afterword   347

Postscript   351

Appendix A   A Transformative Research and Action Agenda
     for Human Freedom in the New Century   353

Appendix B-1   Black Education, Toward the Human,
     After "Man": In the Manner of a Manifesto   357

Appendix B-2   Race and Our Biocentric Belief System:
     An Interview With Sylvia Wynter   361

Appendix C   A Glossary of Terms   367

     Contributing Authors   371

     References   377

     Author Index   421

     Subject Index   431

Foreword

Living long enough gives one perspective to see life not as a series of random events but, rather, as a continuum of sorts that we move along—sometimes smoothly, sometimes slowly, sometimes back and forth and sometimes running in place. We are not functioning in isolated, disjointed episodes. Our learning, our relationships, our careers each represent multiple, multitextured events, times, encounters, and thoughts. Yet, in an attempt to document our stories, be they histories, studies, experiments, or fictions, we look for the "moment," that something or event that places in high relief what we try desperately to express about what matters.

As we try to understand something like the fight for equity and justice in schools, we may point to May 17, 1954, the *Brown v. Board of Education* decision as an event or moment in time, but we know in truth, *Brown* is emblematic of a lifetime of struggle for civil rights and social justice. Indeed, one of the first challenges to separate and unequal schooling took place in Boston in 1849 when Benjamin Cushing sued the Boston School Committee for not allowing him to enroll his daughter in one of the white schools near their home. But, we are focused on the 1954 moment. Viewing life through moments is how we economize both thought and language to create coherence.

And so it is with this volume. It is an artifact, a symbol, a material product of the moment, but in actuality it represents a very long and difficult path of scholarly and social justice work. The fact of this volume may, in some way, occlude the struggle it represents. It appears in a moment, but it was conceived, constructed, and carried out over a long period of struggle within educational research in general and the American Educational Research Association (AERA) in particular. As a result of a publication conflict, the Research Focus on Black Education Special Interest Group mobilized to address ongoing issues of equity and justice in the association.

One outcome of that mobilization was a proposal for the creation of a new division focused on Black education. Although the AERA Council did not approve the proposal, newly elected President Alan Schoenfeld understood the importance of the issues the proposal addressed and solicited another proposal for some significant work that would address the original proposal's concerns.

The Commission on Research in Black Education (CORIBE) is the entity that emerged from that proposal. Its many work products and activities pushed the boundaries of the association and the field. Typically, because of the need to chase scarce social science and education research dollars, the scope of the field and our knowledge are constrained. The university is supposed to be a place where people encounter a wide array of ideas. It is supposed to be a place where there is a dogged pursuit of truths. It is supposed to be a place where minds are opened and perspectives are expanded. This volume represents a return to that central mission of the university and scholarly life.

In 1997, Professor Edmund W. Gordon headed a task force that challenged AERA to examine the epistemological biases that continue to pervade our research and scholarship. Later, James Scheurich (Scheurich & Young, 1997) raised a similar challenge. In 2002, Linda C. Tillman (a contributor to this volume) proposed a culturally sensitive research approach to further expand our perspectives and research paradigms (Tillman, 2002). One might argue that, as an association, AERA has had sufficient admonition about the need to be open to broader, more inclusive forms of research, scholarship, and truth-seeking. However, the canons of orthodoxy die hard. The venues for sharing our research and scholarship are limited and, in some instances, not at all amenable to new thinking or new methodologies.

This volume is symbolic in that as important as it is as a text, its real meaning lay in the epistemological break it makes with past work. Joyce E. King's leadership of CORIBE helped to produce something radically different from the typical convening of scholars and writing of papers. Instead, CORIBE set out to work on and through multiple levels. It expanded the charge to address international issues that were there all along. The commission moved the discourse and knowledge producing from those strictly aimed at the academy, that need to hear them, to the communities who experience the realities of underfunded, underdeveloped education. It produced both products (of which this book is one) and process, something that is typically an afterthought in the academy.

The larger project—the education of Black peoples—is one that should be on the top of the AERA agenda. Many of the education initiatives in the United States have their genesis in Black communities. Title I and other compensatory education programs started in communities serving poor people of color, in which Black children are overly represented.

Worldwide, countries with large numbers of poor Black children need educational assistance from Northern Hemisphere nations that couple foreign aid with research access. In the most recent large-scale federal education initiative in the United States, "No Child Left Behind," the true focus is poor children, many of whom are Black. As we read and examine the body of scholarship that constitutes educational research, we recognize that although the researchers may not identify the students by race or ethnicity, the target population often is Black. However, a large number of our colleagues would not identify themselves with a research agenda focused on Black education. The CORIBE work is designed to point out the way that much of the scholarly work looks to Black communities because much of the general public (and scholars) define Black people, their life situations, their experiences, and their communities as "The Problem."

As Toni Morrison (1989) suggests, we are dealing with "unspeakable things unspoken" (p. 1) that allow us to develop a system of codes and innuendo that represent "Black" and "Blackness." We refer to students who are "low-income," "culturally diverse," and the "achievement gap" and "dropouts," but we really mean Black children. We speak of "welfare moms," "criminal element," and "violent individuals," when we mean Black people. We say "housing projects," "ghetto," and "poor neighborhoods" as proxies for Black communities. There is no language of excellence, hope, and promise aimed at Black people and their circumstances. In those instances in which Black people excel we are quick to identify individuals as exceptions or suggest group excellence is not as significant as other fields of human endeavor. Indeed, excellence in mainstream terms may force people to disidentify with any notion of Black culture. Individuals such as Colin Powell or Condoleeza Rice are to be recognized for their accomplishments in the public sphere, but one might argue that their rise to prominence is predicated on their perceived difference and distance from Black people. Blacks who have accomplished greatness in the arts or athletics find themselves defined as possessing "natural" abilities that connote a genetic advantage as opposed to having worked hard to develop their excellence.

This volume and the effort of CORIBE are designed to disrupt the discourse of Black inferiority and to suggest that the strengths that are already present and are ripe for development among Black peoples are gifts that humankind the world over so desperately needs. When the U.S. Women's movement mobilized in the 1960s, it was able to demonstrate to the nation how wasteful it was not to use women's talents and abilities throughout the society. Similarly, the world cannot afford to squander the human resources that Black people represent.

This volume is both resource and sustenance. By blurring the artificially constructed lines between research and practice, CORIBE has produced a volume that speaks to multiple audiences in multiple ways. It provides a "grammar" of Black education unlike anything mainstream educational research has ever seen. Instead of the dichotomy of cultural deficit versus cultural strength, this volume places the issues facing the world regarding Black people and their education in a robust political, economic, social, historical, and cultural context so that all readers can begin to see the scope of the project and why current legislative and local state reforms cannot truly address the problems.

However, this is not a volume without hope. It moves beyond problem identification and toward solutions—not merely theoretical solutions, but also examples of practice where people are working hard to be the solution they seek. The authors do identify discontinuities, injustices, and bad practices that have been perpetrated on Black people over time, but they also identify the historical legacy of strength and struggle that has allowed Black people to make powerful contributions to their own education and that of others. The volume contains examples from around the world—Australia, Brazil, Haiti, Jamaica, Mali, South Africa, Namibia, Sénégal, Portugal, and the United Kingdom—and at every level of education from early grades to the university as well as community-based independent schools. Most exciting to me is the way the volume incorporates new genres of scholarship, including interviews with pioneers in Black Studies theorizing (Sylvia Wynter) and social justice organizing (Grace Lee Boggs), a readers theatre,[1] technology applications, and a description of the video documentation of the CORIBE initiative, to list a few. For too long we have believed that the only legitimate way to represent our scholarship was through the conventional venues in the conventional ways. This volume demonstrates that we can move outside of old paradigms and create new possibilities in our work and in our attempts to respond to human suffering through education.

This volume also helps us to see that our audiences can be broader and our purposes, grander. Instead of merely talking to ourselves (as scholars), we can speak a more comprehensive language that reaches people in various places in the struggle for quality education. Instead of merely asking scholars to contribute a chapter, this volume represents a more organic process of working through a variety of processes—colloquia, symposia, working conferences, online seminars, community discussions, Web-based research, a participatory evaluation, graduate student apprenticeships, and a Web site—as well as conventional scholarship. This volume represents one of the more ambitious undertakings of AERA and reflects the pulling together of one of the more diverse groups of scholars and scholarly traditions to address a common set of issues.

---

[1] A minimal theater production with narration as the framework of dramatic presentation, it has no full stage sets, no full costumer, and no full costumes. It has no full memorization. Scripts are used openly in performance.

One of the indelible images I retain from the CORIBE experience comes from the working colloquium at St. Simon's Island, Georgia. At the end of a day of panel presentations and group discussions, colloquium members toured the island. One of the places we stopped was Ibo Landing, revered as a place where a group of Africans who believed they were coming to the New World as indentured laborers discovered their horrific fate as slaves. Chained together, the Africans marched into the water and drowned themselves, reminiscent of the line of the old spiritual, "Before I be a slave, I'll be buried in my grave and go home to my Lord and be free." On the banks of that Atlantic Ocean inlet I snapped a photograph of the Chair of the Commission Council of Elders, Dr. Adelaide L. Sanford, Vice Chancellor of the New York State University Board of Regents, and Commission director, Joyce E. King. The two were standing together looking eastward toward the land of beginning. I can remember being overwhelmed with emotion and thinking, "I can see our past and I can see our present, but I cannot see our future." However, as I read this volume, I got a glimpse of our future. As researchers we are standing on the banks of Ibo Landing. We are looking eastward toward the land of beginning and we are charged with the responsibility of making our future.

Gloria Ladson-Billings
University of Wisconsin-Madison
and President-Elect, AERA
April 2004

Acknowledgments

The work of the Commission on Research in Black Education would not have been possible without the support of the American Educational Research Association (AERA). The Elders Council and Commissioners served valiantly, giving generously of their time, their wisdom, and their resources. I am infinitely grateful to our Elders Adelaide L. Sanford, Asa G. Hilliard III, Edmund W. Gordon, Baba Kwame Ishangi (deceased 2004), Thelma L. Spencer, and Frank Bonilla. Finally, the CORIBE Village of Elders, commissioners, scholars, teachers, and community educators has been a continuing source of inspiration for all who, like Sojourner Truth, "stepped into the pool while the water was stirring."

This project benefited from the contributions of many people. My personal heartfelt appreciation is extended to Sharon Parker, DrRashon, Hassimi Maiga, Gloria Ladson-Billings, Etta R. Hollins, Beverly Gordon, Annette Henry, Cirecie A. West-Olatunji, Heidi Lovett Daniels, Linda C. Tillman, Kofi Lomotey, Audrey F. Manley, Mwalimu J. Shujaa, Carol D. Lee, William Franklin, Beverly Lindsay, Fannie M. Haughton, Beverly Daniel Tatum, Mackie V. Blanton, Jean Ishibashi, Shuaib Meacham, A. Wade Boykin, Linda Darling-Hammond, John O'Neal, Greta Gladney, Michèle Foster, Kassie Freeman, William "Bill" Watkins, Petronilha Beatriz Gonçalves e Silva, Ibrahima Seck, Cecile Wright, Terezinha Juraci Machado da Silva, Djanna Hill, Elleni Tedla, Beth Warren, Melanie Schmidt, Jessica Gordon Nembhard, Herb Kohl, Theresa Perry, Bob Moses, Marybeth Gasman, Sara Garcia, Michael Fitzgerald, Al Singleton, Charles Hobson, Tom Piper, Makani Themba, Glenda Price, Alma. H. Young (deceased 2004), Grace Lee Boggs, Jacqueline Jordan Irvine, V.P. Franklin, Garrett Albert Duncan, Valerie Ooka Pang, Carol Faust, Akua Ishangi, James Parker, Karen Buller, Solwasi Olusula, Eugene Garcia, Rosemary Zumwalt, Gwendolyn C. Baker, Cynthia Tyson, Olga Welch, Zakiyyah Muhammad,

Carrie Secret and her "Circle of Learning System Orators," Betty Dopson, and the Board for the Education of People of African Ancestry.

A succession of AERA presidents, including James A. Banks, Alan Schoenfield, Lorrie A. Sheppard, Andrew Porter, Catherine Snow, Robert Linn, Hilda Borko, and Marilyn Cochran-Smith "midwifed" this project; each made a contribution to this effort. In addition, five anonymous reviewers of this manuscript were both encouraging and critical readers. Their comments were extremely helpful.

Finally, the support and resources of Medgar Evers College, CUNY, Spelman College, The CJEES Institute, Agnes Scott College, Georgia State University, and John Henrik Clarke House in the Village of Harlem, New York, are also gratefully acknowledged.

Joyce E. King, PhD
Georgia State University
August 2004

Preface

Imperialism, like the prehistoric hunter, first killed the being spiritually and culturally, before trying to eliminate it physically. The negation of the history and intellectual accomplishments of Black Africans was cultural, mental murder, which preceded and paved the way for their genocide here and there in the world.... Today each group of people, armed with its rediscovered or reinforced cultural identity, has arrived at the threshold of the postindustrial era. An atavistic, but vigilant, African optimism inclines us to wish that all nations would join hands in order to build a planetary civilization instead of sinking down to barbarism.

—Cheikh Anta Diop (1981/1991, p. 10)

Transforming education for and about people of African ancestry in order to go beyond "inclusion into a burning house," as James Baldwin once put it, is a formidable task. To attack the roots of our miseducation, cultural annihilation, and economic subordination, we must undo the entrenched system of thought that has justified our predicament.

—Joyce E. King, http://www.coribe.org

"Excellence, Superior Quality, Perfection, Knowledge, Critical Examination": these highly valued terms are unlikely to be used by researchers, educators, students, parents, or policy decision makers to describe Black education anywhere in the world.[1] Indeed, for most Black students, particularly those attending dysfunctional, resource-starved schools in the United States, a leader among "civilized" nations, Black education is synonymous with underachievement and academic failure. In Africa, where, in the minds of many, "civilization" is still doubtful, education is generally considered a catastrophe in the midst of misery, warfare, and numbing

---

[1] These terms define the CORIBE logo, *Hwehwemudua*, the Adinkra symbol from the culture of the Akan people of Ghana, West Africa.

poverty. This book is about this crisis in Black education in the United States, in other Diaspora contexts, and in Africa; it is also about transformative possibilities for addressing this crisis. Although the prevailing orthodoxy in academic scholarship and the popular media blames these deplorable conditions on Black people's culture, behavior, or historical circumstances, this state of affairs is ultimately a crisis of knowledge—a crisis that calls into question the vaunted pronouncements of the "civilizers": "We know what's best for you" (West-Olatunji, Chapter 19).

By addressing the fundamental roots of the crisis in Black education, "the entrenched system of thought that justifies our predicament," this book offers an alternative to hegemony and miseducation: the findings and recommendations of the Commission on Research in Black Education (CORIBE). The AERA, the most prominent professional organization advancing educational research and its practical application, established CORIBE to stimulate research and policy making to improve education for and about people of African ancestry (1999–2002). The evidence of a transformative role for culture in Black education and research presented in this volume counters orthodox interpretations of the state of Black education, including the refurbished 19th-century genetic inferiority argument that persists in academic scholarship and the popular imagination. For instance, the popular "Bell Curve hypothesis" posits that something lacking in Black students, in their motivation to achieve, in Black people's cultural practice or worse, that something congenitally defective in "blackness" accounts for the crisis in Black education. If the unfinished business of "Brown" has become clearer (Bell, 2004) so, too, have the contradictions of "New World Order" policies and legislation such as "No Child Left Behind" become suspect. Culturally and intellectually liberating approaches to Black education that can benefit all students are an alternative to inclusion in this "burning house." At a time when U.S. educational models are being exported abroad with promises of democracy and freedom, it is still necessary to challenge the unfreedom that exists within inequitable education. The exemplary research and educational practices in this volume offer a critical challenge to orthodox thinking and research about Black education and also suggest ways to achieve a more democratic and "civilized" country—that even "a new world is possible." This volume also challenges the justifications for the "civilizing mission" (and the horrendous consequences of colonialism) in Africa that have negated the intellectual, social, and spiritual contributions of African people to human history. This exclusion distorts our knowledge and understanding of *humanity's* stunning achievements.

Thus, the orientation of this book is informed by Cheikh Anta Diop's (1981/1991) brilliant juxtaposition of "Civilization or Barbarism" in his efforts to dislodge another orthodoxy of Western scholarship: the relentless interpretation of Egypt as a White civilization. Diop's method is both instructive and relevant to the purposes of this book. At once a question, a declaration, and a warning, *Civilization or Barbarism: An Authentic Anthropology* is the title of Diop's highly scientific challenge to establishment scholarship and myth-making. The consummate scientist, Diop assembled a formidable body of interdisciplinary evidence that declares not only the facts of Western civilization's origins in Africa but also warns of the inexorable consequences of "sinking down to barbarism" foreshadowed in Western scholarship's pernicious distortions of human history. The struggle continues. It was only recently "discovered," for example, and the "news" merited a press release, that the centuries-old manuscripts in the libraries of the fabled (and very real) city of Timbuktu in present-day Mali *were actually written by Africans*—literate, multilingual learned men and women, poets, and scholars—who wrote not only in Arabic but also who composed these scientific, political, philosophical, historical, and literary texts in Songhoy-Senni, the language of the Songhoy Empire, as well as other indigenous African languages.

The perpetuation of concepts of civilization and humanity that exclude Africa and Africans represents the Janus face of the worldwide crisis in Black education. This volume puts forward an alternative vision in the chapters that follow. Using a broad-based "process-building" methodology and rigorous scholarly inquiry, four critically important premises shaped the inquiries and outreach activities that enabled the Commission to develop the Transformative Research and Action Agenda presented in this volume. These premises, discussed briefly later, are supported both by theoretical analyses and various kinds of evidence assembled in this volume.

First, truthful, equitable, and culturally appropriate education is understood to be a basic human right and not only as a condition of Black people's individual success and collective survival but is also fundamental to civilization and human freedom. A second premise that influenced the work and the findings of the Commission is that African descent people share broad cultural continuities and our survival as an ethnic family, in other words, our peoplehood, is at stake in educational and socialization processes. As the analyses in this volume demonstrate, these shared cultural continuities are assets, sources of strength and resilience, which can be used to transform educational research and to design learning environments that meet the needs of African students at all levels. That is why participants at the Commission's working colloquium on St. Simon's Island were asked to consider the question: *"What has happened to the Black Education and Socialization Agenda?"* In fact, the current state of Black education represents an historical reversal that pales in comparison to the long tradition of educational and cultural excellence that generations of African people established in the normal course of our human experience.

These well-documented traditions of excellence extend as far back as the "Mystery Schools" of Egyptian antiquity, to the classical universities of the Songhoy Empire in Gao, Djenné, and Sankoré (Timbuktu) and also include independent institutions of learning, socialization, and benevolence organized in the Diaspora before and after the Holocaust of our enslavement ended, during and since the era of legalized apartheid in the United States and South Africa that followed.

A third premise is that Black education has been understudied from perspectives that recognize these educational excellence traditions and a positive role for culture in learning. Conversely, Black education also has been overstudied from mainstream establishment epistemological perspectives, including those that predominate within AERA—perspectives that typically have produced less than beneficial results. Fourth, formal education, abetted by ideological pedagogical content knowledge, has been organized not only for miseducation but also to elevate and maintain the control of dominant groups. For example, contemporary data in U.S. schools as well as the historical and comparative analyses in this volume show how state supported public education for people of African descent worldwide has been denied adequate and appropriate fiscal and human resources. These patterns of material, cultural, and spiritual deprivation in the education that Black people experience is indicative of this systemic and hegemonic control that is global in scale. The consequences are nothing short of catastrophic.

This volume, written for both a scholarly and a general audience, demonstrates a transformative role for research and education practice that use culture as an asset—in classrooms, the academy, in community and cross-national contexts. The goal is to enable educators, policy decision makers, and community leaders to understand, to value, and to use the strengths of African people's cultural heritage more effectively to address the crisis in Black education that also threatens our "planetary civilization." Therefore, we are called to a specific task: to understand the "causes of causes of common problems, [to] think out solutions and organize ways to apply them" (Armah, 1995). That is why the Commission also asked: *How can educational research become one of the forms of struggle for Black education?* The commissioners, Elders, scholars, and others who gave generously of their time and resources to participate in this initiative—many are contributors to this volume—helped to articulate an alternative standpoint from which to challenge hegemony and ideology in Black education and research. This standpoint is articulated in the transformative vision of Black Education discussed in Chapter 1 and embodied in the Commission's "Declaration of Intellectual Independence for Human Freedom," which is presented in Chapter 2. This Declaration of vital principles of Black education and socialization responds to the degradation of Black people—and Africa—that takes place in academia, in the research enterprise, in national and international policies of exclusion, and in alienating structures of inclusion, all of which are logical outcomes of the core belief system of Western civilization's bourgeois culture and history.

Sylvia Wynter's culture-systemic theoretical analysis, which deciphers this belief system, provides an interpretation of the crisis in Black education that informed the Commission's deliberations. According to Wynter's analysis, intellectuals or scholars in any social order reproduce the knowledge needed to sustain the prevailing belief system. That human nature is biologically determined, or "biocentrism," is the prevailing belief system of Western bourgeois culture. Embodied in the construct of "race" and expressed in the practice of racism, this belief system puts the interests of a particular conception of what it means to be human, "ethno-class 'Man'," or "the global middle classes," above the general well-being of all people in the society. This category now assimilates, that is, absorbs middle-class Black individuals as exceptions, as well as some Latino/as and Asians as "honorary whites." (See Wynter's concise statement of this culture-systemic theoretical analysis in Appendix B-1 and B-2.) Wynter suggests that the way out of this system of thought is to recognize in humanity's earliest beginnings in Africa that it is not biology alone (biocentrism) but also culture (sociogeny)—systems of meaning and language developed in our relationships with others—that makes us human. The role of scholars and educators, therefore, who wish to overturn this belief structure that defines our present age and end the oppression of groups that are subordinated by it, is to decipher rather than be controlled by the limited conceptions of what it means to be human within the terms of this belief system. This is "what Africa offers us," according to Wynter. The land of humanity's earliest beginnings offers profoundly human alternatives to biocentrism's limited and unjust conception of "Man"—as life either "worthy" or "unworthy of life," that is to say, the jobless, homeless, incarcerated, and AIDS afflicted "wretched of the earth" (Wynter, Appendix B-2).

Like the proverbial miner's canary (Guinier & Torres, 2002), the crisis in Black education is a harbinger of humanity's descent into barbarism in this new century. Certainly, individual Black people are making tremendous strides as professionals, artists, leaders, and productive citizens. However, the systematic denial of education and, therefore, material and spiritual well-being, for the masses of Black people and other racially excluded groups needs to be understood as a logical *outcome* of the worldwide capitalist economic system that, within the terms of a specific belief system, necessarily privileges and even "multiculturalizes" the global middle classes. Thus, Wynter's culture-systemic analysis suggests that White supremacy racism is an *effect* of this belief system. Therefore, *knowledge is the problem*. However, this is not to argue for Afrocentrism to counter the West's "biocentrism" and the new forms of imperialism in which this belief system is manifested. Rather, by virtue of our humanity, our collective dispossession, the suffering of diverse others as well as the degradation of the planetary environment that we all share must also be our concern. Commission scholar Carol D. Lee expresses the reality of and transformative possibilities inherent in our human interconnectedness succinctly: "Once we learn to teach poor Black children, we will likely learn better how to educate all children."

THE COMMISSION ON RESEARCH IN BLACK EDUCATION

In 1999 AERA commissioned a group of scholars to investigate major issues that hinder the education of Black people. It also was determined that the scope of this investigation would include the education of people of African ancestry in a global context. Through this initiative, AERA sought to place issues of Black education and research practice, which affect all sectors of society, in the forefront of the association's agenda. Moreover, among the various issues that precipitated this initiative are gaps in the research knowledge base, concerns about research training and the professional socialization and intellectual orientation of graduate students and younger scholars, as well as questions about equity in publishing opportunities within AERA, advocacy issues in the public policy arena, accountability issues in research practice, and epistemological tensions within the Association.

It was important to develop a research and action agenda broad enough to address these complex issues. Since the historic *Brown vs. Board* decision that declared segregated and unequal schools in the United States illegal, the research establishment's preoccupation with Black people's presumed cultural deficits has produced negligible enduring positive effects. Therefore, a central CORIBE concern has been: *How can education research effectively improve the lives of Black people and advance human understanding*? What began as a quest for answers to very urgent problems in Black education in the United States, in Africa, and throughout the African Diaspora created opportunities for collaborative dialogue among education professionals, policy decision makers, and community educators from diverse backgrounds and representing a range of diverse viewpoints and experience.

The Transformative Research and Action Agenda that CORIBE developed benefited from broad-based input from the members of the Commission who are leaders in education, business, and government, as well as dialogue across academic disciplines, from comparative, historical, and intergenerational perspectives and exchanges among scholars and community educators including White American, Native American, Asian American, and Latino/a American and Black scholars in the United States and other countries. Invited commentaries with up-to-date reports on the state of Black education in their countries prepared by these educators from South America, Africa, and the United Kingdom augmented the original research that was specially prepared for the Commission. In addition, CORIBE's inquiry activities included innovative education and outreach efforts such as an online research training institute for graduate students, demonstration research projects, forums in various cities, as well as symposia at the Congressional Black Caucus Education Braintrust conferences that Congressman Major R. Owens, a member of the Commission, organized.

THE ORGANIZATION OF THE BOOK

This book is divided into eight sections followed by concluding reflections in the Afterword and a Postscript. In Part I, "Theorizing Transformative Black Education Research and Practice," Joyce E. King (Chapters 1 and 2) situates the Commission's research and outreach within theoretical perspectives and epistemological concerns in the Black intellectual tradition. Chapter 1 defines the principles and methods of transformative research and Chapter 2 further delineates the underlying theory by highlighting relevant scholarship and research exemplars. In Part II, "Taking Culture into Account: Learning Theory and Black Education," Carol D. Lee (Chapters 3 and 4) examines the state of research knowledge in Black education and demonstrates how the emerging "science of learning" paradigm, in contrast to deficit view of Black students as learners, is consistent with certain principles of culturally responsive research. Lee's two-part analysis also includes an emphasis on programs led by African American researchers.

In Part III, "Expanding the Knowledgebase in Black Education and Research Globally," William H. Watkins and Kassie Freeman examine historical and continuing challenges in education on the continent and in nations where African populations are in the minority. Watkins (Chapter 5) addresses the devastation of Africa's colonial past and finds in colonialism's lingering effects meaningful historical comparisons with education designed for Black people in the United States. Kassie Freeman (Chapter 6) examines factors that are common in the exclusion of Black people from education in Australia, France, Great Britain, Portugal, and the United States. Freeman's research identifies economic as well as psychological, monetary, and nonmonetary costs of cultural alienation and annihilation in these countries in which the "controlling population is non-Black."

Hassimi Oumarou Maiga and Beverly Lindsay address vestiges of colonialism in schools in West Africa and postapartheid postsecondary institutions in southern Africa in Part IV, "Engaging the Language and Policy Nexus in African Education." Maiga (Chapter 7) and Lindsay (Chapter 8) examine links between current policy implementation efforts to overcome the ways that curriculum and the language of instruction, for an example, in colonial and apartheid periods, have been used as political and cultural mechanisms in processes of domination in African education. Maiga also explores the potential of African language study for African American students, a research demonstration project supported by the Commission.

The focus on policy and pedagogy within the context of the economy in the next section addresses systemic inequities in U.S. schools and workplaces that are ignored in prevailing "top-down" accountability reforms. Part V, "Situating Equity Policy and Pedagogy in the Political Economic Context," identifies teacher quality and certification, student assessment, and curriculum access as areas in which policy is needed to ensure equitable learning opportunities, as well as the knowledge and skills the global "new economy" requires. Linda Darling-Hammond (Chapter 9) marshals an array of evidence documenting the limitations of standards-based and high-stakes testing policies that ignore such inequity in school resources and funding, the assignment of qualified teachers, and curriculum content. Jessica Gordon Nembhard (Chapter 10) presents innovative pedagogical solutions that can address systemic inequity in the economic arena by preparing Black students not only for employment but also to rebuild Black communities and to democratize the workplace.

In further contrast to "top-down" education reforms, Part VI, "Humanizing Education: Diverse Voices," demonstrates the importance of critical consciousness and transformative spiritual values in community struggles for education and justice. Joyce E. King and Sharon Parker (Chapter 11) draw on activist-scholar Grace Lee Boggs's incisive social analysis to frame selected highlights of the discussion of research priorities that CORIBE organized among a diverse group of citizens in Detroit. This panel included a college president, researchers, activists, administrators, community educators, students, and practitioners. Their conclusions illustrate key points raised in Chapter 9: "bottom-up" reforms are crucial for fundamental change, that is, to rebuild and "respirit" our communities and to "grow our souls." Zakiyyah Muhammad (Chapter 12) addresses the history and spiritual foundations of African American Islamic education that also has roots in Detroit. In a reflective analysis that draws on her combined experience as a teacher, school administrator, and Islamic scholar, Muhammad stresses the unity of educational and spiritual excellence in the long struggle for Black self-respect in community building efforts that now include immigrant Muslims from other nations. Both chapters identify tensions and opportunities for human growth within diversity.

The commentaries by the international scholars who participated in the CORIBE initiative in Part VII, "Globalizing the Struggle for Black Education: African and Diaspora Experiences," affirm research prepared especially for the Commission (Carol D. Lee, William H. Watkins, Kassie Freeman, Chapters 3–6). Ibrahima Seck (Sénégal), Cecile Wright (U.K.), Terezinha Juraci Machado da Silva, and Petronilha Gonçalves e Silva (Brazil) also provide relevant analytical reflections (Chapters 13–16) on research and education in their respective countries. These chapters present examples of historical and continuing domination of African people in familiar patterns of resource inequity and negative representations of "blackness" in schooling that colonization and slavery helped to produce in Africa and the Diaspora. These scholar-activists also offer eloquent testimonies of a role for research-based knowledge in resistance to domination in their communities and schools.

Finally, in four concise chapters that close this book, CORIBE scholars who participated in various research and education outreach activities organized by the Commission address new possibilities for transformative applied research and professional development within the academy. In Part VIII, "*Ore Ire*—Catalyzing Transformation in the Academy: Our Charge to Keep," Linda C. Tillman, Annette Henry, and Cirecie West-Olatunji (Chapters 17–19) demonstrate how culturally sensitive research, evaluation, and technology-related demonstration projects also can provide professional development apprenticeship experiences for graduate students and faculty. In the final chapter, Djanna Hill (Chapter 20) recapitulates the CORIBE experience in an analytical discussion of the Commission's documentary video: "A Charge to Keep." The title, from a traditional African American hymn (composed by the British evangelist Charles Wesley in the 1700s), alludes to a higher spiritual calling in one's life and work. Many of the participating scholars, practitioners, commissioners, and Elders make cameo appearances in this documentary video that concludes with an engaging interview with Sylvia Wynter, as she discusses her theoretical analysis of the crisis in Black education.

VIDEOS AND INTERACTIVE CD-ROM RESOURCES RELATED TO THIS VOLUME

Here are brief descriptions of the multimedia resources CORIBE produced and information for ordering these videos and the CD-ROM related to this volume.

A Charge to Keep. This 50-minute video documents the findings and recommendations of the Commission on Research in Black Education (CORIBE), including exemplary educational approaches that CORIBE identified, candid commentary by Adelaide L. Sanford, Lisa Delpit, Gloria Ladson-Billings, Kathryn Au, Donna Gollnick, Asa G. Hilliard, Edmund W. Gordon, Frank Bonilla, and others as well as an extended interview with Sylvia Wynter. ISBN 0-8058-5626-9

A Detroit Conversation. In this 20-minute video documentary, "A Detroit Conversation" (the subject of Chapter 11), a diverse panel of educators—teachers, administrators, professors, a "reform" Board member, and parent and community activists—offer concrete suggestions for research and practice. Participants engage in a "no-holds-barred" conversation about testing, teacher preparation, and what works in Detroit schools. ISBN 0-8058-5625-0

CORIBE CD-ROM: *Research & Best Practices 1999–2001.* Informed by diverse perspectives and voices of leading researchers, teacher educators, and classroom teachers, this rich, interactive CD-ROM contains an archive of the empirical findings, recommendations, and best practices assembled by the Commission on Research in Black Education. Dynamic multi-media presentations document concrete examples of transformative practice that prepare Black students and others to achieve academic and cultural excellence. ISBN 0-8058-5564-5

CONCLUDING COMMENT

In conclusion, the analyses and empirical findings assembled in this volume link the crisis in Black education to research and academic scholarship and the system of thought that often justifies the deplorable state of Black education. The contributions to this volume, informed by diverse perspectives and voices, demonstrate the need to consider the state of Black education globally and the importance of culture as an asset in Black education and research. As a commitment to the education of Black children and youth and to African people's development here and elsewhere in the world, this extraordinary collaborative experience also affirms that the problems of Black education that undermine the life chances of African people are not a "minority" issue that can be addressed through ameliorative reforms aimed at incremental expansion of the "global middle classes." Rather, as history has taught us, our "particular wrong" is a reflection of the more general state of injustice, here and elsewhere, that calls us to action.

Part I

Theorizing Transformative Black Education Research and Practice

INTRODUCTION

If the white man has inflicted the wound of racism upon Black men, the cost has been that he would receive the mirror image of that wound into himself.

—Wendell Berry

In contrast to prevailing explanations of the crisis in Black education that attribute "school failure" to presumed deficiencies in Black students' culture, behavior, attitudes, or their families and communities (in the United States and elsewhere), the theoretical analyses presented in the first section of this volume transcend this omnipresent mainstream discourse. Part I demonstrates powerful culturally nurturing educational practice and research paradigms in analyses that project what is *transformative* about Black education, not only for people of African ancestry but for humanity more generally as well. What do transformative Black education and research mean in practice? Transformative refers to fundamental requisites of human freedom that are implicated in the educational and life circumstances of people of African descent. One important implication is a primary focus of this volume: The abysmal state of Black education on a global scale indicates not Black people's deficiencies but the actual extent rather than the West's espoused values of freedom, humanism, and democracy.

Joyce E. King begins her examination of two crucial questions that delineate this transformative vision of Black education in Chapter 1, "A Transformative Vision of Black Education for Human Freedom." In this chapter, King discusses alternatives to inclusion in the prevailing hegemonic cultural system that is sustained by the processes of schooling. The first

1

question King discusses is: "*What has happened to the Black education and socialization agenda?*" This chapter describes the cultural alienation and annihilation in education and educational research as principal factors that have undermined educational excellence traditions that African people have instituted and practiced as part of our human experience. Next, in Chapter 2, King addresses the second question: *How can research become one of the forms of struggle for Black education?* Chapter 2 presents the fundamental consensus that emerged during the Commission's deliberations: a "Declaration of Intellectual Independence for Human Freedom." This declaration consists of Ten Vital Principles of Black Education and Socialization and four precepts that are illustrated by scholarship and research exemplars under the headings of these Articles: (1) *Expanding Human Understanding*; (2) *Nurturing Cultural Consciousness*; (3) *Resisting Hegemony/Domination/Dispossession Culturally*; and (4) *Using a Liberatory Cultural Orientation as an Analytical/Pedagogical Tool*. A Glossary of Terms found in Chapters 1 and 2 is presented in Appendix C (Hill & King).

1

A Transformative Vision of Black Education for Human Freedom

Joyce E. King
Georgia State University

I knew nothing about my own historical reality, except in negative terms that would have made it normal for me, as Fanon points out, both to want to be a British subject and, in so wanting, to be anti-black, anti-everything I existentially was. I knew what it was to experience a total abjection of being. A Foucault would never have experienced that, in those terms.

—Sylvia Wynter (Scott, 2000, p. 188)

[A]t the very time when it most often mouths the word, the West has never been further from being able to live a true humanism—a humanism made to the measure of the world.

—Aimé Césaire (2000, p. 42)

INTRODUCTION

This chapter introduces the vision of transformative Black education—understood as a fundamental requirement of human freedom in a civilized world—that shaped the work of the AERA Commission on Research in Black Education (CORIBE). The abysmal state of Black education in the United States and globally is an inhumane situation that calls into question the values and pronouncements of Western "civilization." The

3

research and educational practice assembled in this volume illustrate two critical elements of this vision. First, the educational and life experiences of African descent people are historically and culturally interconnected. Second, the well-being of humanity is inextricably linked to the material and spiritual welfare of African people. This understanding of Black education in the context of African cultural continuity and larger civilizational issues (Munford, 2001) is missing from the mainstream discourse on education reform in the United States; it is absent in models of "development" for Africa and Latin America, where the African presence is gaining increasing attention, and this perspective is largely lacking in multicultural education approaches as well.

Historically, the economic and social development of Europe and the Americas, even "the very idea of freedom" (Wilder, 2000) and "civilization" (Césaire, 2000), have turned on the status of African people (Robinson, 2000). Neither the commonalities among African people, including our educational experiences, or humankind's dependence on the welfare of African people for their well-being—human freedom to be more precise— are recent phenomena. Human freedom in this new millennium remains inextricably bound up with the life chances, and, therefore, the education of African people "here and there in the world" (Diop, 1981/1991). Thus, the theoretical underpinning of this understanding of Black education, and the possibilities for human freedom that depend upon ending our dispossession, suggests a critical question addressed in this chapter: *What has happened to the Black education/ socialization agenda?*

BRINGING OUR DISPOSSESSION TO AN END: A CULTURE-SYSTEMIC THEORETICAL FRAMEWORK

The conception of human freedom advanced in this book is grounded in the culture-systemic theoretical framework Sylvia Wynter developed. A Professor Emerita of Spanish and Portuguese and African and African American Studies at Stanford University, Wynter proposes a very specific role for intellectuals and educators in ending our dispossession. Her "culture-systemic" analysis of the *cultural logic* of the social order builds on the contributions of Frantz Fanon, a psychiatrist and theoretician of the anticolonial Algerian revolution from the former French colony of Martinique, and African American historian Carter G. Woodson (1933) who wrote the classic *Miseducation of the Negro*. Referring to herself as a "Woodsonian," and drawing on her personal experience of subordination growing up as a former British colonial subject in Jamaica, Wynter's analysis shows how mainstream education functions in the domination of subordinated groups and works against the interests of human freedom (King, 1997; Wynter, 1968/1969).

In an interview, which recapitulates her entire intellectual biography—spanning her career as a writer, actress, dancer, Black Studies scholar, and literary theorist beginning in the 1950s—Wynter explains that:

> ... intellectuals and artists who belong to a subordinated group are necessarily going to be educated in the scholarly paradigms of the group who dominates you. But these paradigms, whatever, their other emancipatory attributes must have *always already* legitimated the subordination of your group.... Must have even induced us to accept our subordination through the mediation of *their* imaginary. (Scott, 2000, p. 169)

Clearly, this is one way to understand what *hegemony* means. If, as Holt (2000) suggests, however, "racism is a form of knowledge," then Black education and research practice that produce knowledge and understanding of the process(es) of domination and dispossession, which Wynter refers to as a "new science of the human," also can create possibilities for liberating thought and social action. As Wynter further observes:

> In every human order there are always going to be some groups for whom knowledge of the totality is necessary, seeing that it is only with knowledge of the totality that their dispossession can be brought to an end. (p. 188)

In fact, it is human consciousness and identity that are also distorted by these hegemonic structures of knowledge (King, 1992). Therefore, from this perspective of the inherent liberatory potential of Black education, the ultimate object of a transformative research and action agenda is the universal problem of human freedom. That is, a goal of transformative education and research practice in Black education is the production of knowledge and understanding people need to rehumanize the world by dismantling hegemonic structures that impede such knowledge. The Commission's focus, therefore, producing knowledge and understanding of the *universal human interests* in the survival and development of African people, represents a fundamental engagement with what Césaire (2000) called "a humanism made to the measure of the world" (p. 42). This is precisely why the work of the Commission is not a narrow, self-interested racialized project that ignores the diversity among people of African descent or "essentializes" matters of race. The Commission's examination of Black education globally, historically, and systemically underscores that planetary interests of humankind are at stake.

From the perspective of this transformative understanding of Black education and to stimulate improvements in research and policy making, the Commission explored a number of questions: What forms of knowledge, inquiry, and social action should be the goal of transformative research in Black education? How can such a transformative research and action agenda continue the intellectual tradition of visionary Black thought and collective action? Are there models of exemplary research and practice that merit emulation, support, and wider dissemination? Are some aspects of such an agenda beyond the responsibility of AERA and, therefore, should be taken up independently of the Association? What constitutes a more transformative role for AERA with respect to Black education? What opportunities exist or need to be developed in alliance with other groups and organizations such as with policy decision makers, practitioners, scholars in other disciplines, artists, and community constituents, including parents and students? Is there a role for the Internet and cybertechnology in mobilizing paradigm changing research and action in Black education and socialization—here and globally? Finally, two of the most crucial questions that guided the Commission's inquiries and activities are addressed directly in this chapter and in several of other chapters in this volume:

1. What has happened to the Black education and socialization agenda, here, throughout the Diaspora and in Africa? and
2. How can education research become one of the forms of struggle for Black education?

WHAT HAS HAPPENED TO THE BLACK EDUCATION/SOCIALIZATION AGENDA?

This question was first posed as a challenge to the CORIBE working colloquium participants by one of the CORIBE Elders. The late Baba Kwame Ishangi literally chided us to reflect more deeply on our role as intellectuals and to take more responsibility for addressing the effects of racism, hegemony, as well as the work we do as educators. Baba Ishangi's challenging question is a reminder that epistemological matters have tangible effects on our souls, on the material and spiritual well-being of our people and humanity in general. In essence, "We have a charge to keep."

This "charge" emanates from the contradictions that gave rise to the Commission. CORIBE was established amid recurring tensions around the politics of knowledge within AERA. In 1997 the task force convened by the AERA Committee on the Role and Status of Minorities, chaired by Edmund W. Gordon (1997), produced a compelling report that describes these tensions as an "epistemological crisis" within the association. Epistemology can aptly be described as a "power-knowledge-economics regime" (Vinson & Ross, 2001). In other words, epistemological concerns have to do not only with the nature, origin, and boundaries of knowledge, but also with whose knowledge counts (for funding, for instance), and which research paradigms and "ways of knowing" the research establishment validates. This establishment (or regime) includes the legitimating power and prestige of AERA (B. Gordon, 1990).

Functioning like Kuhn's (1970) "normal science paradigm," by "blaming the victim," this establishment research regime has generally not acknowledged the ways that Black education and socialization have been destabilized and undermined through the processes of schooling (King & Lightfoote-Wilson, 1994; Shujaa, 1994), hegemonic processes of teacher education (Meacham, 2000), and research itself. For instance, Lee demonstrates in Chapters 3 and 4 that much of the research that she and Michèle Foster reviewed for the Commission, which regards African/African American cultural practice as an asset to be used in the design of education interventions and pedagogical practice, is marginalized and remains "on the fringe" of education research discourse. Another example of how this "normal science" paradigm functions is the National Research Council (NRC) publication, "Improving Student Learning: A Strategic Plan for Education Research and Utilization." Introduced to the public with great fanfare at the 1999 AERA annual meeting, this prestigious state-of-the-knowledge report shows how establishment research, by conceptualizing Black students as "disadvantaged" and "at risk," can have the colonizing effect of "othering" these students by placing them outside a normative standard. This is not an inclusive, universal standard; rather, it is culturally specific and ethnocentric: It represents the generic White middle-class norm that Sylvia Wynter refers to as the category of "ethno-class 'Man'." Of course, the use of such concepts by the National Institute on the Education of At-Risk Students, sponsored by the Office of Educational Research and Improvement (OERI), reflects the conceptual framework of the sponsoring agency. Regardless of the race or background of the scholars involved, use of this language and the "deficit" thinking behind it reveal the fundamental problem of epistemological bias and hegemony in research and its application. This is part and parcel of the epistemological crisis within AERA, a kind of paradigm bias that affects:

- How research in Black education is conceptualized
- Whose research agenda gets funded and supported for empirical investigation and replication
- Which research is accepted as "scientific" and validated (that is, legitimated or rejected by prestigious sponsors (like OERI, NSF) and professional associations like AERA
- What kinds of research gets disseminated widely (or not at all) and used (or ignored) in policy decision making, by practitioners as well as parents and the news media and
- How teachers, administrators, researchers, and professors are trained.

Professional Research Training—A Schizophrenic Bind?   These problems of intellectual hegemony exist in graduate school training across the disciplines (King, 1999). For instance, graduate students of color in a doctoral program in sociology describe their experiences with conceptual, methodological, and ideological constraints in a *Harvard Education Review* article entitled "The Department Is Very Male, Very White, Very Old, and Very Conservative" (Margolis & Romero, 1998). Edmund W. Gordon (1999) acknowledges that "many minority scholars find themselves in the schizophrenic bind of using ethnocentric paradigms that are generally accepted as scientific truisms, but are lacking validation" in the experiences of scholars of color and/or their intuitions (p. 178). Likewise, Africana scholars (people of African descent) on the continent and in the Diaspora also are concerned about this kind of alienation. In his inaugural address to the Ghana Academy of Arts and Sciences, *Professor Kwesi Yankah (2000) laments the "complete alienation of scholarly authority" of indigenous (African) intellectuals in favor of the "western academy" and the marginalization of their own academic agenda. Professor Yankah asks an unsettling question: "Who wants to be an alien in a new world academic order?" As Yankah further observes:

> ... in conceding to so-called globalization trends within the academy, we often forget that "globalization" is merely the promotion of another local culture and knowledge to the world stage. The question of whose local knowledge is centralized as the standard and whose should be designated peripheral borders on the politics of knowledge: "Who is in control"? (Yankah, 2004, p. 7)

Historically, many Black intellectuals as well as other scholars of color have experienced their academic and professional preparation as this schizophrenic bind—problems of epistemological bias, hegemony, and scholarly alienation—as an "either–or" choice between the normative paradigm of supposedly objective, detached, and impartial scholarship versus an ethic of community-mindedness, "a charge to keep" in which education and socialization reflect the interests of our communities (Foster, 1998; Garcia, 2001; Meacham, 1998; Tedla, 1997). The quality of knowledge the mainstream research establishment produces is implicated in the historical and continuing domination of African people in the United States, the Diaspora and on the African continent as well as in the "scholarly" justifications of the poverty and other racialized disparities that enslavement and colonial domination introduced. Besides the "achievement gap" that has gained widespread attention recently, a knowledge gap also exists in terms of the preparedness of Africana researchers, educators, and parents to address the root causes of this crisis.

The Crisis of the Black Intellectual.   The late Jacob Carruthers (1994) concluded that "the failure of contemporary Black intellectuals to address

---

* This address has also been published in the United States under the same title. (See Yankah, 2004.)

the problem in their own thinking" is at the heart of this crisis in Black education. "These problems," Carruthers argued with great insight, are:

> ...directly attributable to schooling founded on European-centered constructions of knowledge. The crisis in Black education will not be resolved until Black intellectuals achieve intellectual freedom and re-construct Black education on an African-centered foundation. These are the pre-conditions to the real liberation of the African race all over the world. (p. 41)

Producing the knowledge and understanding needed to address this crisis is both an historical necessity and a moral obligation that are not without precedent (Childs, 1989; King, 1995). This activist intellectual task has a long history—at least as far back as David Walker's *Appeal* in 1830, Woodson's (1933) *Miseducation of the Negro* a century later—followed by the courageous campaign and petition presented to the United Nations in 1951, *We Charge Genocide,* led by William Patterson (1951).

Many Black scholars within AERA, who feel an obligation to this intellectual struggle most acutely, are engaged not only because the well-being of people of African descent is concerned, but also because *human* freedom from these dehumanizing structures of hegemony is in the balance. In this tradition of radical, incisive African thought and engaged social action, the Commission's work envisions Black education as a precondition of global social justice that is only possible if the survival and enhancement of people of African ancestry everywhere are advanced. This is an admittedly daunting vision. However, it is imperative because in the global world order increasingly dominated by the West, the incessant and obsessive degradation of Black life and culture that takes place in the classroom, which Woodson (1933) documented seventy years ago, and which Wynter's culture-systemic theoretical framework permits us to decipher in the academy today, persist to the detriment of humankind.

Furthermore, as a result of the globalization of markets and the corporate media, people everywhere are being induced to identify with the normative category of the "whitewardly mobile middle-class" (Chavetz, 2001), which now assimilates "token Blacks" and some Chicano/a and Asians as "honorary Whites" or "model minorities." The way some South Asian immigrant groups are being assimilated to this category of White middle-classness (in academic scholarship and in the popular media) is reminiscent of the path taken by other non-African groups (e.g., Irish, Italian, and Jewish immigrants). In a recent issue of *Newsweek* magazine, Kantrowitz and Scelfo (2004) tout the "model minority" success of wealthy, well-educated immigrants from India, Pakistan, Bangladesh, Sri Lanka, and Nepal, and others born here. However, in his analysis of "Afro-Asian connections" Prashad (2001) complicates this rosy picture by pointing out the aversion toward Black people that is also part of the South Asian immigrant experience. "Since," as Prashad observes, "white supremacy reigns . . . and blackness is reviled," he wonders:

> . . . why would an immigrant, of whatever skin color, want to associate with those who are racially oppressed, particularly when the transit into the United States promises the dream of gold and glory? The immigrant seeks a form of vertical assimilation to climb from the lowest, darkest echelon on the stepladder of tyranny into the bright whiteness. In U.S. history the Irish, Italians, Jews, and—in small steps with some hesitation on the part of White America—Asians and Latinos have all tried to barter their varied cultural worlds for the privileges of whiteness. (p. x)

In fact, skin color matters a great deal *within* these communities and among other non-Black people who are not quite "White." In further contrast to the celebratory image of multicultural "South Asian chic" extolled in the *Newsweek* cover story, Zakiyyah Muhammad (2003; see also Chapter 12) discusses the everyday reality of anti-Black tensions that negatively charge the learning atmosphere in some Islamic schools founded by South Asian immigrant Muslims. Thus, this situation is both volatile and dynamic. It is also worth noting that scholars, policy decision makers, and business leaders within the United States and hemispherically are paying more attention of late to the potential for a "black-Hispanic" alliance, given that "1.7 million of the 38.8 million Hispanics [in the U.S. Census] identified themselves as both Hispanic and of African descent" (Esdaille & Hughes, 2004, p. 111; see also Moore, Sanders, & Moore, 1995). Moreover, the Organization of Africans in the Americas estimates that one third of the total population of Latin America, or 150 million people, is of African descent (OAA, 2000). As the evidence presented in this volume documents, African people worldwide share the enduring legacy of exclusion from the "privileges of whiteness"—cultural dispossession and annihilation—that disrupts our agenda for education and socialization, as well as our capacity for self-liberation and collective success. Reconstructing Black education on foundations that transcend this contradiction and recuperating research from the normative anti-Black cultural model will be beneficial for ending our dispossession and extricating humanity from the perverse effects of this soul-wounding Black-White binary.

HOW CAN RESEARCH BECOME ONE OF THE FORMS OF STRUGGLE FOR BLACK EDUCATION?

Black education is the lifeblood and economic mainstay of the education research establishment. Massive investments have been made in educational research since *de facto* (and unequal) segregated schooling replaced legally separate (and unequal) disenfranchisement of African Americans in U.S.

schools (Smith, 1999). Since the historic *Brown v. Board* decision, the research establishment's predominate focus on Black education has produced negligible lasting positive effects for the benefit of Black people. As noted in the 1998 AERA proposal that led to the establishment of the Commission:

> Indeed, much research conducted by AERA members bears directly on issues of Black education. Research on Head Start, Chapter I, early literacy, mathematics education, urban education, school desegregation, cooperative learning, and many others all have their foundation in Black communities and schools. (Ladson-Billings, 1999, p. 7)

Scholars have built careers interpreting and managing Black education, which, nevertheless, remains in perilous condition, whether in the inner-city, rural, or suburban communities—or the prisons in which the failures the education system produces are warehoused for further exploitation of their labor at low or no wages and high profits. There is abundant empirical evidence that Black students in the United States, regardless of their socioeconomic circumstances, continue to experience profoundly unequal "opportunities to learn" (Darling-Hammond, Chapter 9; The College Board, 2000). The following indicators suggest the dimensions and depth of the crisis in Black education in the United States:

- Alienating school knowledge, or what is (and is not) taught—about African history, culture, and the significance of the contributions of African people to world development, community building, and economic development
- Reduced national and local financial support for public education and unequal school funding, physical facilities, and access to technology
- Adverse affects of standards-based education reform and mandatory "high-stakes" testing of students and teachers
- Unavailability of health care and counseling services
- Less qualified teachers
- Tracking, that is, more frequent assignments to "lower" curriculum tracks
- Privatization, for example, "hostile takeovers"—the seizure and selling of urban schools
- Racial bias in special education, including the misplacement and over-representation (particularly of Black males) in classes for the emotionally disturbed and mentally retarded, often with inadequately trained teachers
- Underrepresentation in classes for the gifted and talented, the sciences, and advanced mathematics courses, particularly with respect to "gatekeeper" courses such as Algebra

- Abuse of Black athletes
- Higher rates of suspensions, truancy, and expulsions
- Cultural alienation and disengagement from school and from learning
- Overrepresentation of Black (and Chicano/a) students in segregated, failing, and dysfunctional urban schools
- The persistent "achievement gap" and "high-stakes" testing gap
- Increasing school segregation and limited opportunities to learn the skills and values of tolerance and cultural identity needed for engaged global citizenship
- Higher dropout or "push-out" rates; lower grade point averages; lower levels of participation in higher education and lower retention and graduation rates
- Judicial assaults on affirmative action in higher education admissions and attempts to shut down and merge historically Black colleges and universities (HBCUs) with traditionally white institutions
- Too few Black teachers, administrators, and higher education faculty members, and
- The lack of parent education for community building and sustainable development and parent training that is too often limited by the lack of emphasis on visionary social change.

A number of these indicators of the crisis in Black education in the United States also are cited in the research commentaries invited scholars from Africa, Brazil, and the United Kingdom prepared for the Commission (Chapters 7 and 13–16).

Also, with respect to alienation, the urgent need to include African language study in Black education globally emerged in consultation with these invited scholars and others who participated the AERA 1999 annual meeting symposium on "Issues of Epistemology, Teaching and Research for Black Folks Here and There from an African Worldview Perspective" in Montreal, Canada. This recognition of the importance of African language study as a focal point for research and practice prompted the Commission's Songhoy-Senni (language) and culture online demonstration research project. (See Maiga, Chapter 7, for a discussion of the results; see also Tillman's discussion of the CORIBE evaluation in Chapter 17.) It is worth noting that in a 1984 report titled, "Saving the African American Child," the National Association for Black School Educators, Inc. recommended that "acquisition of competence in an African language should be made available as an option" for African American students (NABSE, 1984, p. 35).

The State-of-the-Emergency. It is important to acknowledge, in spite of these above indicators of the perilous state of Black education, that individual Black "successes" abound—from Dr. William "Bill" Cosby to Black college and university presidents and Black educators at every level, not to mention the Black presence in AERA, as well as astronauts, scientists, artists, athletes, doctors, politicians, attorneys, and skilled artisans in every trade. Such success is an undeniable part of the African/Diaspora experience. Nevertheless, Angela Davis (1998) is among those who recognize that for the masses that have not been so fortunate, "the deterioration of public education, including prioritizing discipline and security over learning in public schools located in poor communities, is directly related to the prison 'solution' " (p. 14). Indeed, the United States imprisons one quarter of the world's prisoners—almost 2 million people; more than 70% are people of color. In the past 20 years, the number of Americans incarcerated has risen by almost 400% as a result of "get tough on crime" policies that have disproportionately affected the Black male population and the number of incarcerated Black women and girls is increasing at an alarming rate (The Urban League, 2003). Educational opportunities within prisons have been drastically cut back. At the same time, some schools appear to serve as "feeder" institutions for what has come to be called the "prison industrial complex." For example:

> During the ten years following 1982, the number of prisons in New York state rose from 34 to 69. In [places like] Attica, Dannemore, Greenhaven, and Clinton, the number of inmates soared from 24,798 to 62,209, of whom 85 percent were Black and Latino, nearly all drawn from just seven neighborhoods in New York City. (Munford, 1996, pp. 326–227)

It also appears that both these "public" institutions—prisons and schools—are increasingly serving as lucrative private profit centers as dysfunctional "prison track" schools literally feed the prison industrial complex, which includes more money for new prison construction than is available for education (Staples, 2004). This situation in turn creates economic benefits for mostly White, economically depressed rural communities. These alarming trends in the United States have roots in plantation slavery and the share cropper labor system that followed, as is poignantly demonstrated in the documentary film, "The Intolerable Burden" (Icarus Films, 2003). Moreover, a disturbing connection between high-stakes testing, the so-called accountability requirements of the "No Child Left Behind Act," and possible profit motives in the privatization of public education is gaining increasing attention (Kohn, 2004).

A logical question follows from reflection on the privatization of education that is taking place globally: *Are privatized schools [and prisons] for the poor and subordinated groups the next economic boons for the few on a global scale?* Relatedly, the official publication of the United Nations Educational, Scientific, and Cultural Organization, the *UNESCO Courier*, focused on global education issues under the headline: "Education: The Last Frontier for Profit" (Hallak, 2000). A cautionary editorial by UNESCO's Assistant

Director-General for Education opens this issue of the journal with an appeal to uphold the common purposes of schooling. By contrast, within the market logic of globalization, and in the context of a worsening worldwide economic crisis, at least for the "have-nots," the privatization of public schools and the abysmal state of Black education seem to go hand-in-hand. This crisis represents not only a state-of-emergency for the masses of Black people but also a highly profitable *global market opportunity* for the establishment. If this is so, then it is perhaps not at all hyperbole to argue, as Staughton Lynd has suggested, that matters of life and death are at stake. According to Lynd:

> The ultimate destiny of the Afro-American is likely to be extermination, not assimilation. His situation is less like that of the European immigrant than like that of the American Indian. Black militants have not fully understood the economic basis of what they perceive, but in prophesying genocide they have accurately grasped the end to which the logic of automation leads. (Lynd, 1970, p. xi; cf., Hilliard, 2000a, pp. 14–15)

Indeed, there is much concern today about the "digital divide" worldwide, particularly the disparity within and among nations and regions of the world in access to and facility with computer technology and between middle-class/higher-income families and low-income families in the United States, many of whom are Black. As will be discussed later, and as Carol D. Lee notes in Chapter 4, technology is one of the areas in which research and transformative practice can contribute to the struggle for Black education. Many programs seek to address the disparities in technology by making computers and computer-based activities available in public spaces (libraries, schools, after-school program sites, community centers, etc.). However, making the content of computer-based learning programs, as well as math and science instruction, relevant to the lives of low-income or Black youth remains a pioneering effort and was an important focus in several CORIBE inquiries and activities (see Henry, Chapter 18, for example, on technology impediments in the academy).

To develop a transformative research and action agenda that addresses these broad dimensions of the crisis in Black education the Commission created multiple, overlapping opportunities to identify and demonstrate groundbreaking alternatives to the research establishment's normative approaches and to identify best practices in Black education. The Commission's approach contrasts with the competitive individualism, emotional detachment, presumed objectivity, cultural neutrality, and the "illusion of the mainstream [research paradigm] as universal" (Meacham, 1998, p. 403). Many participants declared that their experiences with the Commission were inspired by and produced significant engagement with the Black intellectual/Black Studies traditions (Bogues, 2003) as well as

African/African American spirituality. This is in contrast to just how disheartened our community constituency is by the lack of pragmatic, effective results when it comes to research and educational interventions. For instance, a New Orleans teacher who attended the Commission's AERA 2000 annual meeting symposium wondered: "*If there are this many Black Ph.D.'s in a room this size, why can't the problems of our children be solved?*" (Haughton, http://www.coribe.org). Consider also an activist inner-city pastor's indictment of Black intellectuals. In a *Boston Review* article, with uncompromising bluntness, Reverend Eugene Rivers contrasts the "stunning disparity between the grim state of Black America and the recent successes (and privilege) of the Black intelligentsia" (Rivers, http://www.yesamerica.org/NTLF). To address this schizophrenic double bind between scholarly alienation and alienation from the community (O'Connor, 2003), the Commission designed several innovative professional socialization apprenticeship experiences for graduate students and younger faculty (see Chapters 17–19). In effect, the theoretical perspective that informed the Commission's work and the culturally nurturing methodological approach, discussed in the next section, serve to explicate, by means of empirical investigation and catalytic validation (King & Mitchell, 1995), a way out of this schizophrenic bind. The CORIBE initiative demonstrates "*how research can become one of the forms of struggle for Black education*" in the best interests of our common humanity.

CORIBE: A CULTURALLY NURTURING PROCESS-BUILDING METHODOLOGY

CORIBE created vital opportunities to affirm the diverse voices and perspectives of many who share a commitment to Black people's collective survival and advancement. Not surprisingly, CORIBE participants repeatedly used the word "healing" to describe their experience of the uncensored liberated spaces the Commission created—at AERA annual meetings (2000–2002) and other venues. The methodology also is consistent with the "profound indigenous pedagogical" tradition of excellence in the history of African people. As CORIBE Elder Asa G. Hilliard (1985) has observed: "An important component of African indigenous pedagogy is the vision of the teacher [and researcher] as a selfless healer intent on inspiring, transforming, and propelling students to a higher spiritual level" (pp. 69–70). Thus, the CORIBE methodology created various contexts or spaces in which to examine the state of Black education research and practice that also point to transformative directions in research. In these inspiring, "liberated" spaces Africana cultural practice and the knowledge and wisdom of our elders were honored and respectfully incorporated in our work. Reverence for elders is a cultural constant in Africana/Diaspora societies. The scholarship, lived experience, and wisdom of CORIBE Elders contributed significantly to the Commission's inquiry processes and other learning opportunities, and the viewpoints of practitioners and community activists also were invaluable to the CORIBE initiative. (Chapter 11 presents the highlights of a panel discussion about research priorities among practitioners and community activists in Detroit, for example.)

Scholars from Brazil, the United Kingdom, Haiti, and West Africa— Ghana, Mali, Nigeria, and Sénégal —as well as other participants of diverse backgrounds (Native Hawaiian, Haitian American, Puerto Rican American, Mexican American, Asian American, and Euro American) enthusiastically described the benefits of their participation in CORIBE activities. The methodology for *building* this broad-based, dynamic participatory process—a process that also served a culturally nurturing *pedagogical* function—is one of the Commission's most significant accomplishments. Participation in the CORIBE *process* enhanced the capacity of many of those involved in various Commission-supported inquiry and outreach activities—colloquia, research presentations, demonstration projects, and apprenticeships—by providing opportunities for collaborative reflection and imaginative empirical inquiry (often grounded in an Africana worldview perspective), cross-cultural and cross-national dialogue as well as other collective action. In addition, this process-building methodology affirms the values of reciprocity, mutuality, and truth-telling in African American cultural practice (King & Mitchell, 1990/1995).

CONCLUDING COMMENTS

CORIBE's process-building methodology included theorizing and action, that is, a form of *cultural praxis* that shares certain "Africanist principles" with a Black aesthetic performance mode in the arts and music (Gottschild, 1996). As a culturally nurturing *pedagogical process* this methodology involves ways of seeing, knowing, and working together that incorporates these jazz-like qualities: (a) *embracing the conflict* or tensions arising in a given situation; (b) *the aesthetic of "coolness"*—relaxing about not getting it right the first time, "embracing the error and going on"; as well as (c) *overlapping polycentrism*—a nonlinear overlapping polycentric approach with simultaneous, multiple centers of activity that, like jazz music, combine discipline, improvisation, and individuality (Woods, 1998).

Brenda Dixon Gottschild (1996) identifies "embracing the conflict" and the "aesthetic of coolness" as invisibilized Africanist influences on American culture and performance, "on stage and in everyday life," which shaped (post)modern American (and European) dance as well as blackface minstrelsy, an original form of theatre in the United States (p. xiii). CORIBE's research and inquiry activities, which were conducted and shared in various venues, including a Readers Theatre "Minstrel Performance" (Chapter 19), also exemplify *overlapping polycentrism*, the construct Clyde Woods (1998) uses to define the blues, another African-influenced indigenous American performing art. Like jazz, according to Woods, the blues, as both a form of folk theory and music genre, represents an alternative "vision of society that is 'dialectically polyrhythmic,' a democracy where both cooperation and individual expression thrive" (p. 288).

These qualities also apply to the CORIBE methodology in so far as this process-building approach, in contrast to the mainstream paradigm, also democratizes the research process. The implications of this democratization of research are reflected in the *Declaration of Intellectual Independence for Human Freedom*, presented in the next chapter.

2

A Declaration of Intellectual Independence for Human Freedom

Joyce E. King
Georgia State University

I don't want nobody to give me nothing. Open up the door. I'll get it myself.
Don't give me integration, give me true communication.
Don't give me sorrow, I want equal opportunity to live tomorrow.
Give me schools and give me better books, So I can read about myself and gain my truer looks.
I don't want nobody to give me nothing. Open up the door. I'll get it myself.
We got talents we can use on our side of town. Let's get our heads together and build it up from the ground.

—James Brown, The Godfather of Soul[1]

Issues of power and agency, as framed by ongoing racialized disparity, enter the discussion.

—Brenda Dixon Gottschild (1996, xiii)

---

[1] "I don't want nobody to give me nothing" by James Brown © 1960 (Renewed), Dynatone Publishing Company. All rights adminstered by Unichappell Music Inc. All rights reserved. Used by Permission. Warner Brothers Publications U.S. Inc., Miami, Florida 33014.

Shakur Afrikanus, a community scholar who resides in Harlem, New York, assisted with the translation of these song lyrics from the Gullah dialect into Standard English.

INTRODUCTION

Chapter 2 presents examples of transformative scholarship and empirical inquiries that demonstrate how research can become one of the forms of struggle for Black education. These exemplary approaches show that intellectual freedom from hegemony is imperative. This is the fundamental consensus reached by the Commission on Research in Black Education that is stated in the form of "*A Declaration of Intellectual Independence for Human Freedom.*" Also the title of this chapter, this declaration consists of Ten Vital Principles for Black Education and Socialization and four Articles that indicate the Commission's concerns about both the quality of knowledge research has produced and the effects of research practice on the material and spiritual well-being of African people.

TEN VITAL PRINCIPLES FOR BLACK EDUCATION AND SOCIALIZATION

1. We exist as African people, an ethnic family. Our perspective must be centered in that reality.
2. The priority is on the African ethnic Family over the Individual. Because we live in a world in which expertness in alien cultural traditions (that we also share) have gained hegemony, our collective survival and enhancement must be our highest priorities.
3. Some solutions to problems that we will identify will involve differential use of three modes of response to domination and hegemony: (a) *Adaptation*—adopting what is deemed useful; (b) *Improvisation*—substituting or improvising alternatives that are more sensitive to our culture; and (c) *Resistance*—resisting that which is destructive and not in the best interests of our people.
4. The "ways of knowing" provided by the arts and humanities are often more useful in informing our understanding of our lives and experiences and those of other oppressed people than the knowledge and methodologies of the sciences that have been privileged by the research establishment despite the often distorted or circumscribed knowledge and understanding this way of knowing produces.
5. Paradoxically, from the perspective of the education research establishment, knowledge production is viewed as the search for facts and (universal) truth, whereas the circumstances of our social and existential condition require the search for meaning and understanding.
6. The priority is on research *validity* over "inclusion." For research validity, highest priority must be placed on studies of: (a) *African tradition* (history, culture, and language); (b) *Hegemony* (e.g., uses

of schooling/socialization and incarceration); (c) *Equity* (funding, teacher quality, content, and access to technology); and (d) *Beneficial practice* (at all levels of education, from childhood to elderhood).

7. Research informs practice and practice informs research in the production and utilization of knowledge; therefore, context is essential in research: (a) cultural/historical context; (b) political/economic context; and (c) professional context, including the history of AERA and African people.

8. We require power and influence over our common destiny. Rapid globalization of the economy and cybertechnology are transforming teaching, learning, and work itself. Therefore, we require access to education that serves our collective interests, including assessments that address cultural excellence and a comprehensive approach to the interrelated health, learning, and economic needs of African people.

9. The Universal Declaration of Human Rights proclaims, and the UNESCO World Education 2000 Report, issued in Dakar, Sénégal, affirms that "education is a fundamental human right" and "an indispensable means for effective participation in the societies and economies of the twenty-first century."[2] We are morally obligated to "create safe, healthy, inclusive and equitably resourced educational environments" conducive to excellence in learning and socialization with clearly defined levels of achievement for all. Such learning environments must include appropriate curricula and teachers who are appropriately educated and rewarded.

10. African people are not empty vessels. We are not new to the study of and practice of education and socialization that is rooted in deep thought. We will not accept a dependent status in the approach and solution to our problems.

These vital principles are further elaborated in the following four Articles:

- Article 1: *Expanding Human Understanding*
- Article 2: *Nurturing Cultural Consciousness*
- Article 3: *Resisting Hegemony/Domination/Dispossession Culturally*
- Article 4: *Using a Liberatory Cultural Orientation as an Analytical/Pedagogical Tool.*

This declaration suggests criteria or guidelines for alternatives to establishment approaches and ameliorative practices that have failed to alleviate the crisis in Black education. The chapter concludes with a discussion of the

---

[2] It is worth noting that the U.S. Constitution does not guarantee education as a human right; see Smith (1999) and Spring (2001).

significance of the Transformative Research and Action Agenda the Commission submitted to the American Educational Research Association (see Appendix A).

Article 1: Expanding Human Understanding

> Traditionally America has turned its immigrants (except those who look African-American) into white people.... No matter how people identify themselves, what counts is how they are identified by society.... Eventually America treats all its ethnics as whites–except blacks.... [A] permanent fault line runs between the perennially disadvantaged descendents of African slaves and everybody else, in various stages of upward (i.e., whiteward) mobility.
>
> —Zev Chafets (2001, p. 4)

Sylvia Wynter's seminal scholarship (2003) explains why the CORIBE Agenda "will have to call in question, dismantle and deconstruct" the "mode of being human" of our social order and the forms of knowledge and representation, such as racism, that sustain it. This is a profound challenge. Wynter (2000) further explains why, as middle-class academics and teachers, we are normally able to know the social reality only in terms that are "adaptive" or supportive of the status quo and its present White middle-class "mode of being human."

> [B]ecause (as intellectuals) ... our task is to elaborate, guard and disseminate the kind of knowledge [that is] able to ensure the well-being of our present mode of the human, *Man*, which represents its well-being as if it were that of the human itself, we cannot normally address the contradictions to which this over-representation leads. (See Appendix B-1, B-2)

Conversely, transformative research expands human understanding and consciousness of societal contradictions such as the social costs of creating categories of "worthless," homeless, jobless, miseducated, alienated, or otherwise expendable people (Hilliard, 2000a; Herrnstein & Murray, 1994) warehoused in prisons, those dying of the AIDS pandemic or the strife of war, and so on in Africa. The transformative perspective asks: *Would an equitable racial distribution or parity among such categories of "worthlessness" be an acceptable solution?*

CORIBE Elder Asa G. Hilliard has produced a body of scholarship that is also profoundly important in articulating this perspective. In his research and writing Hilliard stresses that we must recognize our peoplehood— that we belong to the African family and that we are either uninformed or have lost our collective memory of the fact that we are people with a long tradition of excellence in education, socialization, and mastery of our environment and life circumstances (Hilliard, 2002). We need to know ourselves in order to address the *real* problems that are masked by hegemony and ideological processes. In a paper that he presented at the AERA 2000 annual meeting, Hilliard (2000a) argues:

> To grasp the *real* state of education of African people everywhere, including in America, we must examine the intersection of culture and power. A *global* system of power distribution has dictated and continues to dictate the nature of the education and socialization processes. *Slavery, colonization, apartheid/segregation and the rationalizing ideology of white supremacy are centuries old challenges, really aspects of a global hegemonic system.* That system interrupted and largely destroyed the flow of *thousands of years* of powerful and independent African education/socialization excellence, about which most of us are totally uninformed. (emphasis added, pp. 3–4)

Edmund W. Gordon, another CORIBE Elder whose scholarship was decisive in the Commission's deliberations, observes that "the education research community has at least two responsibilities":

> The first is to produce knowledge that has relevance for education. The second is to pursue understanding of that knowledge and its consequences for the human condition. (Gordon, 2000, p. 302)

An explanatory case study analysis of ideology in education that I undertook as a consequence of the California history textbook adoption controversy in 1991 addresses the tasks Wynter, Hilliard, and Gordon discuss.

Understanding and Consciousness. This analysis of the textbook controversy demonstrates a role for research in the struggle against miseducation (King, 1992). Also explained is the ideology of "race" and how it functions, which is fundamental to expanding knowledge, understanding, and human consciousness, as defined thusly:

> As a social relations construct, human consciousness is more dynamically and *transformatively* inclusive than any single category of existence. In comparison to class, race, or gender consciousness, for example, human consciousness grasps the 'essential nature' of society including Black people's multiple identities as well as the specific ways that racism and other 'isms' work. (emphasis added, p. 320)

Noting the positive uses of the textbook controversy for community learning and action, this analysis discusses how a Black Studies critique of textbook ideology—textbooks that were widely touted as "multicultural"—helped to focus the attention of teachers and parents on the forms of knowledge and understanding that students need in order to resist textbook bias that promotes assimilation and cultural annihilation.

This article identifies specific counterknowledge that Black students need to be able to critique alienating ideological representations in the textbook narrative of "how slavery began" in Africa, for example. The assertion of "Africans selling Africans" into slavery as the root cause of the African Holocaust is precisely what Wynter's deciphering culture-systemic analysis challenges. She points specifically to the absence of a sense of "African" identity among the diverse national groups at that time and she identifies the missing dynamic of lineage-based servitude, enslavement, or prisoner of war captivity in Africa that is omitted in the textbook narrative. As explained in the article:

> The transatlantic slave trade went through several phases. However, it did not begin with chiefs selling their own people to Europeans ... the diversity among the African peoples involved is a factor of major significance that is generally overlooked ... there was no concept of "Africans" among these diverse peoples at that time; rather, the peoples of Africa identified with their lineage (family or kinship), clan, or descent group, and not with the continent. (p. 329)

Subsequent research on pedagogical strategies for teaching Songhoy-Senni, that is, Songhoy language (King, 2004), to African Americans, which developed out of the CORIBE demonstration project, provides linguistic support for Wynter's second point. The Songhoy-Senni word for "slave" is "baaɲaa"; literally, this word means someone "who does not even have a mother"—who is, therefore, a "lineageless" person. This research experience supports the conclusion set forth in the earlier case study: Such textbook representations "cannot enable Black students and others to understand the root causes of the historical and contemporary injustices people continue to endure, nor can they prepare them for the continuing struggle for social transformation" (p. 328). Thus, although underdeveloped and underfunded, African language study and research in this area can potentially serve as a vital resource for pedagogical knowledge and the search for meaning and understanding validated within the global Black experience, not only in terms of "intuitions" (Gordon, 1999) but also at the empirical level of explicating cultural practice.

Article 2: Nurturing Cultural Consciousness

> The priority is on the African ethnic Family over the Individual. Because we live in a world in which expertness in alien cultural traditions (that we also share) have gained hegemony, our collective survival and enhancement must be our highest priorities.
>
> —CORIBE Vital Principles

In order to construct societies based on social and economic justice, a new form of consciousness must emerge.

—Clyde Woods (1998, p. 2)

Cultural consciousness and identity are integral to human understanding. Therefore, a second goal of a transformative agenda in Black education and research is to produce knowledge and understanding of ways to dismantle the "tremendous array of aggressive negative beliefs, behaviors and strategies" of domination deployed against cultural consciousness, in particular. These strategies include negative representations of blackness in the societal cultural apparatus including language, the corporate media, as well as textbooks. Asa G. Hilliard (2000b) emphasizes that people of African ancestry "must keep in our consciousness that domination involves structures and systematic *practices founded on ideology*" that is organized to:

> *suppress the history of the victims; destroy the practice of their culture; prevent the victims from coming to understand themselves as part of a cultural family; teach systematically the ideology of white supremacy; control the socialization process; control the accumulation of wealth; and perform segregation or apartheid.* (pp. 24–25, emphasis in original text)

One empirical question to be addressed, therefore, is: *What forms of research and education practice can help to (re)construct what Hilliard refers to as the "normal nurturing" of (African people's) cultural identity and consciousness?*

Education as a Human Right. It is noteworthy that Native American educators in the United States and indigenous educators in other countries have made great strides in creating curriculum and Web-based materials and educational interventions that meet their needs in this regard. (See National Indian Telecommunications Initiative <http://www.niti.org> and the Northwest Indian Applied Research Institute <http://www.niari.org> at The Evergreen State College, Olympia Washington.) By transcending the limitations of national borders, while also affirming the importance of tribal identity, much has been accomplished in defining indigenous education as a human right—independently of the research establishment. The "Coolongatta Statement" of the World Indigenous People's Education Conference (http://www.wipcehawaii.org) is one outcome of this global WIPEC conference movement. This movement illustrates a "bottom-up" educational intervention that nurtures the collective consciousness and identity of indigenous peoples in ways designed to counter cultural annihilation and accommodation.

In New Zealand, in order "to acknowledge and resist the rapid and ongoing assimilation of Maori language, knowledge, and culture" by the dominant ("Pakeha") society, Maori educators, in partnership with members of their community, are advancing "Kaupapa Maori Theory"—an indigenous, organic theory of change or transformative praxis (Smith, 2002, p. 22). Kaupapa Maori refers to "the practice and philosophy of living a 'Maori,' culturally informed life" (p. 3). According to Graham Hingangaroa Smith, Kaupapa Maori is "more than an innovative approach towards language revitalization and intervention in educational underachievement." Smith's explanation of the emphasis Kaupapa Maori places on "structuralist concerns (economic, ideological and power structure) as well as culturalist responses (related to agency)" merits consideration. Smith writes:

> These concerns about assimilation of culture also extend to other areas such as land loss, and the social and economic marginalization of disproportionately high levels of the Maori population. However, the Maori position here should not be misinterpreted as a total rejection of Pakeha culture or a retrenchment to a "traditional Maori" cultural existence; rather, what is being advanced is the meaningful recovery and development of Maori language, knowledge and culture as well as access to world knowledge, language, and skills. It is not a "one or the other" choice for Maori...However...the cultural capital that has been historically denied, marginalized or "sanitised" within the Pakeha dominant education context, has been that intellectual and cultural capital pertaining to Maori. This is what is often described in the contemporary discourse as "assimilation," "colonization," "eurocentrism," "exploitation" and "oppression" (p. 3). (See also G. H. Smith, 2004.)

International cultural heritage law recognizes cultural rights as human rights that are, therefore, subject to international protection. Native Americans are using these legal conventions in the international human rights arena to their advantage. Indeed, UNESCO recognizes human/cultural diversity as a universal human treasure that should be preserved with the economic benefits of cultural preservation and promotion accruing to the peoples themselves. However, these international conventions never identify African Americans among the cultural groups subject to the protection and development provided for in this body of international law. The book-length petition the coalition led by William Patterson (1951) submitted to the United Nations, *We Charge Genocide: The Crime of the Government Against the Negro People*, set an historic precedent for taking the case of Black Americans into the international legal human rights arena and before the "conscience of mankind" (p. 57). This petition cited evidence of economic subjugation, racial disparities in the penal system (e.g., debt peonage), lynching, and police brutality as well as "denial of education as a matter of public policy," which is specifically identified as contributing to "genocide by forcing Negroes into dangerous industries and poorly paid work, by systematically reducing their income and depriving them of decent housing, medical care, food and clothing" (p. 130). Parallels between these historical and the contemporary circumstances of African Americans and Native Americans in their experience of oppression and miseducation, as well as possibilities for collective social action and collaboration in the development of international policy and education research practice, are worth pursuing.

Language, Consciousness, and Cultural Identity.   Language is fundamental to culture, consciousness, and identity. CORIBE identified several exemplary research projects that build on the primacy of language in nurturing the cultural consciousness and identity of students (parents and teachers) in order to counter what Kassie Freeman's research identifies as cultural annihilation and dominating structures of representation and miseducation (Freeman, Chapter 6). Four examples are presented here.

First, the National Indian Telecommunications Initiative (NITI) has produced online curriculum materials that include interactive math lessons in Navajo (http://www.niti.org). As stated on the organization's Web site, the goal of NITI is "to employ advanced technology to serve American Indians, Native Hawaiians and Alaska Natives in the areas of education, economic development, language and cultural preservation, tribal policy issues and self-determination."

Second, in Boston TERC's Chèche Konnen research group has demonstrated cognitive advantages for student learning in science when students engage in critical thinking and discourse in their home language, Haitian Creole (Hudicourt-Barnes, 2003; see also Lee, Chapter 4). Third, Theresa Perry and her colleagues at Wheelock College's Beaufort, South Carolina, Teacher Preparation project use Gullah culture effectively in teacher and student development. This project is enlarging the pool of Black teachers in that community and is enhancing the capacity of teacher educators to use the material and nonmaterial culture of the local community, including the Gullah language, as an asset in teacher development. Student academic performance in these programs, even on standardized tests, affirms specific benefits of the value added by the cultural asset approach Lee examines in her research for the Commission (Chapters 3 and 4).

Fourth, one of CORIBE's culturally nurturing demonstration research projects, the Songhoy-Senni (or Soŋay-Senni) language and culture online course, proved to be a powerfully motivating learning experience for students in the pilot assessment of the model Web-enhanced lessons that were developed. These animated lessons were based on the textbook, *Conversational Soŋay Language of Mali* (Maiga, 2003/1996). (*Soŋay* and *Songhoy* refer to the same people of West Africa.) The research question that guided this pilot demonstration study is as follows:

> In what ways does reimmersion in African culture, using Web-based learning to study African language: (a) broaden the epistemological, axiological, and ontological perspectives of students; (b) motivate their learning experience;

and (c) reorient their energies toward acceptance of diversity as a tool for global problem solving?

The results of the pilot assessment of six interactive Web-enhanced, multimedia lessons indicate that students found learning Songhoy-Senni (language) terms and concepts (e.g., greetings, counting, proverbs, etc.), and this virtual cultural "immersion" experience both meaningful as well as cognitively and emotionally engaging. A year later, students who participated in the pilot implementation still greeted each other and their teacher-counselor in *Soŋay-Senni* (Songhoy language) and asked if the program will ever be offered again. Interestingly, Songhoy culture embodies the integration of Africa's diversity (Maiga, in press). Such study also offers significant possibilities to enable students of African ancestry to experience an inclusive approach to their identity, heritage, and culture rather than ethnic chauvinism. As several chapters in this volume also demonstrate, language and identity are important factors in education policy making in Africa (see Chapters 7 and 8).

Cultural Consciousness in Indigenous Community Knowledge.   During the "Educational Excellence Expo" that CORIBE organized at the 2001 AERA annual meeting, scholars of diverse backgrounds presented a number of best practices identified by the Commission. An intriguing exchange of linguistic and historical information between two scholars, Josianne Hudicourt Barnes, from Haiti, and Hassimi Maiga, from Mali, about their cultural heritage illustrates the need for research that documents indigenous community knowledge. Hudicourt-Barnes informed Maiga that Haitian Creole speakers use a word that sounds like the Songhoy-Senni word for "earth" or "soil": "labu" (or might this be "la boue," the word for "mud" in French pronounced with a Creole accent?).

Another linguistic clue that deserves further research points to a possible historical connection between the Songhoy people and the Africans who were captured and taken from Benin to be enslaved in Haiti. Maiga's (in press) research on the Songhoy oral tradition and analyses of primary source documents in Arabic and French strongly suggest that the grandfather of Toussaint L'Ouverture, leader of the Haitian Revolution, may have Songhoy roots (Benin or Dahomey is the acknowledged origin of many Africans enslaved in Haiti). The origin of this powerful Haitian family of warriors may be Gao, Mali, the cradle of the Songhoy Empire, also known for its military prowess and warrior tradition. Toussaint's grandfather's name is recorded as: "Gao-Genu," a possible transformation of "Gunu," a word that identifies a branch of the Songhoy people (Maiga, 1996). Using indigenous community knowledge to uncover such interconnections could help to recover forgotten historical links among the "amnesiacs" of the African Diaspora. As Randall Robinson (2000) argues so forcefully, knowing "who we were and, therefore, are" is important to Black people's collective success today and in the future. Such research also has important implications for curriculum content and the professional development of teachers and scholars in this domain—here and globally.

A goal of culturally nurturing transformative education and research practice, then, is to reconnect students to their identity as members of the global African family in ways that also increase their motivation and engagement with the learning process. Teachers with this orientation and understanding are able to create powerful learning opportunities that build on students' prior funds of cultural knowledge as well as the untapped knowledge that is available within their communities and their cultural heritage (Goodwin & Swartz, 2004). The students Carol Lee has taught in her "Cultural Modeling" applied research program using African American discourse as cognitive scaffolding pedagogy, "remember" their culturally grounded rhetorical abilities as they acquire new interpretive skills in responding to literature. Such research, conducted in uncensored, "liberated space" free from hegemonic categories of the research establishment, can serve as a form of social action to enable students (and teachers) to reclaim lost identities and memories.

In conclusion, the invited commentaries in this volume prepared by scholars in Africa, Brazil, and the United Kingdom all suggest further research that is needed in their countries. Both the TERC group and the Wheelock College teacher education program, also featured at the 2001 "Educational Excellence Expo," provide examples of the benefits of community-mediated education and research practice for student and teacher learning. Extending this research to include cross-national collaboration is a logical next step. However, the question is: Where is the funding for education and research in the interest of nurturing and rebuilding the cultural consciousness of the people of the African world? Or for oral history investigations and the translation of primary documents in which such knowledge is to be found?

Article 3: Resisting Hegemony/Domination/Dispossession Culturally

We require power and influence over our common destiny. Rapid globalization of the economy and cyber-technology are transforming teaching, learning and work itself. Therefore, we require access to education that serves our collective interests, including assessments that address cultural excellence and a comprehensive approach to the interrelated health, learning and economic needs of African people.

—CORIBE Vital Principles

It is a reproductive and circular system, a power-knowledge-economics regime in which the financial gains of a few are reinforced by what can count as school (thus social knowledge), and in which what can count as knowledge is determined so as to support the financial greed of corporations.

—K. D. Vinson & E. W. Ross (2001, p. 38)

Powerful interlocking relationships and structures connect the control of education and the economy, locally and globally. A transformative research and action agenda in Black education addresses this social totality and asks how African people can and are resisting hegemony, domination, and dispossession *culturally*. Precise language and constructs are needed to decipher and illuminate the social totality. For example, the relationship among privatizing schools and prisons, mass incarceration in the United States, and the abandonment of the social infrastructure in the spaces African people occupy—whether in the central cities in the United States, other parts of the Diaspora, or the African continent—need to be explicated and communicated in ways that permit "ordinary" people, as well as researchers, educators, and policy makers, to understand what is at stake and what is causing such social misery throughout the world, but, particularly, in the global South. Undoubtedly, such explication and social explanation will challenge myths and folk beliefs in the popular imagination and in academic scholarship that suggest that poverty and underdevelopment (including crime and violence), for example, in Africa and Diaspora communities, are the inevitable result of Black people's biological (natural) degeneracy, genetic defectivity, congenital laziness, and failure to internalize the "virtues" of middle-class/Western civilization or their "fears of acting White." Claude Steele's (1992; Steele & Aronson, 1995; Steele et al., 2002) experimental research on how "stereotype threat" undermines Black student performance and engagement in school and the "acting White" explanation (Fordham & Ogbu, 1986) of Black student failure to achieve have attained the status of near orthodoxy in teacher education. (For alternative interpretations of the "disidentification" hypothesis and "oppositional-culture" explanations of racial disparities in educational achievement—which do not receive the same level of media attention—see, for example, Foley, 1991; Horvat & Lewis, 2003; King, 1994; Morgan & Mehta, 2004.)

An important area for applied research and action that CORIBE explored is the development and assessment of intergenerational learning-by-doing pedagogical tools for educating young people about and for engaging youth in alternative strategies for community economic empowerment using local knowledge and cultural practice as an asset (Nembhard, Chapter 10). That is to say, it is necessary to go beyond the benign volunteerism of the service learning movement in education. Participants in the "Detroit Conversation," a research priority panel discussion that CORIBE convened, cited numerous examples of the benefits of community-based learning. (King & Parker, Chapter 11, discuss the CORIBE documentary video: "A Detroit Conversation.") Empirical research is needed to investigate what happens to our understanding and consciousness (including teacher and student motivation) when euphemisms like "at-risk" students that mask the structures of domination and ideology are replaced by constructs such as: "miseducation," or "imperialism" for "globalization," or "structural joblessness" or "never-employed" for "unemployment." Instead of "structural adjustment," for instance, do terms such as "reconcentration and monopolization of wealth" deepen our understanding (Petras, 2001)? For that matter, what difference does it make to human consciousness and understanding if schools are said to be "under-resourced" rather than "resource-starved"?

Democratic Alternatives. With the practical insight of a teacher-turned economist, Jessica Gordon Nembhard's research (see also Chapter 10), analyzes interconnections between cooperative economic development strategies and school reform. She has been "investigating the theory and practice of democratic economic participation and wealth creation, and economic strategies for the sustenance of humane community." Her research suggests that cooperative education and education about cooperative economic principles "enhances school curricula and gives teachers more strategies with which to motivate students to achieve, and prepare them to be productive members of their community" (personal communication, February 2001). Nembhard and Curtis Haynes (1999) conclude that:

> Conditions for cooperative economic action, therefore, exist in urban areas, particularly when understood as an extension of the rich history of self-help in both immigrant populations and among African American communities. Combined with the numerous attempts by African Americans to implement self-determination through collective actions, deliberate and coordinated cooperative economic activity becomes a rational (even promising) strategy for economic revitalization in inner-cities. Moreover, economic development can be built on a collective and cooperative movement that has always been a part of the "American tradition," whether organized through religious, worker, ethnic or racial groupings. (p. 57)

An excellent example of transformative Black Studies scholarship that could inform this pedagogical approach can be found in Clyde Woods's (1998) analysis of the historical emergence of the "blues tradition" as an alternative culturally democratic, sustainable, and cooperative development path in contrast to the "arrested development" of the plantation regime in the Mississippi Delta region. Woods provides this illuminating interpretation of the origins and social significance of the blues:

Emerging out of the rich tradition of African song-centered orature, and under conditions of intense censorship, secular and sacred songs became fountainheads of cultural transmission and social explanation. Furthermore, as a result of the extremely hierarchical class structure of Southern plantations, African American working-class thought would come to find its fullest expression in the blues: "a collective expression of the ideology and character of Black people situated at the bottom of the social order in America." (p. 56, *c.f.,* Barlow, 1989, p. xii)

Woods also suggests that: "This rich blues tradition remains as relevant today as it was two centuries ago. It is the only basis upon which to construct democratic, sustainable, and cooperative communities" (p. 272).

Not only are the blues, or this interpretation of African sacred and secular music, not usually taught in schools or in teacher education programs, the historical tradition of cooperative enterprise development and wealth creation by African people, in the United States, in other Diaspora regions, and in Africa, are also not taught. For instance, the complex economic infrastructure within the classical West African empires (Ghana, Mali, Songhoy)—not just their roles as "trading states," the economic prowess and ingenuity of African market women, Madame C. J. Walker's million dollar business conglomerate, the phenomenal economic success *and* the horrific destruction of Tulsa, Oklahoma's "Black Wall Street" (Wilson & Wallace, 1992), as well as the southern Black farmers' cooperative movement are notable examples. As a result of such omissions, neither students nor teachers can develop an appreciation of the *economic* genius that is also part of the heritage of African people.

If Woods is right, then transforming the curriculum, creating alternative uncensored liberated learning spaces, like the Freedom Schools of the Civil Rights era, and identifying and supporting programs that may already be so engaged also are priorities for transformative research and social action (Perlstein, 1990). UNESCO recognizes the importance of preserving and promoting culture and heritage as a basis *for group self-development;* however, the U.S. curriculum and pedagogy lag behind in this crucial area and further applied research and policy development are needed.

Global Cultural Dispossession.   In Mali, youth are enthralled by daily television images of Tarzan (produced by a Spanish company), Brazilian soap operas, and the *Fresh Prince of Bel Air,* an American export with (White) French voiceovers. Camille O. Cosby's (1994) research documents the devastating impact of "television's imageable influences" on the group self-perceptions of Black youth in the United States. To prepare youth of African descent in these apparently different contexts to face common impediments to our collective success in the new century applied research is needed to address how our youth can learn to create wealth in their communities (and countries) using alternative culturally nurturing, cooperative community building strategies rather than remain captives of the global consumer-driven, corporate-controlled hip-hop industry's celebrity model of generating wealth for a few individuals (or the NBA "superstar" basketball route to individual wealth). The popular illusion, fed by corporate media distortions, that Black people (and the entire African continent) are economically obsolete (and morally dissolute) contributes to young people's enchantment with "ghetto fabulous" economic fantasy. Moreover, it is generally the case that the appropriation of African and African American (material and nonmaterial) cultural products, in particular, is extremely viable economically—but not for the benefit of Black people or communities. The profits hip-hop artists and films *about* Black people generate for others, especially in foreign markets, is indicative of this viability. It also is worth noting that the Hollywood film industry has used ethically questionable research and marketing methods to test-market violent X- and R-rated films, movie trailers, restricted video games, and commercials, targeting not only children as young as 9 years old but also African American and Latino youth in particular (see "How the Studios Used Children to Test-Market Violent Films," 2000).

As participants at the CORIBE working colloquium emphasized, *economic illiteracy* obstructs this generation's opportunity and responsibility to become engaged in cooperative economic development in the collective interest of the African community-family. Therefore, the economic arena cannot be neglected if transformative education research and practice, and human freedom, are the goals. Interconnections between the profits the prison industrial complex generates and the profits corporations are seeking via privatized urban schools and welfare "reform" should not be overlooked. As Brent Staples (2004) observes in the *New York Times*: "The business of building and running the jailhouse has become a mammoth industry with powerful constituencies" and many states are forced to choose between "building jails and building schools". Historical parallels between the business interests involved in the state-sponsored system of debt peonage, which was the milieu in which the blues emerged, and state-sanctioned privatized prisons operated as for-profit businesses today, the milieu in which hip-hop has emerged, are worth considering. If debt peonage opened the door to both imprisonment and disenfranchisement in 1875, do school failure, mass incarceration, and a pseudoeconomic draft today serve the same hegemonic social functions of exclusion and political containment? How can education and research practice contribute to the potential for resistance that cultural forms of expression often represent? Indeed, to paraphrase the renowned Trinidadian radical scholar C.L.R. James (1970): the capacities of men and women are always "leaping out of the confinements of the system" (p. 138).

Article 4: Using a Liberatory Cultural Orientation as an Analytical/Pedagogical Tool

> The "ways of knowing" provided by the arts and humanities are often more useful in informing our understanding of our lives and experiences and those of other oppressed people than the knowledge and methodologies of the sciences that have been privileged by the research establishment despite the often distorted or circumscribed knowledge and understanding this way of knowing produces.
>
> —CORIBE Vital Principles

> Can you hold the title of *human* without having a consideration for the development of humanity?
>
> —KRS-ONE (2003, p. 42)

In her research for the Commission, Carol D. Lee refers to the importance of a "community calling" in Black education and pedagogy that can include teacher preparation as well as research practice. Like Elleni Tedla's (1995, 1997) emphasis on *Yelougnta*, which means "community-mindfulness" in the Amara language of Ethiopia, privileging community well-being, and the welfare of humanity, is at the conceptual and methodological center of transformative research and action in Black education. Literally, *Yelougnta* means: "What will they say?" Tedla explains that in "cultivating community mindfulness":

> ... we need to regularly ask ourselves: "Are my actions/ thoughts /motives beneficial?" "If the community knew my thoughts/actions /motives, what would they say?" "If the earth, the plants, animals, birds, fish and insects could speak, what would they say about our/my relation with them?" "Have our/my actions been beneficial to them?" (p. 23)

Because, as Lee points out in Chapter 4, "the African American community is and has been under political and cultural assault," and although the struggle for freedom has changed over time, "the need for continuous struggle has not." Therefore, producing knowledge and understanding for "socializing and apprenticing" African American students (at all levels) "to participate in the struggle for the continuing liberation of the African American community" (and the Africana community) are explicit goals of transformative research and action in Black education. That is to say, "our collective survival and enhancement must be our highest priorities" (CORIBE Vital Principles). Thus, research-based pedagogy in the area of sustainable, environmentally sound community development is another important element of an agenda for transformative research and action in Black education, here in the United States and on a global level. If this ethic of community-mindfulness is applied to the education and socialization of all students, then prospective teachers, in the normal course of their liberal arts studies, also will have opportunities for truthful engagement with their own heritage and with the heritages of diverse others as well (King, 1997). Moreover, all students will be prepared for real democracy, for more effective and engaged citizenship.

A LIBERATORY CULTURAL ORIENTATION

Providing education that engages community-mindfulness and rebuilding the community, physically, spiritually, and culturally, is one of the strongest recommendations that emerged from the research priority discussion the Commission convened in Detroit in 2000 (Chapter 11). The diverse panel of educators and activists suggested that research is needed to support and to document the effect of community-oriented education experiences on student learning and engagement *for the benefit of humanity*. For example, Grace Lee Boggs, one of the co-conveners of this community dialogue, commented that:

> ...a high school in Brooklyn, New York, founded by a former member of the Young Lords...patterned on the Black Panthers and which is called the El Puente Academy for Peace and Justice [is]where the young people do rehab[ilitation] work in the community and plant community gardens. Everybody notices that this gets their cognitive juices racing. In Detroit, we have teachers working with the Detroit Agricultural Network, like Paul Weertz, who has his students planting fruit trees and working on his Hay and Honey Farm. In my neighborhood there is a Kwanzaa Garden that was founded by a parent and science teacher at a school based on the Kwanzaa principles of Cooperative Economics and Collective Self-Determination ("A Detroit Conversation").

Chapter 11 includes the voices of practitioners and community activists who participated in this conversation. The chapter includes Grace Boggs's analysis of transformative thinking and action that are needed to rebuild and "respirit" our communities based on her more than half a century of "living for change" in Detroit (Boggs, 1998).

Lee's research for the Commission draws attention to impressive student learning gains that activist scholars Paula Hooper, Alan Shaw, and Nichole Pinkard have produced using a community-minded cultural approach to instruction in technology-based environments they have designed. These young scholar-activists have designed pioneering technology-based applications that use African American cultural content to bridge cultural practice, cognition, and community. The dissertation work of both Hooper and Shaw, African American graduates of the prestigious Massachusetts

Institute of Technology Media Lab, has been showcased at CORIBE presentations. Hooper and Shaw cite Bob Moses and the Algebra Project, another CORIBE exemplar (see Lee, Chapter 4) as a source of inspiration. Legendary Civil Rights movement activist and Algebra Project founder Bob Moses describes The Algebra Project as "organizing in the spirit of Ella Baker" (Moses & Cobb, 2001).

A recent conference of the National Association of Minorities in Cable notes that the "digital divide" may be because of the lack of relevant online content more so than simple lack of access. The Commission was explicitly interested in exploring a role for technology in transformative Black education and research. Several model programs that CORIBE identified, developed by African American and Native American innovators, were presented at the Education Braintrust of the Congressional Black Caucus (CBC). A recent doctoral research project funded by IBM and Intel at the Georgia Institute of Technology demonstrates other impressive possibilities for developing community-mindfulness using a technology-based pedagogical tool. Jason Ellis's (2003, Ellis & Bruckman, 2002) dissertation, *Palaver Tree Online*, involves the design and implementation of an online community that supports youngsters interviewing elders to build up a shared oral history database. Within this environment, youth and elders work together to explore the life stories of the elders and to build artifacts online that share these stories with the world.

Consistent with the liberatory cultural ethos of the Africana worldview perspective, the interactive Website (http://www.coribe.org), Web-enhanced demonstration projects, and research-based graduate student apprenticeships that CORIBE developed explored new online content and inquiry methods that include a "community calling." For instance, participants entering the OnLine Graduate Research Training Institute course site experienced a visually and aurally powerful multimedia presentation of the traditional Negro hymn, "A Charge to Keep." While a choir sings this powerful song, an animated presentation of the names of African Americans who made significant contributions to the world in various fields—revered ancestors—scrolls across the screen. This emotionally moving presentation enacts the interrelationship between spiritual and intellectual ways of knowing and being in the Black experience and affirms their importance in the struggle to overcome mainstream cultural denial and scholarly alienation (Meacham, 2000). The remark of one scholar, in the idiom of the Black church experience, after her first visit to the site ("I didn't know I was going to have to shout") validates the intended message.

Annette Henry and Cirecie West-Olatunji (Chapters 18 and 19) describe two other technology-enhanced projects (the Online Institute and a Web-based study of the experiences of Black academics). With the aid of technology, the CORIBE initiative also reached far beyond AERA and the borders of the United States. The invited research commentaries contributed to this volume by scholars in Africa, Brazil, and the United Kingdom could only have been completed using the Internet and electronic mail. Also, the interactive online Database on Culture and its Transmission in the African World (DCTAW) that CORIBE scholars Mwalimu Shujaa and Nah Dove developed at Medgar Evers College with CORIBE support now operates as a fully functional searchable database of scholarly journals, many of which are not available in mainstream electronic indexes. This project, now housed at the African World Studies Institute at Fort Valley State University (http://www.dctaw.org), has established mutually beneficial partnerships with African institutions and scholars and is precisely the kind of research tool that Inter-Diaspora collaboration requires.

Another stunning convergence of global common interests underscores the importance of creating cross-national community-based education and research opportunities. A collaboration that began with a workshop on social change music in Mali, West Africa, and in Alabama has produced an ongoing exchange among grassroots "Black Belt" education activists in the United States and popular educators in Mali. Building on this collaboration, the former Malian Minister of Education (1992–1999), Adama Samassekou, and the Institute for Popular Education in Mali, in partnership with Rose Sanders and the 21st Century Youth Leadership Movement in historic Selma, Alabama, convened an "Inter-Diaspora Conference" in Bamako, Mali, in 2002. CORIBE Elder Asa G. Hilliard participated in this conference, entitled "Reclaiming Excellence through Rebuilding Education for the African Child Everywhere," which examined issues of "miseducation in Mali and in the Black Belt." Participants planned further collaborative learning and change strategy activities in preparation for future Inter-Diaspora meetings. With adequate support and the use of advanced technologies to overcome language barriers, such a conference movement/program, like the World Conference(s) on Indigenous People's Education (WCIPE), could provide new contexts and tools to expand cross-national pedagogical research, knowledge production, and exchanges between educators and grassroots activists in the United States, Africa, and other parts of the Diaspora (see for example, Moore et al., 1995; Rashidi & Van Sertima, 1995; Walker, 2001).

The Commission concluded that there is a significant role for cross-national initiatives in closing the "digital divide" in order to address Black education globally, through socially engaged learning and exchanges that focus on common problems and community building. Support for community-based learning in the arts (music, dance, theatre, museums, etc.) as well as development funding for African language study *with a liberatory pedagogical cultural orientation* are also critical. Teachers can easily link such study to content standards in history and global education as well as other disciplines. Such Inter-Diaspora learning, if it is to combat the corporate media's identity-destabilizing effects, requires new pedagogical tools to overcome language barriers and to bridge technology gaps. In addition, research and pedagogy in the area of sustainable and environmentally sound community economic development is another important element of an agenda for transformative research and action in Black education here in the United States and on a global level. It is particularly urgent to find ways to engage youth in such action-oriented grassroots research. The Internet, distance learning, and advanced technologies (e.g., video teleconferencing) can support cross-national exchanges and sharing among African people that are especially designed to involve youth in developing solutions to real and pressing social, environmental, and economic problems in their communities. (A program developed by the Links, Inc., with UNICEF and the Embassy of South Africa in New York, demonstrates effective use of video teleconferencing to link youth in the United States and Africa in an annual exchange of views about common concerns. This annual video teleconference commemorates the "Day of the African Child" and the Soweto massacre in South Africa.)

RESEARCH INNOVATIONS AND INNOVATORS

Two recent empirical investigations—one focused on students and the other on curriculum and pedagogy—illustrate conceptually and methodologically innovative research approaches that are pertinent to understanding and supporting the kind of teaching and learning that Grace Lee Boggs and Carol Lee also describe. First, Daniel Solorzano and Dolores Delgado Bernal (2001) use a Critical Race Theory framework, qualitative inquiry and "counterstorytelling" methods to examine the construct of Chicano/a student resistance. The authors suggest that this construct has been "overlooked and understudied in sociology of education research." They contrast this study with previous investigations in resistance literature that are marred by theoretical and conceptual limitations. That is, earlier studies of student resistance have focused on the self-defeating oppositional behavior of working-class White males rather than forms of resistance among Chicano/a that can lead to social transformation. This study extends the concept of resistance "to focus on its transformative potential and its internal and external dimensions" (p. 308). The authors analyze transformational resistance from a panethnic Chicano/a Critical Race Theory perspective that takes multidimensional Chicano/a identity into account. This study reveals new possibilities with regard to a *pedagogical role* for transformative research in developing a deeper understanding of and support for resistance to societal injustice.

Second, Vernon Polite (2000) conducted a study of effective Catholic High Schools that serve predominantly African American student populations. Among the characteristics of these schools that contribute to Black student learning and development, Polite identifies a four-category curriculum continuum that is especially noteworthy: From (Category 1) education to teach basic knowledge and appreciation of African American culture and history (particularly as it pertains to the Catholic Church) to (Category 4) education to prepare agents of social change for the betterment of African American people (particularly Catholics of African descent in the United States). Of particular relevance is the fact that Polite found no schools in Category 4, which "represents an ideal of education to promote social change or relief to social problems affecting the African American community" (p. 151). Nevertheless, Polite chose to include this category in order *to illuminate further transformative possibilities*: "The goal is to prepare students to become productive adults with the knowledge of true social justice and the skills needed to transform the African American community economically, politically, socially, and spiritually" (p. 151).

The Freedom Schools of the civil rights era constitute another precedent for community-minded social justice teaching in Black education (Perlstein, 1990; see also King & Parker, Chapter 11). African-centered schools throughout the United States (Lee, Chapter 3) and the Islamic Clara Muhammad Schools (Muhammad, Chapter 12), exemplify the liberatory tradition of cultural excellence and resistance in independent and religious-based education Black communities have organized historically (Akom, 2003). The role of spirituality in Black education in various settings merits further investigation (Nasir & Kirshner, 2003).

Finally, the arts and humanities, particularly the work of activist artists in schools and community contexts, constitute another untapped reservoir for promoting understanding and developing pedagogical tools for students and teacher development that support community-mindfulness (Washington, 1982). The Color Line Project, a community-based oral history theatre program that is conducted collaboratively with university academics and local activists, is an outstanding example of transformative education through the arts. Mediated by community knowledge and collective African American cultural memory, this project is the brainchild of the activist actor John O'Neal, Founding Director of Junebug Productions, Inc., who is also a founding codirector of the Free Southern Theatre, and like Bob Moses, also is a former Student Non-Violent Coordinating Committee (SNCC) organizer. The Junebug Web site states: "Cultural development and community development are inter-dependent" (http://home. gnofn.org/~junebug/about.html#anchor155022). The Color Line Project involves performing and archiving Civil Rights movement stories that are collected transgenerationally in various communities. Besides demonstrating the importance of identifying and making use of important sites, or "lieux de mémoire" for community memory (King, 1992), this project also illustrates an innovative strategy for creating culturally nurturing pedagogical tools. Better understanding of student learning, motivation, and engagement in the arts through research-as-pedagogy in extracurricular settings also can provide opportunities for teacher development and may lead to improved instruction and curricula in school as well as in after-school contexts.

A TRANSFORMATIVE RESEARCH AND ACTION AGENDA FOR HUMAN FREEDOM

The inquiries and activities of the Commission on Research in Black Education served to mobilize paradigm changing thought and action that advance a vision of Black education and research beyond a narrow focus on "closing the achievement gap," the urgency of this issue notwithstanding. In their e-book, entitled *American Schools*, Dwight Allen and William (Bill) Cosby (Allen & Cosby, 2002, http://www.bn.com) envision an expanded role for the federal government in education and for *better* research ("about teaching kids to read," for example). Their proposal for establishing a multibillion dollar federal agency, the National Experimental Schools Administration, to finance and oversee the production of this research differs markedly from the orientation of the current educational establishment. Noting that we need help to "evaluate and use" research appropriately (p. 44), Allen and Cosby conclude that "we must define experimental agendas that are bold, try out alternatives, and go beyond what we have tried in the past" (p. 237). Currently, the federal government's unprecedented expanded role in and priorities for education, codified in the dubious "No Child Left Behind Act"—though seemingly seeking equity and accountability—constitute a fundamentally different and more dangerous approach to education and "scientifically based research" (Bracey, 2004; Sunderman & Kim, 2004). The Commission proposed, and the American Educational Association accepted, an agenda for transformative research and action in Black education that is globally inclusive and that takes culture into account. This agenda also takes into consideration the experiences African descent people share with other historically subordinated groups in the United States, Africa, and in the global South (see Appendix A).

As the Commission considered the questions discussed in Chapters 1 and 2, a number of concerns influenced the articulation of this agenda. These concerns, many of which are addressed in the following chapters, include: access to higher education in the United States, Africa, and the

Diaspora; the particular challenges facing Black males and females as they move through the education system, including education in two-year colleges; the demands of the "new economy," economic development, and community building in the context of corporate globalization; the quality of teacher preparation and the inequitable distribution of qualified teachers; curriculum access and bias; educational implications of the diversity among African descent peoples, including the Afro Chicano/a populations in the United States, Puerto Rico, other parts of the Caribbean, Mexico, and Latin America; as well as possibilities for "teledigital mobilization" within the Diaspora and alliances with others, including other communities of color. Supporting the development of the knowledge and understanding needed to address these complexities of the global educational crisis is one of the challenges facing members of AERA and the worldwide community of Black educators as well.

Although much progress has been made in articulating multicultural education standards (Banks, 2001) as well as the knowledgebase for effective teaching in urban schools (Goodwin & Swartz, 2004; Irvine, 2003), still unresolved within AERA are concerns about the role of non-Black researchers in Black education. As the 1997 AERA task force report (Gordon, 1997) noted:

> Minority researchers voiced a particular concern over the proliferation of research conducted by White researchers on minority populations and showcased at AERA meetings and in AERA journals. There was an outcry for ethical guidelines that will ensure that investigators who are conducting such work have adequate familiarity with the populations studied and that encourage collaborations between majority and minority researchers when research is conducted on minority populations. (p. 50)

A plethora of community-based organizations exist that are promoting alternatives to and challenging mainstream educational "reform" efforts. Many of these organizations can be reached through the Internet. For instance, the Center for Applied Research has developed standards in the form of a digital "Social Justice Report Card" for grading schools that can be downloaded from the "ARC" Web site (http://www.arc.org). Through its Web site the Advocacy Center for Children's Educational Success with Standards (http://www.accessednetwork.org), a national initiative of the campaign for fiscal equity, "seeks to strengthen the links between school finance legislation, public engagement, and standards-based reform." Local communities and non-Black researchers can benefit from the establishment of a "Clearing House" that provides information regarding these kinds of resources as well as contact with those producing best practices in research in Black education.

CONCLUDING COMMENTS

This chapter demonstrates the praxis of a transformative vision of Black education for human freedom in a civilized world and the research and action agenda that can actualize this vision. The CORIBE "Declaration of Intellectual Independence for Human Freedom" sets authoritative and authentic standards for putting this culture-systemic and global approach toward the crisis in Black education into action. AERA, educators in the academy and the community, and policy decision makers are encouraged to implement the recommendations for research and outreach, which are indicated by the Commission's inquiries and findings explicated in the chapters to follow. As we commemorate the 50th anniversary of the *Brown v. Board* decision and the 40th anniversary of the Mississippi Freedom Schools, James Brown's prescient lyrics offer further epistemological clarity about what remains to be done: "We got talents we can use on our side of town, let's get our heads together and build it up from the ground."

Part II

Taking Culture Into Account:
Learning Theory and Black
Education

INTRODUCTION

The long-standing affair the education research community has had with the idea that the experiences of being poor, a person of color (particularly African American and Latino), living in a community of people of color, predict failure in school achievement generally ignores the literature that documents the richness and complexity of experiences within such communities and families.

—Carol D. Lee, http://www.coribe.org

The chapters in Part II demonstrate how theoretical conceptions from the perspective of a "culture-systemic" analysis of Black education and a science of learning paradigm contrast with deficit perspectives that continue to predominate in establishment research and in prevailing views of Black students. Chapter 3, "The State of Knowledge About the Education of African Americans," introduces Carol D. Lee's two-part critical examination of learning theory and the implications for the education of African American children and adolescents. (The analysis continues in Chapter 4). In Chapter 3, Lee provides an incisive summary of emerging paradigms about learning rooted in the cognitive sciences and sociocultural learning theory, or "learning sciences." Lee explores how the state of research knowledge on learning intersects with the cultural orientation of many researchers of color and ways that conceptions of race inform how educational research considers the education of Black youth. Her analysis indicates the need for the powerful exemplars of culturally nurturing pedagogy that she also discusses.

Lee defines Black education along two dimensions: systematic efforts to teach Black children, particularly in the public sector, and the quality of education the Black community has historically organized itself around and particularly with respect to issues of cultural responsivity and community political empowerment. Historical and contemporary models of self-reliant education within the African American community, which have attended not just to cognitive but to affective, social, and moral development as well, provide evidence that learning can occur despite poverty and limited resources. Lee argues that Black children's readiness for school is highly underrated and that the longer they remain in public school, the weaker their skills become. In both Chapters 3 and 4 Lee suggests that technology is one of the areas where research and culturally grounded intervention can contribute to the struggle for Black education.

Next, in Chapter 4, "Intervention Research Based on Current Views of Cognition and Learning," Lee examines research programs in which African American scholars serve as principal investigators of projects with direct links between domain specific cognition and culture. The exemplary research Lee discusses demonstrates the usefulness of attending to culture and the relevance of students' prior knowledge in the design of pedagogy and learning environments for African American students, as well as for other students. Lee also notes that Black students are part of an international multilingual population group that includes speakers of African American Vernacular English (AAVE).

Also presented are seminal research programs of Euro American scholars that are grounded in cognitive theory and that take culture and equity into account. Finally, Lee discusses differential benefits between culturally responsive ways of teaching and other more generic pedagogical approaches, including Direct Instruction. Lee concludes that we need more discussion and collaboration among those researchers examining the influence of culture on learning and those who are studying advances made in the academic disciplines. Given the evidence presented in these chapters, that schools, programs, and proven pedagogy that offer effective instruction for African American students exist, Lee poses a question that merits urgent attention: *Do we have the will to educate all children to high standards?*

3

The State of Knowledge About the Education of African Americans

Carol D. Lee
Northwestern University

Our children have no idea who they are. How can we tell them? How can we make them understand who they are before the ocean became a furnace incinerating every pedestal from which the ancient black muses had offered inspiration? What can we say to the black man on death row? The black mother alone, bitter, overburdened, and spent? Who tells them that their fate washed ashore at Jamestown with twenty slaves in 1619?

. . .

Culture is the matrix on which the fragile human animal draws to remain socially healthy. As fish need the sea, culture with its timeless reassurance and its seeming immortality, offsets for the frail human spirit the brevity, the careless accidentalness of life. An individual human life is easy to extinguish. Culture is leaned upon as eternal. It flows large and old around its children. And it is very hard to kill. Its murder must be undertaken over hundreds of years and countless generations. Pains must be taken to snuff out every traditional practice, every alien world, every heaven-sent ritual, every pride, every connection of the soul, gone behind and reaching ahead. The carriers of the doomed culture must be ridiculed and debased and humiliated. This must be done to their mothers and their fathers, their children, their children's children and their children after them. And there will come a time of mortal injury to all of their souls, and their culture will breathe no more. But they will not mourn its passing, for they will by then have forgotten that which they might have mourned. (Robinson, 2000, pp. 217–218)

INTRODUCTION

The quality of education for African American K–12 students has been in a state of crisis since the close of the Civil War, when educating African Americans became legal. Through Jim Crow and inadequately resourced segregated schools, African Americans struggled to make education a tool to support community political empowerment and economic advancement for families. Now, in the 21st century, the demands of what it means to be educated are more rigorous and demanding than ever before. The capital of the 21st century is, without doubt, knowledge. Teaching to such rigorous standards is a fundamental challenge to the field of education, and a special challenge to the field is to learn to meet the needs of those who have been underserved by public education (Oakes, 1985, 1990).

The central question with which Chapters 3and 4 grapple is the state of research knowledge in Black education. Black education is defined along two dimensions. The first is the most obvious: systematic efforts to teach Black children in the United States, particularly in the public sector. The second dimension has to do with the quality of education that the African American community has historically organized itself around while considering issues of cultural responsivity and community political empowerment.

These chapters make a conceptual argument using empirical studies involving African American student learning as evidence. The claim explored in Chapter 3 is that explications of the current state of what some have come to call "the science of learning" is consistent with many of the principles that African American culturally responsive educational researchers and philosophers have argued. This chapter examines current paradigms in the science of learning that offer meaningful ground for dialogue among research communities that have been largely separate. The chapter begins with a focus on views of Black children's readiness to learn and then provides historical background on the education of African American children and adolescents. This review illustrates the antecedents of calls to link the cognitive goals of schooling with cultural and political empowerment goals (Bond, 1935, 1976; King, 1990). A summary and critique of the emerging paradigms about learning that are rooted in the cognitive sciences and in sociocultural theory follows. The goal is not to provide an extensive literature review but, rather, to explore how the state of research knowledge on learning intersects with the cultural orientation of many researchers of color. The goal is also to explore the ways that conceptions of race inform how the field of educational research considers the education of Black youth (Lee, 2003a).

VIEWS OF THE BLACK CHILD

In studies of Kikuyu infants from Kenya, East Africa, on mental and motor tests Geber (1958) concluded:

> [their] . . . precocity was not only in motor development: it was found in intellectual development as well. . . . Although most of the African children had never seen anything resembling the test material, they used it in the same way as European children and succeeded in the tests earlier than those children. (cited in Wilson, 1992, pp. 37–38)

Bayley (1965) and Leiderman (1973) reconfirmed Geber's findings. Jackson and Jackson (1978) reviewed numerous studies evaluating the mental and physical precocity of children and concluded that "overall, the greatest precocity has been found in Black infants, both in Africa and in the United States, followed by Indian infants in Latin America and infants in Asia.[1] Caucasian infants rate lowest on the precocity scale." The point here is not to argue for the superiority of any group of children over another but, rather, to argue that Black infants come into the world well equipped to learn.

Scores reported on motor/social skills, the Peabody picture test and verbal memory in the National Longitudinal Survey of Youth: Children 1986–1992, Females 1979–1992 show no significant difference in the motor/social development and verbal memory abilities between African American preschoolers and the total sample. For both African Americans and the total sample, girls score slightly better than boys. For the purposes of this argument, our interest is in the relative comparability of the achievement levels of African American preschoolers and the total sample. The only area in which there is a significant difference is vocabulary knowledge represented in the Peabody Picture test. This test is certainly the measure that is most culturally influenced. It is consistent with many other indices that African American vernacular and standard English practices are viewed more as deficits than assets (Cazden, 1988; Demeis & Turner, 1978; Smitherman, 1977). It is also not clear that the Peabody in its design takes into account language differences. Figure 3.1 summarizes the results from these measures.

Thus, on infant developmental scales as well as on measures of the verbal memory of preschoolers, the overwhelming evidence suggests that African American students come to school prepared to learn; this is despite

[1] I will use both the terms Black and African American. Black will be used more generically to those anywhere in the world who are phenotypically or self identified as a person of African ancestry. African American will be used specifically to refer to Blacks in the United States.

Test Scores of Preschoolers

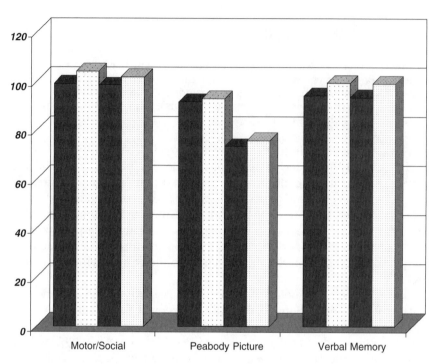

FIG. 3.1. Comparison of Black and White pre-schoolers.
Source: The National Longitudinal Survey of Youth. Children 1986–1992, Females
1979–1992 (cited in Nettles & Perna, 1997, *The African American Education Data Book,
Volume II*).

the perception of some teachers who have been known to report that poor
African American children are not prepared for kindergarten because they
do not know the alphabet or some other form of declarative knowledge.
This is not meant to suggest that knowledge of the alphabet provides no
advantage in reading readiness as children enter kindergarten. Rather, the
argument here is that a lack of such knowledge does not pose an insur-
mountable challenge to learning to read between kindergarten and grade
one. (This point is taken up again in Chapter 4.)

Observations by some teachers are also inconsistent with the reports of
parents taken from the National Household Education Survey of 1993. In
this survey, there is little significant difference in what African American
and the total sample of parents report in terms of parent participation in
(1) telling children stories, (2) helping children with letters and words, or
(3) going to plays or concerts (Nettles & Perna, 1997). In addition, Figure 3.2

**Reading Levels of 5-year-olds as
reported by their parents: 1992**

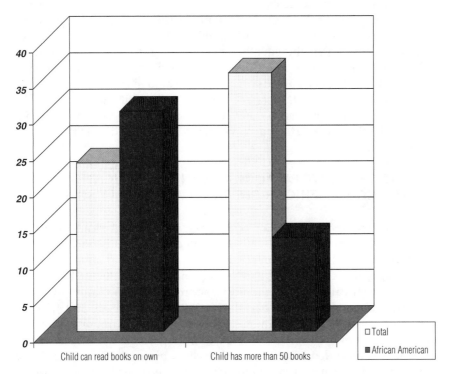

FIG. 3.2. Parent reports of children's reading.
Source: Nettles & Perna (1997, p. 22).

includes the self-report data from parents from that same survey. These parents reported that their 5-year-olds could read books on their own. However, there is a significant difference between the percentage of African American parents and those in the total sample who report that their child owns more than 50 books. This contrast can most likely be attributed to differences in economic resources as well as the distribution of bookstores in poor Black neighborhoods.

The question is not whether the perceptions of these parents are accurate. What is important is that the parents believe it to be so. In fact, it would appear from the results shown in Figure 3.2 that African American parents had higher expectations regarding their children than the mean of the total sample.

When one considers the relative comparability of the developmental levels of Black children from early childhood on, and looks with dismay at the huge differences in achievement once the children enter school, one wonders about the broad impact of U.S. public schooling on African American children and adolescents (Phillips et al., 1998). Dreeban and Gamoran (1986) found "that when black and non-black first graders are exposed to similar instruction, they do comparably well" (p. 667). Although there is clear evidence that the gaps between Black and White children (and other children of color—outside of some Asian American groups) have narrowed over the last 20 years, there is equal evidence that the gap is still huge and unacceptable (National Center for Education Statistics, 1997d). One could reasonably argue that the longer African American students stay in school, the worse their achievement becomes, relative to their white counterparts.

CRITICAL HISTORICAL ISSUES IN THE EDUCATION OF AFRICAN AMERICAN CHILDREN AND ADOLESCENTS

Any considerations of the state of research regarding African American children and adolescents need to be situated within a historical and political context. (Although issues in postsecondary education are of equal importance, this chapter will focus solely on issues related to K–12 education.) Historical and contemporary racism are symbiotically linked to the institutions of schooling and the institutions that shape and support educational research. In addition, a historical context is important for understanding the enduring questions surrounding the quality of educational experiences provided largely in public schooling for African Americans. The African Holocaust of enslavement perpetuated one of the most horrific devastations of humans in history. As part of the culture of enslavement, it was against the law for Africans to learn to read and write. Africans were known to have hands chopped off and were subjected to other forms of disfigurement when those who claimed to own African human beings discovered these enslaved persons engaged in learning to read or write.[2] Despite these unbelievable conditions, Africans hid books under the wooden slats of the floors of their meager cabins and in the dark of the night with the light of candles they would risk life and limb to read. After emancipation, the Freedman's Bureau sent representatives into the deep South to set up schools for the newly freed African Americans. There is an interesting

---

[2] I have consciously chosen not to use the term slave owner here. The use of the term African Holocaust to replace slavery is an attempt to lexicalize, to name the depravity of the historic event, a value judgment not represented in the term slavery. In a similar vein, the term slave owner attributes agency to those who claimed to own these African human beings, but at the same time denies agency to the enslaved human beings. Africans from the onset of this Holocaust resisted their enforced status as slaves and in myriad ways affirmed their humanness. My refusal to use the term slave owner is my attempt to acknowledge and honor that resistance.

question as to when to begin to refer to these Black people as African Americans as they did not become citizens until 89 years after the United States was established as a nation-state, following its equal decimation of the native population of this country. The Freedman's Bureau discovered that these newly freed persons had already established their own schools and resisted any interference from Whites.

John W. Alvord, national superintendent of schools for the Freedman's Bureau, reports in 1886 there were "at least 500 schools of this description . . . already in operation in the South" (Anderson, 1988, p. 7). Buchart (1980) attributes these self-help educational initiatives to African American communal values. In addition to secular schools, they also established what were called Sabbath schools, which operated in the evenings and on weekends providing basic instruction in literacy for those who could not attend regular schools during weekdays. In 1869, Alvord's field agents estimated, "1,512 Sabbath schools with 6,146 teachers and 107,109 pupils" (Anderson, 1988, p. 13). Whereas the segregated school systems that evolved under Jim Crow were clearly seriously under-resourced in contrast to white schools, Siddle-Walker (1993, 1996) documents how the segregated school served a communal function above and beyond that of pure academics. She describes the history of the Caswell County School where teachers and parents worked cooperatively to attend to the developmental, moral, as well as educational needs of young people. Political and economic dilemmas facing the community were negotiated with the school as the hub site for communication and school personnel serving pivotal roles. In discussing what Irvine and Irvine (1983) call the "historic Black community," Billingsley (1968) comments on the ways in which the community and the school served as dual socializing agents:

> In every aspect of the child's life a trusted elder, neighbor, Sunday school teacher, school teacher, or other community member might instruct, discipline, assist, or otherwise guide the young of a given family. Second, as role models, community members show an example to and interest in the young people. Third, as advocates they actively intercede with major segments of society (a responsibility assumed by professional educators) to help young members of particular families find opportunities which might otherwise be closed to them. Fourth, as supportive figures, they simply inquire about the progress of the young, take a special interest in them. Fifth, in the formal roles of teacher, leader, elder, they serve youth generally as part of the general role or occupation. (Billingsley, 1968, p. 99)

There is no question that conditions within the Black community have changed since the period Billingsley describes: the highest incidence of single-parent families in African American history, the greatest concentration of young African American men incarcerated, the most intense levels of violence within poor urban African American communities. In addition, teachers no longer live in the communites of the public schools they serve. As a consequence they are less likely to know parents and assume a personal responsibility for the academic social, and moral development of students. This is not to suggest that under-resourced segregated schools represent some kind of pure ideal toward which we should return (Edgar Epps, *personal communication*). Rather, it is to suggest that as we consider how to address the tremendous challenges of achieving equity in our schools, interventions that take community organizing and community partnerships as foundational to school reform, like The Comer Project (Comer, 1980, 1988) and The Algebra Project (Moses, 1994; Moses et al., 1989; Moses & Cobb, 2000), may well be models that need further investigation and funding. There are debates as to whether "fixing" the economic disparities between African American communities and middle-class White communities or "fixing" schools independently provide the most powerful solutions. There is no simple answer to this question. However, the historical models of the tradition of self-reliant education and socialization within the African American community provide evidence that learning can occur despite limited resources. This claim is made with the caveat that the intellectual and moral rigor of academic and community expectations in schools during the period from 1865 through the 1960s were clearly different from the emerging standards of expertise expected of schools today.

During this early era of African American education, there also were debates within and outside the Black community regarding the best pedagogy. Anderson (1988) and Lee and Slaughter-Defoe (1995) have argued for the following three models of education for African Americans: Euro-Classical Liberal Curriculum, Industrial Education Hampton/Tuskegee model and Education for Black Self-reliance. Table 3.1 summarizes pedagogical assumptions of each model: their manifestations during the period from 1865 through the 1930s and their contemporary manifestations.

THE RESPONSE OF AFRICAN-CENTERED SCHOOLS TO THE EDUCATIONAL DILEMMA

There is another approach to the education of African American students that may not be well recognized within mainstream research but is clearly rooted in the history of African American education. These efforts range from the illegal attempts of Africans under enslavement to learn to read and write, under threats of death and severe physical punishment (Harding, 1981), to the schools established after Emancipation by the newly "freed" Africans (Anderson, 1988), to the freedom schools of the Civil Rights movement (Howe, 1965; Clark, 1962). African Americans established these schools for the purpose of educating Black children, adolescents, and adults not only for personal intellectual development and economic

TABLE 3.1
Historical Models of Education Appropriate for African Americans 1860–1935 and Contemporary Parallels

Educational Models	Euro-Classical Liberal Curriculum	Industrial Education Hampton/Tuskegee	Education for Black Self-Reliance
Supporters	Northern missionary societies; White liberals; Blacks who supported liberal education	Booker T. Washington; northern capitalists; national, state and local White political leaders	W.E.B. Du Bois, William Monroe Trotter, Ida. B. Wells, Martin Delaney, Carter G. Woodson, Mary McLeod Bethune
Historical Sites of Operation	Black land-grant colleges; normal schools; missionary colleges	Black land-grant colleges; southern county school system; Hampton Institute; Tuskegee Institute	Schools set up by formerly enslaved Africans; Sabbath Schools; Black Literary Societies (Porter, 1936)
Key Characteristics	• Curriculum content drawn from Euro-classical traditions • Belief that understanding foundations of Western civilization is a necessary prelude to participation in democracy	• Train workers who are dutiful, hard working, and capable of contributing to the growing labor needs of the postwar South • Do not focus on politics and oppression • Train teachers for public schools	• Administration controlled by Black people • Curriculum reflecting African and African American cultural and historical traditions • Explicit goals related to political empowerment • Education to challenge existing political and cultural norms
Contemporary Parallels	Movement to integrate public schools without an explicit focus on the content and delivery of instruction that is culturally diverse and sensitive	Tracking in vocational programs and inequitable tracking in less challenging academic courses and special education	Freedom schools of the Civil Rights movement; Black independent school movement; Black Studies in higher education; Afro-centric curriculum movement; Rites of Passage movement

Source: Lee & Slaughter-Defoe (1995, p. 352).

opportunities but also as a tool in community efforts at empowerment (Lee, 1992, 1994; Lee et al., 1991; Siddle-Walker, 1993, 1996; also see Muhammad, Chapter 12, for a discussion of African American Muslim schools). African-centered schools exist as independent schools, as charter schools, as public schools, and through educational efforts of community-based organizations, including rites of passage programs (Ratteray-Davis, 1994; Ratteray & Shujaa, 1987; see also Lee & Slaughter-Defoe, 2003, for a review of this historical movement).

Rites of passage are based on traditional African systems of socialization through which young people are apprenticed to the roles they will be expected to carry out as adults in the community, including the knowledge base they are expected to master in order to carry out those roles (Warfield-Coppock, 1990, 1992, 1994a, 1994b). Rites of passage programs are being successfully carried out in cities and towns across this country by churches, community organizations, social clubs, and social networks. Although little in the form of formal research has been conducted on the impact of this movement, it is a clear sign of health and agency within the African American community. Rites of passage programs are also a model that some schools adopt as part of their socializing efforts and may well offer lessons about attending wholistically to students in ways that might meet some of the needs that traditional schooling in this country has not been successful in addressing (Tedla, 1995).

In one sense, the most direct legacy of the Freedom Schools of the Civil Rights Movement is the Independent African-Centered School Movement (Lee, 1993; Lee, 1994; Lee et al., 1991). The philosophies of these institutions are very much rooted in the intellectual legacies of Frederick Douglass, Anna Julia Cooper (1988), Carter G. Woodson (1933/1969), and W.E.B. Du Bois (1973). Current theorists of African-centered education and pedagogy include Haki R. Madhubuti (1990), Maulana Karenga (1993), Molefe Asante (1988), Asa Hilliard (1995), Kofi Lomotey (1990), Mwalimu Shujaa (1994), and Agei Akoto (1992, 1994), among others.

Many of the independent African-centered schools work under the umbrella of the Council of Independent Black Institutions (CIBI) (Lomotey & Brookins, 1988). CIBI was founded in 1972 and has schools in most major cities in the country. CIBI hosts an annual science fair in which K–12 students demonstrate their scientific understandings and relate their scientific investigations to concrete needs in the Black world. CIBI hosts professional development activities for member and non-member schools, includes a system of accreditation for its member schools and publishes African-centered curriculum materials (Council of Independent Black Institutions [CIBI], 1990). A testament to the longevity of these institutions, alumni from CIBI schools can be found in prestigious colleges and universities around the country. CIBI institutions take pride in their attention to cognitive, social, moral, and civic dimensions of children's development.

Other independent Black institutions are not members of CIBI but claim similar goals. One notable example is the Marcus Garvey School in Los Angeles. Garvey is recognized nationally for the extraordinary achievement of its students on standardized tests. Garvey includes both elementary and high school programs. Sankofa Shule in Lansing, Michigan, the Betty Shabazz International Charter School of Chicago and Aisha Shule of Detroit (discussed in Chapter 11) are African-centered charter schools, another growing category of African-centered K–12 schools. All also boast high achievement on standardized measures. This perspective on the education of African American children deserves further attention from the research community (Ratteray & Shujaa, 1987; Slaughter & Johnson, 1988). These institutions offer interesting examples of schools as communities, schools that are culturally responsive and schools that are proactive in conceptualizing the holistic developmental needs of children.

The lessons from this historical view of critical issues in the education of African Americans offer insights for consideration in current educational debates. First, from a traditional African American perspective, academic achievement is intricately linked to issues of political and economic empowerment, not simply for individuals, but rather for the national African American community. Second, traditional pedagogies in historically Black schools always attended to multiple dimensions of development, not just cognitive, but affective, social, and moral development as well (see, for example, Muhammad, Chapter 12).

The focus of this chapter will now shift to a discussion of the state of understanding of what has come to be called the science of learning. I believe principles that provide the foundation for this science are both sound and highly relevant to the design of learning environments for African American students. I also believe that the cognitive orientation seriously underconceptualizes affective and social aspects of the learning process and in so doing does not involve sufficient attention to issues of culture. Although the cognitive literature considers professional and domain specific cultures, the everyday practices, language uses and routines that are the stuff of ethnic experience are relatively ignored (Lee, 2003a, 2003b).

CURRENT UNDERSTANDINGS OF HOW PEOPLE LEARN: IMPLICATIONS FOR THE EDUCATION OF AFRICAN AMERICAN CHILDREN AND ADOLESCENTS

Two recent reports from the National Research Council (Bransford et al., 1999; Donovan et al., 1999) capture current understandings about how the mind works and how best to design environments to support learning. What is coming to be referred to as the learning sciences is a multidisciplinary framework that includes cognitive science, anthropology and linguistics (particularly sociolinguistics and discourse analysis). Learning sciences attempt to take into account the situated nature of learning and in the literature may be referred to as situated cognition (Lave & Wenger, 1991). For the purposes of this analysis, sociocultural theory is coupled as a handmaiden of situated cognition. Sociocultural theory (Rogoff, 1990; Vygotsky, 1978, 1987; Wertsch, 1991), which may also be referred to as cultural-historical activity theory (Cole, 1996), also shares much with what has been referred to as cultural psychology (Stigler et al., 1990). There is no question that theoreticians within these frameworks articulate the nature of their differences (Greeno, 1997). However, the interest here is not so much in the minutiae of their differences but, rather, in their sources of commonality. Thus, this section will summarize key findings and discuss some of the implications of this work for the education of African American children and adolescents.

Broadly speaking, the cognitive sciences provide the intellectual backbone for the findings in the reports *How People Learn: Brain, Mind, Experience and Schools* (Bransford et al., 1999) and *How People Learn: Bridging Research and Practice* (Donovan et al., 1999). Recent brain studies have allowed researchers to document structures in the brain that are utilized as people engage in active learning. This brain research, coupled with basic research in cognitive psychology, contributes to our emerging understandings about human mental functioning. However, Bruer (1999) cautions that many of the pedagogical pronouncements that claim to be supported by basic brain research are more wishful thinking than empirically supported. For example, from this perspective what human beings "know" is stored in long term memory. The meaning that we impose on experience helps us to build neural connections and to enhance connections across existing neural pathways. Thus, the coherence we impose on experience has much to do with how stable and structured our understandings are. The nature of this coherence and structure mark important differences between how experts and novices problem solve (Chi et al., 1981; Larkin, 1981, 1983; Wineburg, 1998). These differences tend to be very subject matter or domain specific. Thus, expertise in one domain does not necessarily increase the likelihood of expertise in another.

Another set of findings indicates that infants are born with the capacity to reason, with what appear to be certain domains that are privileged for development. These include physical and biological causality and number concepts. Learning is enhanced as people learn to monitor and self regulate their emerging understandings through meta-cognitive processes and strategies. Finally, the ability to translate understanding of one category or task to another depends on the extent to which the learner perceives lines of similarity across tasks. These broad principles represent a very attenuated summarization of what the field of educational research officially views as the state of the science of learning. Several broad overarching themes emerge from this body of work that are relevant to issues related to the education of African American children and adolescents. First, there is a fluid notion of the potential for human learning embedded in current theories. Second, prior knowledge plays a major role in learning. A third premise concerns the context in which learning is constructed. Each of these premises is discussed later.

Learning as Dynamic versus Traditional Conceptions of IQ. The idea that learning is fluid is a double-edged sword within the cultural and political arenas surrounding African American education. Static theories of IQ do not seem to fit this model. Static theories of intelligence as a finite capacity measurable by standardized measures have historically been used to categorize Black people as inferior (Scarr, 1981; Shuey, 1966) leading to lower, highly watered down academic standards. Current theories imply that as humans we come predisposed to learning, even from infancy on. Although clearly some people are born at the extremes of genetically influenced capacities (from persons with physically attributable mental retardation to persons with special giftedness in music or mathematics, for instance), most people, as understood from current views, are born with a broad band of capacities that are anchored in part by the built-in human proclivities for learning, in part by their own genetic configuration and in part by the coherence they construct from experiences in the world. Thus, our capacities to learn are dynamic and interactive (Frederiksen, 1986; Gould, 1981; Hilliard, 1976; Perkins, 1995).

The logical implications of these current understandings of the science of learning are that no class or group of people can be classified as being unable to learn because of innate capacity. Whereas, it may seem spurious to some to even raise this as a question, it is clear that at least in the United States, we are not beyond genetic inferiority assumptions. Progressives might feel some comfort in viewing Ku Klux Klan–like extremists as a fringe element; however, *The Bell Curve* (Herrnstein & Murray, 1994), as an academic publication, is merely a continuation of a long line of such pseudoscientific inquiries. In *The Black-White Test Score Gap,* Jencks and Phillips (1998), along with the other contributors to the volume, take a serious stab at addressing the question of genetic inferiority as a basis for the consistent gap in test score achievement between Blacks and Whites. In the broad sense, the volume assumes the progressive position that genetics are not the substantive basis for the difference in test score achievement. However, the mere fact that whether Black people are genetically inferior in terms of native abilities stands as a question worthy of systematic inquiry makes the strongest statement that the notion of Black inferiority remains a stable cultural theory within the belief systems of communities within the United States, North America, and Western Europe. If such assumptions were merely antiquated naïve folk beliefs, a mere legacy from the African Holocaust of enslavement, they would not continue to be the subject of serious academic investigations. We can hardly imagine investigations testing whether persons of Jewish ethnic descent are genetically equal to other human beings. It is an absurd question to pose.

Several comments in the Jencks and Phillips volume flag the continuing underlying assumptions about Black genetic inferiority. In the Introduction, Jencks and Phillips cite findings from the 1990 General Social Survey:

> The 1990 General Social Survey (GSS) asked respondents to rate various groups on a scale that ran from 1 ("unintelligent") to 7 ("intelligent"). Among white respondents, 31 percent gave blacks a score of 3 or less, 16 percent gave southern whites a score of 3 or less, and 6 percent gave all whites a score of 3 or less.... In 1977, 26 percent of whites agreed that... ["most blacks have less inborn ability to learn"] was one possible explanation for black poverty. In 1994, just before the publication of *The Bell Curve*, only 14 percent agreed. In 1996, only 10 percent agreed. This question almost certainly understates the percentage of whites who entertain doubts about blacks' intellectual ability... some whites probably think blacks are unintelligent for environmental reasons, and others are probably reluctant to report politically incorrect views. Nonetheless, we believe the downward trend is real. (p. 36)

Although it is heartening that Jencks and Philips believe such views to be on the decline, they nonetheless assert that such assumptions are still a real issue in the U.S. body and cultural politic. In the article "Race, Genetics and I.Q." (1998), Nesbitt summarizes and critiques the research that directly addresses a possible genetic basis to explain the difference in IQ test scores between Blacks and Whites. These studies address the possible genetic basis of such differences by studying the IQ and test score academic achievement data on "mixed race" children born from a Black and a White parent and on Black children raised by White families in White neighborhoods. Other studies, according to Nesbitt, address indirect arguments for the genetic basis for differences in IQ scores between Blacks and Whites. These studies interrogate the following warrants in the indirect arguments for genetic differences in native abilities:

1. "at every level of socioeconomic status, Blacks have lower IQ's than whites";
2. "Blacks and whites have different ability profiles.... For example, Blacks having an IQ of 105 are likely to be better than either low or high socioeconomic status whites at recalling digit strings, but they tend to be worse at solving mazes"; and

3. "Blacks do well or better than whites on tasks involving complex memory or reaction time. . . . The same racial difference applies to more obviously cognitive skills, such as form perception . . . and vocabulary" (p. 97).

Nesbitt concludes, "the most relevant studies provide no evidence for the genetic superiority of either race, but strong evidence for a substantial environmental contribution to the IQ gap between Blacks and whites" (p. 101).

Arguing from the construct of race to the construct of IQ leads to the problematic circle of research that has at its center questions regarding the very humanity of people of African ancestry. Hilliard (1976, 1991) makes a compelling argument regarding the unscientific basis of the construct of race. Deciding who is Black and who is not cannot be determined by either skin color or other phenotypic attributes alone nor by family history. That is, how much African ancestry does one need to be defined as Black? Hilliard argues that the construct of ethnicity is a more accurate and defensible category, one that captures everyday routine practices and the belief systems that surround them. Yet, ironically, the range of routine practices, belief systems and uses of language that are reflected in the cultural experiences of African Americans are as much under fire and suspect as presumptions of limited native abilities.

The Role of Prior Knowledge in Learning.   Such views about African Americans lead to the second problematic of the double-edged sword that surrounds the idea that knowledge is constructed from experience and that abilities may not be constrained by the assumptions of the normal curve distribution. I have noted that current theories of learning acknowledge both the power of the mechanisms for learning that are innate in all human beings and argue for a dynamic construct of ability that is tied to experience and effort. However, the significance of experience has also been racially problematized in educational research. Whereas the dominant pseudoscientific constructs about learning and ability from the nineteenth century forward were deeply rooted in assumptions of genetic inferiority, elements of the progressive educational research community from the 1960s forward argued not on the basis of genetic inferiority but, rather, that African Americans grew up in a deficit culture (Bereiter & Engelmann, 1966) that did not prepare children from this community to do well academically in school.

To make the point that what we are grappling with here is a strong cultural model, or belief system, this discussion incorporates evidence from both the educational research literature and the evidence of public schooling trends from the general society. Within the cognitive literature, experience is largely couched as prior knowledge. In a recent survey teachers complained that poor children came to school without knowing the alphabet, numbers, colors, or their full names. The extensive literature on the low expectations that many teachers hold of African American students is another aspect of this same cultural model of deficits within the African American cultural experience (Anyon, 1981; Baron et al., 1985; Demeis & Turner, 1978; Rist, 1970). These beliefs were fore grounded in the recent polemical debate over Ebonics that took place not only within the educational community but also was taken up by the general public (Delpit & Dowdy, 2002; Perry & Delpit, 1998; Smitherman, 2000b).

The argument is that prior knowledge has a major influence on learning. Prior knowledge provides learners with conceptual or mental models that we use to filter new knowledge. Depending on how it maps onto new knowledge to be learned, prior knowledge can either enhance learning by embedding new knowledge in a richer context; or it can be the source of misconceptions or naïve concepts (DiSessa, 1982). When learning environments do not provide explicit opportunities for learners to directly engage with the discontinuities between their misconceptions and the new target of knowledge, the abiding misconceptions remain stable, even after extensive teaching to the contrary. One often cited example is in the area of physics where high school and college physics students, despite formal coursework in physics, continue to use naïve theories regarding force (Clement, 1982).

This understanding of the crucial role that prior knowledge plays in supporting or constraining learning becomes racially problematized in relation to African American students. On the one hand, this principle regarding the role of prior knowledge offers opportunities to design knowledge building environments and artifacts to support learning that explicitly draw on the cultural funds of knowledge (Moll & Greenberg, 1990) of African American students. Ironically, research studies carried out by African American researchers that address prior knowledge as a support for learning tend not to have the visibility and level of funding as research carried out by largely European-American researchers who also take culture seriously in their design efforts. On the other hand, there has been a long tradition of educational research that views the prior knowledge constructed out of the cultural experiences of African American students as a deficit to be overcome, rather than as a resource. To make this distinction is not to imply that all forms of prior knowledge rooted in African American cultural experiences are of equal semiotic value to promote academic learning across domains.

As is the case with any human experience, such prior knowledge may be sources of rich connections for learning or may be sources of misconceptions or unproductive habits of mind that need to be overcome. The challenge has to do with having a flexible view on the question of prior knowledge of African American students, using criteria for determining the value of the prior knowledge that does not reflect a Eurocentric bias—a view that takes a deep understanding of subject matter expertise into account. This second criteria is offered in response to negative assessments of young African American children. For example, there are claims that some are not ready to learn to read because they come to kindergarten not knowing their letters and colors. Such observations reflect a very limited view of reading prerequisites. Whether such children recognize letters of the alphabet in isolation, it is highly unlikely in such a media-rich age that they do not have meaningful emergent literacy constructs that are useful resources for learning to read. (At the same time, we must acknowledge that circumstances of illiteracy do exist as documented in the Purcell-Gates [1995] study of some Appalachian families in which children had virtually no access to print.) In a similar vein, a criticism laid on low-income African American families was that many did not read to children at home. Using a set of middle-class norms, this criticism is not sensitive to the range of rich oral experiences available within the African American Vernacular English speech community (Champion, 1998; Heath, 1983; Morgan, 1993, 1998; Smitherman, 1977).

Although one set of warrants for the underachievement of African American students is based on the cultural deficit orientation toward experience, another argument is based on analyses of the political constraints on schools serving largely African American and poor students. A systems analysis makes the case that a complex of inequities institutionalized within U.S. society highly constrains the quality of educational opportunities for African American students. Several chapters in this volume explore these constraints in the United States (see, for example, Chapters 9–12) and in global contexts (Chapters 5–8). These inequities and systemic obstacles have persisted well after *de jure* segregation ended. For instance, demographics, especially in large metropolitan areas, demonstrate that urban and rural areas continue to be highly segregated by race and socioeconomic status (SES). According to the 1993–1994 Schools and Staffing Survey (cited in Nettles & Perna, 1977), 53.89 percent of urban schools have an African American enrollment of 50 percent or more, whereas 82.5 percent of rural schools have no African American enrollment (pp. 68–69). These patterns of school segregation are similar to more recent findings by Orfield (2001). Analyses attributing educational inequities to political and economic factors tend to be made by educational scholars with a leftist political orientation (Apple, 1982; Bowles & Gintis, 1976; McLaren, 1989). Historically, African American scholars and activists have made such analyses (Asante, 1988; Bond, 1976; Cooper, 1988; DuBois, 1973; Gordon, 1993; Hilliard, 1995; King, 1990; Madhubuti, 1990; Shujaa, 1994; Woodson, 1969). It is ironic, however, these African American voices of political resistance are not at the center of institutionalized conversations about the sources of inequity in the educational opportunities for African American students. This silencing of the voices of African American educational researchers, activists, and scholars has not been limited to those who focus on the structural roots of racism in education. As the analysis presented here is intended to demonstrate, such silencing has permeated the discourse within educational research. Delpit (1988) raised this very issue in her highly acknowledged article in the *Harvard Educational Review*, "The Silenced Dialogue."

This silencing is reflected in the percentages of African American tenured faculty in major research universities, the low percentages of articles published in major research journals, including all the journals of AERA, as well as the citations within the recent summaries of the state of the science of learning by the National Research Council, by the percentages of African Americans being funded by major private foundations and public funding agencies such as the National Science Foundation (NSF) and the Institute of Education Sciences. Although there is no question that these numbers are impacted by the overall low quality of educational experience available to the majority of African American K–12 students, even among the existing pool of African American Ph.D. holders in education and education related fields, the proportion tenured in major research institutions, published in major educational research journals and funded with major capital is extraordinarily small. To some degree, the unstated principle seems to be to identify a small constellation of African American educational research stars whose research is the work to be cited, usually uncritically. The converse principle seems to be to gain insight into one important finding about Black youngsters as learners and that finding then serves as a place holder to obfuscate the need for future research.

For instance, the findings of Michaels (1981) may serve to illustrate this observation. Primary level teachers organize a routine activity called sharing time where students bring in an object from home and tell oral stories about the object in front of their peers. The purpose of the activity is to give the teacher authentic opportunities to provide students with feedback on their oral stories. The goal is to lead the children to conceptualize the need for coherence and detailed description that will eventually be incorporated into an academic essay format. With a small sample size, Michaels discovered that low-income African American kindergartners told stories that did not center on a central topic. Teachers did not understand the point of the African American children's stories and therefore did not provide these students with feedback. Michaels came to call this storytelling style topic-centered. Despite more recent studies that have documented expanded storytelling repertoires for young African American students

(Champion, 1998, 2000; Hicks, 1991; Hyon & Sulzby, 1994), there has been a broad acceptance of this limited conception of oral competencies among African American young children. Michaels's argument, later expanded by Gee (1989), was a powerful one; namely that there were aesthetic strengths in the topic-centered storytelling style that needed to be scaffolded. My colleagues and I (Lee, Rosenfeld, Mendenhall, Rivers, & Tynes, 2003) have taken up one of the challenges from this work through the design of a curriculum that explicitly draws on oral storytelling strengths of African American children to promote narrative compositions in an academic setting. However, the generally unexamined assumption for several decades, that one oral narrative strategy based on a small sample size would be assumed to characterize millions of African American children, highlights the limiting way that research within the dominant educational research community has and continues in many ways to operate in relationship to African American students.

The Social Contexts of Learning. A third broad premise emerging from current views of the science of learning emphasizes the importance of the social contexts in which learning is constructed. In many respects, this third premise may be the most radical, reflecting a significant paradigm shift. Social contexts are extraordinarily complex, interactional, and dynamic. Currently, we do not have adequate research methodologies or analytical tools to study the social contexts of learning. Majority researchers align themselves with emerging frameworks, some called situated cognition (Lave & Wenger, 1991), everyday cognition (Rogoff, 1990, 1995), cultural psychology (Stigler et al., 1990), sociocultural theory (Wertsch, 1991), and cultural historical activity theory (Cole, 1996). Although there are clearly differences in some of the assumptions within these various frameworks (Greeno, 1997), they do share a set of fundamental attributes. This focus has been highly influenced by the work of the Russian psychologist Lev Vygotsky and his colleagues from the 1930s, and taken up by U.S. psychologists during the 1970s and 1980s (Wertsch, 1985), as well as by the work of psychologists who began to engage in cross-cultural studies of cognition in context (Lave, 1977; Posner, 1982; Rogoff, 2003; Saxe, 1991; Scribner & Cole, 1981; Serpell, 1982). However, ironically again, Black psychologists from that same time period—completely independent of the neo-Vygotskian and cross-cultural programs of research—developed a discipline called Black Psychology (Boykin, Franklin, & Yates, 1979; Jones, 1980; McAdoo & McAdoo, 1985; Nobles, 1980, 1986). Black Psychology argued from its inception that prior knowledge, cultural artifacts and belief systems and the interactions within social contexts were a central foundation for learning. To this day, the work of these Black psychologists is not reflected in the mainstream literature on situated cognition or sociocultural theory.

Apprenticeship

Rogoff (1995) has characterized learning within and through social contexts as analyzable on three interrelated planes: apprenticeship, guided participation and participatory appropriation. Apprenticeship includes the constructs, artifacts, tools and ways of reasoning that a society or cultural group inherits. Apprenticeship has historical dimensions. Wertsch (1991) asserts that what we inherit as apprenticeship models constitutes a kind of psychological tool kit that is flexibly available to us as we engage in problem solving. Bruner (1990) invokes a similar metaphor when he talks about the communal tool kit that narrative practices make available. Bruner argues that narrative practices within a culture provide us with tools through which to make sense and impose meaning and order on disparate experience. Such cultural groups may include professional communities like the international community of physicists or mathematicians; ways of acting that characterize organizations with intergenerational longevity such as the Girl Scouts (one of Rogoff's examples); or particular communities of practice within ethnic and language communities.

This last example is consistent with the argument that many African-centered psychologists, educational researchers and philosophers have repeatedly made (Ani, 1994; Asante, 1988; Du Bois, 1968; Karenga, 1993; King, 1976; Nobles, 1986; Stuckey, 1987). These scholars speak in terms similar to that of Boykin (1994; Boykin & Allen, 1988), who argues for what he calls an Afro-cultural ethos. Consistent with the earlier anthropological work of Herskovitz (1958), the argument is that Black people in the United States, in fact in the Western Hemisphere, have inherited and negotiated certain forms of social organization. These include: the extended family and the rituals and social networks characteristic of the traditional Black church (Billingsley, 1968); uses of language—African American English in its vernacular and standard varieties as well as the various creoles and pidgins (Mufwene, 1993; Vass, 1979) spoken, for example, in Caribbean nations—art forms (all the variations of music inspired and created originally within the Black community such as the spirituals, the blues, jazz, rock and roll, rhythm and blues), and other art forms such as dance (Asante, 1990)—all anchored to indigenous African, largely West African, cultural legacies.

These scholars have argued that a majority of African American students (including those whose families have migrated from the Caribbean as well as from Central and South America)—particularly, those who live in majority Black neighborhoods and communities—engage in everyday practices, language uses and belief systems that differ from the assumed mainstream of American, that is, United States cultural life. Consistent with the dialogic views of African philosophical traditions, being African and being American are not necessarily mutually exclusive. That is to say, Black children and adolescents can both live in interdependent cultural worlds that do not erase the influence of one or the other. Du Bois (1968) acknowledges this interdependence as an ever-present double consciousness among African Americans. This question of the cultural core of African American life is at the heart of the debates over how culture should be considered in the schooling experiences of Black children (Heath, 1999). Gutierrez and Rogoff (2003), however, argue that caution should be taken. All members of a cultural community do not share equally in the funds of knowledge and belief systems that may be seen to characterize group membership. Therefore, the relevance of experience to schools should be based on analyses of practice rather than solely on presumed cultural membership.

The metaphor of apprenticeship has been very pivotal in educational research informed by situated cognition and sociocultural theory. This metaphor of apprenticeship leads curriculum and intervention designers to focus on authentic problem based learning in which students learn through practice on real problems to take on the modes of reasoning and uses of strategies that characterize experts in academic domains. The idea is for students to learn to think and problem-solve like mathematicians (Ball & Bass, 2000; Lampert, 1990), like physicists (White & Fredericksen, 1997), or like historians (Seixas, 1993; Wineburg, 1998). Technology has been widely used to provide students with some of the tools for visualization and modeling that experts in the field use. In many respects, this analogy to apprenticeship is the dominant metaphor in current curricular design research. However, the way in which the apprenticeship metaphor has been adopted by many Euro American educational researchers does not take into account that there are communities of practice that are rooted in African American cultural norms that may well be relevant to the development of disciplinary knowledge for K–12 students. There are some lines of research by both Euro American and African American scholars that do explicitly explore such cultural resources and these will be discussed in Chapter 4.

Guided Participation

The second plane of analysis Rogoff identifies is guided participation. Focusing on the activity in which learning takes place, guided participation considers the role of social interaction within that activity, with special attention to the role that others play in supporting learning for individuals and for the group involved in the activity. The others may include less or more knowledgeable peers as well as experts such as teachers, parents and professionals. The idea is that people do not learn in isolation by themselves as individuals. According to Bahktin (1981), when people speak, even if by and to themselves, they are continuing a dialogue that began before them, using language, tools and modes of reasoning that, on the one hand, they have inherited from others and, on the other hand, that each individual appropriates in unique ways. Current cognitively inspired educational research argues for scaffolding and fading as principles that should be followed in designing support for guided participation (Bruner, 1959; Collins, Brown, & Newman, 1989). Intervention programs like reciprocal teaching for reading instruction (Palinscar & Brown, 1984) is one example of scaffolding and fading as explicit features of the design. Reciprocal teaching has been highly effective with low-income students, which presumably include significant percentages of African American students (Slavin & Madden, 1996).

The study of social interactions in classrooms has a long history of research related to the schooling opportunities for African American students. To a large degree, the research on mismatches between the cultural practices of classrooms and those of communities has focused on the norms for discourse among participants in classroom activity. Interactional norms evidenced by African American children in classrooms have been shown to influence low expectations held by teachers (Cazden, 1988; Delpit, 1986, 1995; Michaels, 1981). More recent research in discourse analysis offers new possibilities for understanding the complex, dynamic, and longitudinal nature of interactions within classrooms. Green and her colleagues in the Santa Barbara Discourse Group (Green & Dixon, 1994) have developed analytical tools for studying how participatory spaces are constructed over time. This dimension of time is crucial because the ability to identify moments in which African American students, for example, are silenced in classrooms does not tell us how patterned these moments are or the particular ways that such silencing is constructed as part of the norms of classroom life.

Gutiérrez, Rymes, and Larson (1995) have identified the scripts that teachers employ to direct the discourse in classrooms, whereas students who are not engaged by such scripts construct what Gutierrez calls counter scripts. Insufficient attention has been paid to what can be learned by investigating the counter scripts of students—what beliefs and values they hold, the ways in which they recognize the silencing co-created with teachers. What Gutiérrez calls the third space is a set of interactional norms in which teachers and students co-construct what is mutually meaningful and productive. Important in these observations on interactional norms is that what goes on in classrooms is never fully predetermined by teachers, by curriculum designers, by public policy makers, but, rather, is co-constructed within classroom life by teachers and students together. This sociocultural view helps us understand that neither teachers nor students come into the space called the classroom as blank slates. Rather each constituency brings both their individual characteristics and priorities as well as forms of prior knowledge and belief systems that they inherit from community life. From an African American cultural perspective, the analytical plane of guided participation calls on researchers to take seriously such cultural funds of knowledge as language use, as well as assumptions about schooling and knowledge construction.

Participatory Appropriation

The third plane Rogoff identifies is participatory appropriation, which focuses on the role that individual effort and intention play in how people come to appropriate learning. This plane of analysis is one on which too little research has been conducted by both mainstream and African American educational researchers. The efficacy of the individual seems to be lost on both those who ignore African American culture in the design of learning environments as well as those who advocate strongly for a cultural focus in educational design. Irvine (Irvine & York, 1995; Shade, 1982) warned against reliance on the literature on learning styles of African American children and adolescents to stereotype all African American students. Taking up the cultural argument from a learning styles perspective does not tell teachers, for example, that every African American student who sits before them will talk, act or think in a certain way (Gutierrez & Rogoff, 2003). Conversely, the cultural argument does assert that there are cultural funds of knowledge and ways of acting in the world that provide reasonable degrees of freedom in which to understand a pattern of variation among members of the African American community (Lee et al., 2003).

NEW METAPHORS FOR COMPLEX PROCESSES

This chapter has attempted to capture the central propositions of the emerging science of learning and important intersections between culture and cognition. The perspective on learning and cognition that emerges from this sociocultural paradigm shift takes into account the complex contexts in which learning is constructed and acknowledges the interactive and dynamic social supports for such learning. However, this conception of learning is not reflected in the folk beliefs to which, at least, the U.S. public ascribes. Behaviorist assumptions about learning, for example, pervade our discourse about teacher learning. Thus, the intellectual experiences that are expected to prepare students to become teachers are labeled "teacher training."

The argument is that a logical extension of the sociocultural perspective on cognition would lead educational researchers to think carefully about the experiences shaped by ethnicity and language use as they may be relevant to opportunities to learn. Such a perspective also would lead researchers to consider how students' funds of prior knowledge can be related to the knowledge to be learned in school contexts. It also would lead to reflection on culturally responsive kinds of interactions that expand opportunities for learning. This latter issue has been addressed to some extent in the sociolinguistic literature (Cazden et al., 1972; Cook-Gumperz, 1986; Gee, 1990; Gumperz, 1982), but not necessarily translated into standard pedagogical practices. Once the culturally situated experiences, language uses and everyday practices that are historically passed down and negotiated within the African American community become the target of focus in public discourse about education, the racism endemic to this country inevitably surfaces to shape tensions that arise.

Thus, under these circumstances the importance of expanding opportunities to learn through a focus on students' cultural assets—as the sociocultural paradigm suggests—becomes a very delicate argument to construct. On the one hand, Heath (1999) has recently cautioned that the public and educational researchers should not stereotype African Americans by ameliorating them into a unitary experience or language. As has been pointed out earlier, there is much diversity within the African American community—as with any other community. Heath is absolutely correct that both research and educational decisions need to create spaces for that diversity and to plan with that diversity in mind. Still, at least two issues are equally important. As with any other community, ongoing debate and tension exist within the community over definitions of identity and perspectives. That debate is healthy and helps to assure a range of propositions about what it means in this case to be African American. On the other hand, there is equally no question that within that diversity there are boundaries that define a uniquely and historically situated African American identity, range of language practices, forms of social practices, and communal belief systems to which I would argue a majority of African Americans subscribe. The public appetite, including that of the educational research community, to expect a singular African American face is fueled out of the legacy of racism in this country, more so than out of a political agenda of African American activists.

Moreover, we do not have appropriate language or metaphors to capture adequately the complexity of the dynamic model that the sociocultural paradigm suggests. This is partly because we do not sufficiently understand the dynamic quality of learning that the paradigm implies. Conversely, the lack of appropriate language or metaphors limits how we think about the question. Shuaib Meacham in "Threads of a New Language: A Response to Eisenhart's 'On the Subject of Interpretive Review'" (1998) offers a generative model that merits consideration. Although the subject of

Meacham's article is the genre of the research review, his comments apply as well to a research agenda or research design. Meacham says:

> ... research [should challenge] ... our perceptual habits and extend the language through which we construct and study educational questions and problems ... given the interconnected quality of many of our educational issues and problems, many disciplines need to be brought together simultaneously. (p. 405)

The sociocultural paradigm discussed here considers interconnectedness. The existing literature considers connections among individuals, groups, modes of reasoning, interactions within activity, and the role of tools, artifacts, and ideas in extending mental functioning. However, implicit in much of the literature is a univocal voice, a voice of homogeneity that does not take into account the ways that history, conceptions of race, ethnicity, language use, gender, and socioeconomic class weave inside and around individuals, groups, modes of reasoning, and so on. Many disciplines must be brought to bear on the educational issues that research attempts to address—cognitive science, anthropology, linguistics, human development, the academic disciplines (i.e., science, mathematics, literature, history, etc.), public policy, sociology, economics—but also different perspectives. Needed are the perspectives, for example, of Black psychology and the African-centered perspectives of many scholars and educators who believe that African and African American experiences need to be central in our queries and considered on their own terms. (Linda Tillman, Annette Henry and Cirecie A. West-Olatunji, in Chapters 17, 18, and 19, respectively, describe applications of African-centered perspectives in several research components the Commission on Research in Black Education supported.) As such perspectives come together in common inquiry efforts—that is, disciplinary perspectives alongside differing cultural perspectives—they interact in a kind of weaving, to use Meacham's metaphor.

Meacham (1998) goes on to say, "the connections are not inherent to the strands or predetermined, but would connect in improvisational response to specific contextual issues or conditions" (p. 405). Meacham suggests that the jazz metaphor of improvisation is a useful way to think about the research review, and by extension I suggest the enterprise of research. Meacham quotes from Berliner (1994) on the semiotic potential of improvisation:

> ... improvisers constantly strive to put their thoughts together in different ways, going over old ground in search of new.... By ruminating over formerly held ideas, isolating particular aspects, examining their relationships

to the features of others, and perhaps, struggling to extend ideas in modest steps and refine them, thinkers typically have the sense of delving more deeply into the possibilities of their ideas. There are, of course, also the rarer moments when they experience discoveries as unexpected flashes of insight and revelation. (p. 216)

Within the culture of jazz, improvisation requires that players share both a common vision of the music, while at the same time creating as part of their routine practice space, even supports for difference, difference that is both distinct and complementary. Improvisation requires attentiveness to the other. In a similar vein, Gutierrez (Gutierrez et al., 1999) has argued that hybridity—a conversational and ideational space in which difference meets—opens up new and creative possibilities for discovery that would not be accessible any other way.

CONCLUDING COMMENTS

This chapter has argued that the focus on social context offers perhaps the most radical paradigm shift in the emerging science of learning. This shift is radical largely because our levers for understanding and analyzing learning now cannot be simply situated on one plane: culturally inherited patterns of a group, social interactions within a group, or individual efforts. What is emerging is a dynamic and interactional model in which each of these planes contributes to learning and each is influenced by the other. That is, what a culture or group inherits is changed by the participation in activity, the norms of an activity are constrained by the artifacts, tools, and ideas that inform the work, and individuals change groups and cultural ways of knowing while individuals themselves are changed. We do not have adequate metaphors with which to conceptualize such dynamic interactions. As a field we are still tethered to behaviorist and experimental models that require the control of variables. Even though statistical modeling now can capture nested relationships and bidirectional moderators of outcomes, we still do not have in the social sciences adequate tools to capture the dynamic nature of human ecological systems (Lee, 2003a; Orellana & Bowman, 2003). However, as is the case with the shift from Newtonian physics to quantum physics—where light can be a particle or a wave depending on how one interacts with it—we need systematic ways to analyze dynamic systems (Holland, 1998; Wilinsky & Resnick, 1999).

As one example of the schisms in both traditional and current approaches to human learning, those who focus on cognition tend not to consider issues of human development; similarly, the developmentalists do not generally incorporate issues of cognition (Lee, Spencer, & Harpalani, 2003). When developmentalists do consider cognitive questions, they often operate on very stripped down notions of cognition and evidence of learning. Chapter 4 will present examples of intervention research that takes culture into account and that has been shown to be effective with African American students. Included are citations from the developmental literature of research by African American psychologists. For example, Wade Nobles, A. Wade Boykin, and others are among those African American psychologists who have consistently called on educators to attend to the affective and spiritual dimensions of learning. If the emerging model of learning just described holds, certainly how we impose meaning and significance on experience—a crucial element influencing what knowledge structures we hold in long term memory—must be influenced by emotional states, affective dimensions, including spirituality, as well as age and gender influences.

In some respects, the evidence presented in this chapter and the next suggests that taking up the mantle of the "silenced dialogue," as articulated by Delpit (1988), may be the lift our field needs to try to understand the truly complex nature of human learning and development.It may well be the case that what educational researchers, practitioners and public policy makers want to understand about this complex activity we call *learning for all*—rich and poor, Black and White, speakers of English and speakers for whom English is a second language—will be most enriched when we engage difference; difference in our research teams, in our research methods, in our research sites, in the way we conceptualize our disciplines. Once we learn to teach poor Black children, we will likely learn better how to educate all children.

4

Intervention Research Based on Current Views of Cognition and Learning

Carol D. Lee
Northwestern University

INTRODUCTION

This chapter continues the examination of "the science of learning" begun in Chapter 3. In this chapter the argument is that current views regarding the science of learning are not inconsistent with the frameworks invoked by African American educational researchers and others who have argued that culture, as defined by the experiences of ethnicity and language use, are valuable levers to support learning. Research programs in which African American scholars serve as principal investigators are examined in order to illustrate the ways the research of these scholars both links to current paradigms of learning and offer a critique of missing elements in those paradigms. The focus in this chapter is on African American students, but the principles apply across other ethnic and language groups. The purpose is to draw our attention as a field to the development of analytical tools and conceptual frameworks that take into account the dynamic interactions among cultural funds of knowledge, activity structures, and the individual's intentional maneuvering through the activity of learning across contexts. Learning in the real world is situated in a dynamic system, not one in which single variables are a deciding factor, nor ones in which participants in the activities of learning (both in and out of school) are passive blank slates or wells filled with useless knowledge, beliefs and feelings. This understanding of learning is not only the challenge for the effective education of African American children but of all children.

This chapter begins by examining the complementary perspectives between the learning sciences paradigm and interventions by African American researchers and educators that bridge culture and cognition. Two discipline specific cases, mathematics and literacy, as well as technology exemplars are presented next. The next section presents research that illuminates cultural resources that support academic engagement and coping for African Americans across the life span. A discussion of direct instruction and inquiry based approaches that are effective for African American students is followed by examples of small and large scale research by mainstream researchers that take culture into account in math and science teaching. The chapter concludes with a critical interrogation of assumptions and folk beliefs about culture and learning and addresses the need for culturally responsive pedagogy.

COMPLEMENTARY PERSPECTIVES BETWEEN THE SCIENCE OF LEARNING AND INTERVENTIONS BY AFRICAN AMERICAN RESEARCHERS

The following principles represent the state of our knowledge about the science of learning. The next several sections will discuss pivotal research agendas that illustrate the ways in which some researchers are designing educational interventions, curricula and professional development that embody these principles:

1. By connecting intentional learning or instruction to prior knowledge, learners enrich and contextualize new knowledge or learn to grapple with naïve understandings or misconceptions that could limit the development of deep understanding of the new knowledge;
2. The meaning or significance that learners impose on experience shapes how and whether knowledge is stored in long-term memory;
3. The ability to invoke relevant prior knowledge to new but related tasks—the problem of transfer—is highly contextualized and affected by the learner's conception of the target task;
4. The ways in which we represent our understandings may be domain specific, but are not limited to predetermined domain strategies—see, for example, the dieter who figures out three fourths of 1/2 cup of cottage cheese, not by invoking a formal mathematical algorithm but by putting 1/2 cup of cottage cheese in a circle on the table, dividing it into four equal pieces and taking out one fourth (Lave, Murtaugh & de la Rocha, 1984);

5. Ability is not static and finite. Thus, as human beings we literally build our brains through our engagement with experience; although there are pivotal periods when the brain seems more pliable to learn in areas like language development and periods where our cognitive development seems to move at a faster pace (i.e., young children versus the aged), there is no point at which as humans we are not capable of learning, no point when learning is impossible;

6. Through effort, monitoring our understandings and taking steps to adjust our strategies when we do not understand—that is, meta-cognition—we as humans exert influence over what and how we learn; such strategies and habits of mind are teachable.

Researchers in the studies cited below not only draw on the earlier stated principles but also utilize these principles in their analyses through a culturally responsive framework, taking African American cultural funds of knowledge explicitly and seriously as a foundation in some cases and as an integral part in others. These studies have African American students as participants and show positive results. They go against the grain of educational trends that show the longer African American students stay in school, the less they learn as measured by standardized assessments. Although there is no question that such assessments, on the whole, test isolated and less complex understandings (The Education Trust, 1999; Wolf, Bixby, Glenn, & Gardner, 1991), there is some relationship between one's ability to demonstrate competence in basic skills and to demonstrate competence in complex problem solving. At the same time, it is understood that the circumstances of testing—that is, timed tests and multiple choice question formats—also constrain how well one demonstrates competence.

CULTURE AND COGNITION

In the examples presented in the following sections, all of which address both current views of cognition as well as culture and the educational needs of African American students, research in which African American scholars are the principal investigators is discussed separately from research by scholars of other ethnic backgrounds. This separation is done in order to highlight: (a) the work of these African American scholars who in many cases are not well known or at least are not well cited within more mainstream journals; and (b) the multiple dimensions invoked by these research programs related to cognition, affect as well as empowerment. These multiple dimensions are more characteristic of the research of African American and other scholars of color and their research offers useful models for conceptualizing the multidimensionality of our challenges in the field of education.

The two research programs discussed below address direct links between cognition and culture in ways that are domain specific. The first, representing the Mathematics Case, is The Algebra Project, headed by Bob Moses. The second, The Cultural Modeling Project headed by Carol D. Lee, represents the Literacy Case.

The Mathematics Case: The Algebra Project. Ethnomathematicians such as Ascher (1991), Frankenstein (1995), Lumpkin (1990) and Zavlasky (1979) have demonstrated the constructions of mathematical knowledge within different cultural traditions across history. These researchers make a convincing case that mathematical patterns and relationships are represented in artifacts and routine practices in non-Western societies. I have argued (and incorporated in my pedagogical practice when I taught second graders at an independent African-centered school that I cofounded in 1972) that to teach children multiple representations of the division algorithm or of different base systems enriches children's understanding of the core constructs underlying mathematics (Lee, 1992). When I taught second graders the Yoruba counting system along side the base 10 system, these African American children learned several important lessons:

1. Mathematics is socially, culturally, and historically constructed; it is not a set of finite facts and operations located between the pages of a math textbook or mysteriously located in the teacher's head;
2. African people, as have other peoples historically, responded to their own cultural and geophysical reality to construct mathematical representations and systems to meet their needs; and
3. There is more than one way to group quantities—not only bases other than 10 (the Yoruba have a base 20 system), but besides additive systems (i.e., $10 + 1$, $10 + 2$, two sets of $10 + 1$, two sets of $10 + 2$), there are subtractive systems (i.e., $20 - 1$, $20 - 2$, two sets of $20 - 6$, two sets of $20 - 5$).

Each of these understandings, I would argue, is pivotal to developing deep conceptual understanding of numbers, counting, and the operations of addition and multiplication. In addition, the understanding that mathematics is socially, culturally, and historically constructed is one of the powerful differences between mathematicians and passive consumers of school mathematics. There is no question that in this era of international communication systems, there is a universal language of mathematics. That universal language of mathematics does not preclude Brazilian children selling candy on the streets or negotiating profits and pricing through the use of unconventional mathematical strategies (Nunes, Schliemann, & Carraher, 1993; Saxe, 1991); nor does it preclude market sellers across

Asia from using the abacus, with its base 5 system, to calculate (Stigler & Baranes, 1989); nor does it eliminate the mathematical representations in African games like Mancala or in the patterns on Inca or Maori cloth (Ascher, 1991). These mathematical understandings are not trivial in the sense that they are invoked effectively by large numbers of people across the earth. The intention is not to argue naively that what the mathematics community calls everyday/practical mathematics (Lave, Murtaugh, & de la Rocha, 1984; Scribner, 1984) or that the examples in ethnomathematics should replace the formalisms that characterize either the traditional or the reform mathematics curriculum. Rather, the argument is that the mathematical representations in peoples' understandings (both current and historical) provide useful opportunities to make connections across mathematical ideas as they are operationalized in the real world.

Stigler and Baranes (1989) provide an extensive overview of the ways in which mathematical knowledge has been constructed and represented in culturally specific arenas. Their overview includes examples of Puluwat navigation and Mfantse fish sellers. However, the only reference these researchers make to anything African or related to African Americans is Orr's (1987) controversial book *Twice As Less*. Orr argues that African American children who speak African American Vernacular English are inhibited in learning mathematics because features of the language are counterintuitive to certain mathematical constructs. Baugh (1988) attacks Orr's claims by arguing that what she does not address is the quality of the mathematical teaching she describes and the clear limitations of her understanding of African American Vernacular English (AAVE). Equally important is how in this otherwise stellar and important research review article, in an AERA publication, the only reference to African Americans or Africans and mathematics is this deficit view.

In contrast, the civil rights activist Bob Moses decided in 1982 that as algebra is a gatekeeper to higher mathematics and mathematics is a gatekeeper to opportunities to explore fields in the sciences and technology, learning algebra was a political agenda to be engaged as fervently as civil rights activists had pursued the right to vote throughout the 1960s. Moses engaged in a careful analysis of the domain of algebra and concluded that naive conceptions carried over from the study of arithmetic worked against children's understanding of integers necessary to comprehend positive and negative numbers. For Moses, the learning potential of African American children, largely living in poverty, toward which he directed his organizing efforts, was never in question. He did not have to engage in a series of studies of Black children living with White parents and children of mixed race backgrounds to come to an empirical conclusion that these children had tremendous potential. He saw that potential, in part, in the funds of knowledge they had constructed from their home and community experiences. Moses looked for models in the lived experiences of these students that mapped onto key features of the rational number system. He came to the metaphor of the urban transit system. In the curriculum he and others designed, middle school students would leave the school building and take trips on the public transit system, which they knew quite well. The students would be supported in constructing their own problems: I am at stop A and I want to go to stop H; how many stops will I need to travel and in what direction to get to stop H?

> A ride on the subway becomes the basis for understanding displacements, stories about 'making do' become the basis for understanding the difference between equivalence and equality. The concepts of displacements and equivalence provide a new approach to understanding integers. (The Algebra Project Web site: http://www.sirius.com/~casha/curric.html)

Moses had a clear understanding of the role of prior knowledge and how to link naive conceptions to formal constructs in the discipline of mathematics. He also had a powerful understanding of the semiotic role of language as a representational and mediational system. Thus, in The Algebra Project, students first construct these problems meaningful to them in their first language—be that AAVE, Spanish, or Haitian Creole. They then learn to translate these problems into a pictorial representation and finally into a formal, algorithmic, abstract representation. More recent efforts have included the development of a unit of instruction on ratio and proportion involving the rhythms of traditional African drumming as the metaphor and anchor. Currently, The Algebra Project operates in 22 sites in 13 states across the South, the West coast, the Midwest, and the Northeast, serving over 40,000 students. The Algebra Project has achieved great success (Moses & Cobb, 2003; Moses, 1994; Moses et al., 1989; Silva et al., 1990). As with any large-scale intervention, there continue to be challenges as efforts are made to scale up to support teachers to implement the project with the success of the initial efforts (Martin, 2000).

Another important element of the work of The Algebra Project is community organizing. In a vein similar to another important large-scale intervention focused successfully on African American students, The Comer Project (Anson, Cook, & Habib, 1991; Haynes & Comer, 1993), Moses and his colleagues believe strongly that parents and community residents must be partners in learning. (Although this chapter focuses largely on research programs on which there has been less attention in mainstream educational literature, I do want to acknowledge the power of The Comer Project as a model for school reform. It addresses the developmental as well as the academic needs of children, helps teachers to learn to take those needs into account, includes a meaningful parent education component and brings parents into the schools as educational partners.) At every Algebra Project school, councils of parents and community residents are active in the organization of the project and its implementation. In addition, The Algebra Project takes student empowerment seriously. At a recent meeting, I talked with David Dennis, Director of the Southern Initiative of The Algebra Project. He emphasized the need to bring students in as partners, to understand how they view the work. As part of their commitment to the holistic development of young people, not simply a goal of developing students who are competent in mathematics, the project has also developed The Young People's Project, a private company, founded by the youngsters themselves. Through The Young People's Project, students develop leadership skills and engage in economic empowerment by providing services to The Algebra Project network.

Although the work of The Algebra Project is used here as the exemplar of domain specific approaches in mathematics to bridge culture and cognition, it is important to mention briefly the work of other African American scholars in mathematics education who take a culturally responsive perspective. William Tate (1993, 1994) has raised pivotal questions about the economic and political tensions within the reform based mathematics movement as relates to equity issues in mathematics learning by African American students. He also points to the important role of social context in mathematics learning, citing the following example (Silver, Smith, & Nelson, 1995, p. 41):

> Yvonne is trying to decide whether she should buy a weekly bus pass. On Monday, Wednesday and Friday, she rides the bus to and from work. On Tuesday and Thursday, she rides the bus to work, but gets a ride home with her friends. Should Yvonne buy a weekly bus pass? Explain your answer.
>
> Busy Bus Company Fares
> One-Way $1.00
> Weekly Pass $9.00

Teachers at a Philadelphia school in the QUASAR Project gave students this question, which the teachers interpreted as a straightforward multi-step word problem. The teachers had not considered the social contexts of the students' lives that influenced how the students interpreted the problem. The teachers expected a response of "one-way tickets." The students assumed that more than one family member could use the weekly pass and that the pass could be used on weekends as well. Tate (1993) offers other examples of how African American students' opportunities to participate in mathematical discourse in classrooms are constrained because teachers do not take the lived world of students into account. Tate goes on to argue that to teach African American and other poor students of color effectively, teachers must understand not only the mathematics—the argument made by the mathematics reform community—but they must also understand the prior knowledge and experiences of their students in terms of how those prior understandings impact learning specific concepts. The challenge remains for teachers not to view what poor Black students bring from their home and community experiences as deficits, but rather as resources. Tate cites Carter G. Woodson (1933), who recognized as early as 1933 the necessity that mathematics education is situated in the social reality of students:

> And even in the certitude of science or mathematics it has been unfortunate that the approach to the Negro has been borrowed from a "foreign" method. For example, the teaching of arithmetic in the fifth grade in a backward county in Mississippi should mean one thing in the Negro school and a decidedly different thing in the white school. The Negro child, as a rule, comes from the homes of tenants and peons who have to migrate annually from the plantation, looking for light, which they have never seen. The children from the white planters and merchants live permanently in the midst of calculations, family budgets and the like, which enable them sometimes to learn more by contact than the Negro can acquire in school. Instead of teaching such Negro child less arithmetic, they should be taught more of it than white children. (p. 4)

In 1970, S. E. Anderson wrote the article "Mathematics and the Struggle for Black Liberation" in *The Black Scholar* in which he states:

> ... as a matter of fact, it should be our goal to have *every* black student take at least one year of calculus and analytic geometry. ... It should be stressed that this is necessary *not* because American capitalism's advanced forms of technology require this background, but because the Black Liberation Struggle ... requires knowledge of 20th century technology. In other words, to paraphrase Brother Frederick Douglass, we are struggling to learn so that we can learn to struggle. (p. 25)

The point here is that there is a long tradition connecting achievement in mathematics and the sciences to African American community empowerment. The goal articulated from Carter G. Woodson through S. E. Anderson, from Robert Moses through William Tate and others, is that achievement in mathematics is not simply a challenge to meet the demands of the labor market, not simply opportunities for individual economic uplift, but rather a tool in the arsenal of African American historical struggles. This perspective is not captured in the mainstream math reform efforts, although there are certainly mainstream scholars who call for equity in mathematics education (Frankenstein, 1995; Malloy & Jones, 1998; Secada, Fennema, & Adajian, 1995; Silver, Strutchens, & Zawojewski, 1996; Silver et al., 1995; Zavlasky, 1979).

The Literacy Case: The Cultural Modeling Project.   In the area of literacy, the gap in achievement on standardized measures between African American students and their White counterparts narrowed between 1970 and 1980. However, the gap remains unacceptably large and stable. The 1996 National Assessment of Educational Progress (NAEP) reports 40 percent of fourth graders in contrast to 69 percent of African American fourth graders reading below the basic level. The basic level is defined as demonstrating "an understanding of the overall meaning of what they read, being able to make relatively obvious connections between the text and their own experiences, and extend the ideas in the text by making simple inferences" (NAEP, 1994b, p. 42). Between 1992 and 2003 in grades 4 and 8, the gap between Black and White students in reading achievement has remained relatively stable. Low-income students have been shown to fall behind in reading achievement from first grade through third grade, regardless of their achievement levels in first grade (Herman & Stringfield, 1997; Puma, Karweit, Price, Ricciuti, Thompson, & Vaden-Kiernan, 1997; Snow, Burns, & Griffin, 1998). In focusing on the discrepancies in Black-White achievement, some inadvertently "ghettoize" the problem. By contrast, in the work cited later, researchers consider that the problem of achieving rigorous literacy standards, particularly at the high school level, is endemic across ethnic and class populations within the United States.

In Figure 4.1, 1999 NAEP results show the discrepancies in achievement across ethnic groups, while at the same time highlighting the fact that on the most challenging literacy tasks (the specialized level on the chart in Figure 4.1), a very small percentage of Black, Chicano/a, and White

	African American	Latino	White
Make Generalizations	95%	97%	98%
Partial Skills	66	68	87
Understand Complicated Information	17	24	46
Learn from Specialized Materials	1	2	8

FIG. 4.1. 1999 NAEP reading results for 17-year-olds.
Source: National Center for Education Statistics (2000). Washington, D.C.: U.S. Department of Education, 2000.

students at the twelfth-grade level achieve at expected levels. It also must be acknowledged that, on international assessments, U.S. students score relatively well, in contrast with their scores on comparable measures in math and science (Elley, 1992; Snow et al., 1998). This finding suggests that attending to rigorous standards for the lowest achieving students is likely to have a positive impact on the achievement of most students.

In the area of literacy, my own work in Cultural Modeling (Lee, 1993, 1995a, 1995b, 2000, 2001) is presented. Cultural Modeling is a framework that conceptualizes design principles by which to connect domain specific learning to the funds of knowledge that students bring from their home and community experiences, with a special attention to uses of language. Current work in Cultural Modeling focuses on literacy in two areas, response to literature and narrative composition. The principles underlying design in Cultural Modeling are as follows:

1. Detailed task analysis of problem solving in the domain;
2. Determining what constructs and strategies are most generative to problem solving in the domain;
3. Analysis of routine everyday practices in the lives of students that have relevance to problem solving in the domain;
4. Design of learning activities and classroom routines that help students make conscious connections between their everyday knowledge and the domain specific knowledge.

In response to literature, deciding on what core constructs and strategies were most generative to the domain required a radical revamping of the traditional literature curriculum at the secondary school level.

Traditional literature curriculums are organized around either a thematic approach or a chronological approach. When genres are taught, they tend to be taught in the freshman year, focusing on the short story, poetry, fiction and plays. The problem I and others have argued (Lee, 2003c; Smagorinsky & Gevinson, 1989; Smith & Hillocks, 1988) is that recognizing the characteristics of a short story versus a play in itself is of little use to the novice reader in negotiating the interpretive problems posed by the texts. Rather, we argue that core interpretive problems in the domain of response to literature include, but are not limited to, problems of satire, irony, unreliable narrators, symbolism, highly specialized genres such as stream of consciousness, as well as archetypal themes such as the journey of the epic hero and character types such as the picaresque hero (Booth, 1974; Rabinowitz, 1987; Smagorinsky & Gevinson, 1989; Smith & Hillocks, 1988). This reconsideration of the scope of curriculum has parallels in reform movements in other domains. In mathematics, for example, based on international comparisons, the reform community has argued that algebraic and geometry concepts should be integrated from kindergarten forward, that too much time in the middle grades is spent repetitively on the algorithms of long division, that statistics should be integrated across the curriculum and that the underlying focus should be on conceptual understanding (National Council of Teachers of Mathematics, 2000; National Center for Education Statistics, 1997c; Schoenfeld, 1994; Silver, 1998).

Although there have been major reforms in the literacy curriculum, most have been at the elementary school level, making use of the cognitive research on reading and focusing the curriculum on teaching those reading comprehension strategies that characterize better readers (Dole, Duffy, Roehler, & Pearson, 1991; Palinscar & Brown, 1984). At the secondary level, most of the attention of reform has been on reader response in literature (Rosenblatt, 1978). The idea is that students should be empowered to bring their personal responses to works of literature to the fore. The problem I find with this orientation is that if readers cannot make sense of the work, they are likely to have either a negative personal response to the work or at best a very unembellished response. Much of the reader response focus in current literature anthologies provides for only superficial consideration of students' response to themes in a work, as opposed to helping students learn how to figure out the themes themselves.

In our analysis of everyday practices, we have found that African American adolescents who are speakers of African American Vernacular English (AAVE), routinely produce and interpret irony, satire, and symbolism in their everyday talk, especially in the speech genre of signifying (Smitherman, 1977; Mitchell-Kernan, 1981; Morgan, 1993, 1998). Signifying is a kind of talk that may involve ritual insult, such as in playing the dozens ("... *yo mama so skinny she could do the hoola hoop in a cheerio.*") and always involves double entendre. In signifying the words are not to be interpreted literally. Speakers of AAVE bring a powerful habit of mind to language use that is central to problem solving in response to literature (Lee, 1993, 2000). They have a highly embedded appreciation of language play, a love of playing with language as an aesthetic end in itself, as opposed to a strict utilitarian tool of communication. Use of rhythm, alliteration, metaphor, irony, and satire are routine in the language practices of this speech community.

These same norms are picked up and expressed in the artistic productions of the hip hop community. Young people listen to rap music. Whereas I reject rap lyrics that are misogynistic and that advocate wanton violence, there is also a great deal of highly innovative music with lyrics that have high literary quality and socially redeeming themes. In such lyrics, listeners routinely are interpreting problems of symbolism, irony, satire and unreliable narrators. In both the case of signifying and the case of rap music, participants engaged in these practices often make use of tacit knowledge. Students can tackle the interpretive problems posed by the language in signifying or rap, but they cannot articulate the strategies they use. Thus, when these students meet analogous problems in canonical literature, they are unable to bring to bear either the habits of mind, that is, appreciation for language play as an end in and of itself, or strategies they have already made use of in other contexts. Mahiri (1996, 1998) also has investigated the semiotic potential in the cultural funds of knowledge of African American adolescents for supporting literacy learning, including in the area of rap music. Other scholars engaged in similar work include Ernest Morrell and Jeff Duncan-Andrade (Morrell & Duncan-Andrade, 2002) and Shuaib Meacham (1998, 2001).

What I have just described represents the classic problem of inert knowledge (Whitehead, 1929) and is one central challenge around the question of transfer of knowledge from one context to another (see also Chapter 3). Interestingly enough, in our work with teachers, we have found that teachers' knowledge (and we suspect of many other readers as well) of the strategies they invoke when reading is equally tacit. We have asked teachers to read and interpret a short story. When we ask teachers how they came to this interpretation, why they underlined certain phrases and paid special attention to certain passages, they could not articulate reasons why. It may be fine for someone who reads a lot not to be able to articulate the strategies they use, but for teachers such tacit knowledge is not helpful. If teachers cannot articulate how one attacks a category of problem, how can they help others to learn to do it? Thus, as a field, to the extent that we become better at teaching students who have been traditionally underserved by public schooling, we will likely come to understand the disciplines we teach better and to understand the complexities of learning as a process better.

The Cultural Modeling Project has designed a full four-year literature curriculum that has been implemented in a high school in a large, urban midwestern school district. One of the challenges, among others, has been in negotiating what we call meta-cognitive instructional conversations (Lee, 2001) in the early phases of instruction. A central activity in Cultural Modeling is the analysis of what we call cultural data sets. Cultural data sets are texts from the lived experiences of students that pose interpretive problems similar to those that are the focus of a unit of instruction. Such cultural data sets may include samples of signifying dialogues, rap lyrics, rap videos, or other videos. So, for example, in a unit on symbolism, students may study the lyrics of "The Mask" by The Fugees. In each stanza of the song, we meet a new character who wears a mask. No student listening to this song believes that the mask is literal. Every student knows the mask represents a state of mind. The challenge has been to help teachers understand how to focus the discussions of these works, not so much around what the mask represents, but how the students know the mask is not literal, and once they reject a literal interpretation, what clues do they use to figure out what the mask represents. Such conversations are not easy to coordinate because we are simply not used to talking about our own thinking processes. After the modeling phase of instruction, students will have articulated a set of strategies for attacking the target interpretive problem. Thus, when they meet the canonical texts that follow, they have available to them a set of generative and conscious strategies on which to draw to make sense of the technical problems of these texts.

Texts are selected first on the basis of the category of interpretive problems that are central to understanding the texts. If the unit is on symbolism, all the texts selected will be those in which symbolism is a central problem posed across the text. In addition, when working with African American students, we sequence the first canonical text as a work of African American literature. In addition to needing technical knowledge of how to attack particular kinds of interpretive problems in a text, the reader must also be able to negotiate the social codes of the text. If the social world of the text is far removed from the experience of the reader, he or she will have a more difficult time making sense of the text. We begin with African American canonical texts because we believe African American students generally will have relevant prior knowledge of the social world of the texts. Thus, students begin with texts in which they have prior knowledge of the text's social codes, while they are beginning to practice use of the strategies they have used. Then they move to texts for which they have less prior knowledge of the social codes of the text, but have greater experience using the strategies they will need.

This approach represents a radical turn in the organization of literature curriculum at the secondary level. There is no core literature anthology (excluding strictly African American literature anthologies) in which units of instruction revolve around African American texts. In a unit on symbolism for seniors, Toni Morrison's novel *Beloved* served as the core text, with readings by William Faulkner, Amy Tan, John Milton, and William Shakespeare as spokes around *Beloved*, the wheel. In addition, texts are selected because they are expected to engage the students with questions of cultural identity and to provide them with opportunities to struggle with questions about historical African American experiences. In The Cultural Modeling Project, we expect that students will consider critically personal dilemmas with the insights of the griot-authors who offer no simple solutions. In this sense, the selection of texts is meant to serve a socializing function as well as an intellectual function (Lee, Spencer, & Harpalani, 2003).

As part of this early work in Cultural Modeling, I taught in the high school where our curriculum was being implemented. For three years, I taught one English class at the high school in addition to my university-based work. Although the full story of the implementation is complex, students with low standardized reading scores engaged rigorous literary texts. The modeling activities prepared them such that they knew the rules of the game. In my own teaching experiences, on numerous occasions students saw meanings which I had not anticipated in the texts. We developed assessments that involved students in interpreting, both in multiple choice and short answer formats, short stories they had not read in class. Students at all grade levels achieved well beyond what their standardized reading scores would have predicted. As would be expected, individual teachers made a difference. Those teachers whom we knew were implementing Cultural Modeling as we had anticipated achieved the highest gains, while teachers who were less skilled achieved gains as well. Figure 4.2 provides the results from the 1996–1997 assessment for freshmen on an open response test aligned to the Iowa Test of Basic Skills used by the district.

Cultural Modeling also has been applied to narrative composition, which draws on African American students' oral competencies in storytelling to construct bridges to students' academic writing. This work is a direct response to Michaels's (1981) and Cazden's (Cazden, Michaels, & Tabor, 1985) research on topic-centered storytelling styles among African American children and Gee's (1989, 1990) challenge to understand the literary elements and creative aspects of this storytelling style. In addition,

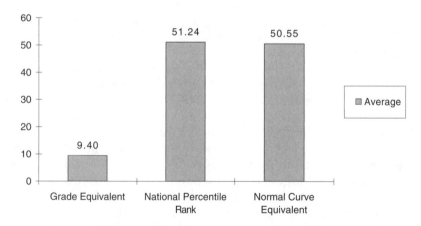

FIG. 4.2. 1996–1997 Assessment data for freshmen.
Source: Lee, C. D. (forthcoming). *Conducting our blooming in the midst of the whirlwind: Understanding culture as a lens for impacting learning and development.* New York: Teachers College Press.

this research is influenced by the work of Ball (1992, 1995b, 1999), who discovered preferences in expository styles of African American adolescents. These expository styles are rooted in African American oral traditions. Ball (1995a) has developed a curriculum that helps students make explicit use of these tacit preferences to improve their expository writing. Smitherman (2000a) conducted an extensive review of results of the writing component of the NAEP from 1969 through 1988/89. Smitherman found that the greater the concentration of features of what she calls the African American rhetorical tradition, the higher the score of the students' writing. These findings are powerful as a post hoc analysis. It is clear that the raters were not consciously considering use of African American rhetorical features as criteria for judging the quality of students' writings. However, Smitherman's analysis makes clear that these features represent characteristics of good writing and implies that focusing on these cultural elements in instruction can prove useful. Results from the Cultural Modeling in Narrative Project show that the use of cultural data sets as prompts for writing results in high quality narratives. Students in grades 3 and 6 were able to draw on cultural scripts to produce writing with vivid details, imagery, and dialogue (Lee, Rosenfeld, Mendenhall, Rivers, & Tynes, 2003).

IMPLICATIONS OF THE CULTURAL CASES IN MATHEMATICS AND LITERACY

One point of these examples in mathematics and literacy is to demonstrate the usefulness of attending to culture in the design of learning environments for African American students, and by extension, other students. The challenge of such work is to avoid superficial conceptualization of the relevance of students' prior knowledge. This requires a very careful analysis both of students' everyday experience as well as of the generative tasks and constructs in the domain. Although clearly not enough, still in mathematics and literacy there is more work being done to link students' prior cultural funds of knowledge with constructs and strategies in the domains (Ball, 1995a, 1995b, 1999; Gilyard, 1991; Hooper, 1996; Mahiri, 1998; Majors, 1998, 2001; Malloy & Jones, 1998; Martin, 2000; Moss, 1994; Nasir, 2002; Pinkard, 2000). Very little is being done from such a framework in science and history. However, the culturally responsive work in science education of Chèche Konnen is discussed in a later section of this chapter.

One challenge often raised to culturally specific orientations in design has to do with classrooms that have a diverse mix of students. Although such classrooms pose additional challenges, this diversity does not mean an approach that ignores culture is the default. Gutierrez's (Gutierrez, Baquedano-Lopez, & Tejeda, 1999) research on hybrid discourses in classrooms is relevant to how such design work should be approached. Gutierrez argues that environments in which conflicting perspectives are negotiated make possible greater opportunities for learning and development. Although research on relationships between culture and cognition has been well studied in cross-cultural contexts (Scribner & Cole, 1981), much less work has been conducted on the U.S. context (Greenfield & Cocking, 1994; Nasir & Saxe, 2003). Conducting such work requires that educational researchers recognize the cultural diversity within the United States. That is, while we are American citizens, with an extant U.S. culture, we also exist within cultural enclaves that are distinct. This is particularly the case with African Americans. As reflected in Du Bois's (1968) construct of double consciousness, African Americans are both uniquely African and African American as well as American. This is a complex cultural construct to understand, but a necessary one if we are to take seriously where students are and where we want them to become academically.

TECHNOLOGY, CULTURE, AND COGNITION

Studies focusing on technology, culture, and cognition are highlighted next, in part because so little work is being done in the area that explicitly addresses African American students, and in part because computer based digital technologies are powerful tools to support learning and will without doubt be central to educational efforts in the future. This is of particular importance considering what has been called the "digital divide" between more affluent and poor communities regarding access to and uses of technology (Goslee, 1998; Piller, 1992).

Much of the work involving designing software environments to support learning draw on current understandings in cognition (much of which has been summarized in the Chapter 3) with a special emphasis on findings from artificial intelligence. The research discussed in this section implicitly challenges the underlying ethos within the community of educational researchers using technology for the design of educational interventions and curricula (Lee, 2003b). That ethos very rarely attends to cultural variation. It makes claims for authentic problem based learning that implicitly assumes novice learners can be defined by what the current literature addresses as misconceptions of generic age grade children within academic disciplines (Chi, Feltovitch, & Glaser, 1981). For example, the literature suggests that children develop certain understandings of physical causality or of biological mechanisms based on what they visually perceive in the physical environment they occupy. That literature, however, does not account for the differences in the experiences of the physical world by children in different communities (Luria, 1976). Conceptions of biological mechanisms may be very different for children growing up on a family farm as opposed to those growing up in a rain forest. In part because this research does not have a large cross-cultural base and tends to focus on small samples of White children, what the implications may be as the pool of children varies more is not clear. Nevertheless, there are important insights to be gained. For example, when Piagetian scholars began to engage in cross-cultural research in Africa, some of their assumptions about children's cognitive development were challenged. (Also see Greenfield and Cocking [1994] for other examples of cross-cultural developmental studies.) I make this critique not because I do not value the research foundation that informs the work of colleagues who address technology as a tool to support cognitive development. Rather, I do not believe we can move toward a more ecologically valid set of constructs about learning if we do not critique ourselves and expand the sites of our research (Lee, 2003a; Lee, Spencer, & Harpalani, 2003).

Learning science researchers who focus on technology as a tool (Pea & Gomez, 1992) argue that technology is powerful in its ability to provide opportunities to:

1. Manipulate data and construct multiple representations of what one understands;
2. Use modeling and visualization tools employed by experts in fields in the sciences and mathematics;
3. Communicate across physical borders;
4. Engage in problem solving in school settings that otherwise would be very expensive or dangerous to do in the real world; and
5. Gain access to huge sources of information that might not be available at one's school site.

In the early stages of work in this area, intervention and curricula tended to be implemented in White, middle-class suburban schools and districts. Much to the credit of this emerging field, a good deal of current educational research using technology is increasingly being implemented in urban school districts, which means increasing numbers of African American students are having access to these resources. Although this is encouraging and laudatory, it also raises the challenge of whether these research programs are looking carefully at the equity issues involved in their implementations.

To what extent do they begin to disentangle differential outcome and process gains between Black, White, Chicano/a, and other students in their programs? I became sensitive to this issue when I visited a Schools for Thought (Bruer, 1993) site in an urban setting a few years ago. As I listened to group discussions, I observed African American students who were quiet and only peripherally involved, whereas their White and Asian

American counterparts actively managed the group conversations. As an experienced classroom teacher and researcher, I understand clearly the limitations of a single visit to a classroom. At the same time, this observation raised what I think is a serious question that tends not to be addressed in the project-based science work that focuses on technology as a tool.

A recent effort by the Cognition & Technology Group at Vanderbilt (1997) who developed the Jasper Series is encouraging. They added the sociolinguist David Bloome (Bloome & Egan-Robertson, 1993) to their team to study classroom interactions with an eye toward how the culture of the classrooms is constructed and how issues of equity may or may not arise. Lin (1999) makes a convincing case that such artifacts as the Jasper Series are not culturally neutral and may be appropriated in culturally specific ways by different communities of learners. Lin followed a teacher in Hong Kong who implemented the Jasper program in ways very different from that initially conceptualized by the Cognition and Technology Group.

The two research programs highlighted below illustrate two ways that we might conceptualize and address ways that culture mediates how African American children make use of software environments designed to support learning. Paula Hooper illustrates how students in an African-centered school appropriate Logo Writer. Nichole Pinkard illustrates another proactive stance on this question. Pinkard addresses culturally responsive principles for the design of computer-based environments to support learning.

Hooper is the first African American female to graduate with the Ph.D. from the prestigious Media Lab at MIT. Papert (1980, 1993), Resnick (1994) and colleagues at the Media Lab propose that through the activities of learning to program with Logo languages, even young children can learn to explore not only mathematical concepts, but are also apprenticed into powerful habits of mind. They propose a conceptual framework on cognition they call "constructionism." Accordingly, Kafai and Resnick (1996) state:

> One of the main tenets of constructionism is that learners actively construct and reconstruct knowledge out of their experiences in the world. It places special emphasis on the knowledge construction that takes place when learners are engaged in building objects. Constructionism differs from other learning theories along several dimensions. Whereas most theories describe knowledge acquisition in purely cognitive terms, constructionism sees an important role for affect. It argues that learners are most likely to become intellectually engaged when they are working on personally meaningful activities and projects. In constructionist learning, forming new relationships with knowledge is as important as forming new representations of knowledge. Constructionism also emphasizes diversity: It recognizes that learners can make connections with knowledge in many different ways. Constructionist learning environments encourage multiple learning styles and multiple representations of knowledge. (pp. 2–3)

From a constructionist perspective, learning how to learn is just as important as the content of learning.

An African-centered scholar, Hooper (1996) decided to explore what it meant for African American children who were being socialized in an African-centered school to appropriate the programming tools of Logo Writer. Logo Writer allows a child to program in a narrative structure, animating and creating stories where characters and the setting can move, make sounds and be active in ways that children as designers decide to program. Hooper followed a group of 8- to 11-year-old students at Paige Academy in Boston as they learned to program in several Logo languages. In the tradition of many other African American scholars, Hooper assumed the role of activist and researcher. She taught part time at Paige Academy instructing the children in Logo programming. Her studies of these children reveal several important points. The children learned to become very successful and enthusiastic programmers. The Media Lab provided opportunities for the students to visit the lab. A number of students in the group have indicated they want to become computer engineers as a future profession. Hooper tells the story of Shamia (not her real name), an 8-year-old girl who wanted to create a program to draw a rainbow for the sky in a scene from her story featuring a character the class had created called "Elephantbird." Shamia had to create a procedure that would produce the image she wanted. She eventually called her procedure the rainbow maker and in the process demonstrated her evolving algebraic thinking: "understanding . . . an inverse relationship between the number of times to repeat and the turning angle for each arc" (Hooper, 1996, p. 251). In this sense, Shamia fulfills the expectations of the designers of Logo Writer; through designing an artifact of her choice, she explores geometry and algebraic concepts, programming procedures and learns to assume a level of control over her own learning and exerts significant effort to learn from her earlier failed attempts.

However, Hooper also found very interesting ways that this group of children learned to appropriate the tools of Logo Writer. As an African-centered school, Paige Academy incorporates the Nguzo Saba into the routine practices of classroom life. The Nguzo Saba are the seven principles that form the foundation of the African American celebration of Kwanzaa (Karenga, 1988). These principles include unity, self-determination, collective work and responsibility, cooperative economics, creativity, purpose, and faith. Hooper discovered that without explicit prompting, these students worked cooperatively in groups as they constructed problems on which to work and programming strategies to tackle the problems on which they focused. Hooper's observation is consistent with Boykin's (1994) findings across repeated controlled experiments that African American children in his studies prefer to work in groups cooperatively not for external reward but for the value of the social interaction with their peers as an end it itself. In addition, in analyzing the animated stories the children created with Logo Writer, Hooper found that the children incorporated: (a) themes consistent with the Nguzo Saba in their stories and (b) African American rhetorical (Smitherman, 2000) and vervistic (Boykin, 1994) traditions into the music they choose, the way characters dressed, moved, and spoke. Similar to Dyson's (1997, 2000, 2003) findings looking at literacy practices of multiethnic children, including African American children, in an urban primary level classroom, these children, appropriated themes from the popular media—a story that takes off from the *Little House of Horrors* movie—but also reappropriate these themes in ways that are culturally specific to their own experiences.

Likewise, another Media Lab graduate, Alan Shaw, extends the construct of constructionism to what he calls social-constructionism. Shaw (1996) asserts, "Social constructionism extends the constructionist view by explicitly including as constructions the social relations and social activities that become shared outcomes and artifacts at work in the developmental cycle" (p. 177). Shaw took the importance of community empowerment as a serious site of development parallel to that of the school. Shaw designed a networking system that allowed community residents and organizations to communicate electronically around issues of community development. Both Shaw and Hooper explicitly acknowledge the inspiration of the work of Bob Moses, connecting mathematical literacy to community empowerment. It is important to emphasize again the ways that a culturally focused research program aimed at enhancing the academic achievement of African American students is for many more than an exploration of cognitive theory, but indeed a passion that is fueled by concerns for equity and constrained by the rigors of systematic research design and analysis.

Pinkard's (2000, 2001) work offers another but related perspective on the role technology can play to bridge culture and cognition. Drawing in part on the principles of Cultural Modeling (Lee, 1995a) and the design principles of goal based scenarios (Schank, Kass, & Riesbeck, 1994), Pinkard has developed two software environments to teach beginning literacy skills. The first is called "Rappin Reader" (Pinkard, 2001). In "Rappin Reader," children assume the role of a music producer. The lyrics of a series of rap songs that the children would know become mixed up and the children must reconstruct the lyrics. In the process, children learn onset rhyme patterns and sight vocabulary. They use reference tools like the dictionary and thesaurus and construct their own lyrics. In the second system, "Say Say Oh Playmate" (Pinkard, 2001), girls living in a housing project have the task of reconstructing the lyrics to the songs that accompany traditional African American girls' clapping games, such as "Miss Mary Mack." As an activist scholar like Paula Hooper and Alan Shaw, Pinkard began to develop these systems while volunteering in the Cabrini Green public housing project on the west side of Chicago. Surrounded by the wealthy "Gold Coast" in Chicago, Cabrini Green was an island of extreme poverty with a history of some of the worst performing schools and most dangerous neighborhoods in Chicago. Pinkard designed the interface for "Say Say Oh Playmate" with Cabrini Green and the children with whom she worked in mind. In a very moving video clip of two girls using the "Say Say Oh Playmate" system together, one of the girls asks who is the female character on the screen. The researchers volley the question back to the girl who then responds that the character on the screen is pretty and so it must be her. Over several iterations, students have achieved gains as large as 25 percent in sight word recognition after minimal explorations in the system (Pinkard, 1999).

Pinkard has argued that the African American children with whom she works in schools in Chicago and Detroit are deeply engaged with these systems, not simply because the goal based scenario design asks the children to assume roles to solve authentic problems with supports built into the system, but also because the interface reflects the culture of the children. The music they hear is music that moves them; the characters and settings look like the children; the tasks are culturally specific and include texts that the children know intimately (not the traditional basal reader). She also has developed a feedback support for teachers to have flexible access to data on what children are learning within the system, what kinds of errors they make and what reading strategies they invoke. In her ethnographic observations of these systems in use, Pinkard (Pinkard & Kleinman, 1999) has discovered that children, especially boys, who may be acting out and unengaged in classroom tasks, become very engaged in these software environments and teachers learn to look on these previously disengaged children with different eyes.

Underlying these two software systems is an architecture that Pinkard (2000) calls "Lyric Reader." Programmed in such a way that tools with the same underlying structure—use of music as lyrics and design of authentic tasks for students to employ their knowledge of the lyrics to explore print awareness and comprehension strategies—"Lyric Reader" can easily be developed, even by nonprogrammers. Pinkard has launched a convincing argument for the importance for designers of computer based learning environments to be sensitive both to issues of interface (i.e., what one sees on the screen) and the nature of the tasks (i.e., that they should be culturally responsive to the students who will be using the system). With an architecture like "Lyric Reader" designers can create multiple versions of software environments with the same underlying pedagogical structure, but with different interface and task structures, without beginning a new programming challenge each time. The National Science Foundation acknowledged Pinkard's work with an Early Career Award.

ENGAGEMENT AND COPING MECHANISMS AS FACTORS THAT SUPPORT LEARNING

The next section will consider a line of research that is rarely discussed in the mainstream literature on cognition. This work speaks to what I believe is an understated aspect of learning that is acknowledged in the cognitive literature but is rarely central; that is, how the design of learning environments can explicitly take into account the promotion of engagement not simply by a generic appeal to authenticity, but in ways that are culturally responsive, particularly to African American students. The construct of concern here is that of coping. How does the ability to cope with challenges and adversity interact with one's engagement in learning, particularly in the context of schooling? This issue is particularly important because no matter how much reform we are able to achieve in schools, it is unlikely that this country will ever eliminate poverty, racism and the violence that surrounds the lives of so many children, especially African American children. Thus, how to cope with adversity has been and continues to be a necessary staple in the socialization of African American students and a prerequisite correlate of academic learning (Lee & Slaughter-Defoe, 1995; Spencer, 1987; Spencer, Swanson, & Cunningham, 1991).

Cultural Resources, Coping Strategies, and Academic Support.   As part of the work of the Center for Research on the Education of Students Placed at Risk (CRESPAR) at Howard University, Sanders (1996) reports on the ways that family support, teacher support and church involvement provide a social ecology in which academic self-concept, school behavior, and academic ideology interact to influence academic achievement among African American urban eighth graders. Sanders found that the combined support from these institutional supports on achievement was greater than the independent effects of any one of the supports. In case study interviews drawn from the larger participant pool of 826, students reported on the specific kinds of activities and social interactions that contributed to their perceptions of their development. In contrast to other studies (Eccles & Midley, 1988), which report that young adolescents experience a decline in academic motivation, behaviors, and self-perceptions that contribute to academic achievement, Sanders found just the opposite with the African American young adolescents in this study. Sanders (1996) concludes:

> This study illustrates how students' attitudes, outlooks and behaviors work as processes that promote achievement. These important processes are directly affected by home, school, and church support, and students benefit most when all three contexts are working toward the same goal of helping them succeed in school. (p. 12)

The argument here is that many of the attitudes, outlooks, and behaviors into which these students are socialized can be classified within the developmental literature as coping mechanisms.

Wade Nobles, Director of the Center for Applied Cultural Studies and Educational Achievement (CACSEA) at San Francisco State University, has drawn on nine cultural themes identified by researchers as central in the lives of large numbers of African Americans:

1. *Spirituality*—... based on the belief that all elements of the universe are of one substance (Spirit) and all matter, animate or inanimate, are merely different manifestations of the God force (Spirit).
2. *Resilience*—is the conscious need to bounce back from disappointment and disaster and to have the tools of humor and joy to renew life's energy. Verve is desire for creative extemporaneousness—a sense of utter antipathy for the mundane and monotonous, the ability to focus on and handle several issues at once...
3. *Humanism*—describes the African view that the whole world is vitalistic (alive) and that this vitality is grounded in a sense of goodness.
4. *Communalism*—denotes awareness of the interdependence of people. One acts in accordance with the notion that the duty to one's family and social group is more important than individual privileges and rights.
5. *Orality and verbal expressiveness*—refers to the special importance attached to knowledge that is passed on through word of mouth and the cultivation of oral virtuosity....
6. *Personal style and uniqueness*—refers to the cultivation of a unique or distinctive personality or essence and putting one's own brand on activity—a concern with style more than with being correct or efficient. It implies approaching life as if it were an artistic endeavor.
7. *Realness*—refers to the need to face life the way it is without pretense....
8. *Emotional vitality*—expresses a sense of aliveness, animation and openness conveyed in the language, oral literature, song, dance, body language, folk poetry, and expressive thought.
9. *Musicality/rhythm*—demonstrates the connectedness of movement, music, dance, percussiveness and rhythm, personified through the musical beat. (CACSEA, 1996).

A number of educational researchers have made similar observations (Boykin, 1979, 1982, 1983; Boykin & Toms, 1985; Gay, 1995, 2000; Foster, 1987, 1999; Hale, 1994; Hale-Benson, 1986; Ladson Billings, 1994, 2001), as have anthropologists (Herskovitz, 1958; Morgan, 1993), historians (Bennett, 1964; Stuckey, 1987), and sociologists (Du Bois, 1968).

Many would argue that it is through everyday practices and institutional social structures, including those within the family and the church, in African American communities that this nexus of interrelated cultural models or belief systems are constructed. (I can imagine the blank gazes of my cognitive scientist colleagues who want to know what has spirituality, musicality, humanism and orality got to do with anything?) Very few who have worked for any length of time in an all African American school setting or neighborhood will not have noticed these themes operationalized in the activity, attitudes, and practices of these students. The challenge may be that we have limited analytical tools available to unpack the dynamic relationships among these themes in the lives of African American children and adolescents, particularly those living in conditions of intergenerational poverty.

The proposition put forth here is that these cultural resources work as part of a psychological tool kit of coping strategies in the African American community that are not mere reactions to historical oppression, but are the bricks out of which senses of identity and group membership are constructed. At the same time, this is not to suggest that every African American man, woman and child will make application of these resources in their routine activities, language use, and belief systems (Gutierrez & Rogoff, 2003; Lee et al., 2003). However, the point is that along a continuum, if one is living in, working in or conducting research in a neighborhood or organization that is majority African American, it is highly likely that one will observe these resources in operation. This is arguably the case regardless of socioeconomic status. For researchers, this existential reality represents not a recipe for design decisions, but rather a pool of resources to be considered in design work. Nor is this to claim that the only way for African American children to learn is in environments that reflect some combination of this resource use. The idea of coping strategies and such developmental constructs as locus of control is that students with strong coping strategies and a well developed internal locus of control will likely be in a better position to negotiate environments that are not consistent with their affective expectations. In the Talent Development Model, A. Wade Boykin and his colleagues at CRESPAR argue that addressing the cultural resources that African American and other children and adolescents bring to classroom settings from their home and community experiences only adds to the repertoire of pedagogical tools available to teachers and administrators (Boykin, 2000a, 2000b; Boykin & Bailey, 2000).

The point is not to replace a generic one-size-fits-all approach with a culturally specific one-size-fits-all approach. Rather, the argument is that what is needed is to expand the repertoire of educative tools available to teachers and educational researchers regarding African American children and adolescents. Because I argue that these themes are most directly captured in the literature on coping, two illustrative lines of research by African American psychologists are addressed in the following section: Philip Bowman's research on role strain and adaptation by Black men across the life cycle and Margaret Beale Spencer's theory of developmental, adaptive coping strategies among Black youth.

Research on Role Strain and Adaptation. Bowman (1989) acknowledges the tremendous role strain on Black males in this country: "Race, gender and class appear to interact in complex ways to place Black males at disturbing risks for persistent school failure, familial estrangement, homicidal violence, stress-related illness and a range of other psychosocial problems" (p. 117). Bowman also asserts that many African American men somehow learn to cope and adapt to these strains, excelling in academics, work, family and community life. Bowman critiques the dominant paradigm of studying maladaptive, pathological behavioral patterns among Black men. As is the case in studies of African Americans in other arenas, gross generalizations are made from small sample sizes and populations with extreme psycho-social problems. Bowman takes a life cycle framework, looking at the critical role strain processes from pre-adult years through early adulthood through eldership. He argues that the roles African American men are expected to carry out and the strains attached to those roles change across the life cycle. Bowman's analysis shows how what he calls adaptive ethnic resources across the adult life cycle serve to buffer and help more successful African American men to cope with adversity. These ethnic resources include community networks such as rites of passage rituals for pre-adults and self-help support groups for early adulthood. Table 4.1 summarizes Bowman's findings.

PVEST: Cultural Ecology Research. Margaret Beale Spencer (1987, 1999, 2001; Lee et al., 2003; Spencer et al., 1991; Spencer et al., 2001) has developed the Phenomenological Variant of Ecological Systems Theory (PVEST). PVEST is grounded in an ecological approach to development (Brofenbrenner, 1979) as well as a sociohistorical perspective on African American cultural history (Boykin, 1994; Du Bois, 1968; Elder, 1985; Franklin, 1985). Whereas Bowman focuses primarily on African American male development from adolescence through elderhood, Spencer considers both African American males and females through the entire life course development span from childhood through late adulthood. In the PVEST model, within and across each developmental age group, influenced by socialization into gender roles, African American males and females experience risks. Some of these risks are direct outgrowths of racism, others of poverty and still others part of the array of tensions inherent in life. The net stress levels of individuals are mediated through social supports.

TABLE 4.1
Adaptive Ethnic Resources Across the Adult Life Cycle

	Community Networks	Familial Relationships	Personal Belief Systems
Pre-Adult Years	Rite of passage Rituals	Race-related Socialization	Ethnic achievement orientations
Early adulthood	Self-help support Groups	Flexible family Ties	Racial consciousness and system blame
Middle adulthood	Para-kin Relationships	Cohesive family Bonds	Religion
Old age	Indigenous Institutions	Consanguineous relationships	Spirituality

Source: Bowman (1989, p. 138).

From these experiences, individuals develop coping strategies that may be adaptive or maladaptive. Over the course of a life span, individuals develop stable coping responses that are part of one's emergent identity. These stable coping strategies may be positive or negative. Thus, the experience of risks may be either productive or unproductive based on the coping strategies one constructs.

The relationships among these variables are not linear or hierarchical. Rather they are interactive and bidirectional. For example, one's experience of risks is influenced by one's coping strategies. Coping strategies are constructed over time with adaptive or maladaptive coping strategies shaping one's reactions to the risks of the moment. Also the patterns of risks at a particular stage in the life cycle in turn influence an emergent identity and vice versa. That is, across the life span one's sense of identity also influences one's patterns of coping reactions.

This model of development of identity and associated patterns of stable coping strategies is situated in a cultural ecology that is influenced by parents, siblings, grandparents and extended family, peers, social, and community institutions such as the church and the school and the influences of the media, including popular culture. The individual child or adolescent is influenced by these social influences and in turn influences these social supports. This interaction between patterns of coping and emerging identities is gendered in Spencer's model. For example, attitudes about violence as manly, callous attitudes about sex and attitudes toward danger as exciting are (a) more characteristic of males than females and (b) have a developmental trajectory, as attitudes of young adolescents and older

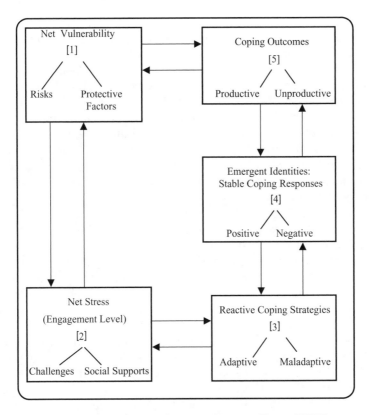

FIG. 4.3. Phenomenological Variant of Ecological Systems Theory PVEST.

adolescents change over time. Spencer further argues that these develop-mental patterns are also racialized in the sense that African American males and females experience violent threats during adolescence at rates greater than the general population. In addition, African American parents feel a necessity to prepare their children for the stresses of learning to cope with racism and poverty (Bowman, 1989). Figure 4.3 provides a graphic over-view of the PVEST model.

Although neither Bowman nor Spencer directly discusses issues of schooling and learning, there are clear implications of these ecological models for the education of African American K–12 students. There is no question that African Americans face specialized and enduring hardships related to the experiences of racism and poverty. Much of our reform ef-forts in education have been directed at either providing social services (i.e., Headstart, breakfast programs, school-based health-care services) or curricular designs that focus squarely on the cognitive demands of the academic domains. The Comer Project and The Algebra Project are two notable exceptions. However, very little has been done to design educational interventions in ways that address both the cognitive and the affective dimensions of development (Lee et al., 2003). Less friendly classroom atmospheres characterize ineffective schools (Teddli et al., 1989). Catherine Snow and her colleagues (1998) report studies in which school readiness and achievement were correlated with closeness and warmth in teacher-student relationships (Howes & Hamilton, 1992; Howes & Matheson, 1992). The affective dimension, I would argue, includes the construction of a stable identity with a repertoire of coping strategies, a sense of an internal locus of control and the array of self-concepts that are part of the identity stable of human beings.

It is worth adding that the way the developmental literature has contrasted internal and external loci of control may not reflect an African view of development (Ani, 1994; Grahams, 1994; Nobles, 1980). It may well be the case than an African view of development suggests variants of external loci of control, some productive and others non- or less productive. In this sense, an external locus of control would include the idea that one is symbiotically linked with others, especially family and that one's ability to grapple with difficulty may well depend on one's relationship with others. (Whereas I suspect, for example, that developmental measures would classify me as a person with an internal locus of control, I cannot imagine that I could have accomplished what I have in life without my mother, my husband, my family, and my extended family. When I grapple in the moment, I think automatically about what social supports I can seek to help me overcome difficulty.)

DIRECT INSTRUCTION: DON'T THROW OUT THE BABY WITH THE BATHWATER

Because of the complexity of maintaining sustained institutional educational reform resulting in widespread academic achievement for African American students and others, debates abound regarding the pedagogical underpinnings for design that can accomplish these ends. Direct instruction and inquiry-based instruction are often pitted against one another. The now classic debate among reading researchers between direct phonics based instruction and whole language is one example of the tension (Chall, 1990; Schickedanz, 1990; Stahl & Miller, 1989). From a cognitive perspective, the question is about the relationships between declarative knowledge and procedural knowledge and how they interact to support conceptual understanding. These debates have become highly polemical and conversations across camps are generally unproductive. Lisa Delpit's (1986, 1995) often cited article on the ways that process writing approaches do not address more basic forms of knowledge, what she calls the language of power, highlights the debate.

However, to the extent that standardized achievement measures are used to validate growth in learning, the field cannot ignore the gains that direct instruction advocates have made with low-income African American students (Sizemore, 1985). The noted senior scholar Barbara Sizemore used a direct instruction approach coupled with intensive professional development with several of the most low achieving elementary schools in the Pittsburgh school system (Sizemore, 1988). Under Sizemore's direction, these elementary schools became two of the highest achieving schools in the Pittsburgh system. Sizemore's work is consistent with that of Ron Edmonds (1979) who argued for characteristics that high achieving schools demonstrate. Sizemore renewed that work in Chicago with the establishment of the School Achievement Structure (SAS) at DePaul University, where she served as Dean until her retirement. SAS worked as instructional partners with some of the lowest achieving and difficult schools, both high schools and elementary, in the Chicago public schools. Although the SAS gains have not been as stark across all sites as those in Pittsburgh, many of the schools working with SAS have achieved a steady and significant growth in academic achievement. Sizemore, along with Asa Hilliard, developed a video series on low-income schools—most serving either largely African American and Hispanic students. From this body of work, Sizemore (1995) has articulated routines that schools need to institutionalize in order to overcome long histories of low achievement. These routines address the following areas:

- Assessment of skills
- Student placements
- Monitoring of implementation
- Pacing of instruction
- Measurements of mastery
- School and classroom discipline
- Instructional routines
- Teacher evaluation
- Staff development routines
- Decision making routines.

The challenge to inquiry based instruction—as with most educational interventions—is that of scale. Scale involves developing institutionalized routines and deployment of resources that help to build an intellectual community within the school, such that ways of teaching and assessing are intellectually rigorous across classrooms. The High Performance Learning Community Project headed by Lauren Resnick and colleagues at the

Learning, Research and Development Center (LRDC) at the University of Pittsburgh has also addressed the question of systemic reform with success in New York City's District Two, but this time with an inquiry based instructional model.

RESEARCH BY MAINSTREAM RESEARCHERS THAT TAKES CULTURE INTO ACCOUNT

In this section, I will discuss several research programs by non-African American researchers that draw on the cognitive and sociocultural frameworks I have defined, while taking culture as a lens. These examples are clearly in no way either exhaustive or representative. Rather, I have selected exemplars in the disciplines of science and mathematics where attention to culture is much less fore grounded in a good deal of the research literature and reforms.

Science Learning for ESL Students Who Are Black.   Often underconceptualized is the fact that Blacks in the United States represent an international group. There is a large population of Black people in Puerto Rico and some communities such as New York City have Puerto Rican populations with significant numbers of Black students. There are large Black populations in Cuba, Panama, Costa Rica, Honduras, the Dominican Republic, Belize, Brazil, and other countries in Central and South America (Moore, Sanders, & Moore, 1995). These Black populations are the legacy of the trade of human beings from Africa to be enslaved in the western Diaspora. Therefore, when we talk about the Chicano/a population, we also may be talking about portions of that group who are Black and carry with them African cultural inheritances. In addition, the Caribbean populations of Jamaica, Haiti, and so on, are predominantly Black. In many communities there is also a growing population of immigrants and U.S. citizens from Africa whose first language is not English. Thus, the Black immigrant population from countries other than Puerto Rico, which is a territory of the United States, is a fairly diverse group.

Chèche Konnen is a research group from the Technical Education Research Center (TERC) in Boston, which includes teachers from the Cambridge, Massachusetts school system (Hudicourt-Barnes, 2003; Warren & Rosebery, 1996; Warren et al., 2001). In Haitian Creole Chèche Konnen means search for knowledge. This research team designs supports for ESL (English as a Second Language) students to become scientifically literate. Their work includes learning to appropriate the discourses of science. Literacy is more than reading and writing. Literacy involves learning related sets of language practices, beliefs, and modes of reasoning that characterize a particular community. Such communities may be speakers of AAVE, speakers of Haitian Creole, as well as practicing scientists, often with distinct disciplinary boundaries—That is, physicists reason and use language in ways that differ from evolutionary biologists (John-Steiner, 2000; Ochs et al., 1994; White & Fredericksen, 1997). Team members are often bilingual teachers who are themselves native speakers of one of the languages of their students. Students in the schools with which they work speak Amharic, Cape Verdean Creole, Haitian Creole, Chinese, Gujarati, Hindi, Korean, Portuguese, Spanish, Tigrina, and Vietnamese. What is reported here is their work with Haitian Creole and Cape Verdean Creole speakers who are Black.

In the design work, students use both their first language and English to negotiate their understanding of scientific concepts. In one study with Haitian Creole speakers (Ballenger, 1997), students were studying digitized representations of sound waves. The conceptual issue was one of understanding scientific inscriptions, technical representations of knowledge and concepts. Similar to the ratio and proportion unit using African drums in The Algebra Project, students used their extensive knowledge of drumming to make sense of representations of different drumming techniques as digitized waves on a computer screen. Not only did students move back and forth between English and Haitian Creole, but they also used the language of drumming and their knowledge of the structures of drumming to scaffold their learning in the scientific domain. This work is unique in the research literature on science education. Most of the science learning literature with a cognitive base looks at expert practices of professional scientists as the cultural reference group to which students are being apprenticed. Very little work in this arena assumes that from everyday practices in their communities students of color are constructing knowledge that shares attributes with practices in scientific domains. The work of Chèche Konnen is largely ethnographic and small in scale, although the group has been working together for over 10 years. The scale question is very complicated, involving deep-seated beliefs about language use and beliefs about how children and adolescents learn science. Public policy on the whole has remained relatively conservative in these matters. Recent decisions limiting the time students can remain in bilingual education in states such as California and districts such as Chicago are examples of this conservatism.

In a second study, to test near and far transfer of knowledge, students engaged in talk aloud protocols on two problems related to the ecology unit being studied (Conant, 1996). Students were able to talk through their reasoning in their native languages. Students' responses in September, before instruction, involved more circular reasoning in which they attributed the ecological problems that were the target of their reasoning to persons or argued that the source of the problem was the problem itself. At the end of the school year, students' reasoning was more scientific: their reasoning was organized in terms of hypotheses, experiments, and explanations. They used their knowledge of water pollution and aquatic ecosystems to generate explanations. Students used the conditional language of scientific reasoning as evidence of their appropriation of scientific discourse. Ongoing research, including the work of Haitian teacher-researcher Josianne Hudicourt-Barnes (2003), represents a contribution to the body of ESL literature, moving from learning appropriate syntactic structures and vocabulary in English, to learning the disciplinary discourses that characterize rigorous domain-specific academic knowledge. Educators tend not to associate ESL issues with Black students. The challenges around uses of African American Vernacular English bear some relationship to the challenges of speakers of Haitian Creole, Amharic, or Cape Verdean learning to reason and communicate using the discourses of science, of mathematics, of history, or of literary response.

Large-Scale Projects That Take Culture and Language Into Account.   In mathematics, two large-scale projects will be discussed that explicitly take culture and language use into account in their design. The first, Children's Math World (CMW), is headed by Fuson (1990, 1996, 1997) of Northwestern University and the second, the QUASAR Project was headed by Silver (Silver et al., 1995) and colleagues at the University of Pittsburgh. Both projects have been implemented in large urban school districts and by default include African American students as participants. CMW focuses largely on children who speak Spanish. Although the Spanish-speaking students in the Chicago schools using CMW are largely Mexican American, as this work expands to other urban areas, such as New York, Spanish-speaking students will include Black students.

Children's Math World

CMW focuses on primary grades to help children master number sense and the conceptual bases for the core operations of addition, subtraction, multiplication and division. Fuson argues that children who speak Spanish, as well as children speaking a number of Asian languages like Korean, in their early linguistic development learn a language of numbers in which the base ten system is evident in the language. So in Spanish, speakers will say, "diez y cinco," 10 and 5, to represent the number: 15. English, Fuson argues, is a counterintuitive language when it comes to number sense. In addition, CMW builds problems for students that are situated in everyday practices of the communities from which the children come. For example, there are a series of activities associated with El Mercado, buying and selling. Problems are presented to children in Spanish and English and the classroom discourse patterns include moving back and forth fluidly from Spanish to English. Fuson understands the complexities of incorporating everyday practices into classroom routines. She acknowledges that although the children are highly engaged in the El Mercado activities, they also understand the differences between El Mercado in the classroom and their buying and selling activities outside of school. In addition to drawing on funds of knowledge that Spanish-speaking children bring from their home and community experiences, CMW has begun to develop classroom routines based on the African American discourse norms of call and response. This move by CMW shows the flexible nature of their design principles and that their design work is not merely about children who speak Spanish as their first language, but about being responsive to the children being taught, whoever they are, with increasing numbers who are African American. CMW has achieved tremendous success with students. CMW students have been shown to achieve at levels equal to children from Taiwan on the same problem-solving tasks. Fuson also makes explicit the need to address both declarative and procedural knowledge, blurring the boundaries between direct instruction and inquiry-based instruction.

The QUASAR Project

The QUASAR Project operated out of the Learning, Research and Development Center at the University of Pittsburgh until 1995. Among the Principal Investigator leadership was noted mathematics educator Edward Silver. QUASAR is an acronym for Qualitative Understanding: Amplifying Student Achievement and Reasoning. QUASAR operated in six sites in California, Georgia, Massachusetts, Oregon, Pennsylvania, and Wisconsin, in schools serving a diverse population of low-income students. Two sites served predominantly African American and two serve primarily Chicano/a students. QUASAR focuses on middle school mathematics, working with schools to strengthen their attention to problem solving and reasoning. The project articulates an explicit interest in issues of equity. Silver, Smith, and Nelson (1995) observe:

> Fortunately, there is reason to be hopeful that the.... [crises in mathematics education] can be addressed in efforts that combine attention both to improving the quality of the mathematical experiences offered to the nation's students and to increasing the relevance of those experiences to their lives and cultures. (p. 15)

The QUASAR Project addresses this question of the relevance of school mathematics experiences for students by

> ...find[ing] appropriate mathematical problem contexts in the everyday lives of children; connecting mathematics to topics or persons in history, art, music, or other areas of cultural relevance to the ethnic and social groups to

which children belong; and using mathematics to analyze problems of deep concern and relevance to members of various ethnic or social communities, such as the analysis of systematic patterns of racism in housing, banking, or colonialist foreign policy decisions. (p. 25)

QUASAR provided a framework for the middle school mathematics curriculum, principles for mathematics pedagogy and for professional development. However, each school site developed its own local plan for implementation, including specific activities to teach concepts and problem solving.

QUASAR sites have incorporated a cultural orientation in their mathematics teaching through using rap music to promote communication in the classroom and use of West African mathematical games such as Wari and Mancala. One site uses the African American Baseline Essays developed in the Portland, Oregon School District (Hilliard & Leonard, 1990). The African American Baseline Essay in mathematics (Lumpkin, 1990) describes the rich contributions of African civilizations to the storehouse of mathematical knowledge as well as those of African American mathematicians, inventors, scientists, and scholars. This essay also includes descriptions of the ways that mathematical thinking is represented in everyday artifacts and practices both within African and African American communities.

ASSUMPTIONS ABOUT CULTURE AND COGNITION

Allington and Woodside-Jiron (1999) offer a comprehensive critique of the credence attributed to a 1997 report by Grossen, citing National Institute for Child Health and Human Development-funded (NICHD) researchers, arguing that a particular form of phonics based direct instruction represented the consensus of empirical research on emergent reading. The Allington and Woodside-Jiron critique also has strong implications for current declarations about the state of the science of learning:

> Benveniste (1977) indicates that in the political use of expertise, policy advocates consolidate a monopolistic position by promoting the appearance of an external professional consensus on a policy issue, often achieved by using highly selective research teams whose advice may not be easily dismissed. Since "widespread professional consensus may be impossible to achieve" (p. 153), Benveniste notes that by selecting like-minded scholars as the "experts," one can produce a research consensus document that can be used as a policy lever, while also providing advocates of that particular policy agenda a substantial "lead time" advantage. In other words, the selected expert(s) produces a friendly interpretation of the research that can be widely distributed but that cannot be easily disputed in a short period of time. (Allington & Woodside-Jiron, 1999, p. 11)

This same critique can be applied to the discourse that surrounds the emerging science of learning. There is a tendency in the mainstream educational research community to adopt several minority scholar stars to serve as tokens on decision-making bodies and major research teams. Many major research teams have no people of color in research positions or as principal investigators. I am defining major research teams as ones with significant research dollars, often federally funded and representing large-scale national school reform efforts. There is no question that critics of my critique will cite exceptions. However, my observations are based on what I perceive as the norm.

I do not believe the community of African American scholars who advocate a cultural framework nor the mainstream community of largely Euro American scholars by themselves are either monolithic or have the answer to the challenges of achieving real equity in African American education. The limitations of each can be complemented by collaboration. This has implications for funding priorities, especially by such large-scale agencies as the NSF and The Institute of Education Sciences. In personal communications, program officers from both agencies have lamented the small number of minority researchers that they fund.

Equally pervasive challenges are assumptions about the intersections between culture and cognition. In U.S. society (and I believe in much of the Western world), there are stable folk beliefs about ability. Despite current propositions regarding the situatedness of learning, IQ tests still play a significant role in placements and tracking of students. IQ presumes a stable and finite ability. Vygotsky's (1978, 1987) construct of the zone of proximal development, by contrast, suggests that learning should always be ahead of ability, with the assumption that zones change as one learns more. As a society, we have come to equate poverty and race with ability and assume that ability is largely innate and measurable as stable. Research on teacher expectations and the abundant use of the term "at risk" in both the educational and public policy literature often associate low expectations and being "at risk" with living in poverty, being a speaker of a first language other than English or a nonmainstream dialect of English (such as African American Vernacular English). Both because of the historical legacy of racism from the African Holocaust of enslavement as well as the fact that African Americans are represented in large numbers in the ranks of the poor and of speakers of nonstandard dialects as well as languages other than English (i.e., the large number of Black people of Hispanic heritage, first generation Haitian Americans, Ethiopian Americans, Cape Verdean Americans, to name a few), "at risk" is routinely associated with African Americans.

Yet, individual measures of SES are not significantly correlated with achievement (Snow et al., 1998; White, 1982; Walberg & Tsai, 1985). That is, in studies analyzing correlations between the SES of individuals and their corresponding measures of achievement, correlations have been between 0.22 and 0.23. By contrast, for correlations between the SES levels of schools as the unit of analysis with achievement, the average size of the correlation was 0.68 (Byrk & Raudenbush, 1992; Snow, Burns, & Griffin, 1998; White, 1982). Although some may argue that the predictability of low achievement by the levels of poverty of students in schools may be due to the concentration of some set of factors associated with family practices or genetic abilities that run in families, I argue that the levels of poverty in schools more often than not are a stand in for the quality of teaching and restricted opportunities for learning. In the report from the National Academy of Education *Preventing Reading Difficulties in Young Children,* Catherine Snow and her colleagues (Snow et al., 1998) acknowledge that although many studies point to the relationship of home literacy environments and reading achievement or reading readiness among young children, "few studies have derived overall measures of the quality of the preschool home environment" (p. 122). In part because of this presumed relationship, assumptions abound declaring the language deficits of children from low-income families whose first language is other than English and children who speak non-standard English dialects. According to Snow et al. (1998), "language-rich experiences in the home are typically associated with activities (like book reading, shared dinner table conversations) that themselves show only modest predictive value" (p. 122). Such normative assumptions imply that young, poor children whose parents do not read to them at home or whose dinner time conversations do not resemble so-called middle class norms (which themselves may be a stereotyped assumption) are less prepared for learning to read in school. Such children may be less prepared for a particular kind of instruction in reading, rather than not being prepared to learn to read. This important distinction apparently escapes many researchers.

Ironically, Snow and her colleagues go on to say, "It is possible, too, that the effects of differences in verbal interaction may not show up until after the primary grades, that is, when more high-level comprehension is required" (p. 122). This observation obfuscates the responsibility of the quality of instruction after the primary grades, the point at which reading in content areas plays a central role in both the elementary and high school experiences of students. It also implies that the vocabulary and the complexity of reading, for example, in content area reading is somehow more closely aligned with the quality of talk in middle-class homes (another possible fiction). Research on the unique qualities of disciplinary discourses and modes of reasoning suggest it is unlikely that verbal patterns in informal home environments, regardless of SES, resemble the discourses of the disciplines (Graves & Fredericksen, 1996; John-Steiner, 2000; Wineburg,

1998). The point here is that the long-standing affair the educational research community has had with the idea that the experiences of being poor, a person of color (particularly African American and Chicano/a), living in a community of people of color, predict failure in school achievement generally ignores the literature that documents the richness and complexity of experiences within such communities and families. The issue may not be that children from these communities are not ready for schools, but rather that schools are not ready for these children (Cazden et al., 1972).

THE NEED FOR CULTURALLY RESPONSIVE PEDAGOGY AND CURRICULUM

This issue—the readiness of schools and teachers—leads to my final area of concern. Existing research points to schools that are successful with concentrations of low-income students of color. Ron Edmunds's research on effective schools, Sizemore's Scholastic Achievement Structure, Hilliard and Sizemore's video series on effective schools for poor youth, as well as a report from the U.S. Department of Education, "Hope for Urban Education: A Study of High-Performing, High-Poverty Elementary Schools" (1999), all describe the characteristics of such schools. Not surprising, there are many commonalties among what all these scholars have observed in high performing schools serving poor children of color. Although its methods are not explicitly cultural, many regard Success for All, operating out of 450 schools in 120 districts in 31 states, as one of the largest and most successful whole school reform efforts (Slavin & Madden, 1996; Slavin & Oickle, 1981). The research literature on this program does not indicate that Success for All focuses on bridging children's funds of knowledge constructed out of their experiences of community and family life in any explicit ways. Eighty-five percent of SFA schools report 50% or more of their children receive free or reduced lunch. Many of these schools serve predominantly African American and Latino populations. SFA researchers report:

> ...Success for All first graders exceed controls by three months in reading; by fifth grade, their advantage is more than a full grade equivalent. Effects are particularly strong for the most at-risk students and for reducing special education placements. (Cooper, Slavin & Madden, 1997)

It is important to note the ongoing debate in which the research supporting these claims is vigorously challenged (Pogrow, 2000, 2002). However, the point is:

1. there is no one size fits all approach for African American students;
2. good systematic teaching works with African American as well as other children; and

3. there is a substantive range of ways of teaching within a broad band-width that defines effective teaching.

The major elements of the SFA program are very much like what Barbara Sizemore does in SAS or the characteristics of effective schools Edmonds (1979) called for or the range of effective schools documented in a recent U.S. Department of Education report on high achieving schools serving poverty populations.

In this study from the former U.S. Department of Education, schools were chosen with at least 80% low-income students, and high achieve-ment data was available for at least 3 years. Six of the nine schools in the case studies were African American. Only two of these schools used nationally known comprehensive school reform models (the Accelerated School Program and Success for All). Some schools achieved success with little turnover in teaching staff, while others made significant changes in teaching staff. These schools were characterized by the following attributes, reflected in other studies of such high achieving schools:

1. high expectations for all students;
2. a school wide coordinated focus on achievement;
3. focusing on one achievable academic outcome at a time;
4. providing school wide explicit and ongoing instructional support for teachers and students;
5. aligning academic goals with state and district standards;
6. building a sense of community with common goals among all stake-holders (including students, teachers, staff and parents;
7. time on task, including additional instructional time and
8. persistence through setbacks.

What No School Can Do.   The spirit of these findings stands in contrast to an article in the January 19, 2000, issue of the *New York Times Magazine.* I point to the source of this publication—it is not an academic journal—because articles on education in such media strongly reflect broad folk beliefs in U.S. society. In the article, "What No School Can Do," James Traub (2000) argues that the enduring social problems associated with poor neighborhoods are so great that schools cannot be expected to overcome the way these problems are assumed to interfere with school learning. He cites as evidence the work of Coleman (1966) and Jencks (1972) arguing that schooling is unlikely to overcome the influences of parents and community on students. Traub further buttresses his argument with findings regarding two federal programs representing large scale attempts to use schools as a site to help the children of the poor, Head Start and Title I.

> Researchers have known from the virtual outset of the program that Head Start had no effect at all on IQ scores. A 1985 study by the Department of Health and Human Services concluded that 'in the long run, cognitive and socio-emotional test scores of former Head Start students do not remain superior to those of the disadvantaged who did not attend Head Start.' A 1997 study conducted for the Department of Education concluded that 'there were no differences in growth' between students who did and did not receive Title I assistance. (Traub, 2000, p. 55)

What neither these evaluations of Head Start nor Traub take into account is the quality of the instruction Head Start children receive, especially after the primary grades, or the quality of instruction supported by programs funded under Title I. Unless one has reliable, representative, and potentially longitudinal data on the quality of instruction during and after these federal supports for low-income students, one cannot reasonably conclude that continuing low achievement is attributable to the experiences of the children's homes and neighborhoods. I do not by these comments mean to suggest that low-income neighborhoods and communities in large urban and rural areas are idyllic locations. However, I want to point out that poverty and academic or life failures are not synonymous.

Traub acknowledges that there are exceptions to the dismal picture he presents. However, he says if achieving scale in reform must depend on stars such as Jaime Escalante, it is unlikely that schools can successfully overcome the obstacles poor children bring to school. I contrast this observation by Traub with an article in *American Educator* entitled "Knowing and Teaching Elementary Mathematics" (Askey, 1999). In this article middle school teachers discuss the mathematics that underlie why, for instance, we invert numerator and denominator and multiply in problems involving the division of fractions with unlike denominators, as in the following example:

$$1/2 \div 4/6 = 1/2 \times 6/4 = 6/8 \quad \text{or} \quad 3/4.$$

When reading the article, I was struck by the mathematical knowledge of the unnamed middle school teachers. I kept wondering, where did the author find these teachers? Midway through the article, it was stated that these middle school mathematics teachers are from Mainland China, interviewed by Liping Ma (1999).

What then accounts for the fact that a country like China, with a higher percentage of its population living at low economic levels, with its own realities of diversity (at least fifty national minorities speaking mutually unintelligible dialects), is able to educate teachers like those cited in the *American Educator* article? One reason is the difference in folk epistemologies: the Chinese believe in the power of effort and Americans believe in the power of ability, as represented, for example, in our love affair with the construct of IQ (Stevenson & Stigler, 1992). Another reason is a strong belief in the professionalism and the intellectual demands of teaching, translated in the nature of teachers' preservice professional development and even more so in the nature of the professional development opportunities and experiences of Chinese teachers. Teachers in China are expected to publish, to write curriculum, and to have extended periods of time within the regular school day to devote to the intellectual focus of effective pedagogy. Schools in China have master teachers on site who work with newer teachers to help them further refine their practice. Instead of continuing to blame the poor, and by extension large numbers of African American students and families, for the problems of low academic achievement, perhaps as a research and public policy community, we need to interrogate ourselves, our epistemologies, our biases. "What no school can do" alone is to undo these deeply held beliefs that affect how we educate children in this society.

The Emancipatory Dimension of Teaching.   Moreover, there are important differential benefits between culturally responsive ways of teaching and other more generic ways of teaching. The African American community is and has been under political and cultural assault since Africans were kidnapped, enslaved, and brought to the Americas. Although the dimensions of the struggle for freedom have changed over time, the need for continuous struggle has not. Issues of identity and community calling are very much at the heart of such instruction. It is not at all clear that reforms like Success for All, Reading Recovery, The Coalition for Essential Schools, the Small Schools Networks, and so on, have as explicit goals socializing and apprenticing African American students to learn to participate in the struggle for the continuing liberation of the African American community.

This observation is not cited as a fault, but as a fact. By contrast, programs like the Center X headed by Jeannie Oakes at UCLA, The Algebra Project, including The Young People's Project or The Comer Project appear to be much closer to addressing emancipatory aims as part of their reform efforts. In addition, the scholarship of Foster (1994, 1997), Hollins (1996b, Ladson-Billings (1994), and Siddle-Walker (1993) on effective teachers of African American students certainly points to the emancipatory dimension of the work of teachers. In line with this set of propositions, recent research by Darling-Hammond (1999) and others (Ferguson & Ladd, 1996; Gallagher & Bailey, 1999; Greenwald, Hedges, & Laine, 1996) argues that the quality of teachers is the strongest predictor of student achievement. In Darling-Hammond's analysis, the strongest predictor of NAEP student achievement scores in Grade 4 reading, Grade 8 mathematics, and Grade 4 mathematics—controlling for student poverty rate and the percent of limited English proficiency students in reading—was found to be the quality of the teaching force. Quality here was measured as the percent of teachers with full certification and a major in the field. (See also Darling-Hammond, Chapter 9.)

On a 4-hour plane ride to the West Coast, I watched the film Music of the Heart about a White female music teacher who developed an extraordinary program to teach elementary-aged children in Harlem to play the violin. Although I was very moved by the story (I was embarrassed by the tears streaming out the side of my eyes, while people on the plane looked at me in surprise), I was equally struck by the opening scenes in Harlem and in the Harlem school filled with African American and Chicano/a children, loud, raucous, unruly. It dawned on me or more appropriately reinforced my understanding that the stereotypes of the Black (or any of its colored variations, i.e., those folk who are not classified as "White") as unruly, undisciplined, ultimately defined as uncivilized, and, by extension, somewhat less than human, is the archetypal folk belief on which the sense of the humanity of those societies who classify themselves as White depends. This archetypal theme is represented in film media in certain identifiable ways with which many of us are very familiar. However, I realized that these stereotypes are also represented in the genre of the research article equally often but differently, say, than in film. Instead of narratives depicting the Black male gangster (who can be anywhere from 5 years of age to 50) or the sexually loose Black female, the research articles begin by posting the statistics that indicate the demographics of the United States are changing drastically. More colored people are coming—which doesn't mean more Black people of African descent, but more of those who are colorized by the construct of Whiteness, that is, those coming to the United States from South and Central America, from the continent of Asia, or, ironically, from Eastern Europe. They will be poor. They will not speak English. They will be a problem. Because in this archetypal narrative, to be non-White, to be poor, to have another language or language variety other than English as your first language is inherently problematic. Because such populations are inherently problematic, we must develop specialized reforms, specialized curricula, and specialized methods of teaching to address their needs.

On one level, that is exactly what I argue, both in my own research and in this chapter—the need for culturally responsive curriculum and pedagogy. However, maybe these "culturally diverse" students can be taught well with instruction that is culturally responsive and perhaps they can be taught well (I would argue with different consequences) with instruction that is not culturally responsive, but which reflects high expectations, affirms their humanity, is focused on generative knowledge in the academic subjects and that is enacted in stable ways across the school and across their educational careers in K–12 institutions. Instruction reflecting the latter case may not specifically address issues of ethnicity, for example, but certainly does not ignore the fact that kids are Black, and is not color blind. In either case, I want to caution that it may well be that the problems in education are not so much with students from these populations, or with their families or with the communities in which they live, but rather with those who assume formal responsibility for the education of the poor: federal, state, and district level policy makers; teachers and school administrators; educational researchers; those who "train" teachers before and after they enter the profession (Irvine, 1990).

CONCLUDING COMMENTS

In this chapter, I have argued that the voices of researchers who take the issue of culture seriously have been relatively silenced by the academy and within major research institutions, professional organizations and academic journals; they remain on the fringe. This is not a call to add to the constellation of stars in the galaxy of educational researchers. Rather, it is a call to take seriously the politically empowering and moral dimensions of the formal experience we call schooling. It is a call to take into account the affordances as well as the constraints of the experiences of poor children. Therefore, we must return to the question of will. Asa Hilliard (1991) formulates the problem as a question: *Do we have the will to educate all children to high standards?* That remains an open question. What keeps teacher education programs from teaching preservice teachers to be Jaime Escalantes? What keeps school districts in large urban and poor rural areas from paying to attract Jaime Escalantes? Unfortunately, as we consider what research helps us understand about educating African American children and as we consider the practices of schooling—both in K–12 schools where the majority of the students are African American and poor or working class or where African American students, often middle class, are integrated in schools serving a majority White student population, often middle and upper class—the answer to Hilliard's question is: Probably not.

Perhaps what we need is not another individual to be roared up, royalized, routed— but lots of the Littles, understanding the strength of clear cooperation, responsibility.

—Gwendolyn Brooks, *Family Pictures*

Part III

Expanding the Knowledgebase in Black Education and Research Globally

INTRODUCTION

Our charge, in the research tradition inspired by Cheikh Anta Diop, is to define an image of Africa reconciled with its past and preparing for its future. Culture transmission is the link between the past, present, and future of the African world

—Mwalimu J. Shujaa, http://www.coribe.org

The chapters in Part III were prepared expressly for the Commission in order to expand the knowledgebase on Black education and research globally. The first of the Commission's "10 Vital Principles for Black Education and Socialization" asserts: "We exist as African people, an ethnic family. Our perspective must be centered in that reality." In Chapter 5, "Colonial Education: Retrospects and Prospects," William H. Watkins reviews the historical foundations of colonialism on the African continent. Chapter 6, "The Costs of the Underutilization of Black People Globally," prepared by Kassie Freeman, examines monetary and non-monetary costs associated with various ways that Black people are excluded from education in "other-than-African" countries in which the controlling population is not Black.

In Chapter 5, Watkins demystifies the destructive processes of colonial rule in Africa. This analysis also addresses significant parallels in the education systems established in colonial African societies as compared to historical developments in Black education in the southern United States. Watkins reviews the role of Western banks and debt bondage as major contributors to the deforming of African economic and social life, including education (in "British Tropical Africa"). In a section on modernization and educational attainment, this chapter also examines theorizing and failed efforts at "development." Missing from these approaches, Watkins concludes, is a community and social justice orientation—a theme Carol Lee also stresses in Chapter 3. Taking pedagogy into the politics and socioeconomic realities of globalization's impact on the world economy, Watkins's overarching conclusion is that Western models of development and mass education cannot be beneficially imposed on the African reality. Hopeful and realistic possibilities to address the crisis in Black education and colonial dependency in Africa are also suggested.

In Chapter 6, Kassie Freeman provides evidence of commonalities and differences among in Black populations in Australia, Great Britain, Germany, Portugal, and the United States. This chapter offers concrete observations regarding research that is needed to address the monetary and nonmonetary costs of cultural alienation and annihilation and underutilization of Black people's skills and talents in these contexts. Numerous parallels between the forms of exclusion and alienation African Americans and Black people in other countries experience are cited. Freeman concludes that it is not enough for countries to assess the national costs of underutilization but rather strategies to address the societal and individual costs of underutilization of Black citizens are needed as well.

5

Colonial Education in Africa: Retrospects and Prospects

William H. Watkins
University of Illinois at Chicago

INTRODUCTION

In a world of plenty, Africa starves. Located on top of an ocean of oil and precious minerals, much of this continent languishes in desperate poverty and stagnation. The "cradle of civilization" is on the precipice of catastrophic ruination. Colonialism, conquest, greed, and inhumanity have arrested the development of one seventh of the earth's human population.[1] Unfortunately, the history, politics, economics, and dynamics of imperialist conquest and subjugation are not known to all. In America, for example, concepts of emergent Western civilization obfuscate the historical plunder and pillage of the "third world."

Deculturalization and the "civilizing" of indigenous people were undertaken in large measure through colonial schooling. Early models of colonial education in British Tropical Africa resembled those of the southern United States (King, 1971). My focus here is to explore salient aspects of education in colonial and contemporary sub-Saharan Africa. The intention of this chapter is to problemitize and situate public education within a sociopolitical and historical context.

---

[1] http://en.wikipedia.org/wiki/Africa

It is hoped that this examination will contribute to a new framework of understanding and discourse. This examination is organized into several sections. First, a brief summary on the historical establishment of colonialism reveals the devastating social, economic, and cultural consequences to a continent left crippled. Second, an inquiry into colonial education finds that the accommodationist model employed in Africa is similar to that launched in the southern United States. The third section looks at the aftermath of direct colonialism, the brief window of hope for education and the subsequent return to dependency and decline. Next, exploring the current state of African education finds a gloomy picture of reverses and major problems caused by debt and new international financial policy. Finally, this chapter explores realistic possibilities, models, and work in progress for meaningful educational and curriculum change.

THE POLITICS OF EDUCATION IN COLONIAL AND POST-COLONIAL AFRICA

Colonialism in Africa cannot be oversimplified. Many different European countries participated in the process. Thus, the models, methods, languages, school formations, and other manifestations of colonial rule differed by region. Space does not permit idiosyncratic treatment of every country in this short analysis. Sub-Saharan Africa occupies a special place in today's world. It is not just a place; it is a symbol of inhumanity and exploitation of the apocalyptic kind. As a politically constructed phenomenon, education in colonial and postcolonial Africa has taken on added significance and complication. Under colonialism, the ruling regime needs education for obedience, docility, and acceptance. The subject people want education for uplift. In the postcolonial setting, regimes need education to centralize disparate peoples and to legitimize authority. Again the masses look to education for economic uplift and expanded participation in society. Education, then, has many meanings for different constituencies and different political interests. As such, discussions of education in Africa must go beyond the pedagogical and into the political.

As colonial education in Africa is better understood, perhaps we can gain a clearer understanding of the (mis)education of nonvoluntary peoples in the United States. Achievement is more a function of history and state politics than genetic predisposition or biological inheritance. For nearly four centuries, people of color in our country have either been falsely pathologized or pronounced intellectually unfit. While contemporary standardized test scores indicate an achievement gap, the reasons have absolutely nothing to do with genetics and everything to do with access. The politics of colonialism intentionally stifled the development of African people on the continent as well as those in the new world. Miseducation and conquest are inextricably linked.

COLONIALISM AND EDUCATION: HISTORY AND FOUNDATIONS

The literature on colonialism in Africa has approached the topic from different angles. The psychological, for example, Fanon (1968); the political, for example, Rodney (1974) and the many cultural approaches are among the most common perspectives. Each has focused on different ramifications of colonial occupation and devastation. I would like to present a socioeconomic orientation as a starting point here.

The mid-19th century found Western European nations furiously expanding their mercantile enterprises after a long period of feudalism and stagnation. By the last quarter of that century the "scramble for Africa," and any other location for favorable profit-making ventures, was well underway. The Berlin Conference, 1885–1886, allowed European powers to partition Africa "peacefully", although other complications soon ushered in World War I. Whereas traditional nineteenth century mercantilism primarily involved commodity production and exchange, a key feature of colonialism and emerging imperialism was the increased significance of banks. During the last one third of the 19th century, the rapid expansion of industry increased the importance of the agencies by which that expansion would be financed. The merging of bank capital with industrial capital created "finance capital," a growth enterprise thriving on lending. Traditional capitalism evolved into imperialism, the highest and final stage of capitalism (Lenin, 1916; Nkrumah,1965). Imperialism and colonialism became inextricably connected.

The key banking houses acted as the negotiators and promoters of foreign expansion. Prior to 1930, the investment bankers functioned directly as lenders and floaters of foreign securities. After World War II, banks handled the massive credits extended by the U.S. government. As principal holders of government bonds, the banks (along with some insurance companies) received the bulk of the interest on the national debt. Their massive reservoirs of money capital now allow Western banks to anchor the World Bank, the International Monetary Fund, and, ultimately, act as the financiers of the world. Accumulations of capital enable them to be the main source of finance for the impoverished "third world" holding debtor countries in perpetual debt. The historical effect of debt will be addressed.

Whereas the quest for profits fueled imperialistic relationships in the 20th century, those relationships also were expressed in the political, social, educational, and cultural sphere. For the imperialistic relationship to endure, victim countries were forced to remain subservient and incapable of exploiting their own resources. The controlling countries tightly managed competing businesses, labor relations, self-governance, and education. The resulting hegemony is the establishment and maintenance of a power relationship favoring the "metropole" or dominant country. The notion of "underdevelopment" emerged.

Underdevelopment means that the institutions of the victim countries must be made to serve the imperial relationship. The free development of a nation's character is thwarted to conform to this unequal power relationship. Indigenous institutions of a victim country, especially schools, are retarded and deformed. The culture of indigenous people is either destroyed or significantly defaced. Social relations become "fossilized" (Rodney, 1974). The social, political, and intellectual development of such countries becomes arrested. These economic and political arrangements provide context to help understand schooling. Four overarching propositions describe how the colonial legacy impacts education.

First, the intrusive effects of colonialism were overwhelming as disparate tribal (ethnic) groups were forced into nationhood by artificially drawn boundaries. Natural resources were looted. Foreign governors were imposed. Religion, customs, and social institutions were all imposed. The entire indigenous social structure was made to serve the colonial relationship. Second, the colonial relationship distorted the development of societal relations. Rodney (1974) describes how the British cut off northern Nigeria from the remainder of the Muslim world. He goes on to assert that the colonial arrangement leads to "atavism," whereby the tribal groups were set against one another, giving rise to antagonism and violence.

Third, under colonialism, economic, political, and social relations serve the colonial relationship. Education is engineered for maintenance. A select group of indigenous people is trained to manage the interests of the foreign corporations. This group, the *compradors*, benefits financially and forms the basis of the indigenous support for the colonial relationship. Finally, an imprisoning dependence dominates the colonized nation. Unable to develop their resources, utilize technological advancement, accumulate capital, eliminate debt, or expand their intelligentsia, such countries languish in a state of prolonged underdevelopment and indebtedness.

EDUCATION: THE "CIVILIZING" MISSION

Colonial education was widely practiced in the southern United States. General Samuel Armstrong, son of Hawaiian missionaries, founded Hampton Normal School in Virginia in 1868 (Anderson, 1988). It was at Hampton where the theory, curriculum, and ideology of educating subject peoples were ironed out (Watkins, 1994, 1993, 1989c). Political accommodationism, character training, and industrial education were fostered at Hampton. Financed by missionary societies, it became the model for funded education of African Americans. Hampton-style education also was found on the African continent as those same missionary societies internationalized their activities. Colonial education in Africa became indistinguishable from colonial education in the southern United States (King, 1971; Watkins 1989).

Missionary schools in Africa undertook to Christianize indigenous people while teaching rudimentary reading and writing. In most cases, the language and culture of the oppressing country was taught. Missionary organizations enjoyed absolute autonomy and management of educational endeavors in colonized sub-Saharan Africa (Boyle, 1999). Despite the ending of direct colonialism, European curriculum continues to dominate many countries of Africa.

POST-COLONIAL EDUCATION AND SOCIAL ORGANIZATION

Education was among the immediate demands of the postcolonial period. Patrice Lumumba of the Congo, Kwame Nkrumah of Ghana, and Julius Nyerere of Tanzania were passionate advocates of education for Africans. Nigeria's Universal Primary Education (UPE) became a model. The demand for universal education resonated throughout the continent. From 1960 to 1980 the African continent experienced greatly expanded public schooling. World Bank (1988) data indicate that between 1960 and 1970 Cameroon, Kenya, and the Congo increased enrollment by percentages from 57% to 89%, 47% to 58%, and 54% to 88%, respectively. Throughout sub-Saharan Africa, in general, enrollment increased from 36% to 76% within all school-age groups between 1960 and 1980. Other important data such as per pupil expenditure, number of graduates, and rise in literacy rates also show positive growth during the period. Reverses were clearly discernible after 1980 coinciding with debt and the continuing problems of economic stagnation.

ONE STEP FORWARD, TWO STEPS BACK

Since the end of colonialism, the world has changed dramatically. There has been an electronics-technological revolution in the West, the world's wealth has been further concentrated into the hands of the few, and the final consolidation of bank hegemony has taken place. The last three decades have seen a major realigning of world power. What has happened in Africa in this period? What has shaped her future, the future of her people, and the future of her institutions?

We turn first to governance because it provides context and determines much of what happens in the intellectual life of a people. The post–World War II independence movements sweeping the continent, and the world, held out hope for the democratization of society. By the 1970s, formerly colonized Nigeria, Ghana, Kenya, and other nations were free of direct colonial rule. By the early 1990s, multiparty elections were held in Angola, Benin, Cameron, Ivory Coast, Mali, Niger, Lesotho, and Malawi. Between 1990 and 1994, 41 out of 47 countries in sub-Saharan Africa underwent political liberalization in their governance process (Harber, 1997). There have been many reverses in those countries, as exemplified by the December 1999 coup in the Ivory Coast. If democracy and liberalization are important conditions for mass education, it is important to understand the status of democracy in sub-Saharan Africa.

Recent scholarship has questioned the romanticizing of democratic participation in traditional and contemporary African society. Simuyu (1988) argues traditional African society was authoritarian and feudalistic but "colonialism unleashed such violence, discrimination and exploitation that Africans, young and old, educated and uneducated, soon forgot the violence and undemocratic practices of their traditional rulers" (pp. 51–52). The extension of that argument suggests a weak foundation and questionable legacy on which to build democratic participation. Chazan (1993) argues that the anticolonial movements opposed foreign domination but "nationalism in many parts of Africa was not, in any fundamental sense, liberal" (p. 75). Harber (1999) points out that ethnic divisions, impaired national consciousness, political instability, "limited managerial and technical talent," and a weak economic infrastructure have lessened possibilities for democratic participation. He concludes that many leaders view the political state as a source of personal enrichment making it difficult for democracy to proceed. Mazrui (1978) writes: "the African state is sometimes excessively authoritarian to disguise the fact that it is inadequately authoritative" (p. 293). Jackson and Rosberg (1982) note the "removal of constitutional rights and protection from political opponents" whereby strong leaders have centralized power and curtailed open party politics (pp. 23–24). To justify their actions, authoritarian leaders have proffered the notion of a single strongman or chief. They claim strongman regimes are necessary for discipline and development. Sklar (1986) wrote about the "developmental dictatorship."

Finally, the issue of external aggression has become another factor working to slow the democratic process. The existence of heavily armed, well-organized guerrilla movements, sometimes supported by foreign countries, has been answered by fierce military response, austerity, and the curtailment of citizen rights. Beyond civil war, some conflicts have caused significant regional realignments, interventions, and bloody turmoil. Now, in the new century, events in Rwanda, the Congo, and Sudan have created destabilization in East Africa. Those events represent a harbinger for the future.

Authoritarian governments manipulate education. Autocratic leaders desire docility, a stupefied population, and little opposition. Liberal education produces the opposite effect. In recent years, the demand for greater democracy has been linked to the demand for expanded education. In Nigeria, for example, students, teachers, and intellectuals have been at the forefront in the movements for democracy.

THEORIZING ON DEVELOPMENT, MODERNIZATION AND EDUCATION

Africa's economic status raises questions about "development," "modernization," and education that have occupied theorists for many years. Pertinent questions relate to opportunities for modernizing a society. What exactly are the processes of development? How are institutions constructed? How is citizen participation expanded? What is the role of schooling in this process? How do education and political development relate?

During colonialism there was little talk of development or modernization emanating from the West, as those countries profited from the exploitation of Africa. Early postcolonial thinking about modernization was scattered and often overly optimistic. Notions of self-sufficiency, human capital development, government efficiency, expanded education, and democracy were believed key to development. Many believed if people and agencies are cultivated, progress can occur. Money and aid were seen as instrumental in this process. Lyndon B. Johnson's "Great Society" was considered the model for the remediation of social ills. Because independence occurred at the height of the Cold War, Western powers were committed to keeping Africa insulated from Soviet influences. Indigenous African opposition to dependence was overshadowed by the anti-Communism of the West. Patrice Lumumba's plans for expanded education and the nationalization of precious metals and minerals was answered by his swift assassination.

The West had few explanations to assist educational and social development in Africa. American "experts" scampered to construct theory that might help rationalize African society. Political scientists connected to the influential Social Science Research Council's Committee on Comparative Studies promoted a new discourse (Harber, 1997). Among that group's influential people were James Coleman who edited *Educational and Political Development* (1965) and Gabriel Almond who wrote (with

S. Verba) *The Civic Culture* (1963) and (with B. Powell) *Comparative Politics: A Developmental Approach* (1966). Although theoretical and practical application differed, "modernization theory" emerged.

The early "modernization theory" of Coleman and Almond explored how education contributed to expanded social participation. It called attention to modern society where education was primary. Second-wave modernization theorists, such as Alex Inkeles (1969), placed more emphasis on the place of the modern individual in bureaucratic rationality (Harber, 1997). Inkeles found schooling important, not for the fostering of democracy but, rather, for preparation of the citizen in the efficient bureaucratic society. Harber (1997) described the changed modernization theory:

> In his empirical research Inkeles (Inkeles & Smith, 1974) found education to have the strongest relationship of all variables with the possession of modern (i.e., bureaucratic) attitudes, values and behavior as described above. The explanation for this is the congruence between the bureaucratic nature of "modernity" and the bureaucratic nature of school organisation. For example, the pupil at school learns new skills such as reading, writing and arithmetic so that he or she will later be able to "read directions and instructions and to follow events in the newspaper" and this produces a heightened sense of personal efficacy. Most revealing of all, however, is the way in which pupils learn impersonal rules from the hidden curriculum of school organization. (p. 32)

Harber (1997) concludes that modernization theory has come full circle with the focus back on democracy; however, events in the intervening years have significantly changed the course of political history. The new world order profoundly altered the circumstances for Africa.

CONSERVATISM AND THE REORDERING OF THE WORLD

Historians might, one day, see 1980 as the watershed of a new economic and political world order. America, Africa, and the entire world were affected. Several dramatic events occurred. First, the technological revolution became firmly established. The computer chip, introduced in the 1970s, forever altered human labor and human relations. The "chip," which could activate machinery, signified that for the first time, production, the basis of all economies, could occur without human labor. Traditional concepts of employment, wages, and value were scrapped as millions were and are soon to be displaced. Chip technology accompanies fiber optics, lasers, and magnets in the creation of a new world.

Second, the globalization of the world's economy has profoundly affected the marketplace. Expanded productive capacity has created fierce competition and reliance on high-tech methods. Industrial production, once concentrated in the West, has been dispersed and compartmentalized throughout the world. The only rule is that production moves to its cheapest source. "Third world" children now manufacture many of our daily commodities for pennies per day and so-called American jobs are exported abroad. There no longer exists a logical or balanced relationship between production and consumption. Those who manufacture goods often can never buy those goods.

Third, the emergence of speculative capitalism has significantly altered world commerce. As mentioned earlier, banks have become all-powerful in the 20th century. Recent changes have affected the flow of money. Financial speculation in stocks, bonds, and ventures has reorganized the distribution of wealth. Nearly $1.5 trillion passes through clearinghouses every day. Financial "ventures" have become the source of great profit, and, sometimes, great disappointment. A redistribution of the wealth is underway where now the top 1% of the population in the United States controls nearly half the nation's wealth. A handful of the richest men in the United States now control more wealth than all of sub-Saharan Africa, excluding South Africa.

The political expression of this shift was evidenced in the changing world leadership. The year 1980 represented an end to traditional politics in the United States. For example, the traditional division between liberal and conservative is now a dead issue, as the major political parties have become indistinguishable from one another. No one now speaks for the downtrodden and dispossessed. The emergence of Reagan, Thatcher, Gorbachev, and the so-called conservative restoration have altered world history. Small people and small countries no longer have allies. Humanitarianism is rapidly giving way to a new greed that victimizes those least able to help themselves. It is within this new context we find Africa drowning in debt.

TROUBLE ON THE CONTINENT: DEBT BONDAGE AND THE POLITICS OF "STRUCTURAL ADJUSTMENT"

In the modern world, debt overshadows and influences every aspect of social and political life. Over 100 years ago, Karl Marx wrote about the political impact of debt. He explained the binding nature of debt and how the creditor/debtor relationship forged economic and political relationships. It was, he argued, much more significant than any buyer/seller relationship. Debt has become the central issue defining the status of individuals, families, and nation-states. It provides the essence of neocolonial dependence. The "structural adjustment" policies now strangling Africa are not widely understood. Major Western banks and financial consortiums with billions to loan employ adjustment programs. The international media sometimes talks of the "Paris Club" to describe creditor nations.

Since the mid-1970s, most "third world" debtor nations, especially in Africa, have defaulted on the repayment of their loans. "Paris Club" banks have taken to adjusting, or refinancing, their loans. The banks claim inefficient economies and overspending in the public sector are the causes of stagnation. To avoid financial catastrophe, indebted countries have turned to the International Monetary Fund (IMF) and the World Bank for new loans. IMF "stabilization" loan bailouts are accompanied by harsh conditions including currency devaluation, public expenditure cutbacks, the elimination of state subsidies, wage restraints on public sector jobs, and credit limitations (Graham-Brown, 1999). Adjustment theory holds that private sector expansion will "grow" these nations out of crises. The net effect of structural adjustment policies has been the devastation of government-funded projects. Infrastructures, public health, relief programs, and schools have been especially hard hit.

Human Costs.   Adjustment policies have taken a drastic toll on populations least able to absorb adversity. Cutbacks in government spending have affected state subsidies forcing prices up for consumers. Additionally, governments are restricted in assisting housing, transportation and medical care. Wages, benefits, and the safety net are profoundly affected. Inflation, high unemployment, stagnation, and recession accompany structural adjustment in sub-Saharan Africa. The burden of adjustment policies has not been shouldered evenly. The rural poor and lower classes have suffered inordinately. Indigenous economies have experienced inflationary pressures to maintain production. The hope for self-sufficiency is rapidly eroding. Zambia, for example, which produces maize, a national staple, suffers pressures from the increased cost of fertilizer, fuel, and farm implements (Graham-Brown, 1999). Women's wages, already low, have been even further depressed. Children, the hope of the future, are often pressed into labor and otherwise ill served by near bankrupt local economies. Employment is a major casualty of "structural adjustment." Restricting public sector spending has not lead to expansion in private sector production. Rural communities are filled with "workers in waiting" relegated to "informal" or subsistence level survival. Beyond economic problems, the quagmire of war and ethnic conflict drain what little resources are available to create modern employment.

THE SPECTER OF CONTINENT-WIDE CONFLICT

The most deleterious effect of structural adjustment has been civil and regional conflict. Having suffered decades of recession, struggles for power and privilege are inevitable. Beyond the traditional tribal and ethnic squabbling conditioned by century-old artificial boundaries, new and dangerous military intrigue and adventure have emerged in the East. Recent events in Rwanda and the Congo have drawn neighboring countries into perilous alliances threatening future stability. Areas throughout Africa possessing some of the planet's richest soil have experienced food riots. The complications of border disputes, religious and cultural conflict, AIDS, and scarcity condemn Africa to a long period of difficulty.

Structural Adjustment and Schooling.   Although private education exists, schools in Africa remain primarily a state enterprise. Cutbacks in public sector spending have had devastating consequences where poverty already prevails. Between 1975 and 1985, government expenditures in Africa on teaching materials was nearly halved—from 7.6% to 4.2%. Studies conducted in the 1980s found, for example, that 20% of all schools in Sudan had no water, whereas over half had no toilets. In Tanzania, 42% of schools had no water and 10% had no toilets. Schools throughout the continent frequently operate without textbooks, desks, chalk, pencils, or chairs. (The chapters in Part IV and VII provide up-to-date analyses of current conditions in West Africa and Southern Africa.)

The training and maintenance of teachers has been a critically important issue. Eleven countries including Kenya, Zambia, Zimbabwe, and Sénégal experienced teacher salary cuts of 10% or more in the 1980s. Teachers frequently work double shifts, teach classes with enormous numbers of students and operate with minimal resources. In some nations, the figures are staggering. The Congo, for example, spent 20.4% of its national budget on education in 1970. By 1990, that percentage slipped to 6.4%.

The consequences of structural adjustment are leading to deschooled societies in sub-Saharan Africa. Some children are leaving after only a few years of schooling. Public education in Africa is collapsing (Boyle, 1999). A United States Agency for International Development (USAID) report in 1995 stated:

> Most African education systems are characterized by stagnating or declining enrollments, evaporating non-salary expenditures, eroding quality of instruction, and growing inefficiency in resource and personnel management. (Boyle, 1999, p. 29)

The politics and economics of structural adjustment have profoundly influenced "development" and modernization in this part of the world. Beyond knowledge acquisition of the citizenry, these policies have forged societies where stratification, inequality, elitism, privilege, and corruption abound. Oppression by region, tribe, class, gender, religion, language, and culture threaten to rip apart the continent. Questions about education in increasingly stratified Africa are crucial to understanding and improving conditions.

EDUCATION, SOCIETAL DEVELOPMENT, AND CULTURE

African societies are perhaps the most historically and politically manipulated. Thrown together into artificially bounded nation-states, governed by foreigners, and stripped of wealth-generating resources, African social development is both unnatural and impaired. Thus, the issue of societal organization is a crucial one. What can be said of social development in sub-Saharan Africa? Emile Durkhiem (1899) asked how it was that societies hold together? What are the salient and binding sociocultural, economic, and political issues in modern African life? What is the place of schools in contemporary African society?

Fundamental for any society are questions about property and economic stratification. How are wealth and power divided? Who benefits from what? Who goes to school and who doesn't? Who eats and who does not? Long known for its traditional communal social fabric, African society has evolved a class structure with rigid delineation. Colonialism created a *compradore* or middle class with access to education and status. Just as America developed a "slave aristocracy" (Bullock, 1967), colonialism created an indigenous elite. By independence, the elite was clearly identifiable and, more important, possessors of social and economic privilege.

The role of education in societal development is crucial in Africa. The hope for uplift of the bottom has not occurred. Instead, educated and privileged Africans provide the core of a state-dependent African bourgeoisie (Sklar, 1979). Some scholarship on elite formation in Africa suggests education as the central variable. Boyle (1999) surveyed assorted views on questions of the relationship of elitism to popular education in Africa. Coleman (1965), for example, linked education to elite status in the African context. Challenges to linkage theories argued that increased access to education in the early 1970s did not seem to alter fundamentally status relationships. Beyond the inability to influence status, Boyle argues that the expansion of education in the 1970s failed to fuel economic development. Newly educated citizens, including those who obtained graduate degrees abroad, found only limited employment opportunities. Because education has not been the "motor" for development, Boyle suggests we look to other dynamics to help understand social development in sub-Saharan Africa. Although a complicated motif of sociocultural and economic variables further explains social development in African society, what can be concluded about the current state of schools?

SCHOOLING IN SUB-SAHARAN AFRICA:
SELECTED ISSUES

As in any setting, the examination of schools is an exhaustive undertaking given to the idiosyncrasies of history, ethnicity, funding, and politics. Comprehensive discussions of African education, by Africans and Westerners alike, do exist. Interested readers may want to consult, for example, Abernathy's (1969) *The Political Dilemma of Popular Education: An African Case*, Clinget and Foster's (1966) *The Fortunate Few*, and other works. What follows is a discussion of selected issues in schooling in sub-Saharan Africa.

The Authoritarian School. If self-determination, social justice, democracy, and actualization are desirable goals of education, then notions of order, discipline, and school structure must be examined. Whether they are located in Japan, the United States, England, or Angola, the "authoritative" school is often a reality. The colonial experience left African schools rigid and authoritarian. Studies conducted by Fuller (1991), Mbilinyi (1977), and Harber (1989) in several countries indicate similar findings. Teachers are revered, and, as such, their lecture style dominates. Student interaction and inputs are mostly absent in the African classroom. Mbilinyi (1979) argues the "banking" approach provides the norm in most classrooms.

Beyond the classroom, African school systems tend to be both centralized and bureaucratized. Colonial administrators set about to establish hierarchical central authority to guarantee control. Africa's bureaucratized schools are characterized by hierarchy, order, rule imposition, lack of elections, and secrecy. Beyond the control so important to former colonial educators, contemporary African states utilize the authoritarian bureaucratic model of schools to appear modern. Fuller (1991) argues that the "fragile" and "shallow" authority of the postcolonial state demands that governments appear sturdy, legitimate, and modern. The centrality of public schools in development makes them important showcase agencies. Fuller (1991) describes this dynamic:

> The younger, more fragile state, common across the Third World, plays a much stronger role in importing and legitimating the bureaucratic structure and moral order of the Western school. Bureaucratic rationalized organizations or firms are still a novel form. Here the visible contours and symbols of "modern organization" take on enormous power. The Third World school may fail to hold deep effects on children's acquired literacy or secular values. But the fact that the school is tightly administered—with tidy accounts, a sharp schedule of classes and attractive gardens—signals the attributes of modern organisation. The institution is recognised by local parents as a concrete instrument of modernity, even if the school's technical objective of raising literacy is rarely accomplished. (pp. 43–44)

Teaching styles are often connected to the authoritarian school and class-room. Serpell's (1999) study in Zambia found "condescending" teaching where the teacher controlled and directed classroom discussions and most importantly, the correctness of answers. Serpell wrote:

> [the] style of classroom management favoured in most African schools still resembles the "chalk and talk" model of early twentieth century Western schools. Largely content free drills are used pervasively to impart much of the curriculum, with an apparent rationale of memorisation. Progress is assessed by the criterion of accurate recitation of the alphabet, the times table and "factual" lesson-notes copied from the blackboard into exercise books. Moreover, most teachers administer their classes in a highly directive (didactic) manner, demanding deferential silence from their students except when called upon to answer specific questions, and enforcing the adherence to right procedural routines with authoritarian discipline. (pp. 93–94)

Authoritarian schooling is deeply entrenched in sub-Saharan Africa. It has gained legitimacy, is seldom challenged, appears consistent with the culture, and is continuously reproduced (Harber, 1997). Education scholars have argued that Africa's authoritarian schools mitigate against democratization of the society at large. Perhaps more insidious and deleterious is the content of the curriculum.

Textbooks: Issues and Problems.   Within the formal curriculum, the textbook is one of the critical learning tools as it organizes and rations the materials to be engaged. Issues surrounding textbooks in African schools date to the beginning of the twentieth century. Because of scarcity, poverty, illiteracy, and difficult communications avenues, the textbook takes on even greater importance as it represents portable knowledge and information. Textbooks allow information to reach areas difficult to access and bring schooling to the community. Production and ideology are two important issues surrounding textbooks.

Production issues include the often-difficult task of the procurement of raw materials in an environment where wood pulp, ink, printing and binding equipment, and so on are scarce. Absent the requisite resources, the graphics and design of textbooks can be challenging. In countries lacking efficient transportation infrastructures, distribution provides major problems. More complex production issues involve securing copyrights, intellectual property and other legal matters, updating editions, supplying teacher manuals, and providing supplementary materials (Altbach & Kelly, 1988).

Beyond those problems are the far more challenging ideological questions involving the content of what goes into the texts. Textbooks are among the most contested and political aspects of public schooling. They provide both a sociohistorical worldview and a body of thought about existing power arrangements. They shape the ever-changing culture of societies in transition. Beyond sacred books, school texts may be the closest to providing "official" knowledge. Additionally, they are subject to intense scrutiny and often censorship. No regime or "party in power" will allow an antithetical worldview to undermine its authority.

Altbach and Kelly (1988) list many questions important to investigate about both the productive and ideological aspects of text-making: What are the pedagogical and philosophical foundations of the text? What will be the language of publication? Who will publish the texts, the state or private firms? How will they be distributed? Will books be purchased or supplied free? How will teachers be trained to use the books? How will books be evaluated and revised? They go on to describe the enormous task of text publishing in poor countries.

The World Bank and UNESCO have studied text publishing in Africa and other "third world" nations. They point to several problems experienced by such countries, including miscalculation of financial feasibility, inadequate planning systems, inadequate management resources, confusion between publisher and printer, failure to coordinate textbooks with prescribed curricula, failure to understand the connection of textbook industry with larger publishing world, and so on. The web of ideological problems surrounding the text is complex. No issue is more difficult than the nature of the content. Social Studies education and texts have been frequently examined in African schools. Watkins (1986) researched frequently used secondary Social Studies textbooks in Nigeria. Watkins concludes:

> The textbook curriculum, as it is now constituted, is a group of generalized standard lessons, which fail to explore Nigeria's unique and significant subservience to the West, which colors its entire social, economic, and political fabric. The problem-solving approach promised by some texts fails to materialize. Rather than engage the student in meaningful social inquiry vis-à-vis politics, economics, and international affairs, the texts generally lapse into exercise of socialization.... The ideological posture of the textbook material is easily discerned. Its tone suggests that one must be reconciled to the political and economic environment. Seldom is the student viewed as a force for inquiry and change. (p. 190)

INTO THE NEW MILLENNIUM: LESSONS FOR CHANGE

As a new century begins, the prospects for oppressed people the world over are not bright. Realistic appraisals and programs are needed to improve, if not radically alter, the lives of Africa's 800 million people. The policies of structural adjustment continue to beat down people already at subsistence. Capital, desperately needed to modernize, is monopolized by a cabal of secretive and avaricious Western financiers with little concern for economic equality or social justice. The World Bank, IMF, and World Trade Organization are quietly reordering and restructuring the entire world before our very eyes. "NAFTA for Africa" will make the continent an economic free fire zone for European and American commercial endeavors. There are no easy formulas or answers for a continent on the verge of apocalyptic collapse. By contrast, the human spirit persists. Africa and her scattered people have endured the harshest treatment imaginable at the hands of colonists and evildoers. It is this human spirit, agency, and intelligence on which we can rely to seek out avenues for progress and justice.

Inhuman treatment will continue, Africa will continue, and education will continue. With no panacea in sight, areas for change must be sought out. There is much ideological and practical work to be done. Social reformers, philanthropists, scholars, educators, altruists, missionaries, and international agencies outside the continent desire to provide support. They need to know where help can be most effective in promoting change. We all need to understand the policies and "models" for change which have possibility. Unfortunately, far too much energy has been wasted.

Scrase (1997) argues the traditional politics of "Fordism," embraced in the West, and applied to economic, social, and educational problems alike, cannot work in Africa. Fordism, a quantity-based approach named for Henry Ford's assembly line/efficiency model, looks at mass production and mass consumption for answers to social problems. It suggests that financial allocations to projects, factory subsidies, and the building of new schools, for example, will pay off and ultimately contribute to an expanding economy. This idea is predicated on a notion that financial accumulation and long-term growth are inevitable. It is a quantity-oriented "remedy" that assumes that infusing capital automatically creates improvement. Here is how Scrase (1997) summarizes the results of Fordism in Africa:

> The rhetoric and ideology of the market (in the form of the ideas of the Chicago school) have permeated both the discourse and practice of government policies, leading to a further deterioration in the living conditions of ordinary people in developing nation. Under the influence of Western financial institutions, such as the IMF and the World Bank, the development ideology embodied in the trickle down and human capital theories, so popular in the 1950s and 1960s, has given way to structural adjustment and the wholesale reduction of government services in an effort to repay the burgeoning debt burden. Over the past decade or more, governmental attempts to satisfy the "debt squads" have led to a decline in the provision of basic levels of social and educational programs for the mass of the population. The immediate beneficiaries of this decline in the provision of programs for the majority of the population have been the middle classes. (p. 38)

The problem with Fordism and most other Western models of development and educational attainment is their lack of "community" and social justice orientation. Africa is not likely to "grow" economically in such a way that problems of want are erased. There is no industrial revolution underway. There are no great accumulations of wealth over the horizon. For the immediate future, African will likely remain rural, agricultural, and poor. What does that mean for education? Do we need a Freirian model of literacy and consciencization? Is vocational education the answer? Because of persistent ethnic rivalries, do we need multicultural education? Because of ongoing sexism, does Africa need feminist pedagogy? Is liberation theology a viable option for the continent? What about Social Reconstructionism?

The expansion of schooling into mass schooling is now a major consideration for Africa. Murky state politics must be brought in line with that objective. Fuller (1991) cautions us to explore political contradictions in mass education. His notion of the "fragile state" in Africa suggests that state forces may utilize mass education to elicit centralization, socialization, and "ideological commitment" to a central authority. He notes that although democratic in rhetoric, many promote education for class privilege.

CONCLUDING COMMENTS: AN AGENDA FOR CHANGE

The complications of state politics in Africa are immense. It is very likely that meaningful educational change will come from local efforts. Without extensive resources and with little fanfare, many communities have launched initiatives for change. The research community needs to know more about them. One such project is the Gao School Museum in Mali, West Africa (Maiga, 1995). Conceptually grounded in experientialism, culturally relevant pedagogy, and social activism, the Gao School Museum approach represents true community and collaborative learning.

The Gao School Museum is neither a conventional school nor a conventional museum. Rather, it is a process of inquiry in which teachers and students come together to construct a living curriculum. The curriculum is connected to their community and the students' lives. It is designed to bridge the gap between theory and practice. Students and teachers form research teams that jointly engage themselves and the people in the community in the research. There is no restriction on the type of research. Projects can be scientific, for example, seeking out minerals; or they might be vocational, such as exploring occupations or they might be mechanical, such as building a structure. Goals of the Gao School Museum are to engage in relevant inquiry, promote the value to collaborative research, encourage creativity, encourage scientific research, help students analyze learning experiences, identify learning resources in the community, and to share and exchange experiences with other learners. This approach is one of many alternative local projects operating outside the entanglements of power politics in Africa. Its credo of learning by doing prepares students for living and for social change. It could be that innovations like the Gao School Museum represent true and doable models for social change in Africa deserving of support and continued research.

6

Black Populations Globally: The Costs of the Underutilization of Blacks in Education

Kassie Freeman
Dillard University

INTRODUCTION

Beyond the details of oppressions, one purpose of this chapter is to explore what educators and researchers should know about the educational challenges that Black people encounter globally in their quest for education. Several questions need to be considered in order to understand better and to address these challenges. First, what are the similarities in the experiences of Black people in various contexts with regard to their participation in education, particularly when the controlling populations are non-Black? Second, what can be learned from research that connects the experiences of Black populations globally that will help illuminate the patterns of exclusion or limitation of Black participation in education? Most important, how is examining the shared experiences of Black populations, both during education and in the workplace, useful for understanding the individual and societal costs of the underutilization of Blacks in different countries?

In this chapter, Black populations are defined using a racial designation. That is, the physical characteristics that identify Black peoples, for example, color, hair and/or other distinguishing physical features that define "race." Although more recently ethnicity has been used to define group identities and experiences in educational research, the construct race is used here because in comparative and international research race more accurately describes the similarity of Black experiences. To be sure, there are similarities in the experiences of Black populations globally. Yet, understandably, there are also notable differences. As Audre Lorde (1992), in reference to the differences among Afro-German women and other Black women, indicated, "particular histories have fashioned our particular weapons, our particular insights" (p. xiii). Yet, in also indicating our sameness, Lorde posed a fundamental question: "As members of an international community of people of color, how do we strengthen and support each other in our battles against the rising international tide of racism?" (p. xiii). In response to this question, she stated, "to successfully battle the many faces of institutionalized racial oppression, we must share the strengths of each other's vision as well as the weaponries born of particular experience" (p. xiii). In no arena is the battle more apparent and similar for Black populations than in their pursuit of education.

From countries as diverse as Australia, Great Britain, France, Portugal, the United States, and New Zealand, Black populations always have had to fight for the right to participate in education. Black people have always realized, as a recent writer in *The Economist* (1999) stated, "the ultimate ladder of opportunity is education" (p. 18). Recognizing the liberating power of education, Black people have held the goal and expressed their desire to participate in education, but across societies throughout the world, they have encountered opposition from their national governments. As Martin Carnoy (1992) indicates, implicit in every discussion of education, there is the invisible hand of the state, determining who will participate and who will not. Globally, at the beginning of the 21st century, countries now find themselves grappling with the individual and societal costs associated with having uneducated and undereducated segments of their populations resulting from centuries of denying educational opportunities to Black populations. Thus, there is now a unique opportunity to study education as a commodity when comparing and contrasting the experiences of Black populations in the United States with Black people in other countries.

This chapter focuses on Black populations in countries external to Africa in which the controlling population is non-Black, for example, Australia, Great Britain, Germany, Portugal, and the United States. There have been substantial research studies on Black Americans in their struggle to participate in education, but very little on Black populations in other countries. Even fewer comparative studies have been done on the educational experiences of Black people after accessing participation. Therefore, the research presented in this chapter examines similarities in the experiences of Black people in their quest to participate in education and assesses the nonmonetary costs associated with the underutilization of Black populations in education.

Across cultures, there are common issues in Black people's pursuit of education relative to the underutilization of their potential. To examine these issues, this chapter addresses four broad themes:

1. the contrast of the historical experiences of Black people's pursuit of education;
2. the pattern of cultural alienation and annihilation on the part of the dominant population in the underutilization of Black people in the education process;
3. the "culture of exclusion" that exists in the participation of Black populations in education and
4. the nonmonetary costs to societies in their underutilization of Black populations in education—the social (societal) and private (individual) costs.

DIFFERENT COUNTRIES, SIMILAR
HISTORICAL EXPERIENCES

As James Anderson (1988, 1999) has so rightly indicated in numerous publications and speeches, to understand the educational experiences of Black people, it is necessary to examine the historical context of their existence. Although, as Audre Lorde (1992) indicated, Black populations in different countries have experienced particular histories, across societies Black populations have had similar experiences relative to their humanity and their pursuit of education. The common historical linkage among Black people in the Diaspora is captured by Opitz, Oguntoye, and Schultz (1992), who refer to Afro-Germans: "In the course of colonial exploitation, enslavement and domination, 'Negro' (from Latin niger, i.e., black) became an especially negative epithet. The thinking underlying this label attempted to link physical characteristics with intellectual and cultural ones" (p. 7). Across cultures, being Black has historically been thought of as being intellectually inferior and being without a culture or having a primitive or uncivilized culture.

Although often not recognized, Black people have been a part of European societies longer, in most cases, than they have been a part of American ones. For example, Fryer (1992), who wrote what would be considered the seminal work on Black people in Britain, indicated that African descendants have been in Britain for centuries; as a group they "have been living in Britain for close on 500 years. They have been born in Britain since about the year 1505" (p. ix). That would mean that, based on American history, Black Britons as a group were in England more than one hundred years before the arrival of Black people in America in Jamestown, Virginia, in 1619 (Clarke, 1972). Although Opitz, Oguntoye, and Schultz (1992) indicate that "there is no precise method of determining when the first Africans came to Germany and when the first Afro-Germans were born," the authors note that "several paintings have survived from the twelfth century that depict Africans living in Germany" (p. 3). Although their exact arrival across cultures may be unclear, what is certain is that by the mid-16th and 17th centuries, Black people were settled in countries around the globe. For example, "in the mid-sixteenth century, one-tenth of the population in the Portuguese capital were Black, and, as in France and England, it was probably also true in Germany" (Opitz, Oguntoye, & Schultz, 1992, p. 3).

Black people in different countries faced similar treatment in the portrayal of their culture. Blackness was associated with evilness, inferiority in every way, and sub-humanism. In Britain, for example, "Africans were said to be inherently inferior, mentally, morally, culturally, and spiritually, to Europeans" (Fryer, 1992, p. 7). Likewise, in Germany, Blacks were portrayed negatively. In general, "Africans were seen as the lowest human form, thought to be related to the highest animal form, the monkey" (Opitz, Oguntoye & Schultz, 1992, p. 8). At that time, "most Portuguese seem to have thought that blacks as a people were innately inferior to whites in physical beauty and mental ability and moreover, that they were temperamentally suited to a life in slavery" (Saunders et al., 1982, p. 166). Although on a different continent, Black people in the United States were experiencing the same devaluation of their humanity. In the United States, this statement about the use of Slave Codes best captures how Black people were viewed:

> There were variations from state to state, but the general point of view expressed in most of them [Slave Codes] was the same, that is: slaves are not persons but property, and laws should protect the ownership of such property, and should also protect the whites against any dangers that might arise from the presence of large numbers of Negroes. (Franklin & Moss, 1988, p. 114)

According to Clarke (1972), this devaluation of Black culture caused Africans the world over to begin, by the 19th century, to search for a definition of themselves.

Another similar link in the historical experiences of Black populations was the exploitation of their labor. As Clarke (1972) indicates, "The story of the African slave trade is essentially the consequences of the second rise of Europe.... They were searching for new markets, new materials, new manpower and new land to exploit. The slave trade was created to accommodate this expansion" (p. xvii). Just as Black people in America were relegated to working the land and working as servants to increase the wealth of this country, so were Blacks in European countries. For example, according to Fryer (1992), "the majority of the 10,000 or so black people who lived in

Britain in the eighteenth century were household servants—pages, valets, footmen, coachmen, cooks, and maids—much as their predecessors had been in the previous century" (p. 73). Although working menial jobs, Fryer conceded that as a Liverpool writer declared in 1893, "it was the capital made in the African slave trade that built some of our docks and the price of human flesh and blood that gave us a start" (p. 66). Similarly, in Germany, Black people were used for menial labor. They were, for example, "forced to cultivate export products or to work on the plantations and in the mines of whites" (Opitz, Oguntoye, & Schultz, 1992, p. 25). The same was the case in Portugal. According to Saunders (1982), "the nobility employed— or underemployed—large numbers of slaves solely as domestic servants" (p. 63).

Even when Black people were interested in working higher status jobs, they were forbidden. For example, in London after 1731, they were not allowed to learn a trade. In fact, on September 14, 1731, the Lord Mayor of London issued the following proclamation prohibiting apprenticeships for Black people:

> It is Ordered by this Court, That for the future no Negroes or other Blacks be suffered to be bound Apprentices at any of the Companies of this City to any Freeman thereof; and that Copies of this Order be printed and sent to the Masters and Wardens of the several Companies of this City, who are required to see the same at all times hereafter duly observed. (cited in Fryer, 1992, p. 75)

Although there were some Black people in the United States who possessed some skills, especially the few slaves who lived in towns, the great majority of the responsibilities of the enslaved were divided between two distinct groups: house servants and field hands (Franklin & Moss, 1988). According to these researchers, the enslaved had little opportunity to develop initiative because their responsibilities were proscribed for them. Therefore, the idea that Black people did not want to work and, thus, played a role in having their skills underutilized was not the case. Understandably, the exploitation of labor is and has always been intricately linked to lack of educational opportunities. To keep groups uneducated or undereducated has been a formula across societies for the underutilization of their talents. Nkrumah, the son of the late African leader, describes it as a sort of worldwide formula by which African descendants everywhere have been relegated to the bottom educationally and economically. As such, the idea has been to prevent Black people from being empowered intellectually, culturally, and economically.

As Anderson (1988) has indicated, it is through education that individuals begin to feel empowered and African Americans were active agents in their right to be educated. From slavery until now, African Americans have had to struggle for the opportunity to participate in any form of education. According to Anderson, "Blacks emerged from slavery with a strong belief in the desirability of learning to read and write" (p. 5). As an example of the intensity of anger that enslaved Africans held for keeping them illiterate, Anderson quotes a former slave: "There is one sin that slavery committed against me which I will never forgive. It robbed me of my education" (p. 5). Restrictive legislation had been passed to prohibit the enslaved from learning to read and write (Fleming, 1976). According to Fleming, from 1850 to 1856 less than 5% of African Americans out of a population of 4.5 million could read and write. Just as Black people in America were forbidden to learn to read and write, the same was true in other countries where the controlling population was non-Black. For example, in Portugal, very few Black people were able to read and write (Saunders, 1982).

As Opitz, Oguntoye, and Schultz (1992) indicate relative to Afro Germans, "the limitations of educational opportunities concurrent with the favoring of some individuals led to hierarchical structures that undermined the solidarity of the community" (p. 33). In that sense, not only has the lack of educational opportunities been utilized to limit the use of the talent and skills of Black people, but education has also been used as a force to destabilize communities. That is, education as a commodity has been used as a means to favor some intra-group members over others as a way to undermine community relationships and solidarity. In Portugal, for example, mulattoes were thought to be more conversant "with Portuguese customs, were supposed to be more gifted intellectually than were blacks from Africa" (Saunders, 1982, p. 172). Therefore, the commonality of the Black historical experience in countries where non-Blacks are the dominant population has been the underutilization of the potential of Black people by demeaning their humanity through enslaving them, destabilizing their communities, exploiting their labor and/or limiting their educational opportunities. However, even when Black people were allowed to participate in education, a process of cultural alienation, or annihilation was implemented.

CULTURAL ALIENATION AND ANNIHILATION

According to Claude Anderson (1994), one way the use of power over a less powerful group takes form is "the group with the greater power annihilates the powerless group or drives them out of the territory" (p. 82). Thus, cultural alienation and annihilation can be defined as that process that controlling populations use to minimize or eradicate the culture of minority populations. Generally, this process is synonymous with assimilation, acculturation, or deracination (the term Mankiller (1993) used to describe the mission of boarding schools to annihilate American Indian culture)—that is, the uprooting or destruction of a race and its culture.

More specifically, as Wilma Mankiller (1993) states, "the primary mission of Sequoyah and the other boarding schools was a full-scale attempt for the children to leave everything behind that related to their native culture, heritage, history, and language" (p. 8).

For Black people to assimilate into the dominant culture in different countries, they were often separated (alienated) from their own cultural group, or an attempt was made to eliminate (annihilate) their culture altogether. Clear examples of cultural alienation and annihilation can be found across Black populations. In Australia, for example, "between 1910 and 1970 it [Australian Government] forcibly stole up to 100,000 Aboriginal children from their families to live with whites in an attempt at forced integration—'to breed the black out,' as politicians of the day expressed it" (Evenson, 1998, p. A10). In Australia, as in other countries, children who were forcibly taken from their families were, in many instances, children, who because of rape, had white fathers. Doris Pilkington (1996), whose aboriginal name is Nugi Garimara, wrote an intriguing account of the assimilationist policy of Australia that took her mother and her mother's sisters, Daisy and Grace, away from their families. (Pilkington's family story has been dramatized in the film, "Rabbit Proof Fences".) Pillington recounts:

> Patrol officers traveled far and wide removing Aboriginal children from their families and transported them hundreds of kilometers down south. Every mother of a part-Aboriginal child was aware that their offspring could be taken away from them at any time and they were powerless to stop the abductors. (p. 40)

The aboriginal experience was not unlike that of Black Britons and African Americans. As it relates to the experience of Black Britons, Fryer (1992) indicates that most Black Londoners "had been torn from their parents and ethnic groups while still children. They were atomized in separate households, cut off from the cultural nourishment and reinforcement made possible by even the most inhumane plantation system" (p. 70). As a Black Briton recently stated in the popular press (Kogbara, 1999): "I have done a lot of thinking about issues of assimilation and national identity. And I'm beginning to suspect that immigrants can only blend totally into their host environment if they are the same colour as the host or dominant population" (p. 58). Similarly, African American families were divided. Franklin and Moss (1988) describe the process of dividing enslaved Black families in the United States:

> Since the domestic slave trade and slave breeding were essentially economic and not humanitarian activities, it is not surprising to find that in the sale of slaves there was the persistent practice of dividing families. Husbands were separated from their wives, and mothers were separated from their children. (pp. 106–107)

Although the division of families may have been justified for economic reasons, it also served the function of cultural annihilation or alienation. That is, when families were divided, they had to reconstruct their social institutions into new forms.

Education has been used as one of the primary channels through which cultural alienation and annihilation have occurred. As Pilkington (1996) notes about the Aboriginal girls who were taken from their family, the belief was that "part-Aboriginal children were more intelligent than their darker relations and should be isolated and trained to be domestic servants and labourers" (p. 40). In a like manner, in America, Blacks were treated to educational opportunities differently by color. For example, according to Franklin and Moss (1988), mulattoes had more of a chance of schooling than others.

In addition to using education as a divisive tool based on color among Black people, cultural alienation and annihilation have occurred through the transmission of education. That is, the way in which education has been transmitted (teaching style) and the content of educational materials (curriculum) have discounted Black people's social and cultural capital (consciously or subconsciously), and have, therefore, minimized the culture of Black populations globally. Researchers such as DiMaggio and Mohr (1985) suggest that cultural capital is specialized social behaviors that make one accepted at different levels of society; whereas some theorists (e.g., Coleman, 1990) argue, that although social capital is related to cultural capital, social capital is more related to relations among persons. For example, Coleman (1988) explains social capital as the networks that provide information, social norms and achievement support. In simplest terms, the concepts of cultural and social capital mean assets, in the form of behaviors, on which individuals or families can draw to meet a certain set of established values in a society (Freeman, 1997).

As I note elsewhere (Freeman, 1997), these societal values are generally established by majority groups in society and encompass behaviors such as the way individuals speak and the way they dress. The more individuals are able to meet these established standards, the more they are accepted by different institutions (e.g., schools) in society. There is no doubt that the cultural and social capital that students bring to the classroom has tremendous implications for how they will be accepted, treated, and provided with necessary information. According to Cicourel and Mehan (1985), students are provided different educational opportunities because students come to school with different types of culture capital. Black students typically come to school with different cultural capital; and schools, therefore, attempt to eradicate their cultural values in order to make them assimilate.

Who has taught, what has been taught, and how it has been taught over time has severely eroded the cultural identity and educational opportunities of Black populations. Although this has been the case historically, Black educators and researchers, particularly in the United States, are currently critically examining and discussing ways to undo the intellectual damage to Black children by demonstrating the importance of valuing Black culture practice rather than eradicating it. The specially commissioned research papers that Carol D. Lee prepared for this volume (Chapters 3 and 4) examine the state of knowledge in Black education and best practices, including how Black students are being taught. Other researchers and educators have written about the influence of the curriculum (what is being taught) on the education of Black children (Banks, 1988; Freeman, 1999; Hollins, 1996a; King, 1995). Petronilha Gonçalves e Silva and Terezinha Juraci Machado da Silva, as well as Cecile Wright, Hassimi Maiga, and Ibrahima Seck present describe the challenges educators face in Brazil, Great Britain, Mali, and Sénégal (see their respective chapters in Part IV and Part VII this volume).

The school curriculum, as defined by Hollins (1996), is "in fact that package of knowledge, skills, and perspectives that prepares us to develop the attributes of thought and behavior that comply with the prescribed norms" (p. 82). Inconsistencies in compliance with these norms by different cultural groups, in this case Black populations, can lead to various group members questioning their identity, being turned off to learning or underperforming academically. The curriculum validates individuals' culture, history, and sense of self—sense of what is possible. Therefore, when Black culture is not included in the very heart of the school experience, the feeling within students that something is missing is created. As James Banks (1988) describes:

> It is important for students to experience a curriculum that not only presents the experience of ethnic and cultural groups in accurate and sensitive ways, but that also enables them to see the experiences of both mainstream and minority groups from the perspectives of different cultural, racial, and ethnic groups. (p. 161)

Chris Searle (1994), a White British educator with close ties to the Black British community, mirrors Banks's statement. In reference to the national curriculum of Britain, Searle states:

> The national curriculum, with its gradinian sequence of learning and testing, the narrow cultural chauvinism of its approach to knowledge and human experience and its blatantly racist exclusion of cultures, histories, languages and perspectives of Britain's black people, is already creating a tedium and uniformity which will do nothing to spark the interest and motivation of young people to learn. (p. 26)

It is as though the fact that many Black students have underachieved is completely divorced from the curriculum. Linkages have clearly been established between the curriculum and its effect on African American students' achievement (Hollins, 1996; King, 1995). For African American children, the "discontinuity between the home-culture and school learning ultimately disrupts the learning process for many children and the resulting failure may lead them to reject the Euro American culture and school learning as well" (Hollins, 1996, p. 84).

Aside from what has been taught (e.g., the curriculum), as a way to stem the tide of alienation and annihilation of Black culture through education, Black educators have also more recently focused their research on who has been doing the teaching and how Black children have been taught. For example, researchers/educators such as Foster (1997), Irvine (1990), Ladson-Billings (1994), and Siddle-Walker (1996) have examined the role of culturally relevant pedagogy and the cultural perspectives of Black teachers in Black students' achievement. More specifically, these researchers articulate the importance of understanding the historic and present role of Black teachers in helping Black students achieve.

At the same time, Black educators in the United States have focused their research on the inclusion of a Black perspective and valuing Black culture in the educational system, Black researchers in other countries have also begun to address these issues. Bridges (1994), a Black educator in Great Britain, indicates that more Black teachers were employed as a way "of counter-balancing the underrepresentation of black teachers in the borough and, through this, to attack the real problems of underachievement among black children" (p. 4). Searle (1994) supports Bridges's observation. About the British system, Searle states, "the ignorance of teachers and the school system generally about the communities whom they serve is still a vital factor which promotes conflict and misunderstanding between teachers and students" (p. 25).

Cultural alienation and annihilation have had a devastating effect on Black students' participation in education. Over time, the process of trying "to breed the black out" (assimilation), whether through the devaluation of Black people's cultural capital or the what and who of the transmission of knowledge, has severely impacted Black students' sense of self and achievement. There should be little doubt that cultural alienation/annihilation has lead to a "culture of exclusion" for Black populations globally.

CULTURE OF EXCLUSION

Even when Black populations have had the opportunity to participate in education, relating to Black British, Searle (1994) indicates, a "culture of exclusion" has existed. Searle describes the "culture of exclusion" as it relates to Black Britons in this way: "There is much mystification surrounding the word 'exclusion' in education parlance. Schools do not refer to 'expulsions' now, even though almost all parents would know what that means. The preferred term is 'permanent exclusion,' but it comes to the same thing" (p. 19). Searle reports that secondary schools "in Nottingham, Reading, Bristol and the north London borough of Brent showed that black students were up to six times more likely to be suspended from school than their white peers" (p. 24). Drawing on the research of Searle and Bridges (1994), a culture of exclusion, then, can be defined as that process whereby Black children are excluded from schooling, whether through suspension or expulsion or placement in the lower tracks of schooling—which would be referred to as "internal expulsion" (p. 11). Educational expulsion (suspension) is a phenomenon that is similarly faced by Black populations globally. For example, the honorable Fernando Ka (1998), in a report on the conditions of Black people in Portugal, indicates that

> the black community in general—and the children and young people in particular—are victims of educational expulsion. The number of those that manage to complete compulsory education (up to the 9th grade) is frightfully low, and even worse if we consider the number of those who manage to complete secondary education (12th grade). (p. 2)

In the United States, as in Britain and Portugal, a greater number of Black children are subjected to suspension or expulsion. For example, a comprehensive study conducted by the Children's Defense Fund (1975) reported the following:

> No one is immune from suspension, but black children were suspended at twice the rate of any other ethnic group. Nationally, if they had been suspended at the same rate as whites, nearly 50 percent or 188,479 of the black children suspended would have remained in school. Although black children accounted for 27.1 percent of the enrollment in the districts reporting to OCR, they constituted 42.3 percent of the racially identified suspensions. (p. 12)

In support of these earlier findings, in a more recent study, Morris and Goldring (1999) cite studies that concluded that "desegregation was often accompanied by an increase in the overall student suspension as well as a high disparity between black and white student suspension" (pp. 60–61), with the greatest number of African American students subject to "internal expulsion." A recent report (Klenbort, 1999) in the Southern Regional Council periodical presents, as an example, a statement from a high school sophomore who spent his schooling in the lower-level track and who stated, "You live in the basement, you die in the basement. You know what I mean?" Researchers, such as Oakes (1985), Wheelock (1992), and Braddock II and Slavin (1995), support this student's description of tracking or what can be referred as internal expulsion. Page and Page (1995) describe how tracking became the norm following desegregation: "Schools in the region [Southern region] became increasingly resegregated through the use of tracking, with the majority of African American students assigned to lower tracks and the majority of Caucasian students assigned to higher tracks" (p. 73).

Oakes (1985) and Braddock II and Slavin (1995) best capture how tracking can be thought of as internal expulsion. For example, Braddock II and Slavin found that students in lower tracks performed significantly less well than similar low achievers in untracked schools and were much more likely to end up in non-college-preparatory programs by 10th grade. This effect, they suggest, "being in the low track in eighth grade slams the gate on any possibility that a student can take the courses leading to college" (p. 8). Oakes suggests "lower-track students are more alienated from school and have higher drop-out rates" (p. 9). These researchers also find that tracking hurts students' self-esteem, causing them to feel inferior. Based on the findings of these researchers, then, the effects of tracking on students' life chances are tantamount to exclusion. That is, Black students who are in tracks are in school, but because they are more likely to drop out or to have limited opportunities beyond secondary school, the school has, in a sense, excluded them. Morris and Goldring (1999), in their study on disciplinary rates of African American and White students in Cincinnati magnet and nonmagnet schools, explain the situation in this way:

> The overall effect of disciplining students, which involves removing them from the classroom, will drastically impact students' acquisition of educational materials presented by the teacher. Other long term effects might include African American students falling behind academically, or worse, dropping out of school altogether. (p. 64)

Whether internally excluded or suspended or expelled, Black students globally share similar experiences. At least, as described in Britain, Portugal, and the United States, Black students comprise the majority of students facing a "culture of exclusion." This "culture of exclusion" has led to the underutilization of Black populations, their talents, and their potential in education, which, in turn, has implications for societal and individual costs.

NONMONETARY COSTS OF UNDERUTILIZATION OF HUMAN POTENTIAL

Through the historical experiences of Black populations, the pattern of cultural alienation and annihilation and the culture of exclusion surrounding their schooling, a clear pattern emerges as to how their human potential has been underutilized. The underutilization of Black people's human potential has not been without costs to individuals or societies. What is the underutilization of potential and how has it been manifested as it relates to Black populations?

The underutilization of human potential is narrowly defined as talents (what constitutes merit), the inappropriate matching of abilities with tasks (underemployment), or the lack of use of talents (unemployment), which prevents individuals or groups from maximizing their capabilities and/or productivity (Freeman et al., 1999). The underutilization of human potential takes on many dimensions across cultures. For example, it can occur in the case of discrimination, differential educational opportunities among individuals or groups, inappropriate training for the market, or a division in the distribution of technological knowledge—digital divide. Consider Schultz's (1961) comment on one aspect of this issue of the underutilization of human potential in the early 1960s: "Human capital deteriorates when it is idle because unemployment impairs the skills that workers have acquired" (p. 320). Additionally, he remarks that there are many hindrances to the free choice of professions because of discrimination, whether ethnic, class, gender, or religious. Understanding the underutilization of human potential is important because it can facilitate greater insight into educational inequality, the underemployment and unemployment of different groups, the differences in roles in societies, and the economic division between the "haves" and "have-nots."

Farrell (1992) outlines a four-point model in which inequality related to educational opportunity is likely to occur: (a) *Access*: the differences in children from different groups getting into the school system; (b) *Survival*: once in school the differences in children from various groups staying in the school system to some defined level, usually the end of a cycle (primary, secondary, higher); (c) *Output*: the differences in children from different groups learning the same things to the same levels, and (d) *Outcome*: the differences in children from different groups living relatively similar lives subsequent to and as a result of schooling (having equal income, having jobs of the same status, having equal access to positions of political power, etc.).

Drawing on Farrell's (1992) research, other researchers (Freeman et al., 1999) have found that there are four points at which the underutilization of human potential typically occurs: (a) the transition of students into schooling; (b) the experiences of students within the educational setting; (c) the transition of students to the labor market; and (d) the experiences in the workplace. In a recent cross-cultural study, these researchers found that minority groups tended to be underutilized across societies at each of these four points. Moreover, at each of these points, the underutilization of potential occurs for Black populations because the definition of merit is too narrow and because the power to define merit for different groups is narrowly situated within the society's dominant group. That is, at the point of entrance to schooling, the culture of Black populations undergoes a process of being discounted, whether through alienation or annihilation. This, in turn, leads to a culture of exclusion in which students are turned off from schooling, and that limits labor market opportunities. As demonstrated in this research, this cycle of underutilization has historically been and continues to be the case with Black populations globally. Understandably, this cycle of underutilization of human potential has enormous costs for individuals and societies.

Theorists of economics of education typically divide the costs and benefits of education into monetary and nonmonetary (Johns, Morphet, & Alexander, 1983; Merisotis, 1998; Schultz, 1961;Thurow, 1972). They generally assess monetary and nonmonetary costs in terms of societal and private/individual factors (Johns, Morphet, & Alexander, 1983). The monetary costs (i.e., unemployment and underemployment which lead to lower productivity and reduced tax revenue) associated with the underutilization of the potential of Black people have been well documented (Carnoy, 1994; Schultz, 1961; Thurow, 1972). In fact, Levitan, Magnum, and Marshall (1972) report that "underutilization and underdevelopment not only deprive Black people of opportunities to improve their material welfare but also cost the nation the economic contribution they could make if they had better employment and income opportunities" (p. 427). However, the current costs associated with the unemployment and/or underemployment of Black people continue to be extremely expensive for societies.

In Australia, for example, a recent article in the *Daily Telegraph* reported that the unemployment rate among Aborigines (23% unemployment rate) was three times the general rate and was growing twice as fast. Although the Australian government subsidizes approximately 70% of Aboriginals who work, the article concluded that instead of subsidies, "better education and training are needed" (*Daily Telegraph*, 1999, p. 10). The monetary costs associated with the underutilization of the potential of Aboriginals are not unlike the costs other countries with Black populations, such as Portugal and the United States, are facing. In Portugal, concerning the Black population's participation in the labor market, Ka (1998) states, "It is not easy for a Black person to find a decent job in this country, even if s/he has good academic and/or professional qualifications. The colour of the skin is always a barrier, often difficult to transpose" (p. 7). Similarly, a recent report from the United States Department of Labor (1999) indicates that although the unemployment rates for African Americans and Hispanics declined in the 2-year period preceding the report, the "unemployment rate of African American men is still twice that of white men. For African American teens, unemployment has fallen dramatically over the past 6 years but remains around 25 percent or higher" (pp. 11–12).

Although the monetary costs associated with the underutilization of the potential of Black people have been documented, considerably less has been written about the non-monetary costs associated with education, particularly in relation to the underutilization of Black populations. This is particularly troubling given that the nonmonetary costs to societies and individuals are much more difficult to penetrate and eradicate. What are the nonmonetary costs associated with the underutilization of Black people's human potential? Nonmonetary costs are usually those costs that are more indirect and occur over time. Merisotis (1998) defines nonmonetary costs as costs that accrue to individuals, to groups of people, or to society broadly that are not directly related to economic, fiscal, or labor market effects. As with monetary costs, nonmonetary costs can be assessed by societal and individual factors.

SOCIETAL NONMONETARY COSTS

Societal nonmonetary costs would include such things as a lack of benefits of intergenerational effect, increased crime, and decreased adaptability to lifelong learning and use of technology—that is, mismatch between skill levels (Johns, Morphet, & Alexander, 1983; Merisotis, 1998). The very nature of nonmonetary costs makes it difficult to affix a particular price tag. Nonetheless, as Bowen (1977) indicates, the importance of better understanding the nonmonetary benefits to societies and individuals is crucial:

> The monetary returns alone, the forms of enhanced earnings of workers and improved technology, are probably sufficient to offset all the costs. But over and above the monetary returns are the personal development and life enrichment of millions of people, the preservation of the cultural heritage, the advancement of knowledge and the arts, a major contribution to the national prestige and power, and the direct satisfactions derived from college attendance and from living in a society where knowledge and the arts flourish. These non-monetary benefits surely are far greater than the monetary benefits—so much greater, in fact, that individual and social decisions about the future of higher education should be made primarily on the basis of non-monetary considerations and only secondarily on the basis of monetary factors (p. 458).

Although there are clearly more costs associated with the underutilization of Black potential, these are highlighted because they are considered among the most important.

Intergenerational Effect.   Intergenerational effect, according to Johns, Morphet, and Alexander (1983), can be understood as a process whereby the quality of life of children whose parents have attended college and

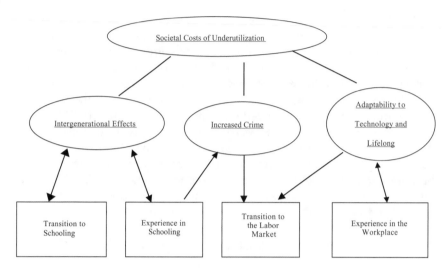

FIG. 6.1. Linkages between societal costs of underutilization and the four points of underutilization.

value education is transmitted between generations. That is, the higher the level of the parents' education, the higher the value of education that parents instill in their children. For example, college choice theorists (e.g., Hearn, 1991; Hossler & Gallagher, 1987) have well documented that the children of college-educated parents are more likely to choose higher education participation than those of parents who have not participated in higher education. Therefore, the fact that Black families have been under-educated is costly to societies because it causes generations of children to be underutilized primarily at the transition of students into schooling and their experiences once in school. The transition into school and the experience in schooling have a reciprocal impact on the intergenerational effect (see Figure 6.1).

Because generations of Black parents have not been the beneficiaries of education, in many cases, they are unable to transmit education to their children, which impacts students' transition into school and their experiences once in school (e.g., different cultural capital and lack of information), which, in turn, impacts the educational outcomes of future generations. This would be considered a nonmonetary cost because what is hurt most is the ability of generations who are uneducated to instill the aspiration and motivation to continue schooling.

In addition, Merisotis (1998) indicates that children whose parents are educated are more likely to have higher cognitive development and have a better quality of life in general. For example, daughters of college-educated mothers are "considerably less likely to become unmarried teen parents" (p. 3). As an example of how this process is currently working, the U.S. the Labor Department (1999) reports "African Americans continue to lag behind in college attendance. This means that these minority groups lack access to many of the skills that higher education provides" (p. 5). The same is the case in Portugal. Ka (1998) states about the conditions of Black participation in education in Portugal that "Black people have scarce means of access to education, particularly higher levels of education. It is distressing the number of Black students in Portuguese higher education" (p. 2). Furthermore, as Ka indicates, "families are subjected to enormous deprivation which determines a high rate of low achievement" (p. 3).

If, as college choice theorists (e.g., Hearn, 1991; Hossler & Gallagher, 1987) assert, parents have the biggest influence on students choosing or not choosing to participate in higher education, then the costs associated with the historical system of undereducating Black populations, who are in, turn, unable to pass on the motivation and aspiration to participate in education to their children, are being realized at all levels of schooling across societies. To understand better across societies how to increase dramatically the number of Black students participating in education at all levels so that future generations will not lose the effects or benefits of education is a challenge, but a highly necessary challenge to undertake.

Increased Crime. Increases in crime rates in communities with less-educated populations are also associated with underutilization of human potential and, therefore, increased costs to society. For example, Merisotis (1998) suggests "there are far fewer prisoners with at least some college education compared with those with high school or less" (p. 3). It should be no surprise that with a "culture of expulsion," more Black students become disinterested in schooling. As Figure 6.1 demonstrates, the schooling experience is directly linked to increases in crime, which impacts on students' inability to transition to the labor market. For example, when *The Economist* (1999) discussed British Prime Minister Tony Blair's war on poverty, the article indicated that the government's micro-initiative would be aimed at trouble spots such as "crime and educational failure" (p. 2). It is widely accepted across societies that increased crime among different segments of the population is associated with decreased educational opportunity. In speaking about social costs related to poverty and education, Carnoy (1994) sums up the linkage between social costs, education, and crime:

> The middle class is a "hostage to worry" about crime, and spends more and more each year on guns, self-defense courses, and other paraphernalia related to warding off assailants.... All this means that whatever the costs

of increasing crime, they are being privatized, and they are rising.... The rising social costs of poverty should be convincing argument for the need to reduce racial inequality. (pp. 240–241)

Adaptability to Lifelong Learning and Technology. Individuals who are adaptable to changing skills and understanding of techniques of life-long learning while being acutely aware of technology are what all societies will increasingly require. Because the potential of Black populations has been underutilized at all four points, societies face enormous costs associated with increasing Black students' motivation and aspiration to participate in higher levels of schooling at the same time that higher skills are already necessary. These societal costs also have had consequences for Black individuals across societies. According to a report from the U.S. Labor Department (1999):

> In the information-based, skills-intensive economy of the twenty-first, one thing is clear: knowing means growing.... While many workers will continue to be in occupations that do not require a bachelor's degree, the best jobs will be those requiring education and training.... Lifelong learning for workers will become more important as a result. (pp. 4–5)

This report indicates that because African Americans lag behind Whites in college attendance, this group lacks access to many of the necessary skills that higher education provides. Similarly, in Portugal, Ka (1998) notes, "few are the Black persons that can benefit from adequate professional training, although Portugal has been one of the European Union countries that received the largest amounts in subsidies for that end" (p. 5). Therefore, it is easy to see how, relative to adaptability to lifelong learning and technology, the potential of Black populations has been and continues to be underutilized at the points of transition into the labor market and in the labor market itself (see Figure 6.1).

INDIVIDUAL NONMONETARY COSTS

Relating to benefits of education to the individual, Bowen (1977) notes that "education should be directed toward the growth of the whole person through cultivation not only of the intellect and practical competence but also of the affective dispositions, including the moral, religious, emotional, and esthetic aspects of the personality" (p. 38). Unfortunately, as pointed out historically, education has not necessarily served Black individuals in this way. In fact, individual costs to Black people would include psychological barriers or affective dispositions, such as decrease in motivation and aspiration to participate in education (Freeman, 1997) and what Steele (1999) refers to as "stereotype threat." Having their talents

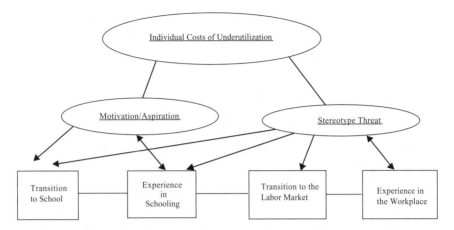

FIG. 6.2. Linkages between individual costs of underutilization and the four points of underutilization.

underutilized over centuries has impacted their psychological being, including self-esteem and self-confidence, because the costs of underutilizing their potential has gone to the heart and soul of Black people. Overcoming this phenomenon will not be easy.

Aspiration and Motivation.   In a qualitative study that I conducted (Freeman, 1997) among Black high school students to assess college choice (i.e., why some African Americans choose to participate in higher education and some do not), a student responded: "They lose hope" (p. 537). As Figure 6.2 suggests, that sense of loss of hope impacts on students' desire to transition to the next level of schooling. The experiences within school affect students' motivation and aspiration, which impacts on their acquiring the skills to transition to the labor market and also can impact on their experiences once in the labor market.

Aspiration and motivation are obviously tied to intergenerational effect, explained earlier, and are associated with academic achievement (Freeman, 1995). Children who do not perform well academically are obviously more prone to disconnect from schooling. Also, motivation and aspiration are closely linked to cultural affinity. That is, the more individuals there are of the same culture not participating in education, the more unmotivated individuals from the same group there are likely to be. For example, one starts to assume that if other like-individuals who have participated in the labor market have not obtained positions commensurate with their level of schooling, why should one bother? The costs to societies of individuals who lose their motivation and aspiration to participate in schooling at any level, although difficult to assess, are high. The questions become: How do societies go about impacting motivation and aspiration; and, how do societies place a price tag on impacting the change of a process that has been historically implemented and systemically maintained?

Stereotype Threat. In the same way that Black individuals' motivation and aspiration have been adversely affected by the underutilization of Black populations over time, Steele (1999) more recently has documented a process that he refers to as "stereotype threat" that also can influence the costs of underutilization of Blacks people's potential. Steele describes stereotype threat as "the threat of being viewed through the lens of a negative stereotype, or the fear of doing something that would inadvertently confirm that stereotype—something external, the situational threat of being negatively stereotyped" (p. 45). As depicted in Figure 6.2, stereotype threat influences students at the point of transition to schooling and their experiences in school and shows that students' experiences in school have a reciprocal impact on stereotype threat. Through this research, Steele reports that Black students taking an experimental test "under 'stereotype threat' seemed to be trying to [sic] hard. . . . The threat made them inefficient on a test that, like most standardized tests, is set up so that thinking long often means thinking wrong, especially on difficult items like the ones we used" (p. 50). Steele's findings cut across social class and, in fact, he indicates: "What exposes students to the pressure of 'stereotype threat' is not weaker academic identity and skills but stronger academic identity and skills" (p. 50).

In addition to the academic costs to Black people that accompany "stereotype threat," Steele (1999) states: "Sadly, the effort that accompanies 'stereotype threat' exacts an additional price. . . . We found the blood pressure of Black students performing a difficult cognitive task under 'stereotype threat' was elevated compared with Black students who were not under 'stereotype threat' or white students in either situation" (pp. 50–51).

Unlike societal nonmonetary costs, individual costs are often ignored or underestimated. Certainly, there are enormous costs associated with the damage exacted on the individual psyches of Black people by having their potential underutilized. Unless and until individual costs are addressed, programs or models will be difficult to effectuate. As Henry Levin once stated, "individuals act on what they perceive not necessarily on what others say is . . . " (personal communication). Through a society's underutilization of the human potential of their Black population, the nonmonetary costs have been high and the effects are still growing. How do all of these pieces tie together to demonstrate the composite costs associated with the underutilization of Black populations globally? How do these pieces fit together to make the case for an expanded research agenda?

BLACKS IN EDUCATION: THE CASE FOR AN EXPANDED RESEARCH AGENDA

As pointed out in this review of the extant research, Black populations in different countries have had similar historical experiences and it is important for these to be examined collectively to determine where similar programs and models might be instituted. When cultural differences are taken into consideration, the wheel might not have to be reinvented. This analysis, consistent with James Anderson's position, suggests that to understand better the experiences of Black populations, a more in-depth comparison must be made of their historical experiences and the impact of these experiences on the construction of the current educational phenomenon in which Black people find themselves.

Another area of research suggested here is the examination of the educational experiences of Black populations across disciplinary boundaries as well as across national and international borders. Better linkages between the different research agendas, whether K–12, higher education, or different aspects of educational phenomena, need to be established as this research demonstrates how each aspect of the Black experience impacts each experience and level of schooling. Regarding the barriers constructed across cultures that underutilize the human potential of Black populations in countries where non-Black groups are the controlling populations, much more research needs to be conducted. Specifically, this research should entail a deeper exploration of each point where underutilization occurs. To enhance national understanding of how everyone within the society is losing, it is imperative for these countries to understand the costs, particularly the nonmonetary costs described by Bowen (1977), associated with the underutilization of Black potential in the society.

CONCLUDING COMMENTS

Finally, it is not enough for countries to assess the costs associated with the underutilization of the potential of Black populations, for the research discussed in this chapter suggests that at each point in the educational and economic systems Black people have been underutilized. At the beginning of the 21st century, it is necessary for countries to develop strategies to address the societal and individual costs associated with Black people's underutilization while simultaneously increasing the utilization of the potential of Black people. For example, Carnoy (1997) offers that:

> the vicious cycle of increasing social costs will gradually break. Down the road, as early-childhood investment reduces spending on adult social problems, more public funds will become available for general education and other activities that improve worker productivity and growth rates. (p. 241)

However, countries have not yet been able to develop a formula for assessing these individual and societal costs and, therefore, have been unable to appropriately target their spending on improvements. In this new century, if the potential of all of citizens is to be utilized, different paradigms and players have to be a part of the research agenda, and the research agenda has to be expanded.

Part IV

Engaging the Language and Policy Nexus in African Education

INTRODUCTION

We require power and influence over our common destiny. Rapid globalization of the economy and cybertechnology are transforming teaching, learning and work itself. Therefore, we require access to education that serves our collective interests, including assessments that address cultural excellence and a comprehensive approach to the interrelated health, learning, and economic needs of African people.

—CORIBE Vital Principles

Presenting first-person perspectives on initiating transformation in education in Africa, the chapters in Part IV address comparative, historical, sociolinguistic, and policy analyses of the impact of colonialism and apartheid across the educational spectrum in West Africa and Southern Africa, respectively. For instance, students in these contexts are obliged to master European colonial/apartheid languages in order to proceed with their studies. Hassimi Oumarou Maiga (from Mali) and Beverly Lindsay (from the United States) address the language and policy nexus in their examination of education policy interventions in Mali, Namibia, South Africa, and Zimbabwe. Their insights and conclusions complement the analyses of Watkins and Freeman in the preceding section and Maiga and Lindsay also draw meaningful interconnections regarding Black education globally.

In Chapter 7, "When the Language of Education Is Not the Language of Culture: The Epistemology of Systems of Knowledge and Pedagogy," Maiga reports the results of two language interventions, one in Mali and the other in the United States. The first is an assessment of the effectiveness of Mali's postindependence national language policy, instruction in local languages, in this case: Soŋay-Senni (Songhoy language) and Tamasheq. The other involves the introduction of African American students to the study of African language and culture (Soŋay-Senni) using multimedia online lessons, a CORIBE pilot demonstration. The chapter begins with an analysis of the roots of West Africa's contemporary education crisis in the colonial systems of epistemology and pedagogy and neocolonial manipulations. Maiga indicts the language of instruction as a vestige of colonial epistemology that limits the ability of educators to tackle current problems of cultural alienation, miseducation, and the "standstill" situation in Africa.

In Chapter 8, "Initiating Transformations of Realities in African and African American Universities," Beverly Lindsay analyzes and synthesizes two recent publications concerning African education. One identifies structure and policies needed to transform postsecondary education in postapartheid South Africa and to eliminate racism and discrimination in South African and Namibian universities. The other examines globalization's effects on education in less developed nations. Both publications demonstrate the need for development paradigms that take into account the dynamic interconnectivity among individual, institutional, and global realities in Africa. Apartheid regime policies that segregated schools by language are implicated in the "language gap" that compromises the quality of education available for Black South African students in institutions in which Afrikaaner is the language of instruction. Lindsay offers the life and work of Nobel Laureate Ralphe J. Bunche to underscore the "dynamic integration of scholarship and policy" needed in transforming the academy and world developments for the public good.

An interesting paradox is that Maiga identifies positive outcomes of instruction that builds on students' home languages and, in the case of African Americans, students' cultural heritage and African identity. By contrast, policy efforts Lindsay identifies that are intended to ensure "nonracial," equitable characteristics of postapartheid South African universities may actually exclude instruction in indigenous languages that previously were the basis for substandard, segregated education.

7

When the Language of Education Is Not the Language of Culture: The Epistemology of Systems of Knowledge and Pedagogy

Hassimi Oumarou Maiga
University of Bamako, Mali

> There is very little that is more important for any people to know than their history, culture, traditions and language; for without such knowledge, one remains naked and defenseless before the world.
>
> —Marcus Tillus Cicero (106 B.C.E—43 B.C.E.)

INTRODUCTION

The central question this chapter addresses is what happens when the epistemology of systems of knowledge and pedagogy—or the language of education—is not the language of culture? Recognizing that the common problem of miseducation that African people share includes the misrepresentation of our cultural heritage and the marginalization of contemporary African realities—if they are addressed at all—it is important to search for solutions. A goal is to demonstrate a role for research in possible solutions using empirical findings from two inquiries that focus on language instruction: the implementation of national languages in Mali (West Africa) and a pilot research demonstration implementing Web-enhanced instruction in Soŋay-senni (language) and culture designed for African American students. These investigations illustrate what can happen when the language of education *is* the language of culture, that is to say, when students in Africa and African Americans in the United States can see themselves and their realities in the learning process.

As the first Regional Director of Education in Gao, Mali (Deputy Minister) for 10 years (1981–1991), I supervised the development and implementation of the national indigenous languages (Soŋay-Senni and Tamasheq) curriculum and pedagogy in the public schools in the Gao region in Mali. (Songhoy, Songhai, Sonrai, Somrai, or Songhay all refer to the Soŋay or Soŋoy people of West Africa [Mali, Niger, Benin, Nigeria, Ivory Coast, Togo, Ghana, and Burkina Faso]. Soŋay-senni or Soŋoy-senni is the language.) In 1982–1983, for the first time students in schools in this region of northern Mali had the opportunity to learn in their home languages as a foundation for academic study rather than learning only French, the colonial language.

From my vantage point as an African educator, with extensive research and teaching experience in both my home country of Mali and the United States, I will discuss the roots of contemporary challenges in African education that lie in the colonial systems of knowledge and pedagogy. I also will discuss historical interconnections that have produced significant problems of miseducation that African people, including continental Africans and African Americans in the United States and the Diaspora, share. To explore the historical and epistemological connections underlying the miseducation of African people on the continent and in the United States this chapter begins with a comparison of colonial schools in West Africa and in the U.S. colonies.

This chapter concludes with a brief discussion of an alternative to prevailing systems of knowledge and pedagogy that I developed in Mali: the Gao School Museum (Maiga, 1993, 1995). This innovative integrated learning-by-doing pedagogical approach, which suggests new directions for research and teaching, is particularly responsive to the urgent social and economic problems that educated people must be able to address.

WHAT COLONIAL SYSTEMS OF KNOWLEDGE AND PEDAGOGY HAVE PRODUCED

Today, all over Africa students and parents, teachers, school administrators, and staff from kindergarten to the universities are in a standstill situation, sitting around, waiting to see what will happen next. The problem they are facing is that there are no ready-made alternatives or solutions for those students who:

- Have earned a formal education degree in a predominantly nonformal market society, that is, in a "no-job" context in Africa where their degrees do not lead to employment;

- Are still attending school but who have absolutely no hope given what is happening to the degree holders whom they are aspiring to become; or
- Have just enrolled in school but are dropping out because of the language barrier (in French-speaking countries, for example) or because of the lack of parental support due to financial constraints and/or their lack of faith in the prevailing educational systems in Africa.

Consequently, as William H. Watkins states so conclusively in Chapter 5:

> In a world of plenty, Africa starves, located on top of an ocean of oil and precious minerals, much of this continent languishes in desperate poverty and stagnation. The "cradle of civilization," is on the precipice of catastrophic ruination. Colonialism, conquest, greed and inhumanity have arrested the development of one sixth of the human race (p. 117).

This is an accurate description of the reality that we face in Mali and throughout West Africa as education researchers in search of solutions.

Language has served as the bedrock of colonial domination in Africa and Euro American hegemony in the United States. Today in what is called "Francophone" West Africa or French-speaking African countries such as Mali, Ivory Coast, and Sénégal, for example, students must master the colonial language, French, before they proceed to the study of school subject matters and higher levels of learning. In the United States, Euro American hegemony contributes to forms of cultural annihilation that take place in schools, which results, as Kassie Freeman points out in her research for the Commission (Chapter 6 in this volume), in an academic performance gap between Black students and White students. This gap is viewed by many as an indication of mental retardation or other forms of unreadiness to learn. Clearly, for African people much of the educational experience is intended to increase one's hate against oneself and anger against one's own family or community and, more important, against one's own people as a race. European and Euro American hegemony functioned initially through colonial and neocolonial educational systems of knowledge and pedagogy that overtime have instilled a very narrow, linear way of thinking that has made it impossible for generations of very capable African educators to think for themselves and to take a comprehensive, holistic approach to solving our common problems.

WHEN THE LANGUAGE OF EDUCATION IS NOT THE LANGUAGE OF CULTURE

The African continent was divided among the colonial powers of Europe at the Berlin Conference of 1984–1985 (Shillington, 1995, p. 305). One of the most far-reaching obstacles to be overcome in the economic and social development of postcolonial nations in Africa, and for African people everywhere, is the psychological effects of domination or the split between the mind and the body. This split produces what the celebrated Kenyan writer Ngugi Wa Thiong'o (1981) describes in his book, *Decolonising the Mind* as: "nations of bodiless heads and headless bodies." Wa Thiong'o states:

> Berlin of 1884 was effected through the sword and the bullet. But the night of the sword and the bullet was followed by the morning of the chalk and the blackboard. The physical violence of the battlefield was followed by the psychological violence of the classroom. . . . In my view language was the most important vehicle through which that power fascinated and held the soul prisoner. The bullet was the means of physical subjugation. Language was the means of spiritual subjugation. (p. 9)

However, there is no recognition in any European educational system of the need to minimize the contradiction that results from the fact that students of African ancestry are not educated in the language of their original, that is, indigenous cultures. What kind of reliable, effective education can be provided to African nations and people when all the latest developments in science, technology, health, media, business, finance, and other forms of knowledge and skills of survival are stored in foreign languages? In other words, what happens when the language of education is not the language of culture?

A clear understanding of history in general and the history of education in particular is required to address these questions (Power, 1970). The significance of an historical juxtaposition of colonial English America and Francophone Africa and the educational process that colonization implemented in both areas is summed up in this observation made by William H. Watkins in Chapter 5 of this volume:

> The mid-nineteenth century found western Europeans nations furiously expanding their mercantile enterprises after a long period of feudalism and stagnation. By the last quarter of that century, the "scramble for Africa" and any other location for favorable profit-making ventures, was well underway. (p. 119)

Juxtaposing historical contexts—colonial America and colonial Africa—is a place to begin the analysis.

A COMPARATIVE HISTORICAL ANALYSIS PARADIGM

The following colonial schools were established in the New England colonies of North America in the 17th century:

• *The Dame Schools.* These schools were extensions of the home's teaching function.

- *The Town Schools.* The curriculum of the Town School consisted of writing and arithmetic. This form of schooling was also a continuation of the scribal tradition in education in which the school's main purpose is to educate clerks. With the Massachusetts Act of 1647 establishing a permanent precedent in American educational law, the Town School became a Reading School. The prior goal of the Town School was to impart the three Rs of the 17th century: Reading, Writing, and Religion. Arithmetic was thought to be a mercantile skill and was not commonly taught except in the towns that enjoyed a commercial status.
- *The Latin Grammar School.* The Boston Latin Grammar School, which was the first one established in colonial New England, was first and foremost a religious institution. The Latin Grammar School's curriculum contained the usual classical subjects. This school catered to the so-called better classes, that is, the elite; it maintained an exclusive policy for admission; and it was a school exclusively for boys (Power, 1970, p. 549).
- *The College.* A year after the Latin Grammar School was established, the General Court of Massachusetts Bay Colony was granted an appropriation of 400 pounds and founded the first college in English America. This school became Harvard College. Dedicated to fundamental Puritanism, Harvard's first mission was to produce future ministers. Harvard divinity students followed a curriculum resembling the ancient liberal arts: Grammar, logic, rhetoric, geometry, astronomy, ethics, metaphysics, natural sciences, and sometimes some Hebrew, Greek, and ancient history. Latin occupied its familiar position as a prominent subject for study *and as the language of instruction.*

In addition to Harvard, other colonial colleges were established, as follows:

1693—The College of William and Mary
1701—Yale
1746—Princeton
1754—Columbia
1755—The University of Pennsylvania
1756—Brown
1766—Rutgers
1769—Dartmouth (Power, 1970, page 552).

Each of these schools had a counterpart in Europe and each transplanted instructional practices originating in Europe, especially in Great Britain. Using a similar pedagogy and system of knowledge, the same colonizers (e.g., British, French, etc.) established early colonial schools in Africa. For example, in West Africa some of the schools the French colonizers created are:

1816	The Mutual School of St. Louis
1847	The School of Hostages
1857–1895	The Schools of Podor, Sedhiou, Bakel, Dakar, Longa, Rufisque, Matam, etc.
1887–1896	The School of Haut-Sénégal Niger (Mali)
1896	The School of Guinea, Ivory Coast, Dahomey
1903	The School of Faidherbe
1903	The Normal School of Saint-Louis
1903	The Professional School of Pinct-Laprade, Dakar.

In 1903, the Lieutenant Governor of Sénégal, M. C. Guy, Agrégé de l'Université (a university appointment of distinction), presented the first official report to the Council of the Colonies of West Africa. Signed by Governor General Roumain on November 24, 1903, this report regulated and organized the colonial schools in West Africa as follows:

- Primary/elementary schools
- Professional schools
- Primary education/Commercial education
- Schools for girls' education
- Normal schools for teacher training
- Schools for European staff/indigenous staff.

After 10 years of experience, the colonizers became more precise as far as the outcomes of these schools were concerned. As a result, the schools were reorganized in 1912 and the curriculum became more focused on the training of secretaries/translators, business agents, health care specialists/nurses, veterinarians, teachers/substitute teachers, specialized manpower, and so on (Moumouni, 1998, pp. 39–42, translated by H. Maiga).

It is worth noting that among all the academic disciplines taught in these colonial schools, good handwriting and excellent French language mastery were thought to be the most rewarding above all subjects. This emphasis continues to influence the employment situation even today, including standards for promotion and social consideration as well. Indeed, mastery of French language is still a key prerequisite for school success rather than the knowledge and skills that reflect the contemporary needs in our countries. It is no wonder then that Wa Thiong'o (1981) concludes: "Learning, for a colonial child, became a cerebral activity and not an emotionally felt experience" (p. 17). In "Worldwide Conspiracy Against Black

Culture and Education" (Chapter 13 of this volume) Ibrahima Seck makes this point with respect to the situation in Sénégal, another former French colony. This comparison of the characteristics of colonial schools in Africa and the U.S. colonies suggests the following conclusions:

- The nature of the early schools established here and there is a result of similar social and political motives.
- The content areas of the respective curriculum (or curricula) in these colonial schools were an extension of the colonizers' home country education, their system of knowledge and pedagogy, their culture, and even their religion.
- The knowledge and skills of the students trained in these early schools reflect the labor needs of the colonizers.
- The educational policies implemented in these schools were consistent with the colonizers' goals of control, domination and exploitation.
- Last, but not least, the language of instruction is the language and culture of the European colonizer.

It is also important to point out that wherever a group of people dominates and imposes its own language on another group as a medium of instruction and communication, the subordinated group assimilates but with resistance. The linguistic outcome of the process of domination is never the total adoption of a language that is identical to the original language imposed. The following examples are worth noting:

- The British language produced American English in America (British colonizers versus the various national languages of European peoples);
- American English in its turn during the period of slavery produced the Gullah language and what is known today as Ebonics or African American Vernacular English (White Americans versus the various national languages of African peoples);
- The French language has produced Patois, Cajun, and Creole languages (French colonizers versus African peoples in the Caribbean, Louisiana, or in Africa).

WEST AFRICA'S CONTEMPORARY EDUCATIONAL CRISIS

As a result of this colonial past and the neocolonial manipulations just discussed, the four most critical issues of West Africa's contemporary educational crisis are: (a) education in the context of economic realities, (b) educational finance and planning, (c) the struggle for rural education, and

(d) curriculum development and educational policy making. Each of these issues is discussed briefly here.

1. *Education in the Context of Economic Realities.* In recent years, various social and economic crises have profoundly shaken West African countries, including: low prices for the raw materials West African countries produce and low wages for both white-collar and manual workers as a result, as well as a low rate of food production. In some areas there has been no production at all because of the lack of rain with terrible consequences for human beings, cattle-raising, and agricultural production.

2. *Educational Finance and Planning.* In West Africa, education has always been sponsored and financed for the most part by the State. This means if the State has a financial problem, education is directly endangered. And that is usually the case because of drought and the economic problems just described. Most of the countries, therefore, have already identified their spending priorities as food production, health care, and cattle-raising techniques. That support for early child development techniques has not been a major priority is reflected in governmental budgets. Likewise, long-term rational planning using the results of research data, also related to the available financial resources, also has been inconsistent at best.

Financing education remains unpredictable and erratic. The financial support usually dedicated to education has been cut back and in some cases the masses have been required to contribute to help support the cost of education. Such support is never adequate given the tremendous educational needs of the children and the limited resources available to local populations, on the one hand, and the low rate of schooling in most African countries, on the other hand. Where can additional pennies be found to support much-needed educational programs and literacy campaigns or community building projects? It is in the context of this dilemma that loans from the World Bank and the IMF come into play and the story is well known. That is why educational planning and finance are such urgent issues in our countries.

3. *The Struggle for Rural Education.* The majority of the population lives in villages in rural areas in African countries. Most of these villages have no water supply or electricity. Thus, health and education become critical because of their importance and their costs. Moreover, most of the governmental rural development strategies in these countries rely on village structures in order to implement education and development projects. To serve the masses of people at the village level effectively, adult literacy programs must be developed and implemented in national (indigenous) languages.

4. *Curriculum Development and Educational Policy Making.* In general, curriculum implicitly or explicitly serves the economic function of preparing young people for the type of work that increasingly characterizes the adult

working world. In fact, all the problems just discussed are structural in nature; that means they are related to the prevailing needs of the economy for different types of adult workers at a given point in time. The organization of the curriculum and educational policy making flow directly from this reality.

Most African countries find it difficult to provide distinctly different curricula, in terms of the focus, balance, and orientation of what is taught, to different groups of students as well as an academic foundation for tomorrow's workers. Because the economic base of African societies, which underlies the prevailing curriculum, has been so severely shaken, it is not surprising that the present curriculum (curricula) of our schools is not relevant for the future of the young people who are still attending school. Nor is it surprising that the new degree holders search for jobs where there are in fact no work places ready to employ them.

Furthermore, it is urgently necessary to call to the world's attention that the imposition of foreign languages in *every* African society has been a main cause of school failure and dropping out of school, underdevelopment, and social stagnation throughout the continent. Professor Kahombo Mateené (1966), senior staff member from the Organization of African Unity in charge of linguistic politics (Niamey, Niger), emphasized that the large majority of the African population does not need to deal with foreign countries (p. 143). The minority of African people who speak foreign languages may use these languages for diplomatic and commercial purposes and foreign languages should be kept in schools but as a second language. Certainly, no one would argue against the importance of learning any other language if possible, as language learning always opens a new door to a new culture. This is an enrichment all by itself. However, Professor Mateené (1996) added that because of the necessity to master the French language in order to succeed in schools in West Africa, less than 15% of young Africans have the chance to accomplish this goal. Now, the question is: Shall we give up or try harder to find solutions? The introduction of indigenous languages in Malian schools, using a scientific approach to assess the impact of this innovation, represents one attempt to search for a solution.

WHEN THE LANGUAGE OF EDUCATION IS THE LANGUAGE OF CULTURE

In 1962, 2 years after the nation's independence from French colonial rule, a national decree required instruction in national (indigenous or home) languages of Mali. Since the 1960s the National Ministry of Education-DNAFLA (The National Office of Functional Literacy and Applied

Linguistics) has produced a number of research and specialized linguistic documents as well as curriculum materials to support instruction in Soŋay-Senni and Tamasheq (Haidara et al., 1992; IPN–DNAFLA, 1999; Ministère de l'Education de Base–DNAFLA, 1995, 1997). The introduction of indigenous national languages for instruction in the schools in the Gao Region of northern Mali, as developed by the Direction Nationale de l'Alphabétisation Fonctionnelle et de la Linquistique Appliquée (DNAFLA–National Office of Functional Literacy and Applied Linguistics), began in 1982–1983, when I was the Regional Director of Education in Gao.

This pedagogical innovation was also an outgrowth of my previous experiences in the 1970s as Section Chief for Pedagogical Research and Technical Advisor for indigenous and second language instructional methods and materials development at the National Institute of Pedagogy (IPN) under the direction of the National Ministry of Education (MEN) in Bamako. By 1985, after 3 years of implementation, my office conducted a formal evaluation of the effectiveness of this experiment (Maiga, 1986). A brief description of this pedagogical innovation and a discussion of the outcomes and impact follow.

Experimenting With National Language Instruction in Mali.   The field study that we conducted in Gao in 1985 compared the results of instruction for two groups of students, one in conventional public schools and the other in experimental schools, as they moved through Grades 1 through 3 (First Form to Third Form) (Maiga, 1986). Instruction for students in the conventional (nonexperimental) schools began in French. Students in the experimental national languages schools in the First Form (grade) began learning in Soŋay-Senni or Tamasheq language, the two indigenous languages spoken in the Gao region. These students were introduced to French in the second quarter of the First Form and as oral language only; they were not permitted to write in French during this period.

Five (5) of the 96 schools in the Gao Region were the first to implement the national language policy of instruction in the home language. To conduct the study the experimental schools were matched with five (5) conventional schools. All 10 schools were located in the same general area. The teachers in these schools had the same formal training, professional degrees as well as the same type of certification and pedagogical preparation. Both groups of schools shared the same challenges with respect to the lack of equipment and shortage of teaching materials and supplies and teachers experienced the same working conditions. The only difference between the teachers in these two groups of schools was preparation for teaching the indigenous languages: teachers in the experimental schools completed a special in-service training to prepare them to teach their own language.

The Regional Office of Education evaluation research team examined six indicators of effectiveness in the five experimental schools (3 taught Songhoy-Senni; 2 taught Tamasheq) compared to the outcomes in the conventional (nonexperimental) schools. These are the indicators of instructional effectiveness examined in this study:

- Change in class size
- Student pass rates from the First Form to Third Form
- Frequency/percentage of students repeating a grade
- Frequency/percentage of students expelled from school
- Frequency/percentage dropping out of school and
- School attendance rates (Maiga, 1986).

The data reported below were collected for the years 1983–1985 by the Regional Office of Education evaluation team under my supervision. Tables 7.1 through 7.6 show the results for each of the above indicators for the cohorts of students who entered the First Form at the start of the 1982–1983 school year and who completed the Third Form at the end of the 1984–1985 school year.

Outcomes and Impact Assessment

Class Size.   In the experimental schools, 768 students enrolled in the First Form at the beginning of the year and 870 enrolled in the selected conventional schools (see Table 7.1).

Table 7.1 also shows a general decreasing pattern: the number of student in each type of school decreased each year even though the conventional schools began and ended with more students than the experimental schools over the 3-year period. However, the conventional schools started each year with a larger number of students and retained a much higher proportion of their students than the experimental schools.

Pass Rates.   Table 7.2 presents the pass rates by type of school. The date indicate a higher pass rate in the experimental schools as compared to the conventional schools at all grade levels (from 16.02%; 22.39%; 46.67%)

TABLE 7.1
Class Size From 1983 to 1985

Year	1983	1984	1985		
Grades	1st	2nd	3rd	Total	Percentage
Experimental Schools	768	307	86	1,161	11.19 %
Conventional Schools	870	554	492	1,916	56.55 %

TABLE 7.2
Pass Rate by Type of School

Year	1983	1984	1985	Percentage
Grades	1st	2nd	3rd	Mean
Experimental Schools	58.05	72.28	84.92	71.75%
Conventional Schools	42.03	49.89	38.25	43.39%
Difference	16.02	22.39	46.67	

TABLE 7.3
School Repeaters by Type of School

Year	1983	1984	1985	Percentage
Grades	1st	2nd	3rd	Mean
Experimental Schools	32.23	24.47	18.50	25.06 %
Conventional Schools	48.77	28.58	26.27	34.54 %
Difference	16.54	4.11	7.77	

from the First through the Third Form. This effect steadily increases each year until, by the end of the third year, the pass rate in the experimental schools more than doubled the pass rate in the conventional schools (84.92% compared to 38.25%).

School Repeaters. Not surprisingly, the rate of school repeaters is consistent with this outcome.Table 7.3 presents the frequency and percentage of school repeaters, that is, the students who failed to pass to the next grade. The data presented in this table indicate that more students repeated a grade in conventional schools than in experimental schools each year in all grade levels.

Expulsions. The rate of expulsion, which is shown in Table 7.4, increased each year in the conventional schools. In the experimental schools, the rate of expulsion not only decreases, there were no expulsions at all in the experimental schools during the third year. The rate of expulsion decreased from 3.44% to 1.62% to 0 for students in the experimental schools. In the conventional schools, the rate of expulsion, which was higher than the rate in the experimental schools each year, fluctuated from 10.62% in the first year to 8.83% in the second year, and reached a high 12.34% in the third year. Based on this indicator of effectiveness, the difference between the schools is significantly striking.

Dropout Rate. Table 7.5 shows the dropout rate by type of school. In contrast to an increase in the percentage of dropouts in the second year,

TABLE 7.4
Rate of Expulsion by Type of School

Year	1983	1984	1985	Percentage
Grades	1st	2nd	3rd	Mean
Experimental Schools	3.44	1.62	0	1.68 %
Conventional Schools	10.62	8.83	12.34	10.59 %
Difference	7.18	7.21	12.34	

TABLE 7.5
Dropout Rate by Type of School

Year	1983	1984	1985	Percentage
Grades	1st	2nd	3rd	Mean
Experimental Schools	0.29	0.81	0	0.36 %
Conventional Schools	2.27	0.72	0.22	1.98 %
Difference	1.98	0.09	0.22	

the experimental schools had no dropouts in the third year. The percentage of students dropping out also decreased each year in the conventional schools; however, these schools had a higher dropout rate than the experimental schools each year (from 2.27% to 0.72% and a low of less than 1%).

School Attendance Rate. Finally, Table 7.6 presents the attendance rate for each cohort. Consistently, the experimental schools have a higher rate of attendance than the conventional schools, as the percentage of attendance in both types of schools increased each year. The data also show a steadily increasing rate of attendance in the experimental schools that was not matched in the conventional schools.

It is also interesting to note that while the experimental schools achieved a near perfect rate of attendance (95.65%), and the conventional schools improved their attendance rate from 65% to a little over 80% after the first year, the difference between the two types of schools in rate of attendance increased over the 3-year period.

Discussion

In general, the experimental schools demonstrated a greater degree of effectiveness in terms of the higher percentage of students moving on to the next grade at the end of the year, fewer repeaters, fewer expulsions, and fewer dropouts as compared to the conventional schools. Better class attendance also was reported in the experimental schools in comparison

TABLE 7.6
Average Rate of Attendance by Type of Schools Each Year

Year	1983	1984	1985	Percentage
Grades	1st	2nd	3rd	Mean
Experimental Schools	75.50	86.11	95.65	85.75 %
Conventional Schools	65.09	83.04	83.19	76.44 %
Difference	10.41	4.07	13.46	

with the conventional schools. A number of factors may have contributed to the dramatic decrease in the number of students in the experimental schools by the end of the 3rd year (from 768 initially enrolled to 86). First, the conventional schools were already in existence and as a result, these schools were well known to parents. The experimental schools, however, were newly constructed, had just opened and, as is often the case with any innovation, these new schools were adversely affected by a number of uncertainties and challenges. For instance, there was strong opposition to the teaching of national languages. There was fear, for example, that students would not be able to get a job or be able to further their studies if they did not learn French in the conventional way. Second, teachers who were inexperienced with the new pedagogy were not strong advocates of this new policy. As a result of resistance among teachers who opposed this innovation and tremendous negative propaganda, parents became increasingly doubtful about the validity of instruction in home languages for school success and students were not convinced of the benefits either.

The only explanation possible for the overwhelming success of the experimental schools as measured by all other indicators, however, is the use of national languages as a medium of teaching and learning. What would be the impact of an educational program that uses African languages for instruction from kindergarten through the 12th grade? As Wa Thiong'o (1981) stated clearly: "The association of the child's sensitivity" would then be in harmony with "the language of his experience of life" (p. 14).

WHEN THE LANGUAGE OF EDUCATION BUILDS ON STUDENTS' CULTURE

The Commission on Research in Black Education supported a pilot research demonstration to explore the benefits of African language and culture study for African American students. (Study of African language instruction was recommended as a focus for the work of the Commission Research in Black Education by a panel of African and African American scholars attending the AERA annual meeting in Montreal in 1999.) I code-veloped six Web-enhanced online Soŋay-Senni (language) and culture lessons and in April 2000 implemented a pilot implementation and assessment of these lessons at Medgar Evers College in Brooklyn, New York.

Implementing a Pilot Research Demonstration. The intent was to use the Internet (Web-enhanced lessons) to present new cultural content and historical information including positive information about and vibrant images of contemporary African life today as well. In contrast to prevailing negative images of Africa and African people in the media, the six lessons we developed are visually attractive, dynamic, multimedia, multi-disciplinary, and interactive. These lessons introduce students to African history, language, values, and cultural practice. Thus, in the case of this pilot demonstration project, the language of education builds on students' culture. The following research question guided this demonstration research project: *In what ways does reimmersion into African culture, using Web-based learning to study African language*:

1. Broaden the epistemological, axiological, and ontological perspectives of students;
2. Motivate their learning; and
3. Reorient their energies toward acceptance of diversity as a tool for global problem solving?

A long-term goal suggested by the findings of this pilot research demonstration is to create a complete online course package including curriculum materials that can be made available to students in after school settings such as libraries, community centers, and other locations in which computers and the Internet are available.

In the six model lessons, language is presented in naturally occurring everyday events in which students experience African traditions, values, and cultural practices through important social activities, such as a wedding and the installation ceremony for the Songhoy Chief. These lessons, which were supported by Blackboard.com courseware, included the following topics:

1. Introduction to the Lessons
2. *"Black Is . . . "*
3. Alphabet & Pronunciation
4. Greetings
5. Introducing Yourself
6. Counting.

This lesson content is adapted from a textbook for English speakers, *Conversational Soŋay Language of Mali* (Maiga, 1996/2003). Although also keeping the focus on language learning, these interdisciplinary lessons and the pedagogical approach used integrate African language with folklore, philosophy, proverbs, culture, history, geography, and politics in Songhoy traditional culture. The lesson entitled "Black Is . . . " exemplifies this integrated pedagogical approach. In contrast to the concept of "blackness" in the English language, the meanings associated with "black" in Soŋay-Senni are extremely and consistently positive. For instance, this lesson presents an animated sequence of definitions, proverbs, and a folk tale that explain the meaning of:

- "black water" (hari bibi)
- "black earth" (labu bibi) and
- "black sun" (wayne bibi) in Soŋay-Senni.

The definitions of these terms include: where to get potable (black) water from the deepest part of the Niger River, when to plant crops (when the earth is black) and being mindful of the effects of the (black) sun, at midday when it is brightest. In addition to these examples of cultural knowledge and practices related to the concept of blackness in Soŋay-Senni, the lively folktale about a "choosey Hyena" who learns to appreciate the value and enduring quality of the color black illustrates Soŋay proverbial wisdom. In sum, this lesson displays African thought and values in the worldview of the Soŋay (Songhoy) people, for example, their conceptions of beauty and qualities of character that appeal to young people's concerns and interests in everyday cultural practices.

Using original footage from Gao, Mali, the design team (Hassimi Maiga, Joyce King, and TekAfrika Digital Media) produced these lessons in a multimedia Web-enhanced format to explore the potential of this instructional medium and to introduce students to an online learning experience that builds on and draws them into a deeper understanding of their own cultural heritage as people of African descent. We pilot tested these lessons with a group of middle school students from the Liberty Partnership Program at Middle College High School of Medgar Evers College, CUNY. This after school program serves youngsters with a range of academic abilities and interests. Eight students and a teacher/counselor participated in the after school "cultural enhancement workshop" that was designed expressly for the purpose of implementing and assessing the impact of these lessons on student learning, motivation, and engagement. The workshop was spread over 4 days including an orientation meeting. Parent permission was secured and the workshops were held in the Faculty Computing Room at Medgar Evers College, where each student was seated at his/her own computer terminal. To eliminate the time required to download the lessons, which include short digital movie clips, graphics, and animation, each student manipulated the lessons in CD-ROM format.

Outcomes and Impact Assessment

At the end of the workshop students completed an evaluation of the experience. The evaluations indicate that this experience was a creative way to engage students in an interactive mode of learning. For example, during the first session the students settled down right away and learned quickly how to move through material in sync with each other and with the instructor. That is, each student viewed the "pages" and completed various steps required to navigate the structure of the lessons simultaneously on the same page or screen by clicking the mouse. With each workshop session, the students' interest and fascination increased. The students were engaged in reading, oral practice of the language and there was a great deal of discussion. The performance of the students during the workshops as well as their evaluation forms indicate that what they learned was extremely meaningful. In addition, they were very enthusiastic about the material presented and expressed a desire to continue this kind of learning experience.

Designing and implementing the (Soŋay-Senni) online lessons provided a new opportunity to illuminate and uncover hidden connections among African people by means of an integrated pedagogical process. New cultural content, such as the material presented in the "Black Is . . ." lesson, allowed students to consider "blackness" from an African worldview perspective that is positive. For another example, the "Counting" lesson offered students a close-up view of an exciting social event, a marriage, which was of great interest to African American teenagers. A video clip presents a Songhoy *garasa* (griot) singing and counting the wedding gifts at a courtyard reception for a bride-to-be. The guests are dressed in richly colored, flowing robes and the women wear elaborately wrapped matching headscarves. The traditional Songhoy cultural practice of giving the tenth wedding gift to the sisters in the family of the husband-to-be served as a contemporary, living social context for uncovering enduring African values such as generosity that these students also recognize as a shared cultural connection. In this lesson, students reported that they were able recognize African people expressing conceptions of beauty and enacting valued social graces on their own cultural terms.

We determined that the impact of these images is quite powerful, especially in comparison to the prevalent media depictions of starving, emaciated African children in filthy conditions covered with flies. The "Greetings" lesson was especially memorable and meaningful for these students who learned that Songhoy people place great emphasis on "respect," as demonstrated in the way they greet each other. Students reported that this aspect of Songhoy culture is a reminder of how important it is to them not to be "dissed" (i.e., disrespected).

Discussion

Student responses to the evaluation are summarized in the Appendix at the end of this chapter. As part of his apprenticeship in qualitative research, CORIBE Scholar William Franklin prepared and independent evaluation of this pilot implementation. Preliminary results, which were reported in the CORIBE evaluation (see also, Tillman, Chapter 17), confirm the findings just discussed. In addition, the interactive style of learning about culture and language enhanced classroom communication and the nature of the content—images of real people, natural sound, lively activities, and action embedded in short narrative stories about everyday occurrences in Africa today—brings the subject matter to life in ways the students can identify with. This project also demonstrates the potential of a Web-enhanced, interactive multimedia approach for developing new cultural content that satisfies current academic standards (e.g., the National History Standards; Global Studies on the New York State Regents Exam). Students also found the content and mode of presentation very enticing and personally engaging. Thus, the design and teaching of these model African language online lessons was a tremendous achievement. To summarize, use of multimedia Web-enhanced lessons allows:

- The instructor to organize the learning process in an active, interactive, and dynamic mode that is engaging and attractive for adolescents;
- The students to interact, react, and communicate directly with the teacher;
- The instructor to make language teaching more relevant and real by incorporating movie clips and animation into text-based lessons;
- Students to encounter the language in naturally occurring settings, scenes, and social events in contemporary Soŋay (Songhoy) life that would not ordinarily be found in textbooks; and
- Students to immerse themselves in the sights and sounds of a living African cultural context through language study and engagement with knowledge across the disciplines.

In conventional classrooms, communication between the students and the teacher is vertical. In the Songhoy Online Course, the teacher functions in a different mode of communication with the students: the vertical one-way relationship is broken down and a horizontal, two-way communicative mode takes place between the teacher and the students and among the students. This mode of communication sets up the platform for individualized assistance and group work that also permit the students and the teacher to express their views whenever they feel like it.

These lessons were demonstrated for teachers in other settings (at Southern University in New Orleans and the College of Staten Island, CUNY). Given the now well-known "digital divide," it is also important to note that these teachers who also experienced these online multimedia lessons agreed that they learned more about using the computer through this experience than ever before.

WHAT IS TO BE DONE HERE AND THERE?

The field study comparing two systems of knowledge and pedagogy in Mali—teaching national indigenous languages as compared to instruction in French—is just an indication on a small scale of what it could be like in Africa today when the language of education is in fact the language of culture. Likewise, there is great potential underlying the pilot demonstration of African language and culture instruction for African American students, which can be deepened, broadened, and expanded to a full-length course. After further development of curriculum materials, full implementation and evaluation of this next stage, we will have a clearer understanding of all the dynamics of an interactive Web-enhanced language and culture class—from the technological underpinnings to the pedagogical elements, as well as the evaluation or assessment components.

Furthermore, the implementation of the Soŋay-Senni pilot research demonstration gives us confidence to move forward with the development of other well structured, lessons that articulate selected themes/topics across the disciplines. Lessons that address science content, for example, could demonstrate the relevance of African language to the social, economic, and development needs of people here and there. Urgent social, economic, and environmental crises and calamities in the United States and on the continent are creating an unprecedented educational predicament—a predicament that requires the development of the kind of human competence that will permit people to see themselves as capable of solving these challenging problems. These pedagogical experiments in two different contexts of Black education suggest the potential of African language and culture study for the development of such human competence in Africa and the United States.

It is also important to note broader learning implications of Soŋay-Senni instruction. In Gao we observed that learning in home languages creates a context in which indigenous systems of knowledge and thought are made available as a pedagogical resource for problem solving (e.g., student identification with their heritage, appreciation of cultural diversity, etc.). In other words, integrating the cultural knowledge embedded in students' home languages into the curriculum and pedagogy enhances student learning. My observations of the impact of indigenous language instruction inspired the development of the Gao School Museum methodology, an integrated pedagogical approach that I developed as a result of my research, observations, and evaluation studies in Gao (Maiga, 1993, 1995). A brief description of the relevance of this approach for the development of human competence follows.

DEVELOPING HUMAN COMPETENCE: THE GAO SCHOOL MUSEUM METHODOLOGY

The Gao School Museum methodology was created as a tool for action. That is, this approach links indigenous community knowledge and empowerment with social action. As stated in the book that documents the development of this methodology:

> The philosophy of this approach is based on the idea of infusing relevant cultural knowledge and practical experience into the existing school curriculum so that what students are learning (content) and why they are learning it (intent) [are] more closely linked to the country's human resource needs and to its scientific, economic and ecological environment. (Maiga, 1993, p. 24)

Thus, this methodology does not refer to a typical museum where "historical objects" are displayed. Rather it is a place inside the school or a classroom "where curriculum-related objects and documentation collected or made by the students . . . have been identified . . . classified and labeled for use in planning and implementing particular lessons" (Maiga, 1993, p. 34). As these pedagogical supports are integrated into the instructional process, the teachers and students can "see themselves and their lives reflected" in lessons that use this resource bank produced through their collaborative inquiry activities (p. 23).

CONCLUDING COMMENTS

The two research experiences presented in this chapter demonstrate a role for research in the quest for possible solutions to the problems African people have experienced when the language of education is not the language of culture—here and there. The examination of the historical interrelationships and current crises in education—in Africa and the United States—suggests the need for an integrated approach to common problems in the search for solutions. The interrelated historical roots of these commonalities can be recognized in contemporary manifestations.

For example, I have taught both French and "Songhoy Language and Culture" in U.S. universities. In my French courses at Southern University in New Orleans, I was amazed to find that African American students at a historically Black university had so little confidence in their ability to learn another language. In Africa, it is not unusual for children to grow up speaking several languages. I speak five languages: two Songhoy (Songhoy/Zarma) corelated languages, one of which is my first language, and Bambana, another language spoken in Mali. I also am fluent in French and English, my fifth language, which I was also prepared to teach in normal school as a second language (ESL) in Mali. Because my African American students also had such little knowledge of but a strong desire to learn more about their history and heritage, I developed a Soŋay-Senni (language) course that incorporates knowledge of African thought and culture in language instruction in new ways. I taught this course in New Orleans using the textbook that I developed for English speakers, which is based on this pedagogical innovation (Maiga, 1996/2003).

My expertise includes the discipline of psychopedagogy, the history of education, curriculum development and evaluation as well as language teaching. In addition, I have served for 36 years as a classroom teacher, teacher educator, researcher, and professor of higher education in my country and in the United States as well. I have also taught multicultural education and educational psychology courses in the teacher education program at Medar Evers College of the City University in New York—in Brooklyn— where my students were from several countries in Africa (e.g., Ghana, Nigeria), the Caribbean (e.g., Barbados, Haiti, Jamaica, and Trinidad) as well as the United States. Their scanty knowledge of our shared African heritage stood out as something all these students have in common. Thus, it seems that wherever we are, African descent peoples are struggling for survival by annihilating awareness of our indigenous cultures so that we can assimilate into the "modern" global mainstream culture. Increasingly, this global culture is epitomized by the culture of the United States, which is often represented in the media through glamorous images of African Americans living the "good life" in sports, music, and other forms of consumer success and entertainment. The realities of the African American situation are less well known and understood, if at all, in Africa, on the other hand, and African Americans, like the students whom I have taught, are cut off from their African cultural heritage. They are also denied opportunities to be informed and concerned about realities in Africa today. In other words, they are denied the opportunity to search for solutions. The European (and American) colonial systems of knowledge and pedagogy have inexorably produced these results.

The research findings presented in this chapter suggest the importance of language as one dimension of the educational experience that people of African ancestry share—here and there. As the empirical inquiries discussed above demonstrate, beneficial effects are produced when the language of education is the language of culture, that is, when the content and pedagogy permit students to see themselves and to experience their cultural heritage in the curriculum. Thus, we are well advised to remember the words of Dr. Abdou Moumouni (1998), professor of physical sciences who created the first office of solar energy in Mali, West Africa:

> It is clear that as long as African languages are set aside and the actual teaching structure maintained as it is, there can be no serious illiteracy programs nor true educational development nor any safeguard of African originality and personality except as a myth or simply as an abstract mysticism. (p. 94, translated by H. Maiga)

APPENDIX

Soŋay-Senni Language & Culture OnLine Course:
"The People Who Could Fly"
Selected Student Evaluation Data
Eight students completed the evaluation. Their responses are summarized below.

1. Tell us what you learned about Soŋay language and culture (and about Africa) in this class that you didn't know before.
   - *Students reported that they learned some elements of Soŋay language: Alphabet, greetings, proverbs and numbers.*
2. How is "blackness" defined in Soŋay language?
   - *Blackness is defined as having a positive meaning to it.*
   - *Some good things are connected to the color "Black" in Soŋay language. It is more positive in Africa than in United States.*
3. Is it important for young people here to know about African culture and language? Why or why not?
   - *Yes, because Black children growing up in a White world need to know who our ancestors were not what the White man thinks they were . . . and we need to know that we are important being Black."*
4. Why do Soŋay people take so much time greeting each other?
   - *The Soŋay people take time to great each other to show respect and consideration.*
5. How will this Soŋay online class affect you as a student, as a learner?
   - *The Soŋay class helped me to use the computer better.*

- *We enjoyed learning via computer and Internet because it took teaching to a new level.*
- *It will help me to talk with other people and get along with people from here and there.*

6. What can students do if they take a class like this on Soŋay language and culture?
   - *With this education of Soŋay language you can use it to speak to African people.*
   - *You can use it as a way to identify with the culture in order to learn a lot and know yourself better.*
7. What are you going to do with what you learned in this class?
   - *We are going to teach others what we have learned.*
   - *We will tell our friends about the language for we know now that being Black is a great opportunity.*
8. Write a Soŋay-Senni proverb below:
9. Explain what this proverb means in your own words.
   - *Each student was able to write his or her favorite proverb and explain it in his/her own words (in English).*
10. On the other side please tell us: What did you like best about this class? What didn't you like about this class? How can this class be improved?
    - *We like the class and would not change anything about it.*
    - *This Sonay class was excellent because it taught me to use the computer better, speak a new language.*
    - *I like what was different from what I used to learn in English; and all opinions were accepted.*
    - *No answers were wrong.*
    - *There wasn't anything to dislike and I hope the size of the class does not increase.*
    - *The class can be improved by having more sessions.*

8

Initiating Transformations of Realities in African and African American Universities

Beverly Lindsay
Pennsylvania State University

INTRODUCTION

This chapter addresses the need for and possibilities for transformation of higher education in Southern Africa. During summer and early fall 2003, I was a Senior Fulbright Specialist assigned to the Institute of Peace, Leadership and Governance and Africa University in Mutare, Zimbabwe. For much of the past 5 years, Zimbabwe and neighboring countries in the Southern African Development Community (SADC, which is roughly similar to the European Union regarding regional economic cooperation) have been on the radar screen of scholars of African affairs, often because of the tremendous sociopolitical and educational challenges confronting Zimbabwe and other Southern African nations. Based on insights from the field and a review of recent analyses that contextualize processes of transformation and globalization in Africa, this chapter considers how alternative paradigms and policies can assist university personnel in Zimbabwe and other African nations meet their professional responsibilities and help to focus postsecondary institutions on the public good. The chapter concludes with a discussion of the thought and life example of Nobel Laureate and global statesman Dr. Ralph Bunche, which epitomizes the dynamic integration of scholarship and policy applied to pressing academic and social problems to support peace and development.

Central to my Fulbright portfolio was working with African and other international professionals to examine conditions that contribute to and/or impede peace and progressive development via university enterprises. In a region where economic stagnation and inflation are twin challenges, their impact on the university system were quite evident as witnessed by the recent strikes of University of Zimbabwe faculty and professionals whose salaries cannot enable them to purchase very basic necessities. Such conditions were a sharp contrast to my observations in South Korea during fall 2002 when I undertook my first Senior Fulbright Specialist grant. South Korea was a developing nation during much of the 1950s and 1960s as were most African nations. Now South Korea is one of the tiger economies of Asia and its gross domestic product places the nation among the top 12 in the world.

Although universities in Zimbabwe and South Korea are experiencing vastly different economic realities, postsecondary institutions in both countries are still called on to provide sound quality education in a range of disciplines for students and faculty who are eager to engage in scholarship and outreach to local or regional communities. Simultaneously in the United States, African immigrants and African Americans are debating about different ways to influence American transnational and foreign policy toward Africa so the realities of nations on the continent move toward more authentic economic and sociocultural viability as those such as South Korea have experienced. Deliberations among African immigrants and African Americans, that are taking place in venues such as the annual conference of the Congressional Black Caucus Foundation (CBC), highlight issues for debate within the scholarly and public policy communities regarding phenomena affecting both. Conferences such as the 2003 CBC session entitled "The U.S. and Africa: Continuing Challenges, New Approaches" posit salient educational policies needed to address these challenges. Specific examples of these phenomena and possible solutions via a role for research and policy alternatives will be addressed following a consideration of development paradigms and a review of recent scholarship.

CONTEXTUALIZING CURRENT PARADIGMS OF DEVELOPMENT

A number of scholars articulate various theoretical frameworks regarding the interaction among capitalism, class, and race (Amin, 1997; Drucker, 1993; Wilson, S., 1990), the role of educational institutions in nation building (Carnoy, 2000; Dzvimbo, 1991; Lindsay & Poindexter, 2003; Stromquist & Basile, 1999) and the sociopsychological effects of racism and gender discrimination on individual Africans and African Americans (Fanon, 1967; Lorde, 1995; Steele, 1998; Tatum, 1999). In Chapter 5 of this volume, William H. Watkins presents conceptual frameworks regarding colonialism, neocolonialism, dependency theory, and modern economic theory—the dominant paradigms for the last 30 to 50 years in international relations. Now that we are in the postmodern era, different structural formulas are being employed in the international development arena, such as structural adjustments and debt relief. However, indebted countries do not have the means to resolve their outstanding debt given the few viable economic resources within a "developing" society, and this realization is critical when incredible social and educational needs exist. Another factor that Watkins discusses in this chapter is that 20% of the Gross National Product (GNP) of many African countries has been spent on education. However, if 20% is spent on education, what does that mean for the other components in the society that rely on the economic infrastructure? How do other sectors obtain government appropriations for societal development in this postmodern era? Such questions are critical areas of inquiry for scholars and policy makers who focus on developing nations.

Keeping these frameworks in mind, two recent publications, *Apartheid No More*, edited by Reitumetse Obakeng Mabokela and Kimberly King (2001), and *Education in a Globalized World* by Nelly Stromquist (2002), also are helpful in exploring the dynamic interconnectivity among individual, institutional, and global challenges as well as new factors that manifest themselves in contemporary milieus on the continent. These recent volumes provide foundations for considering three significant questions that contextualize the social, political, and economic pressures shaping current paradigms of development in Africa.

First, although universities in the new South Africa have become officially open to all students, it is important to ask what hidden obstacles impede the progress of African students and faculty as they attempt to meet their professional and social responsibilities? Second, how do national financial allocations influence the effectiveness of social and educational institutions when the intrigues of political realities continually appear? Finally, to what extent do the pervasive effects of globalization and its various manifestations necessitate new paradigms and subsequent policies to address continuous and emerging problems of economic power, technological innovations, and new knowledge? In essence, can meaningful institutional transformations occur in higher education so that the personal and collective lives of people will be enhanced?

CONTEMPORARY CHALLENGES IN SOUTH AFRICAN
AND NAMIBIAN UNIVERSITIES

Frequently, knowledgeable lay audiences tend to view education as primarily teacher training and pedagogy. Mabokela's and King's anthology, *Apartheid No More*, quickly moves beyond that perspective as the contributors to this volume attempt to portray lucid nexuses between the elimination of political apartheid for the nations of South Africa and Namibia *and* the remnants of apartheid in the universities. The cadre of emerging scholars that Reitumetse Obakeng Mabokela and Kimberly Lenease King have assembled represents the fields of sociology, intercultural studies, history, philosophy, and educational policy studies, as well as higher education. These scholars explicate and analyze the post-1948 Afrikaaner elections resulting in a series of repressive laws: notably the Prohibition of Mixed Marriages Act (1949); the Population Registration Act (1950) requiring a pass, which limited physical mobility; the Reservation of Separate Amenities Act (1950) obligating specific residential locales for the races; and the Bantu Education Act (1953), which restricted the types and levels of educational access and attainment. Hence, the rights of Black and Colored people were severely curtailed by solidifying public and educational policies of apartheid throughout South Africa and the former South West Africa, now Namibia.

This anthology examines these historical laws in terms of subsequent laws and measures of the 1990s and early 2000s designed to eliminate apartheid and its multifaceted vestiges. That is to say, this volume points to hidden impediments facing African students and faculty. The chapters throughout the volume maintain that sociopolitical and economic forces are integrally linked to educational policies and programs, to the psychological reactions of university students in intergroup and interracial relations, and to subtle, lingering vestiges of apartheid that prevent the recruitment and retention of African faculty. Indeed, these emerging scholars contribute to the body of works of senior scholars such as Nelly Stromquist and Kassie Freeman.

Freeman's research, prepared at the request of the Commission on Research in Black Education (see Chapter 6 in this volume), which focuses on Black populations in Australia, Great Britain, Germany, Portugal, and the United States, examines cultural alienation and annihilation, that is, the "process that controlling populations use to minimize or eradicate the culture of minority populations" (p. 140). Freeman further postulates that Black populations globally find themselves in a "culture of exclusion" via cultural alienation and annihilation. Mabokela and King's anthology presents a series of case studies of several universities that complement Freeman's analysis. Scrutinizing the necessity for and means of structural and policy transformation, this anthology discusses the historical positions of universities and the marginalized positions of Black universities (comparable to peripheral positions of other social institutions such as hospitals, social welfare agencies, and labor organizations).

Language and the Politics of Repression.   In their introductory chapter, Mabokela and King assert that a comparative sociological analysis of apartheid and segregation in Hitler's Germany, the American South, and the Japanese occupation of Korea illuminates the dynamics of racism and political oppression in South Africa. What is noteworthy about this assertion is the comprehension of the political and cultural means employed to exert domination (Mazuri, 1996; Wilson, W., 1987). The post-1948 apartheid provisions of South Africa may be compared to the 1896 U.S. Supreme Court decision in *Plessy v. Ferguson* and the policies and laws spawned thereby. In both instances, separate facilities were designed ostensibly to provide quality services—a situation far from reality because the separate institutions were vastly unequal.

Ten historically White universities were created in South Africa, from 1829 to the 1960s as compared to five for Black, Colored and Indian students, although Whites comprised well under 30% of the population. Sociocultural and linguistic features were visible in the six Afrikaan-language universities and the four English-medium sites. Similar divisions existed for Indians (University of Durban, Westville), University of Western Cape (for Colored students), University of North (for Sotho- Venda- Tsongan-speaking individuals), the University of Zululand (for Zulu-speakers), and the historical University of Fort Hare (the oldest Black university designed for Xhosa-speaking Africans). Historical sociolinguistic realities were used to separate groups and lessen possibilities for creating solidarity among groups who separately desired a democratic society.

The languages of instruction, the social studies curriculum, and the composition of the faculty limited cross-cultural interactions. The Extension of University Act (1959), in some regards, had the same effect at the university level as the Bantu Education Act had for primary and secondary education since it established or further solidified postsecondary education along ethnic lines. Some proponents contended that the Act enabled Blacks to attend postsecondary institutions that they otherwise would not have attended, especially in the Bantustans, which were established to create semiautonomous states for particular ethnic groups (Academy for Educational Development, 1992). In some instances, proponents asserted that these political entities were comparable to neighboring states of Lesotho and Swaziland. The nexus between sociopolitical and public educational policies, again, becomes evident. Absent the politically charged enactments by the South African Parliament, segregated universities would not have been established and forced to provide substandard instruction due to differential funding.

The national government established and then justified differential university funding formulas, especially prior to the 1990s, based on the number of student matriculants, the percentage of students who were successful in their academic studies (certainly influenced by their level of preparation in segregated secondary institutions), enrollments in scientific fields in contrast to the humanities, and graduate student enrollment. Hence as Mabokela and King portray, the University of Cape Town (an English-medium White site) garnered 71% of its budget from the government compared to 46% of that at the University of the Western Cape (an English-speaking Colored university situated in the same metropolitan area). The repercussions of social and political realities play out in various dimensions as the case studies demonstrate inadequate infrastructures, different academic credentials of White, Black, Colored, and Indian faculty, and limited instructional and curriculum material.

Post-Apartheid Social Transformation Matters.   With the advent of a democratic majority government in the early 1990s, the several case studies address new transformation concerns. Working constructs or definitions of transformation were not adequately provided in several chapters. However, Anne Austin (2001) offers notable components in her chapter, "Transformation through Negotiation," that illuminate points articulated in the University of Port Elizabeth Strategic Master Plan. This plan states that "negotiated transformation is a process in which the systemic features of the institutions are modified . . . which include structural, cultural and interactional dimensions" (pp. 5–7). Structural transformation would include a shift in power arrangements so that all faculty, not based on demographic characteristics, would be participants in transparent decision making. Equally important for universities are the cultural transformations that refer to the ideals, ideologies, knowledge, and values of the university and their transmission to graduates who, in turn, can effect transformations in their careers and in provincial and national policy making.

Doria Daniel's (2001) chapter, "Crossing the Divide: Black Academics at the Rand Afrikaans University," examines and summarizes university documents wherein transformation is "defined as a human phenomenon characterized by a reorientation of attitudes of individuals as well as groups of people working at the institutions" (p. 39). Key to the success of social transformation defined in this way are the attitudes of the university population including students, support workers, professional staff, and administrators. In another chapter, "Higher Education Transformation in Namibia," Rodney K. Hopson (2002) discusses impediments to the "transforming nature of higher education" due to the lingering roles of "of cultural hegemony [as] the process where ruling classes are able to exert general predominance over subordinate classes" (pp. 124–125).

Collectively, Austin, Daniel, and Hopson offer constructs that provide perspectives of transformation in the aftermath of the formal apartheid epoch. The challenging task then becomes combining the various elements of transformation into concrete policies and programs that reflect the new national constitutional provisions within university settings and simultaneously help ensure that universities contribute to social transformation. The new South African constitution specifies nonracial and nonsexist conditions and requires affirmative action. How will these constitutional requirements be planned, initiated, evaluated, and altered in postsecondary institutions so that comprehensive transformation occurs?

Several chapters in Mabokela and King offer pertinent examples. For instance, Mabokela (2001) notes in "Selective Inclusion" that faculty at the University of Stellenbosch struggle with language as the medium of communication and instruction since many Black students do not understand Afrikaans sufficiently to participate fully in university life. In essence, a transformation in language policy is necessary to ensure that non-racial university characteristics are safeguarded. In "Oh Sorry, I'm a Racist: Black Student Experiences at the University of Witwatersrand," Rochelle Woods (2001) describes how White faculty dismiss or ridicule the questions of Black students, how White students avoid Black students outside formal classroom interactions, and how perceptions that White students (and some faculty) are afraid of or feel intimidated by Black students persist. In one instance, Woods reports that a White male student sent an e-mail to a student asking her if she would like to talk. The woman student replied that she is Black, whereupon the White male student replied, "Oh, sorry, I'm a racist" (Woods, p. 101).

Such interpersonal attitudes portray blocks in transformational processes. Faculty and other professionals, for instance, at the postsecondary level are aware of the plans of the government and university executives to initiate affirmative action so more Black people and women will be represented in the faculty and professional ranks. Identifying promising undergraduate and graduate students and young faculty is one method of "growing one's own" to join the professional ranks. As Daniels's chapter observes, once these same Black faculty or women enter the professional cadre, many report that White faculty still believe they were appointed simply because of affirmative action, not because of their academic qualifications and experiences. Several of the chapter authors conclude, unfortunately, that limited progress is being made in the transformation process due to such individual attitudes—attitudes that are buttressed by external sociopolitical forces. However, there is an irony at play because many historically White institutions now have a majority Black student body, which is a major indicator of progress toward social and educational transformation.

As *Apartheid No More* went to press, the President's Office and the Ministry of Education had commissioned a series of White Papers designed to consolidate or amalgamate postsecondary institutions in the same geographical locale to avoid duplication and to use fiscal and human resources most effectively. Several of the newer Black institutions (created under rigid apartheid) were fighting for their survival. In a conversation with one former university senior executive, I asked, "What about the preservation of historical institutions such as Fort Hare University, the alma mater of President Nelson Mandela?" She replied that historical origins are not a current rationale for sustaining less viable institutions. The changes that could occur through consolidations (for example, the University of Durban-Westville [n historical Indian university] and the University of Natal [n historical White institution], both located in Durban) could become a transformative process. It remains to be seen how well the various demographic groups will be represented in all spheres of consolidated university life.

GLOBALIZATION AND ITS IMPACT ON EDUCATION

Nelly P. Stromquist's volume, *Education in a Globalized World: The Connectivity of Economic Power, Technology, and Knowledge*, delineates revised sociopolitical and economic paradigms for comprehending contemporary manifestations of global phenomena (i.e., jobs, wages and working conditions, and intellectual property), especially as such issues affect people of color in the United States and people of Africa and other developing nations. As a senior professor of international development whose research is steeped in sociological frameworks, Stromquist seeks to move beyond existing paradigms associated with dependency, neocolonialism, and postmodern theories by developing and refining components and policy definitions of globalization. She begins with the premise that globalization compels a multidisciplinary examination built on the frameworks of economics, political science, sociology, psychology, anthropology, communications, and technology.

To appreciate the comprehensive effects of globalization, Stromquist cites descriptive economic statistics from the United States and other settings affected by an international labor market where about 500,000 American workers each year are displaced as a result of imports and about one third of these workers will be reemployed with no substantial decrease in lifetime earning. About 33% will experience severe reductions. Simultaneously, labor conditions and compensation in developing nations means meager existence, including malnourishment, in the very countries that export goods to the United States and other developed nations. Furthermore, income distribution levels are widening, rather than narrowing, with increased globalization. So, ratio discrepancies between developed and developing nations rose from 30:1 in 1960, 60:1 in the early 1990s, and then 71:1 by the late 1990s. With reference to the world's wealthiest 200 individuals, their net worth doubled between the early and late 1990s totaling over $1 trillion.

Globalization is a multidimensional and multilevel phenomenon initiated by industrialized countries and pursued via formal and informal structures. Stromquist further posits that the G-8 countries (the United States, Japan, Germany, Great Britain, France, Italy, Canada, and Russia) set in motion and sustain economic conditions (including international trade, labor, and intellectual property rights) that affect all sectors of individual societies and international relations. Also, consideration should be paid to the kinds of contemporary conditions caused by historical appropriations the European Union (EU) nations, the World Bank, or the U.S. government have provided to different countries. For instance, the United States spends less than 2% of its federal budget on international matters, excluding military appropriations. In other words, only 2–3% of the total national budget directed to international funding will move into development.

Stromquist points out that the influences or roles of transnational corporations (TNCs) and the media are also critical to the globalization process. Her assertions about transnational corporations would be strengthened if she clearly differentiated their characteristics from those of large multinational corporations that seem to be the same entities as TNCs. The media, according to Stromquist, convey messages and symbols about business products and commodities that promote economic exchanges. Moreover, the sociocultural messages reinforce the predominant views of G-8 countries and the TNCs headquartered therein.

Whereas the media convey sociocultural messages, Stromquist explicates how the interactive effect of TNCs and the media are perpetuating "new knowledge" that is created by collaborations between TNCs and universities (for example, TNC-funded research grants to universities). The new knowledge is usually not developed in emerging nations of Africa and elsewhere in the global South. Indeed, the obliteration or eradication of indigenous knowledge common to African ethnic groups prevents the maintenance of their traditional sociocultural practices and modes of learning. Simultaneously, in the North or developed countries, knowledge creation (in a range of fields) is patented by copyrights to protect Western intellectual property. To what extent should knowledge production and intellectual property be available to all, and under what conditions, with new forms of dissemination via the Internet and other technological modes

(Lindsay & Poindexter, 2003)? After all, if indigenous knowledge is eradicated and African universities are not integrally involved in the intellectual property equation, then African citizens are not likely to be equal beneficiaries of globalization. (See Chapter 1 for a discussion of the progress Indigenous peoples, including Native Americans in the United States, are making in this arena, globally.)

Herein lie the crux of Stromquist's arguments regarding globalization: there is a convergence, rather than a divergence, of economic, sociocultural, political, and educational benefits to nations of the global North. Even when there are some beneficial results in developing nations, these usually accrue to select societal sectors and, in some cases, these so-called benefits have deleterious effects on poor African Americans and other people of color in the United States. For example, when technological positions are transferred overseas, or "outsourced," instead of preparing Black and Hispanic Americans for such positions, the work is often transferred to select Asian nations and often, the individuals who acquire these jobs have spent time or undertaken training in Northern nations as noted in very recent documentation (Auchard, 2003).

Transforming structural economic and sociocultural conditions within developed nations so that globalization reaps benefits for all, especially in African nations and comparable areas of the global South, is a daunting endeavor. Stromquist devotes especial attention to the roles of nongovernment organizations (NGOs). NGOs are social and political groups that carry out resistance to the status quo. Stromquist maintains that although they vary in their altruistic goals, the majority of NGOs pursue a public good by seeking the social inclusion of people who are marginalized and by drawing attention to market patterns and government structural policies that are not beneficial. We should bear in mind, however, that many NGOs in developing nations are funded by international organizations and assistance agencies from G-8 nations, which will allow some policy alterations but radical structural changes are not the goals of agencies in G-8 nations.

In her final analyses, Stromquist suggests that resistance to adverse effects of globalization (such as labor displacement, low salaries, deplorable working conditions, and environmental degradation) must take into account the interconnected components of economic power, technology, and new knowledge. In addition, individuals, labor unions, women's organizations, university students and faculty, and the United Nations should buttress resistance—a contention that is very similar to that of Wilson (1999) for linking domestic and international economic inequities. Stromquist cites Jubilee 2000 (a coalition of NGOs, religious groups, and celebrities) as an illustration of initial success in beginning to change structural conditions by seeking writeoffs of debts for 52 African and 4 Latin American nations.

The United Nations' introduction of the "Global Compact," which 44 TNCs signed, ostensibly commits them to respect human, labor, and environmental rights.

The final chapter of *Education in a Globalized World: The Connectivity of Economic Power, Technology, and Knowledge* provides a comprehensive framework for synthesizing the analyses Stromquist presents in this volume as well as important tenets contained in the Mabokela and King book. Reframing the future means advocating the alteration or creation of intellectual and disciplinary paradigms that help professionals in the social sciences, humanities, technology, and sciences address pressing global and domestic issues—and the interconnectivity between the global and domestic issues—in order to propose and implement alternative sociopolitical, cultural, and educational policies. The scholarly analyses discussed in this chapter suggest alternative policies are needed in language, sponsorship of research, and so on to ensure that universities are engaged in enhancing the personal and collective lives of people in the communities they serve. To accomplish alternatives such as those proposed in these volumes and in this chapter, university faculty in Africa and the global North should consider how the formal and informal aspects of their disciplinary frameworks examine globalization and domestic issues, how globalization affects their disciplines through issues associated with intellectual property and the like, and how their disciplines and scholarly work are part of the public good.

CONCLUDING COMMENTS

Ralph J. Bunche: Historical Inspiration for Fostering Dynamism

The intellectual contributions and experiences of the late Nobel Laureate Dr. Ralph J. Bunche offer historical frameworks and inspiration regarding the public good. Nearly 65 years ago, Dr. Bunche maintained that universities are part of the public good and must prepare students and faculty to address concrete problems and pose solutions. He further asserted that universities have a great responsibility in trying times. Windows of truth must be at the center; yet he declared: "Too often our search for Truth becomes an escape device. We may come to conceive of the quest after Truth as an end in itself and fall *in the unconscious error of assuming that there is no connection between the Truth and the practical and that it is not academically respectable to tackle the practical.*" (Bunche, 1995, p. 222, emphasis added). Tackling the practical so that sound educational policies emerge would be a major link on the chain of transformation.

During his Harvard graduate school tenure (where he completed his PhD while teaching at Howard University) and his administrative and scholarly career at Howard, Bunche espoused clear nexuses between the life of university and the need to address policy and programmatic solutions to pressing academic problems. Bunche made important contributions to the monumental publication, *An American Dilemma*, headed by the Swedish sociologist Gunnar Myrdal, a research project that articulated the salient connections between the presence of segregation and discrimination and the principles of democracy. From his youth to his diplomatic United Nations career, Bunche continually espoused and then implemented the integration of concrete problematic challenges with the role of academy and the life of the scholar.

Bunche concluded that universities often produced B.A.s—"Babes in Arms"—who, failing to obtain insight, often turn to radical and lunatic fringe organizations. Bunche argued that it is absolutely necessary for any university to equip its graduates with skills for an intelligent comprehension of the world and its multiple and competing forces, institutions, and ideologies (Bunche, 1995, p. 223). When such comprehension occurs in conjunction with active engagement with civic groups and organizations, then multidisciplinary intellectual knowledge can assist students and faculty in initiating sociopolitical and cultural transformations.

Building on Bunche's perspective, this chapter concludes by articulating the necessity for evolving dynamic paradigms to support peace and progressive development through university enterprises. If universities in Africa, other developing nations, and the global North are to move in concert toward authentic viability, we must simultaneously address macro-, intermediate, and micro-level analyses using interdisciplinary and multidisciplinary analytic frameworks and methods of research. As we accomplish this dynamic integration, our research can become more valuable, not only to those of us within the educational community, but also to the policy decision makers at the state, national, and international levels.

Part V

Situating Equity Policy and Pedagogy in the Political Economic Context

INTRODUCTION

[I] propose as the next step which the American Negro can give to the world a new and unique gift. We have tried song and laughter and with rare good humor a bit condescending the world has received it; we have given the world work, hard, backbreaking labor and the world has let black John Henry die breaking his heart to beat the machine. . . . It is now our business to give the world an example of intelligent cooperation so that when the new industrial commonwealth comes we can go into it as an experienced people and not again be left on the outside as mere beggars . . . if leading the way as intelligent cooperating consumers . . . we become pioneer servants of the common good, we can enter the new city as men [sic] and not mules.

—W.E.B. Du Bois, 1933

Part V situates education policy and pedagogy for equity and democracy within the context of systemic inequality in U.S. schools and workplaces and increasing skill requirements of the "new economy." Transcending the "rhetoric of standards-based reform" and policies aimed merely at closing achievement gap, a transformative vision of equality of opportunity and human freedom informs the analyses in Part V. Chapters 9 and 10 examine unequal funding, inequitable learning opportunities and curriculum content, workplace discrimination, and the changing requirements of the postindustrial global economy. These chapters also demonstrate new possibilities not only for access to high quality teaching and learning in schools but also Chapter 9 argues for education that prepares students to participate in democratizing the postindustrial economy.

Chapter 9, "New Standards and Old Inequalities: School Reform and the Education of African American Students," by Linda Darling-Hammond, presents quantitative evidence that "standards-based" reform does not address systemic structural disparities in school funding, the assignment of qualified teachers, or the quality of instruction, that is, curriculum and pedagogy. Darling-Hammond argues that "policy for equality" and resources are needed that go beyond high-stakes testing, content standards, and standardization that ignore these structural impediments to equal opportunities for learning and achievement. Such impediments can be linked to students' race and social status. More likely than charter schools or vouchers to address systemic impediments to equity and democracy, such policies at the state and federal level are needed to: recruit and retain a qualified teaching force, equalize funding, and change curriculum and testing requirements in order to ensure that students are prepared for available opportunities in the "new economy."

Jessica Gordon Nembhard's analysis in Chapter 10, "On the Road to Democratic Economic Participation: Educating African American Youth in the Postindustrial Global Economy," considers the achievement gap in relation to racialized wage disparities and changing economic opportunities. Nembhard situates the relationships between pedagogy and political economy within the devastating effects of institutional racism and other societal contradictions. Both Nembhard and Darling-Hammond note that schools are not organized to prepare most African American students for the kind of "thinking work" that the new economy requires. Nembhard concludes Chapter 10 with exemplars of cutting-edge educational experiences that foster the kind of learning the new economy requires—problem solving, team building, learning by doing, and developing leadership skills. Nembhard demonstrates that such learning can also prepare youth to participate in community building and to transform the economic system—"to humanize and democratize it—so that it serves everyone well."

9

New Standards and Old Inequalities: School Reform and the Education of African American Students[1]

Linda Darling-Hammond
Stanford University

INTRODUCTION

The education reform movement in the United States has focused increasingly on the development of new standards for students. Virtually all states have begun to create standards for graduation, new curriculum frameworks to guide instruction, and new assessments to test students' knowledge. Many have put in place high-stakes testing systems that attach rewards and sanctions to students' scores on standardized tests. These include grade retention or promotion as well as graduation for students, merit pay awards or threats of dismissal for teachers and administrators and extra funds or loss of registration, reconstitution or loss of funds for schools. School districts across the country are weighing in with their own versions of standards-based reform, including new curricula, testing systems, accountability mechanisms, and promotion or graduation requirements.

---

[1] This chapter has been updated from an earlier, longer version that appeared in *The Journal of Negro Education*, 69(4) (2000), 263–287.

To be sure, there are other kinds of reforms being proposed. Sprinklings of charter schools and a few voucher programs aim to create new options for some students' education. "Bottom-up" reforms of curriculum and assessment in some schools aim to provide more thoughtful and authentic learning experiences that challenge and excite students' interests and develop higher order thinking and performance skills. (See Chapter 11, for example). Reorganization of schedules and new school designs sometimes provide options for more in-depth study and longer-term relationships between adults and students. School-to-work programs promise greater options for some students who are enabled to connect more directly to the workplace. However, all of these efforts are partial and scattered. The constant of reforms today is standard-setting for student achievement. The variable is educational opportunity.

The rhetoric of "standards-based" reforms is appealing. Students cannot succeed in meeting the demands of the new economy if they do not encounter much more challenging work in school, many argue, and schools cannot be stimulated to improve unless the real accomplishments—or deficits—of their students are raised to public attention. There is certainly some merit to these arguments. But standards and tests alone will not improve schools or create educational opportunities where they do not now exist. The implications for students who have not received an adequate education are suggested by such recent headlines as this one in the Raleigh, North Carolina, *News and Observer*: "Twenty Percent of Wake Seniors Could Fail Competency Test." The article states: "Among this year's ninth graders, 40% of Black students have met the eighth-grade competency requirement; among 12th-graders, 66% have" ("Twenty Percent," 1997). That large proportions of students might fail to graduate and lose access to their futures due to these policies is suggested by recent findings in Texas, where the use of test-based accountability for the past decade is associated with graduation for African American and Latino students of less than 50% (Haney, 2000).

Reforms such as charters and vouchers are unlikely to help many minority students, although they may provide an escape hatch for a few. Although spurring innovation in schools is a worthwhile idea, in the context of dramatic inequalities that exist among U.S. schools in quality of staffing and resources, proposals to develop charters or other kinds of model schools promise to enhance the capacities of a very few while doing little to help the other 99%. Thousands of innovative schools already exist. What is needed are the policies and resources that can support the spread of their practices to tens of thousands of others. Unless charter advocates can use what is learned in these schools to transform the policies that guide the rest of the system (and few seem aware of this connection), charters will go the way of the experimental schools of the 1930s and the alternative schools of the 1960s. They will live briefly, dying out when leaders change, and affect the system and the educational experiences of most students little or not at all.

Similarly, allowing parents to choose schools for their children is a useful idea and one that has many potential benefits in securing commitment to a community and allowing diverse approaches to flourish. A number of public school choice plans that have been part of broader reforms have proved productive in these ways. However, unless such a plan is accompanied by policies that explicitly concentrate on building the supply of good schools, choice does not help the large majority of students who cannot get into the limited slots available in schools they want to choose. Neither does it help improve the schools that are not desirable and desperately need improvement. Increasing competition without increasing the capacity of schools to offer good education—a capacity that is tightly tied to the supply of knowledgeable and skillful teachers and principals—will produce improved education for only a few and greater segregation and inequality for many.

The bottom-line question for students, especially those of color, is whether investments in better teaching, curriculum, and schooling will follow the press for new standards or whether standards built on a foundation of continued inequality in education will simply certify student failure with greater certainty, reducing access to future education and employment.

THE SOCIAL AND ECONOMIC CHALLENGE

The requirements of success in today's knowledge-based economy are indeed changing. Before the end of the first decade of the 21st century, nearly 50% of all jobs will require the higher levels of knowledge and skill once reserved for the education of the few. Only about 10% of jobs will offer the kind of routine work factories once provided for low-skilled workers, and these will pay far less than what such jobs offered only 20 years ago (Drucker, 1994). Only college-educated workers have come close to holding their own economically over the last 2 decades, whereas those with a high school education or less have steadily lost real income as previously well-paid factory jobs have become automated or moved overseas. Studies of high school graduates show that among individuals with the same degrees, those with higher levels of skill increasingly have greater earning capacity. Surveys of employers indicate that even entry-level jobs require workers who have mastered higher levels of basic skills, are technologically literate and can plan and monitor much of their own work (Murnane & Levy, 1996).

More than ever before in our nation's history, education is not only the ticket to economic success but to basic survival. Whereas a high school dropout had two chances out of three of getting a job in 1970, today he has less than one chance out of three, and the job he can get pays less than half of what he would once have earned (W.T. Grant Foundation, 1988). The effects of dropping out are much worse for African American young people than for Whites. In 1996, a recent school dropout who was Black had only a one in four chance of being employed, whereas the odds for his white counterpart were about 50% (NCES, 1998, p. 100). Even recent graduates from high school struggle to find jobs. Among African American high school graduates not enrolled in college, only 42% were employed in 1996, as compared to 69% of White graduates (p. 100). Those who do not succeed in school are becoming part of a growing underclass, cut off from productive engagement in society. In addition, working-class young people and adults who were prepared for the disappearing jobs of the past teeter on the brink of downward social mobility.

Because the economy can no longer absorb many unskilled workers at decent wages, lack of education is increasingly linked to crime and welfare dependency. Women who have not finished high school are much more likely than others to be on welfare, while men are much more likely to be in prison. National investments in the last decade have tipped heavily toward incarceration rather education. Nationwide, during the 1980s, federal, state, and local expenditures for corrections grew by over 900%, and for prosecution and legal services by over 1000% (Miller, 1997), while prison populations more than doubled (U.S. Department of Commerce, 1996, 219). During the same decade, per pupil expenditures for schools grew by only 26% in real dollar terms, and much less in cities (NCES, 1994). The situation has grown worse in some parts of the country. While schools in California have experienced continuous cutbacks over the last decade, for example, the prison population there has increased by more than 600%.

In 1993, there were more African American citizens on probation, in jail, in prison, or on parole (1,985,000) than there were in college (1,412,000) (see Tables 281 and 354 of U.S. Department of Commerce, 1996, for complete data). Increased incarceration, and its disproportionate effects on the African American community, is a function of new criminal justice policies and ongoing police discrimination (see, e.g., Miller, 1997) as well as lack of access to education that could lead to employment. More than half the adult prison population has literacy skills below those required by the labor market (Barton & Coley, 1996), and nearly 40% of adjudicated juvenile delinquents have learning disabilities that were went undiagnosed and untreated in the schools (Gemignani, 1994).

Meanwhile, schools have changed slowly. Most are still organized to prepare only about 20% of their students for "thinking work"—those students who are tracked very early into gifted and talented, "advanced" or honors courses. These opportunities are least available to African

American, Latino, and Native American students. As a consequence of structural inequalities in access to knowledge and resources, students from racial and ethnic "minority" groups in the United States face persistent and profound barriers to educational opportunity. As described later, schools that serve large numbers of African American students are least likely to offer the kind of curriculum and teaching needed to meet the new standards. They are typically funded at lower levels than schools serving a whiter and more affluent population, and they often lack the courses, materials, equipment, and qualified teachers that would give students access to the education they will need to participate in today's and tomorrow's world.

Serious policy attention to these ongoing, systemic inequalities is critical for improving educational outcomes. If Americans do not recognize that students experience very different educational realities, policies will continue to be based on the presumption that it is students, not their schools or classroom circumstances, that are the sources of unequal educational attainment.

CLOSING THE GAP: CHANGES IN EDUCATIONAL ACHIEVEMENT

The struggle to close the gap in educational achievement between African American and White students could be enhanced by the current reforms or it could be seriously undermined. Although overall educational attainment for Black Americans increased steadily between 1960 and 1990, this trend is reversing in some states that have imposed graduation exams. By 1997, 87% of Black Americans between the ages of 25 and 29 had completed high school with a diploma or an equivalency (NCES, 1998, p. 80)—a trajectory that has closed much of the gap with White Americans in this regard. Dropout rates for 16- to 24-year-old Black male students declined steadily between 1975 and 1990, but they have been increasing since 1990, reaching 13.3% in 1997 (NCES, 1999, p. 124). As discussed later, this trend may be related to the increasing use of exit examinations and the return of policies encouraging widespread grade retention without investment in improved teaching.

On national assessments in reading, writing, mathematics, and science, Black students' performance continues to lag behind that of White students, with uneven progress in closing the gap. In reading, large gains in Black students' performance throughout the 1970s and 1980s have actually reversed since 1988, with scores registering declines for 13- and 17-year-olds since then. Scores in writing have also declined for eighth, grade and eleventh-grade Black students since 1988. Although there have been slight improvements in mathematics and science for 9- and 13-year-olds, the achievement gap has stayed constant or widened since 1990 (NCES, 1998, pp. 68–74). The lack of progress in student achievement during the 1990s is not surprising, as the situation in many urban schools has deteriorated over the decade. Drops in real per pupil expenditures have accompanied tax cuts and growing enrollments. Meanwhile, needs have grown with immigration, growing poverty and increased numbers of students requiring second language and special educational services. In many cities, increasing numbers of unqualified teachers have been hired since the late 1980s— teachers who are even less prepared to deal with these needs than was the case when the teaching force was more stable.

In addition, many urban systems have focused their curriculum more on rote learning of "basic" skills than on problem solving, thoughtful examination of serious texts and ideas, or assignments requiring frequent and extended writing (Cooper & Sherk, 1989; Darling-Hammond, 1997). As the new tests in many states (and the National Assessment of Educational Progress) focus more on higher-order skills, problem solving, analytic, and writing ability, they diverge from the lower level skills taught in many texts and tested by multiple-choice examinations. Students whose education is guided mostly by the basal readers and workbooks compatible with basic skills tests find themselves at a growing disadvantage when they confront the more challenging expectations of new standards and the assessments that accompany them.

INEQUALITY AND ACHIEVEMENT

Curricular inequalities are exacerbated by Black students' lack of access to qualified teachers, high-quality materials, equipment, and laboratories, among other things. Despite the rhetoric of American equality and the effects of school desegregation and finance reform, the school experiences of African American and other "minority" students in the United States continue to be substantially separate and unequal. Nearly two thirds of "minority" students attend predominantly "minority" schools, and one third of Black students attend intensely segregated schools (90% or more "minority" enrollment) (Orfield, Monfort, & Aaron, 1989, cited in Schofield, 1992, p. 336), most of which are in central cities.

As of 1995, 56% of all students in central city schools were Black or Hispanic (NCES, 1998, p. 134). This concentration facilitates inequality. Not only do funding systems and tax policies leave most urban districts with fewer resources than their suburban neighbors, but schools with high concentrations of "minority" students receive fewer resources than other schools within these districts. Tracking systems exacerbate these inequalities by segregating many "minority" students within schools, allocating still fewer educational opportunities to them at the classroom level. In their review of resource allocation studies, MacPhail-Wilcox and King (1986) summarize the resulting situation as follows:

> School expenditure levels correlate positively with student socioeconomic status and negatively with educational need when school size and grade level are controlled statistically.... Teachers with higher salaries are concentrated in high income and low minority schools. Furthermore, pupil-teacher ratios are higher in schools with larger minority and low-income student populations.... Educational units with higher proportions of low-income and minority students are allocated fewer fiscal and educational resources than are more affluent educational units, despite the probability that these students have substantially greater need for both. (p. 425)

Although some progress has been made since *Brown v. Board of Education*, dramatic disparities persist. Little positive change has occurred since Jonathan Kozol's 1991 *Savage Inequalities* described the striking differences between public schools in urban settings—schools whose population is between 95 and 99% non-White—and their suburban counterparts. While Chicago public schools spent just over $5,000 per student in 1989, nearby Niles Township High School spent $9,371 per student. While central city Camden, New Jersey schools spent $3,500 that year, affluent suburban Princeton spent $7,725 per student. Schools in New York City spent $7,300 in 1990, while those in nearby suburbs such as Great Neck spent over $15,000 per student for a population with many fewer special needs (pp. 236–237). Ten years later, school finance lawsuits continued to document wealthy suburbs spending two or three times what poor cities could afford in those states and others.

Savage Inequalities (Kozol, 1991) is replete with familiar yet poignant stories: MacKenzie High School in Detroit where word processing courses are taught without word processors because the school could not afford them (p. 198); or East St. Louis Senior High School whose biology lab had no laboratory tables or usable dissecting kits (p. 28). Meanwhile, children in neighboring suburban schools enjoyed features like a 27-acre campus (p. 65), an athletic program featuring golf, fencing, ice hockey, and lacrosse (p. 157) and a computer hookup to Dow Jones to study stock transactions (p. 158).

The students notice. As one New York City 16-year-old noted of his school, where holes in ceilings expose rusty pipes and water pours in on rainy days, in comparison with others:

> You can understand things better when you go among the wealthy. You look around you at their school, although it's impolite to do that, and you take a deep breath at the sight of all those beautiful surroundings. Then you come back home and see that these are things you do not have. You think of the difference. (p. 104)

His classmate added:

> If you . . . put White children in this building in our place, this school would
> start to shine. No question. The parents would say: "This building sucks.
> It's ugly. Fix it up." They'd fix it fast—no question. . . . People on the outside
> may think that we don't know what it is like for other students, but we *visit*
> other schools and we have eyes and we have brains. You cannot hide the
> differences. You see it and compare. (p. 104)

The disparities in physical facilities are just the tip of the iceberg. Shortages of funds make it difficult for urban and poor rural schools to compete
in the marketplace for qualified teachers as well as to provide the equipment and learning materials students need. When districts do not find
qualified teachers, they assign the least able individuals to the students
with the least political clout. In 1990, for example, the Los Angeles City
School District was sued by students in predominantly minority schools
because their schools were not only overcrowded and less well funded
than other schools; they were also disproportionately staffed by inexperienced and unprepared teachers hired on emergency credentials. Unequal
assignment of teachers creates ongoing differentials in expenditures and
access to educational resources, including the knowledge well-prepared
teachers rely on in offering high-quality instruction (*Rodriguez et al. v. Los
Angeles Unified School District*, Superior Court of the County of Los Angeles
#C611358. Consent decree filed August 12, 1992).

In 1999, students in California's predominantly "minority" schools were
still 10 times more likely to have uncertified teachers than those in predominantly White schools (Shields et al., 1999). A recent lawsuit brought
in California documents the conditions in dozens of schools serving
"minority" students where facilities are unsafe and inadequate; textbooks
and other supplies are unavailable and most of the staff is untrained and
uncertified (*Williams et al. v. State of California*, Superior Court of the State
of California, filed June, 2000). This description of one San Francisco school
serving African American and Latino students is typical of others in the
complaint.

> At Luther Burbank, students cannot take textbooks home for homework in
> any core subject because their teachers have enough textbooks for use in class
> only. . . . For homework, students must take home photocopied pages, with
> no accompanying text for guidance or reference, when and if their teachers
> have enough paper to use to make homework copies. . . . Luther Burbank is
> infested with vermin and roaches and students routinely see mice in their
> classrooms. One dead rodent has remained, decomposing, in a corner in the
> gymnasium since the beginning of the school year. The school library is rarely
> open, has no librarian, and has not been updated recently. The latest ver-
> sion of the encyclopedia in the library was published in approximately 1988.

Luther Burbank classrooms do not have computers. Computer instruction and research skills are not, therefore, part of Luther Burbank students' regular instruction. The school no longer offers any art classes for budgetary reasons. Two of the three bathrooms at Luther Burbank are locked all day, every day. When the bathrooms are not locked, they often lack toilet paper, soap, and paper towels, and the toilets frequently are clogged and overflowing. Ceiling tiles are missing and cracked in the school gym, and school children are afraid to play basketball and other games in the gym because they worry that more ceiling tiles will fall on them during their games. Eleven of the 35 teachers at Luther Burbank have not yet obtained regular, non-emergency teaching credentials, and 17 of the 35 teachers only began teaching at Luther Burbank this school year. (Complaint, pp. 22–23)

Recent studies of resource allocations in New York found similar patterns. By virtually any resource measure—state and local dollars per pupil, student-teacher ratios and student-staff ratios, class sizes, teacher experience, and teacher qualifications—districts with greater proportions of poor and minority students receive fewer resources than others (Berne, 1995; New York Study Group, 1993). These disparities became the source of a school-funding suit in New York, which eventually led the state's highest court to declare the funding system unconstitutional.

Such disparities in resources are largely a function of how public education in the United States is funded. In most cases, education costs are supported by a system of general taxes—primarily local property taxes, along with state grants-in-aid. Because these funds are typically raised and spent locally, districts with higher property values have greater resources with which to fund their schools, even when poorer districts tax themselves at proportionally higher rates. In Texas, for instance, the 100 wealthiest districts taxed their local property at an average rate of $0.47 per $100 of assessed worth in 1989; at that level of effort, they were able to spend over $7000 per student. Meanwhile, the 100 poorest districts, taxing themselves at a rate of over $0.70 per $100, were able to raise only enough to spend some $3000 per student (Kozol, 1991, p. 225).

These disparities translate into real differences in the services provided in schools: higher spending districts have smaller classes, higher paid and more experienced teachers, and greater instructional resources (Hartman, 1988), as well as better facilities, more up-to-date equipment, and a wider range of course offerings (ETS, 1991). Districts serving large proportions of poor children generally have the fewest resources. Thus, those students least likely to encounter a wide array of educational resources at home are also least likely to encounter them at school (ETS, 1991). As Taylor and Piche (1991) demonstrate:

Inequitable systems of school finance inflict disproportionate harm on minority and economically disadvantaged students. On an *inter*-state basis, such students are concentrated in states, primarily in the South, that have the lowest capacities to finance public education. On an *intra*-state basis, many of the states with the widest disparities in educational expenditures are large industrial states. In these states, many minorities and economically disadvantaged students are located in property-poor urban districts, which fare the worst in educational expenditures. In addition, in several states economically disadvantaged students, white and black, are concentrated in rural districts, which suffer from fiscal inequity. (pp. xi–xii)

WHAT DIFFERENCE DOES MONEY MAKE?

Efforts to rectify these inequalities have often been stymied by legal arguments that money "does not make a difference" in educational outcomes. The relationship between educational funding and educational achievement was placed in question in 1966, when James Coleman (1966) and a team of researchers issued *Equality of Educational Opportunity*, which later came to be known as the "Coleman Report." Although the report pointed out sources of inequality that it argued should be remedied, its statement that "[s]chools bring little influence to bear on a child's achievement that is independent of his background and general social context" (as cited in Ferguson, 1991, p. 468) became widely viewed as a claim that school funding does not affect school achievement. As later analyses pointed out, it is in part the high correlation between students' backgrounds and their schools' resources that makes it difficult in macro-analytic studies to identify an independent effect of schooling on achievement (see e.g., MacPhail-Wilcox & King, 1986). The "no effects" finding in the Coleman report also was a predictable result of the use of gross measures of inputs and outcomes aggregated to the school level, a shortcoming of the data also noted by the report's authors.

Recent studies, however, have provided solid evidence that money *does* make a difference, especially for African American children. Analyzing a data set covering 900 Texas school districts, with data more extensive than that available to Coleman and his team of researchers, Ronald Ferguson (1991) found that the single most important measurable cause of increased student learning was teacher expertise, measured by teacher performance on a state certification exam, along with teacher experience and Master's degrees. Together these variables accounted for about 40% of the measured variance in student test scores. Holding socioeconomic status (SES) constant, the wide variation in teachers' qualifications in Texas accounted for almost all of the variation in Black and White students' test scores. That is, after controlling for SES, Black students' achievement would have nearly equaled that of Whites if they had been assigned equally qualified teachers.

Ferguson (1991) also found that class size, at the critical point of a teacher-student ratio of 1:18, was a statistically significant determinant of student outcomes, as was small school size. Other data also indicate that Black students are more likely than White students to attend large schools with much larger than average class sizes (NCES, 1997a, p. A-119), and confirm that smaller schools and classes make a difference for student achievement (for a review, see Darling-Hammond, 1997).

Ferguson and Ladd (1996) repeated this analysis in Alabama and again found sizable influences of teacher expertise and smaller class sizes on student achievement gains in reading and mathematics. They found that 31% of the predicted difference in mathematics achievement between districts in the top and bottom quartiles was explained by teacher qualifications and class sizes, whereas 29.5% was explained by poverty, race and parent education.

Both of these findings are confirmed elsewhere (for a review, see Darling-Hammond, 2000). For example, Strauss and Sawyer (1986) found that North Carolina's teachers' average scores on the National Teacher Examinations (a licensing test that measured basic skills, and teaching knowledge) had a strikingly large effect on students' failure rates on the state competency examinations. A 1% increase in teacher quality (as measured by NTE scores) was associated with a 3 to 5% decline in the percentage of students failing the exam. This influence remained after taking into account per-capita income, student race, district capital assets, student plans to attend college, and pupil-teacher ratios. The authors' conclusion is similar to Ferguson's:

> Of the inputs which are potentially policy-controllable (teacher quality, teacher numbers via the pupil-teacher ratio and capital stock), our analysis indicates quite clearly that improving the quality of teachers in the classroom will do more for students who are most educationally at risk, those prone to fail, than reducing the class size or improving the capital stock by any reasonable margin which would be available to policy makers. (p. 47)

Far more than any other factor, teacher quality made the difference in what children learned. Unequal access to well-qualified teachers, a major side effect of unequal expenditures, is one of the most critical factors in the underachievement of African American students.

WHAT MATTERS IN TEACHING?

Unfortunately, policy makers have nearly always been willing to fill teaching vacancies by lowering standards so that people who have had little or no preparation for teaching can be hired, especially if their clients are "minority" and low-income students. Although this practice is often excused by the presumption that virtually anyone can figure out how to teach, a number of reviews of research have concluded that fully prepared and certified teachers are more highly rated and more successful with students than teachers without full preparation (Ashton & Crocker, 1986, 1987; Darling-Hammond, 1992, 2000; Druva & Anderson, 1983; Evertson, Hawley, & Zlotnik, 1985; Greenberg, 1983). Teacher education is also related to the use of teaching strategies that encourage higher-order learning and the use of strategies responsive to students' needs and learning styles. Thus, policies that resolve shortages in poor districts by supporting the hiring of unprepared teachers serve only to exacerbate the inequalities low-income and "minority" children experience.

A number of studies have found that teachers who enter without full preparation are less able to plan and redirect instruction to meet students' needs (and less aware of the need to do so), less skilled in implementing instruction, less able to anticipate students' knowledge and potential difficulties, and less likely to see it as their job to do so, often blaming students if their teaching is not successful (Bents & Bents, 1990; Bledsoe, Cox, & Burnham, 1967; Copley, 1974; Grossman, 1989; 1990; Rottenberg & Berliner, 1990).

How this occurs is revealed by the experiences of bright young entrants into teaching like those recruited by Teach for America (TFA) who are placed in classrooms after only a few weeks of summer training. As Yale University graduate Jonathan Schorr (1993) explained:

> I—perhaps like most TFAers—harbored dreams of liberating my students from public school mediocrity and offering them as good an education as I had received. But I was not ready.... As bad as it was for me, it was worse for the students. Many of mine ... took long steps on the path toward dropping out.... I was not a successful teacher and the loss to the students was real and large. (pp. 317–318)

Schorr argued that "sending recruits into the classroom with just 8 weeks of training ... may be long enough to train neighborhood clean-up workers or even police auxiliaries but [it isn't] enough for teachers." Others agreed:

> I felt very troubled about going into an elementary classroom having had 6 weeks [of training]. I didn't even know where to start. I was unprepared to deal with every aspect.... I had a lot of kids who were frustrated and I was frustrated because I wanted to help them and I didn't have the training to do that (A recruit who left after the first year and later entered a teacher preparation program)

> I could maybe have done a bad job at a suburban high school. I stood to do an awful job at a school where you needed to have special skills. I just didn't have the tools, and I didn't even know I needed them before I went in. I felt like, OK, I did the workshops. I know science; and I care about these kids.... You know, I had the motivation to help, but I didn't have the skill. It's sort of like wanting to fix someone's car and not having nay idea how to

fix a car. I wasn't equipped to deal with it, and I had no idea. (A recruit who left in the first year and went to medical school)

Similar concerns are reflected in Gomez and Grobe's (1990) study of the performance of alternate route candidates hired with only a few weeks of prior training in Dallas. The performance of these candidates was much more uneven than that of trained beginners, with markedly lower ratings on their knowledge of instructional techniques and instructional models, and with a much greater proportion of them (from 2 to 16 times as many) likely to be rated "poor" on each of the teaching factors evaluated. The proportions rated "poor" ranged from 8% on reading instruction to 17% on classroom management. The effects of this unevenness showed up most strongly on students' achievement in language arts, where students of the alternate route teachers scored significantly lower than students of fully prepared beginning teachers after adjusting for initial achievement levels.

The reasons for this are no mystery. Dorothy Strickland (1985) stresses that good teachers of beginning reading must understand the nature of language and language development as well as the child growth and development in order to accommodate a variety of cognitive styles and learning rates. Recent data from the National Assessment of Educational Progress (NAEP, 1994a) show that the kinds of classroom practices associated with higher reading scores—use of trade books and literature rather than basal readers and workbooks, frequent discussions and writing, group projects, and oral presentations—are more frequently found in the classrooms of teachers with more training in education and in the teaching of reading. Unfortunately, the same report shows that these practices and better-trained teachers are less likely to be available to urban and "minority" students.

Access to Good Teaching.   Disparities in teaching quality are a long-standing reality for African American students. In "Closing the Divide," Robert Dreeben (1987) describes the results of his study of reading instruction and outcomes for 300 Black and White first graders across seven schools in the Chicago area. He found that differences in reading outcomes among students were almost entirely explained, not by SES or race, but by the quality of instruction the students received:

> Our evidence shows that the level of learning responds strongly to the quality of instruction: having and using enough time, covering a substantial amount of rich curricular material, and matching instruction appropriately to the ability levels of groups.... When Black and White children of comparable ability experience the same instruction, they do about equally well, and this is true when the instruction is excellent in quality and when it is inadequate. (p. 34)

However, the study also found that the quality of instruction received by African American students was, on average, much lower than that received by White students, thus creating a racial gap in aggregate achievement at the end of first grade. In fact, the highest ability group in Dreeben's sample was in a school in a low-income African American neighborhood. These students, though, learned less during first grade than their lower-aptitude White counterparts because their teacher was unable to provide the quality instruction this talented group deserved.

Curricular differences like these are widespread, and they explain much of the disparity between the achievement of White and minority students and between those of higher and lower-income levels (Lee & Bryk, 1988; Oakes, 1985). When students of similar backgrounds and initial achievement levels are exposed to more and less challenging curriculum material, those given the richer curriculum opportunities outperform those placed in less challenging classes (Alexander & McDill, 1976; Gamoran & Behrends, 1987; Oakes, 1985).

Most studies have estimated effects statistically based on natural occurrences of different tracking policies. However, one study that randomly assigned seventh-grade "at-risk" students to remedial, average, and honors mathematics classes found that at the end of the year, the at-risk students who took the honors class offering a prealgebra curriculum outperformed all other students of similar backgrounds (Peterson, 1989). Another study of African American high school youth randomly placed in public housing in the Chicago suburbs rather than in the city found similar results. Compared to their comparable city-placed peers, who were of equivalent income and initial academic attainment, the students who were enabled to attend largely White and better-funded suburban schools had better educational outcomes across many dimensions. They were substantially more likely to have the opportunity to take challenging courses, receive additional academic help, graduate on time, attend college, and secure good jobs (Kaufman & Rosenbaum, 1992).

These examples are drawn from carefully controlled studies that confirm what many other studies have suggested. Much of the difference in school achievement found between African American students and others is because of the effects of substantially different school opportunities, and in particular, greatly disparate access to high quality teachers and teaching (see e.g., Barr & Dreeben, 1983; College Board, 1985; Darling-Hammond & Snyder, 1992; Dreeben & Barr, 1987; Dreeben & Gamoran, 1986; Oakes, 1990).

The Unequal Distribution of Teachers.   Minority and low-income students in urban settings are most likely to find themselves in classrooms staffed by inadequately prepared, inexperienced, and ill-qualified teachers because funding inequities, distributions of local power, labor market conditions, and dysfunctional hiring practices conspire to produce teacher shortages of which they bear the brunt. The data confirm that these difficulties continue to be structural conditions of urban schooling. By every measure of qualifications—certification, major or minor in the field taught or preparation for secondary assignment field—unqualified and underprepared teachers continue to be found disproportionately in schools serving greater numbers of low-income or "minority" students (NCES, 1997a). In 1994, just over 25% of newly hired public school teachers were hired without having met regular certification requirements (NCTAF, 1997). The vast majority of these teachers were assigned to the most disadvantaged schools in central city and poor rural school districts.

Districts with the greatest concentrations of poor children, "minority" children and children of immigrants are also those in which incoming teachers are least likely to have learned about up-to-date teaching methods or about how children grow, learn, and develop—and what to do if they are having difficulties. In addition, when faced with shortages, districts often hire substitutes, assign teachers outside their fields of qualification, expand class sizes, or cancel course offerings. These strategies are used most frequently in schools serving large numbers of students of color (NCES, 1997a; NCTAF, 1997). No matter what strategies are adopted, the quality of instruction suffers.

This situation is partly a function of real shortages but is also due to urban district hiring practices that are often cumbersome, poorly managed, insensitive to teacher qualifications, and delayed by seniority transfer rules and a variety of other self-inflicted procedures (NCTAF, 1996). Furthermore, as many of the more expert and experienced teachers transfer to more desirable schools and districts when they are able, new teachers and those without training are typically given assignments in the most disadvantaged schools that offer the fewest supports (Murnane, Singer, Willet, Kemple, & Olsen, 1991; NCTAF, 2003). Because they confront challenging assignments without mentoring or other help, attrition rates for new teachers, especially in cities, average 30% or more over the first 5 years of teaching (NCTAF, 1996; NCES, 1997b).

This adds additional problems of staff instability to the already difficult circumstances in which central city youth attend school. Where these practices persist, many children in central city schools are taught by a parade of short-term substitute teachers, inexperienced teachers without support, and underqualified teachers who know neither their subject matter nor effective teaching methods well. The California Commission on Teaching (1985) concluded that disproportionate numbers of minority and poor students are taught throughout their entire school careers by the least qualified teachers. This sets up the school failure that society predicts for low-income and minority children—a failure that it helps to create for them by its failure to deal effectively with the issues of teacher supply and quality.

Oakes's (1990) nationwide study of the distribution of mathematics and science opportunities confirmed these pervasive patterns. Based on teacher experience, certification status, preparation in the discipline, degrees, self-confidence, and teacher and principal perceptions of competence, it is clear that low-income and "minority students" have less contact with the best-qualified science and mathematics teachers. Students in high-minority schools have only a 50% chance of being taught by a math or science teacher who is certified at all, and an even lower chance of being taught by one who is fully qualified for their teaching assignment by virtue of the subject area(s) they prepared to teach. Oakes concludes:

> Our evidence lends considerable support to the argument that low-income, minority, and inner-city students have fewer opportunities. . . . They have considerably less access to science and mathematics knowledge at school, fewer material resources, less-engaging learning activities in their class-rooms, and less-qualified teachers. . . . The differences we have observed are likely to reflect more general patterns of educational inequality. (pp. x–xi)

This difference matters greatly for student achievement, as teachers who lack preparation in either subject matter or teaching methods are significantly less effective in producing student learning gains than those who have had a full program of teacher education.

Access to High-Quality Curriculum.   In addition to being taught by less-qualified teachers than their White and suburban counterparts, urban and minority students face dramatic differences in courses, curriculum materials, and equipment. Unequal access to high-level courses and challenging curriculum explains much of the difference in achievement between minority students and White students. For example, analyses of data from the High School and Beyond surveys demonstrate dramatic differences among students of various racial and ethnic groups in course-taking in such areas as mathematics, science, and foreign language (Pelavin & Kane, 1990). These data also demonstrate that, for students of all racial and ethnic groups, course-taking is strongly related to achievement. For students with similar course-taking records, achievement test score differences by race or ethnicity narrow substantially (College Board, 1985, p. 38; Jones, 1984; Jones, Burton, & Davenport, 1986).

One source of inequality is the fact that high-minority schools are much less likely to offer advanced and college preparatory courses in mathematics and science than are schools that serve affluent and largely White populations of students (Matthews, 1984; Oakes, 1990). Schools serving predominantly "minority" and poor populations offer fewer advanced and more remedial courses in academic subjects, and they have smaller academic tracks and larger vocational programs (NCES, 1985; Rock, Hilton, Pollack, Ekstrom, & Goertz, 1985). The size and rigor of college preparatory programs within schools vary with the race and socioeconomic status of school populations (California State Department of Education, 1984). As plaintiffs noted in the New Jersey school finance case, wealthy and predominantly White Montclair offers foreign languages at the preschool level, whereas poor and predominantly Black Paterson does not offer any until high school—and then, relatively few. And whereas 20% of 11th and 12th graders in wealthy Moorestown participate in Advanced Placement courses, none are even offered in any school in poor and predominantly Black Camden and East Orange (ETS, 1991, p. 9).

When high-minority, low-income schools offer any advanced or college preparatory courses, they offer them to only a very tiny fraction of students. Thus, at the high school level, African American, Hispanic and Native American students traditionally have been underrepresented in academic programs and overrepresented in general education or vocational education programs, where they receive fewer courses in areas such as English, mathematics and science (Oakes, 1990). Even among the college bound, non-Asian minority students take fewer and less demanding mathematics, science, and foreign language courses (Pelavin & Kane, 1990).

The unavailability of teachers who could teach these upper level courses, or who can successfully teach heterogeneous groups of students, reinforces these inequalities in access to high quality curriculum. Tracking persists in the face of growing evidence that it does not substantially benefit high achievers and tends to put low achievers at a serious disadvantage (Hoffer, 1992; Kulik & Kulik, 1982; Oakes, 1985, 1986; Slavin, 1990), in part because good teaching is a scarce resource, and thus must be allocated. Scarce resources tend to get allocated to the students whose parents, advocates or representatives have the most political clout. This results, not entirely but disproportionately, in the most highly qualified teachers teaching the most enriched curricula to the most advantaged students. Evidence suggests that teachers themselves are tracked, with those judged to be the most competent, experienced, or with the highest status assigned to the top tracks (Davis, 1986; Finley, 1984; NCTAF, 1996; Oakes, 1986; Rosenbaum, 1976; Talbert, 1990).

Tracking exacerbates differential access to knowledge. Although test scores and prior educational opportunities may provide one reason for differential placements, race and SES play a distinct role. Even after test scores are controlled, race and SES determine assignments to high school honors courses (Gamoran, 1992), as well as vocational and academic programs and more or less challenging courses within them (Oakes, 1992; Useem, 1990). This is true in part because of prior placements of students in upper tracks in earlier grades, in part because of counselors' views that they should advise students in ways that are "realistic" about their futures, and in part because of the greater effectiveness of parent interventions in tracking decisions for higher-SES students (Moore & Davenport, 1988).

Tracking in U.S. schools is much more extensive than in most other countries. Starting in elementary schools with the designation of instructional groups and programs based on test scores and recommendations, it becomes highly formalized by junior high school. From "gifted and talented" programs at the elementary level through advanced courses in secondary schools, teachers who are the most skilled generally offer rich, challenging curricula to select groups of students, on the theory that only a few students can benefit from such curricula. Yet, the distinguishing feature of such programs, particularly at the elementary level, is not their difficulty, but their quality. Students in these programs are given opportunities to integrate ideas across fields of study. They have opportunities to think, write, create, and develop projects. They are challenged to explore. Although virtually all students would benefit from being similarly challenged, the opportunity for this sort of schooling remains acutely restricted. The result of this practice is that challenging curricula are rationed to a very small proportion of students, and far fewer U.S. students ever encounter the kinds of curriculum students in other countries typically experience (McKnight et al., 1987; Useem, 1990; Usiskin, 1987; Wheelock, 1992).

In many instances, the reasons for restricting access to challenging courses is the scarcity of teachers who can teach in the fashion such curricula demand. In addition, schools continue to believe that few students need or will profit from such demanding instruction. Those beliefs are especially strong with respect to students of color. The disproportionately small enrollment of non-Asian minority students in gifted and talented programs is widespread. In most districts, though there are exceptions that result from different policies, African American and Hispanic students are represented in such courses at well under half their representation in the population (College Board, 1985, pp. 31–33). Statistical patterns are brought alive by descriptions of sorting like those offered by Kozol (1991) of a school in New York City.

> The school is integrated in the strict sense that the middle- and upper-middle class white children here do occupy a building that contains some Asian and Hispanic and black children; but there is little integration in the classrooms. (p. 93)

He describes how minority children are disproportionately assigned to special education classes that occupy small, cramped corners and split classrooms, whereas gifted and talented classrooms, exclusively White and a few Asian students, occupy the most splendid spaces, filled with books and computers, where they learn, in the children's words, "logical thinking," "problem solving," "respect for someone else's logic," and "reasoning." Students are recommended for these classes by their teachers and parents as well as by their test scores. Kozol wrote in his notes:

> Six girls, four boys. Nine white, one Chinese. I am glad they have this class. But what about the others? Aren't there ten black children in the school who could enjoy this also? (p. 97)

Meanwhile, students placed in lower tracks are exposed to a limited, rote-oriented curriculum and ultimately achieve less than students of similar aptitude who are placed in academic programs or untracked classes (Gamoran, 1990; Gamoran & Mare, 1989; Oakes, 1985, 1990). Teacher interaction with students in lower track classes is less motivating and less supportive, as well as less demanding of higher order reasoning and responses (Good & Brophy, 1987). These interactions are also less academically oriented, and more likely to focus on behavioral criticisms, especially for minority students (Eckstrom & Villegas, 1991; Oakes, 1985). Presentations are less clear and less focused on higher order cognitive goals (Oakes, 1985).

In addition, many studies have found that students placed in the lowest tracks or in remedial programs—disproportionately low-income and minority students—are most apt to experience instruction geared only to multiple-choice tests, working at a low cognitive level on test-oriented tasks that are profoundly disconnected from the skills they need to learn. Rarely are they given the opportunity to talk about what they know, to read real books, to write, to construct and solve problems in mathematics, science, or other subjects (Cooper & Sherk, 1989; Davis, 1986; Oakes, 1985; Trimble & Sinclair, 1986). Cooper and Sherk (1989) describe how such worksheet-based instruction focused on the discrete "skill" bits featured on multiple-choice tests impedes students' progress toward literacy:

> When hundreds of these worksheets, each of which presents a small, low-level skill related to reading, have been completed, children are said to have completed the "mastery" skills program. Often, these children still cannot read very well, if one defines reading as the ability to discern connected prose for comprehension.
>
> [Furthermore], worksheets are devised in such a way, teachers are told, that the material teaches itself. As a result, the amount of oral communication between pupil and teacher and between pupil and pupil is drastically reduced. . . . [Yet] if children are to learn language, a part of which is reading,

they must interact and communicate. They must have some opportunity to hear words being spoken, to pose questions, to conjecture, and to hypothesize. (p. 318)

Their discussion of what teachers should be able to do to support children's literacy development reflects what is known about the knowledge base for effective instruction generally. Good teachers construct active learning opportunities involving student collaboration and many uses of oral and written language, help students access prior knowledge that will frame for them the material to be learned, structure learning tasks so that students have a basis for interpreting the new experiences they encounter and engage students' higher-order thought processes, including their capacities to hypothesize, predict, evaluate, integrate, and synthesize ideas (Cooper & Sherk, 1989; see also Bowman, 1993; Braddock & McPartland, 1993; Garcia, 1993; Resnick, 1987).

POLICY FOR EQUALITY: TOWARD EQUALIZATION OF EDUCATIONAL OPPORTUNITY

The common presumption about educational inequality is that it resides primarily in those students who come to school with inadequate capacities to benefit from what education the school has to offer. The fact that U.S. schools are structured such that students routinely receive dramatically unequal learning opportunities based on their race and social status is simply not widely recognized. If the academic outcomes for minority and low-income children are to change, reforms must alter the caliber and quantity of learning opportunities they encounter. These efforts must include equalization of financial resources; changes in curriculum and testing policies; and improvements in the supply of highly qualified teachers to all students.

Resource Equalization. Progress in equalizing resources to students will require attention to inequalities at all levels—between states, among districts, among schools within districts, and among students differentially placed in classrooms, courses, and tracks that offer substantially disparate opportunities to learn. As a consequence of systematic inequalities at each of these levels, minority and low-income students are frequently "at risk," not from their homes or family factors but from the major shortcomings of the schools they attend.

Special programs such as compensatory or bilingual education will never be effective at remedying underachievement so long as these services are layered on a system that so poorly educates "minority" and low-income children to begin with. The presumption that "the schools are fine, it's the children who need help" is flawed. The schools serving large concentrations of low-income and minority students are generally not fine, and many of their problems originate with district and state policies and practices that fund them inadequately, send them incompetent staff, require inordinate attention to arcane administrative requirements that fragment educational programs and drain resources from classrooms, and preclude the adoption of more promising curriculum and teaching strategies.

Current initiatives to create special labels and programs for "at-risk" children and youth—including mass summer school programs and mandatory Saturday classes for the hundreds of thousands of students who are threatened with grade retention under new promotion rules—are unlikely to succeed if they do not attend to the structural conditions of schools that place children at risk. In the pursuit of equity, our goal should be to develop strategies that improve the core practices of schooling rather than layering additional programs and regulations on foundations that are already faulty. The pressures to respond to special circumstances with special categorical programs are great, and the tradition of succumbing to those pressures in an add-on fashion is well established, in education as in other areas of national life. But special programs, with all their accoutrements of new rules and procedures, separate budgets, and fragmented, pullout programs will be counterproductive as long as the status quo remains unchanged in more significant ways.

As the 1992 report of an independent commission on Chapter 1 observed: "Given the inequitable distribution of state and local resources, the current notion that Chapter 1 provides supplemental aid to disadvantaged children added to a level playing field is a fiction" (Commission on Chapter 1, 1992, p. 4). The Commission proposed that each state be held accountable for assuring comparability in "vital services" among all its districts as well as in all schools within each district. Among these vital services, perhaps the most important is highly qualified teachers, not just for specific Chapter 1 services, but for all classrooms.

Ferguson's (1991) recommendation that equalization focus on district capacity to hire high-quality teachers is an important one. In addition to the weight of evidence indicating the central importance of qualified teachers to student learning, there is real-world experience with the positive effects on teacher quality and distribution of such policies. When Connecticut raised and equalized beginning teacher salaries under its 1986 Education Enhancement Act, shortages of teachers (including those that had plagued urban areas) evaporated. By 1989, most teaching fields showed surpluses. The state raised standards for teacher education and licensing, initiated scholarships and forgivable loans to recruit high need teachers into the profession (including teachers in shortage fields, those who would teach in high need locations, and minority teachers), created a mentoring and assessment program for all beginning teachers and invested money in high quality professional development, with special aid to low-achieving districts. The state also developed a low-stakes, performance-oriented assessment program focused on higher-order thinking and performance skills, which is used to provide information to schools and districts, but not to punish children or teachers. By 1998, Connecticut had surpassed all other states in fourth-grade reading and mathematics achievement on the NAEP and scored at the top in eighth-grade mathematics, science, and writing. Although Connecticut still has an achievement gap it is working to close, Black students in Connecticut score higher than their counterparts in many other parts of the country.

The new wave of school finance lawsuits that are challenging both within-state and within-district resource allocation disparities also are promising. These suits are increasingly able to demonstrate how access to concrete learning opportunities is impaired by differential access to money, and how these learning opportunities translate into academic achievement for students. As standards are used to articulate clearer conceptions of what students need to learn to function in today's society and what schools need to do to support these levels of learning, lawsuits such as ones recently won in Alabama and New York may be linked to definitions of the quality of education that is "adequate" to meet the state's expectations for student achievement. Such cases are requiring remedies that link levels of funding to minimum standards of learning and teaching. As suits brought on the adequacy theory establish that learning experiences depend on resources and influence outcomes, they establish a principle of "opportunity to learn" that could allow states to define a curriculum entitlement that becomes the basis for both funding and review of school practices.

Opportunity-to-Learn Standards. The idea of opportunity-to-learn standards was first developed by the National Council on Education Standards and Testing (NCEST), which argued for student performance standards but acknowledged they would result in greater inequality if not accompanied by policies ensuring access to resources, including appropriate instructional materials and well-prepared teachers (NCEST 1992, E12–E13). The Commission's Assessment Task Force proposed that states collect evidence on the extent to which schools and districts provide opportunity to learn the curricula implied by standards as a prerequisite to using tests for school graduation or other decisions (NCEST 1992, F17–F18).

Opportunity-to-learn standards would establish, for example, that if a state's curriculum frameworks and assessments outlined standards for science learning that require laboratory work and computers, certain kinds of coursework, and particular knowledge for teaching, resources must be allocated and policies must be fashioned to provide for these entitlements.

Such a strategy would leverage both school improvement and school equity reform, providing a basis for state legislation or litigation when opportunities to learn are not adequately funded.

Such standards would define a floor of core resources, coupled with incentives for schools to work toward professional standards of practice that support high-quality learning opportunities. Enacted through a combination of funding commitments, educational indicators, and school review practices, such standards would provide a basis for:

- state legislation and, if necessary, litigation that supports greater equity in funding and in the distribution of qualified teachers;
- information about the nature of the teaching and learning opportunities made available to students in different districts and schools across the state;
- incentives for states and school districts to create policies that ensure adequate and equitable resources, curriculum opportunities, and teaching to all schools;
- a school review process that helps schools and districts engage in self-assessments and peer reviews of practice in light of standards;
- identification of schools that need additional support or intervention to achieve adequate opportunities to learn for their students.

Curriculum and Assessment Reform.   As I have noted, the curriculum offered to many students, and to most African American students, in U.S. schools is geared primarily toward lower-order "rote" skills–memorizing pieces of information and conducting simple operations based on formulas or rules—that are not sufficient for the demands of modern life or for the new standards being proposed and enacted by states and national associations. These new standards will require students to be able to engage in independent analysis and problem solving, extensive research and writing, use of new technologies, and various strategies for accessing and using resources in new situations. Major changes in curriculum and resources will be needed to ensure that these kinds of activities are commonplace in the classrooms of Black students and others.

These efforts to create a "thinking curriculum" for all students are important to individual futures and our national welfare. They are unlikely to pay off, however, unless other critical changes are made in curriculum, in the ways students are tracked for instruction and the ways teachers are prepared and supported. Although mounting evidence indicates that low-tracked students are disadvantaged by current practice and that high-ability students do not benefit more from homogeneous classrooms than from heterogeneous grouping (Slavin, 1990), the long-established American tracking system will be difficult to reform until there is an adequate supply of well-trained teachers. Students need teachers who are both prepared to teach the more advanced curriculum that U.S. schools now fail to offer most students and to assume the challenging task of teaching many kinds of students with diverse needs, interests, aptitudes, and learning styles in integrated classroom settings.

Other important changes concern the types and uses of achievement tests in U.S. schools. As a 1990 study of the implementation of California's new mathematics curriculum framework pointed out, when a curriculum reform aimed at problem solving and the development of higher-order thinking skills encounters an already mandated rote-oriented basic skills testing program, the tests win out (Cohen et al., 1990; Darling-Hammond, 1990a). As one teacher put it:

> Teaching for understanding is what we are supposed to be doing . . . (but) the bottom line here is that all they really want to know is how are these kids doing on the tests? . . . They want me to teach in a way that they can't test, except that I'm held accountable to the test. It's a Catch 22. (Wilson, 1990, p. 318)

Students in schools that organize most of their efforts around the kinds of low-level learning represented by commercially developed multiple-choice tests will be profoundly disadvantaged when they encounter more rigorous evaluations like those being developed by states, the College Board, and the federal government that require greater analysis, writing, and production of elaborated answers. Initiatives to develop richer curriculum and more performance-oriented assessments that develop higher-order skills have begun to address this problem in states such as Connecticut, Vermont, and Kentucky and cities such as New York and San Diego. Unfortunately, most cities continue to rely heavily on multiple-choice tests used for many purposes such as promotion and track or program placement for which they were not designed and are not valid.

The issue of how tests are used is as important as the nature of the tests themselves. The professional associations that set standards for test use—the American Psychological Association, American Educational Research Association, and National Council on Measurement in Education—clearly state that no high-stakes decision should ever be made based only on a test score and that other indicators of performance such as class work and teacher observations should always be factored in. This is because no test is a foolproof predictor of ability or future performance. Most predict much less than 50% of the variance in future performance in real-life settings, misleading those who would rely on tests alone as the indicator for major decisions. Furthermore, grade retention as an answer to low performance has been found consistently to decrease achievement and increase dropout rates (Darling-Hammond, 2001).

If new assessments are used, like current tests, primarily for sorting, screening, and tracking, the quality of education for African American students is unlikely to improve. Qualitatively better education will come only from creating more adaptive approaches to teaching, which means using assessment, not as a sorting and labeling device, but as a tool for identifying student strengths and needs as a basis for adapting instruction more successfully (Glaser, 1981, 1990). Robert Glaser (1990) argues that schools must shift from an approach "characterized by minimal variation in the conditions for learning" in which "a narrow range of instructional options and a limited number of paths to success are available" (p. 16), to one in which "conceptions of learning and modes of teaching are adjusted to individuals—their backgrounds, talents, interests, and the nature of their past performances and experiences" (p. 17).

Thus, the outcomes of the current wave of curriculum and assessment reforms will depend in large measure on the extent to which developers and users of new standards and tests employ them to improve teaching and learning rather merely reinforcing the historic tendency to sort and select those who will get high-quality education from those who will not (Watson, 1996). They also will need to pursue broader reforms to improve and equalize access to educational resources and support the professional development of teachers, so that new standards and tests are used to inform more skillful and adaptive teaching that enables more successful learning for all students (Darling-Hammond, 1997). During the 1990s, the highest achieving states in the United States, both before and after controlling for student poverty and language background, were distinguished by the fact that they had the most well qualified teaching forces and they did not use high-stakes testing. Those that had state assessment systems at that time used them only for informational purposes and instructional improvement, rather than selecting, sorting, and punishing students and schools (Darling-Hammond, 2000).

Investments in Quality Teaching. A key corollary to this analysis of inequality is that improved opportunities for minority students will rest, in large part, on policies that strengthen the teaching profession by boosting attractions to teaching while increasing teachers' knowledge base and skills. This means providing *all* teachers with a stronger understanding of how children learn and develop, how a variety of curricular and instructional strategies can address their needs and how changes in school and classroom practices can support their growth and achievement.

There are two reasons for this approach. First, professionalizing an occupation raises the floor below which no entrants will be admitted to practice. It eliminates practices of substandard licensure that allow untrained entrants to practice disproportionately on underserved and poorly protected clients. Second, professionalization increases the overall knowledge base for the occupation, thus improving the quality of services for all clients, especially those most in need of high-quality teaching (Darling-Hammond, 1990b).

The students who have, in general, the poorest opportunities to learn—those attending the inner-city schools that are compelled by the current incentive structure to hire disproportionate numbers of substitute teachers, uncertified teachers, and inexperienced teachers and that lack resources for mitigating the uneven distribution of good teaching—are the students who will benefit most from measures that raise the standards of practice for all teachers. They also will benefit from targeted policies that provide quality preparation programs and financial aid for highly qualified prospective teachers who will teach in central cities and poor rural areas, including teachers of color and teachers in shortage fields. Providing equity in the distribution of teacher quality requires changing policies and long-standing incentive structures in education so that shortages of trained teachers are overcome, and schools serving low-income and minority students are not disadvantaged by lower salaries and poorer working conditions in the bidding war for good teachers.

Building and sustaining a well-prepared teaching force will require local, state, and federal initiatives. To recruit an adequate supply of teachers, states, and localities will need to upgrade teachers' salaries to levels competitive with those of college graduates in other occupations, who currently earn 25 to 50% more, depending on the field. This should occur as part of a general restructuring effort, which places more resources as well as decision-making authority at the school level and allocates a greater share of education dollars to classrooms rather than to large bureaucracies that oversee them (see e.g., Darling-Hammond, 1997).

Incentive structures must be reshaped to encourage the provision of highly qualified teachers to low-income and minority students. Some models are emerging. North Carolina's Teaching Fellows Program has encouraged more than 4,000 high-ability college students—a disproportionate number of them male and minority—to enter teaching by underwriting their entire teacher preparation program in state universities. More than 75% have stayed in teaching (Berry, 1995). In New York City, dynamic groups of teachers and principals were invited by Chancellor Joe Fernandez to develop proposals to launch new schools. More than 250 new small schools were started during the 1990s with significantly better outcomes for students (Darling-Hammond, 1997). In such experiments, and in the policy changes they incorporate, lays one part of the hope for equalizing opportunities to learn.

States also must strengthen teacher education and certification. In almost all states, teacher education is more poorly funded than other university departments (Ebmeier, Twombly & Teeter, 1990). It has long been used as a revenue producer for programs that train engineers, accountants, lawyers and future doctors. Rather than bemoaning the quality of teacher training, policy makers must invest in its improvement; require schools of education to become accredited and create assessments that allow teachers to demonstrate they can teach diverse students as well. As in Connecticut's successful reforms, shortages must be met by enhanced incentives to teach rather than by lowering standards, especially for those who teach children in central cities and poor rural schools.

The federal government can play a leadership role in providing an adequate supply of well-qualified teachers just as it has in providing an adequate supply of well-qualified physicians for the nation. When shortages of physicians were a major problem more than 25 years ago, Congress passed the 1963 Health Professions Education Assistance Act to support and improve the caliber of medical training, to create and strengthen teaching hospitals, to provide scholarships and loans to medical students and to create incentives for physicians to train in shortage specialties and to locate in underserved areas. Similarly, federal initiatives in education should seek to:

1. *Recruit new teachers*, especially in shortage fields and in shortage locations, through scholarships and forgivable loans for high quality teacher education.
2. *Strengthen and improve teachers' preparation* through improvement incentive grants to schools of education and supports for certification reform.
3. *Improve teacher retention and effectiveness* by improving clinical training and support during the beginning teaching stage when 30% of them drop out. This would include funding internship programs for new teachers in which they receive structured coaching and mentoring, preferably in urban schools supported to provide state-of-the-art practice.

If the interaction between teachers and students is the most important aspect of effective schooling, then reducing inequality in learning has to rely on policies that provide equal access to competent, well-supported teachers. The public education system ought to be able to guarantee that every child who is forced to go to school by public law is taught by someone who is prepared, knowledgeable, competent and caring. That is real accountability. As Carl Grant (1989) puts it:

> Teachers who perform high-quality work in urban schools know that, despite reform efforts and endless debates, it is meaningful curricula and dedicated and knowledgeable teachers that make the difference in the education of urban students. (p. 770)

When it comes to equalizing opportunities for students to learn, that is the bottom line.

10

On the Road to Democratic Economic Participation: Educating African American Youth in the Postindustrial Global Economy

Jessica Gordon Nembhard
University of Maryland, College Park

INTRODUCTION

In the postindustrial global era, or the Information Age, a high school diploma no longer assures you a decent job or even a livable wage. There are fewer and fewer of the "good" manufacturing and government jobs that once were stable, provided benefits and were unionized. The nature of work has changed. The rewards to knowledge and highly technical skills have skyrocketed while rewards for traditional craft skills have stagnated or declined. The need for flexibility or versatility, good communication skills, some level of self-management, and other, often called "soft skills," also has increased. Soft skills, those that are not particularly technical or industry specific, are more "people-oriented"—including customer service, team building and collaboration, problem solving, learning by doing, and leadership skills. A college degree is now more often the signal that an applicant has the required skills or the ability to attain them; yet it is more difficult and more costly to earn than a high school diploma. At the same time, contrary to conventional wisdom, racial and ethnic job discrimination has actually increased in some cases because the latter types of skills are more difficult abilities to discern and are subject to stereotyping (see Darity & Mason, 1998; Nembhard, 2000; Williams, 2000). Moreover, the "hard" technical as well as the "soft" people skills are not evenly taught or evenly acquired across different populations (for a variety of reasons discussed later). The consequences of this shift in the nature and requirements of work in the "new" global Information Age are particularly severe for African American youth, and in general young people of color, because they continue to be left behind both academically and economically.

This chapter addresses three aspects of the consequences that relate to preparation and opportunity. Given the increasing skill requirements of the Information Age, we must first be concerned with young people's educational achievement and the quality of the credentials they earn. Those of us concerned with African American youth achievement and prosperity, for example, must be concerned about how we prepare our young people to be active, productive, and successful economic players. Earning the appropriate credentials and achieving the necessary skills are the first priority. Second, we must still concern ourselves with issues of inequality and discrimination. Contrary to optimistic predictions at the beginning of the last economic boom (late 1990s) the so-called new economy has not eliminated discrimination and oppression, and still does not deliver prosperity to all. Therefore, it is important to understand the nature of the economic system in which we must function, and the variety of opportunities available and the challenges that one must always face (even if we are prepared). I argue that given the nature of the globalized information economy, young people need not only the new highly technical skills associated with the Information Age, but also networking, problem-solving, and leadership skills that will allow them to take advantage of changes in industrial organization, participate in economic decision making and be proactive about democratizing our economic system. Finally, with the increasing globalization and the movement of industry and finance across national borders, many of the localities in the United States in which African Americans are concentrated are experiencing decreased economic activity and a loss of resources. Many central city areas, for example, have few jobs, little formal official economic activity, and even fewer financial services (see Nembhard, 2002a and 1999). Our young people can be encouraged to fill that void by becoming involved in community building and community-based economic development. Such activity begun as early as middle school and high school also may help young people feel more connected to their communities and society, and provide additional motivation for academic achievement (Nembhard & Pang, 2003).

This chapter begins by delineating some of the characteristics of the postindustrial global economy and discusses the kinds of skills that are rewarded and not rewarded. The next section provides a cursory discussion of the inequality in credentials between African American young people and European American youth, and summarizes a much larger debate about the Black–White "skills gap" and the role of the achievement gap in the analysis of racial and ethnic economic inequality. In the third section, I discuss some changes in industrial organization that open a space for increased workplace democracy, which helps to address both how the economic system might become more democratic, and to illustrate an area in which more creative thinking and problem solving can lead to making change. I explore some alternative ways to approach the concern about the achievement gap and ways in which thinking about alternative democratic community-based economic development strategies helps to address issues of pedagogy and achievement for African American youth. The chapter concludes with a few examples of educational and community-building experiences for young people, which may help simultaneously to catalyze community-based economic development and youth academic achievement. (Nembhard & Pang, 2003, also explore some of these issues and provide a variety of examples of leadership and economic development projects initiated and run by youth of color.) These examples also suggest directions for a new millennium research and action agenda in Black education for the postindustrial economy.

CHARACTERISTICS OF THE POSTINDUSTRIAL ECONOMY

The change from a manufacturing-based national economy to a service-based global economy with increased international competition over the past 30 years has led corporations in the United States to consolidate their power at home and to follow cost-cutting, antilabor policies. Wages and benefits have decreased as transnational corporations force U.S. workers to compete with the lowest paid jobs around the world. This has been a period in which growth "generates inequality" (Williams, 2000), even during "good times," as were the late 1990s (Collins & Yeskel, 2000; Persuad & Lusane, 2000). All measures of income inequality in the United States, for example, show increased inequality since the late 1960s (Left Business Observer, 1993, and U.S. Census Bureau, 2002, Table IE-6). Households with the highest incomes continue to do better and better. Households with the lowest incomes tend to lose ground (except for during a very short period at the height of booming times). Middle-income jobs dwindle, as has the middle class in the United States (Nembhard, Pitts, & Mason, 2005). Some types of knowledge production and technological skills receive a high premium, whereas the majority of jobs pay pittances and may be more discriminatory. This dichotomization is particularly strong in the service sector, which has been the fastest growing sector over the past 20 years. If one, therefore, does not qualify for the high-wage jobs, the only other option is very low-wage jobs with little mobility. The service sector also increasingly hires more contingent workers, or casual or temporary workers, whom they do not hire full time, do not train, and to whom they do not give employee benefits. (For more on the characteristics of the postindustrial global economy, particularly the service sector, see Nembhard, 2000; Persuad & Lusane, 2000; Williams, 2000.)

Wright and Dwyer's (2000/2001) study of what they describe as "The American Jobs Machine" illustrates the way economic growth of the 1990s increased inequality, particularly African American inequality.[1] They develop a measure of job quality based on the median earnings of full-time hourly employees, to determine the proportion of high-middle-, and low-quality jobs created during the expansion of the 1990s. Twenty percent of new jobs came from the highest decile (those high earning occupations that in 1992 were 10% of all jobs). They matched this with the 17% of job growth generated by the worst decile (those low-earning occupations that in 1992 were 10% of all jobs). The middle to upper echelon of the job distributions (deciles 2 through 5), which represented about 40% of all jobs in 1992, only represented 14% of job growth during the expansion. This "hourglass" pattern of job creation (the very good jobs and the very poor jobs grow, but the middle-level jobs dwindle) is starkly different from the pattern in the 1960s. During that decade of growth, the lowest decile contributed less than 2% of total growth and the job creation from the four lowest deciles (20%) was roughly equivalent to the contribution of the worst decile during the expansion of the 1990s. The 1960s labor market experienced strong growth in both the upper and middle ranges of job quality and little growth in the worst jobs, which decreases inequality.

The starkly different outcomes across the decades were also matched by a stark difference in the racial (and gender) distribution of jobs. (Note that the 1960s data uses Whites as a unit of analysis; in 1990s, non-Hispanic Whites are the point of reference.) In the 1960s, for Black and White men, a smaller number were working in the worst jobs at the end of the decade compared to the beginning of the decade. In contrast, for Black women and White women, the four worst deciles represented approximately half of all job growth (52%; 48%, respectively). In the 1990s, this gender pattern of job distribution was replaced by a racial pattern of job distribution. For Black men and women, approximately one quarter of employment growth came from the worst two deciles (28%; 25%, respectively). For White men

---

[1] Thanks to Steven C. Pitts, PhD, Center for Labor Research and Education, University of California, Berkeley, for introducing me to this research. We presented this in an early draft of Nembhard, Pitts, & Mason, 2005.

and women, these deciles represented a much lower proportion of group job growth (4%; 15%, respectively; Wright & Dwyer, 2000/2001).

In addition, according to the U.S. Bureau of Labor Statistics (2004) Employment Projections for 2002–2012: "Professional and related occupations and service occupations—two groups at opposite ends of the educational and earnings ranges—are projected to increase the fastest and to add the most jobs, accounting for more than half of total job growth over the 2002-2012 decade" (p. 2). This dichotomy, more "good" jobs and more "poor" jobs, appears to persist, and is projected to persist.

In terms of returns to a credential, between 1974 and 1993 the ratio between what a high school graduate earned and what a college graduate earned decreased from 70% to 57% (Rodgers, 1999; also see Uchitelle, 2000). This ratio rose slightly to 60% by 2000 (author's calculations from the U.S. Census 2000, http://www.uscensus.gov). In addition, wage inequality grew even among workers with the same level of education (Rodgers, 1999).

There is a paradox. Although high-wage jobs increasingly depend on a college degree, the greatest growth in employment is not necessarily in high-wage industries or occupations, particularly for African Americans and Latinos. Therefore, the greatest demand for workers has not been in areas that reward high educational attainment. Professional, technical, and managerial jobs, for example, which pay the highest wages in the service sector and employ college educated workers, accounted for only 23% of job growth in 1992 (Williams, 2000, from the U.S. Bureau of Labor Statistics). According to the latest projections of growth (U.S. Bureau of Labor Statistics, 2004, p. 2), jobs that are growing the fastest are in health (medical assistants, physicians assistants, social and human service assistants, home health aides, for example) and computer (information technology) occupations, where there is a wide range of educational requirements.

Although an Associate or Bachelor's degree is the "most significant source of postsecondary education or training" for 6 of the 10 fastest growing occupations (in health and computers), short-term on-the-job training is the most significant source of postsecondary education or training for 6 of the 10 occupations with the largest job growth, those which employ the most people (U.S. Bureau of Labor Statistics, 2004, p. 2). This means that the majority of the occupations that are expected to show the most growth in employment do not require a Bachelor's or Associate's degree. In particular, the occupation with the largest projected job growth, registered nurses, only requires an Associate's degree. A Bachelor's degree is needed only for the eighth occupation with the largest job growth, general and operations managers. Only the second occupation with the largest job growth, postsecondary teachers, requires a doctoral degree. The other 7 of the 10 occupations with the largest job growth require only on-the-job training—6 require short-term and one requires moderate-term on-the-job training. These occupations are retail salespersons; customer service representatives; combined food preparation and serving workers, including fast food; cashiers, except gaming; janitors and cleaners, except maids and housekeeping cleaners; waiters and waitresses; and nursing aides, orderlies, and attendants (U.S. Bureau of Labor Statistics, 2004, Table 3c). Most of these are low-wage jobs, and some do not even require a high school diploma, but they account for most of the growth in employment. Most of the high-wage jobs are not growing very fast. Competition within the high-wage, high-growth occupations is therefore stiffer as there are so few of them. At the same time, it is much easier to obtain a low-wage job that requires few credentials. The dilemma then is, that in most cases, to earn a high salary a person needs the proper (and often increasingly higher) credentials; however, those good jobs are more difficult to obtain. There is no guarantee that having the credential ensures a job.

THE ISSUE OF CREDENTIALS AND THE "SKILLS GAP" DEBATE

There was hope that more education and high test scores would translate into higher wages for all, which would equalize wages and solve the problem of income inequality. During the past 20 to 30 years, African Americans aged 25 and older have been closing the gap with European Americans in completion of a high school education. In 2002, 34.8% of Black men (25 and older) had a high school diploma compared with 31.5% of "non-Hispanic White" men (McKinnon, 2003, from the March 2002 "Current Population Survey"). For African American women, 33.3% were high school graduates compared with 34.3% of white women in 2002 (McKinnon, 2003). One of the paradoxes is that more African Americans are attaining high school diplomas at a time when a high school education does not provide enough of the technological skills or enough of the "soft" skills necessary for the new "good" jobs.

College enrollment continues to be quite competitive and costly, so is out of the reach of many young people, particularly African Americans, Latinos, and Native Americans. Although more African American men, for example, have an Associate's degree or some college (27.3% compared with 25.2% of White men), only 16.4% of Black men have a Bachelor's degree or higher, compared with 31.7% of "non-Hispanic White" men. African American women have slightly higher percentages of attainment of an Associate's degree or some college (28.2%) and a Bachelor's degree or more (17.5%) than Black men, but lag behind White women in Bachelor's degree or higher (27.3% for "non-Hispanic White" women; McKinnon, 2003). In addition, since 1976, college costs have more than doubled while government loans and other financial support for students have remained essentially the same (Collins & Yeskel, 2000).

Economists and sociologists struggle with the difficulties of identifying and verifying correlations between academic performance and its various components, on the one hand, and economic performance and its various modes of success on the other. We know with certainty that those with few or no up-to-date skills tend not to be in the official economy—are usually unemployed, in the informal sector, or in jobs at the bottom rung (low paying, least secure, poorest benefits). We also know that certain credentials help provide a signal to employers about what skills to expect in potential employees. Uchitelle (2000) observes that:

> ... in the high-technology economy, employers say they value a college degree as evidence that a job applicant has learned to think and to master new ways of working, and is also sufficiently disciplined to work hard. The high school diploma no longer sends that message to employers. (p. 1)

By contrast, good training is not always enough. Political economic analyses suggest that there are questions about who gets trained, for what, and why—and who does not. Although academic achievement is increasingly necessary for economic prosperity, it is not sufficient. A focus only on academic achievement can be a smoke screen, obscuring increased and subtler discrimination, because it seemingly leaves the onus of who can participate in the economic system on the individual. The focus on academic achievement assumes that a meritocracy exists, and is fair and masks the enduring power of personal connections, inheritance, previous endowments, structural inequalities, institutional racism, and stereotyping in our economic system. All of these complications and contradictions surface in the postindustrial global economy.

Concern about the quality of education and continuing wage and income gaps has led researchers to investigate disparities in the skills different groups bring to the labor market and the relationships between testable skill levels and wages. Recent research compares the wages of African Americans and "non-Hispanic Whites," for example, who have the same education, experience, and test scores (Rodgers, 1999). Educational credentials and test scores are proxies used to decide or "expose" who is trained to participate in this new economic era and who is perceived not to be capable or worthy of participation or reward. However, educators know that assessing capacity, training, and knowledge is not unidimensional, but multidimensional and complex—there is no one perfect measure.

There is a continuing debate among those researchers who find test score differences to explain almost completely the Black–White wage gap and those who find that a significant portion of the wage gap cannot be explained by test scores (see Nembhard, 2000, for some of this data and

Darity & Mason, 1998, and Rodgers, 1999). From his recent study, Rodgers (1999) concludes: "At any point in time, the black-white wage gap is mostly due to labor market discrimination and not to test score differences that supposedly point to racial skill gaps" (p. 179). Rodgers also discusses problems with the tests that have been used and his previous work in this area. He contends that the challenge is to "construct instruments that truly sort individuals on the basis of their knowledge and skills, instead of the context in which questions are asked" (p. 179). Therefore, increasing education levels and test scores, while important, do not necessarily end economic inequality.

Although the Black–White wage gap between full-year and full-time employed men decreased between the mid-1970s through 1979, during the 1980s the gap expanded again, even among workers with the same education (Rodgers, 1999). More striking, the wage gap between Black and White college graduates was virtually zero in 1979 but expanded to 17% by the middle of the 1980s. (See also Bond and Freeman, 1992, cited by Rogers, 1999.) An increasing number of studies suggest that differences in educational attainment, although important, are less significant than racial and ethnic discrimination in explaining differences in earnings and occupations (see, for example, Stewart, 1997; Darity & Mason, 1998; Mason, 1999; Rodgers, 1999; also Nembhard, 1998). Indeed, Mason (1999) finds that "all other things being equal, African Americans will accumulate 0.29 *more* [emphasis added] years of education than whites" (p. 71), but still earn less. Mason notes that when he controls for differences in family values, class, and a number of demographic factors to explain racial inequality in wages, hours, and education, race is statistically significant (p. 71). Similarly, Gyimah-Brempong and Fichtenbaum (1997) find that "the contribution of human capital to the wage differential is in favor of black males" (p. 162). In other words, if returns to human capital were the only factor that differed between White men and Black men in the labor market, "black male wages would exceed white male wages" (p. 155).

In an extensive study of the effect of childhood family environment on young adult years of educational attainment, wage rates, and annual hours of employment, Mason (1999) finds that "class explains a higher percentage of variation in economic well-being than family values" (p. 74). In family environment, Mason includes values such as aspirations, economizing, achievement motivation, visible reading material in the home, index of trust or hostility, religion and commitment to extended family, class, family status, and other standard demographics. Mason concludes that,

> . . . racial discrimination within the labor market continues to be a major determinant of well-being, explaining at least 40% of the hourly wage differential and 80% of the difference in hours of employment. However, greater effort among African Americans reduces the educational gap by 33%. (p. 77)

Although the difference in skills and credentials between African American and European American young people is still too large and disturbing, scholars do find that racial discrimination and economic inequality continue to exist, even when skills are well measured and matched between groups. Therefore, we cannot examine the global economy and its skill requirements without examining other aspects of the global economy, particularly discrimination.

Finally, wealth inequality is more disturbing than income inequality and has been increasing (see, for example, Oliver & Shapiro, 1997; Conley, 1999). Wolff (2001) found that wealth inequality between the rich and the poor in general increased throughout the 1980s and 1990s (also see Collins & Yeskel, 2000). In 2001, the difference between Black and White wealth holdings actually increased compared with the 1998 figures. The Black–White ratio for median net worth was a mere 0.162 in 2001 (Aizcorbe, Kennickell, & Moore, 2003, p. 8). In addition, about 27.4% of Black households actually possess zero or negative net worth, meaning the value of their debts exceeds the value of their assets (Wolff, 2001, p. 50). This is almost twice the percentage of comparable White households. The magnitude of wealth inequality has many consequences (Conley, 1999), and suggests that the strategy of obtaining the right credentials and training for a high paying job is not sufficient. Real economic prosperity depends on wealth accumulation and increased ownership of assets that appreciate.

ECONOMIC INNOVATIONS, NEW FLEXIBILITY, AND WORKPLACE DEMOCRACY

Along with fierce competition and increasing skills needs, industrial organization paradigms in the global economy are changing in favor of more teamwork, management-labor cooperation, integrated production, and sometimes profit sharing. These require problem solving skills, flexibility, and collaboration. Are we educating young people of color to participate in such forms of workplace democracy? The nature and direction of economic innovations have important implications for how we educate young people. Current innovations in many competitive businesses increase employee participation in decision making at all levels of the corporation, and increase the possibilities for meaningful work, returns to schooling, and economic security for workers. Here the need may not be as much in highly technical skills but, rather, in problem solving and critical thinking skills. Rosenzweig (2000), for example, suggests that:

> There is emerging evidence that schooling does not always have payoffs, and just where and when schooling does augment productivity suggests some answers to our puzzles. One long-standing hypothesis is that schooling

augments productivity by enhancing the ability to learn, which implies that
where profitable learning opportunities exist, schooling is most productive.
(p. 229)

Schooling, in some cases, may be more important because of the learning
attitudes, habits and opportunities created (or not created), rather than any
specific skills or techniques imparted per se.

Many competitive companies around the world now rely more on
entrepreneurial strategies, which combine competition and cooperation,
than on hierarchical relations (see Haynes & Nembhard, 1999, for example). These methods often gain them market share. Today's successful industries, for example, use strategies that are more production-based, focused on organizational practices that facilitate continuous improvement
in methods, products, and processes. Many successful businesses practice varying degrees of worker participation and require much more flexibility in organizational relationships. There is increasing documentation
that democratic firms, which practice flexibility, teamwork, decentralized
control, and participatory governance, are more effective and competitive
(Levine & Tyson, 1990).

In her study of democratic companies, for example, Fenton (2002) finds
that as a result of a more democratic culture and organizational design,
companies can increase productivity, profitability, sales, and efficiency;
improve customer service; attract and retain top talent; decrease turnover;
increase levels of trust and communication; increase flexibility and ability
to adapt to both external and internal changes; and heighten a company's
awareness of its surrounding community and its opportunities for civic engagement. In other words, these companies are productive, competitive,
and profitable. Case's (2003) profile of democracy at work in Atlas Con-
tainer Corporation reveals similar benefits. "The open books and democracy are ways to shape a company that can do things that its competitors
can't" (p. 82). In the long run, costs are cheaper because the culture created
by workplace democracy and "open book" accounting "obviates the need
for an army of frontline managers"—"we have people here that run the
plant themselves" (p. 82). In addition, the employee retention rate of about
85% is much higher than the industry average (an estimated 50%), and
employees "buy into tough decisions instead of the kind of grousing that
undermines morale and performance at a lot of companies" (p. 82).

Economic benefits of various forms of democratic economic participation include: giving workers a stake in expanding company productivity; promoting feelings of ownership and pride in high-quality workman-
ship; fostering creativity and critical thinking; increasing productivity and
professionalism; improving self respect, happiness, health, and the environment; personal growth; wage security; preserving and creating jobs;

and family and community orientation (Krimerman & Lindenfeld, 1992). Democratic enterprises often give women control of economic resources, more leadership, and managerial training and opportunities (Weiss & Clamp, 1992).

Cooperatives are companies democratically owned by their members, the people who use their services—consumer-owned, producer-owned, or worker-owned. Cooperatives promote pooling of resources, sharing risks and profits and the production, distribution, or acquisition of affordable high-quality goods and services. Cooperative businesses operate according to a set of principles about democratic governance, open membership, returns based on use, continuous education, and concern for community (see for example, National Cooperative Business Association, n.d.). Cooperatives often develop and survive as a response to market failure and economic marginalization. Groups of people come together to form democratically owned businesses in order to provide goods and services they may not otherwise be able to obtain or afford; to distribute, market, or process their products under more favorable conditions; and to control their own workplaces and income generation. Cooperatives also anchor economic activity in a local community and exemplify local economic development. More than 100 million people in the United States are members of 47,000 successful cooperatives that operate in almost every kind of industry (as of 2000; see National Cooperative Business Association Web site, http://www.ncba.coop).

African Americans have a history of cooperative ownership that is not particularly well known, ranging from farms, to processing and distribution cooperatives, food co-ops, credit unions, mutual insurance companies, taxi cab companies, security services companies, sewing enterprises, catering businesses, and home health-care agencies (Du Bois, 1907; Haynes, 1994; Haynes & Nembhard, 1999; Nembhard, 2004 and Shipp 2000). Several African American scholars and leaders have advocated for economic cooperation as an important strategy for Black economic empowerment including the scholar-activist W. E. B. Du Bois, the businesswoman Nannie H. Burroughs, the activist and businessman Marcus Garvey, the activist Ella Jo Baker, the journalist George Schuyler, the pastor Vernon Johns, the scholar E. Franklin Frazier, and the (former) Jackson State College President Jacob Reddix (Nembhard, 2002-a, 2004; also see Demarco, 1974; Du Bois, 1933, 1975; Haynes, 1993; Shipp, 1996). Before he became president of Jackson State College (now University) Reddix (1974), for example, was a founder of The Consumers' Cooperative Trading Company in Gary, Indiana, in 1932. The Trading Company developed a complex of stores and had an extensive educational program (see later). Given the economic needs in African American communities and the characteristics of the global economy, local cooperative business ownership is a promising strategy.

MODELS OF CURRICULUM DEVELOPMENT
FOR DEMOCRATIC ECONOMIC TRANSFORMATION

With proper preparation and more opportunities—traditional and nontraditional—young people can be active participants in democratic enterprises and in democratizing the global economy. Participation in such alternatives and cutting-edge economic processes require both opportunity and preparation, formal and informal education, ability to be flexible, engage in critical thinking, good communication skills, and continuous learning habits. Standard achievement measurements are often a proxy for such "skills" and here again lack of high achievement can put students and people of color at a disadvantage. However, such "skills" are not just learned in a formal education setting and can be acquired, developed, and nurtured through a variety of experiences. Schools can promote this kind of learning but also can facilitate experiences that develop good learning habits and creative, flexible thinking.

Curriculum development sensitive to the needs of democratic businesses can combine teaching critical thinking, problem solving and team building, along with technical skills, and at the same time provide experiences that foster learning-by-doing, flexible thinking, creativity, and democratic participation. Moreover, as one of the characteristics of the global Information Age is to leave a void of economic activity in certain communities, school-based and other kinds of experiences for youth can focus on the local economy and community economic development. Nembhard and Pang (2003), for example, suggest

> ... youth can learn to be economic innovators in a changing economy that relies more on information, technology and technological change, problem solving, and team work and collaboration than ever before. At the same time, they can be exposed to new forms of economic organization and management that put people and communities more in control. (p. 190)

Below I provide four examples of programs or curricula for youth that both help motivate them to be academic achievers and provide real world experiences where they learn by doing and participate democratically, as well as develop leadership, advocacy, or entrepreneurial skills.

An early example is the young people's branch of the Gary Indiana Consumers' Cooperative Trading Company. In addition to the grocery store, a branch store, a filling station and a credit union, the cooperative supported a young people's branch that operated its own ice cream parlor and candy store (Reddix, 1974). Jacob Reddix is quoted as saying that the "most important single factor" in the cooperative's progress "has been our education program" (Hope, 1940, p. 40). They held weekly educational meetings for 18 months before opening any of the businesses. In 1933, they instituted a cooperative economic course in Roosevelt High School's evening school in Gary. By 1936, it was the largest academic class in the school (Hope, p. 41). The Education Committee published a 5-year plan for "Uplifting the Social and Economic Status of the Negro in Gary" (Hope) in 1934. The Consumers' Cooperative Trading Company provides just one example of how important education about cooperative principles, organization, and business management is to the development of cooperatives, especially the development of African American cooperatives in the 20th century (see Nembhard, 2004).

The Youth Warriors Environmental Justice After School Program in Baltimore, Maryland (started in 1998) focuses African American 13- to 18-year-olds on learning about and becoming active in addressing local environmental injustices. Such advocacy also engages the students in community service and leadership development at the same time that they learn environmental science and communication skills. The program also makes sure their homework is done (for more details, see Nembhard & Pang, 2003).

The Federation of Southern Cooperatives/Land Assistance Fund (FSC/LAF) is a network of rural cooperatives and cooperative development centers in the southern United States (FSC/LAF, 2002). The FSC/LAF youth development arm teaches African American youth about economic paradigms, cooperatives, and business development. One strategy used is to help young people make connections between democratic economic concepts and their own cultural and family values (Nembhard, 2002-b). FSC educators remind students, for example, of the principles celebrated during the Kwanzaa festivals (in particular "Ujamaa" or cooperative economics). Another strategy is to point out everyday paradigms or systems, discuss them, and show how they can be changed (see Nembhard, 2002-b and Nembhard & Pang, 2003, for more details). Only after these preliminaries do the programs then discuss democratic economic structures and how young people can begin to create their own businesses and cooperative enterprises. The FSC/LAF provides workshops and summer programs for youth.

The University of Pennsylvania has partnered with the West Philadelphia Partnership and Philadelphia Public Schools on a school-based community health promotion collaboration, the Urban Nutrition Initiative (UNI). The interdisciplinary program uses college students learning horticulture and nutrition to teach high school students, to teach middle school students, to teach elementary school students about health, nutrition, and business development. This is a learning-by-doing experience for all involved, at every level. It is a "dynamic educational process based on experiential learning and community problem-solving" integrated with public service (UNI, 2002, p. 3). The program combines a community health curriculum, school-based urban gardens and entrepreneurial and business development. The program's goals are to:

- create and sustain an interdisciplinary pre-K through 16+ curriculum that focuses on improving community health and simultaneously results in increased educational skills and abilities;
- work with university faculty, public school teachers, and community residents to effectively engage students as agents of school and community change; resulting in
- students' increased sense of control over their lives and their futures, and in
- mobilization of substantial and effective resources (youth) to improve community health (Center for Community Partnerships, 2003; and UNI, 2002).

Students (mostly African American) combine learning about nutrition, teaching it to others, growing healthy food and creating businesses to sell and market the food. The businesses they create are cooperative purchasing clubs, food co-ops, and farmer's markets. The young participants develop entrepreneurship and many related skills (math, science, marketing, communication). Students engage in school and community service through a "democratic collaborative process" (UNI, 2002, pp. 8, 3; see also Nembhard & Pang, 2003, and Center for Community Partnerships, 2003).

Giving young people opportunities to build their communities, the chance to be involved in leadership development, and study and practice economic democracy in action involves them early in economic activity and may motivate them to be academic achievers. Because the global economy removes resources and activity from communities and also requires higher levels of learning and training, such combinations can be powerful.

CONCLUDING COMMENTS

Although African American students (actually all students) need more credentials and more skills for this "new" economy, that will not be enough. We must begin to educate them to be "movers and shakers" in the economy, to challenge, problem solve, and change paradigms—particularly in their own communities. Analyzing the achievement gap from a political economic perspective broadens our notions about the relationships between pedagogy and political economy and the importance not just of opportunity and preparation, but also of inclusion and motivation. In some cases, it is not the achievement gap per se that is the biggest problem (it may be the reverse of what we think), in other cases, it is the kind of achievement gap that matters (what skills do some have that others need and what really are the necessary skills?). In still other cases, starting with economic development, and economic opportunity and participation contributes to our understanding of how academic achievement is rewarded and what may help to motivate it.

Although those who can will continue to make superhuman achievements in education to cash in on higher returns in the labor market, we still live in a world where they also need to do so to compensate for continued discrimination. Increased education and better test scores are necessary but not *sufficient* conditions for increased economic well being. We must consider that one of the things we should be educating our youth for is to transform the economic system—humanize and democratize it—so that it serves everyone well. It is important to study the ways in which engagement of young people in community building and economic development and entrepreneurship activities motivates and enhances their positive academic experiences and achievement, prepares them to be productive members of the economy, and also launches them into the world of advocacy and movement building.

I worry that in some communities the connections between academic achievement, or scholarship, and economic reward and success are so remote that our young people are making pragmatic even rational decisions not to invest in schooling. More and more of us are finding that they can be drawn back in with innovative curricula that are participatory and activist, and involve them early on in economic development (see Nembhard & Pang, 2003, for example). In addition, competitive democratic firms require learned and thinking participants, with participatory experience (or at least those who can learn-by-doing quickly). Perhaps, even more important, low resourced, marginalized, underdeveloped, often abandoned communities need local community-based economic development. School settings can be training grounds for alternative democratic community-based economic development (and for the skills needed to design, develop, and manage such enterprises). Students can learn entrepreneurial, cooperative business skills, along with other necessary skills and attitudes, and at the same time have experience building and running democratic economic enterprises in their neighborhoods.

Part VI

Humanizing Education: Diverse Voices

INTRODUCTION

Each of us needs to undergo a tremendous philosophical and spiritual transformation. Each of us needs to be awakened to a personal and compassionate recognition of the inseparable interconnection between our minds, hearts and bodies, between our physical and psychical well-being, and between our selves and all the other selves in our country and in the world.

—Grace Lee Boggs

Part VI presents diverse voices of educators who are grappling with some of the most challenging questions of our times. Chapters 11 and 12 address the rhetoric versus the reality of "top-down" reforms and alienating educational philosophy that constrain teachers, teaching, and the viability of communities. In Chapter 11, "A Detroit Conversation: These Are the Times that Grow Our Souls," Joyce E. King and Sharon Parker have organized a presentation of the model community dialogue the Commission on Research in Black Education convened to demonstrate *democratic* accountability in the education research enterprise. During this 3-hour dialogue (selected excerpts from the transcript of the CORIBE video documentary are presented in Chapter 11), grassroots leaders, education professors, veteran public and private school administrators and teachers, a student teacher as well as researchers and a college president engaged in an agenda-setting conversation about effective education practice, research, and reform. The near-legendary Chinese American activist educator Grace Lee Boggs's analytical commentary frames the selected highlights of this "Detroit Conversation."

The questions Boggs poses in this commentary delve deeply into the social crisis and the possibilities for transformative, humanizing education that can "grow our souls":

> How are we going to make our livings in an age when hi-tech and the export of jobs overseas have brought us to the point where the number of workers needed to produce goods and services is constantly diminishing? Where will we get the imagination, the courage and the determination to reconceptualize the meaning and purpose of Work in a society that is becoming increasingly jobless? ... How, then, are we going to build a twenty-first century America in which people of all races and ethnicities live together in harmony, and Euro-Americans in particular, embrace their new role as one among many minorities constituting the new multi-ethnic majority?

This chapter concludes with several questions intended to spark conversation in other communities using the documentary videotape of this conversation.

The Commission convened a number of forums in which researchers, practitioners, community educators, and parents of diverse backgrounds discussed research, education, and social justice praxis. The diverse participants in the Commission's working colloquium recommended developing a transformative agenda that would prioritize:

> *Applied research* that is *inclusive of the entire Black community* (churches, parents, advocacy organizations, artists, writers, actors, etc.); that utilizes *advanced technology in various ways*; and that *addresses Black education globally*. In addition, *the importance of recognizing and embracing a role for spirituality in Black education research and practice* was also affirmed.

In Chapter 12, "Faith and Courage to Educate Our Own: Reflections on Islamic Schools in the African American Community," Zakiyyah Muhammad, an African American Muslim scholar, teacher, and school administrator, offers reflections on Islamic education in the historical and contemporary African American experience with particular emphasis on the roles of spirituality, community self-determination, and interethnic relationships. This chapter describes a model of Islamic education following a spiritual tradition embraced by a growing number of Americans of diverse ethnic and racial backgrounds. Muhammad describes the significant self-empowering role this tradition has played in the Black community in the United States during three historic periods. She also outlines an agenda for research and community action in Islamic schools.

From vantage points that valorize the legacies of community-based struggles Chapters 11 and 12 suggest that researchers need to pay closer attention to models for humanizing education that emerged from the Civil Rights movement—the Freedom Schools—and the Clara Muhammad Schools, which represent the African American (Black) Muslim tradition of self-determination, educational excellence, and community empowerment.

11

A Detroit Conversation

Joyce E. King
Georgia State University

Sharon Parker[1]
Claremont Graduate University

INTRODUCTION

In 1999 the Governor of Michigan and the legislature replaced a democratically elected local school board in the City of Detroit with an appointed "reform board." In 2002 the AERA Commission On Research in Black Education (CORIBE) organized a 3-hour conversation among a diverse group of educators, school administrators, and parent leaders in Detroit. The meeting was convened by CORIBE Chair Joyce E. King and Administrator Sharon Parker in collaboration with three local leaders: Grace Lee Boggs, Detroit community activist, educator, and writer; Glenda Price, President of Marygrove College and a member of the "reform board;" and Alma Harrington Young,[2] Dean of the School of Metropolitan, Labor and Urban Affairs at Wayne State University. Dean Alma Young hosted the meeting on her campus. The three Detroit area co-conveners selected the eight

---

[1] Dr. King, who served as CORIBE Chair, and Ms. Parker, who was the CORIBE Project Administrator, organized the Detroit Conversation on behalf of CORIBE. Ms. Parker served as the facilitator for the conversation. The Detroit Conversation was recorded and the discussion later transcribed. King and Parker reviewed and edited the transcript for use as an organizing tool by other educators, parents, and community leaders. This chapter comprises excerpts from the transcript. All participants are identified in the text.

[2] Dr. Young passed away on March 14, 2004.

participants, who represented the ethnic and cultural diversity of the city as well as a broad range of professional and community-based experiences in education.

This chapter presents selected excerpts from the transcript of the video documentary titled "A Detroit Conversation." In order to provide a context for the conversation, excerpts from recent speeches by Grace Lee Boggs have been included. The participants discussed various innovative and alternative school- and community-based programs in which they are involved, such as the Comer Project; the Catherine Ferguson Academy, a public alternative school for pregnant and parenting teens; the Friends School; the Timbuktu Academy, an African-centered school; and Detroit Summer, a grassroots youth program/movement to "rebuild and respirit" the City of Detroit spearheaded by the James and Grace Lee Boggs Center to Nurture Community Leadership. In a "no-holds-barred" conversation the participants shared views about what works in various public and private educational contexts and offered concrete suggestions for the Commission's research and action agenda. It is worth noting that since this conversation took place, "takeovers" of schools and districts have become common place around the country.[3]

VOICES FROM A DETROIT CONVERSATION

President Glenda Price made a brief opening statement. An excerpt follows:

Glenda: I'm here this afternoon for the same reason that I serve on the Detroit Reform Board and that is because I believe that education is the key to the future. Education is that process that allows each of us to grow and to become all that we can be. And if we have educational systems that are not functioning, that are not allowing young people to achieve the American Dream, then we have educational systems that are failing our young people, failing us and ultimately failing society.... [W]e have approximately 167,000 young people in the Detroit public schools. We have close to 20,000 employees in the system ... one of the largest employers

---

[3] Under the state-appointed school board that was imposed in 1999, Detroit public schools student enrollment continued to decline precipitously, 9300 since September 2003 alone. Most just dropped out because they refused to stay in schools that were not meeting their needs. Each student represented a loss of around $7,000 in state funding which has created a $200 million deficit. Because so many dropouts drift into drugs and crime and end up in prison, declining enrollment has also helped to create a culture of violence in Detroit. In 2002 there were 402 homicides in the city; in 2003 there were 366 and there were already 368 on December 20, 2004. On November 2, 2004 Detroiters went to the polls and overwhelmingly voted to return to a traditionally elected board. This decision has provided Detroiters with an unparalleled opportunity to make a much-needed fresh start. (*Personal communication,* Grace Lee Boggs, December 20, 2004.)

in the Detroit Metropolitan area.... [T]he Detroit public schools have a significant economic impact on the Detroit area, just from the employment standpoint, in addition to the educational standpoint. Unfortunately, we have too many young people graduating from high school who are reading at the eighth grade level. I know this to be a fact because we see them at Marygrove College and we are attempting to remediate the deficiencies that they come with.

...So we do have a crisis at one level and we need to understand how we can engage in programs of research and programs of action that are going to allow us to develop systems that are as effective as they can be... where we have an adequate number of certified teachers; where we have buildings that are in good repair; where we have children who are excited about learning and teachers who are excited about teaching and where we have a dynamic interchange with the community that allows for everyone to have appropriate input into the system and allows everyone to feel as though they can make a difference in the lives of these young people, and therefore, ultimately make a difference in the life of this community and the economic growth that that entails.

Grace Lee Boggs, by her own account, has participated in most of the "great humanizing movements of the last sixty years." Her incisive theorizing and analyses of community change have appeared in various publications since the 1970s, including the *Harvard Educational Review* (Boggs, 1974) and *Monthly Review*. Currently she writes a weekly column in the *Michigan Citizen*. The texts of recent public lectures, "These are the Times to Grow our Souls"[4] and "We Must Become the Change,"[5] contextualize the Detroit conversation and the need for "bottom-up" transformative changes in education, in our communities as well in as the larger society, and most especially, in our own thinking and actions.

Grace: In the last sixty years I have had the privilege of participating in most of the great humanizing movements of the second half of the last century: labor, civil rights, Black power, women's, Asian American, environmental justice, anti-war. Each was a tremendously transformative experience for me, expanding my understanding of what it means to be an American and a human being, and challenging me to keep deepening my thinking about how to bring

---

[4] National Exchange on Art and Civic Dialogue, October 9–12, 2003. http://www. americansforthearts.org/animatingdemocracy/resources/grow_our_souls

[5] 16th Annual Martin Luther King Jr. Symposium, University of Michigan, January 20, 2003.

about radical social change. However, I cannot recall any previous period when the issues were so basic, so interconnected and so demanding of everyone living in this country, regardless of race, ethnicity, class, gender, age, or national origin. At this point in the continuing evolution of our country and of the human race, we urgently need to stop thinking of ourselves as victims and to recognize that we must each become a part of the solution because we are each a part of the problem.

Fifteen years ago, in 1988, Coleman Young, Detroit's first black mayor, confronted by mushrooming crime (in 1986 47 young Detroiters had been killed and 365 wounded) decided that what the city needed to replace the jobs lost by deindustrialization was a casino industry. To defeat the proposal, we created Detroiters Uniting, a wide-ranging coalition of ministers, community activists, and cultural workers. During the struggle Young called us "naysayers" and challenged us to come up with an alternative. "Our concern," we said in our brochure, "is with how our city has been disintegrating socially, economically, politically, morally and ethically. We are convinced," we said, "that we cannot depend upon one industry or any large corporation to provide us with jobs. It is now up to us—the citizens of Detroit—to put our hearts, our imaginations, our minds and our hands together to create a vision and project concrete programs for developing the kinds of local enterprises that will provide meaningful jobs and income for all citizens."

Toward this goal, thinking back to Mississippi Freedom Summer and Martin Luther King's advocacy of direct action structure-transforming and self-transforming projects for young people in our dying cities, in 1992, we founded Detroit Summer, a multicultural/intergenerational program involving young people in projects to rebuild, redefine, and respirit our city from the ground up and putting the "Neighbor" back into the "hood." These projects include community gardening to reconnect young people to the earth and to the community, murals to create public space for dialogue with the community, and "rehabbing" abandoned houses. In a desolate neighborhood on the near west side of the city, there is a public high school for teenage mothers called the Catherine Ferguson Academy, where students are learning respect for life and for the earth by raising farm animals, planting a community garden, and building a barn. Across the street from the Catherine Ferguson Academy (CFA) there were a couple of abandoned houses that Detroit Summer bought for a few hundred dollars each and is now rehabbing for emergency use by CFA mothers. On the corner between the two houses we created an Art Park as a meeting and story telling place for neighborhood residents. As a result, this neighborhood is coming back to life.

As I witness and participate in this excitement and contrast our visionary efforts to rebuild Detroit with the multibillion mega-projects of politicians and developers that involve casinos, giant stadia, gentrification, and the 2006 Superbowl, I am saddened by their shortsightedness. On the other hand, I rejoice in the energy being unleashed in the community by our human scale programs that involve bringing the country back into the city and removing the walls between schools and communities, between generations, and between ethnic groups; and I am confident, that just as in the early twentieth century people came from around the world to marvel at the mass production lines pioneered by Henry Ford, in the twenty-first century they will be coming to marvel at the thriving neighborhoods that are the fruit of our visionary programs.

How are we going to make our livings in an age when hi-tech and the export of jobs overseas have brought us to the point where the number of workers needed to produce goods and services is constantly diminishing? Where will we get the imagination, the courage, and the determination to reconceptualize the meaning and purpose of Work in a society that is becoming increasingly jobless? How are we going to redefine Education so that 30 to 50 percent of inner-city children do not drop out of school, thus ensuring that large numbers will end up in prison? Is it enough to call for "Education, not Incarceration"? Or does our top-down educational system, created a hundred years ago to prepare an immigrant population for factory work, bear a large part of the responsibility for the escalation in incarceration?

We live in a very dangerous time because these questions are no longer abstractions. Our lives, the lives of our children and future generations, and even the survival of the planet depend on our willingness to transform ourselves into active planetary and global citizens who, as Martin Luther King Jr. put it, "develop an overriding loyalty to mankind as a whole in order to preserve the best in their individual society." How are we going to build a twenty-first century America in which people of all races and ethnicities live together in harmony, and Euro Americans in particular embrace their new role as one among many minorities constituting the new multiethnic majority? What is going to motivate us to start caring for our biosphere instead of using our mastery of technology to increase the volume and speed at which we are making our planet uninhabitable for other species and eventually for ourselves? What is going to happen to cities like Detroit that were once the arsenal of democracy? Now that they've been abandoned by industry, are we just going to throw them away? Or can we rebuild, redefine, and respirit them as models of twenty-first century self-reliant, sustainable multicultural communities? Who is going to begin this new story?

THE CONVERSATION ABOUT RESEARCH PRIORITIES

Paul Weertz, a 10-year veteran in the Detroit Public Schools, teaches Biology, Earth Science, Anatomy/Physiology, Agri-science, and Home Repair at the Catherine Ferguson Academy. Accomplished in many fields, from pipefitting to home rehabilitation to farming and animal husbandry, he is a member of the Detroit Agricultural Network and the National Science Teachers Association.

Paul: I'm trying to get agri-science into the Detroit public schools. We think of diversity in terms of black and white, in terms of people's colors, but we don't think of it in terms of occupations and trades and ideas. . . . I think we have to get into the make-up of our society and make sure that every child has got an option to be what our society needs, whether it's a food scientist, a farmer, or a computer operator. . . . We have to make sure that all the kids, especially in our urban schools, are prepared in those fields. We tend to leave out a lot of rural models in our urban programs . . . We're very much in jeopardy, if we can't grow our own food. We can always do without a computer or e-mail and a lot of other things. We got through Y2K all right, but how many people can get by without food and water? . . . In teaching history we need to know where we've come from, so we can figure out where we're going. . . . Many students in Detroit don't know a thing about, say, growing plants, but their parents and grandparents do. . . . So when we think of diversity, we have to think of more than just the people but also about ideas.

Marie L. Thornton, civic leader and President, Michigan Parent Advocates for School Reforms, Inc., has been involved in various bottom-up initiatives, including campaigns against vouchers and school takeovers as well as the Civil Rights Commission. She has been recognized by the Detroit Reform Board for her assistance with "on-the-spot" hiring of certified Detroit teachers. She also helped organize the participation of Detroit students in the 35th Anniversary "Right to Vote, Bridge Crossing Jubilee" in Selma, Alabama, in March 2000.

Marie: I just want to mention some bottom up approaches that I am working on with Detroit public school children.... I just took a group of children from Renaissance High School to Selma, Alabama to participate in the 35th anniversary of the Selma–Civil Rights march.... These children were there to get first-hand experience with the Civil Rights movement. While we were there, they saw that people wanted to dump trash (in this area) on the Civil Rights trail. The children learned firsthand about environmental racism and the dumping of trash. They made us take them back to the site where they saw this sign that said "Dumping Trash." So children need to learn first-hand, just like you said, about environmental racism, environmental dumping.

Yusif Barakat, born in Haifa, Palestine, spent summers as a shepherd boy. At the age of 12 he became a refugee and came to the Detroit area where he has been a County Commissioner, an activist for peace and multicultural diversity on a local and global basis, and a psychotherapist in private practice. Currently he works at the W.J. Maxey Boys Training School.

Yusif: You mention "exposure." Education is not only in schools. Academic and formal education take place in schools. But whatever children are exposed to becomes their education. Children are exposed to some horrendous commercials. They are exposed to some awful broadcast programming. I think of myself as a person with a glass of water trying to put out a bush fire and there's this giant with a gasoline tank pouring gas all over the flames. So it seems that the whole society is in crisis. That's because a society is characterized by the way it treats its children and its elderly, and this society is a dismal failure in both. I think we need to look at the larger picture of what children are exposed to as much as what they get in the classroom. I'd also like to pick up on the dehumanizing factor of being taken away from nature. We are basically dehumanized as a society; we are commercialized and standardized. We need to rehumanize. I was one of the people who started Detroit Summer with Grace and her late husband. I think getting back to the earth is very important.

There is a Native American prayer:
Teach your children that the earth is our mother.
Whatever befalls the earth befalls the sons and daughters of the earth.
This we know, the earth does not belong to us. We belong to the earth.
This we know, that all things are connected.
Like the life blood which unites one family. All things are connected.

> *Whatever befalls the earth, befalls the sons and daughters of the earth.*
> *We did not weave the web of life. We are merely a strand in it.*
> *Whatever we do to the web, we do to ourselves.*

Norma Barquet, a founding member of the Hispanic Coalition for Educational Opportunity, the Detroit Bilingual Parent Institute, and the Academy of the Americas, has also served as chair of the Hispanic Referent Group for the Michigan State Superintendent of Public Instruction and on the Advisory Council to the Michigan State Board of Education. As Associate Director of National Origin Equity Programs for Educational Opportunity at the University of Michigan, she coordinates services to K–12 school districts in the six Great Lakes states. Dr. Barquet has taught in both public and private schools and served as department head in the Detroit Public Schools for 10 years.

Norma: The program I work with assists K–12 systems promote equity for children. Part of the reason I was asked to join the conversation is to add to the mix some of the issues and programs available to Latino students here in Detroit as well.... We are a dissemination site for math and science involving parents—"Playtime Science," "Family Math," and "Family Science." It's hands-on, using nature and things that exist around the house.... Because very often we ask families to do things and they don't have the economic resources for certain activities. These are programs that are tailor-made to make sure that all students have access to scientific thinking and mathematical thinking and to reduce the anxiety the parents bring. Most of us are very anxious about learning science and math just as we are anxious about learning a second language. This is one of the ways in which we try to bring in equity issues.... As some people here have said, you have to connect the learning of science and math to conditions that exist in the community, in terms of the air and pollution and water, in terms of civil rights issues, so that children are engaged with meaningful learning that impacts their community, and so that they see themselves powerful enough to bring about a change.

Julia Pointer, a Detroit Public Schools graduate, is enrolled in the University of Detroit-Mercy teacher preparation program and is a veteran of Detroit Summer, the intergenerational, multicultural community-based program designed to rebuild and respirit the city of Detroit.

Julia: When I say "education"... I think of something beyond what it takes to pass a test and...to get a job. I think it involves community;

it involves interaction and exposure to people in the community and also different kinds of knowledge, not only test-taking skills. One of the goals of education right now, when people talk about it on the administrative level, is to give kids the skills they need to take the tests they need to take to get better jobs. But those jobs are often outside of the community. So the goal of education becomes preparing you for a job that takes you away from the community, instead of being exposed to and being able to relate to adults in the neighborhood who might not know how to fill out a census form or might not be able to read a novel but who still have useful information.... [T]he goal should not be to get children jobs outside of the community so that they go away, but to find a way for kids to feel like they can be agents of change in their neighborhoods and where they come from so that they don't view the city as a stepping stone to get a way but a place where they can make a difference.

Ernestine Moore, Director of the Skillman Center for Children, is an attorney and social work professor and Interim Assistant Dean of the College of Urban, Labor and Metropolitan Affairs at Wayne State University. She serves on a number of civic boards and committees including the Citizen's Review Panel for Child Protection and the Governor's Task Force on Children's Justice.

Ernestine: I wanted to pick up on the definition issue because I have a practical definition and I also have a philosophical definition. The practical one is in terms of education for poor children living in an urban environment.... I want them to be able to meet the expectations of the White Man's world so that, in fact, they can succeed in that world. And the philosophical definition of education is to be able to live a life as you see fit: To be able to read, to enjoy, to inquire, to do. If I wanted to be a farmer, I would want to be a good farmer. And there's a lot of science in that. To be a good basketball player, there's a lot of math, a lot of physics.... But we don't incorporate these in our teaching and our education of children so that they can incorporate them into their learning. In the current environment, the one that I expect will exist for our generation and the next two or three, we're not going to see this society change to the point where it accepts the fact that people can be who they choose to be and they can be fed and clothed without any hassle.... And we need to change that [MEAP] test so that in fact what we're measuring is: Do kids know? Can they think? Can they make critical judgments?

Gil Leaf (James G. Leaf), Head of the Friends School in Detroit, has taught History and Literature at the elementary, secondary, and college levels in both public and private schools, has served as principal of four elementary schools in the United States, and worked in Australia and Africa. Dr. Leaf has established numerous school/university curriculum partnerships and recently served as Executive Director of the Children's Museum of Los Angeles.

Gil: There's a huge momentum of centralization at the federal and state level—there's one education for our children and here's the content that's going to be approved. And it's being driven by politics, not even by educators. This is a top-down...boulder that's rolling down the hill....I get so sick of: "We have to wire up every kid in America to meet the corporate needs." What we really need to do is talk about rebuilding neighborhoods...We don't need School Boards, we need Children's Boards—because as Dr. Comer has pointed out to all of us, we've got to get away from this male American thing, of treating pieces of children in different sectors. We really need to look at health, education, recreation, the arts, and the environment in a holistic way....Probably our best shot is after school—from 3 to 6. I feel that we've had it backwards for quite a while. It takes a child to make the village whole. The child is the best force we've got to mobilize and rebuild a neighborhood. We can be taught to hate each other for a thousand years. But in the name of our respective children, we'd better have a dialogue, and that dialogue can be the great power for rebuilding our neighborhoods. It's got to be bottom-up. In the meantime we're looking at the extinction of freedom and independence in education.

I happen to be in an independent school. We need independence much more desperately in our public schools. I'm radical enough to think that a good school depends on good teachers. Right now, the young people coming into our teacher programs come from the bottom 25 percent of their class academically. Now that's not the group that's going to turn our schools around. Who is going to come into a teaching profession who is bright, dedicated, able, and committed to children, if they're given some teacher-proof curriculum which is basically already laid out? Believe me, it's not about standards. People confuse standards with tests. We're talking about tests, and some pretty mediocre ones at best. We're talking about an extraordinary by-passing of the Constitution and Constitutional rights of neighborhoods having some say in the education of children. So, I would hate to have us pointing out 25 wonderful little examples of things that are going great in Detroit [as if] that makes everything OK. Well, I guess I'm getting more radical as I get older.

Jacqueline Jackson is the Representative of the Comer School Development Program at Cooper Elementary School, where she works closely with parents.

Jacqueline: One of the things that the Comer program addresses is engaging the unengaged parent, making them more active and a part of the process in making child-centered decisions. I've been pretty successful at... bringing in our unengaged parents and make them a part of every level of our child-centered decision-making. They sit on... the School Planning Management Team... and we sit down and collaborate and come to a consensus about "What do you want for your child?"... Another aspect of Comer is not just looking at the academic and behavioral aspect of the child but looking at the total child development: the language aspect, the social, ethical, physical, psychological, and cognitive development when we make child-centered decisions about our children. We are not just focusing on the two aspects of cognitive and behavioral.... [Parents] don't just come in to baby-sit the children, tutor, or check papers. They are actually part of the decision-making process. They sit on the panel with the administration, teachers, instructional staff, non-instructional staff. Part of Comer is that every constituency group is represented. Their needs are addressed.

Gloria House is Professor Emerita in the Wayne State University Interdisciplinary Studies Program, where she was on the faculty for 27 years. From 1992-1996, she was Visiting Professor in the English Department and Director of the Partnership with Township Schools at the University of Witswatersrand in Johannesburg, South Africa and is now on the faculty of the University of Michigan-Dearborn. A veteran of the Civil Rights movement in the South, Dr. House is a founding faculty member of the Timbuktu Academy in Detroit, where she directed faculty development.

Gloria: Back in the early 1970s, having just left the south to come to Detroit and become part of this community, I became involved with a small group of educators who decided that we wanted our children to have a different kind of education from the one that they were receiving in the public school system. So we organized one of the early African-centered independent schools here in Detroit. It was first called Crummel School. Then it was called Aisha. Many of you know Aisha from the school for gifted children. Then later on we added a high school unit as well. So there's W.E.B. Du Bois

Academy. My child went to that school. He was one of the first graduates along with a nucleus of students. We felt very proud of the work we were able to do. But we were dealing with a very small group of students. They were our own children whom we had educated in our homes and simply were now schooling them with the same principles and ideas that they were familiar with from the home.

As the years went by, Aisha School and W.E.B. Du Bois Academy struggled to pay their teachers, really struggled—to the point that they took the Charter School option when it became available. So Aisha and Du Bois became a charter school and happily could pay its teachers every payday and people didn't have to starve in order to carry out their commitment to independent schooling. Then we started to get an altogether different student clientele, the children who would have been in the public school but were coming because their parents believed in the philosophy of an African-centered school. But we had a whole different set of issues to deal with now . . .

Our school is K through fifth grade, and for the most part the children K through fourth grade are doing very, very well. We've been able to establish an environment of learning that they have plugged into and are happy with and are thriving in. We have fifth graders, however, who are at the preadolescent stage, who are a different ball of wax altogether. This is where the ideas of the school as community and children as agents of change and participating in structuring their own learning become very valuable. Because it's very clear to me that our preadolescent children are having a very, very difficult time living with the traditional culture of learning, that is, coming in sitting, down quietly, waiting for the teacher to come in and lay out the plans for the day.

They are very fast thinkers. They are astute. They are tuned in. They're very good at analyzing relationships. They are socially adept. But they are not interested in sitting still for your conventional, traditional approaches to learning. So, we are going to have to come up with new forms—a school in movement—a moving school—a school moving in the community. I don't know what shape it's going to take but it's clear that if we want out children to succeed in terms of developing their human potential, we are going to have to find these new structures, these new models. Julia's question, "What is education?" is very relevant. What do we educate our children for? . . .

What can we do with the children who don't already come to school with a culture of learning? They are not going to go up the ladder of education. They are not going to go into corporate jobs. They are more likely to drop out of school. They are more likely to end up in the juvenile detention system. So what can we do about those children? Educating those children requires teachers who make a political commitment. Because that's the only way we are going to really be able to do anything that supports those children. Do we have those teachers who will say, "Sorry about the MEAP, I don't know whether my children are going to fare very well on the MEAP, because I'm spending time teaching them gardening," or "I'm spending time moving around the community to examine the problems of environmental racism." How is that going to factor on the MEAP or the MAP? I don't know. And when we meet this overwhelming centralization that's coming down through the various administrations, you see the major conflict that we're facing in the system. So those are all the things that are going on in my mind as someone responsible for staff development and curriculum in an inner-city school. By the way, Timbuktu is in the poorest neighborhood in our city.

Grace: Gloria, I've never heard you say these things this way and I don't know if it's because you've only recently taken on this job at *Timbuktu*. But it just seems to me that what you're saying is so real. Our children have changed. We talk about changes that have taken place in technology. There are changes that have taken place in our children since the 1960s in this world and we're still trying to act the old way. And when we try something, and it fails, we don't examine why it fails. We try to do more of it.... We try to restrict our children more. We try more tests. We try to do more top-down stuff.... I think there are people, teachers particularly, who are being shafted all over the place. They're being turned into wardens.

JoAnne Isbey, a tenured associate professor in the English Department at the University of Detroit-Mercy, taught college English at the Ford Rouge Plant to both production and skilled trades workers for 12 years. She is involved in the university's initiative to build sustainable community activism, leadership development, women's studies, teacher education, diversity work, and interdisciplinary undergraduate teaching and learning.

JoAnne: I want to resonate with Grace because I have young teachers who walk on water. They're wonderful, but they are being disheartened, they're being frustrated. We're forming a support group to try to see if we can keep them in. And I think that's horrible and it's because of the environment in the schools—from the administration, not from the children and not from the parents. And it's tragic to me if people who are called to teaching drop out because they are not able to teach. We are in the process of change, whether we like it or not. It's happening. All it takes in systems theory is [for] the butterfly to flap its wings a little bit and the whole system is changing. Because we're in it, we don't see it as much.

Alma H. Young is the Coleman A. Young Professor of Urban Affairs and Dean of the College of Urban, Labor and Metropolitan Affairs at Wayne State University. Dr. Young is a political scientist whose areas of research include the political economy of urban development, the gendered perspective of the changing welfare state, race, and poverty, literacy, and community building in the United States, Latin America, and the Caribbean. She has worked in local and state government, with community-based organizations, and she founded and directed the Toyota Families for Learning program in New Orleans, a family literacy program serving preschoolers and their parents.

Alma: I simply wanted to say . . . that this movement, whatever you want to call it, has to include the whole community. It may be child-centered but it is not the child that we have to look to do all these things. There is a role for parents, a role for teachers, and a role for others of us in the wider community to take part in this critique or this movement. . . . As a political scientist, I always start from the question: Why are we having all these group tests, why are we having less freedom? I think it goes back to the changing demographics. Who fears that he or she may be losing power, as someone else gains power? I think we have to put it in a proper context, a proper perspective. In the Civil Rights movement, we saw part of what was going on in the marches, etc. But there was another part going on, consciousness was being raised, the understanding of why things were as they were. So when you got out onto the front lines, you really knew why you were there. You knew what to expect but you had to keep on going. It seems to me that whether we continue with conversations that then lead to something else, we've made a start so that we can raise our consciousness, figure out what the next steps are—because I think there are a lot of steps that we have to be involved in if we are going to understand the situation and then really work to change it in some sustained, systematic way.

Norma: We're talking about . . . the state of education in our country. That's one big issue in terms of what we're doing, what we should be doing, and how we compare with the rest of the world. The other issue has to do with equity in our own society in addition to the issue of education. They're sort of overlapping. We need to sort them out as we discuss them. Our urban centers are overpopulated with children who are poor, who are mostly African American and Latino and poor. . . . We need to look at what's happening in our urban centers and the multiple issues that are surrounding children and families. And we must not be afraid to speak out and say this is what is. . . . Because in our society people who have continue to accumulate resources. We are consumerists. We are consuming not only our own goods but goods from around the planet. This globalization of the economy—people working for us—is the reason why we can get jeans and t-shirts at a certain price. Then, we see what's happening in our communities where there is a social consciousness. Some of the young people are saying, "We've got to do something for our communities." It's like we live in . . . two different worlds, in two different countries. And that's one of the issues that I think we're discussing here and I'm having a hard time in terms of putting my fingers—or my arms around it because it's just bigger.

Gloria: I just wanted to make two points. One is that the children of the ruling class and the managerial class are not in crisis in terms of education. They are doing quite well. They are getting the education they need in order to continue in positions of dominance. So it seems to me that we really need to ask the question: Why are our children in crisis and what is planned for our children in this society? One of the things we need to look at in answering that question is the prison industrial complex and the fact that it continues to get fatter and fatter; more and more of our children are being caught up in it, more and more of our children are being tried and sentenced as adults. It seems to me that's one place we can look to get real clarity about the future that's intended for our children and what we need to do about it.

Grace: My final comment relates to the escalating crisis in public education all over the nation. For more than thirty years, since I was involved in the community control of schools movement in the 1960s, I have been insisting that the time has come to leave behind the top-down factory model of education, which was created at the beginning of the century to supply industry with a disciplined workforce—and make a paradigm shift to a form of democratic education in which children are engaged in solving real questions of their lives and communities.

Forty years ago, during Mississippi Freedom Summer, civil rights activists created Freedom Schools. Two thousand students joined members of the Student Non-Violent Coordinating Committee (SNCC) to create a democratic form of education based upon linking skills training with participation in the ongoing struggle. Children and adults were motivated to learn because they were empowered to view themselves as change agents and citizens. The Freedom Schools created during Mississippi Freedom Summer in 1964 gave us a preview of this new kind of schooling. Since the rebellions of the late 1960s our inner cities especially have needed Freedom Schooling to transform our children from angry rebels into positive change agents and at the same time make our communities safer, healthier, and livelier almost overnight. In the last two years, as a result of Bush's "No Child Left Behind Act," there is a growing interest in Freedom Schooling. Teachers are beginning to resist the "teaching to the test" that the act requires. Administrators are threatened by the punitive measures that the act provides, including closing down their school. Students are beginning to resent the "zero tolerance" (like hall sweeps, suspensions) administrators resort to in order to rid their schools of troublesome students who bring down test scores.

These are the times that grow our souls. Each of us needs to undergo a tremendous philosophical and spiritual transformation. Each of us needs to be awakened to a personal and compassionate recognition of the inseparable interconnection between our minds, hearts, and bodies, between our physical and psychical well being, and between our selves and all the other selves in our country and in the world. Each of us needs to stop being a passive observer of the suffering that we know is going on in the world and start identifying with the sufferers. Each of us needs to make a leap that is both practical and philosophical, beyond determinism to self-determination. Each of us has to be true to and enhance our own humanity by embracing and practicing the conviction that as human beings we have Free Will; that despite the powers and principalities that are bent on objectifying and commodifying us and all our human relationships, the interlocking crises of our time require that we exercise the power within us to make principled choices in our ongoing daily and political lives, choices that will eventually (although not inevitably; there are no guarantees) make a difference. Each of us needs to discover and exercise the power within us that enabled Rosa Parks to choose not to go to the back of the bus without waiting to see if others would join her.

USING THE CONVERSATION
TO FURTHER CHANGE

Grace: ...We could use [this] video to start discussions...

JoAnne: There are tons of images of hope in this discussion. I think we need to bring them together and keep the dialogue open and going.

Marie: How do we reach beyond these walls here, into the grassroots community?...I think people have been talking for years about the same issue of education. I think it's time for a Civil Rights Education movement in the City of Detroit. I think we should rise up and tell society that we won't conform to standardized tests that are not geared to helping our children....Until we hear each other and know that we're not isolated, we'll be weaker.

Norma: Much of the research that is done at the local universities is shared among researchers but very little trickles down to the practitioners. Perhaps one of the recommendations is that AERA [should] look very closely at the research and make sure that there is a social piece to the research agenda that says: "Once we find out what works, we're going to share this in a very meaningful way with communities." Because if you go into certain communities, they are tired of being researched and they hear very little back, in terms of what has been found. The conversation stays with people who are doing the same job.

Gil: Perpetual diagnosis.

Alma: The other piece is teacher training. We need to have a more diverse teaching force. The majority of the teaching force is coming from suburban America, mostly white females. Those teachers need to know about the populations they are going to find in the urban centers in terms of the diversity, but we also need to reach out to the minority populations so they become teachers. Those are two ways higher education can help.

It is clear that all Detroit Conversation participants felt strongly about the failure of education systems to meet the needs of low-income, working class children of all racial/ethnic backgrounds. They intended that other concerned citizens throughout the country should learn from their experiences in Detroit and create a sea-swell of voices demanding change. To spark conversations in other communities, the following questions are suggested to launch awareness and action.

• The Detroit conversation was stimulated by the appointment of a "reform board" to manage education in K–12 schools. Has your school system experienced the imposition of a "reform board?" How is your school system governed? Is it an elected or appointed body? To whom is this body accountable? Who serves on it? How do concerned citizens provide input to it?

• Bottom-up education is mentioned frequently throughout the Detroit Conversation. Another way to think about "bottom-up education" is child-centered education. Would you say that your school system is meeting all the needs of children? In what ways?

• Another theme of the conversation is community. The participants talked at length about making children partners in community building and the importance of experiencing the power of a partnership in relationship to their total education. They mentioned the Comer School Development Program, Detroit Summer, Aisha School, W.E.B. Du Bois Academy, and the Timbuktu Academy. What examples can you give of educational programs launched and supported by your community? Do these programs help round out the education of children? Do they teach concepts of cooperation, collaboration, and pride in caring for the community?

• An overarching theme of the conversation is "What is the purpose of education?" Are children educated merely to become mindless workers in this era of corporate workforces? Or, should they be given the tools to become leaders in all aspects of society? Does education require a standard of conformity that overrides the unique identities of children and their families and communities? What would it mean for public education to develop children to be "agents of change" in their own communities?

• Finally, the Detroit Conversation suggests that institutions of higher education need to take greater responsibility for the educational process of K–12. How can you partner with your local college or university to continue addressing these issues in your community? What is the responsibility of researchers?

12

Faith and Courage to Educate Our Own: Reflections on Islamic Schools in the African American Community

Zakiyyah Muhammad
American Institute on Islamic Education

INTRODUCTION

In the year of the 50th anniversary of *Brown v. Board of Education*, the systemic problem with American education continues to be inequality and the absence of a comprehensive system that educates African Americans as human beings to be independent, and self-sufficient in the struggle for familial, cultural, social, and material well-being. African Americans can only overcome this systemic problem by realizing—as our ancestors did since their captivity and arrival in this hemisphere in 1501—that we must take responsibility for our own circumstances for we will not be educated by others and "set free," we must educate ourselves and "walk to freedom."

This chapter addresses the historical role African American Muslims have demonstrated in fulfilling our religious and commonsense obligation to take responsibility for the education of our children and community. It presents Islamic education as a model for human freedom and community empowerment. My experience with Islamic education, for approximately 30 years, has afforded me invaluable perspectives resulting from my service as principal of an immigrant Islamic school, Director of Education of

[then] 38 Clara Muhammad Schools in the United States and Bermuda, principal of a Clara Muhammad School, and a teacher in the University of Islam. These experiences, balanced with teaching in the American public school system and in the university, have enabled me to personally observe the challenges African American young people face daily in the maze called education.

From my perspective as an Islamic educator, I will offer a redefinition of education for human society using the Islamic education model. I will also: (a) trace the historical development of a successful model of Islamic education in the African American experience; (b) identify a fundamental misunderstanding of human identity in Western educational theory; (c) discuss the significance of contradictions in schools established by immigrant Muslims; and (d) recommend a role for research and community action that addresses the potential of Islamic education as a model for human development. There are other Islamic schools that have contributed to Islamic educational development and several that have assisted Muslims currently engaged in academic careers. This chapter, however, addresses those model schools that have sustained themselves over time and have had the greatest impact on African American and Muslim communities in the United States.

We begin with a brief discussion of Islamic education followed by evidence of the Islamic tradition brought to America by our enslaved ancestors and proceed forward from their arrival on the shores of America to recount three distinct developmental periods that define Islamic education in the African American experience. Observations of current contradictions in some Islamic schools founded by immigrant Muslims—contradictions that are antithetical to the precepts of Islam—follow. The chapter concludes with a brief commentary on recommendations for research and action.

ISLAMIC EDUCATION

The *Encyclopedia of American Education* (1996) defines education in two ways. Education is: (a) the acquisition of knowledge, skills, and values that permit an individual to function and make decisions perceived as self-enhancing; and (b) knowledge acquired through formal instruction (p. 320). It is precisely because this definition does not insure the absence of *duplicity* in the educational process that it is dissimilar to the definition of Islamic education.

Representing a distinctively different worldview—Islamic education is defined as *the perfected process of human development that evolves the consciousness of the human being into the excellence of one's human potential* (Muhammad, 1998, p. 88). This consciousness begins with a spiritual component recognizing that human beings *first* have a role and responsibility to the One that created us and to the physical creation that sustains us and of which we are the guardians/trustees. Islamic education is constructed on the excellence of human nature clarified in the revelation of the Qur'an and exemplified in the life of Muhammad ibn Abdullah, the Last Prophet, Peace Be Upon Him. In *The 100: A Ranking of the Most Influential Persons in History* (Hart, 1978), Muhammad the Prophet is described (by someone other than a Muslim) as the most influential human being in history. The Qur'an Prophet Muhammad brought to human society is the most read book in the world and is not the product or possession of Arabs or Muslims. The Qur'an is the last revealed scripture from The Creator to all humanity, revealed to Prophet Muhammad Ibn Abdullah over a period of 23 years in the Arabic language. In addition, the confusing and conflicting theories that have prevailed for thousands of years relative to human identity, specifically the concepts that the human being is born in sin, that woman is responsible for it and subsequently cursed with childbirth, are clearly and decisively corrected by the revelation of the Qur'an. In its transformative power the Qur'an has nurtured the soul and intellect and guided Muslims to free themselves and humanity from scriptural oppression by declaring that the *human being is created in excellence not sin, that The Creator is not White or Black, male or female, and that women and Black people are not cursed.*

In Islamic education, the spiritual and intellectual dimensions of the human being, although distinct, work in harmony, and the foundation of Islamic education, which is moral consciousness—when practiced— expands the intellect. Inherent in the philosophy of Islamic education are the concept of *Tauheed*, the Oneness of the Creation, the excellence of human nature, the processes by which human excellence can be achieved, and the concept of *fitra*, which represents the inherent *pattern* that is in the order and nature of creation. *Fitra* represents the nexus of human identity and the physical creation; it encompasses the essential moral, spiritual, rational, and intellectual consciousness required for a meaningful educational experience to take place.

From an Islamic perspective, the absence of *fitra,* a critical missing link in American education, contributes to the disconnection, frustration, and rebellion young people experience in school and toward school. In addition, the concept of the excellence and potential inherent in human nature in Islamic educational philosophy precludes a teacher from perceiving youngsters as "at-risk," or "culturally deprived," "urban," "economically disadvantaged" or otherwise limited. Thus, Islamic education philosophy requires a different curricular, teaching methodology and perception of the student being taught (Z. Muhammad, 1998). Educational progress and student development are measured not simply in test scores or grade promotions but in terms of universal standards of what constitutes civilization (Z. Muhammad, 1998).

Civilization As a Universal Standard.   Education and civilization are inseparable, corresponding one to the other. Defined as an advanced state of human society in which a high level of culture and science has been reached (Random House, 1983), civilization includes people, society, nation, culture, development, evolution, and progress. In 1933, Dr. Carter G. Woodson said, "The first essential of civilization is to educate a people so that they can make a living for themselves," (38). In 1993, Imam W. Deen Mohammed said, "In Islamic education the essential additions are the elevation of virtuous life and the elevation of rational life."

THE TRADITION

Islamic education is an integral part of the history of the African American experience. Documentation now confirms that even during the brutal system of slavery in America, Muslims distinguished themselves in self-perception, integrity, humanity, courage, and the continuous struggle for literacy-education (Diouf, 1998, p. 6). The practice and progression of an Islamic education philosophy in the African American experience developed in three distinct periods from 1501 to 2004 (the time of this writing). The first period is the experience of enslavement. The second period was distinguished by the founding of the University of Islam in Detroit Michigan by the Honorable Elijah Muhammad and Fard Muhammad, and the third period is represented by the establishment of Clara Muhammad Schools founded by Imam W. Deen Mohammad, who succeeded his father as the spiritual leader of the majority of African American Muslims. For nearly 30 years, the concepts of Islamic education have been articulated and demonstrated with great success in the Clara Muhammad Schools, in spite of enormous financial hardship. This American Society of Muslims school system, which is an association of 27 elementary, secondary, and high schools throughout the United States and Bermuda, includes in its larger community educational program Jum'ah (Friday religious service for Muslims) and Ta'aleem (public lectures of teaching and learning). Inspired by Imam W. Deen Mohammed, leader of the largest community of African American Muslims in the United States, to address the needs and aspirations of a people still affected by the consequences of enslavement and the lack of cultural and material development, the American Society of Muslims and Clara Muhammad Schools are models of Islamic education that are realizing commendable results. Imam W. Deen Mohammed (1982) has noted: "The psychology for making life better is not in the public schools, it is not in the universities, it is in your Qur'an."

FLAWED WESTERN EDUCATIONAL THEORY

Education (including education research) in America has been conceptualized as an applied science drawing primarily from the disciplines of anthropology, psychology, and sociology. During the last four decades, scholars have uncovered significant flaws in the philosophical assumptions of these disciplines resulting in misinformation and misapplication of educational theory. (Lee offers a critique of mainstream educational theory in Chapters 3 and 4 of this volume.) What is rarely discussed, however, is that the scriptural—distinct from spiritual—underpinning of western educational theory is founded on a misunderstanding of human identity that in turn, influences the perception of Black people globally. "*The Curse of Ham*" is a specific example. For millennia, Black people have suffered under scriptural oppression, asking pressing questions such as these that have haunted them:

"Am I all right with God? Was I cursed by God? Is God White? Am I born inferior? Was I born in sin? Are Caucasians superior to me because God is projected in their skin color and because of their legacy of dominance?"

These are the deep psychological concerns and spiritual yearnings that have troubled and debilitated African Americans in spite of our enormous intelligence and accomplishments. The souls of Black people have been yearning to know, "Am I all right with God?!!" because religious scriptures have been interpreted to state that Black people, as the children of Ham, were indeed cursed by God and condemned to perpetual slavery. According to Goldenberg (2003):

Use of the color black as a metaphor for evil is found in all periods of Jewish literature. Application of the metaphor to the skin color of the black African is made in Jewish Hellenistic and rabbinic literature to a limited extent and in patristic (fathers of the Christian church and their writings) allegory more extensively. (p. 196)

Antiquity notwithstanding, in contemporary society the film industry repeatedly represents God in the skin color of Caucasians. In fact, as of this writing, the movie that has grossed the largest revenue ever, *The Passion of the Christ* continues to project God in White skin, and few have even raised the issue. A consequence of this psychological and spiritual assault has been a propensity among African Americans continually to seek the acceptance of Caucasians and to imitate them to a fault. A consequence for Caucasian Americans is their sense of cultural and racial superiority. Furthermore, negative conceptions of "blackness" have permeated the educational process globally. (See, for example, Juraci Macado da Silva's discussion of negative textbook images in Brazil in Chapter 15.) In the United States, academics and educators are beginning to acknowledge the impact of this "American ethos" on recent immigrants and their interactions with African Americans (Wynter, 2003). Despite the diligent efforts of multicultural education specialists, without a comprehensive approach to education and human development, this fundamental flaw in Western education and its scriptural roots will remain invisible, unaddressed, and debilitating.

Fragmented Academic Disciplines. Moreover, the discipline of education is also fragmented and lacks a comprehensive, holistic understanding of the science of human development. Although scholars provide insights and contributions to the field periodically, the consistent fragmentation of ideologies is damaging. As the Harvard biologist Edward O. Wilson (1998) notes: "The ongoing fragmentation of knowledge and resulting chaos in philosophy are not reflections of the real world but artifacts of scholarship" (p. 8). Wilson continues, "People expect from the social sciences— anthropology, sociology, economics and political science—the knowledge to understand their lives and control their future" (p. 181). Indeed, one would expect that in schools youngsters from elementary to high school should be afforded an understanding of their lives and how to manage their future.

In a statement that shows the consistency between the Qur'anic concept of *Tauheed*—oneness or unity—and the term *Consilience*, which was coined during the European Renaissance and which was inspired by Islamic civilization's impact on Europe, Wilson (1998) recalls:

> It is the custom of scholars when addressing behavior and culture to speak variously of anthropological explanations, psychological explanation biological explanations and other explanations appropriate to the perspectives of individual disciplines. I have argued that there is intrinsically only one class of explanation. It traverses the scales of space, time and complexity to unite the disparate facts of the disciplines by *Consilience*, the perception of a seamless web of cause and effect. (p. 266)

Regardless of this unifying principle, schools of education and classroom teachers vacillate yearly with "new fangled" educational practices of which African American youngsters are the unfortunate experimental target audience (Z. Muhammad, 1993). It is no wonder that by the fourth grade African American boys in particular are turned off from school (Kunjunfu, 1983). The role of educational institutions in the destruction of African American manhood makes the development of Islamic schools that much more a necessity for Muslims (Rashid, 1990).

African American youngsters experience an education that is burdened with notions of the ethnic and cultural superiority of one group over all others. For the majority of Black youth, education in America has resulted in emotional and mental cruelty. Cruelty and the unconscionable failure to prepare these young people to achieve intellectual, social, and material well-being. The crisis in African American education is so pervasive that unless addressed at its origin, African Americans will be either extinct or continually relegated to a permanent slave class.

A COMMUNITY IN PERIL

It is critical to note that the essential cultural fabric of the African American community is unraveling. The renowned psychologist Na'im Akbar (audiocassette) observes, "There is no life for a people who have lost sight of their culture." He further concludes, that just as genes are the biological determinants that bring encoded messages individually from one person to the next, culture is the essential transmitting mechanism by which a people's collective life is ensured (i.e., the rituals that hold a community together) guaranteeing survival through language, critical survival strategies, adaptations, natural reactions, and predetermined immunities. "One of the difficult problems we are experiencing is increasingly confusing the culture of other people with our own culture," observes Akbar (audiocassette). The sense of community, group consciousness, and respect for elders has diminished and the mutual respect and appreciation African American men and women have traditionally demonstrated for each other has been usurped. As a result, marriage and family life have been destabilized and the socialization and character development of African American children are in peril. The institutional establishment of legacies and preservation of wealth within the community for future generations is also threatened. Moreover, it is apparent that families at all levels of the socioeconomic spectrum are one or two paychecks away from poverty.

Those at the lower end of the spectrum are expanding in poverty and ignorance with enormous social dysfunctions resulting in public displays of licentious and obscene behavior fueled by a pseudo culture that is alien to the sense of morality and human excellence in the traditions of African and African American people. It is unprecedented in the history of the African American community to have the sacred expressions of music and dance—which have been so central to our survival—vulgarized and denigrated as they are today in addition to young peoples' disregard for the wisdom and guidance of elders when they speak to the issue of dignified cultural expression.

Culture and *spirituality*, which normally are sources of inspiration and beauty for a people, have been appropriated, manipulated, and misdirected and are now the primary vehicles of destruction. As a result, regardless of significant increases in individual income or high visibility for a few, collective community development and intergenerational ownership of our cultural heritage and resources for the benefit of the masses of African Americans, and the society in general, are minimal to nonexistent. Most insidious, as well, is the punishment and dismissive response scholars and leaders experience for daring to raise these concerns in the public sphere or in academia.

HISTORICAL DEVELOPMENTS: THE CONTINUITY OF ISLAMIC LEARNING

The vehicle for self-empowerment and economic independence for all people has been education. Taking charge of ones destiny has been the tradition of African American Muslims from our experience of enslavement to the present. Muslims have continually led the charge for independent schools that enable African American youngsters to learn in a loving environment supportive of their human dignity and acquisition of skills required to achieve their aspirations. The following discussion of the historical development of Islamic schools brings into focus the circumstances, the voices and directives of our African American progenitors who clearly saw the problems and implemented solutions to address the dire need for education for our people in America.

Early Islamic Learning and Teaching.   Islamic education commenced on southern plantations of the United States (and South America) in the early 16th century and was practiced by approximately 40% of African Muslims who were brought to America and enslaved from 1501 to 1865 (Austin, 1997). According to the Sénégalese scholar Sylvianne Diouf (1998), "Islam in the Americas has been practiced by some people of African descent virtually uninterrupted for the last 500 years" (p. 207). The example of the "Moorish slave," cited by Austin (1997), is worth quoting at length:

> Another proud self-respecting Muslim was the unnamed outspoken "Moorish slave" who was interviewed in 1822, ten years after being brought illegally to work on the Mississippi River. He declared that his homeland was more comfortable and his people more learned than what he had seen in America. He wrote the Fatiha [opening chapter of *Qur'an*] in Arabic for his interviewer. His sympathetic interviewer—a man who traded in pork—said the man "lamented in terms of bitter regret that his situation as a slave in America prevents him from obeying the dictates of his religion. He is under the necessity of eating pork but denies ever tasting any kind of spirits." Clearly the Moor strove to adhere to his religion and ten years of American slavery had not made him think worse of Africa and Islam. (Austin, 1997, p. 35)

Likewise, Edward Wylmot Blyden (1871) offers a related historical example:

> The *Qur'an* is almost always in their hand. It seems to be their labor and their relaxation to pour over its pages. They love to read and recite it aloud for hours together. They seem to posses an enthusiastic appreciation of the rhythmical harmony in which it is written. But we cannot attribute its power over them altogether to the jingling sounds, word-plays and refrains in which it abounds. These it is true please the ear and amuse the fancy, especially of the uncultivated. But there is something higher of which these rhyming lines are the vehicle, something possessing a deeper power to rouse the imagination, mould the feelings and generate action. (p. 67)

In fact, the informal yet organized manner in which enslaved African Muslims endeavored to preserve their spiritual knowledge and connection with The Creator was to establish Qur'an schools or *halaqas*—circles of learning—to read, recite, and teach the Qur'an, their valued source of knowledge and guidance (Diouf, 1998, p. 6). These seemingly simple circles of learning constituted the foundation of Islam in the United States and the first period of Islamic education among the ancestors of African Americans. What is intriguing and commendable about their struggle is the value the enslaved Muslims placed on *community* in their exhaustive efforts to preserve their *dietary laws*, *Islamic dress*, *Qur'anic learning*, and support of each other, irrespective of the most inhumane conditions of bondage. This is not to suggest that slavery was lenient but, rather, that our ancestors were determined to live their faith as much as possible benefiting from cracks in the system.

Although underreported in conventional accounts of the African American experience, Austin (1977) and Diouf (1998) document that enslaved Muslims came to America with knowledge and skills; they were scribes, poets, teachers, judges, students, and scholars. As Diouf (1998) writes:

> Muslims worked inside as well as outside the slavery system and they also worked against it. Muslims were the first to rebel; they played a major role in the only successful slave revolution and organized and led the most threatening slave uprising in urban America. Though individuals of different persuasions attained similar results, the Muslims were the only group that consistently, on a global scale pursued these objectives with tenacity and achieved a high degree of success. (p. 208)

Even with the continued presence of Muslims and the continuity of Islamic learning in America, neither the general society nor the African American community is fully cognizant of Islamic ideals as a philosophical foundation for the institutional establishment of education in the United States. A conscious reconnection with Islam as a practicing *philosophy of education* does not emerge among African Americans until later in the early 1930s.

The University of Islam. The appalling state of education for [Negroes] African Americans in 1933 was brilliantly articulated in Carter G. Woodson's seminal treatise, *The Miseducation of the Negro.* Woodson stressed, "The program for the uplift of the Negro in this country must be based upon a scientific study of the Negro from within to develop in him the power to do for himself what his oppressors will never do to elevate him to the level of others" (page 144). Responding to the multiplicity of needs of African Americans, including protection from murder/lynching and physical assaults, economic deprivation, repair of family life, and the need for an educational experience that was positive, self-empowering, and productive for African American children, the second developmental phase of Islamic education in the African American community also emerged in 1933, with the establishment of the University of Islam, the FOI (Fruit of Islam), and the MGT&GCC (Muslim Girls Training and General Civilization Class) by Fard Muhammad and Elijah Muhammad in Detroit, Michigan. Representing the essential components of the Nation of Islam, these structures comprised a comprehensive system of education that addressed every facet of life necessary for a people to be educated and productive in a nurturing community environment.

In his historic *Message to the Blackman* (1965), the Honorable Elijah Muhammad encapsulated the condition of African Americans then and now. He stated:

> We must begin at the cradle and teach our babies that they must do something for self. They must not be like we, their fathers, who look to the slave-makers' and slave-masters' children for all. We must teach our children now with an enthusiasm exceeding that which our slave-masters used in having our forefathers imbed the seed of dependency within us. We must stop the process of giving our brainpower and wealth to the slave-masters' children. We must eliminate the master-slave relationship. (E. Muhammad, 1965, p. 57)

Speaking to the needs of a people who were still reeling from the effects of enslavement, the Honorable Elijah Muhammad, leader of the Nation of Islam, declared,

> "We must have that which will make us want to do for ourselves as other people want to do for themselves. You ask, "How can this be done?" The religion of Islam makes the so-called Negroes think in terms of self and their own kind. Thus, this kind of thinking produces an industrious people who are self-independent." (E. Muhammad, pp. 57–58)

Through a dignified work ethic, high morals, and a disciplined mind, body, and spirit, Muslims were taught that they were masters of their own destiny and could produce for themselves. The mantra "Knowledge of

Self," "Love Self," and "Do for Self" resounded in The Nation of Islam, a self-empowering collective social movement, and reverberated throughout America and the general African American community that watched from the sidelines and was inspired and strengthened. The Honorable Elijah Muhammad was among the first in this historical period, along with Marcus Garvey, to refer to the Negro as a "Blackman" in a positive way. On the book jacket of *Message to the Blackman*, *Readers Digest* referred to Elijah Muhammad as "the most powerful Blackman in America." A *Readers Digest* writer captured the spirit of this phenomenal movement and noted: "He offers a new way of life. Muhammad prompts even his severest critics to agree when he says he attacks traditional reasons the Negro race is weak" (back cover, *Message to the Blackman*, 1965).

The University of Islam schools the Honorable Elijah Muhammad founded represented the *embryonic phase* of a formal Islamic education system in America. Notwithstanding its humble beginnings, it was a courageous effort for a people denied human dignity. Although not a university as the name implies, the University of Islam was actually an elementary and secondary school that eventually evolved into a high school. It was called a university because the curriculum taught higher concepts in all subjects, particularly mathematics, science, astronomy, and African and African American history. C. Eric Lincoln (1961), the great scholar who completed the first study of Muslims in America, wrote:

> Muslim schools are emphasizing Negro history, Negro achievements and the contributions of Negroes to the world's great cultures and to the development of the American nation. These facts are rarely taught in public schools, and the Muslims may be alone in trying to bring the Negro community to an awareness of racial heritage. (p. 250)

Understanding education to be all-inclusive, the Honorable Elijah Muhammad and the Nation of Islam required every member of the community to engage actively in classes in order to learn knowledge of self. Adult men and women had separate programs for self-development.

The Muslims Girls Training and General Civilization Class (MGT& GCC) was the mandatory 1-day per week class designed for adult women with a separate class for junior girls. They were taught how to cook healthy food—as the African American "soul food" diet was causing great harm and early death—how to sew, improve the home environment, raise children, take care of the husband, and how to act "at home and abroad"— stressing civilization (civilized behavior) as the hallmark of a cultured, dignified people.

The Fruit of Islam (FOI) was the self-development class for adult men. Classes offered for boys were called Junior (Jr.) FOI. These classes taught males self defense, especially karate, work ethics, responsibility, organizational skills, what to look for in a wife, and how to be a good husband. Mandatory classes along with other duties required the men to meet approximately three times per week. Men also were taught various skills to enable them to become self-sufficient. Controversial initially, the male and female classes for adults and youngsters changed the conduct and appearance of African Americans, who were widely perceived as an underclass—although this is a misnomer—and brought great respect to Black men and women and the collective Muslim community.

Little credit has been given to African American Muslims as early forerunners in creating and adhering to a healthy eating regimen that drastically improved the health and appearance of African Americans. Muslims became herbalists and developed their own distinct cultural cuisine and health regimens and created the famous "one meal a day" eating discipline as well. In the context of the conditions that existed in America during this period (e.g., the Depression in the 1930s), this was more than a tremendous accomplishment; it was nothing short of remarkable.

The University of Islam schools, lauded as exemplary models of independent education, influenced numerous later endeavors and expanded to 48 schools throughout the major cities of the United States by 1975, the most notable being in the larger cities of Chicago, Detroit, New York, Philadelphia, and cities in California. These schools were owned and operated by the Nation of Islam and educated thousands of young people in addition to a cadre of professionals who sought viable alternative means to aid the condition of the African American community.

The University of Islam schools were nurtured by a loving mother, the first teacher of the school, Clara Muhammad, wife of Elijah Muhammad and the matriarch of the early Islamic movement among African Americans. She fought for her Muslim children. Like Rosa Parks who *sat* in defiance of legalized discrimination, Clara Muhammad *stood* defiantly—refusing to be intimidated by truant officers and police who demanded that she put her children in public school. A petite woman and mother of eight children, she stood at the door of their humble home trembling, with fists clenched as she said, "I will die as dead as this door rail, before I let you take my children and put them in your schools." The officers tried to intimidate her further by threatening to put her in jail. Clara Muhammad stood, looked them in the eye and repeated her statement. They looked at each other, said she must be crazy and left. They never returned (Mohammed, audiocassette, 1976).

Virtually impoverished, yet with faith in The Creator and a love and commitment to their children, these dedicated parents stood against formidable odds to ensure that their children would be protected from a harmful school environment. Elijah Muhammad said, "We know that kindergarten children and first graders once in Islam cannot be taken into Christian schools without having to suffer mockery and attack from the Christian children and from the Christian teachers who hate Islam, the God of Islam and the Prophets of Islam. Therefore, we believe that to keep peace with the Christians, we must teach our children in their own schools." (E. Muhammad, 1965, p. 214). Although formally educated only to the third grade, the Honorable Elijah Muhammad established a model of education that moved in the tradition of what Carter G. Woodson called for when he said, "Men of scholarship and consequently of prophetic insight must show us the right way and lead us into the light which shines brighter and brighter" (Woodson, 1933, p. 145).

The University of Islam schools modeled unique characteristics, some of which were later adopted as public school policies. First, they were private schools for poor African American Muslim youngsters. This instilled pride and self-confidence in the students, their families and the community. In addition, students began school at 3 years old, before Head Start existed; these schools pioneered instruction of the Arabic language to elementary school students; provided year-round school; separated boys and girls; required students to wear uniforms; provided a disciplined, clean environment; taught African American history; provided a universal worldview; developed their own curricular and textbooks; and trained their own dedicated teachers who made enormous financial sacrifices to support "the cause". The University of Islam schools engendered ownership, pride, and empowerment for the Muslims and African Americans, as many students who attended and adults who supported them were not Muslims.

It was during this period that W.E.B. Du Bois, initially a proponent of integration, began to be disillusioned about integration as a single operating principle. He saw that there was no contradiction in African Americans having their own quality schools (Wilkins, 2002), and stated,

> A separate Negro school, where children are treated like human beings, trained by teachers of their own race, who know what it means to be black is infinitely better than making our boys and girls doormats to be spit and trampled upon and lied to by ignorant social climbers, whose sole claim to superiority is the ability to kick "niggers" when they are down. (p. 329)

From 1933 until 1975 when the Honorable Elijah Muhammad passed away, the University of Islam schools provided not just Muslim but also African American children with a quality education that stressed self-love, self-knowledge, self-discipline, and self-reliance. These achievements generated greater confidence with respect to the perception African Americans had of themselves and their ability to achieve during this period of time. With dedication, commitment and literally nickels and dimes

African American Muslims developed a system of education that brought pride and educational excellence to their community. Although the Nation of Islam had its detractors philosophically and has been marginalized in the scholarship—believed by many to be an effort to minimize a successful model of empowerment for African Americans—this educational model stands, nevertheless, as an extraordinary accomplishment by African American Muslims.

The Clara Muhammad Schools.   The third developmental period of Islamic education for African American Muslims began in 1975, when Imam W. Deen Mohammed assumed leadership of the largest community of African American Muslims in the United States. Acknowledging the extraordinary work of the Honorable Elijah Muhammad and the University of Islam school system, it was understood among the membership that the 40-year cultural tradition of the Nation of Islam ended with the passing of his father. A new period of development had begun guided by the Qur'an and the life example of Muhammad Ibn Abdullah, the last Prophet, which would enable the African American Muslim community to evolve into its full potential. Imam Mohammed stated that the good things the Nation of Islam espoused should remain—love for self and kind, strong family life, cleanliness, integrity, economic development, and so on. "We haven't severed ourselves from our past, only from the things that are improper and not usable" (Mohammed, 1982).

Consistent with the concept of education as that which impacts the whole life of the individual and community, Imam Mohammed stressed the Qur'an as the primary source of knowledge and guidance as did the early Muslim ancestors of African Americans. He made education the number one priority of the community and began a transition of all of the existing University of Islam schools to Clara Muhammad Schools in concert with Qur'anic principles and in dedication to the tireless work and commitment of his mother, Clara Muhammad. While students in the Clara Muhammad schools were to continue to be taught about the African origins of civilization, their religious education was to become consistent with the belief system embraced by over one billion Muslims throughout the world (Rashid & Muhammad, 1992). To support education as the number one priority, Imam W. Deen Mohammed also sought to develop a Muslim Teachers College and purchased the Palmer Memorial Institute in Sedalia, North Carolina, the former private finishing school of Dr. Charlotte Hawkins Brown, (1883–1961), the distinguished African American educator.

As the Islamic education model crystallized, Imam W. Deen Mohammad taught that as valuable as ethnic identity is for African Americans, human identity is greater. He further taught that African Americans are great and blessed not because of their skin color but because of the circumstances they endured during their enslavement and thereafter, and how those circumstances have shaped the soul, consciousness, and humanity of African American people. After years of transitioning the Nation of Islam removing any vestiges of racism, corruption, or debilitating structures, Imam Mohammed brought the African American Muslim community into the universal Muslim *Ummah* (Muslim World), *but not as expected.*

What has been observed for 30 years, but unacknowledged in any significant way by scholars should be hailed as the "religious and human development phenomenon of the century." Imam W. Deen Mohammed— without battles or bloodshed—successfully transitioned millions of African American Muslims—as well as the millions who are influenced by Muslims—from a separatist philosophy that declared that the "Blackman" was god and the "white man" was inherently wicked and the devil, to a balanced, sober middle ground supported by the Qur'an with the following understanding: God is not a man in any color; individuals and their behavior suggests that the best one among all of us is the one who is most righteous in conduct.

What is also profound about this human development phenomenon is Imam W. Deen Mohammed's insistence that the African American Muslim community maintains the integrity of its identity and establishes independent African American thought. This is in concert with the principle that Islam promotes the excellence of every people and their unique cultural expression. As a consequence, the African American Muslim community today representing approximately 53% of the eight million Muslims in America (Project Maps, 2001) has evolved a new cultural identity that has merged the strengths of its African heritage and the African American experience, concomitantly, fostering transformative independent thought that provides unique solutions to the numerous problems confronting the African American community and America, of which one of the most critical is the absence of true education.

For almost 30 years (1975 to 2004), Imam W. Deen Mohammed has held steadfast, refusing significant funding and influence that might undermine the identity of African American Muslims. In sum, Islam offers the African American community a new way to conceive reality and has a historical record to stand on in the United States, in the African Diaspora, and in world civilization. As Aminah McCloud (1998) has observed: "Historically, the myriad of problems facing the African American community—poor education, drugs, unemployment, violence, racism, oppression, police brutality, despair, etc.—and the solutions offered by the Black Christian elite however inarticulate or self defeating are usually accepted as accurately representing the authentic concerns of Black America" (p. 182).

History also records that Islam was the regenerative power that gave new birth to Europe, when, during the Renaissance (from the 14th to the

17th centuries), Europeans witnessed copious artistic endeavors, an unprecedented cultural explosion, and the establishment of outstanding institutions of learning, including the model for the university now copied from Muslims and used in the United States and throughout the world. Likewise, Islam has demonstrated its power to give new birth to the African American community. Islam was the precursor of—and to many the inspiration for—subsequent development in Black Studies and African-centered scholastic/curriculum endeavors. The African American experience in Islamic education has much to offer education in the Muslim world and is currently demonstrating that expertise in interactions among African Americans and immigrant Muslims in many communities in the United States.

IMMIGRANT MUSLIMS, AFRICAN AMERICAN MUSLIMS, AND EDUCATION IN THE MUSLIM WORLD

Immigrant Muslims in the United States come from nearly every country in the world, with the largest groups coming from the Middle East and South Asia. Thus, the American Muslim community is diverse and includes indigenous Muslims both born here and converted who are Caucasian, African American, Asian, Latino, and Native American. Because many Caucasian Muslims usually align with the immigrant community, the African American community often remains independent. Thus, it is not surprising that:

> The divergent perspectives of each community on education, coupled with each one's self-perceptions, have caused the landscape of Islamic schools to resemble the United States before *Brown vs. Board of Education*. (Z. Muhammad, 2003, p. 104)

Various models of Islamic schools serve this diverse community and those established by immigrant Muslims are increasing throughout the United States. Not to be confused with immigrant schools that African Americans often attend, supervise, or teach in, the Clara Muhammad Schools remain consistent with the human aspirations and the tradition of the "freedom struggle" for African Americans. What makes this specific yet broad application possible is the Islamic worldview.

Given current geopolitical tensions, Islamic education has taken center stage. If Islamic education is destabilized, however, by American governmental efforts to export "democracy," pending plans to revive the educational systems of Afghanistan (Gall, 2004) and Iraq (Robelen, 2003) could have devastating consequences for the people and those countries, and doing so also could have serious repercussions in the United States, where the issue of identity is at "the heart of the American Muslim community" (Z. Muhammad, 2003, p. 105). Elsewhere I have suggested that Islamic education that follows the principles of the Qur'an, "as exemplary models of moral, human and academic excellence, could contribute immensely to solving this country's current and continuing education problems" (p. 100). Thus, the education of African American Muslims and immigrant Muslims has implications for developing greater understanding of the potential benefits the Islamic education model offers society more generally and the enhancement of Islamic education and stabilization globally. However, a great deal depends on how the Muslim community in the United States addresses the contradictions that exist within local Islamic schools founded and operated by immigrant Muslims which borders on a bifurcated system (Z. Muhammad, 2003). Rather than acquiesce to what is perceived as acceptable in contemporary U.S. society, Islamic educators, many of whom are African Americans, are often advising local Islamic schools founded by immigrants to become more "representative Islamic school models," free from the racial, class, and gender attitudes that some immigrants bring with them or acquiesce to in this society.

In contrast to many Muslims who immigrated in recent decades to the United States from postcolonial societies, whose relatively more privileged socioeconomic backgrounds may have afforded them opportunities to attend "secular" or missionary schools in their homelands, African Americans are not usually so "enamored of the Western educational model which historically did not educate African Americans" (Z. Muhammad, 2003, p. 104). In fact, one result of the onslaught of colonial domination in these former colonies was the loss of Muslim identity and intellectual thought and the "imitation of the other," that is, British, French, and Western civilization generally. That is why in nearly two centuries of a bifurcated, Westernized, secularized education, the Muslims have produced neither a school, college, university, nor a generation of scholars that matches the West in creativity or excellence. The Western educational model depends ultimately upon a specific vision and is animated by a will to realize that vision. The vision of the West is not the vision of Islam or Muslims. That is why, perhaps, "internal issues of identity . . . beleaguer Islamic schools" (Institute of Islamic Thought, 1982). These issues "stem from colonialism, slavery and the 'dream of whiteness,' the ideal that permeates the ethos of America" (Z. Muhammad, 2003, p. 100).

RESEARCH AND COMMUNITY ACTION

There is a role for research and community action to ensure that the direction of Islamic education in the United States is consistent first with the principles and practices of Islam and guided by the best research available to ensure that all Muslims—African American and immigrant—are afforded institutions of learning that will lend to the stability and advancement of education in the United States. The following research and community action agenda could begin to address the potential of Islamic education for human freedom and development. Research is needed to:

- Assess the methods and outcomes of Islamic education, including an in-depth study of the model used in the education of males and females that has proven to be transformative in the lives of African American Muslims
- Determine the characteristics of effective Islamic schools, including comparison of Clara Muhammad Schools and Islamic schools organized by Immigrant Muslims, focusing particularly on the relationship between nurturing academic excellence and moral development
- Identify best practices, including teacher preparation methods, character education strategies (Nasir & Kirshner, 2003, Nasir, 2004), factors that engage and motivate students to achieve (Akom, 2003), and ways to address racism and prejudice within the American Muslim community, particularly among immigrant Muslims and African American Muslims, and
- Document the accomplishments of graduates from Islamic schools and the factors in Islamic education that contributed to their success.

Community action is needed to:

- Establish ongoing national symposia to share the results of this research with the broader community of scholars, educators, parents, and policy makers, and
- Begin a dialogue between Muslim and non-Muslim educators concerning the important issues identified earlier.

CONCLUDING COMMENTS

The United States of America has made monumental achievements, particularly in science, yet, it is important to keep in perspective that America as an *experiment* in reality is only 228 years old, has yet to evolve into maturity and has failed miserably in its human development because it has not provided quality education to all of its citizens. Global education statistics confirm this observation and the cultural and social fabric of contemporary America further confirms this reality. In the interest of the stability and advancement of the nation and all of its citizens, the fundamental institutions of learning must be transformed so that all citizens may come into their full human rights and reach the excellence of their potential.

With meager resources, an ennobled spirit and in the face of unfath-omable obstacles, African American Muslims have persevered toward hu-man dignity and material establishment, creating new pathways while engendering confidence and courage to a community that was forced to question their human worth. The courage and confidence in their human-ity and ultimate success came from and continues to come from one source, the Qur'an. In an historic address to the First Educational Conference for Imams, Teachers and Administrators of Clara Muhammad Schools held in Sedalia, North Carolina in 1982, Imam W. Deen Mohammed (1982) asked the question, "What made America great?" He answered, "People who had a bigger vision than the present state they were in." He continued, "If we have the same vision that the world has, we will never be leaders. I know most of you want to help America. I know I do, this is my home. My ancestors lived in Africa, but this is my home, America. If you want to rise above that world, you will have to come out of it. Those that rise above American can lead America. Anytime you can latch on to the Qur'an and see its superiority, then you can stand above this world. That's the only way you can help it. The future of our children depends on our ability to step out of the muck and mire of America's (un-American) ideas and walk to an idea of our own" (audiocassette). In conclusion, we must remember that "Our Walk to Freedom" requires faith—in the Creator—and courage.

Part VII

Globalizing the Struggle for Black Education: African and Diaspora Experiences

INTRODUCTION

When a people lose the knowledge of who they are, that is, their culture, they lose the very foundation upon which their individual existence and their society is based. To combat this loss, each African person must be equipped with a "Grand Vision of the Future," a vision extending beyond personal interests such that this vision becomes the embodiment of the *vital interest* and *moral centerhood* of the entire African World Community.

—Anderson Thompson (1997, pp. 9–10)

The crisis in Black education worldwide is a manifestation of Black people's material and spiritual dispossession. Part VII consists of commentaries by African and African-descent scholars who were invited to participate in CORIBE symposia, research, and outreach activities that address this global reality. Depicting current conditions of education for African people in Sénégal, Great Britain, and Brazil, these chapters also provide examples of resistance even as the authors affirm the findings and conclusions in the research Carol D. Lee, William H. Watkins, and Kassie Freeman prepared for the Commission (Chapters 3–6). The authors, teachers, teacher educators, researchers, and activist-scholars, discuss extant research on Black education in their countries; several reflect on their own teaching, research, and activism. Each corroborates the need for cross-national collaboration in the global struggle for Black education.

The global picture of Black education that emerges in these chapters reveals the material and existential conditions of African people's shared dispossession and cultural resistance as well as ways that Black education also serves human freedom. Consistent with other contributions to this volume, the critical observations presented in these chapters affirm the Commission's groundbreaking decision to broaden the knowledgebase in order to address the crisis in Black education globally.

Ibrahima Seck, in Chapter 13, concludes that there is a "Worldwide Conspiracy Against Black Culture and Education," as the title of this chapter indicates. His insights about historical and contemporary challenges in education in Sénégal extend to critical assessments of the vestiges of colonial education, as well as adverse effects of structural adjustment and curriculum deformation—factors William H. Watkins also documents in Chapter 5. In addition to describing some of the ways that classroom teachers and students struggle against these constraints, Seck also recommends that African governments develop a collective response in the struggle to defend Black culture and education, including educational approaches that value local indigenous knowledge, traditions, and expertise.

Chapter 14, "Black Educational Experiences in Britain: Reflections on the Global Educational Landscape," by Cecile Wright, is a concise sociological analysis of Black education and employment opportunities in Britain. Wright cites academic and government research that point to "representations of blackness" as well as historical patterns of exclusion that closely parallel the experiences of African Americans. That is, Black youngsters in Britain, many of whom have family roots in the Caribbean, enter school with "academic potential" equal to or greater than the national average but, the longer they remain in school, the poorer their academic performance, regardless of their socioeconomic status. As is also the case in the United States, Black males are especially vulnerable and although the "inferior" homes and cultural backgrounds of Black British students are similarly maligned in educational research and popular consciousness, Wright describes how Black families have responded by establishing community-based independent Saturday Schools and other alternatives.

Terezinha Juraci Machado da Silva examines "veiled" racism in Brazilian society in Chapter 15, "Black People and Brazilian Education." She demonstrates the need for and describes organized community efforts to educate Afro Brazilians about the dynamics and manifestations of both interpersonal and institutional racism as a "systemic process grounded in everyday life." Referred to as "instruction for consciousness," Machado da Silva explains how she uses children's literature to decipher and demystify racism and exclusion in Brazilian society.

Chapter 16, which further explicates Black education in Brazil, is entitled "A New Millennium Research Agenda in Black Education: Some

Points to Be Considered for Discussion and Decisions," by Petronilha Beatriz Gonçalves e Silva. This chapter describes both historical and contemporary influences of race on Afro Brazilians—in research and education practice. Gonçalves e Silva poses a question that is at the center of the Commission's concerns: "*What must we do to persuade not only schools, but the entire society, that Black Education, as well as other questions concerning the well-being of Africans and African descended people, are very serious problems that involve all of the society?*" She also recommends specific ways to implement a collaborative cross-national dialogue and research agenda that includes "militant" community action as a focus and a context for popular dissemination of knowledge produced from Black perspectives on Black education. In effect, Gonçalves e Silva calls for staking out the territory of Black Education as a field of study. Finally, it deserves emphasis that Carol D. Lee's focus on pedagogy for cultural responsibility and community political empowerment in Chapter 3 finds correspondence in the education and community action these activist-scholars describe in the chapters to follow.

13

Worldwide Conspiracy Against Black Culture and Education

Ibrahima Seck
Cheikh Anta Diop University, Dakar, Sénégal

INTRODUCTION

This commentary addresses the chapters that William H. Watkins and Kassie Freeman prepared for the Commission on Research in Black Education. It is obvious that most of the problems Africans are facing today in their quest for education, which is meant to lead to a better life, originated from political and social unrest generated by the Atlantic slave trade and European colonization. This "trade" in human beings introduced permanent warfare, which resulted in the dislocation of powerful and stable empires into small kingdoms. Traditional rules of succession were discarded. Only firearms opened the way to power. This situation facilitated European colonization. The African continent was divided into new political units separated by artificial boundaries. During the era of African enslavement, Europeans were mainly interested in providing human labor to their American colonies. With colonialism, however, the main goal was to use Africans to work on their own land in order to provide badly needed raw materials to European industries. Railroad tracks were built just like needles reaching the far interior of the African continent, from where all kinds of goods were transported to the coast and then to Europe. New towns mushroomed on the coast and most of them became the capitals of the newly created political entities and the cradle of the colonial schools Europeans established.

As demonstrated by William H. Watkins in Chapter 5, under colonialism, the ruling regime needed education for obedience, docility, and acceptance. Because few Europeans could actually establish themselves in Africa, and also in order to minimize colonial administrative expenses, Africans were introduced to European education in order to serve the colonial masters. Most of the African countries were granted "independence" around the 1960s but the ruling powers managed to leave behind them the tool of permanent subordination, which is the colonial school, as Hassimi Maiga discussed in Chapter 7.

What follows are comments specifically related to education issues in Sénégal. These issues will focus on my own experience as a researcher in African and African American history and also as a teacher of history for 15 years at Lycée Blaise Diagné, an exemplary high school located in Dakar, the capital of Sénégal. I am especially interested in three issues:

1. The two-speed-society created by the colonial school.
2. Problems related to the language used in education and the content of the school curriculum.
3. The impact of the structural adjustments imposed by the International Monetary Fund (IMF) and the World Bank.

THE TWO-SPEED SOCIETY CREATED BY THE COLONIAL SCHOOL

In Sénégal, although the constitution states the right of every citizen to receive an education, about 70% of the children have no access to school. The lack of classrooms and teachers is the main explanation of this situation. Among the 30% who have access to school, a very small percentage manage to enroll in secondary school. Those who reach the university constitute an even smaller percentage. So, many people are condemned to illiteracy and can never expect to get decently paid jobs in the country. Most of these students know very little about their rights, as the constitution and the laws are written in French, the official language in schools and administration.

On the other side of the street, we have the elite, consisting of people educated in French who run the country. This elite often looks down on the majority of the population and often prefers a Western style of life. Western knowledge also has been imposed on the population, whose own traditional knowledge was considered as backward and scorned. No wonder that some say that the first enemy of Africa is its own elite. Interestingly enough, it is also well known that many of the most talented Africans are those who are considered to be illiterate, even though some of them know how to read and write in Arabic. The most successful businessmen in West Africa are from this very group, but they represent a very small number. If our educational policy did not exclude the majority of our population, we might have more successful businessmen and workers with a higher level of productivity. As Kassie Freeman states in her research for the Commission on Research in Black Education (Chapter 6): "to keep groups uneducated or undereducated has been a formula across societies for the underutilization of their talent."

PROBLEMS RELATED TO THE LANGUAGE USED IN EDUCATION AND THE CONTENT OF THE CURRICULUM

William H. Watkins's research clearly describes the impact of colonial rule on education in Africa. Because the entire indigenous social structure was made to serve the colonial relationship, all indigenous institutions of a victim country, especially schools, are retarded and deformed. The culture of indigenous people is either destroyed or significantly damaged. Language is the vehicle by which all the genius and the history of a people are transmitted. Because indigenous groups were forced into artificially drawn national boundaries, the language of the ruling country was used as the base of the colonial school. In Sénégal, French was used as the language of instruction. This is despite the fact that Abbé Boilat, an educational leader in Sénégal in the 19th century, wanted people to be educated in their own language for greater efficiency. However, the authorities in Paris knew that the exploitation of the country depended on the cultural subordination of their colonial subjects. And the best way to achieve that goal was to impose the French language.

Children grow up speaking their own native languages, usually two or even more. All knowledge of the surrounding world and basic education are transmitted to them in those languages. When time comes to go to school, our children are introduced to a totally different language and to a new culture. In "Les Fondements d'un Etat Federal d'Afrique Noire," Cheikh Anta Diop expresses well how troublesome and time consuming it is to master science in a foreign language. For example, to enable an African child to understand the meaning of the mathematical concept of "line," the child has to sit in a classroom for years in order to master the French alphabet and enough vocabulary and grammar.

As a secondary school teacher, working mainly with students in their last year of high school, I understood that, for the majority of the students, education in a colonial school is just a waste of time because most of them can hardly write correct sentences in French. For African children, as for African Americans, the discontinuity between the home culture and school learning ultimately disrupts the learning process for many children and the resulting failure leads them to reject learning itself (see Freeman, Chapter 6). The situation for these children is even worse if we consider the fact that very few skills are taught to them except in a very limited number of specialized schools. Even those who graduate at the university find out that their training most of the time is inappropriate for the market. This has resulted in social unrest, especially with the effects of structural adjustment imposed by the IMF and the World Bank. These impacts are discussed briefly here.

THE IMPACT OF STRUCTURAL ADJUSTMENTS IMPOSED BY THE IMF AND THE WORLD BANK

Since the early 1980s, the IMF and the World Bank have imposed drastic cuts on most African countries. Public health and education have been particularly affected, as they do not represent an immediate source of income that allows African countries to reimburse their debts. For the ministry of education, this has resulted in the diminution of classroom construction and, although few teachers could be recruited, the number of students has increased rapidly. To illustrate this problem, I will consider the case of Lycée Blaise Diagné, the largest high school in Sénégal, a West African country where education is free. This institution was originally designed to host a few hundred students and the total annual budget amounted to 21 million Francs CFA, approximately $35,000. With the IMF and World Bank policy of structural adjustment, this figure has been lowered to 12 million Francs CFA, approximately $20,000. Now Blaise Diagné High School hosts 5,000 students, which means only $4 is spent every year by the state on each student. The increasing number of students per classroom is one of the major problems. The average figure now is 50 students per classroom. This number also can increase to as many as 60 students in the last grade where we usually sympathetically accept some of the students who failed the previous year and who are not officially allowed to attend classes.

The new structural adjustment policy also results in a scarcity of school supplies, especially textbooks. Scientific labs are available but are few in number and these are generally poorly equipped. Chalk and erasers are the tools that one can usually expect to be provided by the school. Without such tools, some teachers have resorted to inventive strategies for the school's survival. For example, they produce readers through their own research to replace missing textbooks that are sold to the students at a very reasonable price just to cover expenses. Students also make maps under the supervision of their teachers.

During the 1960s and the 1970s, textbooks were available in sufficient quantity but were financed by the French government and often these were written by French teachers. As Watkins has noted, it is very important to question what goes into textbooks, the pedagogical and philosophical foundations of the texts, the language of publication, and so on. These questions are of the ulmost importance, especially when history is concerned. During colonial times, African students were taught to undermine their own culture and to praise the culture of the ruling powers. After "independence," many African countries had to rely on the former regime for teachers and school supplies. This was called "cooperation," even though it had no other meaning than the perpetuation of colonial domination.

As a schoolboy in my third year at elementary school, I was provided, like my schoolmates, with a textbook in which African kings were depicted as tyrants and the colonial conquerors as heroes. That book taught me that Andrée Brue, director of the French Company of Sénégal in the late 1600s and early 1700s, led "*une oeuvre civilisatrice*"(a civilizing mission) in Sénégal. But later, as a graduate student in the History Department of the University of Dakar, I realized that he was nothing but the head of a slave trading company who eventually spent some time in jail for trying to impose his control upon one of our local kingdoms. Those who went to elementary school before my generation were taught to praise "*nos ancêtres les Gaullois*" (our ancestors the Gauls). Until this very day, most of the people seem to be programmed or forced to believe in their racial inferiority. Freeman (Chapter 6) clearly shows that the same situation exists throughout the Diaspora, in Europe, and the United States. In my concluding comments, I will suggest opportunities for action.

CONCLUDING COMMENTS

The educational problems of Africans on the continent and Africans of the Diaspora are widely known. Now it is time for action. As a history teacher and researcher, I can say that we know a great deal about the contributions of Black people to the world. This knowledge needs to be turned into textbooks and made available to African students worldwide. Black students everywhere need to be taught from their own worldview perspective. Education is nothing without self-respect and self-confidence. Local initiatives such as the Gao School Museum in Mali that address real community needs through the pedagogical process and content of school curricula must be supported morally and financially (Maiga, 1993, 1995; see also Watkins, Chapter 5, and Maiga, Chapter 7, for brief descriptions of the Gao School Museum methodology). Finally, structures such as the African Union (AU) must host programs dedicated to the African renaissance through education.

14

Black Educational Experiences in Britain: Reflections on the Global Educational Landscape

Cecile Wright
The Nottingham Trent University, United Kingdom

INTRODUCTION

This chapter briefly delineates conditions of education, labor market participation and research issues in terms of the needs of Black people in Britain. (The term "Black" includes students with African and/or Caribbean heritage.) Within the context of Britain, the passion with which education is held among the Black population is clearly evident at every stage of educational process. Many Black people in Britain migrated there in the 1950s and 1960s, arriving primarily from the Caribbean, to give their children the opportunity to succeed in education and to achieve successful labor market outcomes. Indeed, Black students have some of the highest rates of school attendance. Many, especially girls, achieve relatively well at school (Mirza, 1992). Black students are featuring in greater numbers in proportion to their population in further and higher education statistics (Modood, 1998). Yet, paradoxically the successes charted need to be considered against a dominant discourse which links Black educational underperformance and school exclusion with confrontational masculinities and antieducation culture (e.g., Sewell, 1997).

Kassie Freeman's research for the Commission on Research in Black Education (Chapter 6) examines the process by which Diasporic Black populations experience educational and career opportunities and barriers. Freeman argues that despite differences in the educational systems across borders, the apparent lack of educational (and subsequent career) opportunities for Black populations remains a salient feature of the global educational landscape. The commentary below briefly sketches the educational experiences of Black people in Britain.

THE PAST BEHIND THE PRESENT

Early literature on the educational experiences of Black students in Britain stems from research conducted in the 1960s and 1970s by academics (Coard, 1971; ILEA Research and Statistics Group, 1968) and a number of government bodies (Rampton, 1981; Swann, 1985). This research reveals that Black students were underachieving at all levels of the educational system in comparison to other groups. Additionally, the discourse at the time portrayed Black children as coming from inferior cultures and homes (Carby, 1982). Studies undertaken in the 1980s and 1990s among different groups within the educational system illustrate that although Black students at age 5 entered school with an academic potential either greater or much the same standard as the national average, by age 10, however, they had fallen behind academically. At age 16, they achieved less than half the national average of students achieving 5 or higher (e.g., passing) General Certificate of Secondary Education grades (Gillborn & Gipps, 1996; Gillborn & Mirza, 2000). The GSCE is the General Certificate of Secondary Education. It is expected to be taken in up to 10 academic subjects by the vast majority of school students usually at age 16. It is the end of compulsory schooling qualification. The GSCE is graded from "A" to "G", with grades "C" and above referred to as higher grades. Although there are no pass and fail grades, it is grade "C" that is generally accepted as the requirement for advanced study and employment qualification. There is also a grade "U" for those not achieving any grade. In most subjects, 55% of students taking the examination obtain grade "C" and above.

These trends also reveal that underperformance persists even when social class differences are taken into account. There is an established trend within the British education system between social class and educational success. For example, the higher a child's social class background, the greater the child's educational attainments are likely to be. In Britain, the Department for Education and Employment (DFEE) figures for 1977 show that children from the most advantaged social class background were three times more likely to obtain five or higher GCSE grades than their peers from more disadvantaged backgrounds. Furthermore, in a recent study Gillborn and Mirza (2000) assert "inequality of attainment are now evident for Black pupils regardless of their class background" (p. 20). These authors also reported the following: "African Caribbean pupils from working class backgrounds fell behind other working class peers in levels of attainment during the late 1980's and 1990's" (p. 20). Similarly, according to the findings of this research: "African Caribbean pupils from non-manual homes are the lowest attaining of the middle class groups. In some cases they are barely matching the attainments of working class pupils in other ethnic groups" (p. 20).

Additionally, studies have also highlighted differences in attainment between Black males and females (Gillborn & Gipps, 1996; Gillborn & Mirza, 2000). These differences can be further extrapolated along group division with Black males being located at the bottom of the class (Blyth & Miller, 1996; Coffield & Vignoles, 1997). Black males' continuing educational underperformance is also associated with their experience of the exclusion process. (The term "exclusion" refers to the expulsion of a child from school, either permanently or for a fixed period. The decision to exclude is the sole responsibility of the head teacher, but parents have the right to appeal against this action.) Research evidence repeatedly highlights the overrepresentation of Black males in the statistics of those excluded from school (Osler, 1997; Wright et al., 2000). Some researchers argue that the overrepresentation of Black males in the exclusion process is reflective of the institutional culture and wider racialized discourses. For instance, wider societal representations of the Black male as posing a threat and a problem invariably infiltrate the school culture. Studies show that Black males are often portrayed as the sporting hero or are considered irresponsible and unworthy (Westwood, 1990). Within the context of the school, therefore, teachers have been found to hold negative attitudes toward and expectations of Black students (Sewell, 1997; Wright et al., 2000). Black male students, in particular, are more likely to be labeled violent or dangerous even when they display behavior similar to other groups. They are also regarded as being of low ability, disruptive, and in need of frequent reprimanding (Wright et al., 2000).

Research has shown that involvement in the exclusion process not only denies Black students access to education at primary and secondary stages of schooling, but ultimately results in underrepresentation in both further and higher education, lack of employment opportunities and can induce both alienation and disaffection (The Runnymede Trust, 1996). Thus, of the Black students who generally participate in higher education, those categorized as "Black Caribbean" are less likely to be males (Fitzerald et al., 2000). Thus, the weight of evidence highlights race in relation to educational achievement and differences in discipline patterns.

By contrast, research evidence suggests that in contrast with their white peers of the same gender and social class background, Black students tend to value education as much as higher achieving White students and display high levels of motivation and commitment to education. This is demonstrated in their high rates of attendance (Sewell, 1997; Smith & Tomlinson, 1989) and their support for homework (Eggleston et al., 1986). Alongside this finding also has been the encouragement to pursue further education that Black students receive from their families and the young people's continued participation in education, despite the adverse experience within the compulsory sector (DFES, 2003).

RECENT INTERVENTIONS

Over the decades, Black parents have expressed concerns about the persistent lack of access to quality education and the perceived stigmatizing of their children. Essential to Black young people's continued participation in education, despite the negative experience of the compulsory system, has been the application of the social and cultural capital provided by families and community networks. The concept of social capital refers to a variety of less tangible assets such as power association and networks. People of African descent, it can be argued, gain social capital from their acknowledgment of common ancestry and culture, with unity being a significant source of social capital. Also, increasingly, education is being closely linked to social capital (Bourdieu, 1977). Indeed, the family and community networks have both served to challenge and resist the portrayal of Black young people as academic failures and at the same time they have promoted the educational advancement of young people. This has led (some) Black families to set up separate schooling, either in "Saturday Schools" or full-time schooling. These separate provisions, it was felt, would not only reinforce particular cultures, but could provide stringent academic standards (Dove, 1993; Reay & Mirza, 1997).

Given the nature of the crisis in education delineated above for the Black population in Britain, to what extent have the strategies implemented ameliorated this exigency? Since the late 1960s, a range of methods of interventions have been employed to address the poor educational outcomes of Black students. These measures have included providing positive role models for Black students to increase their self-awareness and self-worth, incorporation of a multicultural curriculum, with some writers expressing an explicit need for Black studies, teachers' awareness training, and emphasis on teacher-parent partnerships (The Runnymede Trust, 2000).

The clearest indication of the efficacy of these interventions would be reflected in more recent figures regarding both educational and labor market outcomes. However, one recent report draws attention to low proportions of Black males in further and higher education, suggesting evidence of a continuing problem at the earlier stages of schooling and the poor representation of the Black population in employment and certain sectors of the labor market (Fitzerald et al., 2000). Despite the emphasis on multicultural or antiracist practices, a focus on teacher awareness training and role models, these interventions have not given rise to the desired transformation in Black young people's situation in the British education system. Clearly, there is a need to connect analyses of the Black experience of schooling in Britain to a wider discourse on the role that the educational system plays in the maintenance of current structural inequalities, which, it could be argued, serves to deny Black students both educational and career opportunities.

CONCLUDING COMMENTS

Since the 1960s, the schooling of Black children within Britain (who had been accorded the status of immigrant) had become a political issue. This situation prevails to the present day (DFES, 2003). Examining the experiences of schooling of Black young people in Britain requires an analysis of representations of blackness within the discourses and practices that maintain their high levels of underattainment and underperformance within the education system. Moreover, research suggests that these dynamics represent culturally exclusionary practices that are considered to be sustained by processes such as teachers' stereotypes, White middle-class discourses, institutionalized racism, and Eurocentric histories (DFEE 2001; McPherson, 1999; The Runnymede Trust, 2000). These processes are, in turn, embodied in the macro-politics of everyday encounters.

In conclusion, Black participation in the educational process and the labor market within Britain is characterized by a lack of access to quality education and successful labor market outcomes, particularly for Black males. This brief overview suggests that the structures and the pedagogies of schools and the education system, more generally are, perhaps, in a Durkheimian or Parsonian sense, an extension of the state whose effective structural functioning is dependent on making the Black experiences marginal and marginalized. It is acknowledged that this situation typifies the experience of Diasporic Black populations, thus highlighting a common experience in both the educational and employment sectors that would appear to transcend national borders. Underlying this inherent and persistent global racial inequality that is witnessed through the prism of schooling is a wider discourse concerning social, cultural, political, and economic issues. Examination of this discourse also needs to inform the debates on transforming the education and social situation of Diasporic peoples. Finally, this brief commentary notes research that suggests that counter public spheres of community networks, "alternative learning provision" and family relationships, can encourage empowering narratives of identity and community (Dove, 1993).

15

Black People and Brazilian Education

Terezinha Juraci Machado da Silva
National University of Cordoba, Argentina

INTRODUCTION

This commentary has been prepared to present reflections on the Afro Brazilian reality of education. I have reviewed the research papers prepared for the Commission on Research in Black Education. However, the reflections and observations presented here are not limited to or intended to respond directly to the issues raised in these commissioned papers. Rather, in this chapter, I discuss some of my own research experience and concerns and offer reflections as a Black teacher educator and researcher in Brazil.

FACING THE BRAZILIAN REALITY

The Brazilian people are the result of a mixture of African, Indian, and White groups mainly represented by the Portuguese. This hybridism was supposedly the origin of the proclaimed "racially integrated Brazilian society," in which there are no fundamental differences or racial conflicts. However, this myth of a racial democracy has been questioned more and more and debated openly, revealing the veiled face of racism and discrimination in Brazil.

A recent scientific-journalistic study about racism in Brazil (Institute of Research Datafolha and the *Folha de São Paulo*) presents some interesting data: 89% of Brazilians believe there is racism in the society; only 10% admitted they are prejudiced; 87% manifested some sort of prejudice or admited having had shown discriminatory behavior toward others in the past. The same study also reports: 48% of Black people interviewed agree with the statement "Good Blacks have White souls." These findings provoked a national debate about racism and freedom of expression in Brazil.

This study also suggests that the degree of racism in Brazil and how it is manifested in our society remains unclear because explicit anger and hate are rarely demonstrated in people's behavior toward Black Brazilians and mulattos ("mixed race" people). Racism in Brazil is deeply rooted and subliminal, making it very hard to determine when it is manifested. Even though the racial debate we are experiencing in Brazil shows us that:

> Black people in Brazilian society and culture have suffered long years all kinds of veiled discrimination. Brazilian society doesn't admit that white people are racist and Brazilians used to say that we—African-descendent Brazilians—are much more racist than they are because our organizations are always denouncing them and are paying so much attenton to white speech and other signs of their prejudice. Unfortunately, our laws, in most of the cases, don't permit us to prove we are being insulted. In these situations they (whites) invert the situation and put the responsibility for the problem on our "black shoulders," saying that we are agressive and intolerant.

Manifestations of racism are routinely "swept under the carpet." We must be vigilant regarding the changing faces of racism and we are trying to demystify it through education. Our studies and research are headed in this direction, basically in the educational arena, in which a group of educators is working with Black teachers in particular in elementary schools in our communities, showing them the "new" (but at same time old) expression of racism and oppression in the lives of African-descendent people in Brazil. Their focus is on the forms racism and oppression present, for instance, in children books, in the media, TV programs, pictures, reports, laws, and popular literature, and so on.

LEARNING TO CHANGE OUR CONSCIOUSNESS

Unfortunately, most of the examples of racism just mentioned are not understood by Black people in Brazil. So, whenever we "sit together," we to refer the distinction that has to be made between individual and institutional racism. The former refers to personal prejudice and behavior and the second refers to procedures and regulations that may not even be racist in their intent but which are discriminatory in their impact, effectively reinforcing racial inequality. This distinction gives us the opportunity to demonstrate to our community that Black people are always outside of the context in which regulations and procedures are made because the official societal structure is organized and controlled by Whites. The question then arises: What are we to do?

Our goal at this point is to help our community understand that racial discrimination in Brazil and in the world can be described as a set of economic, political, social, and ideological relations—as a systemic process grounded in everyday life. Because it is so pervasive, in general, racism is tolerated as if it were a "normal" procedure of the dominant (White) culture, as demonstrated by the statistical results mentioned above. All these factors indicate the need for a new strategy against racism, that is, to develop as much as possible, through a global political education strategy, the powerful flame of instruction for consciousness. This is difficult but possible. For all these reasons I decided to introduce into my teaching at the university (Faculty of Dos Rios in Porto Alegre, Brazil) and in the Black community where I have been working for several years, some essential elements for reading and discussion. These include:

- Consciousness of our blackness
- Why self-esteem has been lost over the years by most people in our Black commmunity, and
- How to detect veiled prejudice.

In this way I am trying to show people that racism in Brazil is so subtle that the offenses are almost taken as mere jokes in songs, in textbooks, in illustrations, in poems and other cultural texts and contexts.

I start this community learning process using children's literature where we can find a lot of good examples of exclusion that are not usually noticed by the majority of readers because these publications are seen as "innocent" and "sweet" children's books. What we can see in these children's books?

- Black characters in general do not have a structured family; they live alone. But when the parents appear, they don't work in a respected or profession. The father is a simple laborer, for example, and the mother is a housemaid;
- At school, Black children are always disturbing the order of the classroom and they are punished by the principal;
- In general, Black children in these books are not shown as being intelligent enough to succeed in school, and so they are shown as failures;

- They are poor and receive kindness and sympathy from the White people who are rich or middle-class;
- In many stories Black characters are not called by their Christian names but by some nickname, according to the stereotype created to represent the respective character;
- Rarely are either Black adults or children the heroes in this literature. Kings, queens, and princesses are Europeans, are always blond, with light (clear) skin and they have blue eyes. They are beautiful, tall, and strong—exactly the opposite of the way Black people are portrayed in the majority of the stories written by Whites.

This is just a single aspect of a big universe of racism and exclusion that we can document in our daily lives that I choose to discuss with Black teachers, university and college students, and the community in general, with the goal of demonstrating the inherent problems that exist in our society but that are not discussed or addressed as part of our national public debate on education. Along with other Black leaders in the country, I am personally involved in discussing these issues in schools, at Black programs, and through various nongovernmental organizations (NGOs).

CONCLUDING COMMENTS

In conclusion, we know that if we don't change the history, if we don't restructure our communities, if we don't include Black people in the society's formal knowledge(s), and if we don't stop—by denunciation and/or affirmative actions—the veiled racial discrimination that exists in the public and private Brazilian school system, we will never attain our rightful place in this society. And the myth of White supremacy will endure for "500 (more) years of oppression" in Brazil.

16

A New Millennium Research Agenda in Black Education: Some Points to Be Considered for Discussion and Decisions

Petronilha Beatriz Gonçalves e Silva
Federal University of São Carlos, Brazil

INTRODUCTION

The initiative of the AERA Commission on Research in Black Education (CORIBE) to call together senior researchers and graduate students of African descent in order to identify priorities in Black education research, teaching, and militant activities, is very relevant not only for African Americans but also for Black people all over the world. This was certainly the understanding of the organizers of the Online Research Training Institute, a professional development experience organized for graduate students, in which I also participated as a visiting Faculty Mentor (Jegna) in the CORIBE Professional Development and Training Mini-course (AERA annual meeting, New Orleans, April 24, 2000).[1] My contribution

---

[1] As an Afro Brazilian and a South American scholar, and as a participant in the International Research Group—Cultural Survivals and African Epistemology, led by Joyce E. King (AERA Invited Presidential Session, Montreal, 1999)—I have contributed to the discussion of CORIBE's Transformative Research and Action Agenda. In the same way I have been involved in political efforts to be implemented by research and teaching institutions, by communities, and by groups of the Black movement in Brazil.

to the CORIBE initiative also included reviewing and discussing the commissioned research presented in this volume and preparing this commentary.

This commentary addresses the commissioned research prepared by Kassie Freeman, Carol D. Lee, and William H. Watkins, which appears in this volume. Their chapters show clearly that we, Black people, are still on the road to freedom. Their research demonstrates, although it was not the principal aim of our oppressors, that five centuries of enforced enslavement and colonialism did not definitively extinguish our African conceptions, beliefs, and attitudes. So the work of these scholars can empower the African community and strengthen the argument that it is from our African ethos, from our history on the continent, and in the Diaspora that we can present for the world our propositions for peace and happiness for all human beings. This means that to participate in the struggle for peace in the world, as UNESCO has urged for the new millennium, we need to continue to fight against racial privilege and for respect—to fight in order to assure our civil, social, cultural, and political rights.

These four very powerful contributions furnish a diverse set of data and information that can be used to improve—theoretically, methodologically, and empirically—the research agenda as well as other initiatives in Black education. In this sense, this research is contributing to building a rightful democratic place for this field of scientific, pedagogical, and political knowledge. In different ways, the research prepared for the Commission draws our attention to the contours of Black Education as a field of study and action by pointing out and directly discussing significant questions concerning Black education in the context of:

- racial relations;
- scientific and political recognition of the knowledge produced in this field of research and pedagogical action;
- the examination and criticism of non-African theoretical approaches that are useful for understanding and explaining findings on and for Black Education;
- the human costs of an undemocratic racialized education; and
- similarities and differences in conditions of education offered to Black people in different countries.

In what follows, I will address specific aspects of these preceding chapters in comparison with the social and cultural situation of Afro Brazilians and with research and pedagogical issues for and related to Black people in Brazil.

THE STATUS OF BLACK EDUCATION IN BRAZIL

Before going further, it is necessary to explain that in Brazil Black education is a subject that is discussed only within the context of the Black movement. The principal reason for this situation certainly lies in the fact that Afro Brazilians are, for the most part, outside of schools physically and culturally. Just a few examples will serve to illustrate this point: No more than 3% of the youth between 18 and 24 years of age are students in college (faculties) and the history and literature courses taught neglect African history and African literature, even African literature in Portuguese, the language that we speak in Brazil. (Brazil is a former Portuguese colony.) Another reason that Black education is not a term that has wide currency in Brazil, no less important than the first example, however, is the belief, or perhaps the wish, which is widely disseminated throughout the society, that what we experience in Brazil is a "racial democracy." This myth has been, if not created, strongly reinforced by the work of the internationally recognized Brazilian sociologist, Gilberto Freire (e.g., *Casa Grande e Senzala*). The myth persists in spite of research by Roger Bastide and Florestan Fernandes—commissioned by UNESCO in the 1950s in order to understand how a racial democracy works—which presented evidence that the so-called racial democracy in Brazil was a sham.

It was only 10 years ago that the official curricula for primary and secondary schools began to include material on cultural pluralism. Now, although in a superficial manner, subjects on Black culture and history can be addressed in the school curriculum. The criticism offered by some Afro Brazilian scholars and groups within the Black movement, however, is that the official material on cultural pluralism omits the actual racial problems in Brazil. To fill this void, works of Black scholars and graduate students are being published and disseminated. This includes my book (Gonçalves & Gonçalves e Silva, 1998), which examines different forms and contexts of multiculturalism; another publication (Gomes & Gonçalves e Silva, 2002) organized to infuse analyses of ethnicity and culture in teacher preparation; a book edited by Munanga (1999) in response to a request from the Ministry of Education that consists of contributions by eleven Black researchers and militants, as well as the series "Black Thought on Education," organized by the Black Studies Group (a Black movement group) from Florianópolis in the state of Santa Catarina (*Série Pensamento Negro em Educação* (Black Thought on Education Series, 1996–2004).

It is worth noting that, even though the term Black education is not used in Brazil, it is not possible to know exactly how many educational initiatives Black movement groups have implemented since the abolition of slavery until today. Very well known are the formal and also the nonformal schools carried out by the "äfoxés" in Bahia, such as Ilê Ayê, Olodum, Araketu in Pará by CEDEMPA, in São Paulo, Rio Grande do Sul, and many other states by the Black Pastoral Agents, by the Unified Black Movement in Goiás, Maranhão, and by the Union Movement of Black Consciousness. The community-based activities of the Black Pastoral Agents are guided by the tenets of liberation theology. For another example, the African Brazilian Studies Center of the Federal University of São Carlos (where I teach) has offered relevant courses and seminars for public school teachers in the region of São Carlos, in the state of São Paulo since 1998.

Finally, it is important also to point out that White people in Brazil are very disturbed when they hear the term "Black education." On the one hand, White Brazilians are concerned not to appear to be racist, as for them "Black education" can be only understood as "bad education," that is, as education that is not qualified, as education that is less than excellent. On the other hand, we Black people in Brazil understand there is a fear of losing space, privileges, and control in their expressions of concern.

As in Africa and elsewhere, opportunities for education for Black people, for the poor, and for other marginalized people are guided by unequal power, discrimination, practices of violence, as well as social class and ethnic divisions. School equipment, supplies, and buildings are inadequate and unreliable. In addition, most teachers are unable to deal with Black people's ways of being, living, and thinking. The most frequently used teaching model is the "teacher's talk and chalk" methodology. Textbooks that "represent portable knowledge and information" (Watkins, p. 130) about Africa, and that have been written taking into account only the Euro Brazilian (White) point of view, do not include enough information concerning African and African-Brazilian history and culture. Furthermore, these textbooks usually are very expensive. As Terezinha Juraci Machado da Silva describes in Chapter 15, school (formal education) helps to whiten Brazilian society, thereby alienating Black children and youth from the culture of their people. This process also encourages the adult population, whether illiterate or not, to lose interest in their African roots.

It is certain that after five centuries of contact with African culture, Euro Brazilians have rewritten their way of being, of thinking, of cultural production, having been influenced directly and indirectly by Africans and Afro Brazilians (and Indians, of course), just as their culture has influenced Black culture in Brazil. But, very often, Euro Brazilians do not recognize these influences; they just appropriate them and try to erase their actual roots. For example, during a recent Carnival parade, a White musician commented, in an interview for television, that the Black musical instruments of the "Samba Schools" have been replaced by White instruments that are used for Portuguese rhythms. Now the music of the Carnival parade in Rio is changing from Samba to "Marchas" (a rhythm that is close to military rhythms). It is important to point out that the curriculum guidelines that the National Council of Education approved in March 2004 have created conditions to change this situation.

TOWARD AN AGENDA FOR CHANGE

Research concerning the situation of Black people in the educational system in Brazil—entrance, retention and outcomes—has been undertaken since the 1980s, mostly by White researchers (e.g., Carlos Hasembalg, Fúlvia Rosemberg, Nelson do Valle, and Luís Cláudio Barcelos). With regard to prejudice and discrimination against Black children, we can find studies done in the 1950s, almost all of which were conceived and developed by White researchers (e.g., Amélia Bicudo; F. Fernandes). In the educational field, the first thesis that addresses Black research questions was not completed until 1985, and it was presented by an Afro Brazilian male (Luis Alberto de Gonçalves). In 1987, I presented the first dissertation by and Afro Brazilian woman in the history of the country. Today about 40 theses can be found, most of them conceived and developed by scholars of African descent.

Concerned about the very low level of interest in questions regarding Black people and education on the part of the educational system and educational researchers, the Brazilian Educational Research and Graduate Studies Association in partnership with the nongovernmental organization (NGO) Educative Action and the Ford Foundation in Brazil decided, since 1998, to finance 10 junior researchers who are studying Black education. The aim of this initiative is to increase interest in the field and to stimulate the organization of research in this area in colleges (faculties) and research centers. In collaboration with the Carlos Chagas Foundation, another Brazilian institution, the Ford Foundation is also offering scholarships to support graduate study for Indian (indigenous) people and Afro descendents whose lower socioeconomic status qualifies them for this financial assistance.

In 2004, the National Council of Education, of which I am a member, approved, with no dissenting vote, the "National Curriculum Legislation for Ethnic-Racial Relationships Education and Teaching Afro Brazilian and African History and Culture." This legislation provides for the broad implementation and dissemination of educational programs in school systems for administrators, teachers, parents, students, and others involved the struggle against racism and discrimination. We hope that this national legislation will support the development of institutional programs, materials, and pedagogical activities at all levels of schooling, from elementary to high schools focusing on education to improve "ethnic-racial relationships" and the teaching of Afro Brazilian and African history and culture. In fact, the Brazilian Black movement considers this national legislation as an important political victory. However, Black militants also know that if Black people are not very vigilant, these provisions for curriculum and educational change will not be implemented appropriately.

These very brief reflections on the status of Black education in Brazil are presented to demonstrate the need for governmental, institutional, and community policies regarding Black Education. In the United States and in Brazil, we need to develop proposals and strategies to improve teacher preparation programs that are supported by the best practices for educating African descent populations. Likewise, more research is needed documenting the success of Black teachers and other successful teachers of Black children (Foster, 1995; Gomes, 1995; Gonçalves e Silva, 1993; Ladson-Billings, 1994). We need also to support studies of community-based, non-formal education initiatives organized and promoted by groups within the Black movement as well as other research to address how children of African descent grow and learn in particular settings. It is very important to demonstrate, with empirical data, "how culture is or can be positively exploited in classroom and pedagogical practice" (Foster, 2001, p. 14). Finally, we need to develop pedagogical content across the disciplines that is linked with our age-old struggle for liberation, to create classrooms that are "safe, where students are respectful, respected, encouraged to take risks, free to fail but can only get better, and [are] intellectually challenged" (p. 27).

To accomplish such an agenda for change, a number of research questions need to be addressed. For example, how can we help teachers to improve their ability to teach Black students effectively—especially White teachers, who are in the majority in Brazil? What kinds of strategies must we create in order to motivate the teachers of teachers to include in their agenda of concerns racial questions and the obstacles that affect Black students' school achievement? What data and other elements must we bring together in order to reconceptualize the meaning of educational excellence on our own terms? What must we do to persuade not only schools, but the entire society, that Black Education, as well as other questions concerning the well-being of Africans and African-descended people, are very serious problems that involve all of the society? What kinds of lessons can we include in the courses and seminars offered to teachers that can move them to join us in the fight for Black people's human rights? What kinds of lessons will give them the necessary and appropriate information, methodologies, and attitudes to provide positive education for Black people and for White people that encourages them to be respectful toward Black people and our culture?

As Kassie Freeman demonstrates in Chapter 6, as a result of the ignorance of educators and researchers with regard to Black peoples' worldview perspective, our values, and culture, official educational policies and school curricula work to keep marginalized groups uneducated or undereducated. By trying to make students who come to school with different traditions of learning, such as those rooted in our African heritage, conform to the requirements of a capitalist society, schools create cultural alienation. Fortunately, however, these processes generate resistance as well.

ON THE ROAD TOWARD FREEDOM AND INTELLECTUAL INDEPENDENCE

In his autobiography, *Long Walk to Freedom*, Nelson Mandela (1994) observes that schools have been designed to reduce the capabilities of and to blunt the lives of Black people. That is why, Mandela argues, each Black person is a political militant, whether he or she is conscious of that or not. This reality reinforces the importance of undertaking comparative studies among Africans on the continent and in the Diaspora, as Freeman powerfully illustrates in Chapter 6. Comparative studies are needed that focus on access and success in educational systems; on material, emotional, and symbolic support for learning; on African traditional styles of learning; on African educational thought; on strategies for our cultural survival under conditions of enslavement, colonialism, as well as other forms of oppression and discrimination. It is also important to emphasize that the results of these studies must be disseminated widely within each society, after careful analysis, interpretation, and "translation" of the White language of research, that is, the mainstream research discourse.

Carol D. Lee's substantive analysis of the state of research knowledge about the education of African Americans (Chapters 3 and 4) has important implications for Black education in Brazil. As do other authors in this volume, Lee dialogues with the mainstream research literature of Euro American scholars but interprets this literature using an African-centered referent or point of view as she identifies possibilities for racial misunderstanding. Rejecting what can be used against us and emphasizing European and Euro American theories that offer the best possibilities for understanding human phenomena and the dynamics of learning and teaching, Lee selects those theoretical orientations that are most helpful in explaining research findings concerning the education of Black people. In sum, she identifies those theoretical orientations that are less than helpful to the extent that they contribute to the destruction of our identity, that is, our cultural point of reference.

Lee's approach suggests an important and relevant question to be considered in a transformative research and action agenda for human freedom. How can we achieve the intellectual independence proclaimed by the Commission on Research in Black Education? That is, how can we best engage in a dialogue with the theories of White or mainstream scholars, while presenting on the same level the theories we are constructing from our African cultural point of view—theories that have emerged from our experiences of oppression and resistance? This is not an easy task because, as Sylvia Wynter has observed, we have been educated professionally and scientifically trained within a White mind-set (see Appendix B). By contrast, White people, for the most part, do not give any consideration or validity to what in their minds is classified as primitive, as a nonscientific culture. Thus, another dimension of the question about how to dialogue with the theories of White scholars is that we need to discuss the concerns we have about the sources of our theoretical positions and references. Furthermore, we need to decide how best to communicate these concerns, if they are to be understood by non-Blacks, without reproducing these shortcomings in our own analyses and proposals. In other words, our White colleagues are often not open to producing dimensions of knowledge that are not rooted and grounded in their "own." In my experience, there is a tendency among non-Black scholars to try to agree with or to try to understand our approach(es) but only if there is something in it to benefit them. In this sense, a very challenging question that we have to face is how to find strategies to have our scientific theories and research recognized by the scientific community on our own terms. Therefore, we must find the right way to link our knowledge production to mainstream White approaches without being subsumed by them.

CONCLUDING COMMENTS

In closing, I want to strongly endorse the relevance of the methodology of the online course CORIBE developed for implementing the agenda we are building cross-nationally. I recommend the implementation of a new course that will include Black graduate students from institutions on the continent and in the Diaspora. Such an online course would provide a very unique opportunity for exchanging ideas and information about similar and particular questions; it will be a great opportunity to define more precisely our needs for research and community action. This new online course could be an occasion for the creation of international collaborative research groups and exchanges. Such a collaboration also would challenge us to overcome the language barriers that contribute to our separation and lack of dialogue. A significant theme to be addressed in such a course is the links between research and militant action in our communities. Focusing on community action as a field of study or as a context for research and ways of disseminating research results and applications is of prime importance. In conclusion, I hope that as a result of our participation in the work of the AERA Commission on Research in Black Education and the AERA annual meetings, not only will we better understand our common needs and concerns, but that we also will be able to implement the agenda the AERA Commission on Research in Black Education has put forward. We need to translate our ideas into a work plan, a calendar, and priorities.

Part VIII

"Ore Ire"—Catalyzing Transformation in the Academy: Our Charge to Keep

INTRODUCTION

A charge to keep I have, a God to glorify
A never-dying soul to save, and fit it to the sky
To serve the present age, my calling to fulfill. . . .

—Charles Wesley (1707–1788)

The chapters in Part VIII bring this volume full circle. Four brief commentaries demonstrate how Commission-sponsored research and professional development activities, as well as the documentary video, "A Charge to Keep," address the epistemological issues as well as the larger crisis in Black education that prompted AERA to establish the Commission. Each chapter demonstrates culturally nurturing research and professional development activities that can, by providing an epistemological alternative, counter the "schizophrenic bind" that Black academics and graduate students (and others) experience in the academy. *"Ore Ire,"* which translates (from Yoruba) as maintaining and aligning our African consciousness with our work (see West-Olatunji, Chapter 19), exemplifies that alternative standpoint. This is "our charge to keep"—a "moral mindpath" (Armah, 1995, p. 10) and spiritually engaged intellectual commitment to scientific inquiry in Black education for the survival and enhancement of African people and ultimately, for the benefit of the human family. What, after all, is the denial and debasement of our African heritage if not the denial, debasement, and distortion of the history of humankind?

These commentaries include analytic descriptions of the CORIBE evaluation, the online graduate student research institute, a demonstration research/apprenticeship experience, a component of this institute, and a review of the COBIRE documentary video. In this video, in a lively interview, Sylvia Wynter explains the culture-systemic theoretical analysis that informs the Commission's approach.

In Chapter 17, "Culturally Sensitive Research and Evaluation: Advancing an Agenda for Black Education," Linda C. Tillman describes the participatory evaluation process, a team effort that she directed as an example of culturally sensitive research. Focusing on the methodology employed to assess more than one CORIBE activity, Tillman describes how the evaluation process also served as a professional mentoring experience for a junior faculty member and a doctoral student. As a professional development process this CORIBE component is consistent with Tillman's own research on mentoring faculty of color. The evaluation and other CORIBE activities also provided opportunities to engage cross-cultural dialogues and perspectives in "liberated space."

Next, in Chapter 18, "*Anayme Nti*"—As Long as I Am Alive, I Will Never Eat Weeds: The Online Institute As a Catalyst for Research and Action in Black Education," Annette Henry, Co-Director of the Online Graduate Research Training Institute, presents a critical analysis of this multifaceted professional development project. Henry demonstrates how this research training experience offered graduate students and participating faculty opportunities for significant engagement with technology, both as a means of instruction and for community building within an African-centered worldview perspective. Although Henry acknowledges a number of factors that compromised the overall success of this endeavor, including "technophobia," she also shows how this experience vitalized her own research focus on Black students and technological literacy as a site for struggle.

Cirecie A. West-Olatunji, in Chapter 19, "Incidents in the Lives of Harriet Jacobs's Children—A Readers Theatre: Disseminating the Outcomes of Research on the Black Experience in the Academy," describes an empirical study/research apprenticeship that also was a component of the online institute. West-Olatunji conducted a Web-based investigation of the experiences of Black faculty and administrators in higher education. Interview responses, which were reported to a Web-board that West-Olatunji designed, indicate problems of cultural and scholarly alienation in both White and historically Black higher education contexts. A growing body of scholarship addresses the particular experiences of Black men and Black women in the academy (Jones, 2000; Mabokela & Green, 2001). As affirmed by the responses this presentation generated among the standing-room-only audience that attended the AERA symposium Readers Theatre performance of the data, many scholars fear that such experiences can be neither openly voiced nor empirically investigated with impunity. The excerpts from the Readers Theatre script that portray, in graphic and sometimes painful detail, the everyday realities of how alienating the Black experience in the academy can be, suggest directions for mentoring, methodological innovation, and further research.

Djanna Hill provides a descriptive review of the CORIBE video documentary in Chapter 20, "Answering a Call for Transformative Education in the New Millennium—A Charge to Keep: The CORIBE Documentary Videotape." The commentaries that conclude this volume suggest the continuing need for applied, culturally nurturing inquiries focused on successful strategies for resisting scholarly alienation in academia and other research settings.

17

Culturally Sensitive Research and Evaluation: Advancing an Agenda for Black Education

Linda C. Tillman
University of North Carolina at Chapel Hill

INTRODUCTION

The Commission on Research in Black Education (CORIBE) Evaluation Group, led by Dr. Linda C. Tillman, completed a participatory evaluation of CORIBE's research and professional development activities (1999–2000). This chapter, which presents a brief overview of the evaluation process, demonstrates how this component of the CORIBE methodology functioned simultaneously as a generative research process as well as a culturally nurturing pedagogical experience. The Commission provided culturally nurturing professional development experiences for faculty and graduate student participants in several activities and research contexts. For instance, the Commission's participatory evaluation process featured a faculty-faculty and faculty-graduate student mentoring component, an example of "overlapping polycentrism"—research, professional developing and evaluation taking place simultaneously within the same culturally nurturing activities.

Also, in keeping with concerns about Eurocentric epistemological and cultural perspectives embodied in the term "mentor," a conscious effort was made to incorporate the concept of Jegna in the roles I and other senior scholars undertook to support the professional development and socialization activities that CORIBE initiated. *Jegna* is an Ethiopian (Amharic) word that refers to a relationship that entails commitment, humility and love (Herbert, 1999). In addition, Jegna/Jegnoch (plural) are special people who have demonstrated determination and courage in the protection of their people, land, and culture, who show diligence and dedication to (African/African American) people, produce exceptionally high quality work and dedicate themselves to the defense, nurturing and development of their young by advancing their people, place, and culture.

I served as Jegna for doctoral candidate, Jean Ishibashi, and William Franklin, an assistant professor of educational psychology with expertise in quantitative research. Professor Franklin's goal, to gain qualitative research skills, was accomplished via a "learning by doing apprenticeship" as a member of the Evaluation Group. Our apprenticeship/mentoring triad (experienced faculty member, new faculty member, and graduate student) represents a participatory evaluation process as well as a collaborative professional development (mentoring) experience for an early career faculty member and a graduate student. The participatory evaluation process engaged this triad in a unique collaborative experience. This chapter addresses these professional development learning experiences from the perspective of recent research on mentoring and culturally sensitive research (Tillman, 2001, 2002) and suggests recommendations for future research.

FACING THE EPISTEMOLOGICAL CRISIS IN AERA HEAD-ON

The Africana worldview perspective that Joyce King articulates in Chapter 1 of this volume informed the CORIBE initiative and the participatory evaluation process. As the report the Evaluation Group prepared for the Commission notes, the "epistemological crisis" and attendant "tensions" within AERA led to the development of professional development experiences that were designed "to meet specific research training needs of African American graduate students." These activities provided "opportunities for transdisciplinary discussion and online deliberations among scholars in order to address the perilous condition of Black education in the United States and other contexts" (Tillman et al., 2000, p. 1). The demonstration research projects and professional development activities the Commission supported responded "to a call to AERA scholars to join in a collaborative effort to explore a culturally grounded conceptual and methodological approach to research and Black education" (p. 4).

A GENERATIVE EVALUATION METHODOLOGY

The evaluation research design permitted an exploration of alternative ways to conduct research using an Africana worldview perspective. That is, the evaluators attempted to assess the outcomes of the CORIBE initiatives in a manner that recognizes research as a cultural artifact. More specifically, the methodological design used in this participatory research process was regarded as a cultural artifact of the state of education for Black people as it was examined through the various components of the CORIBE initiative. Through this generative methodology and exploratory evaluation process, the Evaluation Group sought to employ culturally specific and culturally sensitive research procedures (Tillman, 2002). Critical elements of an African-centered ethos implicit in the research activities that were the focus of our research and the theoretical understanding of the universal humanism inherent in the Commission's efforts are evident in the research design.

A generative evaluation methodology evolved as CORIBE's various activities developed during this two and a half year initiative. The Evaluation Group used qualitative research methods to collect, analyze, and interpret data from the following components of the CORIBE initiative: (a) the Online Graduate Research Training Institute, (b) CORIBE demonstration research projects, which included the Songhoy Language and Culture Online Course, as well as (c) the CORIBE Working Colloquium and (d) the graduate student apprenticeships shown here.

The combination of both separate and interconnected or overlapping activities (online instruction and mentoring/apprenticeships versus Working Colloquium versus online Songhoy language and culture pilot course) required an evaluation methodology that was developed on a continuous basis. Rather than implement a fixed research design separately for each component of the evaluation, the evaluators used multiple data collection and analysis procedures that would allow an evaluation of the broad scope of the CORIBE initiative as well as the simultaneous assessment of several components. For example, whereas interviews with graduate student Online Institute participants could be conducted via e-mail, data collection at the Working Colloquium required the evaluators to take extensive field notes and to conduct both structured and unstructured interviews during this two-day meeting.

Procedures used to collect, analyze, and interpret the data included:

1. Using collective and individual cultural perspectives as an analytical lens;
2. Identifying, collecting and analyzing data using the multiple perspectives of the Evaluation Group: an African American female professor with expertise in qualitative research methods, who also served as a Jegna/mentor, an African American male professor, who also was an apprentice/mentee, and a Japanese American female graduate student, who also was an apprentice/mentee and cross-cultural partner;

3. Providing opportunities for African American graduate students to dialogue with one another and with African American faculty—dialogues that many participants felt were absent in their institutions;

4. Maintaining an awareness of and sensitivity to graduate students' career and psychosocial needs related to their growth and development as mature adults and developing scholars;

5. Seeking cross-cultural views by interviewing and engaging participants from diverse races/ethnicities in the United States and other parts of Africa and the Diaspora; and

6. Posing questions that were directly related to participants' lived experiences/realities (in the academy, as researchers, as users of technology, for example).

DATA SOURCES AND ANALYSES

The culturally sensitive research evaluation drew on various triangulation techniques. We triangulated data by using a variety of data sources including interviews with the directors of various CORIBE activities, faculty mentors, graduate students, and CORIBE Commissioners and Elders. Triangulation within the Evaluation Group was accomplished by using evaluation procedures that drew on the perspectives of the lead evaluator/mentor and two mentees. The lead evaluator/mentor helped the mentees to identify critical aspects of the various components of the initiative that were the focus of their assessment, develop interview and observation protocols and develop coding categories/themes for data analysis. Multiple perspectives were also used to accomplish theory triangulation. For example, the graduate student mentee offered a cross-cultural perspective of her experiences in the academy and as a member of the Evaluation Group. Additionally, methodological triangulation was accomplished by using interviews, observations, questionnaires, participant-observation, and document analysis. Technology was a primary method of data collection and the CORIBE Web site and e-mails were used as primary methods of communication. The Web site made it possible to conduct interviews, participate in chat rooms, observe discussion threads, and analyze documents posted on the website.

Analytic codes included but were not limited to the following:

1. *Socialization*: Black graduate students and Black faculty, culture of the department/institution, graduate student, and faculty roles

2. *Mentoring*: Black graduate student and Black faculty needs, availability of mentors, graduate student learning, and development

3. *Distance learning*: Digital divide, technological expertise, use/value of technology as a method of communication across institutions

4. *Research training:* Epistemological concerns, tensions, and paradigm shifts within AERA, graduate student learning and development
5. *Africana worldview perspective*: Importance to Black education, how it is used, opportunities for cross-cultural alliances.

These analytic codes encompassed the entire scope of the CORIBE initiative but could also be applied to specific CORIBE activities or components. For example, the analytic code *mentoring* was used to analyze student and faculty experiences not only in the context of the Online Institute component but also could be applied to the experiences of Black faculty and graduate students in various types of postsecondary institutions. The analytic code *Africana worldview perspective* was used to analyze participants' knowledge of this perspective and how such a perspective shapes their research focus, funding, and so on. The research design and evaluation was consistent with Tillman's (2002) framework for culturally sensitive research approaches: culturally congruent research methods, culturally specific knowledge, cultural resistance to theoretical dominance, culturally sensitive data interpretations, and culturally informed theory and practice.

THE ONLINE INSTITUTE

In Chapter 19, Annette Henry offers an insider's perspective of the Online Graduate Research Training Institute. We asked graduate student participants to provide qualitative reflections about their participation in the various components of this activity, for example, Annette Henry's critical analysis of the AERA annual meeting program apprenticeship experience, other Web-based modules/apprenticeships, and their experiences using technology as the primary mode of communication (see Table 17.1). An analysis of the participants' reflections indicates that the Online Graduate Research Training Institute was perceived as an effective method of: (a) interacting with accomplished African American scholars from various institutions (mentoring); (b) developing new skills; and (c) expanding their knowledge base about research epistemology and methodology from an Africana worldview perspective (research training).

An analysis of the responses of student and faculty Online Institute participants regarding their varied mentoring experiences indicate that both groups valued the collaborative and participatory nature of the relationships they established. These relationships helped to meet students' intellectual and personal needs in terms of socialization into the academy, guidance and direction, development of research skills, understanding how to pose questions and becoming/staying connected to an Africana worldview perspective. The following statements are illustrative of responses

TABLE 17.1
CORIBE Research Apprenticeships

Jegna/Jegnoch	Apprenticeship Focus	Participant Institutions
Dr. Mwalimu Shujaa Medgar Evers College, CUNY Dr. Nah Dove, Medgar Evers College, CUNY	Developing the DIRECT Center online relational database of bibliographic references on intergenerational cultural transmission and identity in the African world (DCTAW)	State University of New York, Buffalo Medgar Evers Colleges, CUNY
Dr. Mwalimu Shujaa Medgar Evers College, CUNY	Editing submissions for the DIRECT Center "Uncovering Connections Conference" and online journal	University of New Orleans, LA
Dr. Cirecie A. West-Olatunji Xavier University, LA	Translating qualitative web-based research data into a Readers Theater –Minstrel Performance for an invited AERA 2000 Division G Symposium	Xavier University of New Orleans, LA
Dr. Annette Henry, University of Illinois, Chicago	Developing a critical analysis of the state of research on Black Education in the AERA 2000 annual meeting program.	UC Berkeley University of Illinois, Chicago
Dr. Linda C. Tillman University of New Orleans	Producing a participatory qualitative evaluation of: (a) the Online Graduate Research Training Institute and (b) the Online Songhoy Language and Culture Demonstration Course	Cal State–LA UC Berkeley

from the evaluation group's online questionnaire as well as interviews with individual graduate student participants:

- "My experiences as a graduate student have been enriching and mentoring has been a tool which has showed me the path. My mentor saw something in me that I was too inexperienced to notice and cultivated that something into a mission."
- "We need a lot of mentoring and direction—a lot of immersion in who we are as African people."
- "My needs as a graduate are to have contact with scholars who talk about the importance of color. The Online Institute helps to make

contacts and creates an awareness about the different theories that are culturally grounded."

The opportunity to become a part of the Commission's deliberations on the "epistemological crisis" in AERA that Edmund Gordon's task force (1997) identified, and to contribute to the development of a changed paradigm within the association, was a significant factor in the graduate students' desire to participate in the CORIBE Online Institute. In addition, during the CORIBE Professional Development and Training Workshop the directors of the Online Institute convened at the 2000 AERA annual meeting, both faculty and student participants affirmed the quality and content of the instruction provided and the ongoing need for this type of research training initiative. Participants also had an opportunity to interact with international scholars who were invited to serve as Jegnoch during this event.

DISTINCTIVE VOICES AND LEARNING BY DOING APPRENTICESHIPS

William Franklin, one of my mentees in the Evaluation Group, completed a qualitative evaluation of the Online Songhoy Language and Culture research demonstration project, with my support. Franklin's evaluation, which triangulated data from several sources (interview and questionnaires), concludes:

> The interviews and student evaluations indicate that this brief demonstration project served as a powerful learning experience. The general consensus is that this kind of learning experience is needed because of its focus on technological literacy skills, language learning and cultural relevance.

I also served as Jegna for Jean Ishibashi, the doctoral student who assisted in developing the coding scheme for the analysis of the various components of the evaluation project and the interview protocol. She also contributed to the selection and analysis of relevant literature.

The distinct voices of the individual members of the triad contributed to a shared perspective on research epistemology and methodology that reflects an Africana worldview perspective and a cross-cultural perspective. The Africana worldview perspective that shaped the Commission's activities also "eschews exclusivity and absolutism: It recognizes that all people have culture and it values the insights of multiple voices" (Evaluation Report, included in the CORIBE Report to AERA, p. 4). The Evaluation Group's report documents the ways in which CORIBE's initiatives constructively engaged epistemological issues using culturally nurturing approaches. In the CORIBE Evaluation Report Jean Ishibashi affirms the importance of the space the CORIBE evaluation methodology provided for sharing cross-cultural perspectives:

> ...As an outsider to the experiences of African Americans and the Diaspora as well as on the Continent, I was privileged to be included in the initial phase of the CORIBE initiative within AERA. As a community educator and activist engaged in coalition and alliance building cross-culturally for several decades, I was excited by the possibility of CORIBE *researching, recognizing, respecting* and *retelling* Africana perspectives within a predominantly Eurocentric space, the American Educational Research Association (AERA).... Although the research was conducted in an academic context dominated by Eurocentric and colonialist legacies such as racial, class, gender, and linguistic hierarchies, participants crossed those hierarchical borders in order to practice Africana worldviews and values. (CORIBE Evaluation Report, http://www.coribe.org)

Ishibashi's observations demonstrate the value of the culturally based, culturally sensitive approach to mentoring (Tillman, 2001) that was a fundamental dimension of the participatory evaluation process. The experience Ishibashi describes is a departure from the dominant paradigm approach to research and is one that Joyce E. King and I have used in another setting (Tillman et al., 1999). In the CORIBE evaluation report, Ishibashi's reflections on her learning experiences support Gonçalves e Silva's observations in Chapter 16 about how "we" can be affected (and limited) by dominant paradigms, often without our conscious awareness:

> ...[A]s an Asian American, I need to *recognize* the "orientalization" of my cultural legacies by Eurocentric and Colonialist frameworks. CORIBE has assisted me in this effort by allowing me to distinguish Africana worldviews from Eurocentric worldviews that would stereotype, commodify and exoticize Africans, the Diaspora and their/our respective cultures.... CORIBE's recognition of the value of the Africana worldview makes possible coalitions and alliances within the academy in ways that cross borders and free our imaginations, memories and knowledge. (CORIBE Evaluation Report, http://www.coribe.org)

In sum, the CORIBE initiative was effective in addressing some of the most crucial and pressing issues that are pertinent to the education and professional socialization of African Americans and other graduate students and faculty of color in higher education.

CONCLUDING COMMENTS

The Evaluation Group identified two outcomes of the CORIBE initiative that are consistent with my earlier research (Tillman, 2001) on African American faculty in predominantly White institutions. This study shows that not only is it important for African American faculty to be provided opportunities to participate in mentoring arrangements, but it is also important that these mentoring experiences be culturally relevant. The data collected from African American faculty who participated in the research apprenticeship that Cirecie A. West-Olatunji (Chapter 19) organized and presented as a Readers Theatre validates the need to form a network of Jegnoch faculty to assist graduate students and beginning, untenured faculty to realize their career and psychosocial goals. Particularly with regard to research, writing, and publishing, respondents indicate the importance of having a relationship with Jegnoch while they are graduate students in order to become socialized to the requirements of the academy and develop and maintain an Africana worldview perspective.

Although mentoring has been found to be important for all untenured faculty, it may be particularly important for African American faculty in predominantly White institutions who continue to be underrepresented in these institutions. According to participants in the earlier study, such mentoring should begin in graduate school and should address both career and psychosocial needs and goals. Mentoring is one way to socialize graduate students to the norms and expectations of the academy. Additionally, it is important that mentoring addresses the professional and social isolation that African American graduate students (and faculty) may experience—issues that contributed to the establishment of the CORIBE initiative. An emergent theme in my research is that mentees seek out same-race mentors with similar personal and cultural backgrounds and who could provide support in coping with feelings of isolation. Both Annette Henry and Cirecie A. West-Olatunji present concrete examples of professional and social isolation in the chapters that follow.

The professional development components the Commission on Research in Black Education initiated can be deemed successful in identifying salient professional, personal and educational issues that affect Black faculty. Needed now are efforts to implement long-term policies and procedures that will focus on an agenda for Black education that includes support for Black faculty and graduate students in the academy as well as a commitment to recruiting, training, and retaining African Americans and other graduate students and faculty of color. Over the last several years, AERA has made significant efforts to assist these groups though grants, scholarships, fellowships, and mentoring experiences. The CORIBE initiative reinforces the importance of this type of support within AERA and presents a framework for the establishment of formal arrangements that can facilitate and advance an agenda for Black education that includes higher education. Our colleagues in other Diaspora countries affirm that a global approach in these efforts as well as online technology would be beneficial.

18

"Anayme Nti"—As Long As I Am Alive, I Will Never Eat Weeds: The Online Institute As a Catalyst for Research and Action in Black Education

Annette Henry
University of Illinois at Chicago

"Anayme nti," an African proverb, expresses the notion of usefulness, integrity, meaning, and value, and perhaps, interpreted thusly, "As long as I live, my life will be useful." Often, our research teaches us, points us toward new and useful connections, or even wakes us up to what is already present but not readily seen. In this brief essay, I discuss the outcomes of the Online Graduate Research Training Institute, one of the many interrelated CORIBE projects. As stated on the opening page of the Online Institute on the CORIBE Web site:

> Through online conferencing with instructors and other participants, Web-based research and assignments, graduate students will critically examine epistemological alternatives to mainstream research and experience culturally nurturing teaching and research paradigm perspectives. They will also develop critical research and writing skills in the context of rethinking disciplinary assumptions. (http://www.CORIBE.org)

In this chapter, I want to discuss how this project has extended my research focus regarding Black students and technological literacy. Outcomes from the Online Institute suggest that it is axiomatic to understand technological literacy as a site of education struggle for Black students.

CONCEPTUAL FRAMEWORK OF THE ONLINE INSTITUTE

Using technology as a methodological tool, Joyce E. King and I conceptualized and designed a pilot project to work with African American graduate student researchers during the summer of 1999. This Online Institute was framed by three broad overarching goals to: (a) invite African American doctoral students to reconceptualize educational research and the educational research community using the World Wide Web; (b) foster collaborative, interactive and perhaps lifelong academic relationships among Black doctoral students working on interrelated issues in African American education, and (c) provide opportunities for dialogue between African American graduate students and scholars doing innovative work. The theoretical framework for this course was that of the CORIBE initiative, which builds on the scholarship of Sylvia Wynter (2003). Hence, the title of the Online Institute: "We Must Sit Down and Talk Together (Online) about a Little Culture," is an adaptation of the title of a seminal Wynter (1968/1969) essay.

The 4-week interactive course was planned to provide online dialogue/mentoring experiences with senior African American researchers such as Gloria Ladson Billings, Etta R. Hollins, Carol D. Lee, William Watkins, and Mwalimu Shujaa, to name a few. These scholars were involved in CORIBE, and several had written papers for the CORIBE symposium at the 2000 AERA annual meeting in New Orleans. The Online Institute was the hub for several modules available to the students, including a critical analysis of the AERA annual meeting program, which I directed. The goal was to critically examine the AERA program in light of participants' research interests using a content analysis approach. Content analysis, an important research tool, has been used in the history of uncovering truths and rewriting the historical and contemporary worlds of Black people. For example, Ida B. Wells (1862–1929) used this method to collect and analyze written documents regarding 728 lynchings. Her published research exposed the purposes and practices for the dominant society of the lynching of Black people. The aim of a critical analysis of the AERA program would be to cull both epistemological and methodological issues regarding the design and execution of research from Africana (or informed Black) perspectives. Participants were to demonstrate capability of searching for relevant material, summarizing it, arranging it by themes, and relating it to their research. Another component of the proposed work included attending

AERA sessions to hear research papers and interact with scholars researching Black issues pertinent to the interests of the graduate students.

MULTILAYERED AND CONTRADICTORY PROCESSES AND FINDINGS

Joyce E. King and I had recruited fifteen doctoral students throughout the
United States through scholars associated with CORIBE. Their preliminary
assignment entailed posting an autobiographical introduction, a response
to the novel *The African* by Harold Courlander (1967), as well a response
to *Lest We Forget*, a multimedia Powerpoint photo-essay. Three students
from Chicago, New York, and Los Angeles, respectively, responded by
logging on to Blackboard, a course management system, and introducing
themselves. For example:

> I am a mother, teacher-scholar and community activist. I entered the research
> arena with hope to gain knowledge that would provide a better understand-
> ing for what I observed teaching children for over 30 years in urban schools.
> My doctoral student experience has been a struggle to maintain integrity and
> focus. I've been able to survive by staying grounded in teaching practice. I
> have continued to be a primary teacher throughout my doctoral studies. I in-
> vestigate African American teaching practices and the relationship between
> theory and practice.

However, this participant and others soon became discouraged with the
project during its preliminary stages.

TECHNOPHOBIA AND THE PARADOX OF COMMUNITY

The novel (*The African*) was out of print. The graduate students showed
disinterest in using Blackboard and became frustrated with the technology. Some were unable to open or download the PowerPoint presentation
(*Lest We Forget*). Those enrolled from my institution complained about the
unavailability/inaccess to high quality computers. Similarly, Online Institute faculty expressed disinterest in learning technological communicative
modes such as Blackboard and PowerPoint. One exclaimed that she was
"paid to be a researcher" and did not have the time for anything else. A few
faculty were clearly embarrassed about their lack of technological facility.
(We learned this after the completion of the project.) CORIBE provided
hands-on, confidential, individualized assistance by appointment and on
demand, via telephone. Heidi Lovett Daniels, an expert instructional technology specialist, also a participating graduate student, provided this cus-
tomized support. This experience confirmed how online activities beyond
e-mail can be alienating in an environment already alienating for many
Black faculty and students.

My co-director and I had assumed that the online approach would be perceived as an opportunity to use an interesting communicative tool to expand a research community. However, for the most part, the graduate students and faculty expressed fear, or "lack of time," to engage in learning new methods. We had overlooked this "technophobia." Paradoxically, the Online Institute was designed to engender community beyond institutional borders, yet it contributed to the already alienating academic environment inhabited by the participants.

GROUP CONVERSATION: SHARING OUR RESEARCH WITH THE COMMUNITY

The project had flopped. Or so I had thought. During the CORIBE professional development and training mini-conference at AERA, 2000, I shared the Online Institute's goals and modus operandi with the group of eight African American doctoral students who had signed on for this workshop, of whom two had been part of the online pilot project. I presented the methodology and contradictory findings. As Linda Tuhiwai Smith (1999) writes, "Sharing is a responsibility of research. For indigenous researchers, sharing is about demystifying knowledge, and information and speaking in plain terms to the community" (p. 160). For Black researchers, sharing the research agenda and the findings with one's community is integral to the integrity of the research. The community members' presence and participation were fundamental to this "process-building methodology" (King, 2001). The process gave us an opportunity for reflexive exchange about the uses, tensions, and possibilities of this project. To my surprise, the graduate students were encouraged by the idea. As one responded, "If I'd known of this opportunity to be mentored by African American researchers, I would have signed up." She confirmed the "face validity" (Lather, 1991) of the project, that is, that the work made sense to others. "It is achieved by checking your analyses, descriptions and conclusions with at least some of the participants in your research" (Ristock & Pennell, 1996, p. 50). Validity in research for the Black community must be achieved through accountability both to the participants and to those who will be affected by the outcomes. As Patti Lather (1991) has written, catalytic validity is achieved when participants and the broader community affected by the research feel energized or reoriented in some way by the project.

REFLECTIONS ON WORKING IN THE COMMUNITY

I have always had ambivalence about the ways in which "technology" is promoted in North American society. As international scholars illustrate, it can act as another kind of cultural imperialism (Hawisher & Selfe, 2000).

Regarding the Online Institute, however, I welcomed an opportunity to examine Web-based instruction. The opportunity to experience new ways of thinking about teaching, and the opportunity to mentor young scholars were seductive reasons to carry out the project.

Researchers have examined the "digital divide" of racial/ethnic groups and the inequality of access to computers in schools along the dimensions of class, gender, and race (Bryson & Castell, 1998; Oquendo-Rodriguez, 1999; Pearson & Young, 2002). I can only speculate the degree to which these elements played in this graduate student apprenticeship/mentoring project. My students bemoaned the conditions of their home computers to download the needed class materials; however, we had two state of the art computer laboratories in the building that houses our college, not to mention other laboratories on campus. Perhaps, the university was already such an alienating environment that the extra step to come onto campus seemed harrowing. The students' technological literacy seemed inadequate for the task. For example, one student did not realize that PowerPoint, the program needed to do the initial *Lest We Forget* assignment, was a feature on all the computers in the College of Education laboratory. Students seemed unable to navigate Blackboard, although there was online and offline help available. Moreover, students' other commitments (academic and otherwise) played a role in their lack of participation. Sharing the experience at the AERA mini-course confirmed the need to continue such work as a way of working with and mentoring graduate students.

NEW CONNECTIONS: CONTINUING THE RESEARCH

The Online Institute precipitated my interest in educational discourses of technological literacies. How are these literacies being defined and taught? To whom, by whom, and from what epistemological/political positions? These questions led me in two directions. First, I began taking courses in Web-based instruction through our university, including a weeklong summer faculty institute at University of Illinois at Urbana Champaign. Second, and more important for this discussion, I began to read voraciously on themes of race, literacy, gender, and technology (since, ultimately, the Online Institute was comprised of female graduate students). A review of the research literature informed me that despite many educational initiatives over the past 20 years, young women, especially those from diverse socioeconomic and ethnocultural backgrounds, are poorly represented in professions and careers related to science, mathematics, and technology (AAUW, 1991; 1999; Barr & Birke, 1998). Girls' and women's participation in these fields appears to be diminishing (AAUW, 2000; Jenson, 1999). Our current information age economy demands a strong foundation in technology, mathematics, and science. Current data reveal that, although women and people of color have made progress in some of these areas, their progress is declining in other areas (Sanders & Peterson, 1999). For example, women earned 37% of the computer science bachelor's degrees in 1984 but only 28% in 1996. Between 1992 and 1996, the full-time enrollment of minority students in engineering decreased by 5% (National Science Foundation, 2000). Technological literacies, then are sites of Black educational struggle (Hooper, 1998; Moses, 2001; Pinkard, 2001; Tate, 2001). According to Bob Moses (2001), the former civil rights activist and founder of The Algebra Project, "economic access and full citizenship depend crucially on math and science literacy" (p. 5). Moses and others such as William Tate (2001) argue passionately for science, mathematics and technology education in urban environments.

I am currently involved in a process-building methodology at a school for girls. The curricular focus is mathematics, science, and technology. I am conducting a multiyear study of teaching and learning in this unique environment in which girls, especially girls from diverse sociocultural backgrounds, learn mathematics, science, and technology (as well as the humanities and social sciences) in cooperative, collaborative classrooms.

The study takes place in a predominantly African American setting (67% Black, 15% Latina). The goal of this research is to investigate teaching and learning activities that contribute to adolescent girls' development of scientific, mathematical and technological literacies. Research in such a setting is significant— girls, especially girls of African descent and girls from diverse socioeconomic and cultural backgrounds, are highly underrepresented in mathematics, science, and technology classes and careers. The challenges of educating Black girls in large urban school districts have never been greater. Quality education has been threatened by teacher shortages, lack of funding, a paucity of resources and cultural incongruences, among other factors.

"ANAYME NTI": AS LONG AS I AM ALIVE, I WILL NEVER EAT WEEDS

The dominant culture teaches us to privilege some ways of knowing and to devalue others. Perhaps the Online Institute contributed to the ever increasing privileging of Web-based instruction without thinking about socioeconomic and sociopolitical factors. The institute and my consequent examination of Black girls and literacy have allowed me to witness that issues of access and equity continue to be embroiled in the new discourses of education, namely, those of technological literacies. Indeed, research can be an effective teacher, guiding us toward new research connections and ways to broaden the discussion of Black educational issues. The Online Institute helped raise issues and directions for my continued research in the African American community.

19

Incidents in the Lives of Harriet Jacobs's Children—A Readers Theatre: Disseminating the Outcomes of Research on the Black Experience in the Academy

Cirecie A. West-Olatunji
University of Florida

INTRODUCTION

Much of the current literature on the African American experience in academia utilizes the deficit model in which the individual is the focus of the study rather than the collective consciousness of the participants (John, 1997). Moreover, current publications in this area lack the thematic link to faculty development and graduate student mentoring programs. The purpose of the study (and research apprenticeship) described in this chapter was to capture the voices and experiences of African American faculty and administrators in academia in order to delineate the implications for mentoring graduate students and faculty. Issues of resiliency as well as personal and collective empowerment are presented within the conceptual framework of culture-centered theory applied to higher education research and practice (Freeman, 1998). As such, this study involves a discussion of the implications of African-centered worldviews (Kambon, 1996; Schiele, 1994; Tedla, 1995), African-centered research (King & Mitchell, 1995), and African-centered acts of resilience and transformation (Ani, 1994) for higher education.

AN OVERLAPPING RESEARCH DESIGN

The methodology used in this study involved WebBoard, an online data collection tool. Data included an initial group interview (via a conference call) with eight African American faculty and administrators. A preliminary analysis of emergent themes guided the development of a Web-based format that was designed to document the experiences of an intentional sample of respondents in selected institutions. WebBoard data was managed by graduate research assistants and was supplemented by elite interviews with selected respondents and data collected from various other sources. A secondary analysis of themes was triangulated with the initial data analysis.

Two graduate students assisted with the implementation of this study as part of the CORIBE OnLine Graduate Research Institute. Incorporated into the research design, this emphasis on involving African American graduate students in the research was a way to sensitize them to issues Black faculty (and others of color) frequently confront in higher education and to facilitate critical awareness of skills correlative with a satisfying academic career. This experience has greatly affected the graduate students involved with the study primarily in that it has provided them with more realistic expectations regarding the academy while highlighting the importance of establishing a support network with individuals who share their cultural and philosophical worldview. More important, students spoke of how the experience reinforced their commitment to the validity of using an African-centered research paradigm.

TENETS OF AN AFRICAN-CENTERED
RESEARCH PARADIGM

African-centered research methodology, a specific form of culture-centered research, was chosen as the framework for this study because of its emphasis on transformation, liberation, and praxis (King & Mitchell, 1995). Traditional research methodology stems from the empirical roots of scientific (and, by extension, social scientific) investigation that evaluates the quality, strength, and rigor of a study based upon the semantic argument of the researcher. This myth of objectivity on the part of the researcher is called into question outside of the realms of positivistic research, mainly by the tenets of qualitative theory (Fine, 1994).

However, culture-centered researchers offer another option for maximizing the trustworthiness of liberating social science by moving from objectivity to transubjectivity in which they generate the research within (as part of) the collective experience of the participants. Transubjectivity allows the researcher to become part of the collective experience of the participant(s). In this manner, the researcher experiences a duality of self that is reflexive, reciprocal, and transformative. Personal commitment, personal contact (physical and spiritual), and personal responsibility to the collective is part of the research process. Specifically, African-centered thought and research suggest a form of knowing that is in the practice of a people. African-centered research also calls into question the assumption that dominant social science research methodology is itself universal. Western research reflects an emphasis on individualism, independence, autonomy, mastery of nature, and materialism. Different forms of being and knowing suggest different forms of defining self in relation to others. Research reflecting values stemming from an African-centered experience evidences reciprocity, interdependence, and a responsibility to transform the collective community. African-centered research establishes transformation as a key element from research design through analysis. At the design stage, African-centered research involves personal commitment, personal contact, and personal responsibility. Analysis and interpretation are subjective behaviors that evidence the responsibility for transformation as an outcome of the research endeavor. These culture-centered methodological protocols were utilized in this study.

A PERFORMATIVE DISSEMINATION PROCESS

We translated the findings into a Readers Theatre script and performed the data in the format of the Negro minstrelsy as an invited symposium at the 2000 annual meeting of AERA. The symposium served as a springboard for scholarly discussion of the content and quality of mentoring experiences needed at each level of academic advancement. The Readers Theatre symposium was entitled, "Incidents in the Lives of Harriet Jacobs' Children in the Academy: A Millennium Minstrel Readers Theatre Performance" (see Box 19.1). The Negro minstrelsy, a distinctive American institution, was born during the 19th century out of the African American experience of enslavement (Toll, 1977; Wittke, 1971). Although popularly misconstrued as a derogatory form of mimicry of Africans by Whites in America, this type of drama is the only original form of theatre in the United States. It provided a literal stage for political commentary and resistance as well as well as economic livelihood for African American entertainers from circa 1830 to the beginning of the 20th century. In the past, minstrel shows provided a new venue for the Brer Rabbit theme of outwitting and outfoxing

---

Box 19.1 *Harriet Jacobs*

Known primarily for her narrative, *Incidents in the Life of a Slave Girl: Written by Herself*, Harriet Jacobs was a reformer, Civil War and Reconstruction relief worker, and antislavery activist. In her autobiographical book, Jacobs describes her life as a Southern slave, her abuse by her master, and involvement with another White man to escape the first, and the children born of that liaison. She also describes her 1835 runaway, her seven years in hiding in a tiny crawlspace in her grandmother's home, and her subsequent escape north to reunion with her children and freedom. During the Civil War, Jacobs began a career working among Black refugees. In 1863, she and her daughter moved to Alexandria, Virginia, where they supplied emergency relief, organized primary medical care, and established the Jacobs Free School—Black-led and Black-taught—for refugees. After the war, they sailed to England and successfully raised money for a home for Savannah's (Georgia) Black orphans and aged. Moving to Washington, DC, she continued to work among the destitute freed people and her daughter worked in the newly established "colored schools," and, later, at Howard University. In 1896, Harriet Jacobs was present at the organizing meetings of the National Association of Colored Women.

---

the "slave master," who held the Africans captive. Moving into the 21st century, this theatre form proves to be an ideal format for the presentation of research findings as it provides a congruency between theory, methodology, and dissemination. This performance genre is thematically consistent with forms of oppression and "masking" that respondents articulated regarding their experience in the academy.

We had hoped that the voices of the Minstrel performers would delineate implications for mentoring new faculty and administrators in the African American tradition. They did. The script/performance generated a discussion of issues of resiliency and empowerment (both personal and collective). The struggles African American faculty and administrators experience in higher education are simultaneously intrapsychic as well as interpersonal. Interpersonal conflicts exist not only between African American academics and their White counterparts but also among African Americans in academia. The intrapsychic conflicts refer to expectations of both the Eurocentric reality of the tenure and promotion processes as well as the internal drive to pursue scholarship steeped in their own often-conflicting realities. The title of the symposium implicates Harriet Jacobs because her life story is an embodiment of acts of empowerment, courage, and resilience (Jacobs, 1988). She is a model for African American academics and her lived experience as a captive who resisted enslavement exemplifies how to navigate through and succeed in the midst of oppression.

FINDINGS AND DISCUSSION

This demonstration research is important because it provides such rich documentation on the quality of experiences among African American academics in diverse institutional contexts. The findings suggest that there are common threads of: (a) pervasive incidents involving exclusion from the mentoring process; (b) the presence of an emergent African consciousness impacting the conceptualization, development, and implementation of research with resulting cultural conflicts in the academic environment (that are interpersonal, intellectual, and systemic); and (c) the desire to pass on what is known to future academics. One overarching theme culled from segments of the script presented here—about struggles of power and oppression in the workplace—can be understood in a context of what bell hooks (1992) calls "White supremacist capitalistic patriarchy." The findings of this study contribute to the knowledgebase in Black education by providing a discussion of future research possibilities that explore culture-centered approaches for enhancing the preparation of African American faculty, administrators, and graduate students.

THE SCRIPT

Streams of Consciousness[1]

Voice #1: I contend that the experiences of African American graduate students is highly analogous to those of African slaves, forced to maintain our culturally based understandings of education within ourselves as we learn the "operative metaphysics" of academic conceptions and dispositions which ignore our cultural strengths and ways of knowing. Particularly in . . . when I started my doctoral program, there was little research which validated culture as a focus of inquiry and perhaps even less which portrayed African Americans as other than dropouts, culturally deficient and a host of other variations on the theme of substandard.

Voice #2: I have often joked about a way to reduce the cognitive and emotional dissonance that arises in my job as an administrator— whether in Black or White institutions. A purse-size six-pack of disposable red bandanas—the headgear that Aunt Jemima used

---

[1] During the performance, members of the cast donned white or black Mardi Gras masks and red headscarves, according to their identities as indicated in the script.

to wear—would be just the thing to tie on lickety-split whenever a situation reaches that dehumanizing level of disrespect
that is so common in these plantation-like institutions.

Voice #3: Well, as a graduate student in a predominantly White institution, I almost always struggled with maintaining my identity
as a Black person/woman and trying to fit in the "politically
correct" way as defined by the institution. That is, as a student
(and now as a faculty member), I was constantly trying not to be
sucked in the "Great White Way" of doing/knowing/thinking/
speaking. But the reality is that if I wanted to survive in that
environment, many times I had to leave some parts of my
"Blackness" and "cultural ways of living" at the door. But I
always picked them up when I left each day. So I think . . . there
is a dissonance between our lived realities and how we are
expected to act in the academy—it's a matter of survival.

Voice #2: As the political climate in the community changed, a high-
ranking Black administrator was forced to resign from a
neighboring school. The message conveyed by administrators
on our campus was:

All Black: Watch yourself. You could be next!

Voice #2: A well-meaning colleague cautioned me not to speak my
mind so freely, reminding me that I am setting myself up
to be "targeted." Sixteen years ago, when I was a beginning
department chair, my Dean invited me to lunch to tell me that
a program that I had planned would upset the Trustees.

White #A "Maybe you're getting ready to fly, fly, fly . . . away from here."

Voice #2: Again, the message was clear. That's when I first started
thinking about marketing those disposable red bandanas.

Voice #1: I remember distinctly, the experience of sitting in qualitative
research methods classes and have professors attempt to
discredit my research ideas because my desire to utilize my
cultural perspective as an analytical perspective persevered
and I attempted to use "repetition and revision" in the process
of "signifying" as a framework through which to understand
the literacy instruction of an African American teacher. Another
qualitative research professor stole my ideas and published
work which used material directly from papers which I had
turned into him. Your presence, your work, as well as that
of the other scholars I mentioned validated my presence and
helped me to know that my inner sensibility related to the true
power of my cultural perspective was not only viable, but that
which was most truly needed in educational research.

Incidents in the Lives...

Voice #A: I am a maid/domestic servant with a Ph.D., expected to validate the White colleagues' research findings, affirm their presence in Black community research settings, and so on. I must validate their ability to "get along" with Black people. One colleague even put on her annual review that...

White #1: [I] "mentor" women faculty of color...

Voice #A: ... (I'm the only Black woman) because she read a manuscript of mine, before I sent it off for review. This is related to the issue of Black students, who want to work with White professors (for their big names, etc.) but then come to me for help with readings, methodology, etc., and complain that the White prof[essor] "doesn't get it". Just this week I let a Black woman know that it was a slap in the face that she is doing a thesis on Black feminism (my area) and working with Mr. Rich White Liberal... that I'm not going to do his work for him, so she should make her choice.

Voice #B: The quote by Anna J. Cooper can be a useful description of the long and often difficult journey when and where individuals who are different from the mainstream by virtue of race enter the tenure track process in the academy. When and where I entered into tenure track positions, the obstacles were already in place. They are familiar: an unsupportive department chair; an isolating cultural environment that relegated my difference to the margin (i.e., never being included in the information flow); an overload of advisees and class preparations while White faculty of the same rank were being protected from too many advisees and classes; a narrowly defined publication channel; and a general lack of support and assistance. Ironically, researchers have concluded that these very familiar obstacles are what prohibit African Americans from being tenured. Yet, the system to deny African Americans tenure is often entrenched and predetermined when and where we enter.

Voice #A: I am a domestic servant/big breast for (disrespectful White) students. In my qualitative research class, a student decided that she didn't want to listen and take notes. She passed around a petition while I was teaching and had students sign it with their email address, requesting that I email them my Powerpoint lectures!! Another woman said...

White #2: "[Missy]..."

Voice #A: (I don't like being addressed this way)...

White #3: "*YOU* need to go to the library and find us some ethnographies. Because I don't have time to go and spend six hours in the library and not find anything because that library sucks!"

Voice #A: I informed her that one of the class assignments provided this information and that just that afternoon I was thinking that certain students expected me to be a big, all-nurturing breast. (That shut her up).

Voice #C: I was hired to teach literature, theory, and composition, that is, to perform in the White academy much as our ancestors were enslaved and cast as mammies to cook for the master and care for his children but were always suspect and never good enough. We sustained and supported the master's children while ours caught the "short end of the stick." My story is one of many years of excellent teaching but no financial or institutional recognition until I resigned to take another teaching position. Only then was I tapped for a teaching excellence award and given a substantial monetary honorarium. This performance is a post–Civil Rights phenomenon that has been repeated at many institutions. White students who have studied with me and who have been primed by me have consistently been admitted to graduate and professional schools. My own "children" are missing from the rosters and when they appear thereon, they have been neglected—trained by post-segregation White institutions—to be second-class intellects. I think I have just been too frightened to tell the story. But I realize that my thirty-six years in the academy leave me no choice but to tell the truth for my own sanity and integrity and for the survival of future generations of our children.

Male #1 & Male #2 (simultaneously):
I was told during an interview with an executive search firm that if I wanted to advance in higher education administration—to become a vice-president, say, or president—I would have to shave off my mustache—that any facial hair on Black males is threatening to White people. My C.V. is ten pages long containing mostly articles published in top refereed journals in my field, experimental psychology. The "'headhunter" had nothing at all to say about my scholarship.

Reflections

Voice ZZ: My graduate experience has been one of disillusionment, transition, and new appreciation and understanding. As a re-entry student I had expected to take some of the hard-won courses not available to me in my previous schooling experience. I was dumbfounded to find our community histories and literature and cultures all framed and code-switched into an academic, dominant Eurocentric, male, middle class points of view.

All Whites: We know what's best for you.

Voice ZZ: I was determined to look for different epistemologies, paradigms, and frameworks and found them in marginalized communities and departments on campus, ethnic studies, women's studies, etc. Even for these courses I had to learn academese to interrogate particular perspectives that were problematic. My transition was, then, to learn this new language while continuing to immerse myself in my community's on-going dialogue that was articulated in non-standard English or different languages entirely. And in order for me to keep being part of my community(ies) I needed to take part in the different ways my life was being shaped by political, economic, social, and cultural forces. There was/is a backlash of anti-immigrant, anti-non standard English, and anti-people of color forces (legislation) in California.

All Whites: We know what's best for you.

Voice ZZ: The latter led me to search for a new understanding of and a realization that academic knowledge was one linear segment or line that made up the immense circle of knowledge and epistemologies that goes largely unrecognized by the academy. That realization gave me a perspective with which to work within the limitations and possibilities of the academy. I was able to re-search different frameworks and see under a different lens my own history/herstory/ourstories.

Voice YY: I realize in retrospect that what I needed most from my committee, and particularly my major advisors, was assistance with publications. And that did not happen. None of my committee members published with their students and I am still paying for that. Most assistant professors who are well published had advisors (or some senior professor) who really helped to prepare them to write, to write well, to write consistently—to be very task-oriented with regard to publications. Well-published assistant professors know the journal editors, they know how to "write like White men," they are very savvy in terms of the whole publication genre.

All Whites: We know what's best for you.

Voice YY: All during my doctoral studies, I was told that I was really a good thinker and writer and that I would have no problem getting published.

All Whites: We know what's best for you.

  Voice ZZ: The system shifts gears; the paradigm shifts so that I always feel destabilized. For example, you're only supposed to write by yourself. Everybody pooh-pooh[ed] theory but now they're on the bandwagon of theory but in a way that doesn't allow every one to participate. I've never ever felt that I am more than a pawn in a game that is already always in motion, where the rules change depending upon who the players are. And the rules change if the players are African American.

All Whites: We know what's best for you.

  Voice ZZ: The profession denies itself the fullness of what we could bring to the profession. If we look like we're going to be too good, the rules change. The profession tends to honor people who fit some kind of mold, but if you step out and bring the fullness of consciousness to the class, to the text, to what you're writing, you have a problem. It's a very select club. I'm struck that people don't realize the degree to which they're being used.

All Whites: We know what's best for you.

POSTSCRIPT: CONCLUDING COMMENTS

Although only three themes were presented in the Readers Theatre format, a total of seven separate themes emerged from the data (see Table 19.1). Over a 24-week period, data was collected from a variety of sources: e-mail correspondence, discussion threads, chats, personal journal entries, telephone conference calls, and interviews. Participants in the study ranged from graduate students, beginning faculty, to seasoned and retired faculty and upper-level administrators ($N = 17$).

The most significant contribution resulting from this investigation was the development of definition, texture, and meaning regarding the Black experience in the academy. Despite the fact that African Americans have been present within both the Historically Black Colleges and Universities (HBCUs) as well as at predominately White institutions, there have not been significant numbers (collectively), that is, critical mass, nor the potential for multigenerational information transmission in the White academy. It may even be argued that the predominate mode of academic theorizing on HBCU campuses mirrors the subjectivity of the White experience.

Of particular interest is the use of technology to unify around one's different-ness. During the study, technology was intentionally used to share a common viewpoint. Technology became the medium for connecting beyond race ("having the commonality of being Black or being Latino

TABLE 19.1
Seven Salient Themes

	Theme	Description
One	"Interaction (Bonding)"	Little or no effort by colleagues to informally and formally theorize, socialize, or intellectualize
Two	"Variables (Streams of Consciousness"	Black academics are often overwhelmed by the multiplicity of micro-aggressions enacted by their White counterparts in the academic workplace
Three	"No Transference of Power/Authority"	Without institutional accountability, neither colleagues nor students acknowledge Black academics as "real" or first-class intellectuals (students continue to challenge grades, never being defined as knowledgeable because of the way in which success is defined in academia, White counterparts' resistance to new perspectives, becoming pariahs)
Four	"Subjective Reality of the White Experience (Reflections)"	Despite the existence of critical inquiry into the perceived universality of the Eurocentric tradition that investigates the hegemony of whiteness and maleness in the Ivory Tower, Black academics articulated the surreality of working among their White colleagues.
Five	"Mutual Benefits of Reciprocity and Transformation"	A sense of hopefulness and expectation that positive outcomes are possible, that multiple centers are beneficial, and that diunital theorizing creates new possibilities for research and praxis.
Six	"Disconnections, Duality, and Divergence"	Understanding the effects of the oppressive academic experience: masking as a form of survival, loss of personal as well as collective identity, impact on their children growing up in the same environment, and the impact on their personal lives.
Seven	"Resiliency"	Despite their experiences in the academy, participants in the study articulated acts of resistance, self-preservation, creativity, resourcefulness, and a pervasive commitment to staying grounded in their own worldview.

isn't enough; there needs to be a common worldview"). The researcher used technology in the methodology and design to facilitate within-group bonding such that participants could share the commonality of the experience of being the "one and only."

The study suggests a potential use of technology to recreate a culturally defined sense of community among African American academics that relies on culture-specific axiology that emphasizes a collective identity (Tedla, 1995). What this may mean is that beginning faculty, such as I, can use technology to develop a strategy for successful navigation in the academic environment by:

a. Anticipating the hegemonic pitfalls by tapping into the wealth of experiences and knowledge of seasoned academic "elders";
b. Getting periodic "reality checks" by maintaining a dialogue with other African American faculty and administrators who are experiencing similar conflicts and challenges regarding the subjective reality of the White experience;
c. Receiving support across disciplines to respond to the challenges in the academic environment by bonding within and across regional and national boundaries; and
d. Believing within one's self that it is possible through the maintenance of personal and collective identity and the realignment of self (*Ore Ire*) and thus encouraging acts of resiliency. "*Ore Ire*" is a West African word from the Yoruba people loosely interpreted as, "realigning of African Consciousness."

ACKNOWLEDGMENT

This study was conducted with the aid of two graduate assistants, Kimberly Frazier, PhD, and Kalpana Saravanan.

20

Answering a Call for Transformative Education in the New Millennium—"A Charge to Keep": The CORIBE Documentary Video

Djanna Hill
William Paterson University

"Woodson in 1935 had looked at the entire educational system and he said that it is set up in such a way as to motivate White students by telling them that they have done everything and to[de] motivate Black students by telling them that they have done nothing. It is the body of knowledge in schools and universities, the system of representation [that we must challenge] that is indispensable to the instituting of our present bourgeois conception of being human."

—Sylvia Wynter (CORIBE Interview, 2002)

INTRODUCTION

"A Charge to Keep: CORIBE 1999–2002" is a powerful video documenting the work of the Commission on Research in Black Education (CORIBE). Recalling the tradition of transcendent inspiration, faith and courage expressed in the hymn from which the title takes its name, this 50-minute tape offers the possibility of a shift to a new worldview—not Afro-centric

or Euro-centric but, rather, evolving from an understanding of humanity beyond today's conception. Viewers are shown this new perspective
through a series of multicultural voices, projects, and events, such as the
preparation and presentation of research papers, a working colloquium
in Georgia's Gullah Land, a demonstration research project that culmi-
nated in the performance of as a Readers Theatre/Minstrel Performance
based on an empirical examination of the experiences of Black educators
in academia, demonstrations of best practices with children of diverse cultural and geographic origins and reflections from renowned educators who
served as members of the Commission, the CORIBE Council of Elders, and
CORIBE scholars.

INTELLECTUAL INDEPENDENCE FOR HUMAN FREEDOM

From its inception in 1999, as an initiative of the American Educational Research Association, CORIBE approached its mission to stimulate research
and policy making to improve education for and about people of African
ancestry with the understanding that issues of Black education are *not* a minority concern but, rather, a reflection of the general state of global injustice.

"A Charge to Keep," the CORIBE video-documentary, has five major
components:

1. A narration and explanation of the "10 Vital Principals of Black Education and Socialization" that CORIBE has presented;
2. A discussion and explanation of the transformative research and action agenda identified and experienced by CORIBE participants (see
   Appendix A);
3. Excerpts of AERA presentations of research or best practices that
   exemplify precepts of the Commission's Declaration on Intellectual
   Independence;
4. A discussion of the systemic conditions that result from a lack
   of meaningful and equitable education, including excerpts from a
   speech by Angela Davis on the prison industrial complex; and
5. An interview with Sylvia Wynter, Professor Emerita at Stanford University, who postulates that the concept of the human, "ethno-class
   'Man'," as currently understood within the Western belief system or
   cultural model of the human, does not fully allow for the interplay
   of biology and sociocultural factors, thereby limiting our awareness
   and freedom as human beings. (See Appendix B-2 for the interview
   transcript.)

The Commission's vital principles, recurring issues, that emerged as
central to CORIBE's concerns about the quality of knowledge and Black

education and socialization, are summarized as follows:

1. Recognition that African people exist as an ethnic family. This perspective is informed by Africana tenets such as interdependence, cooperation, collectivism, synergism, movement, and verve. African-centeredness can be interpreted as a theoretical and methodological orientation that makes possible knowledge about, and understanding of, the cultural history of African people based on their accumulated and shared experiences;

2. A priority of the collective Black family over the individual. For example, an Elders Council, an appointed Commission, diverse academic and community educators, and students completed the work of the Commission with a belief in the importance of collective survival and enhancement;

3. Recognition of three modes of response when dealing with domination and hegemony—adaptation, improvisation, and resistance;

4. The idea that epistemologies or "ways of knowing" provided by the arts and humanities often are more useful in understanding the lives and experiences of oppressed people than the sciences;

5. The need for a research paradigm that emphasizes knowledge production as a search for meaning and understanding, rather than as a search for facts and universal truth;

6. A priority on research validity for studies of African traditions, hegemony, equity, and beneficial practices from the Africana worldview perspective;

7. An emphasis on the importance of context in research building on the notion of praxis in the production and use of knowledge;

8. The urgency of access to education that serves the collective interests of people of African descent;

9. The conviction that education is a fundamental human right that requires appropriate curricula and adequately compensated and qualified teachers to serve the collective interests of African people; and

10. The declaration that African people are not empty vessels and will not accept a dependant status in the approach and solution to our problems.

BEYOND HEGEMONY

The second part of the video presents what a transformative research and action agenda does and addresses why the structure and prevailing epistemological orientation of AERA and the mainstream research establishment impede it. In the video, Asa G. Hilliard, distinguished professor and Commission Elder, addresses this issue: "It isn't that we have not been included, but we have been included in a hegemonic way." A transformative research agenda is about truth-telling, such that "as a people we can recognize ourselves in that truth." Edmund W. Gordon, also a professor of renown and a Commission Elder, advised that paying too much attention to identity concerns, to what "separates us," also could cause us to lose sight of particular ways that we are being exploited. Their remarks were filmed during a panel discussion of Sylvia Wynter's culture-systemic theoretic, chaired by Professor Beverly Gordon, at the CORIBE working colloquium.

In the third part of the video, exemplary educational approaches identified by the Commission illustrate the core precepts of a transformative research and action agenda. The Peachtree Urban Writing Project in Atlanta, GA illustrates "Expanding human understanding." Lisa Delpit, a member of the Commission, addresses the impact of this innovation on student learning and teacher development. The importance of "Nurturing cultural consciousness" is demonstrated by Hassimi Miaga's discussion of CORIBE's online interactive Songhoy Language and Culture course materials. Teacher Judy Richards of Wheelock College's Beaufort, South Carolina, model teacher preparation program describes ways authentic assessment helps students and teachers "Resist hegemony, domination, and dispossession culturally," another precept of intellectual independence that is integral to a transformative research and action agenda. Finally, Paula Hooper's computer-based instructional program, which engages young children in the writing process using an interactive tool, and Robert Moses's Algebra Project are indicative of "Making use of a cultural orientation as an analytical/pedagogical tool," the fourth precept of the Commission's intellectual framework.

Among the other scholars who make brief but memorable appearances in the video are Kathryn Au, Gloria Ladson-Billings, Michèle Foster, Antoine Garibaldi, Donna Gollnick, and Abdulalim Shabazz. CORIBE Elders Adelaide L. Sanford and Frank Bonilla also offer profound observations. A montage of excerpts from interviews and symposia presentations (e.g., the CORIBE "Educational Excellence Expo"), some whose programs have been described in earlier chapters of this volume, complement the observations of the senior scholars. Yvonne Lefcourt and Corinna Luna (the Kamehameha program, Honolulu) and Josianne Hudicourt-Barnes (Chèche Konnen Center), Paula Hooper (Paige Academy) discuss aspects of their teaching. Grace Lee Boggs, student teacher Julia Pointer, and several others in the "Detroit Conversation" (presented in Chapter 11 of this volume) are shown discussing "top-down" versus "bottom-up" reforms.

A "command performance" by the "Circle of Learning Orators," the third grade Prescott Elementary School students of celebrated Oakland, California, teacher Carrie Secret, is a dynamic, "over-the-top" exemplar of academic and cultural excellence. These African American and Chicano/a children perform two resounding "call-and-response" choral recitations, in English and Spanish: "What Makes You So Strong Black People?" and "Mexico Inside Me y Debemos Celebrar (We Must Celebrate)."

Sylvia Wynter's theoretical analysis of the prevailing belief structure of biocentrism, "race," "ethno-class 'Man,'" and the well-being of humans brings "A Charge to Keep" to a close. Wynter's lucid explanation of the causes of the achievement gap, racism, and global poverty demonstrates how rethinking the normative conception of what it "means to be human," including "race" suggests that our challenge as academics is to rewrite knowledge in order to disrupt systemic conditions of hegemony and cultural displacement for the benefit of humanity. "A Charge to Keep" fulfills one important CORIBE goal: To sustain the important conceptual and methodological work that was begun with the Commission.

CONCLUSION

This video is a resource that can be used for professional development for teachers in K–12 classrooms and faculty in postsecondary institutions. It is a must for teacher preparation programs. Elements of "A Charge to Keep" can be used to illustrate transformative applied research, which can help teachers understand the significance of including parents, families, church-based organizations, and community organizations in the education of youth, holding students to a standard to which they have access, and helping students recognize the specific strategies of colonization, domination, and hegemonic control. "A Charge to Keep" also can assist teachers to consider the importance of presenting culturally valid ways of thinking and producing knowledge. This video is useful for those engaged in curriculum planning, as well as collaborative research activities. Centering on transformative practices in the new millennium, "A Charge to Keep" answers Dr. Carter G. Woodson's call by illustrating a collective standard for education, that is, for civilization and human freedom, for our consciousness, and for our future.

Afterword

> ... [S]ome "research" has been subordinated to and corrupted by ideology ... there has been substantial questioning of what educational research should be and a fear that the federal government is moving to a rigid orthodoxy in defining what counts as "science" or "research."
>
> —Gerald Bracey (2004, p. 556)

> "... [T]he state of the education of many African Americans can be seen as a crime against humanity."
>
> —The National State of Black Education Movement

> "Africa is destined to play an expanding role in this new century."
>
> —Chautauqua Institute (2004)

If we are serious about changing the educational experiences of Black students, we must address those obstacles that impede their intellectual stimulation including fundamental problems of perspective bias and conceptual flaws that corrupt education research. CORIBE's approach call attentions to ways the ideological corruption of research, buttressed by the mainstream research orthodoxy, blocks the development of beneficial knowledge, education practice and policy. The findings and recommendations presented in this volume also illuminate the far-reaching social costs of alienating, soul-damaging education—costs that top-down, corporate-driven, for-profit reform efforts fail to address. Ameliorative reforms may facilitate individual economic goals for a few but not our collective advancement and empowerment of Black people and our communities.

Moreover, the evolving "diversity" discourse in the United States too often encourages a false hope in "multicultural chic"—hybridity, inclusiveness, anything but African. Although Europeans are attempting to forge a new pluralism and respect for their multiple heritages and languages,

African people are being cut off from our collective identity and care for each other, strengths that have been so integral to our survival, which is clearly in jeopardy.

Indeed, the news coming out of our communities in the United States, the Diaspora, and out of Africa is cause for alarm: 28% of Black men in the United States will be sent to jail or prison in their lifetime; women and girls of African descent globally are bearing the brunt of the violence and poverty ravaging our communities and villages; of 38 million cases of AIDS in the world, 34 million are in Africa; a genocidal war against the Black population of western Sudan portends the latest of "the world's greatest humanitarian crises" on the continent as the "new scramble for Africa" takes place in the guise of "tribal conflict" (*New Internationalist*, 2004).

In the midst of this global crisis and the abject state of Black education that is painstakingly illuminated in this volume, there are hopeful signs, however. Fifty years after the Supreme Court's landmark Brown decision another watershed event, the 40th anniversary of the Freedom Schools has also been celebrated. During the Civil Rights movement SNCC activists joined with fearless local people in Mississippi under conditions of sheer terror to create these extraordinary liberated spaces for education. In this new century, young artists and activists are bringing educational messages of high moral and socially redeeming value in spite of the massive onslaught of *ghetto-fabulous* cultural capital promoted by the $5 billion "hip-hop economy" (Chuck D, 1997; KRS-ONE, 2003). Reparations, no longer a fringe conversation, has entered even the venerated "halls of ivy" as institutions such as Brown University are using the tools of scholarly inquiry and ethical introspection to reveal more instances of mainstream dependency on "benefits" derived from our "Holocaust of Holocausts" (Moore, Sanders, & Moore, 1995).

Some may wonder about or even object to the attention given to Africa in this initiative. Why focus on learning African language or on what is going on over there, or in Brazil, when "we have so many problems of our own to deal with right here?" Or, "Our children need to pass these tests so they can get a job." Such short-sightedness will not serve us well. This is because our dispossession in the United States is part of a system of global hegemony that transcends both individual opportunities as well as our domestic predicament. Furthermore, the well-being of the human family is also imperiled by these patterns of exclusion and domination.

A recent Chautauqua Institute lecture titled "Why Africa Matters" is also worth mentioning. In this lecture H. J. de Blij (O'Grady, 2004), distinguished professor of geography at Michigan State University, emphasizes the African foundation of our human interconnectedness. "We are all Africans," he observes: "It is where we learned to speak, where we learned to live in communities, where we did our first art, it is where we made our first music. . . . Man [*sic*] would understand himself better if he knew Africa better." Of five reasons why Africa matters (or should matter) to all Americans, the second one that Professor de Blij cites is that eleven percent of the U.S. population is African American. "For that reason alone," he concludes, "we should re-connect."

Re-connect? How? What do "we" need to know to "re-connect?" On whose terms? Sadly, like most of our fellow citizens, as several of the chapters in this volume demonstrate, neither African Americans nor Diaspora Africans are being educated to feel connected to Africa, nor are we sufficiently informed about Africa's best interests to act accordingly. Celebrated hip-hop artist and author Chuck D (1997) sums up the gravity of our miseducation succinctly: "Brothers and sisters in Africa have been lied to about us, just as we have been lied to and misinformed about them" (p. 162). Furthermore, our particular disaffection from our African heritage and identity is a burden that non-Africans do not have to bear. This is the crime against our humanity.

What have we learned from the CORIBE initiative that can address the conditions of Black education? The transformative agenda that CORIBE has distilled shifts the research framework beyond a narrow focus on so-called academic "dis-identification" (the "acting White" hypothesis) or the "stereotype threat," the "achievement gap," the "skills gap", or quick-fix school reforms. Instead, this volume presents research on proven solutions—best practices—that prepare Black students and other students to achieve at high levels of academic excellence and to be agents of their own socioeconomic and cultural transformation. The vision of Black education that CORIBE is advancing is grounded in two important premises: (a) education is a basic human right and (b) humane and equitable education for and about Black people is a condition of humane and equitable education, justice, and human freedom for all.

The globally inclusive approach to Black Education as a field of study, as well as the research and practice presented in this volume, take into consideration the experiences African descent people share with other historically subordinated groups in the United States, in the global South, and in other parts of the world. Racialized disparity and alienation are inexorable outcomes of the "power-knowledge-economics regime" in which White supremacy reigns and corrodes education at every level—for students, teachers, and teacher educators as well as other scholars in academia. More so than studying these matters to produce a conventional report, CORIBE was designed as a broad-based participatory process to reframe our thinking about the issues that created the need for this initiative.

Pointing toward new directions for research, education, and social action, the powerful documentation assembled in this volume demonstrates the expertise of educators who know how to provide culturally nurturing, enriching, and liberating education across the disciplines in schools and community settings. CORIBE's Transformative Research and Action Agenda (Appendix A) underscores the importance of linking research and social action to be undertaken by the global community of African-descent scholars/activists and our allies, within and also independently of AERA. Fortunately, this work has already begun. In the Postscript that follows, "Bill" Watkins affirms the dedication, passion, and hope among those who have stepped fearlessly into the fray. In conclusion, this book and the exemplary work of the Commission on Research in Black Education testify that we are prepared to battle the forces of barbarism—whether ideological, institutional and cultural practices, or policies—that dare to exclude Black children here and there in the world from their rightful futures. Civilization and human freedom in the new century hang in the balance.

. . .

> It may look as if all we ever did was to endure this history of ruin, taking no steps to end the negative slide and begin the positive turn. That impression is false. Over these disastrous millennia there have been Africans concerned to work out solutions to our problems and to act on them. . . .
>
> [E]ven in defeat the creative ones left vital signs. They left traces of a moral mindpath visible to this day, provided we learn again to read pointers to lost ways. Then, connected with past time and future space through knowledge recovered, thinking Africans seeking one another in this common cause will meet the best of humanity for the work ahead: ending the past and current rule of slavers.
>
> We are not after the slave-foreman power that, under the killer's continuing rule, is blind ambition's hollow prize. We are after the intelligent understanding of all our realities, not simply the politics of power. We are after intelligent action to change these realities. For we intend, as Africans, to retrieve our human face, our human heart, the human mind our ancestors taught to soar. That is who we are, and why.
>
> —Ayi Kwei Armah (*Osiris Rising*, pp. 9–10)

Postscript

I spent considerable time in 1999 researching and writing this project. It was a labor of love because I had spent considerable time in Africa. This project allowed me to be both personal and political. When the final product came out in April 2000, I was ambivalent. Buoyed that the essay helped clarify many obfuscated issues, I was saddened that conditions on the "continent" were worsening. My only hope was that the "liberals" then in office would call attention to my motherland.

Fully expecting that kindred "liberals" would replace the Clinton regime, I was hopeful that somebody would notice Africa. It was not to be. The reactionaries and forces of darkness took the election and it became clear that Africa would not appear on their radar screen. Pessimistic about the new "conservative" regime, I had no idea that we would take a giant step backward.

The new imperialists have taken us all back to the visions of Caesar and Napolean. They intend to rule the world. Africa be damned, except for the continued exploitation of its considerable mineral resources and cheap labor. Thus, we are still on square one. As I wrote then, Africa continues to be characterized by continental conflict, atavism, poverty, and decline. Promises of assistance for AIDS have yet to materialize. Those of us committed to equity, justice, and the restoration of Africa's greatness can only hold on. "Change gonna come."

Long Live Africa.

William H. Watkins
April 2004

351

Appendix A

A Transformative Research and Action Agenda for Human Freedom in the New Century

CORIBE's Agenda focuses on the transformative power of using culture as an asset in the design of learning environments that are applicable to students' lives and that lead students toward more analytical and critical learning. This Agenda includes a call for:

I. *Well-funded large- and small-scale research to support and disseminate proven practices* that use culturally relevant schema to organize and enhance instruction in beneficial ways for students at all levels and for teacher and researcher learning and development. This includes:
    * Identifying teachers whose culturally nurturing instruction improves student performance on standardized tests and supporting ways this group of teachers can pass on their knowledge to other teachers.
    * Identifying new models for ongoing in-service teacher development that are powerful enough to change teachers' habits of mind and classroom practices in urban classrooms.
II. *Authentic assessment instruments and methods* informed by broader conceptions of what government mandated high-stakes tests should assess.

    ❖ Such assessments should reflect cultural and academic excellence as well as truthful curricula and instructional approaches that incorporate students' funds of prior cultural knowledge and experience.

III. *Critical assessments of government-mandated reforms and research-based community dialogues* among scholars, practitioners, policy makers, parents, and other stakeholders focusing on issues such as:

    ❖ The benefits and social costs of various national reform models (Success for All, Comer Schools, Accelerated Schools, Professional Development Schools).

    ❖ The content and learning experiences that enable teachers as well as parents or other caregivers to facilitate student literacy acquisition and development.

    ❖ Ways to eliminate inequity and promote democratic inclusion in education with respect to school funding, tracking, expulsions, and suspensions, Special Education, and curriculum content, and textbook adoption standards.

    ❖ Methods for visionary parent education that addresses the relationship between student alienation and achievement.

IV. *Adequately funded and better educational opportunities for incarcerated youth.*

V. *Community building action research that brings researchers, parents, and teachers together* to support and evaluate programs in school and non-school settings that include the arts, service learning, and interrelated health, education, and recreation strategies and which expand student opportunities for learning-by-doing, critical reasoning, and civic engagement. This includes:

    ❖ Creating, opportunities for effective community teachers to share their knowledge with "regular" teachers.

    ❖ Evaluating what and how Black youth and teachers are learning about community economic empowerment and wealth creation strategies.

    ❖ Supporting the efforts and abilities of parents and community elders to work with youth to develop effective strategies to resist negative and unhealthy media messages and influences.

VI. *Policies and practices to ensure that qualified teachers and administrators are adequately prepared and equitably assigned to urban schools.* This includes:

    ❖ Identifying factors that influence African Americans and other teachers of color to enter and remain in the teaching profession.

VII. *Public policy development informed by international comparative research* that enhances the education, survival, and advancement of African descent peoples. This includes:
   * Assessing the impact of African language, culture, and heritage study in motivating student effort and engagement as well as teacher knowledge and development in various African and Diaspora contexts.
   * Examining and supporting ways people of African descent resist domination and societal exclusion.
   * Investigating the extent to which scholars of African descent who embrace a cultural orientation and resistance in their work experience role strain and scholarly alienation and promoting research that addresses ways to alleviate this problem.

VIII. *Productive exchanges with Native American, Asian, and Chicano/a educators* and opportunities for dialogue and collaboration among diverse groups and with international scholars.

IX. *Support for using cybertechnology and the Internet in the best interests of Black education globally.* This includes a focus on access and content to eliminate the "digital divide."

X. *Research, policies, and practices that promote gender equity in education at all levels for Black males and females.*

Appendix B-1

Black Education, Toward the Human, After "Man": In the Manner of a Manifesto

Framing a Transformative Research and Action Agenda for the New Millennium

Commission on Research in Black Education
Working Colloquium June 30–July 2, 2000
St. Simons Island, GA

"Rethinking Origins/Knowledges/The Achievement Gap: Black Education After '*Man*'" Sylvia Wynter in Conversation with Asa G. Hilliard, III and Edmund W. Gordon

> No one would dream of doubting that its major artery (i.e., of the Black student's self-doubt and division) is fed from the heart of those various theories that have tried to prove that the Negro is a stage in the slow evolution of monkey into man.
>
> —Frantz Fanon, *Black Skins/While Masks* (1967)

We who are gathered here, all actualize and embody ethno-class, *Man*, as the first purely secular or nonreligious conception/mode of the human in history. Indeed, the fact that, whatever our religions and cultures of origin, we have all, as middle-class academics and administrators, been socialized in the same "set of instructions" or mode of sociogeny (Fanon, 1967),

357

which institute us hegemonically, as human in the ethno-class (i.e., Western-bourgeois) terms of *Man*, is the fact that provides the indispensable condition of our being able to understand each other.

Because the laws that govern our cognizing behaviors as hybridly nature-culture beings are precisely analogous to those that govern the behaviors of purely organic species, we must, as ethno-class subjects, know our social reality in terms that are *adaptively* advantageous to the realization, production, and reproduction, of the mode of being human that *we* embody and actualize.

Furthermore, because as academics and teachers, our task is to elaborate, guard, and disseminate the kind of knowledge able to ensure the well-being of our present mode of the human, *Man*, one which represents its well-being as if it were that of the human itself, we cannot normally address the contradictions to which this overrepresentation leads. Yet, the phenomenon called the achievement or IQ gap between White and Black, as well as between non-Black and Black, is a direct consequence of this overrepresentation, one of the central contradictions to which it leads.

The hypothesis here is that it is this overrepresentation, together with its corollary subordination of the well-being of the human as a species to the well-being of ethno-class *Man*, that a Black Education Project will have to call in question, dismantle, and deconstruct. To do so to *complete* the Second Emergence of the human (that is, from our subordination, hitherto, to the hybrid nature-culture "set of instructions" that institute us as specific modes of the human, of the/and of the We), as an Emergence that the two scientific revolutions of the West have brilliantly set in motion, with a third scientific revolution. One that, moving beyond the limits of the Human Genome Project, and therefore, of the *natural* sciences, will take as its object of investigation our hybrid nature-culture, ontogeny/sociogeny modes of being human together with their resultant orders of consciousness, including the insights and blindnesses of our present ethno-class own, as its new object of knowledge and of inquiry.

In summary, if the scientific revolutions of the West began with the lay humanists of Renaissance Europe going back to Greece and Rome, in order to find an alternative secular model of being human beyond the limits of the medieval order's then theocentric conception, so, too, in order to find an alternative model to our present biocentric and ethno-class one, our intellectual revolution will begin by going back to the continent of Africa where the event of *singularity* to which I give the name of the First Emergence—that is, our emergence from subordination to the genetic programs which prescribe the behaviors of purely organic life, and our entrance instead into the behavior-programming mechanisms of the Word/of Myth—first took place. Doing so to bring into existence what

Aimé Césaire first proposed in 1946 as a science of the Word, in which the study of the Word (i.e., of the phenomenon to which we give the name *culture*), will condition the study of nature (of the neuro-physiological mechanisms of the brain) as a new science able to complete what he defined as our present "half-starved" natural sciences, and to, thereby, make possible a new "humanism made to the measure of the world."

Sylvia Wynter
June 30, 2002

Appendix B-2

Race and Our Biocentric Belief System: An Interview With Sylvia Wynter

JK: Can you explain what you mean by "our biocentric belief system"?

SW: The central point of biocentrism is that this conception of the human is the first universally applicable conception, which is, since Darwin, that we are biological beings. Race and racism are logical outcomes of the biocentric conception of the human that we elaborate and enact in academia, because in all human cultures this is the role of the intellectuals from the shamans to ourselves—to effect both this inscripting and therefore the lawlike order of knowledge. Therefore, just as a bat knows the world from the perspective of a bat, if you were a feudal Christian, you knew the world in those terms. If now, we are Western ethno-class bourgeois modes of the subject, we know the world in such modes. But the belief is that we are biological beings who then create culture. Whereas my proposal is that we are bioevolutionarily prepared by means of language to inscript and autoinstitute ourselves in this or that modality of the human, always in adaptive response to the ecological as well as to the geopolitical circumstances in which we find ourselves.

FANON'S REVOLUTION

I am making the hypothesis that the modern world has actually been brought into being on the basis of three very powerful revolutions. One was the "Copernican Revolution," which gave rise to the physical sciences. The next was the "Darwinian Revolution," which gave rise to the biological sciences. And Fanon's revolution is the one that will give rise to an entirely new science, which will be that of the nature-culture mode of being human. Notice. This is very important. It's not one or the other (nature versus culture). It is the *co*-relation. Fanon came up with this in his book, *Black Skins, White Masks*. What he suggested is that—he wanted to find out for himself: He said, "Look. In the Caribbean it is normal for the Antillean subject to be anti-Black, to be anti-Negro." But he said, if you went to Africa and you saw the Pygmy in his traditional cultural constellation, there he is the normal human being. And it is impossible for him to experience himself as a Negro because he is the norm, and to be a Negro is to be the opposite to the norm.

Then Fanon made the leap. He said that if a Black person can be aversive to himself, so that—just as the White person is—the White person will shout, "dirty nigger," but the Black person will also have that same response to himself—then this is because, in the case of the human, while Freud spoke about the ontogenetic subject, that is to say, the ontogenetic individual (let us think of the child: it's born as an embryo, the embryo grows—we watch with awe as this beautiful miracle unfolds itself). But, Fanon said that from the moment this is happening, it is also being socialized within the terms of a specific—we have to use the word "culture," we have no better word—a specific cultural conception of what it is to be human; of what it is to be a good man or woman of your kind. And so Fanon says, in the case of the human, besides "ontogeny," there is "sociogeny." And the moment we have said that, we now have moved outside of an entirely biological conception of being which underlies our present conception. We live in a mode of sociogeny, a conception of the human, in which to be human you must be anti-Black. This is the point he is making.

THE WELL-BEING OF THE HUMAN VS. ETHNO-CLASS 'MAN'

We define the human as *homo-economicus*. What we call capitalism is the only mode of production that can produce the material conditions of existence of the definition of the human as *homo-economicus*. That is why, although our economies in the third world want a new economic order, we cannot have a new economic order. This is the best that we can possibly hope for within the terms of the conception of the human as an economic being. But, if we now move toward the conception of the human as being fundamentally a social being, a being that is always instituting itself as social, and we then ask: The economic system we have now functions for the well-being of the ethno-class conception of the human man. What system of economics would we need to function for the well-being, not just of the global middle classes, but of the human itself? People are massively poor in the midst of great abundance. Never before has the productive capacity of humankind been greater. So, therefore, we are faced with a contradiction.

Obviously, the contradiction has to do with distribution. So the question then is: What determines distribution? Adam Smith gave a wonderful clue, when he was attacking the landlord class and he said—you know the landlord has these vast fields and he enjoys the products, but his stomach is limited. So he can not eat all that food, right? So he has to distribute it. But what drives him to distribute that little that he pays his workers is due to his desire to keep up and to reproduce his "economy of greatness." Marx told us the key is the mode of production. I knew he was partly right. And then I realized what is produced is not just the material conditions. What is produced is our conception of being human. Every mode of production is a function of producing that conception. That is why our system of capitalist production, brilliant as it is, cannot deal with the issue of the poor or the impoverished nations. Because its function is to produce for the well-being of the global middle classes—for a conception of the human. And so our great problem now, the great struggle is between the well-being of "Man" or the well-being of the human.

BLACK AS A LIMINAL CATEGORY

In every order, there is always a liminal category. That liminal category is a deviation from the norm. It is through the deviation from norm that the rest of the society can recognize themselves as kin. For example, America is held together on the basis of Whiteness. The middle-class has been able to "sucker" the lower middle-class by bonding it to itself on the fact that "We are all White." So transgender, transrace, transeverything, they are held together by the concept of White. But, "White" is a cultural conception that is only possible as an opiate-triggering reward conception by means of the degradation of the "Black." And by the way, for homosexuals and heterosexuals, it is the same. Heterosexuality also binds the lower classes to the middle classes by saying we are all one against that scapegoat "other." This was also the role of the Jews in medieval Europe and later, of course, the concept of "life unworthy of life" within this dangerous biological conception of the human that there could be life unworthy of life. This is also what is really happening to Blacks in the prison-industrial complex.

The price of our incorporation as middle-class Blacks was their extrusion because they now become the "name of what is evil" rather than the entire Black population, as it had been before.

Somehow the Western bourgeoisie has come to see its own physiognomic being as the only possible mode of being human. Now, this is funny, because this is a late mutation. Genetics have now proved—because there is ethnogenetics, which is *The Bell Curve*, and there is genetics—ethnogenetics is a function of a genetics whose function is to legitimate the structure of the order. Genetics has to move entirely outside that and what it has proved, of course, is the origin of the human in Africa. Africans are the oldest people. The greatest degrees of genetic diversity remain, as has been said, in a small village where there is genetic more diversity than in all the world. And, yet, it is being wiped out by AIDS. When I say that the rest of my life will be dedicated to fighting the belief system of biocentrism, as the obverse of the medieval belief system of theocentrism, you can really see that we don't fight racism. Racism is an effect of the biocentric conception of the human.

WHAT AFRICA OFFERS US

The West has always been arguing about "civilization" because it has always had the belief system that to be "human" is to be "civilized." Civilization is a far later and derivative form of the first mechanisms of what Africa offers us. When we go back to Africa—Egypt is wonderful and I am not putting it down—but the great, the dazzling moment is when you go back 50,000 years ago, you are seeing the first manifestations of the techniques by means of which the human is producing and instituting itself as human. I am suggesting that we should be able to see there the fundamental rules that still govern us today. That is what Africa has to offer. It is a tremendous challenge because this is to say that we make ourselves human through words, through meanings, through institutions. We are not interested in what I call the "I got a shoe, you got a shoe," mentality: "You got a civilization, I got a civilization." Rather, it is the way in which in Africa we can say an "other" exists to what the West calls human. When you are looking at Voudun, we are seeing an "other" to what the monotheistic religions have called "human." We are going back to our very origin as humans and the processes of hominization and that is to me what Africa has to offer, when we look at it this way.

By the way, taking this magnificent body of knowledge that has been built up by the West, but seeing it differently from them because they could not see these ("others") as alternative forms of life. So when Evans Pritchard says so brilliantly about the Azande and their belief in "witchcraft": "It is the very texture of their thought and they couldn't think that their thought was wrong, not as long as they were Azande," so it is with us as the embodiment of ethno-class "Man" in the mode of the Western bourgeoisie. All of our beliefs about IQ, about the Bell Curve, these are the very texture of our thought and we can not normally think that our thought is wrong. So that is what Africa will give us: the fundamental rules. By the way, this wonderful Italian, Vicco, has said that we should look for that institution which is common to all humankind then we will have the makings of a new science, which would be the science that we are talking about—the science of being human, of the Word.

TOWARD THE SCIENCE OF BEING HUMAN

The way out, as Fanon has said, "Besides ontogeny, there is sociogeny." He is giving us a description of ourselves because then we can ask, "What is the mode of sociogeny in which we are?" Do you see? Because we have been doing it. We have been putting it in place but we have been doing this nonconsciously, as a spider spins its elegant web. But the fact is that we have also been changing these conceptions (of the human). All the great movements of history have actually been changes and struggles against (the prevailing) conception. Now, for the first time, we would literally come into full consciousness of the fact that it is we who are the agents and authors of ourselves and that we do it according to rules. And these rules function in the same way for the first human cultures. When we look at circumcision—a biocentric perspective—we see genital mutilation, because we can't afford to see what we are seeing. We see the first "writing" on the flesh, as Nietzsche says: "That tremendous labor of the human upon itself by means of which it was to make itself calculable." So in instituting ourselves, we institute our order of consciousness. As Fanon would say, "We are going to have to become enemies to our own consciousness."

TOWARD A TRANSFORMATIVE RESEARCH
AND ACTION AGENDA

Woodson in 1935 had looked at the entire educational system and he said that it is set up in such a way as to motivate White students by telling them that they had done everything and to de-motivate Black students by telling them they had done nothing. So the question that we have been running away from is the body of knowledge in the university and schools itself. It is not any other extraneous factor. It is the body of knowledge. It is the system of representation. When people have struggled, asking, "Why is there no Black history?" This is not arbitrary. This is indispensable to the instituting of our present bourgeois conception of being human. So, we are all accomplices. We are all in complicity. We can't come up with a "good-guy/bad-guy." We are necessarily in complicity with the order in which we find ourselves. But also, as intellectuals, remember, we are social, but we also have a vocational interest. And so, the Faustian temptation will always drive us, hopefully, to go beyond the immediacy of what would be our social interest in continuing to know the world *adaptively*. Because we want to say, "Oh that's how it works."

Palo Alto, California
June 2000

Appendix C

Glossary of Terms

Djanna Hill and Joyce E. King

Cooperative Economic Development: Promotes pooling of resources, shared wealth, and economic and political enfranchisement that puts community members in control over economic activity and wealth creation through noncompetitive business practices for the collective benefit of all local residents. Parallels one of the seven principles of the African American value system celebrated as KWANZAA that encourages African Americans to build and maintain stores, shops, and other businesses and to profit from them together.

Cultural Annihilation: The destruction of values, practices, beliefs, and language via assimilation or some other form of domination.

Culture-systemic Framework: A theoretical conception of the way a particular order must represent itself in the academic disciplines in order to reproduce itself.

Culturally Nurturing Research: Investigation that produces knowledge and understanding of ways to dismantle the aggressive beliefs, behaviors, and strategies of domination through an affirmation of voices and perspectives of those who share a commitment to Black people's survival and advancement.

Digital Divide: The disparity in access to and facility with computer technology for low-income families and people of color that also includes unequal access to meaningful content in electronic and computer-based formats that are created by and serve the best interests of these groups.

Ethno-class "Man": The first conception of the human or "Man" that is a purely secular or nonreligious conception of being human that came into being with the rise of the modern European state; a Western-bourgeois (and eventually White) middle-class category that purports to represent humanity but is actually a local ethnocentric category of human beingness. A mode of the human that is reproduced through both nature-culture dynamics and that represents its well-being "as if it were that of the human itself."

Ethnocentric Research Paradigms: Dominant research establishment perspectives, beliefs, or practices of the mainstream culture that adhere to supposedly scientific, objective, and politically neutral practice, which constitute, by contrast, nonculturally affirming knowledge production practices, methods, and theories.

Ghetto Fabulous: A colloquialism, refers to the performance of an attitude and public display of conspicuous consumption associated primarily with the way inner-city Black youth mimic the expensive, expansive, and carefree lifestyle of the fabulously "rich and famous"; images often portrayed in hip-hop industry music videos (e.g., MTV, BET) that evoke lavish spending and overnight "success" represented as superwealth, superstardom, and wanton abandon (e.g., women and men in costly furs, jewelry, and luxury cars, in sexually provocative clothing and promiscuous posturing). Reminiscent of the relatively more restrained mimicry of the 19th-century plantation society "Cakewalk" dance exhibitions, an earlier form of Black performance parody of the well-to-do.

Globalization: A component of imperialism, includes the policies, practices, and structures necessary for extending transnational corporate power and hegemony across the globe, irrespective of national boundaries, for the purpose of economic dominion, political influence, control of markets, and the transfer of material, human, and cultural resources outside of national and community localities in order to generate profits for corporate owners.

Hegemony: The maintenance of domination primarily through social practices, social forms, and social structures produced in specific sites—the church, the state, schools, media, the political system, and the family; a struggle in which the powerful win the consent of those who are oppressed, with the oppressed unknowingly participating in their own oppression.

Indigenous Education: Systems of education that reflect, respect, and embrace the cultural values, philosophies, and ideologies of Indigenous people and that have shaped, nurtured, and sustained these population groups for tens of thousands of years.

Prison-industrial-complex: Refers to the massive economic and political interests vested in the construction, proliferation, and maintenance of prisons and the abuse of low and nonpaid prison laborers in the service of corporate sector private industry and the disenfranchisement of disproportionately incarcerated African Americans, Latinos, and other dominated groups. This interrelated complex of interests also threatens democratic processes and liberty for all American citizens, whereas politicians, law enforcement, and other agencies of social control derive economic and symbolic benefits from the "prison solution" for "fighting crime." Parallels in many ways the "military-industrial-complex," the term former President Dwight D. Eisenhower coined to describe the potent nexus of the U.S. military establishment, the corporate and academic sectors, and the federal government, including well-funded defense and security agencies and congressional leadership in defense, national security, and foreign affairs (Flateau, 1966).

Process-building Methodology: Providing multiple opportunities to engage, participate, share, affirm, and produce knowledge and the generation of theory from everyday shared realities by allowing participants to reflect on their own individual experience, and, thereby, make connections with the shared experiences of others through dialogue for the purpose of making society more just for future generations.

Scholarly Alienation: The schizophrenic bind scholars of color often experience as a consequence of using ethnocentric research paradigms that are generally accepted as scientific truisms but are lacking validation in the "minority" scholar's experiences and/or intuition; the nonuse of indigenous (African) intellectual traditions in favor of the Western academy.

Social Totality: A conceptualization of the powerful interlocking relationships and structures that control education and the economy locally and globally, including the corporate media, textbooks, as well as academic scholarship that rationalizes these and other mechanisms that shape identity and consciousness and control the life chances and well-being of individuals and groups.

Transformative Black Education: Education that reconnects students to their identity as members of the global African family in ways that also improve their motivation and engagement with the learning process; education that addresses the goals of expanding human understanding, nurturing cultural consciousness, resisting hegemony, domination, and dispossession culturally and making use of a liberatory cultural orientation as analytical and pedagogical tools.

Whiteward Mobility: One way that conceptual "whiteness" functions in society as a category through which various ethnic groups, except African-descent people, become "honorary Whites" and, thereby, achieve upward social mobility into a higher socioeconomic class, often at the expense of their collective advancement.

Contributing Authors

Linda Darling-Hammond, PhD, is Charles E. Ducommun Professor of Education at Stanford University School of Education. She was the founding executive director of the National Commission on Teaching and America's Future, which produced the 1996 widely cited blueprint for education reform: "What Matters Most: Teaching for America's Future." Darling-Hammond's research, teaching, and policy work focus on educational policy, teaching and teacher education, school restructuring, and educational equity. Among her more than 200 publications is *The Right to Learn*, recipient of the 1998 Outstanding Book Award from AERA, and *Teaching as the Learning Profession*, awarded the National Staff Development Council's Outstanding Book Award in 2000.

Terezinha Juraci Machado da Silva, MA, teaches at the National University of Cordoba in Argentina as a Brazilian Lecturer for the Ministry of International Exchange Relationships. She has taught Children's Literature in the Teacher Education Program at the Faculdades Integradas Ritter Dos Reis (College) in Porto Alegre, Brazil. The title of her Master's thesis research in Portuguese is: "Literatura Infanto-Juvenil Angolana: Cinco Autores Contemporaneos" (Children's Literature from Angola: Five Contemporary Authors). She is a doctoral candidate researching the comparative history of Black people in Brazil and Argentina.

Kassie Freeman, PhD, is the Dean of the Division of Educational and Psychological Studies and Professor of Education at Dillard University. Her research interests include cultural considerations related to African Americans and college choice, and comparative/international issues related to higher education and the labor market. She has edited two books, *African American Culture and Heritage in Higher Education Research and Practice* and, with M. Christopher Brown II, *Black Colleges: New*

Perspectives on Policy and Practice. She is also author of the forthcoming book, *African Americans and College Choice: The Influence of Family and School.*

Annette Henry, PhD, is Associate Professor in Curriculum/Policy Studies in the College of Education at the University of Illinois at Chicago. Her scholarship examines Black women teachers' practice in international contexts as well as race, language, gender, and culture in sociocultural contexts of teaching and learning. Her research interests include alternative epistemologies and methods. Author of *Taking Back Control: African Canadian Women Teachers' Lives and Practice,* she has written extensively about conceptual and methodological issues regarding research with Black women and girls.

Djanna Hill, EdD, is Assistant Professor of Science and Urban Education in the College of Education at William Paterson University. She teaches undergraduate and graduate courses in educational foundations, general methods, and elementary and secondary science methods. Her research interests include Black feminist/womanist theory, multicultural and urban education, the teacher education professoriate, and enhancing qualitative approaches to inquiry. Her recent publications include: *Teachers for Tomorrow in Urban Schools: Recruiting and Supporting the Pipeline* (with coauthor M. Gillette, in press) and "The Poetry in Portraiture: Seeing Subjects, Hearing Voices, and Feeling Contexts" in the *Journal of Qualitative Inquiry,* volume 11(1).

Joyce E. King, PhD, holds the Benjamin E. Mays Endowed Chair for Urban Teaching, Learning, and Leadership at Georgia State University. Previously she served as Provost and Professor of Education at Spelman College, Associate Provost at Medgar Evers College (CUNY), Associate Vice Chancellor of Academic Affairs and Diversity Programs at the University of New Orleans, and Director of Teacher Education at Santa Clara University. Her publications include several books, *Preparing Teachers for Diversity* (Senior Editor), *Teaching Diverse Populations* (with E. Hollins and W. Hayman), and *Black Mothers to Sons: Juxtaposing African American Literature with Social Practice* (with C. A. Mitchell), in addition to articles on Black Studies curriculum theorizing, cultural knowledge, and teacher preparation. Dr. King chaired the CORIBE initiative.

Carol D. Lee, PhD, is Associate Professor of Education and Policy Studies and African American Studies at Northwestern University and Cocoordinator of the SESP Spencer Research Training Program. Lee has developed a theory of Cultural Modeling that provides a framework for the design and enactment of curriculum that draws on forms of prior knowledge that traditionally underserved students bring to classrooms. In addition to numerous articles and book chapters, Lee's books include *Signifying as a Scaffold for Literary Interpretation: The Pedagogical Implications of an African American Discourse Genre*, and she is coeditor (with P. Smagorinsky) of *Neo-Vygotskian Perspectives on Literacy Research*. Active in public school reform, Lee taught in both public and private schools before assuming a university career. She is a founder and former director of an African-centered independent school in Chicago that is 28 years old—New Concept School. She is also a founder of a newly established African-centered charter school, the Betty Shabbazz International Charter School.

Beverly Lindsay, PhD, is the first American to become a Senior Fulbright Specialist in South Korea and Zimbabwe, where she engaged in peace and conflict resolution, initiated executive and faculty leadership development models and fostered strategic planning and program evaluation processes. She is a former dean at Hampton University and Penn State University for international education and policy studies, where she is a Professor and Senior Scientist at the latter university. Her recent books include: *The Quest for Equity in Higher Education* (with M. J. Justiz) and *The Political Dimension in Teacher Education* (with M. Ginsburg).

Hassimi Oumarou Maiga, PhD, holds a Distinguished Research Professorship at L' ISFRA, the University of Bamako, Mali (by Presidential appointment), where he supervises doctoral and masters candidates and teaches the history of education, research methods, curriculum, and evaluation. In the United States, he has taught multicultural education, history of education, educational psychology, French, and Soŋay-Senni (Songhoy language) and culture using his textbook, *Conversational Soŋay Language of Mali*. A recent publication is *Classical Songhoy Education and Socialization: The World of Women and Child Rearing Practices in West Africa*. Formerly Regional Director (Deputy Minister) of Education in Gao, northern Mali, he is founding President of the Askya Mohammed Center for Education and Research, a private school in Gao that includes an Africana Studies curriculum and an international exchange program.

Zakiyyah Muhammad, PhD, is Founding Director of the American Institute on Islamic Education; her area of expertise is Islamic schools in America and she is an experienced teacher-scholar and school administrator. Muhammad has served as Director of Education for the Clara Muhammad Schools and as Principal of Orange Crescent School. She has published in *The Muslim Education Quarterly*, the *Journal of Negro Education* and the *Journal on Religion and Education*, among others. She is the author of "A History of Islamic Education in America" and

"Islamic Schools in the United States: Perspectives of Identity, Relevance and Governance," prepared for the Woodrow Wilson Center of International Scholars Symposium on Muslims in the United States.

Jessica Gordon Nembhard, PhD, is Assistant Professor and Economist in the African American Studies Department and The Democracy Collaborative at the University of Maryland (UMD), College Park. Her current areas of interest include democratic community-based economic development, alternative urban development strategies, cooperative economics, race and economic inequality, wealth inequality, and popular economic literacy. Gordon Nembhard's recent publications include "Cooperatives and Wealth Accumulation: Preliminary Analysis" (*American Economic Review*) and *From Community Economic Development and Ethnic Entrepreneurship to Economic Democracy: The Cooperative Alternative* (coedited with J.M. Feldman).

Sharon Parker, MA, is presently a co-Principal Investigator for a research project on diversity in higher education institutions. The project is based at Claremont Graduate University where Ms. Parker is a visiting faculty member. She is also affiliated with Evergreen State College in Olympia, Washington, where she resides. Ms. Parker served as the CORIBE Administrator (1999–2001).

Ibrahima Seck, PhD, is Assistant professor, History Department, Cheikh Anta Diop University, Dakar, Sénégal. A former high school history teacher, Seck is also the recipient of numerous fellowships from research organizations and programs including the Fulbright Foundation, which supported his research on the blues in Mississippi. Recent publications include "The Illegal Slave Trade between Saint Louis in Sénégal, the West Indies and Louisiana in the 19th Century" and "African Cultures and Slavery in the Lower Mississippi Valley, from Iberville to Jim Crow."

Petronilha Beatriz Gonçalves E. Silva, PhD, teaches in the Department of Teaching Methodologies at the Federal University of São Carlos in the state of São Paulo, Brazil, where she is also a researcher affiliated with the African-Brazilian Studies Center. She completed postdoctoral study in Educational Theory at the University of South Africa in Pretoria. Professor Silva is also an engaged scholar (militant) in the Brazilian Black movement and she is the first Afro Brazilian woman appointed to the National Council on Education. A recent publication is *Experiencias Ethnico-culturais para a Formação de Professores* (with N. Gomes), and she contributed a chapter to *Diversity and Citizenship Education: Global Perspectives* (J. A. Banks, Editor).

Linda C. Tillman, PhD, is Associate Professor in the Department of Leadership at the University of North Carolina, Chapel Hill. A former K–12 and community college educator who also has served on the faculty at Wayne State University and the University of New Orleans, she is a consultant to schools, universities, and boards of regents. She has served on the AERA Social Justice Action Committee. Her research interests include mentoring African American teachers and principals, culturally sensitive research approaches, parental involvement, and leadership theory.

William H. Watkins, PhD, is Professor of Education at the University of Illinois, Chicago. A former high school teacher, Bill is the author of *The White Architects of Black Education* (2001), lead editor and contributor to *Race and Education* (2001) and editor and contributor to the upcoming book, *Black Protest Thought and Education,* in addition to numerous articles, chapters, essays, and reviews in scholarly journals, books, encyclopedias, and the popular press. Dedicated to equality, social justice, and peace, he has lectured and traveled widely throughout North America, Mexico, Central America, South America, Africa, Europe, Asia, and the Caribbean.

Cirecie A. West-Olatunji, PhD, is Assistant Professor of Counselor Education at the University of Florida. Her current research focuses on special education placement, counseling, and culturally diverse young children. West-Olatunji is a nationally recognized speaker, practitioner, and author in the areas of culture-centered theory, research, and practice. She maintains a clinical practice and is a specialist in multicultural family and personal counseling.

Cecile Wright, PhD, is Professor of Sociology at the Nottingham Trent University in the United Kingdom. Her research interests include "race," gender, and social class in education. Wright's most recent book is *"Race," Class, Gender Exclusion from School* (with D. Weekes).

References

AAUW. (2000). *Tech-savvy: Educating girls in the new computer age*. Washington, DC: American Association of University Women Educational Foundation.

Abernethy, D. (1969). *The political dilemma of popular education: An African case*. Stanford, CA: Stanford University Press.

Akbar, N. (n.d.). The need for a cultural revival. (Audio cassette). Tallahassee, FL: Mind Productions & Associates.

Akom, A. A. (2003). Reexamining resistance as oppositional behavior: The Nation of Islam and the creation of a Black achievement ideology. *Sociology of Education, 76*(4), 305–325.

Akoto, A. (1992). *Nation building: Theory and practice in Afrikan-centered education*. Washington, DC: Pan-Afrikan World Institute.

Akoto, A. (1994). Notes on an African-centered pedagogy. M. Shujaa (Ed.), *Too much schooling, too little education: A paradox of Black life in white societies* (pp. 319–340). Trenton, NJ: Africa World Press.

Alexander, K. L., & McDill, E. L. (1976). Selection and allocation within schools: Some causes and consequences of curriculum placement. *American Sociological Review, 41*, 963–980.

Allen, D., & Cosby, W. (2000). *American schools: The 100 billion dollar challenge*. ipublish.com. Retrieved from http://www.bn.com, June 30, 2001.

Allington, R. L., & Woodside-Jiron, H. (1999). The politics of literacy teaching: How "research" shaped educational policy. *Educational Researcher, 28*(8), 4–13.

Almond, G. A., & Powell, G. B. Jr. (1966). Comparative politics: A developmental approach. Boston: Little, Brown.

Almond, G. A., & Verba, S. (1963). The civic culture: Political attitudes and democracy in five nations. Princeton: Princeton University Press.

Altbach, P. G., & Kelly, G. P. (Eds.). (1988). Textbooks in the third world: Policy, content, and context. New York: Garland Pub.

Amin, S. (1997). *Capitalism in the age of globalization*. London: Zed Books.

Anderson, C. (1994). *Black labor–White wealth: The search for power and economic justice.* Edgewood, MD: Duncan & Duncan.

Anderson, J. D. (1988). *The education of Blacks in the South, 1860–1935.* Chapel Hill: The University of North Carolina Press.

Anderson, S. E. (1970). Mathematics and the struggle for Black liberation. *The Black Scholar,* September, 20–30.

Ani, M. (1994). *Yurugu: An African-centered critique of European cultural thought and behavior.* Trenton, NJ: Africa World Press.

Anson, A., Cook, T., & Habib, F. (1991). The Comer School Development Program: A theoretical analysis. *Urban Education, 26*(1), 56–82.

Anyon, J. (1981). Social class and school knowledge. *Curriculum Inquiry, 11*(1), 3–42.

Apple, M. (1979). *Ideology and curriculum.* New York: Routledge.

Armah, A. K. (1995). *Osiris rising: A novel of Africa, past, present and future.* Popenguine, Sénégal: Per Ankh.

Asante, M. K. (1988). *Afrocentricity.* Trenton, NJ: Africa World Press.

Asante, K. W. (1988). Commonalities in African dance: An aesthetic foundation. In M. K. Asante & K. W. Asante (Eds.), *African culture: The rhythms of unity* (pp. 71–82). Trenton, NJ: Africa World Press, Inc.

Ascher, M. (1991). *Ethnomathematics: A multicultural view of mathematical ideas.* Pacific Grove, CA.: Brooks/Cole Publishing Company.

Ashton, P., & Crocker, L. (1986). Does teacher certification make a difference? *Florida Journal of Teacher Education, 38*(3), 73–83.

Ashton, P., & Crocker, L. (1987, May–June). Systematic study of planned variations: The essential focus of teacher education reform. *Journal of Teacher Education, 38,* 2–8.

Askey, R. (1999). Knowing and teaching elementary mathematics. *American Educator, 23*(3), 6–13.

Auchard, E. (2003, July). One in 10 U.S. tech jobs may move overseas, report says. *Yahoo! News* 29 July, 2003, (citing Gartner, Inc. Report, "U.S. offshore outsourcing: Structural changes, Big impact").

Austin, A. (2001). Transformation through negotiation. In R. O. Mabokela & K. L. King (Eds.), *Apartheid no more* (pp. 1–37). Westport, CT: Bergin & Garvey.

Austin, A. D. (1997). *African Muslims in antebellum America.* New York: Routledge.

Ayres, R. L. (1983). *Banking on the poor: The World Bank and world poverty.* Cambridge, MA: MIT Press.

Azicorbe, A. M., Kennickell, A. B., & Moore, K. B. (2003, January). Recent changes in U.S. family finances: Evidence from the 1998 and 2001 survey of consumer finances. *Federal Reserve Bulletin, 89,* 1–32.

Bakhtin, M. M. (1981). In M. Holquist (Ed.), *The dialogic imagination: Four essays by M. M. Bakhtin.* Austin: University of Texas Press.

Ball, A. F. (1992). Cultural preferences and the expository writing of African American adolescents. *Written Communication, 9*(4), 501–532.

Ball, A. F. (1995a). Text design patterns in the writing of urban African-American students: Teaching to the strengths of students in multicultural settings. *Urban Education, 30,* 253–289.

Ball, A. F. (1995b). Community based learning in an urban setting as a model for educational reform. *Applied Behavioral Science Review, 3,* 127–146.

Ball, A. F. (1999). Evaluating the writing of culturally and linguistically diverse students: The case of the African American English speaker. In C. R. Cooper & L. Odell (Eds.), *Evaluating writing* (pp. 225–248). Urbana, IL: National Council of Teachers of English.

Ball, D. L., & Bass, H. (2000). Interweaving content and pedagogy in teaching and learning to teach: Knowing and using mathematics. In J. Boaler (Ed.), *Multiple perspectives on the teaching and learning of mathematics* (pp. 83–104). Westport, CT: Ablex.

Ballenger, C. (1997). Social identities, moral narratives, scientific argumentation: Science talk in a bilingual classroom. *Language and Education, 11*(1), 1–14.

Banks, J. A. (1988). *Multiethnic education* (2nd ed.). Boston, MA: Allyn and Bacon.

Banks, J. A., et al. (2001). Diversity within unity: Essential principles for teaching and learning in a multicultural society. Seattle, WA: Center for Multicultural Education.

Barlow, W. (1989). *Looking up and down: The emergence of blues culture.* Philadelphia: Temple University Press.

Baron, R., Tom, D., & Cooper, H. (1985). Social class, race and teacher expectations. In J. Dusek (Ed.), *Teacher expectations* (251–269). Hillsdale, NJ: Erlbaum.

Barr, J., & Birke, L. (1998). *Common science? Women, science, and knowledge.* Bloomington: Indiana University Press.

Barr, R., & Dreeben, R. (1983). *How schools work.* Chicago: University of Chicago Press.

Barton, P. E., & Coley, R. J. (1996). *Captive students: Education and training in America's prisons.* Princeton, N.J.: Educational Testing Service.

Baugh, J. (1988). Twice as less, Black English and the performance of Black students in mathematics and science: A book review. *Harvard Educational Review, 58,* 395–403.

Bayley, N. (1965). Comparisons of mental and motor test scores for ages 1–15 months by sex, birth order, race, geographic location and education of parents. *Child Development, 36,* 379–410.

Bell, D. (2004). *Silent covenants: Brown v. Board of Education and the unfulfilled hopes for racial reform.* New York: Oxford University Press.

Bennett, L. (1964). *Before the Mayflower: A history of the Negro in America, 1619–1964.* Chicago, IL: Johnson Publishing Company.

Bents, M., & Bents, R. B. (1990). *Perceptions of good teaching among novice, advanced beginner and expert teachers.* Paper presented at the annual meeting of the American Educational Research Association, Boston, MA.

Benveniste, G. (1977). *The politics of expertise.* San Francisco, CA: Boyd and Fraser.

Bereiter, C., & Engelmann, S. (1966). *Teaching disadvantaged children in pre-school.* Englewood Cliffs, NJ: Prentice Hall.

Berliner, P. (1994). *Thinking in jazz: The infinite art of improvisation.* Chicago: University of Chicago Press.

Berne, R. (1995). Educational input and outcome inequities in New York State. In R. Berne & L. O. Picus (Eds.), *Outcome equity in education* (pp. 191–223). Thousand Oaks, CA: Corwin Press.

Berry, B. (1995). *Keeping talented teachers: Lessons from the North Carolina Teaching Fellows*. Commissioned by the North Carolina Teaching Fellows Commission. Raleigh: Public School Forum.

Billingsley, A. (1968). *Black families in White America*. Englewood Cliffs, NJ: Prentice Hall.

Bledsoe, J. C., Cox, J. V., & Burnham, R. (1967). *Comparison between selected characteristics and performance of provisionally and professionally certified beginning teachers in Georgia*. Washington, DC: U.S. Department of Health, Education, and Welfare.

Bloome, D., & Egan-Robertson, A. (1993). The social construction of intertextuality in classroom reading and writing lessons. *Reading Research Quarterly, 28*, 305–333.

Blyden, E. W. (1871, January). Mohammedanism in Western Africa, *Methodist Quarterly Review*, 65–69.

Blyth, E., & Miller, J. (1996). Black boys excluded from school: Race or masculinity issues? In E. Blyth & J. Miller (Eds.), *Exclusion from school: Inter-professional issues for policy and practice* (pp. 20–25). London: Routledge.

Bogues, A. (2003). *Black heretics, Black prophets: Radical political intellectuals*. New York: Routledge.

Bond, H. M. (1935). The curriculum of the Negro child. *Journal of Negro Education, 4*(2), 159–168.

Bond, H. M. (1976). *Education for freedom*. Lincoln, PA: Lincoln University Press.

Bond, J., & Freeman, R. B. (1992, February). What went wrong? The erosion of relative earnings and employment among young Black men in the 1980s. *Quarterly Journal of Economics, 107*, 201–232.

Booth, W. (1974). *A rhetoric of irony*. Chicago: University of Chicago Press.

Bourdieu, P. (1997). The forms of capital. In J. G. Richardson (Ed.), *Handbook of theory and research for the sociology of education* (pp. 46–58). New York: Greenwood Press.

Bowen, H. (1977). *Investment in learning*. San Francisco, CA: Jossey-Bass.

Bowles, S., & Gintis, H. (1976). *Schooling in capitalist America*. New York: Basic Books.

Bowman, B. (1993). Early childhood education. In L. Darling-Hammond (Ed.), *Review of Research in Education, 19* (pp. 101–134). Washington, DC: American Educational Research Association.

Bowman, P. (1989). Research perspectives on black men: Role strain and adaptation across the adult life cycle. In R. Jones (Ed.), *Black adult development and aging* (pp. 117–150). Berkeley: Cobbs & Henry.

Boykin, A. W. (1979). Psychological/behavioral verve: Some theoretical explorations and empirical manifestations. In A. W. Boykin, A. Franklin, & J. Yates (Eds.), *Research directions of Black psychologists* (pp. 351–367). New York: Russell Sage.

Boykin, A. W. (1982). Task variability and the performance of Black and White school children: Vervistic explorations. *Journal of Black Studies, 12,* 469–485.

Boykin, A. W. (1983). On academic task performance and Afro-American children. In J. Spencer (Ed.), *Achievement and achievement motives* (pp. 324–371). Boston: W. H. Freeman and Company.

Boykin, A. W. (1994). Harvesting culture and talent: African American children and educational reform. In R. Rossi (Ed.), *Educational reform and at risk students.* New York: Teachers College Press.

Boykin, A. W. (2000a). Talent development, cultural deep structure, and school reform: Implications for African immersion initiatives. In D. Pollard & C. Ajirotutu (Eds.), *African centered schooling in theory and practice* (pp. 143–162). Westport, CT: Greenwood.

Boykin, A. W. (2000b). The talent development model of schooling: Placing students at promise for academic success. *Journal of Education for Students Placed At Risk, 5,* 3–25.

Boykin, A. W., & Allen, B. (1988). Rhythmic-movement facilitated learning in working-class Afro-American children. *Journal of Genetic Psychology, 149,* 335–347.

Boykin, A. W., & Bailey, C. *Experimental research on the role of cultural factors in school relevant cognitive functioning: Synthesis of findings on cultural contexts, cultural operations and individual differences.* Center for Research on the Education of Students Placed At Risk (CRESPAR) Technical Report #42 Carol Lee (Ed.) Washington, DC/Baltimore, MD: Howard University/John Hopkins University.

Boykin, A. W., Franklin, A., & Yates, J. (1979) (Eds.), *Research directions of Black psychologists.* New York: Russell Sage Foundation.

Boykin, A. W., & Toms, F. D. (1985). Black child socialization: A conceptual framework. In H. P. McAdoo & J. L. McAdoo (Eds.), *Black children: Social, educational, and parental environments* (pp. 33–51). Beverly Hills, CA: Sage.

Boyle, P. M. (1999). *Class formation and civil society: The politics of education in Africa.* Aldershot, England: Ashgate.

Bracey, G. W. (2004, March/April). The trouble with research, Part 1/Part 2. *Phi Delta Kappan, 85*(7), 556–557/*85*(8), 635–636.

Braddock, II, J. M., & Slavin, R. E. (1995). Why ability grouping must end: Achieving excellence and equity in American education. In H. Pool & J. A. Page (Eds.), *Beyond tracking: Finding success in inclusive schools* (pp. 7–19). Bloomington, IN: Phi Delta Kappa Educational Foundation.

Braddock, J., & McPartland, J. M. (1993). Education of early adolescents. In L. Darling Hammond (Ed.), *Review of Research in Education, 19,* 135–170. Washington, DC: American Educational Research Association.

Bransford, J., Brown, A., & Cocking, R. (1999). *How people learn: Brain, mind, experience and school.* Washington, DC: National Academy Press.

Bridges, L. (1994). Exclusions: How did we get here? In J. Bourne, L. Bridges, & C. Searle (Eds.), *Outcast England: How schools exclude Black children* (pp. 1–16). London: Institute of Race Relations.

Brofenbrenner, U. (1979). *The ecology of human development: Experiment by nature and design*. Cambridge, MA: Harvard University Press.

Brooks, G. (1970). *Family pictures*. Detroit: Broadside Press. (Reprinted in Brooks, G. (1991). *Blacks*. Chicago: Third World Press.)

Bruer, J. (1993). *Schools for thought*. Cambridge, MA: MIT Press.

Bruer, J. (1999, May). In search of brain-based education. *Phi Delta Kappan, 80*(9), 648–657.

Bruner, J. (1959). Learning and thinking. *Harvard Educational Review, 29*, 184–192.

Bruner, J. (1990). *Acts of meaning*. Cambridge, MA: Harvard University Press.

Bryson, M., & de Castell, S. (1998). Gender, new technologies, and the culture of primary schooling: Imagining teachers as Luddites in/deed. *Journal of Policy Studies, 12*(5), 542–67.

Bullock, H. (1967). *A history of Negro education in the south: From 1619 to present*. Cambridge, MA: Harvard University Press.

Bunche, R. (1995). The role of the university in the political orientation of Negro youth. In R. Bunche (C. Henry, Ed.), *Selected speeches and writings* (pp. 221–230). Ann Arbor: University of Michigan Press.

Byrk, A. S., & Raudenbush, S. W. (1987). Application of hierarchical linear modes to assessing change. *Psychological Bulletin, 101*(1), 147–158.

California Commission on the Teaching Profession (1985). *Who will teach our children?* Sacramento: California Commission on the Teaching Profession.

California State Department of Education (1984). *California high school curriculum study: Path through high school*. Sacramento: California State Department of Education.

Carby, H. (1982). Schooling in Babylon. In Center for Contemporary Cultural Studies (Ed.), *The empire strikes back* (pp. 182–188). London: Hutchinson.

Carnoy, M. (1992). Education and the state: From Adam Smith to Perestroika. In R. Arnove, P. Altbach, & G. Kelly (Eds.), *Emergent issues in education* (pp. 143–159). Albany: State University of New York Press.

Carnoy, M. (1994). *Faded dreams: The politics and economics of race in America*. Cambridge: Cambridge University Press.

Carnoy, M. (2000). Globalization and educational reform. In N. P. Stromquist & K. Monkman (Eds.), *Globalization and education: Integration and contestation across cultures* (pp. 43–61). Boulder, CO: Rowman & Littlefield.

Carruthers, J. (1994). Black intellectuals and the crisis in Black education. In M. J. Shujaa (Ed.), *Too much schooling, too little education: A paradox of Black life in white societies* (pp. 37–55). Trenton, NJ: African World Press.

Case, J. (2003, March). The power of listening: How does an old-line manufacturer in a stagnant industry manage to grow 25% a year for 10 years? By taking its employees seriously. *Inc Magazine, 25*(3), 77–84, 110.

Cazden, C. (1988). *Classroom discourse: The language of teaching and learning*. Portsmouth, NH: Heinemann.

Cazden, C., John, V. P., & Hymes, D. (1972). *Functions of language in the classroom*. New York: Teachers College Press.

Cazden, C., Michaels, S., & Tabors, P. (1985). Spontaneous repairs in sharing time narratives: The intersection of metalinguistic awareness, speech event and narrative style. In S. W. Freedman (Ed.), *The acquisition of written language: Revision and response* (pp. 51–64). Norwood, NJ: Ablex.

Center for Community Partnerships (2003). The Urban Nutrition Initiative Project. www.upenn.edu/ccp/uni.shtml (accessed 1-13-03).

Césaire, A. (2000). *Discourse on colonialism.* New York: Monthly Review Press.

Chafets, Z. (2001, March 25). Changing races, *New York Daily News*, p. 4.

Chall, J. (1990). *The reading crisis: Why poor children fall behind.* Cambridge, MA: Harvard University Press.

Champion, T. (1998). Tell me something good: A description of narrative structures. *Linguistics and Education, 9*(3), 251–286.

Chazan, N. (1993). Between liberalism and statism: African political cultures and democracy. In L. Diamond, J. Linz, & S. Lipset (Eds.), *Political culture and democracy in developing countries* (pp. 67–105). Boulder, CO: Lynne Rienner.

Chi, M. T. H., Feltovich, P. J., & Glaser, R. (1981). Categorization and representation of physics problems by experts and novices. *Cognitive Science, 5,* 121–152.

Children's Defense Fund. (1975). *School suspensions: Are they helping children?* Washington, DC: Author.

Childs, J. B. (1989). *Leadership, conflict and cooperation in Afro-American social thought.* Philadelphia, PA: Temple University Press.

Cicourel, A. V., & Mehan, H. (1985). Universal development, stratifying practices, and status attainment. *Research in Social Stratification and Mobility, 4*(5), 728–734.

Clark, S. (1962). *Echo in my soul.* New York: E. P. Dutton.

Clarke, J. H. (1972). Introduction. In J. A. Rogers, *World's great men of color.* New York: Macmillan.

Clement, J. (1982). Student preconceptions of introductory mechanics. *American Journal of Physics, 50,* 66–71.

Clignet, R., & Foster, P. (1966). *The fortunate few.* Evanston, IL: Northwestern University Press.

Coard, B. (1971). *How the West Indian child is made educationally subnormal in the British school system.* London: New Beacon Books.

Coffield, F., & Vignoles, A. (1997). NICHE: Widening participation in higher education by ethnic minorities, women and alternatives students, Report 5, Section 1. In R. Dearing (Ed.), *The National Committee of Inquiry into Higher Education: Summary Report* (pp. 30–40). London: HMSO.

Cognition and Technology Group at Vanderbilt. (1997). *The Jasper project: Lessons in curriculum, instruction, assessment, and professional development.* Mahwah, NJ: Erlbaum.

Cohen, D., et al. (1990). Case studies of curriculum implementation, *Educational Evaluation and Policy Analysis, 12*(3). Entire volume.

Cole, M. (1996). *Cultural psychology: A once and future discipline.* Cambridge, MA: The Belknap Press of Harvard University Press.

Coleman, J. S., Campbell, E. Q., Hobson, C. J., McPartland, J., Mood, A. M., Weinfeld, F. D., & York, R. L. (1966). *Equality of educational opportunity.* Washington, DC: U.S. Government Printing Office.

Coleman, J. S. (1965). *Education and political participation.* Princeton, NJ: Princeton University Press.

Coleman, J. S. (1988). Social capital in the creation of human capital. *American Journal of Sociology, 94,* 95–120.

Coleman, J. S. (1990). *Foundations of social theory.* Cambridge, MA: Belknap Press of Harvard University.

College Board. (1985). *Equality and excellence: The educational status of Black Americans.* New York: College Entrance Examination Board.

College Board. (2000). *Reaching the top: A report of the National Task Force on Minority Achievement.* New York: Author.

Collins, A., Brown, J., & Newman, S. (1989). Cognitive apprenticeship; teaching the craft of reading, writing and mathematics. In L. Resnick (Ed.), *Knowing, learning, and instruction: Essays in honor of Robert Glaser* (pp. 453–493). Hillsdale, NJ: Erlbaum.

Collins, C., & Yeskel, F. with United for a Fair Economy (2000). *Economic apartheid in America: A primer on economic inequality and insecurity.* New York: The New Press.

Comer, J. (1980). *School power.* New York: The Free Press.

Comer, J. (1988). Educating poor minority children. *Scientific American, 159*(5), 42–48.

Commission on Chapter 1 (1992). *High performance schools: No exceptions, no excuses.* Washington, DC: Author.

Conant, F. (1996). Drums in the science lab. *Hands On, 19*(1), 7–10.

Conley, D. (1999). *Being Black, living in the red: Race, wealth, and social policy in America.* Berkeley: University of California Press.

Cook-Gumperz, J. (Ed.). (1986). The social construction of literacy. New York: Cambridge University Press.

Cooper, A. J. (1988). *A voice from the South.* New York: Oxford University Press.

Cooper, E., & Sherk, J. (1989). Addressing urban school reform: Issues and alliances. *Journal of Negro Education, 58*(3), 315–331.

Cooper, R., Slavin, R., & Madden, N. (1997). (Report No. 16). Baltimore, MD: Center for Research on the Education of Students Placed At Risk (CRESPAR), John Hopkins University.

Copley, P. O. (1974). *A study of the effect of professional education courses on beginning teachers.* Springfield, MO: Southwest Missouri State University. ERIC Document No. ED 098 147.

Cosby, C. O. (1994). *Television's imageable influences: The self-perceptions of young African Americans.* New York: University Press of America.

Council of Independent Black Institutions. (CIBI). (1990). *Positive Afrikan images for children.* Trenton, NJ: Red Sea Press.

Courlander, H. (1967). *The African.* New York: Henry Holt & Company, Inc.

Chuck, D. (1997). *Fight the power: Rap, race, and reality.* New York: Delta Books.

Daniel, D. (2001). Crossing the divide: Black academics at the Rand Afrikaans University. In R. O. Mabokela & K. L. King (Eds.), *Apartheid no more* (pp. 37–58). Westport, CT: Bergin & Garvey.

Darity, W. A., Jr., & Mason, P. L. (1998, Spring). Evidence on discrimination in employment: Codes of color, codes of gender. *Journal of Economic Perspectives, 12*(2), 63–90.

Darling-Hammond, L. (1990a). Instructional policy into practice: The power of the bottom over the top. *Educational Evaluation and Policy Analysis, 12*(3), 233–242.

Darling-Hammond, L. (1990b). Teacher quality and equality. In J. Goodlad & P. Keating (Eds.), *Access to knowledge: An agenda for our nation's schools* (pp. 237–258). New York: College Entrance Examination Board.

Darling-Hammond, L. (1992). Teaching and knowledge: Policy issues posed by alternate certification for teachers. *Peabody Journal of Education, 67*(3), 123–154.

Darling-Hammond, L. (1997). *The right to learn: A blueprint for creating schools that work.* San Francisco, CA: Jossey Bass.

Darling-Hammond, L. (1999). *Teacher quality and student achievement: A review of state policy evidence.* Seattle, WA: Center for the Study of Teaching and Policy.

Darling-Hammond, L. (2000). Teacher quality and student achievement: A review of state policy evidence. *Educational Policy Analysis Archives, 8*(1). http://epaa.asu.edu/epaa/v8n1.

Darling-Hammond, L., & Snyder, J. (1992). Traditions of curriculum inquiry: The scientific tradition. In P. W. Jackson (Ed.), *Handbook of research on curriculum.* New York: Macmillan.

Davis, A. Y. (1988). Masked racism: Reflections on the prison industrial complex. *Color Lines,* Fall, 12–14.

Davis, D. G. (1986). A pilot study to assess equity in selected curricular offerings across three diverse schools in a large urban school district. Paper presented at the Annual Meeting of the American Educational Research Association, San Francisco.

de Castell, S. (2000). Literacies, technologies, and the future of the library in the information age. *Journal of Curriculum Studies, 32*(3), 359–376.

Delpit, L. (1986). Skills and other dilemmas of a progressive Black educator. *Harvard Educational Review, 56*(4), 379–385.

Delpit, L. (1988). The silenced dialogue. *Harvard Educational Review, 58*(3), 280–298.

Delpit, L. (1995). *Other people's children: Cultural conflict in the classroom.* New York: The New Press.

Delpit, L., & Dowdy, J. K. (2002). *The skin that we speak: Thoughts on language and culture in the classroom.* New York: New Press.

Demarco, J. (1974, March). The rationale and foundation of DuBois's theory of economic cooperation. *Phylon, 35*(1), 5–15.

DeMeis, D. K., & Turner, R. R. (1978). Effects of students' race, physical attractiveness and dialect on teachers' evaluations. *Contemporary Educational Psychology, 3,* 77–86.

Department for Education and Employment (2001). *Reason for exclusion from school.* London: Author.

Department for Education and Skills (2003). *Aiming high: Raising the achievement of minority ethnic pupils.* London: Author.

DiMaggio, P., & Mohr, J. (1985). Cultural capital, educational attainment, and marital selection. *American Journal of Sociology, 90*(6), 1231–1261.

Diop, C. A. (1991). *Civilization or barbarism: An authentic anthropology.* Brooklyn, NY: Lawrence Hill.

Diouf, S. A. (1998). *Servants of Allah: African Muslims enslaved in the Americas.* New York: University Press.

DiSessa, A. (1982). Unlearning Aristotelian physics: A study of knowledge-base learning. *Cognitive Science, 6,* 37–75.

Dole, J. A., Duffy, G. G., Roehler, L. R., & Pearson, P. D. (1991). Moving from the old to the new: Research on reading comprehension. *Review of Educational Research, 61*(2), 239–264.

Donovan, M. S., Bransford, J. D., & Pellegrino, J. W. (1999). *How people learn: Bridging research and practice.* Washington, DC: National Academy Press.

Dove, N. (1993). The emergence of Black supplementary schools: Resistance to racism in the United Kingdom. *Urban Education, 27,* 430–470.

Dreeben, R. (1987, Winter). Closing the divide: What teachers and administrators can do to help Black students reach their reading potential. *American Educator, 11*(4), 28–35.

Dreeben, R., & Barr, R. (1987). *Class composition and the design of instruction.* Paper presented at the annual meeting of the American Education Research Association, Washington, DC.

Dreeban, R., & Gamoran, A. (1986). Race, instruction and learning. *American Sociological Review, 51,* 660–669.

Drucker, P. F. (1993). *Post-capitalist society.* New York: Harper.

Drucker, P. F. (1994, November). The age of social transformation. *Atlantic Monthly,* 53–80.

Druva, C. A., & Anderson, R. D. (1983). Science teacher characteristics by teacher behavior and by student outcome: A meta-analysis of research. *Journal of Research in Science Teaching, 20*(5), 467–479.

Du Bois, W. E. B. (1907). *Economic cooperation among Negro Americans.* Atlanta, GA: Atlanta University Press.

Du Bois, W. E. B. (1933). Where do we go from here? (A lecture on Negroes' economic plight). An address delivered at the Rosenwald Economic Conference, Washington, DC, May 1933. First published in *The Baltimore Afro-American,* May 20, 1933. Reprinted in A. G. Paschal, (Ed.), *A W. E. B. Du Bois reader* (pp. 146–163). New York: Collier Books (1971).

Du Bois, W. E. B. (1935, July). Does the Negro need separate schools? *Journal of Negro Education,* 328–335.

Du Bois, W. E. B. (1968). *The souls of Black folk: Essays and sketches.* Greenwich, CT: Fawcett.

Du Bois, W. E. B. (1973). *The education of Black people: Ten critiques 1906–1960.* New York: Monthly Review Press.

Du Bois, W. E. B. (1975). *Dusk of dawn*. Millwood, New York: Krause Thompson.

Durkheim, E. (1899/1956). *Education and sociology*. Glencoe, IL: Free Press.

Dyson, A. (1997). *Writing superheroes: Contemporary childhood, popular culture and classroom literacy*. New York: Teachers College Press.

Dyson, A. (2000). Linking writing and community development through the children's forum. In C. D. Lee, P. Smagorinsky, et al. (Eds.), *Vygotskian perspectives on literacy research: Constructing meaning through collaborative inquiry* (pp. 127–149). New York: Cambridge University Press.

Dyson, A. (2003). *The brothers and sisters learn to write: Popular literacies in childhood and school cultures*. New York: Teachers College Press.

Dzvimbo, K. P. (1991). The transition state and the dialectics of educational transformation in the Third World: The case of Zimbabwe. *International Studies in Sociology of Education, 1*(1), 43–58.

Ebmeier, H., Twombly, S., & Teeter, D. (1990). The comparability and adequacy of financial support for schools of education. *Journal of Teacher Education, 42*(3), 226–235.

Eccles, J., & Midgley, C. (1988). Stage environment fit: Developmentally appropriate classrooms for early adolescents. In R. E. Ames & C. Ames (Eds.), *Research on motivation in education*, Vol. 3 (pp. 139–180). New York: Academic Press.

Eckstrom, R., & Villegas, A. M. (1991). Ability grouping in middle grade mathematics: Process and consequences. *Research in Middle Level Education, 15*(1), 1–20.

Edmonds, R. (1979). Effective schools for the urban poor. *Educational Leadership, 37*, 15–24.

Educational Testing Service (1991). *The state of inequality*. Princeton, NJ: Author.

The Education Trust. (1999). *Ticket to nowhere* (Vol. 3, Issue 2). Washington, DC: New York Author.

Eggleston, J., Dunn, D., Anjail, M., & Wright, C. (1986). *Education for some: The educational and vocational experiences of 15–18 year-old members of minority ethnic groups*. Stoke-on-Trent, UK: Trentham Books.

Elder, G. (1985). Household, kinship, and the life course: Perspectives on Black families and children. In M. B. Spencer, G. K. Brookins, & W. R. Allen (Eds.), *Beginnings: The social and affective development of Black children* (pp. 29–44). Mahwah, NJ: Erlbaum.

Elley, R. (1992). *How in the world do students read?* Hamburg: The Hague International Association for the Evaluation of Educational Achievement.

Ellis, J. B. (2003). *Palaver Tree Online: Technological support for classroom integration of oral history*. Ph.D. Dissertation, Georgia Institute of Technology.

Ellis, J. B., & Bruckman, A. S. (2002). *What do kids learn from adults online? Examining student-elder discourse in Palaver Tree*. Electronic Proceedings of *CSCL 2002* Conference on Computer Supported Collaborative Learning, Boulder, CO, January 7–11.

The Encyclopedia of American Education. (1996). Facts on File, p. 320.

Esdaille, M., & Hughes, A. (2004, February). The Afro-Latino connection. *Black Enterprise, 34*(7), 111–118.

Evenson, B. (1998, February 23). Land crisis brewing down under: A 1996 court ruling means aboriginals could claim 80 per cent of Australia's landmass. *The Ottawa Citizen*, p. A–10.

Evertson, C., Hawley, W., & Zlotnick, M. (1985). Making a difference in educational quality through teacher education. *Journal of Teacher Education, 36*(3), 2–12.

Fanon, F. (1965/1968). *The wretched of the earth*. New York: Grove Press.

Fanon, F. (1967). *Black skins white masks: The experiences of a Black man in a white world*. New York: Grove Press.

Farrell, J. (1992). Conceptualizing education and the drive for social equality. In R. Arnove, P. Altbach, & G. Kelly (Eds.), *Emergent issues in education* (pp. 107–122). Albany: State University of New York Press.

Federation of Southern Cooperatives/Land Assistance Fund (FSC/LAF). (2002). Thirty-Fifth Anniversary Annual Report-2002: Learning from our history as we plan for our future. East Point, GA: FSC/LAF.

Fenton, T. L. (2002). *The democratic company: Four organizations transforming our workplace and our world*. Arlington, VA: World Dynamics, Inc.

Ferguson, R. F. (1991, Summer). Paying for public education: New evidence on how and why money matters. *Harvard Journal on Legislation, 28*(2), 465–498.

Ferguson, R. F., & Ladd, H. F. (1996). How and why money matters: An analysis of Alabama schools. In H. F. Ladd (Ed.), *Holding schools accountable* (pp. 265–298). Washington, DC: Brookings Institute.

Fine, M. (1994). Working the hyphens: Reinventing self and other in qualitative research. In N. K. Denzin & Y. S. Lincoln (Eds.), *Handbook of Qualitative Research* (pp. 70–82). Thousand Oaks, CA: Sage Publications.

Finley, M. K. (1984). Teachers and tracking in a comprehensive high school. *Sociology of Education, 57*, 233–243.

Fitzerald, R., Finch, S., & Nove, A. (2000). *Black Caribbean young men's experiences of education and employment*. London: Department for Education and Employment Publications, HMSO.

Flateau, J. (1966). *The prison industrial complex: Race, crime & justice in New York*. Brooklyn, NY: Medgar Evers College Du Bois Center for Public Policy.

Fleming, J. (1976). *The lengthening shadow of slavery: A historical justification for affirmative action for Blacks in higher education*. Washington, DC: Howard University Press.

Foley, D. (1991). Reconsidering anthropological explanations of ethnic school failure. *Anthropology and Education Quarterly, 22*, 60–86.

Fordham, S., & Ogbu, J. (1986). Black students' school success: Coping with the burden of "acting White". *Urban Review, 18*, 176–206.

Foster, M. (1987). *"It's cookin' now": An ethnographic study of a successful Black teacher in an urban community college*. Unpublished doctoral dissertation, Harvard University, Cambridge, MA.

Foster, M. (1994). Educating for competence in community and culture: Exploring views of exemplary African-American teachers. In M. Shujaa (Ed.), *Too much schooling, too little education: A paradox of Black life in white societies* (pp. 221–244). Trenton, NJ: Africa World Press.

Foster, M. (1997). *Black teachers on teaching*. New York: The New Press.

Foster, M. (1998). Race, class and gender in education research: Surveying the political terrain. *Educational Policy, 13*(1), 77–85.

Foster, M. (2001). Teaching Black students: Best practices. Paper prepared for the Commission on Research in Black Education. In J. E. King (Ed.), Facing the New Millennium: A transformative research and action agenda in Black Education. Final Report to AERA. Washington, DC: AERA.

Foster, P. (1980, June). Education and social inequality in Africa. *The Journal of Modern African Studies, 18*, 201–236.

Frankenstein, M. (1995). Equity in mathematics education: Class in the world outside the class. In W. Secada, E. Fennema, & L. B. Adajian (Eds.), *New directions for equity in mathematics education* (pp. 165–190). New York: Cambridge University Press.

Franklin, J. H., & Moss, Jr., A. A. (1988). *From slavery to freedom: A history of Negro Americans* (6th ed.). New York: McGraw–Hill.

Franklin, V. P. (1985). From integration to Black self-determination: Changing social science perspectives on Afro-American life and culture. In M. B. Spencer, G. K. Brookins, & W. R. Allen (Eds.), *Beginnings: The social and affective development of black children* (pp. 19–28). Mahwah, NJ: Erlbaum.

Frederiksen, N. (1986). Toward a broader conception of human intelligence. In R. J. Sternberg, & R. K. Wagner (Eds.), *Practical intelligence: Nature and origins of competence in the everyday world* (pp. 84–118). New York: Cambridge University Press.

Freeman, K. (1997, September/October). Increasing African Americans' participation in higher education: African American high school students' perspective. *The Journal of Higher Education, 68*(5), 523–550.

Freeman, K. (Ed.). (1998). *African American culture and heritage in higher education research and practice*. Westport, CT: Praeger Press.

Freeman, K. (1999, Fall). My soul is missing: African American students' perceptions of the curriculum and the influence on college choice. *Review of African American Education, 1*(1), 30–43.

Freeman, K., Carnoy, M., Findlay, H., Joiner, B., & Magyari-Beck, I. (1999). *Economic development and the utilization of human potential: Bridging the gap between higher education, economics, and culture*. Nashville, TN: Vanderbilt University, Department of Leadership and Organizations.

Fryer, P. (1992). *Staying power: The history of Black people in Britain* (6th ed.). London: Pluto Press.

Fuller, B. (1991). *Growing-up modern: The western state builds third-world schools*. New York: Routledge.

Fuson, K. C. (1990). Conceptual structures for multiunit numbers: Implications for learning and teaching multidigit addition, subtraction, and place value. *Cognition and Instruction, 7*, 343–403.

Fuson, K. C. (1996). Latino children's construction of arithmetic understanding in urban classrooms that support thinking. Paper presented at the annual meeting of the American Educational Research Association, New York.

Fuson, K., Smith, S., & LoCicero, A. (1997). Supporting Latino first graders' ten-structured thinking in urban classrooms. *Journal for Research in Mathematics Education, 28,* 738–760.

Gall, C. (2004, December 27). Afghan students are back, but not the old textbooks. *New York Times.* http://www.nytimes.com. (Retrieved December 27, 2004)

Gallagher, K. S., & Bailey, J. D. (2000). *The politics of teacher education.* Thousand Oaks, CA: Corwin Press.

Gamoran, A. (1990). The consequences of track-related instructional differences for student achievement. Paper presented at the annual meeting of the American Educational Research Association, Boston, MA.

Gamoran, A. (1992). Access to excellence: Assignment to honors English classes in the transition from middle to high school. *Educational Evaluation and Policy Analysis, 14*(3), 185–204.

Gamoran, A., & Berends, M. (1987). The effects of stratification in secondary schools: Synthesis of survey and ethnographic research. *Review of Educational Research, 57,* 415–436.

Gamoran, A., & Mare, R. (1989). Secondary school tracking and educational inequality: Compensation, reinforcement or neutrality? *American Journal of Sociology, 94,* 1146–1183.

Garcia, E. (1993). Language, culture, and education. In L. Darling-Hammond (Ed.), *Review of Research in Education, 19,* 51–98. Washington, DC: American Educational Research Association.

Garcia, E. (2001). *Hispanic education in the United States: Raíces y alas.* New York: Rowman & Littlefield.

Gay, G. (1995). Curriculum theory and multicultural education. J. Banks & C. M. Banks (Eds.), *Handbook of research on multicultural education* (pp. 25–43). New York: Macmillan.

Gay, G. (2000). *Culturally responsive teaching: theory, research, and practice.* New York: Teachers College Press.

Geber, M. (1958). The psychomotor development of African children in the first year and the influence of maternal behavior. *Journal of Social Psychology, 47,* 185–195.

Gee, J. P. (1989). The narrativization of experience in the oral style. *Journal of Education, 171*(1), 75–96.

Gee, J. P. (1990). *Social linguistics and literacies: Ideology in discourses.* New York: The Falmer Press.

Gemignani, R. J. (1994, October). Juvenile correctional education: A time for change. Update on research. *Juvenile Justice Bulletin.* U.S. Department of Justice, Office of Juvenile Justice and Delinquency Prevention.

Gillborn, D., & Mirza, H. S. (2000). *Inequality: Mapping race, class and gender—A synthesis of research evidence.* Office for Standards in Education in Education. London: The Stationery Office.

Gillborn, D., & Gipps, C. (1996). *Recent research on the achievements of ethnic minority pupils.* London: HMSO.

Gilyard, K. (1991). *Voices of the self: A study of language competence*. Detroit, MI: Wayne State University Press.

Glaser, R. (1981). The future of testing: A research agenda for cognitive psychology and psychometrics. *American Psychologist, 39*(9), 923–936.

Glaser, R. (1990). *Testing and assessment: O Tempora! O Mores!* Pittsburgh, PA: University of Pittsburgh, Learning Research and Development Center.

Goldenberg, D. M. (2003). *The curse of Ham, race and slavery in Early Judaism, Christianity and Islam*. Princeton, NJ: Princeton University Press.

Gomes, N. L., & Gonçalves e Silva, P. (2002). *Experiencias ethnico-culturais para a formação de professores* (Ethnic-cultural experiences for the education of teachers). Belo Horizonte, Brazil: Autentica.

Gomez, D. L., & Grobe, R. P. (1990). Three years of alternative certification in Dallas: Where are we? Paper presented at the annual meeting of the American Educational Research Association, Boston.

Good, T. L., & Brophy, J. (1987). *Looking in classrooms*. New York: Harper and Row.

Goodwin, S., & Swartz, E. (2004). *Teaching children of color: Seven constructs of effective teaching in urban schools*. Rochester, NY: RTA Press.

Gordon, B. (1990). The necessity of African-American epistemology for educational theory and practice. *Boston Journal of Education, 172*(3), 88–106.

Gordon, B. (1993). African-American cultural knowledge and liberation education; Dilemmas, problems, and potentials in a postmodern American society. *Urban Education, 27*(4), 448–470.

Gordon, E. W. (1997, April). Report of the Task Force on the Role and Future of Minorities in the American Educational Research Association. *Educational Researcher, 44*, 44–52.

Gordon, E. W. (1999). *Education and justice: A view from the back of the bus*. New York: Teachers College Press.

Gordon, E. W. (2000). Production of knowledge and pursuit of understanding. In E. W. Gordon (Ed.), *Advances in education in diverse communities: Research, policy, and praxis* (pp. 310–318). New York: JAI Press.

Goslee, S. (1998). *Losing ground bit by bit: Low-income communities in the information age*. Washington, DC: Benton Foundation.

Gottschild, B. D. (1996). *Digging the Africanist presence in American performance: Dance and other contexts*. Westport, CT: Praeger.

Gould, S. J. (1981). *The mismeasure of man*. New York: W. W. Norton.

Graham, S. (1994). Motivation in African Americans. *Review of Educational Research, 64*, 55–117.

Graham-Brown, S. (1991). *Education in the developing world: Conflict and crisis*. London: Longman.

Grant, C. A. (1989, June). Urban teachers: Their new colleagues and curriculum. *Phi Delta Kappan, 70*(10), 764–770.

Graves, B., & Frederiksen, C. H. (1996). A cognitive study of literary expertise. In R. J. Kruez & M. S. MacNealy (Eds.), *Empirical approaches to literature and aesthetics* (pp. 397–418). Norwood, NJ: Ablex.

Green, J. L., & Dixon, C. N. (1994). Talking knowledge into being: Discursive and social practices in classrooms. *Linguistics and Education, 5*(3 & 4), 231–239.

Greenberg, J. D. (1983). The case for teacher education: Open and shut. *Journal of Teacher Education, 34*(4), 2–5.

Greenfield, P. M., & Cocking, R. R. (1994). *Cross-cultural roots of minority child development.* Hillsdale, NJ: Erlbaum.

Greeno, J. G. (1997). Response: On claims that answer the wrong questions. *Educational Researcher, 26*(1), 5–17.

Greenwald, R., Hedges, L. V., & Laine, R. D. (1996). The effect of school resources on student achievement. *Review of Educational Research, 66*, 361–396.

Grossman, P. L. (1989). Learning to teach without teacher education, *Teachers College Record, 91*(2), 191–208.

Grossman, P. L. (1990). *The making of a teacher: Teacher knowledge and teacher education.* New York: Teachers College Press.

Guinier, L., & Torres, G. (2002). *The miner's canary: Enlisting race, resisting power, transforming democracy.* Cambridge, MA: Harvard University Press.

Gumperz, J. J. (1982). *Discourse strategies.* New York: Cambridge University Press.

Gutiérrez, K., & Rogoff, B. (2003). Cultural ways of learning: Individual traits or repertoires of practice. *Educational Researcher, 32*(5), 19–25.

Gutiérrez, K., Baquedano-Lopez, P., & Tejeda, C. (1999). Rethinking diversity: Hybridity and hybrid language practices in the third space. *Mind, Culture & Activity: An International Journal, 6*(4), 286–303.

Gutiérrez, K., Rymes, B., & Larson, J. (1995). Script, counterscript, and underlife in the classroom: James Brown versus Brown *vs.* Board of Education. *Harvard Educational Review, 65*(3), 445–471.

Gyimah-Brempong, K., & Fichtenbaum, R. (1997). Black-White wage differential: The relative importance of human capital and labor market structure. In J. B. Stewart (Ed.), *African Americans and post-industrial labor markets* (pp. 139–172). New Brunswick, NJ: Transaction Publishers.

Haidara, Y. M., Maiga, Y. B., Maiga, M. B., & Hutchison, J. P. (1992). *Lexique Soŋay-Français: Kalimaway citaabo Soŋay-Annasaara Šenni.* Bamako, Mali: MEN—DNAFLA.

Hale, J. (1994). *Unbank the fire: Visions for the education of African American children.* Baltimore, MD: John Hopkins University Press.

Hale-Benson, J. (1986). *Black children: Their roots, culture and learning styles.* Baltimore, MD: John Hopkins University Press.

Hallak, J. (2000, November). Guarding the common interest. *UNESCO Courier,* 16–17.

Haney, W. (2000). The myth of the Texas miracle in education. *Education Policy Analysis Archives, 8*(41): http://epaa.asu.edu/epaa/v8n41/.

Harber, C. (1997). *Education, democracy and political development in Africa.* Brighton (England): Sussex Academic Press.

Harding, V. (1981). *There is a river: The Black struggle for freedom in America.* New York: Harcourt Brace Jovanovich.

Hart, M. H. (1978). *The 100: A ranking of the most influential persons in history.* New York: Citadel Press.

Hartman, W. T. (1988). District spending disparities: What do the dollars buy? *Journal of Education Finance, 13*(4), 436–359.

Hawisher, G., & Selfe, C. (2000). *Global literacies and the world-wide web.* New York: Routledge.

Haynes, C., Jr. (1993). *An essay in the art of economic cooperation: Cooperative enterprise and economic development in Black America.* Unpublished Ph.D. dissertation. University of Massachusetts, Amherst.

Haynes, C., Jr. (1994, October). A democratic cooperative enterprise system: A response to urban economic decay. *Ceteris Paribus, 4*(2), 19–30.

Haynes, C., Jr., & Nembhard, J. G. (1999, Summer). Cooperative economics: A community revitalization strategy. *The Review of Black Political Economy, 27*(1), 47–71.

Haynes, N., & Comer, J. (1993). The Yale school development program: Process, outcomes, and policy implications. *Urban Education, 28*(2), 166–199.

Hearn, J. C. (1991). Academic and nonacademic influences on the college destinations of 1980 high school graduates. *Sociology of Education, 64*, 158–171.

Heath, S. B. (1983). *Ways with words: Language, life and work in communities and classrooms.* New York: Cambridge University Press.

Heath, S. B. (2000). Island by island we must go across: Challenges from language and culture among African Americans. In D. Pollard & C. Ajirotutu (Eds.), *African centered schooling in theory and practice* (pp. 163–186). Westport, CT: Bergin & Garvey.

Henry, A. (1998b). Speaking up and speaking out: Examining voice in a reading/writing program with adolescent African Caribbean girls. *Journal of Literacy Research, 30*(2), 233–252.

Herbert, T. (1999). The concept of Jegna. *Psych Discourse, 30*(11), 1.

Herman, R., & Stringfield, S. (1997). *Ten promising programs for educating the disadvantaged: Evidence of impact.* Arlington, VA: Educational Research Service.

Herrnstein, R., & Murray, C. (1994). *The Bell-curve: Intelligence and class structure in American life.* New York: The Free Press.

Herskovitz, M. J. (1958). *The myth of the Negro past.* Boston, MA: Beacon Press.

Hicks, D. (1991). Kinds of narrative: Genre skills among first graders from two communities. In A. McCabe & C. Peterson (Eds.), *Developing narrative structures* (pp. 55–87). Hillsdale, NY: Erlbaum.

Hilliard, A. G. (1976). *Alternatives to IQ testing: An approach to the assessment of gifted "minority" children.* Final Report to the Special Education Support Unit. Sacramento: California State Dept. of Education.

Hilliard, A. G. (1991). Do we have the will to educate all children? *Educational Leadership, 49*(1), 31–36.

Hilliard, A. G. (1995). *The maroon within us: Selected essays on African American community socialization.* Baltimore, MD: Black Classic Press.

Hilliard, A. G. (1997). *SBA: Reawakening of the African mind*. Gainesville, FL: Makare.

Hilliard, A. G. (2000a, April). The state of African education. Paper presented at the AERA 2000 annual meeting. New Orleans, LA.

Hilliard, A. G. (2000b). "Race," identity, hegemony, and education: What do we need to know now? In W. H. Watkins, J. H. Lewis, & V. Chou (Eds.), *Race and education: The roles of history and society in educating African American students* (pp. 7–33). Boston: Allyn and Bacon.

Hilliard, A. G. (2002). *African power: Affirming African indigenous socialization in the face of the culture wars*. Gainesville, FL: Makare.

Hilliard, A. G., & Leonard, C. (1990). (Eds.). *African American baseline essays*. Portland, OR: Portland Public Schools.

Hoffer, T. B. (1992). Middle school ability grouping and student achievement in science and mathematics. *Educational Evaluation and Policy Analysis, 14*(3), 205–227.

Holland, J. (1998). *Emergence from chaos to order*. Cambridge, MA: Perseus Books.

Hollins, E. R. (1996a). *Culture in school: Revealing the deeper meaning*. Mahwah, NJ: Lawrence Erlbaum Associates.

Hollins, E. R. (1996b). *Transforming curriculum for a culturally diverse society*. Mahwah, NJ: Lawrence Erlbaum Associates.

Holt, T. C. (2000). *The problem of race in the 21st century*. Cambridge, MA: Harvard University Press.

hooks, b. (1992). *Black looks: Race and representation*. Boston, MA: South End Press.

Hooper, P. K. (1996). "They have their own thoughts": A story of constructivist learning in an alternative African-centered community school. In Y. Kafai & M. Resnick (Eds.), *Constructionism in practice: Designing, thinking, and learning in a digital world* (pp. 241–255). Mahwah, NJ: Lawrence Erlbaum Associates.

Hooper, P. K. (1998). They have their own thoughts: Children's learning of computational ideas from a cultural constructionist perspective. Ph.D. Thesis, Massachusetts Institute of Technology.

Hope, J., II. (1940, First Quarter). Rochdale cooperation among Negroes. *Phylon 1*(1), 39–52.

Hopson, R. K. (2001). Higher education transformation in Namibia. In R. O. Mabokela & K. L. King (Eds.), *Apartheid no more* (pp. 121–138). Westport, CT: Bergin & Garvey.

Horvat, E. N., & Lewis, K. S. (2003). Reassessing the "Burden of 'Acting White'": The importance of peer groups in managing academic success. *Sociology of Education, 76*(4), 265–280.

Hossler, D., & Gallagher, K. (1987). Studying student college choice: A three-phase model and the implications for policymakers. *College & University, 62*(3), 207–221.

(2000, September 27). "How the studios used Children to test-market violent films," *New York Times*, pp. A1, A21.

Howe, F. (1965). Mississippi's freedom schools: The politics of education. *Harvard Educational Review, 35*(2), 144–160.

Howes, C., & Hamilton, C. E. (1992). Children's relationships with caregivers: Mothers and child care teachers. *Child Development, 63*(4), 859–866.

Howes, C., & Matheson, C. C. (1992). Sequences in the development of competent play with peers: Social and social pretend play. *Developmental Psychology, 28*(5), 961–974.

Hudicourt-Barnes, J. (2003). The use of argumentation in Haitian Creole science classrooms. *Harvard Educational Review, 73*(1), 73–93.

Hyon, S., & Sulzby, E. (1994). African American kindergarteners' spoken narratives: Topic associating and topic centered styles. *Linguistics and Education, 6*(2), 121–152.

Icarus Films. (2000). *The intolerable burden.* Brooklyn, NY: Author.

Inkeles, A. (1969a). Participant citizenship in six developing countries. *American Political Science Review, 43,* 1122–1133.

Inkeles, A. (1969b). Making men modern. *American Journal of Sociology, 75,* 208–225.

Institute of Islamic Thought (1982). *Islamization of knowledge: General principles and work plan.* Herndon, VA: Author.

IPN-DNAFLA (1999). *Caw tiira.* (*Grades 3–6*). Bamako, Mali: Author.

Irvine, J. J. (1990). *Black students and school failure: Policies, practices, and prescriptions.* Westport, CT: Praeger.

Irvine, J. J. (2003). *Educating teachers for diversity: Seeing with a cultural eye.* New York: Teachers College Press.

Irvine, J., & York, D. E. (1995). Learning styles and culturally diverse students: A literature review. In J. Banks & C. M. Banks (Eds.), *Handbook of research on multicultural education* (pp. 484–497). New York: Macmillan.

Jackson, F., & Jackson, J. (1978). *Infant culture.* New York: New American Library.

Jackson, R., & Rosberg, C. (1982). *Personal rule in Black Africa: Prince, autocrat, prophet, tyrant.* Berkeley, CA: University of California Press.

Jacobs, H. (1988). *Incidents in the life of a slave girl: Written by herself.* New York: Oxford University Press.

James, C. L. R. (1970). The Atlantic slave trade and slavery: Some interpretations of their significance in the development of the United States and the western world. In J. A. Williams & C. F. Harris, (Eds.), *Amistad 1* (pp. 119–164). New York: Vintage Books.

Jencks, C. (1972). *Inequality: A reassessment of the effect of family and schooling in America.* New York, NY: Basic Books.

Jencks, C., & Phillips, M. (1998). *The Black-White test score gap.* Washington, DC: Brookings Institution Press.

Jenson, J. (2003). Women@work: Listening to gendered relations of power in teachers' talk about new technologies. *Gender and Education, 15*(2), 169–81.

John, B. M. (1997). The African American female ontology: Implications for academe. In L. Benjamin (Ed.), *Black women in the academy: Promises and perils* (pp. 53–63). Gainesville: University of Florida Press.

Johns, R. L., Morphet, E. L., & Alexander, K. (1983). *The economics and financing of education* (4th ed.). Englewood Cliffs, NJ: Prentice Hall.

John-Steiner, V. (2000). *Thought communities: Dynamics of collaboration*. New York: Oxford University Press.

Jones, L. (2000). *Brothers of the academy: Up and coming Black scholars earning our way in higher education*. Sterling, VA: Stylus Publishing.

Jones, L. V. (1984). White-black achievement differences: The narrowing gap. *American Psychologist, 39*, 1207–1213.

Jones, L. V., Burton, N. W., & Davenport, E. C. (1984). Monitoring the achievement of Black students. *Journal for Research in Mathematics Education, 15*, 154–164.

Jones, R. L. (1980). *Black psychology* (2nd ed.). New York: Harper & Row.

Ka, F. (1998). *Black people's situation in Portugal*. Paper prepared for Fisk University Race Relations Institute Conference, Nashville, Tennessee.

Kafai, Y., & Resnick, M. (1996). *Constructionism in practice: Designing, thinking and learning in a digital world*. Mahwah, NJ: Erlbaum.

Kambon, K. K. K. (1996). The Africentric paradigm and African American psychological liberation. In D. A. ya Azibo (Ed.), *African psychology in historical perspective & related commentary*. Trenton, NJ: Africa World Press.

Kantrowitz, B., & Scelfo, J. (2004, March 22). American masala. *Newsweek*, 50–57.

Karenga, M. (1988). *The African-American holiday of Kwanzaa: A celebration of family, community, and culture*. Los Angeles: University of Sankore Press.

Karenga, M. (1993). *Introduction to Black Studies*. Los Angeles: University of Sankore Press.

Kaufman, J. E., & Rosenbaum, J. E. (1992). Education and employment of low-income Black youth in white suburbs. *Educational Evaluation and Policy Analysis, 14*(3), 229–240.

King, J. E. (Ed.). (1990). In search of African liberation pedagogy: Multiple contexts of education and struggle. *Journal of Education, 172*(2).

King, J. E. (1992). Diaspora literacy and consciousness in the struggle against miseducation in the Black community. *Journal of Negro Education, 61*(3), 317–338.

King, J. E. (1994). The purpose of schooling for African American students. In E. R. Hollins, J. E. King & W. C. Hayman (Eds.), *Teaching diverse populations: Formulating a knowledgebase* (pp. 25–44). Albany: SUNY Press.

King, J. E. (1995). Culture-centered knowledge: Black studies, curriculum transformation, and social action. In J. Banks & C. A. Banks (Eds.), *Handbook of research on multicultural education* (pp. 265–290). New York: Macmillan.

King, J. E. (1997). Thank you for opening our minds: On praxis, transmutation and Black Studies in teacher development. In J. E. King, E. R. Hollins, & W. C. Hayman (Eds.), *Preparing teachers for cultural diversity* (pp. 156–169). New York: Teachers College Press.

King, J. E. (1999). In search of a method for liberating education and research: The half (that) has not been told. In C. Grant (Ed.), *Multicultural research: A reflective engagement with race, class, gender and sexual orientation* (pp. 101–119). Philadelphia, PA: Falmer Press.

King, J. E. (2001). *Facing the New Millennium: A transformative research and action agenda in Black Education*. Final Report to AERA. Washington, DC, AERA.

King, J. E. (2004). Cultural knowledge. In. S. Goodwin & E. Swartz (Eds.), *Teaching children of color: Seven constructs of effective teaching in urban schools* (pp. 53–61). Rochester, NY: RTA Press.

King, J., & Lightfoote-Wilson, T. L. (1994). Being the soul-freeing substance: A legacy of hope in AfroHumanity. In M. Shujaa (Ed.), *Too much schooling, too little education: A paradox of life in Black Societies* (pp. 269–294). Trenton, NS: Africa World Press. Inc.

King, J. E., & Mitchell, C. A. (1995). *Black mothers to sons: Juxtaposing African American literature with social practice.* New York: Peter Lang Publishing.

King, J. R. (1976). African survivals in the Black community: Key factors in stability. *Journal of Afro-American Issues*, 4(2), 153–167.

King, K. (1971). *Pan Africanism and education: A study of race, philanthropy and education in the southern states of America and East Africa.* Oxford: Clarendon Press.

Klenbort, M. (1999). *Learning to be Leaders: The Southern Regional Council Leadership Development Experience Through Its Education Programs, 1988–1999.* Southern Regional Council: Atlanta, GA.

Kogbara, D. (1999, August). A sense of elsewhere. *Mail on Sunday*, 58–59.

Kohn, A. (2004, April). Test today, privatize tomorrow: Using accountability to "reform" public schools to death. *Phi Delta Kappan*, 85(8), 569–577.

Kozol, J. (1991). *Savage inequalities.* New York: Crown.

Krimerman, L., & Lindenfeld, F. (1992). *When workers decide: Workplace democracy takes root in North America.* Philadelphia: New Society Publishers.

KRS-ONE (2003). *Ruminations.* New York: Welcome Rain Publishers.

Kulik, C. C., & Kulik, J. A. (1982). Effects of ability grouping on secondary school students: A meta-analysis of evaluation findings. *American Education Research Journal*, 19, 415–428.

Kuhn, T. S. (1970). *The structure of scientific revolutions.* (2nd ed.). Chicago: University of Chicago Press.

Kunjufu, J. (1983). *Countering the conspiracy to destroy Black boys.* Chicago: African American Images.

Kunjufu, J. (2002). *Black economics: Solutions for economic and community empowerment.* (2nd ed.). Chicago: African American Images.

Ladson-Billings, G. (1994). *The dreamkeepers: Successful teachers of African American children.* San Francisco, CA: Jossey-Bass.

Ladson-Billings, G. (1998). Proposal to AERA Council to establish a Commission on research in Black education. Unpublished document.

Ladson-Billings, G. (2001). *Crossing over to Canaan: The journey of new teachers in diverse classrooms.* San Francisco, CA: Jossey-Bass.

Lampert, M. (1990). When the problem is not the question and the solution is not the answer: Mathematical knowing and teaching. *American Educational Research Journal*, 27(1), 29–64.

Larkin, J. (1981). Enriching formal knowledge: A model for learning to solve problems in physics. In J. R. Anderson (Ed.), *Cognitive skills and their acquisition* (pp. 311–334). Mahwah, NJ: Erlbaum.

Larkin, J. (1983). The role of problem representation in physics. In D. Gentner & A. L. Stevens (Eds.), *Mental models* (pp. 75–98). Mahwah, NJ: Erlbaum.

Lather, P. (1991). *Getting smart: Feminist research and pedagogy with/in the postmodern.* New York: Routledge.

Lave, J. (1977). Cognitive consequences of traditional apprenticeship training in West Africa. *Anthropology and Education Quarterly, 8,* 177–180.

Lave, J., Murtaugh, M., & de la Rocha, O. (1984). The dialectic of arithmetic in grocery shopping. In B. Rogoff & J. Lave (Eds.), *Everyday cognition: Its development in social context* (pp. 67–94). Cambridge, MA: Harvard University Press.

Lave, J., & Wenger, E. (1991). *Situated learning.* New York: Cambridge University Press.

Lee, C. D. (1992). Profile of an independent Black institution: African-centered education at work. *Journal of Negro Education, 61*(2), 160–177.

Lee, C. D. (1993). *Signifying as a scaffold for literary interpretation: The pedagogical implications of an African American discourse genre* (Research Report Series). Urbana, IL: National Council of Teachers of English.

Lee, C. D. (1994a). Cultural Modeling in Reading Comprehension: Proposal funded by the McDonnell Foundation's Cognitive Studies in Education.

Lee, C. D. (1994b). The complexities of African centered pedagogy. In M. Shujaa (Ed.), *Too much schooling, too little education: A paradox of Black life in white societies* (pp. 295–318). Trenton, NJ: Africa World Press.

Lee, C. D. (1995a). A culturally based cognitive apprenticeship: Teaching African American high school students' skills in literary interpretation. *Reading Research Quarterly, 30*(4), 608–631.

Lee, C. D. (1995b). Signifying as a scaffold for literary interpretation. *Journal of Black Psychology, 21*(4), 357–381.

Lee, C. D. (2000). Signifying in the zone of proximal development. In C. D. Lee, P. Smagorinsky, et al. (Eds.), *Vygotskian perspectives on literacy research: Constructing meaning through collaborative inquiry* (pp. 191–225). New York: Cambridge University Press.

Lee, C. D. (2001). Is October Brown Chinese: A cultural modeling activity system for underachieving students. *American Educational Research Journal, 38*(1), 97–142.

Lee, C. D. (Ed.). (2003a). Reconceptualizing Race and Ethnicity in Educational Research. *Educational Researcher, 32*(5), 3–5.

Lee, C. D. (2003b). Literacy, technology and culture. In G. Hatano & X. Lin (Eds.), *Technology, culture and education,* Special Issue of *Mind, Culture and Activity 10*(1), 42–61.

Lee, C. D. (2003c, April). Cultural modeling and pedagogical content knowledge of the teacher of literature. Paper presented at the annual meeting of the American Educational Research Association, Chicago, IL.

Lee, C. D. (forthcoming). *Conducting our blooming in the midst of the whirlwind: Understanding culture as a lens for impacting learning and development.* New York: Teachers College Press.

Lee, C. D., Lomotey, K., & Shujaa, M. (1991). How shall we sing the Lord's song in a strange land? The dilemma of double consciousness and the complexities of an African centered pedagogy. *Journal of Education, 172*(2), 45–61.

Lee, C. D., Rosenfeld, E., Mendenhall, R., Rivers, A., & Tynes, B. (2003). Cultural modeling as a frame for narrative analysis. In C. Dauite & C. Lightfoot (Eds.), *Narrative analysis: Studying the development of individuals in society.* Thousand Oaks, CA: Sage Publications.

Lee, C. D., & Slaughter-Defoe, D. (1995). Historical and sociocultural influences on African American education. In J. A. Banks & C. M. Banks (Eds.), *Handbook of research on multicultural education* (pp. 348–371). New York: Macmillan.

Lee, C. D., Spencer, M. B., & Harpalani, V. (2003). Every shut eye ain't sleep: Studying how people live culturally. *Educational Researcher, 32*(5), 6–13.

Lee, V., & Bryk, A. (1988). Curriculum tracking as mediating the social distribution of high school achievement. *Sociology of Education, 61*, 78–94.

Left Business Observer (LBO). (1993). Gini says: Measuring income inequality. http://www.leftbusinessobserver.com/Gini_supplement.htm (first accessed 9-19-2002 at http://www.panix.com/~dhenwood/Gini_supplement.html), 1–3. (Originally published in *Left Business Observer*, October 18, as a supplemental report)

Leiderman, G. (1973). African infant precocity and some social influences during the first year. *Nature, 242*, 247–249.

Lenin, V. I. (1916/1939). *Imperialism: The highest stage of capitalism.* New York: International Publishers.

Levine, D., & Tyson, L. D. (1990). Participation, productivity and the firm's environment. In A. Blinder (Ed.), *Paying for productivity: A look at the evidence* (pp. 205–214). Washington, DC: Brookings Institute.

Levitan, S., Mangum, G., & Marshall, R. (1972). *Human resources and labor markets: Labor and manpower in the American economy.* New York: Harper & Row.

Lin, X. (1999, April). Cultural continuity and technology artifacts: A case study of a 5th grade Hong Kong classroom. *Paper presented at the annual meeting of the American Educational Research Association.* Montreal, CA: Canada.

Lincoln, C. E. (1961). *The Black Muslims in America.* New York: Beacon Press.

Lindsay, B., & Poindexter, M. (2003). The Internet: Creating equity through continuous education or perpetuating a digital divide? *Comparative Education Review, 47*(1), 112–122.

Lomotey, K. (1990). *Going to school: The African-American experience.* Albany: SUNY Press.

Lomotey, K., & Brookins, C. (1988). The independent Black institutions: A cultural perspective. In D. T. Slaughter & D. J. Johnson (Eds.), *Visible now: Black in private schools* (pp. 163–183). New York: Greenwood Press.

Lorde, A. (1992). Foreword to the English Language Edition. In M. Opitz, K. Oguntoye, & D. Schultz (Eds.), *Showing our colours: Afro-German women speak out* (pp. xi–xviii). London: Open Letters.

Lorde, A. (1995). Age, race, class, and sex: Women redefining difference. In P. Rothenberg (Ed.), *Race, class, and gender in the United States: An integrated study* (pp. 432–446). New York: St. Martins Press.

Lumpkin, B. (1990). Mathematics. In A. G. Hilliard & C. Leonard (Eds.), *African American baseline essays*. Portland, OR: Portland Public Schools.

Luria, A. R. (1976). *Cognitive development: Its cultural and social foundations*. Cambridge, MA: Harvard University Press.

Lynd, S. (1970). Preface. In S. M. Wilhelm (1970). *Who needs the Negro?* (p. 14). New York: Anchor.

Ma, L. (1999). *Knowing and teaching elementary mathematics*. Mahwah, NJ: Erlbaum.

Mabokela, R. O. (2001). Selective inclusion. In R. O. Mabokela & K. L. King (Eds.), *Apartheid no more* (pp. 59–72). Westport, CT: Bergin & Garvey.

Mabokela, R. O., & Green, A. L. (2001). *Sisters of the academy*. Sterling, VA: Stylus.

Mabokela, R. O., & King, K. L. (2001). *Apartheid no more*. Westport, CT: Bergin & Garvey.

MacPhail-Wilcox, B., & King, R. A. (1986). Resource allocation studies: Implications for school improvement and school finance research. *Journal of Education Finance, 11*, 416–432.

MacPherson, W. (1999). *The Stephen Lawrence inquiry: Report of the Inquiry by Sir William Macperson of Cluny. Presented to Parliament by Secretary of State for the Home Office Department by Command of Her Majesty*. London: Stationery Office.

Madhubuti, H. (1990). *Black men: Obsolete, single, dangerous?* Chicago: Third World Press.

Mahiri, J. (1998). *Shooting for excellence: African American and youth culture in new century schools*. New York: Teachers College Press and National Council of Teachers of English.

Mahiri, J. (1996). Writing, rap, and representation: Problematic links between text and experience. In G. Kirsch & P. Mortensen (Eds.), *Ethics and representation in qualitative research of literacy*. Champaign/Urbana, IL: National Council of Teachers of English.

Maiga, H. O. (in press). *La contribution du peuple Songhoy en Afrique*. Bamako, Mali: Edition Jamana.

Maiga, H. O. (1986, April). *Quelques aspects de la recherche évaluative en éducation— une étude de cas: L'Education dans la Région de Gao, Mali 1981-1985*. (Some aspects of research & evaluation: A case study of education in the Gao Region). Gao, Mali: Regional Office of Education/Bamako: IPN.

Maiga, H. O. (1987, April). *Enquêtes et musées scolaires: Région de Gao*. (Research studies and the School Museum in the Gao Region). Gao, Mali: Regional Office of Education.

Maiga, H. O. (1993). *From whole to part—The Gao School Museum: Restoring a learning tradition that achieves school success by bridging classroom, curriculum and community*. San Francisco, CA: Aspire Books.

Maiga, H. O. (1995). Bridging classroom, curriculum, and community: The Gao School Museum. *Theory Into Practice, 34*(3), 209–215.

Maiga, H. O. (1996). Our Africana Heritage: A Brief Socio-Cultural Perspective Chart. New Orleans: Murehm Books.

Maiga, H. O. (2003/1996). *Conversational Songhoy language of Mali.* Atlanta, GA: Murehm Books.

Majors, Y. (1998). Finding the multi-voiced self: A narrative. *Journal of Adolescent and Adult Literacy, 42*(2), 76–83.

Majors, Y. (2001). Passing mirrors: Subjectivity in a midwestern hair salon. *Anthropology and Education Quarterly, 32*(1), 116–130.

Malloy, C., & Jones, G. (1998). Investigation of African-American students' mathematical problem solving. *Journal for Research in Mathematics Education, 29*(2), 143–163.

Mankiller, W. (1993). *Mankiller: A chief and her people.* New York: St. Martin's Press.

Margolis. E., & Romero, M. (1998). The department is very male, very white, very old, and very conservative. *Harvard Educational Review, 68*(1), 1–32.

Martin, D. (2000). *Mathematics success and failure among African-American youth: The roles of sociohistorical context, community forces, school influence, and individual agency.* Mahwah, NJ: Erlbaum.

Marx, K. (1867/1967). *Das kapital: A critique of political economy.* Chicago: Henry Regnery Co.

Mason, P. L. (1999). Family environment and intergenerational well-being: Some preliminary results. In W. Spriggs (Ed.), *The state of Black America 1999* (pp. 45–90). New York: The National Urban League.

Mateené, K. (1996, October). Plaidoyer pour les langues nationales à l'école. *Jeune Afrique* (1867–1868), 16–29.

Matthews, W. (1984). Influences on the learning and participation of minorities in mathematics. *Journal for Research in Mathematics Education, 15*, 84–95.

Mazrui, A. (1978). *Political values and the educated class in Africa.* London: Heinemann.

Mazuri, A. (1996). The imperial culture of north-south relations: The case of Islam and the west. In K. Dawish & B. Parrott (Eds.), *The end of the empire? The transformation of the USSR in a comparative perspective* (pp. 218–240). New York: Armond.

Mbilinyi, M. (1977). Basic education: tool of liberation or exploitation? In Prospects: *Quarterly Review of Education, 7*(4), 489–503.

McAdoo, H. P., & McAdoo, J. L. (Eds.). (1985). *Black children: Social, educational and parental environments.* Beverly Hills, CA: Sage.

McCloud, A. (1998). Misunderstood alliance: Louis Farrakhan and the world community of Black Muslims. In A. Alexander (Ed.), *The Farrakhan factor* (pp. 168–183). New York: Grove Press.

McEwan, E. C., Gipps, C. V., & Summer, R. (1975). *Language proficiency, 1968.* ILEA Research and Statistics Group, Inner London Education Authority, London, UK.

McKinnon, J. (2003, April). The Black population in the United States: March 2002. *Current Population Reports P25-541* (pp. 1–8). U.S. Department of Commerce, Economics and Statistics Administration, U.S. Census Bureau. http://www.census.gov/pubs2003/p20-541.

McKnight, C. C., Crosswhite, J. A., Dossey, J. A., Kifer, E., Swafford, S. O., Travers, K. J., & Cooney, T. J. (1987). *The underachieving curriculum: Assessing U.S. school mathematics from an international perspective.* Champaign, IL: Stipes Publishing.

McLaren, P. (1989). *Life in schools.* New York: Longman.

McLoyd, V. (1998). *Children in poverty: Development, public policy and practice.* In W. Damon, I. Sigel & K. A. Renninger (Eds.), *Child psychology in practice: Handbook of child psychology* (5th ed.), *4*, 135–210.

Meacham, S. (1998). Threads of a new language: A response to Eisenhart's "On the subject of interpretive review". *Review of Educational Review, 68*(4), 401–407.

Meacham, S. (2001). Vygotsky and the blues: Re-reading cultural connections and conceptual development. *Theory Into Practice 40*(3), 190–198.

Merisotis, J. P. (1998). Who benefits from education? An American perspective. *International Higher Education.* Chestnut Hill, MA: Boston College, Department of Higher Education.

Michaels, S. (1981). "Sharing time," children's narrative styles and differential access to literacy. *Language in Society, 10,* 423–442.

Miller, J. G. (1997, June). African American males in the criminal justice system. *Phi Delta Kappan,* K1–K12.

Ministère de l'Education de Base—DNAFLA (1995). *Lexiques spécialisés.* Bamako, Mali: Author.

Ministère de l'Education de Base—DNAFLA (1997). *Caw ma hantum. (Grades 1 & 2).* Bamako, Mali: Author.

Mirza, H. S. (1992). *Young, female and Black.* London: Routledge.

Mitchell-Kernan, C. (1981). Signifying, loud-talking and marking. In A. Dundes (Ed.), *Mother wit from the laughing barrel* (pp. 310–328). Englewood, Cliffs, NJ: Prentice Hall.

Modood, T. (1998). Ethnic minorities drive for qualifications. In T. Modood & T. Acland (Eds.), *Race and higher education* (pp. 30–35). London: Policy Studies Institute.

Mohammed, Imam W. D. (Speech, April 9, 1982). Sedalia Education Conference: Educational Concerns. Audio cassette. Sedalia, NC: Office of Imam W. Deen Mohammed.

Mohammed, Imam W. D. (Speech, December, 19, 1993). Civilization and Education. St. Louis, MO. Audio cassette.

Moll, L., & Greenberg, J. B. (1990). Creating zones of possibilities: Combining social contexts for instruction. In L. Moll (Ed.), *Vygotsky and education: Instructional implications and applications of sociohistorical psychology* (pp. 319–348). New York: Cambridge University Press.

Moore, D., & Davenport, S. (1988). *The new improved sorting machine.* Madison, WI: National Center on Effective Secondary Schools.

Moore, C., Sanders, T. R., & Moore, S. (Eds.). (1995). *The African presence in the Americas.* Trenton, NJ: Africa World Press.

Morgan, M. (1993). The Africaness of counterlanguage among Afro-Americans. In S. S. Mufwene (Ed.), *Africanisms in Afro-American language varieties* (pp. 432–438). Athens: University of Georgia Press.

Morgan, M. (1998). More than a mood or an attitude: Discourse and verbal genres in African American culture. In S. S. Mufwene, J. R. Rickford, & G. Bailey (Eds.), *African-American English: Structure, history, and use* (pp. 251–281) New York: Routledge.

Morgan, S. L., & Mehta, J. D. (2004). Beyond the laboratory: Evaluating the survey evidence for the disidentification explanation of Black-white differences in achievement. *Sociology of Education, 77*(1), 82–101.

Morrell, E., & Duncan-Andrade, J. (2002). Promoting academic literacy with urban youth through engaging Hip-Hop culture. *English Journal, 9*(6), 88–92.

Morris, J. E., & Goldring, E. (1999). Are magnet schools more equitable? An analysis of the disciplinary rates of African American and White students in Cincinnati magnet and nonmagnet schools. *Equity and Excellence in Education, 32*(3), 59–65.

Morrison, T. (1989). Unspeakable things unspoken: The Afro-American presence in American literature, *Michigan Quarterly Review, 28*(1), 1–34.

Moses, R. P. (1994). The struggle for citizenship and math/sciences literacy. *Journal of Mathematical Behavior, 13,* 107–111.

Moses, R. P., & Cobb, C. (2001). *Radical equations: Math literacy and civil rights.* Boston, MA: Beacon.

Moses, R. P., Kamii M., Swap, S. M., & Howard, J. (1989). The Algebra Project: Organizing in the spirit of Ella. *Harvard Educational Review, 59*(4), 423–443.

Moss, B. (1994). Creating a community: Literacy events in African-American churches. In B. Moss (Ed.), *Literacy across communities* (pp. 147–178). Cresskill, NJ: Hampton, Press.

Moumouni, A. (1998). *L'Education en Afrique.* Paris: Présence Africaine.

Mufwene, S. (Ed.). (1993). *Africanisms in Afro-American language varieties.* Athens: The University of Georgia Press.

Muhammad, E. (1965). *Message to the Blackman in America.* Chicago: Muhammad's Temple No. 2.

Muhammad, Z. (1993). Introduction to Islamic education: Philosophy, principles and practice. Sacramento, CA: American Institute on Islamic Education. Unpublished Manuscript.

Muhammad, Z. (1998, Winter). Islamic education in America. *Religion and Education, 25*(1/2), 87–96.

Muhammad, Z. (2003). Islamic schools in the United States: Perspectives of identity, relevance and governance. In P. Strum & D. Tarantolo (Eds.), *Muslims in the United States* (pp. 95–112). Washington, DC: Woodrow Wilson International Center for Scholars.

Munaga, K. (1999). *Superando o racismo na escola* (Overcoming racism in the school). Brasília, Brazil: Ministéro da Educação (Ministry of Education).

Munford, C. J. (1996). *Race and reparations: A Black perspective for the 21st Century.* Trenton, NJ: Africa World Press.

Munford, C. J. (2001). *Race and civilization: Rebirth of Black centrality.* Trenton, NJ: Africa World Press.

Murnane, R. J., & Levy, F. (1996). *Teaching the new basic skills.* New York: The Free Press.

Murnane, R. J., Singer, J. D., Willett, J. B., Kemple, J. J., & Olsen, R. J. (1991). *Who will teach? Policies that matter.* Cambridge, MA: Harvard University Press.

Myrdal, G. (1996). *An American dilemma: The Negro problem and modern democracy.* New Brunswick, NJ: Transaction Publishers.

Nadeau, E. G., & Thompson, D. J. (1996). *Cooperation works!* Rochester, MN: Lone Oak Press.

Nasir, N. S. (2002). Identity, goals, and learning: Mathematics in cultural practice. *Mathematical Thinking and Learning, 4*(2/3), 211–245.

Nasir, N. S. (2004). "Halal-ing" the child: Reframing identities of resistance in an urban Muslim school. *Harvard Educational Review, 74*(2), 153–174.

Nasir, N. S., & Kirshner, B. (2003). The cultural construction of moral and civic identities. *Applied Developmental Science, 7*(3), 138–147.

Nasir, N., & Saxe, G. (2003). Ethnic and academic identities: A cultural practice perspective on emerging tensions and their management in the lives of minority students, *Educational Researcher, 32*(5), 14–18.

National Assessment of Educational Progress (1994a). *NAEP Trial State Assessment.* Washington, DC: U.S. Department of Education.

National Assessment of Educational Progress (1994b). *The NAEP 1992 Technical Report.* Princeton, NJ: Educational Testing Service.

National Association of Black School Educators, Inc. (NABSE). (1984). *Saving the African American Child: Report of the Task Force on Black Academic and Cultural Excellence.* Washington, DC. Author.

National Center for Education Statistics (NCES). (1985). *The condition of education, 1985.* Washington, DC: U.S. Department of Education.

National Center for Education Statistics (NCES). (1994). *Digest of education statistics, 1994.* Washington, DC: U.S. Department of Education.

National Center for Education Statistics (NCES). (1997a). *America's teachers: Profile of a profession, 1993–94.* Washington, DC: U.S. Department of Education.

National Center for Education Statistics (NCES). (1997b). *Characteristics of stayers, movers, and leavers: Results from the teacher follow-up survey, 1994–95.* Washington, DC: U.S. Department of Education.

National Center for Education Statistics. (1997c). *Pursuing excellence: A study of U.S. eighth-grade mathematics and science teaching, learning, curriculum, and achievement in international context.* Initial findings from the Third International Mathematics and Science Study (NCES Report 97–98). Washington, DC: U.S. Government Printing Office.

National Center for Education Statistics. (1997d). *Reading and mathematics achievement: Growth in high school. Issue Brief.* Washington, DC: U.S. Government Printing Office.

National Center for Education Statistics. (2000). *NAEP 1999 Trends in Academic Progress.* Washington, DC: U.S. Department of Education.

National Commission on Teaching and America's Future (NCTAF). (1996). *What matters most: Teaching for America's future.* New York: Author.

National Commission on Teaching and America's Future (NCTAF). (1997). Unpublished tabulations from the 1993–94 Schools and Staffing Surveys.

National Cooperative Business Association. (n.d.). *Cooperatives are ... cooperative business in the United States*. Pamphlet, circa 1997. Washington, DC: National Cooperative Business Association.

National Cooperative Business Association. Web site: http://www.ncba.coop.

National Council of Teachers of Mathematics. (2000). *Principles and standards for school mathematics*. Reston, VA: National Council of Teachers of Mathematics.

National Council on Education Standards and Testing (NCEST). (1992). *Raising standards for American education*. Washington, DC: Government Printing Office.

National Science Foundation (2000). *Women, minorities, and persons with disabilities in science and engineering*. HTML document, http://www.nsf.gov/sbe/srs/women/strt.htm.

Nembhard, J. Gordon. (1998, July). Book Review: *African Americans and post-industrial labor markets. Industrial and Labor Relations Review, 51*(4), 714–715.

Nembhard, J. Gordon. (1999). Community economic development: Alternative visions for the 21st century. In J. Whitehead & C. K. Harris (Eds.), *Readings in Black political economy* (pp. 295–304). Dubuque, IA: Kendall/Hunt Publishing Company.

Nembhard, J. Gordon. (2000). Post-industrial economic experiences of African American men, 1973–1993. In C. Yeakey (Ed.), *Advances in education in diverse communities: Research, policy, and praxis, Vol. 1* (pp. 241–261). Stamford, CT: Jai Press.

Nembhard, J. Gordon. (2002-a). Entering the new city as men and women, not mules. Working Paper, University of Maryland, College Park.

Nembhard, J. Gordon. (2002-b). Education for a people-centered democratic economy. *GEO Newsletter* Issue 53–54 (July–October), 8–9.

Nembhard, J. Gordon. (2004). Cooperative ownership in the struggle for African American economic empowerment. *Humanity and society, 28*(3) (August), 98–321.

Nembhard, J. Gordon, & Pang, V. O. (2003). Ethnic youth programs: Teaching about caring economic communities and self-empowered leadership." In G. Ladson-Billings (Ed.), *Critical Race Theory perspectives on social studies: The profession, policies, and curriculum* (pp. 171–197). Greenwich, CT: Information Age Publishing (A Volume in Research in Social Education).

Nembhard, J. Gordon, Pitts, S. C., & Mason, P. (2005). "African Americans, intragroup inequality and corporate globalization." In C. Conrad, J. Whitehead, P. Mason, & J. Stewart (Eds.), *African Americans in the United States economy* (pp. 208–222). New York: Rowman & Littlefield Publishers.

Nesbitt, R. (1998). Race, genetics, and IQ. In C. Jencks & M. Phillips (Eds.), *The Black-White test score gap* (pp. 86–102). Washington, DC: The Brookings Institute.

Nettles, M., & Perna, L. (1997). *The African American education data book. Volume II: Preschool through high school education*: Fairfax, VA: Frederick D. Patterson Research Institute of The College Fund/UNCF.

New Internationalist. (2004, May). "Wars for Africa's wealth". (Theme Issue).

New York Study Group on Outcome Equity. (1993). In R. Berne (Ed.), *The road to outcome equity. Final report of the study group on outcome equity*. Albany, NY: State Education Department.

Nkrumah, K. (1965). *Neo-colonialism: The last stage of imperialism*. New York: International Publishers.

Nobles, W. (1980). African philosophy: Foundations for Black psychology. In R. L. Jones (Ed.), Black psychology, (2nd Ed., pp. 23–36). New York: Harper & Row.

Nobles, W. (1986). *African psychology: Toward its reclamation, reascension, and revitalization*. Oakland, CA: Black Family Press.

Nunes, T., Schliemann, A. D., & Carraher, D. W. (1993). *Street mathematics and school mathematics*. New York: Cambridge University Press.

O'Connor, C. (2002). Black women beating the odds from one generation to the next: How the changing dynamics of constraint and opportunity affect the process of educational resilience. *American Educational Research Journal, 39*(4), 855–903.

Oakes, J. (1983, May). Limiting opportunity: Student race and curricular differences in secondary vocational education. *American Journal of Education, 91*(3), 328–355.

Oakes, J. (1985). *Keeping track: How schools structure inequality*. New Haven, CT: Yale University Press.

Oakes, J. (1986, June). Tracking in secondary schools: A contextual perspective. *Educational Psychologist, 22*, 29–154.

Oakes, J. (1990). *Multiplying inequalities: The effects of race, social class, and tracking on opportunities to learn mathematics and science*. Santa Monica, CA: The RAND Corporation.

Oakes, J. (1992, May). Can tracking research inform practice? Technical, normative, and political considerations. *Educational Researcher, 21*(4), 12–21.

Ochs, E., Jacoby, S., & Gonzales, P. (1994). Interpretive journeys: How physicists talk and travel through graphic space. *Configurations, 2*(1), 151–172.

O'Grady, A. R. (2004). "We Are All Africans"—H. J. de Blij—Lecture. http://www.chautauqua-inst.org/Week%20One/index.html. (Retrieved 5-2-04)

Oliver, M., & Shapiro, T. (1997). *Black wealth/White wealth: A new perspective on racial inequality*. New York: Routledge.

Opitz, M., Oguntoye, K., & Schultz, D. (Eds.). (1992). *Showing our colours: Afro-German women speak out*. London: Open Letters.

Oquendo-Rodriguez, A. (1999). Latina girls of Puerto Rican origin who are successful in science and mathematics high school courses. Ph.D. Thesis, University of Massachusetts–Boston.

Orellana, M. F., & Bowman, P. (2003). Conceptual diversity research on learning and development: Conceptual, methodological, and strategic considerations, *Educational Researcher, 32*(5), 26–32.

Orfield, G. (2001). *Housing segregation: Causes, effects, possible cures*. Cambridge, MA: Civil Rights Project, Harvard University.

Orfield, G. F., Monfort, F., & Aaron, M. (1989). *Status of school desegregation: 1968–1986*. Alexandria, VA: National School Boards Association.

Organization of Africans in the Americas (OAA). (2000). *Quest for inclusion: Realizing Afro-Latin American potential*. Washington, DC. Author.

Orr, E. W. (1987). *Twice as less: Black English and the performance of Black students in mathematics and science.* New York: Norton.

Osler, A. (1997). *Exclusion from school and racial equality.* London: Commission for Racial Equality.

Page, J. A., & Page., F. M., Jr. (1995). Tracking and its effects on African-Americans in the field of education. In H. Pool & J. A. Page (Eds.), *Beyond tracking: Finding success in inclusive schools* (pp. 71–78). Bloomington, IN: Phi Delta Kappa Educational Foundation.

Palinscar, A., & Brown, A. (1984). Reciprocal teaching of comprehension-fostering and comprehension-monitoring strategies. *Cognition and Instruction, 2*(2), 73–109.

Papert, S. (1980). *Mindstorms.* New York: Basic Books.

Papert, S. (1993). *The children's machine.* New York: Basic Books.

Patterson, W. (1951). *We charge genocide: The crime of the government against the Negro people.* New York: Civil Rights Congress.

Pea, R. D., & Gomez, L. (1992). Distributed multimedia learning environments. *Interactive Learning Environments, 2*(2), 73–109.

Pearson, G., & Young, A. (2002). *Technically speaking: Why all Americans need to know more about technology.* Washington, DC: National Academy Press/National Academy of Engineering/National Research Council.

Pelavin, S. H., & Kane, M. (1990). *Changing the odds: Factors increasing access to college.* New York: College Entrance Examination Board.

Perkins, D. (1995). *Outsmarting IQ: The emerging science of learnable intelligence.* New York: The Free Press.

Perlstein, D. (1990). Teaching freedom: SNCC and the creation of the Mississippi Freedom Schools. *History of Education Quarterly, 30*(3), 287–324.

Perry, T., & Delpit, L. (Eds.). (1998). *The real Ebonics debate: Power, language and the education of African-American children.* Boston: Beacon.

Persuad, R. B., & Lusane, C. (2000, July–September). The new economy, globalization and the impact on African Americans. *Race & Class, 42*(1), 21–34.

Peterson, P. (1989). Remediation is no remedy. *Educational Leadership, 46*(60), 24–25.

Petras, J. (2001, March). Left intellectuals and the desperate search for respectability. *Z Magazine, 14*(3), 54–59.

Phillips, M., Crouse, J., & Ralph, J. (1998). Does the Black-White test score gap widen after children enter school? C. Jencks & M. Phillips (Eds.), *The Black-White test score gap* (pp. 229–272). Washington, DC: Brookings Institute.

Pilkington, D. (1996). *Follow the rabbitproof fence.* Queensland, Australia: University of Queensland Press.

Piller, C. (1992). Separate realities: The creation of the technological underclass in America's public schools. *Macworld*, 218–230.

Pinkard, N. (1999). *Learning to read in culturally responsive computer environments.* Ann Arbor, MI: Center for the Improvement of Early Reading Achievement.

Pinkard, N. (2000). Lyric Reader: Architecture for creating intrinsically motivating and culturally relevant reading environments. *Interactive Learning Environments, 18*(1), 1–17.

Pinkard, N. (2001). "Rappin' Reader" and "Say Say Oh Playmate": Culturally relevant beginning literacy in a computer-based learning environment. *Journal of Educational Computing Research, 25*(1), 7–34.

Pinkard, N., & Kleinman, K. (1999, April). Examining gender and technology: A formative study of urban children's computer interests, self-image and software preferences. Paper presented at the annual meeting of the American Educational Research Association, Montreal, Canada.

Pogrow, S. (2002). The unsubstantiated success of Success For All: Implications for policy, practice and the soul of our profession, *Phi Delta Kappan, 82*(8), 596–601.

Pogrow, S. (2002). Success For All is a failure. *Phi Delta Kappan, 82*(7), 463–468.

Polite, V. (2000). Cornerstones: Catholic high schools that serve predominately African American student populations. In J. Youniss & J. Convey (Eds.), *Catholic schools at the crossroads: Survival and transformation* (pp. 127–156). New York: Teachers College Press.

Porter, D. (1936). The organized educational activities of Negro literary societies, 1828–1846. *Journal of Negro Education, 5*(4), 555–576.

Posner, J. (1982). The development of mathematical knowledge in two West African societies. *Child Development, 53*, 200–208.

Power, E. J. (1970). *Main currents in the history of education.* New York: McGraw-Hill.

Project MAPS. (2001). Muslims in American Public Square: American Muslim Poll. Available at http://www.projectmaps.com.

Puma, M., Karweit, N., Price, C., Ricciuti, A., Thompson, W., & Vaden-Kiernan, M. (1997). *Prospects: Final report on student outcomes.* Washington, DC: U.S. Department of Education, Planning and Evaluation Services.

Purcell-Gates, V. (1995). *Other people's words: The cycle of low literacy.* Cambridge, MA: Harvard University Press.

Rabinowitz, P. (1987). *Before reading: Narrative conventions and the politics of interpretation.* Ithaca, NY: Cornell University Press.

Rampton, A. (1981). *West Indian children in our schools.* London: HMSO.

Rashid, H. (1990). *In search of the path: Socialization education and the African American Muslim.* Capital Heights, MD: Imania Publications.

Rashid, H., & Muhammad, Z. (1992). The Sister Clara Muhammad Schools: Pioneers in the development of Islamic education in America, *The Journal of Negro Education, 61*(2), pp. 178–185.

Rashidi, R., & Van Sertiman, I. (1995). *The African presence in early Asia.* New Brunswick, NJ: Transaction Publishers.

Ratteray-Davis, J. (1994). The search for access and content in the education of African-Americans. In M. Shujaa (Ed.), *Too much schooling, too little education: A paradox of Black life in white societies* (pp. 123–142). Trenton, NJ: Africa World Press, Inc.

Rattaray-Davis, J., & Shujaa, M. (1987). *Dare to choose: Parental choice at independent neighborhood schools.* Washington, DC: U.S. Department of Education.

Reay, D., & Mirza, H. S. (1997). Uncovering the genealogies of the margins: Black supplementary schools. *British Journal of Education, 18*(4), 477–499.

Reddix, J. L. (1974). *A voice crying in the wilderness: The memoirs of Jacob L. Reddix.* Jackson: University Press of Mississippi.

Reed, I. (2003). *Another day at the front: Dispatches from the race war.* New York: Basic Books.

Resnick, L. B. (1987). *Education and learning to think.* Washington, DC: National Academy Press.

Resnick, M. (1994). *Turtles, termites and traffic jams: Explorations in massively parallel microworlds.* Cambridge, MA: MIT Press.

Rist, R. (1970). Student social class and teacher expectations: The self-fulfilling prophecy in ghetto education. *Harvard Educational Review, 40*(3), 411–451.

Ristock J., & Pennell, J. (1996). *Community research as empowerment: Feminist links, postmodern interruptions.* Toronto, Canada: Oxford University Press.

Rivers, E. (n.d.). Beyond the nationalism of fools: Toward an agenda for Black intellectuals. http://www.yesamerica.org/NTLF. (Retrieved May 1, 2001)

Robelen, E. W. (2003, May 28). U.S. institutions help shape education in Islamic world. *Education Week,*

Robinson, R. (2000). *The debt: What America owes to Blacks.* New York: Dutton.

Rock, D. A., Hilton, T. L., Pollack, J., Ekstrom, R. B., & Goertz, M. E. (1985). *A study of excellence in high school education: Educational policies, school quality, and student outcomes.* Washington, DC: National Center for Education Statistics.

Rodgers, W. M., III. (1999). A critical assessment of skills explanations of Black-White employment and wage gaps. In W. Spriggs (Ed.), *The state of Black America 1999* (pp. 167–184). New York: The National Urban League.

Rodney, W. (1974). *How Europe underdeveloped Africa.* London: Bogle-L'Ouverture.

Rogoff, B. (1990). *Apprenticeship in thinking: Cognitive development in social context.* New York: Oxford University Press.

Rogoff, B. (1995). Observing sociocultural activity and three planes: participatory appropriation, guided participation, and apprenticeship. In J. Wertsch, P. del Rio & A. Alvarez (Eds.), *Sociocultural studies of mind* (pp. 139–164). New York: Cambridge University Press.

Rogoff, B. (2003). *The cultural nature of human development.* New York: Oxford University Press.

Rosenbaum, J. (1976). *Making inequality: The hidden curriculum of high school tracking.* New York: Wiley.

Rosenblatt, L. (1978). *The reader, the text, the poem: The transactional theory of the literary work.* Carbondale: Southern Illinois University Press.

Rosenzweig, M. R. (2000). Schooling, learning, and economic growth. In R. Marshall (Ed.), *Back to shared prosperity: The growing inequality of wealth and income in America* (pp. 229–237). Armonk, NY: M. E. Sharpe.

Rottenberg, C. J., & Berliner, D. C. (1990, April). Expert and novice teachers' conceptions of common classroom activities. Paper presented at the annual meeting of the American Educational Research Association, Boston, MA.

The Runnymede Trust. (1996). *This is where we live.* London: Author.

The Runnymede Trust. (2000). *Curriculum 2000: Monocultural or multicultural?* London: Author.

Sanders, J. P., & Peterson, K. (1999). Close the gap for girls in math-related careers. *Education Digest, 65*(4), 47–49.

Sanders, M. G. (1996). *School-family-community partnerships and the academic achievement of African American, urban adolescents.* Washington, DC: Center for Research on the Education of Students Placed At Risk (CRESPAR), Howard University.

Saunders, A. et al. (1982). *A social history of black slaves and freedmen in Portugal 1441–1555.* Cambridge, England: Cambridge University Press.

Saxe, G. (1991). *Culture and cognitive development: Studies in mathematical understanding.* Hillsdale, NJ: Erlbaum.

Scarr, S. (1981). *Race, social class, and individual differences in IQ.* Mahwah, NJ: Lawrence Erlbaum Associates.

Schank, R. C., Kass, A., & Riesbeck, C. K. (1994). *Inside case-based explanation.* Hillsdale, NJ: Erlbaum.

Scheurich, J., & Young, M. D. (1997). Coloring epistemology: Are our research epistemologies racially biased? *Educational Researcher, 26*(4), 4–16.

Schickedanz, J. A. (1990). The jury is still out on the effects of whole language and language experience approaches for beginning reading: A critique of Stahl and Miller's study. *Review of Educational Research, 60*(1), 127–132.

Schiele, J. H. (1994). Afrocentricity: Implications for higher education. *Journal of Black Studies, 25*(2), 150–169.

Schoenfeld, A. (1994). *Mathematical thinking and problem solving.* Hillsdale, NJ: Erlbaum.

Schofield, J. W. (1991). School desegregation and intergroup relations. In G. Grant (Ed.), *Review of Research in Education, 17,* (335–409). Washington, DC: American Educational Research Association.

Schultz, T. W. (1961). Investment in human capital. *American Economic Review, 51,* 1–17.

Scott, D. (2000, September). The Re-enchantment of humanism: An Interview with Sylvia Wynter. *Small Axe, 8,* 119–207.

Scrase, T. J. (Ed.). (1997). *Social justice and third world education.* New York: Garland Publishing Inc.

Scribner, S. (1984). Studying working intelligence. In B. Rogoff & J. Lave (Eds.), *Everyday cognition: Its development in social context* (pp. 9–40). Cambridge, MA: Harvard University Press.

Scribner, S., & Cole, M. (1981). *The psychology of literacy.* Cambridge, MA: Harvard University Press.

Searle, C. (1994). The culture of exclusion. In J. Bourne, L. Bridges & C. Searle (Eds.), *Outcast England: How schools exclude black children* (pp. 17–28). London: Institute of Race Relations.

Secada, W., Fennema, E., & Adajian, L. B. (1995). *New directions for equity in mathematics education.* New York: Cambridge University Press.

Seixas, P. (1993). The community of inquiry as a basis for knowledge and learning: The case of history. *American Educational Research Journal, 30*(2), 305–326.

Serpell, R. (1982). Measures of perception, skills and intelligence: The growth of a new perspective on children in a Third World country. In W. W. Hartup (Ed.), *Review of Child Development Research* (Vol. 6). Chicago: University of Chicago Press.

Serpell, Z., & Bozeman, L. A. (1999). Beginning teacher induction (microfilm): A report on beginning teacher effectiveness and retention. Washington DC: National Partnership for Excellence and Accountability in Teaching: U.S. Dept. of Education, Office of Educational Research and improvement, Educational Resources Information Center.

Sewell, T. (1997). *Black masculinities and schooling: How Black boys survive modern schooling*. Stoke-on-Trent, England: Trentham Books.

Shade, B. (1982). Afro-American cognitive style: A variable in school success. *Review of Educational Research, 52*, 219–244.

Shaw, A. (1996). Social constructionism and the inner city: Designing environments for social development and urban renewal. In Y. Kafai (Ed.), *Constructionism in practice: Designing, thinking, and learning in a digital world* (pp. 175–206). Mahway, NJ: Erlbaum.

Shields, P. M., Esch, C., Humphrey, D. C., Young, V. M., Gaston, M., & Hunt, H. (1999). *The status of the teaching profession: Research findings and policy recommendations. A report to the Teaching and California's Future Task Force*. Santa Cruz, CA: The Center for the Future of Teaching and Learning.

Shillington, K. (1995). *History of Africa*. New York: St. Martin's Press.

Shipp, S. C. (1996, March). The road not taken: Alternative strategies for Black economic development in the United States. *Journal of Economic Issues, 30*(1), 79–95.

Shipp, S. C. (2000, March). Worker-owned firms in inner-city neighborhoods: An empirical study. *Review of International Cooperation 92–93*(4/99–1/00), 42–46.

Shuey, A. (1966). *The testing of Negro intelligence*. New York: Social Science Press.

Shujaa, M. (1994). *Too much schooling, too little education: A paradox in black life in white societies*. Trenton, NJ: Africa World Press.

Siddle-Walker, E. V. (1993). Caswell County Training School, 1933–1969: Relationships between community and school. *Harvard Educational Review, 63*(2), 161–182.

Siddle-Walker, E. V. (1996). *Their highest potential: An African American school community in the segregated south*. Chapel Hill: University of North Carolina Press.

Silva, C. M., Moses, R. P., Rivers, J., & Johnson, P. (1990). The Algebra Project: Making middle school mathematics count. *Journal of Negro Education, 59*(3), 375–392.

Silver, E. (1998). *Improving mathematics in middle school*. http:www.enc.org/change/01fram/3atimss/131000/silver.htm: Eisenhower National Clearinghouse.

Silver, E., Smith, M. S., & Nelson, B. S. (1995). The QUASAR Project: Equity concerns meet mathematics education reform in the middle school. In W. Secada, E. Fennema, & L. B. Adajian (Eds.), *New directions for equity in mathematics education* (pp. 9–56). New York: Cambridge University Press.

Silver, E. A., Strutchens, M. E., & Zawojewski, J. S. (1996). NAEP findings regarding race/ethnicity and gender: Affective issues, mathematics performance, and instructional context. In P. A. Kenney & E. A. Silver (Eds.), *Results from the sixth mathematics assessment of the National Assessment of Educational Progress*. Reston, VA: National Council of Teachers of Mathematics.

Simuyu, V. (1988). The democratic myth in the African traditional societies. In W. Oyugi, E. Atieno, M. C. Odhiambo, & A. Gitonga (Eds.), *Democratic theory and practice in Africa* (pp. 49–70). London: James Currey.

Sizemore, B. (1985). Pitfalls and promises of effective schools research. *Journal of Negro Education, 54*, 269–288.

Sizemore, B. (1988). The Madison elementary school: A turnaround case. *The Journal of Negro Education, 57*(3), 243–266.

Sizemore, B. (1995). *Ten routines for high achievement*. Chicago: School Achievement Structure, DePaul University.

Sklar, R. L. (1979). The nature of class domination in Africa. *The Journal of Modern African Studies, 17*, 531–552.

Slaughter, D. T., & Johnson, D. J. (Eds.) (1988). *Visible now: Blacks in private schools*. New York: Greenwood Press.

Slavin, R. E. (1990). Achievement effects of ability grouping in secondary schools: A best evidence synthesis. *Review of Educational Research, 60*(3), 471–500.

Slavin, R. E., & Madden, N. A. (1996). Scaling up: Lessons learned in the dissemination of Success for All. Report No. 6. Baltimore, MD: Center for Research on the Education of Students Placed At Risk (CRESPAR), John Hopkins University.

Slavin, R. E., Madden, N. A., Dolan, L. J., & Wasik, B. A. (1996). *Every child, every school: Success For All*. Newbury Park, CA: Corwin.

Slavin, R., & Oickle, E. (1981). Effects of cooperative learning teams on student achievement and race relations: Treatment by race interactions. *Sociology of Education, 54*, 174–180.

Smagorinsky, P., & Gevinson, S. (1989). *Fostering the reader's response: Rethinking the literature curriculum, grades 7–12*. Palo Alto, CA: Dale Seymour Publications.

Smith, D., & Tomlinson, S. (1989). *The school effect: A study of multi-racial comprehensives*. London: Policy Studies Institute.

Smith, G. H. (2002, April). Kaupapa Maori Theory: An indigenous theory of transformative praxis. Paper presented at the annual meeting of the American Educational Research Association, New Orleans.

Smith, G. H. (2004). Mai i te Maramatanga ki to Putanga mai o te Tahuritana: From conscientization to transformation, *37*(1), 46–52. Special Edition edited by M. Maaka. *Educational Perspectives: Journal of the College of Education/University of Hawaii at Manoa*.

Smith, L. T. (1999). *Decolonizing methodologies: Research and indigenous peoples*. London: Zed Books.

Smith, M., & Hillocks, G. (1988). Sensible sequencing: Developing knowledge about literature text by text. *English Journal* (October) 44–49.

Smith, P. J. (1999). Our children's burden: The many-headed hydra of the educational disenfranchisement of Black children. *Howard Law Journal, 42*, 133–239.

Smitherman, G. (1977). *Talkin and testifyin: The language of Black America*. Boston, MA: Houghton Mifflin.

Smitherman, G. (2000a). African American student writers in the NAEP, 1969–1988/89 and "The Blacker the berry, the sweeter the juice". In G. Smitherman, *Talkin that talk: Language, culture and education in African America* (pp. 163–194). New York: Routledge.

Smitherman, G. (2000b). Ebonics, King, and Oakland: Some folks don't believe fat meat is greasy. In G. Smitherman, *Talkin that talk: Language, culture and education in African America* (pp. 150–162). New York: Routledge.

Snow, C., Burns, M. S., & Griffin, P. (1998). *Preventing reading difficulties in young children*. Washington, DC: National Academy Press.

Solorzano, D., & Delgado Bernal, D. (2001). Examining transformational resistance through a Critical Race and LatCrit Theory framework: Chicana and Chicano students in the urban context. *Urban Education, 36*(3), 308–342.

Spencer, M. B. (1987). Black children's ethnic identity formation: Risk and resilience in castelike minorities. In J. Phinney & M. Rotheram (Eds.), *Children's ethnic socialization: Pluralism and development* (pp. 103–116). Newbury Park, CA: Sage.

Spencer, M. B. (1999). Social and cultural influences on school adjustment: The application of an identity-focused cultural ecological perspective. *Educational Psychologist, 34*(1), 43–57.

Spencer, M. B. (2001). Identity, achievement orientation and race: "Lessons learned" about the normative developmental experiences of African American males. In W. Watkins, J. Lewis & V. Chou. (Eds.), *Race and education* (pp. 100–127). Boston, MA: Allyn & Bacon Press.

Spencer, M. B., Noll, E., Stoltzfus, J., & Harpalani, V. (2001). Identity and school adjustment: Revisiting the "Acting White" assumption. *Educational Psychologist, 36*(1), 21–30.

Spencer, M. B., Swanson, D. P., & Cunningham, M. (1991). Ethnicity, ethnic identity, and competence formation: Adolescent transition and cultural transformation. *Journal of Negro Education, 60*(3), 366–387.

Spring, J. (2001). *Globalization and educational rights: An intercivilizational analysis* Mahwah, NJ: Lawrence Erlbaum.

Stahl, S., & Miller, P. (1989). Whole language and language experience approaches for beginning reading: A quantitative research synthesis. *Review of Educational Research, 59*, 87–116.

Staples, B. (2004, December 27). Why some politicians need their prisons to stay full. *New York Times*. http://www.nytimes.com. Retrieved December 27, 2004.

Steele, C. M. (1992). Race and the schooling of Black Americans. *Atlantic Monthly, 269*(4), 68–78.

Steele, C. M. (1998). Stereotyping and its threat are real. *American Psychologist, 53*(6), 680–681.

Steele, C. M. (1999). Thin ice: "Stereotype threat" and Black college students. *The Atlantic Monthly, 284*(2), 44–54.

Steele, C. M., & Aronson, J. (1995). Stereotype threat and the intellectual test performance of African Americans. *Journal of Personality and Social Psychology, 69,* 797–911.

Steele, C. M., Spencer, S. J., & Aronson, J. (2002). Contending with group image: The psychology of stereotype and social identity threat. In M. P. Zanna (Ed.), *Advances in experimental psychology* (Vol. 34, pp. 379–440). Amsterdam, NY: Academic Press.

Stevenson, H. W., & Stigler, J. W. (1992). *The learning gap: Why our schools are failing and what we can learn from Japanese and Chinese education.* New York: Simon & Schuster.

Stewart, J. B. (1984, December). Building a cooperative economy: Lessons from the Black community experience. *Review of Social Economy, 62*(3), 360–368.

Stewart, J. B., (Ed.). (1997). *African Americans and post-industrial labor markets.* New Brunswick, NJ: Transaction Publishers.

Stigler, J. W., & Baranes, R. (1989). Culture and mathematics learning. *Review of Research in Education, 15,* 253–306.

Stigler, J. W., Shweder, R. A., & Herdt, G. (1990). *Cultural psychology: Essays on comparative human development.* New York: Cambridge University Press.

Strauss, R. P., & Sawyer, E. A. (1986). Some new evidence on teacher and student competencies. *Economics of Education Review, 5*(1), 41–48.

Strickland, D. (1985). Early childhood development and reading instruction. In C. Brooks (Ed.), *Tapping potential: English and language arts for the Black learner.* National Council of Teachers of English.

Stromquist, N. P. (2002). *Education in a globalized world: The connectivity of economic power, technology, and knowledge.* Lanham, MD: Rowan & Littlefield Publishers.

Stromquist, N. P., & Basile, M. L. (Eds.). (1999). *Politics of educational innovations in developing countries.* New York: Falmer Press.

Stuckey, S. (1987). *Slave culture.* New York: Oxford University Press.

Sunderman, G., & Kim, J. (February 4, 2004). *Inspiring vision, disappointing results: Four studies on implementing the No Child Left Behind Act.* Cambridge, MA: Harvard Civil Rights Project. http://www.civilrightsproject.harvard.edu/research/esea/call_nclb.php?Page=2. Retrieved 3-19-04.

Sutton, R. E. (1991). Equity and computers in the schools: A decade of research. *Review of Educational Research, 61*(4), 475–503.

The Swann Report. (1985). *Education for all.* London: HMSO.

Swartz, E. (1999). Continuing white reign: Essay review. *Encounter, 12*(2), 63–73.

Talbert, J. E. (1990). *Teacher tracking: Exacerbating inequalities in the high school.* Stanford, CA: Center for Research on the Context of Secondary Teaching, Stanford University.

Tate, W. (1993, March). Can America have a colorblind national assessment in mathematics? Paper presented at the annual meeting of the American Educational Research Association, Atlanta, GA.

Tate, W. (Guest Editor). (1996). Urban schools and mathematical reform: Implementing new standards. *Urban Education, 30*(4).

Tate, W. (2001). Science education as a civil right: Urban schools and opportunity-to-learn considerations. *Journal of Research in Science Reaching, 38*(9),1015–1028.

Tatum, B. D. (1999). *Why are all the Black kids sitting together in the cafeteria? And other conversations about race.* New York: Basic Books.

Taylor, W. L., & Piche, D. M. (1991). *A report on shortchanging children: The impact of fiscal inequity on the education of students at risk.* Prepared for the Committee on Education and Labor, U.S. House of Representatives. Washington, DC: U.S. Government Printing Office.

Teddlie, C., Kirby, P., & Stringfield, S. (1989). Effectiveness vs. ineffective schools: Observable differences in the classroom. *American Journal of Education, 97*(3), 221–236.

Tedla, E. (1995). *Sankofa: African thought and education.* New York: Peter Lang.

Tedla, E. (1997). Sankofan education for development of personhood. *Raising Standards, Journal of the Rochester Teachers Association* (Spring/Summer), pp. 19–25.

The Random House Dictionary. (1983). New York: Author, p. 166.

Thurow, L. C. (1972). Education and economic equality. *Public Interest, 28,* 66–81.

Tillman, L. C. (2001). Mentoring African American faculty in predominantly White institutions. *Research in Higher Education, 42*(3), 295–325.

Tillman, L. C. (2002). Culturally sensitive research approaches: An African American perspective. *Educational Researcher, 31*(9), 3–12.

Tillman, L., King, J., Wallace, L., Richardson, L., Lovett, H., & Vegas, J. (1999). *Mapping university assets for public scholarship and the praxis of community partnering.* (ERIC Document Reproduction Service No. ED431369)

Tillman, L., Fracklin, W., & Ishibashi, J. (2000). On evaluation of the selected activities of the Commission on Research in Black Education: On initiative of the American Educational Research Association.

Toll, R. (1977). *Blacking up: The minstrel show in nineteenth-century America.* New York: Oxford University Press.

"Tony Blair's war on poverty." (1999, September 25). *The Economist, 352*(8138), 18–19.

Traub, J. (1999, January 16). What no school can do. *New York Times Magazine,* pp. 52–56.

Trimble, K., & Sinclair, R. L. (1986). Ability grouping and differing conditions for learning: An analysis of content and instruction in ability-grouped classes. Paper presented at the annual meeting of the American Educational Research Association, San Francisco.

Turner, C. (Interview, 1992). Empowering communities of color. In L. Krimerman, F. Lindenfeld, C. K., & J. Benello (Eds.), *From the ground up: Essays on grassroots & workplace democracy by C. George Benello* (pp. 185–192). Boston, MA: South End Press.

Uchitelle, L. (2000, July 23). The classroom ceiling: Making sense of a stubborn education gap. The Week in Review – The Nation. *New York Times,* Sunday, Late edition-Final, Section 4, p. 1, column 1.

The United States Department of Labor. (1999). Labor Day 1999 executive summary. *Future work: Trends and challenges for work in the 21st century.* Washington, DC: Author.

U.S. Bureau of Labor Statistics. (2004). BLS Releases 2002-12 Employment Projections. *News.* Press Release USDL 04-148. Washington, DC: United States Department of Labor, February 11, 2004. http://www.bls.gov/emp/home.htm.

U.S. Census Bureau. (2000). htpp://www.uscensus.gov.

U.S. Census Bureau. (2002). Table IE-6. Measures of Household Income Inequality: 1967 to 2000. Last revised 22 August 2002. http://www.census.gov/hhes/income/histinc/ie6.html.

U.S. Department of Commerce (1996). *Statistical abstract of the United States: 1996.* 116th Edition. Washington, DC: Bureau of the Census.

U.S. Department of Education. (1999). *Hope for urban education: A study of high-performing, high-poverty elementary schools.* Austin: University of Texas.

Urban Nutrition Initiative (2002). Annual Report May 2001–May 2002. Philadelphia: University of Pennsylvania, Center for Community Partnerships. www.upenn.edu/ccp/uni.shtml (accessed 1-13-03).

Useem, E. L. (1990, Fall). You're good, but you're not good enough: Tracking students out of advanced mathematics. *American Educator, 14*(3), 24-27, 43–46.

Usiskin, Z. (1987). Why elementary algebra can, should, and must be an eighth grade course for average students. *Mathematics Teacher, 80,* 428–438.

Vass, W. (1979). *The Bantu speaking heritage of the United States.* Los Angeles: UCLA, Center for Afro-American Studies.

Vinson, K. D., & Ross, E. W. (2001, March). What we can know and when we can know it. *Z Magazine, 14*(3), 34–38.

Voss, J. (1988). Problem solving and the educational process. In A. Lesgold & R. Glaser (Eds.), *Foundations for a psychology of education* (pp. 251–294). Hillsdale, NJ: Erlbaum.

Vygotsky, L. S. (1978). *Mind in society: The development of higher psychological processes.* Cambridge, MA: Harvard University Press.

Vygotsky, L. S. (1987). *Thinking and speech.* New York: Plenum.

W. T. Grant Foundation, Commission on Work, Family and Citizenship (1988). *The forgotten half: Non-college youth in America.* Washington, DC: Author.

Wa Thiong'o, N. (1981). *Decolonising the mind: The politics of language in African literature.* London: James Currey.

Walberg, H. J., & Tsai, S. (1985). Correlates of reading achievement and attitude: A national assessment study. *Journal of Educational Research, 78*(3), 159–167.

Walker, S. (Ed.). (2001). *African roots/American cultures: Africa in the creation of the Americas.* New York: Rowman & Littlefield.

Warfield-Coppock, N. (1990). *Afrocentric theory and application. Volume 1: Adolescent rites of passage.* Washington, DC: Baobob Associates.

Warfield-Coppock, N. (1992). The rites of passage movement: A resurgence of African-centered practices for socializing African American youth. *Journal of Negro Education, 61*(4), 471–482.

Warfield-Coppock, N. (1994a). *Life cycle rites of passage: African-American development strategies.* Washington, DC: Baobob Associates.

Warfield-Coppock, N. (1994b). The rites of passage: Extending education into the African American community. M. Shujaa (Ed.), *Too much schooling, too little education: A paradox of Black life in white societies* (pp. 377–393). Trenton, NJ: Africa World Press.

Warren, B., & Rosebery, A. (1996). "This question is just too, too easy!" Students' perspectives on accountability in science. In L. Schauble & R. Glaser (Eds.), *Innovations in learning* (pp. 97–126). Mahwah, NJ: Erlbaum.

Warren, B., Ballenger, C., Ogonowski, M., Rosebery, A., & Hudicourt-Barnes, J. (2001). Rethinking diversity in learning science: The logic of everyday sense-making. *Journal of Research in Science Teaching, 38,* 529–552.

Washington, M. H. (1982). Teaching black-eyed Susans: An approach to the study of Black women writers. In G. Hull, P. Scott, & B. Smith (Eds.), *But some of us are brave* (pp. 208–217). New York: The Feminist Press.

Watkins, W. (1986). The political sociology of postcolonial social studies curriculum development: The case of Nigeria, 1960–1980. Unpublished Ph.D. Dissertation. Chicago: University of Illinois.

Watkins, W. (1989). On accommodationist education: Booker T. Washington goes to Africa. *International Third World Studies and Journal, 1,* 137–143.

Watkins, W. (2001). The white architects of black education. New York: Teachers College Press.

Watson, B. C. (1996). *Testing: Its origins, use and misuse.* Philadelphia: Urban League of Philadelphia.

Weiss, C., & Clamp, C. (1992). Women's cooperatives: Part of the answer to poverty? In L. Krimerman & F. Lindenfeld (Eds.), *When workers decide: Workplace democracy takes root in North America* (pp. 229–232). Philadelphia: New Society Publishers.

Wertsch, J. (1991). *Voices of the mind: A sociocultural approach to mediated action.* Cambridge, MA: Harvard University Press.

Wertsch, J. (Ed.). (1985). *Culture, communication and cognition: Vygotskian perspectives.* New York: Cambridge University Press.

Westwood, S. (1990). Racism, Black masculinity and the politics of space. In J. Hearn & D. H. Morgan (Eds.), *Men, masculinities and social theory* (pp. 60–71). London and Winchester: Unwin Hyman.

Wheelock, A. (1992). *Crossing the tracks: How "untracking" can save America's schools.* New York: The New Press.

White, B. J., & Frederickson, J. R. (1997). *The Thinker/Tools Inquiry Project: Making scientific inquiry accessible to students.* Princeton, NJ: Center for Performance Assessment, Educational Testing Service.

White, K. R. (1982). The relation between socioeconomic status and academic achievement. *Psychological Bulletin, 91,* 461–481.

Whitehead, A. N. (1929). *The aims of education.* New York: MacMillan.

Wilder, C. (2000). *A covenant with color: Race and social power in Brooklyn.* New York: Columbia University Press.

Wilensky, U., & Resnick, M. (1999). Thinking in levels: A dynamic systems perspective to making sense of the world. *Journal of Science Education and Technology, 8*(1), 3–19.

Wilkins, R. (2002, Winter). The importance of *Brown v. Board*. In P. Strum (Ed.), *Brown v. Board: Its impact on education and what it left undone* (pp. 14–16). Washington, DC: Woodrow Wilson International Center for Scholars.

Williams, J. D., et al. (2001). Consumer racial profiling: Bigotry goes to market. *Crisis, 108*(6), 22–25.

Williams, R. (2000, May). If you're Black, get back; if you're Brown, stick around; if you're White, hang tight: Race, gender and work in the global economy. Working Paper for the Preamble Center. University of Maryland, College Park.

Wilson, A. (1992). *Awakening the natural genius of Black children*. New York: Afrikan World InfoSystems.

Wilson, E. O. (1998). *Consilience, the unity of knowledge*. New York: Knopf.

Wilson, J. J., & Wallace, R. (1992). *Black Wall Street: A lost dream*. Tulsa, OK: Duralon.

Wilson, S. (1990). A conflict of interests: Constraints that affect teaching and change, *Educational Evaluation and Policy Analysis, 12*(3), 309–326.

Wilson, W. J. (1987). *The truly disadvantaged: The inner city, the underclass, and public policy*. Chicago: University of Chicago Press.

Wilson, W. J. (1999). *The bridge over the racial divide: Rising inequality and coalition politics*. Berkeley: University of California Press.

Wineburg, S. (1998). Reading Abraham Lincoln: An expert-expert study in the interpretation of historical texts. *Cognitive Science, 22*, 319–346.

Wise, A. E., Darling-Hammond, L., & Berry, B. (1987). *Effective teacher selection: From recruitment to retention*. Santa Monica, CA: The RAND Corporation.

Wittke, C. F. (1971). *Tambo and bones*. New York: Greenwood Publishing (Originally published 1930).

Wolf, D., Bixby, J., Glenn, J., & Gardner, H. (1991). To use their minds well: Investigating new forms of student assessment. In G. Grant (Ed.), *Review of Research in Education, Volume 17* (pp. 31–74). Washington, DC: American Educational Research Association.

Wolff, E. N. (2001). Recent trends in wealth ownership, 1983–1998. In T. Shapiro & E. Wolff (Eds.), *Assets and the disadvantaged: The benefits of spreading asset ownership* (pp. 34–73). New York: Russell Sage Foundation.

Woods, C. (1998). *Development arrested: The blues and plantation power in the Mississippi Delta*. London: Verso.

Woods, R. (2001). "Oh sorry, I'm a racist": Black student experiences at the University of Witwatersrand. In R. O. Mabokela & K. L. King (Eds.), *Apartheid no more* (pp. 91–110). Westport, CT: Bergin & Garvey.

Woodson, C. G. (1933). *The mis-education of the Negro*. Washington, DC: Associated Publishers.

Working towards a solution. (1999, May 26). *The Daily Telegraph*, p. 18.

World Bank. (1988). *Education in sub-Saharan Africa: Policies for adjustment, revitalization and expansion*. Washington, DC: Author.

World Bank. (1990, 1989, 1988). *Annual reports*. Washington, DC: Author.

Wright, C., Weekes, D., & McGlaughlin, A. (2000). *Race, class and gender in exclusion from school*. London: Falmer Press.

Wright, E. O., & Dwyer, R. (2000/2001). The American jobs machine. http://bostonreview.mit.edu/BR25.6/wright.html (first accessed 8-23-2002), 1–17. Originally appeared in *Boston Review 25* (6, December/January).

Wynter, S. (1968/1969). We must learn to sit down together and talk about a little culture: Reflections on West Indian writing and criticism. *Jamaica Journal, 2*(4), December, 1968, Volume 3, 23–32/March, 1969, Volume 1, 27–42.

Wynter, S. (1995). Breaking the epistemological contract on Black America. *Forum NHI, 2*(1), 41–57.

Wynter, S. (2000, June 30). Black education: Towards the human, After "Man": In the manner of a manifesto. Presented at the CORIBE Working Colloquium, St. Simon's Island, GA.

Wynter, S. (2003, Fall). Unsettling the coloniality of being/power/truth/freedom: Towards the Human, after Man, its overrepresentation—An argument. *The New Centennial Review, 3*(3), 257–357.

Yankah, K. (2000, November, Inaugural Lecture). Scholarly authority and the quest for a new world academic order. University of Ghana–Legon.

Yankah, K. (2004). Scholarly authority and the quest for a New World Academic Order. *The Journal of Culture and Its Transmission in the African World, 1*(2), 1–42.

Zaslavsky, C. (1979). *Africa counts*. New York: Lawrence Hill Books.

FURTHER READING

Academy for Educational Development. (1992). *South Africa: Tertiary education sector assessment*. Washington, DC: Academy for Educational Development.

Anderson, S., Cavanagh, J., (with T. Lee), & The Institute for Policy Studies (2000). *Field guide to the global economy*. New York: The New Press.

Benello, G. (1992). Economic democracy and the future. In L. Krimerman, F. Lindenfeld, C. Korty, & J. Benello (Eds.), *From the ground up: Essays on grass-roots & workplace democracy by C. George Benello* (pp. 81–88). Boston, MA: South End Press.

Bethune, M. M. (1939). The adaption of the history of the Negro to the capacity of the child. *Journal of Negro History, 29*, 9–13.

Blake. J. (n.d.). Preliminary study into the advisability of development of a new standard-setting instrument for the safeguarding of intangible cultural heritage (Traditional culture and folklore), UNESCO.

Bradley, W. (2000, Spring). Speech at the Harlem democratic debate, New York: Apollo Theater.

Bratton, M. (1989, April). Beyond the state: Civil society and associational life in Africa. *World Politics, 41*, 407–430.

Bray, M., Clarke, P. B., & Stephens, D. (1986). *Education and society in Africa*. London: Edward Arnold.

Buchart, R. E. (1980). *Northern schools, southern Blacks, and reconstruction: Freedmen's education, 1862–1875*. Westport, CT: Greenwood Press.

Carnoy, M., & Samoff, J. (Eds.). (1990). *Education and social transition in the third world*. Princeton, NJ: Princeton University Press.

Carruthers, J., & Harris, L. C. (1997). *African world history project: The preliminary challenge*. Los Angeles, CA: Association for the Study of Classical African Civilization.

Congressional Black Caucus Foundation Annual Conference (2003). Symposium—The U.S. and Africa: Continuing challenges, new approaches. Washington, DC: Author.

Fafunwa, A. B. (1974). *History of education in Nigeria*. London: Allen & Unwin.

Fugard, A. (1964). *Blood knot*. New York: Samuel French, Inc.

Ginwright, S. A. (2004). *Black in school: Afrocentric reform, urban youth, and the promise of hip-hop culture*. New York: Teachers College Press.

Green, J., & Harker, J. (Eds.). (1988). *Multiple perspective analyses of classroom discourse*. Norwood, NJ: Ablex.

Grissmer, D. W., & Kirby, S. N. (1987). *Teacher attrition: The uphill climb to staff the nation's schools*. Santa Monica, CA: Rand Corporation.

Henry, A. (1998a). *Taking back control: Black women teachers' activism and the education of African Canadian children*. Albany: State University of New York Press.

Irvine, R. W., & Irvine, J. J. (1983). The impact of the desegregation process on the education of Black students: Key variables. *Journal of Negro Education, 52*(4), 410–422.

Johnson, J. H., Jr., Bienenstock, E. J., & Stoloff, J. A. (1997). An empirical test of the cultural capital hypothesis. In J. B. Stewart (Ed.), *African Americans and post-industrial labor markets* (pp. 39–59). New Brunswick, NJ: Transaction Publishers.

Lloyd, P. C. (1966). *The new elites of tropical Africa*. London: Oxford University Press.

Marc, F. (2003, July 29). A portrait of injustice in Black and White, *Washington Post*, B-1.

Author Index

A

Aaron, M., 202
Abernethy, D., 129
Adijian, L. B., 80
Akbar, N., 267
Akom, A. A., 38, 39, 278
Akoto, A., 54
Alexander, K., 148, 149
Alexander, K. L., 210
Allen, B., 64
Allen, D., 39, 40
Allington, R. L., 106
Almond, G. A., 123, 124
Altbach, P. G., 130, 131
Amin, S., 184
Anderson, C., 140
Anderson, J. D., 51, 52, 120, 137, 139
Anderson, R. D., 208
Anderson, S. E., 80
Ani, M., 64, 100, 330
Anjail, M., 294
Anson, A., 78
Anyon, J., 60
Apple, M., 61
Armah, A. K., v, xxiv, 309, 350
Aronson, J., 30
Asante, K. W., 64
Asante, M. K., 54, 61, 64
Ascher, M., 76, 77
Ashton, P., 208
Askey, R., 111
Auchard, E., 192

Austin, A., 188, 189, 268, 269
Azicorbe, A. M., 233

B

Bailey, C., 96
Bailey, J. D., 112
Bakhtin, M. M., 65
Ball, A. F., 87
Ball, D. L., 65
Ballenger, C., 102, 103
Banks, J. 88, 143
Banks, J. A., 40, 143
Baquedano-Lopez, P., 70, 87
Baranes, R., 77
Barlow, W., 31
Baron, R., 60
Barr, J., 327
Barr, R., 210
Barton, P. E., 200
Basile, M. L., 185
Bass, H., 65
Baugh, J., 77
Bayley, N., 47
Bell, D., xxii
Bennett, L., 95
Bents, M., 208
Bents, R. B., 208
Benveniste, G., 106
Bereiter, C., 59
Berends, M., 210
Berliner, D. C., 208
Berliner, P., 69

Berne, R., 205
Berry, B., 211, 222
Berry, W., 1
Billingsley, A., 51, 64
Birke, L., 327
Bixby, J., 75
Bledsoe, J. C., 208
Bloome, D., 93
Blyden, E. W., 269
Blyth, E., 293
Boggs, G. L., 34, 35, 241, 244, 245
Bogues, A., 14
Bond, H. M., 46, 61
Bond, J., 232
Booth, W., 82
Bourdieu, P., 294
Bowen, H., 149, 152, 155
Bowles, S., 61
Bowman, B., 216
Bowman, P., 70, 97, 98, 99
Boykin, A. W., 64, 91, 92, 95, 96, 97
Boyle, P. M., 121, 127, 128
Bozeman, L. A., 130
Bracey, G. W., 40, 347
Braddock, J., 216
Braddock, J. M. II, 145, 146
Bransford, J., 55, 56
Bransford, J. D., 55, 56
Bridges, L., 144
Brofenbrenner, U., 97
Brookins, C., 54
Brooks, G., 114
Brophy, J., 215
Brown, A., 55, 56, 66, 83
Brown, J., 19, 66
Bruckman, A. S., 35
Bruer, J., 56, 89
Bruner, J., 64, 66
Bryk, A., 210
Bryson, M., 327
Bullock, H., 128
Bunche, R., 193, 194
Burnham, R., 208
Burns, M. S., 81, 82, 100, 107, 108
Burton, N. W., 212
Byrk, A. S., 108

C

Campbell, E. Q., 110, 206
Carby, H., 292

Carnoy, M., 136, 147, 148, 151, 155, 185
Carraher, D. W., 76
Carruthers, J., 8
Case, J., 234
Cazden, C., 47, 66, 68, 86, 109
Césaire, A., 3, 4, 5, 359
Chafets, Z., 9, 22
Chall, J., 100
Champion, T., 61, 63
Chazan, N., 122
Chi, M. T. H., 56, 88
Childs, J. B., 9
Chuck D., 347, 349
Cicero, M. T., 156159
Cicourel, A. V., 142
Clamp, C., 235
Clark, S., 52
Clarke, J. H., 137, 138
Clement, J., 60
Clinget, R., 129
Coard, B., 292
Cobb, C., 35, 52, 78
Cocking, R., 55, 56
Cocking, R. R., 88, 89
Coffield, F., 293
Cohen, D., 220
Cole, M., 56, 63, 88
Coleman, J. S., 110, 123, 128, 142, 206
Coley, R. J., 200
College Board, 11, 210, 212, 214
Collins, A., 66
Collins, C., 227, 231, 233
Comer, J., 52, 78
Conant, F., 103
Conley, D., 233
Cook, T., 78
Cook-Gumperz, J., 68
Cooney, T. J., 214
Cooper, A. J., 54, 61
Cooper, E., 202, 215, 216
Cooper, H., 60
Cooper, R., 109
Copley, P. O., 208
Cosby, C. O., 32
Cosby, W., 39, 40
Courlander, H., 325
Cox, J. V., 208
Crocker, L., 208
Crosswhite, J. A., 214
Crouse, J., 50
Cunningham, M., 94, 97

D

Daniel, D., 188, 189
Darity, W. A., Jr., 226, 232
Darling-Hammond, L., 112, 202, 207, 208, 210, 211, 220, 221, 222
Davenport, E. C., 212
Davenport, S., 214
Davis, A., 12, 13
Davis, D. G., 213, 215
de Castell, S., 327
de la Rocha, O., 74, 77
Delpit, L., 60, 62, 66, 71, 100
Demarco, J., 235
DeMeis, D. K., 47, 60
DiMaggio, P., 142
Diop, C. A., xxi, xxii, 4
Diouf, S. A., 264, 268, 269
DiSessa, A., 60
Dixon, C. N., 66
Dole, J. A., 83
Donovan, M. S., 55, 56
Dossey, J. A., 214
Dove, N., 294, 295
Dreeben, R., 209, 210
Drucker, P. F., 184, 199
Druva, C. A., 208
Du Bois, W. E. B., 54, 61, 64, 65, 88, 95, 97, 195, 235
Duffy, G. G., 83
Duncan-Andrade, J., 84
Dunn, D., 294
Durkheim, E., 128
Dwyer, R., 228, 229
Dyson, A., 92
Dzvimbo, K. P., 185

E

Ebmeier, H., 222
Eccles, J., 94
Eckstrom, R., 215
Edmonds, R., 101, 110
Egan-Robertson, A., 93
Eggleston, J., 294
Ekstrom, R. B., 213
Elder, G., 97
Elley, R., 82
Ellis, J. B., 35
Engelmann, S., 59
Epps, E., 52

Esch, C., 204
Esdaille, M., 10
Evenson, B., 141
Evertson, C., 208

F

Fanon, F., 119, 185, 357, 358, 362
Farrell, J., 147
Feltovich, P. J., 56, 88
Fennema, E., 80
Fenton, T. L., 234
Ferguson, R. F., 112, 206, 207, 217
Fichtenbaum, R., 232
Finch, S., 293, 295
Findlay, H., 147
Fine, M., 330
Finley, M. K., 213
Fitzgerald, R., 293, 295
Flateau, J., 369
Foley, D., 30
Fordham, S., 30
Foster, M., 8, 95, 112, 144, 306
Foster, P., 129
Frankenstein, M., 76, 80
Franklin, J. H., 138, 139, 141, 142
Franklin, V. P., 97
Franklin, W., 319
Frederickson, J. R., 65, 103
Frederiksen, C. H., 108
Frederiksen, N., 57
Freeman, K., 142, 143, 147, 152, 153, 329
Freeman, R. B., 232
Fryer, P., 137, 138, 139, 141
Fuller, B., 129, 133
Fuson, K. C., 104

G

Gall, C., 276
Gallagher, K., 150, 151
Gallagher, K. S., 112
Gamoran, A., 210, 213, 215
Garcia, E., 8, 216
Gardner, H., 75
Gaston, M., 204
Gay, G., 95
Geber, M., 47
Gee, J. P., 63, 68, 86
Gemignani, R. J., 200
Gevinson, S., 82

Gillborn, D., 292, 293
Gillborn, G., 292, 293
Gilyard, K., 87
Gintis, H., 61
Gipps, C., 292, 293
Glaser, R., 56, 88, 221
Glenn, J., 75
Goertz, M. E., 213
Goldenberg, D. M., 265
Goldring, E., 145, 146
Gomes, N. L., 303
Gomez, D. L., 209
Gomez, L., 89
Gonçalves e Silva, P., 303
Gonzales, P., 103
Good, T. L., 215
Goodwin, S., 28, 40
Gordon, B., 6, 61
Gordon, E. W., 6, 8, 23, 24, 40, 41, 319
Goslee, S., 88
Gottschild, B. D., 16, 19
Gould, S. J., 57
Graham-Brown, S., 126
Grant, C. A., 223
Graves, B., 108
Green, A. L., 310
Green, J. L., 66
Greenberg, J. B., 60
Greenberg, J. D., 208
Greenfield, P. M., 88, 89
Greeno, J. G., 56, 63
Greenwald, R., 112
Griffin, P., 81, 82, 100, 107, 108
Grobe, R. P., 209
Grossman, P. L., 208
Guinier, L., xxv
Gumperz, J. J., 68
Gutierrez, K., 66, 67, 96
Gutiérrez, K., 70, 87
Gyimah-Brempong, K., 232

H

Habib, F., 78
Haidara, Y. M., 168
Hale, J., 95
Hale-Benson, J., 95
Hallak, J., 13
Hamilton, C. E., 100
Harber, C., 122, 123, 124, 129
Harding, V., 52

Harpalani, V., 70, 85, 89, 97
Hart, M. H., 263
Hartman, W. T., 205
Hawisher, G., 326
Hawley, W., 208
Haynes, C., Jr., 234, 235
Haynes, N., 78
Hearn, J. C., 150, 151
Heath, S. B. 99, 65, 68
Heath, S. B., 61
Hedges, L. V., 112
Herbert, T., 314
Herdt, G., 56, 63
Herman, R., 81
Herrnstein, R., 22, 57, 364
Herskovitz, M. J., 64, 95
Hicks, D., 63
Hilliard, A. G., 14, 22, 23, 25, 54, 57, 59, 61,
    106, 114
Hilliard, A. G. 85, 15
Hillocks, G., 82
Hilton, T. L., 213
Hobson, C. J., 110, 206
Hoffer, T. B., 213
Holland, J., 70
Hollins, E. R., 112, 143, 144
Holt, T. C., 5
hooks, b., 333
Hooper, P. K., 87, 91, 328
Hope, J. II, 236, 237
Hopson, R. K., 188, 189
Horvat, E. N., 30
Hossler, D., 150, 151
Howard, J., 52, 78
Howe, F., 52
Howes, C., 100
Hudicourt-Barnes, J., 26, 102, 104
Hughes, A., 10
Humphrey, D. C., 204
Hunt, H., 204
Hutchison, J. P., 168
Hymes, D., 68, 109
Hyon, S., 63

I

Inkeles, A., 124
Iracklin, W., 314
Irvine, J., 67
Irvine, J. J., 40, 114
Ishibashi, J., 314

J

Jackson, F., 47
Jackson, J., 47
Jackson, R., 122
Jacobs, H., 332
Jacoby, S., 103
James, C. L. R., 33
Jencks, C., 57, 58, 110
Jenson, J., 327
John, B. M., 329
John, V. P., 68, 109
Johns, R. L., 148, 149
Johnson, D. J., 55
Johnson, P., 78
John-Steiner, V., 103, 108
Joiner, B., 147
Jones, G., 80, 87
Jones, L., 310
Jones, L. V., 212
Jones, R. L., 63

K

Ka, F., 145, 148, 151, 152
Kafai, Y., 93
Kambon, K. K. K., 330
Kamii, M., 52, 78
Kane, M., 212, 213
Kantrowitz, B., 9
Karenga, M., 54, 64, 91
Karweit, N., 81
Kass, A., 92
Kaufman, J. E., 210
Kelly, G. P., 130, 131
Kemple, J. J., 211
Kennickell, A. B., 233
Kifer, E., 214
Kim, J., 40
King, J., 320
King, J. E., xxi, 4, 5, 7, 9, 15, 16, 23, 24, 30, 34, 39, 46, 61, 143, 144, 326, 330
King, J. R., 64
King, K., 117, 121
King, K. L., 185, 186, 188, 189
King, R. A., 203, 206
Kirby, P., 100
Kirshner, B., 39, 278
Kleinman, K., 93
Klenbort, M., 145
Kogbara, D., 141

Kohn, A., 13
Kozol, J., 203, 204, 205, 214, 215
Krimerman, L., 235
KRS-ONE, 33, 347
Kulik, C. C., 213
Kulik, J. A., 213
Kunjunfu, J., 266

L

Ladd, H. F., 112, 207
Ladson-Billings, G., 11, 95, 112, 144, 306
Laine, R. D., 112
Lampert, M., 65
Larkin, J., 56
Larson, J., 66
Lather, P., 326
Lave, J., 56, 63, 74, 77
Lee, C. D., 43, 46, 52, 53, 54, 55, 63, 67, 70, 76, 82, 83, 84, 85, 86, 87, 88, 89, 92, 94, 96, 97, 100
Lee, V., 210
Leiderman, G., 47
Lenin, V. I., 119
Leonard, C., 106
Levin, H., 154
Levine, D., 234
Levitan, S., 148
Levy, F., 199
Lewis, K. S., 30
Lin, X., 93
Lincoln, C. E., 271
Lindenfeld, F., 235
Lindsay, B., 185
LoCicero, A., 104
Lomotey, K., 54
Lorde, A., 136, 137, 185
Lovett, H., 320
Lumpkin, B., 76, 106
Luria, A. R., 88
Lusane, C., 227, 228
Lynd, S., 14

M

Ma, L., 111
Mabokela, R. O., 185, 186, 188, 189, 310
MacPhail-Wilcox, B., 203, 206
MacPherson, W., 295
Madden, N., 109
Madden, N. A., 66, 109

Madhubuti, H., 54, 61
Magyari-Beck, I., 147
Mahiri, J., 84, 87
Maiga, H. O., 27, 28, 133, 160, 168, 169, 174, 178, 179, 289
Maiga, M. B., 168
Maiga, Y. B., 168
Majors, Y., 87
Malloy, C., 80, 87
Mandela, N., 307
Mangum, G., 148
Mankiller, W., 140, 141
Mare, R., 215
Margolis, E., 8
Marshall, R., 148
Martin, D., 78, 87
Marx, K., 125
Mason, P., 227
Mason, P. L., 226, 232
Mateené, K., 167
Matheson, C. C., 100
Matthews, W., 213
Mazrui, A., 122
Mazuri, A., 187
Mbilinyi, M., 129
McAdoo, H. P., 63
McAdoo, J. L., 63
McCloud, A., 275
McDill, E. L., 210
McGlaughlin, A., 293
McKinnon, J., 230
McKnight, C. C., 214
McLaren, P., 61
McPartland, J., 110, 206
McPartland, J. M., 216
Meacham, S., 7, 8, 14, 36, 68, 69, 84
Mehan, H., 142
Mehta, J. D., 30
Mendenhall, R., 63, 67, 87, 96, 97, 100
Merisotis, J. P., 148, 149, 150, 151
Michaels, S., 62, 66, 86
Midgley, C., 94
Miller, J., 293
Miller, J. G., 200
Miller, P., 100
Ministère de l'Education de Base-DNAFLA, 168
Mirza, H. S., 291, 292, 293, 294
Mitchell, C. A., 15, 16, 330
Mitchell-Kernan, C., 83
Modood, T., 291

Mohammed, C., 272
Mohammed, W. D., 264, 274, 279
Mohr, J., 142
Moll, L., 60
Monfort, F., 202
Mood, A. M., 110, 206
Moore, C., 10, 102, 347
Moore, D., 214
Moore, K. B., 233
Moore, S., 10, 102, 347
Morgan, M., 61, 83, 95
Morgan, S. L., 30
Morphet, E. L., 148, 149
Morrell, E., 84
Morris, J. E., 145, 146
Morrison, T., xv
Moses, R. P., 35, 52, 78, 328
Moss, A. A., Jr., 138, 139, 141, 142
Moss, B., 87
Moumouni, A., 164, 180
Mufwene, S., 64
Muhammad, E., 270, 271, 273
Muhammad, Z., 10, 262, 263, 264, 266, 274, 276, 277
Munanga, K., 303
Munford, C. J., 4, 13
Murnane, R. J., 199, 211
Murray, C., 22, 57, 364
Murtaugh, M., 74, 77

N

Nasir, N., 88
Nasir, N. S., 39, 87, 278
Nelson, B. S., 79, 80, 104, 105
Nembhard, J. G., 30, 31, 226, 227, 228, 231, 232, 234, 235, 236, 237, 238, 239
Nesbitt, R., 58, 59
Nettles, M., 48, 49, 61
Newman, S., 66
Nkrumah, K., 119
Nobles, W., 63, 64, 100
Noll, E., 97
Nove, A., 293, 295
Nunes, T., 76

O

Oakes, J., 46, 145, 146, 210, 212, 213, 214, 215
Ochs, E., 103

O'Connor, C., 15
Ogbu, J., 30
Ogonowski, M., 102
O'Grady, A. R., 347
Oguntoye, K., 137, 138, 139, 140
Oickle, E., 109
Oliver, M., 233
Olsen, R. J., 211
Opitz, M., 137, 138, 139, 140
Oquendo-Rodriguez, A., 327
Orellana, M. F., 70
Orfield, G., 61
Orfield, G. F., 202
Orr, E. W., 77
Osler, A., 293

P

Page, F. M., Jr., 146
Page, J. A., 146
Palincsar, A., 66, 83
Pang, V. O., 226, 227, 236, 237, 238, 239
Papert, S., 93
Patterson, W., 9, 26
Pea, R. D., 89
Pearson, G., 327
Pearson, P. D., 83
Pelavin, S. H., 212, 213
Pellegrino, J. W., 55, 56
Pennell, J., 326
Perkins, D., 57
Perna, L., 48, 49, 61
Perry, T., 60
Persuad, R. B., 227, 228
Peterson, K., 328
Peterson, P., 210
Petras, J., 30
Phillips, M., 50, 57, 58
Piche, D. M., 205, 206
Pilkington, D., 141
Piller, C., 88
Pinkard, N., 87, 92, 93, 328
Pitts, S., 227
Pogrow, S., 109
Poindexter, M., 185
Polite, V., 38
Pollack, J., 213
Posner, J., 63
Powell, G. B., Jr., 123, 124
Power, E. J., 162, 163
Prashad 01, 9, 10

Price, C., 81
Puma, M., 81
Purcell-Gates, V., 61

R

Rabinowitz, P., 82
Ralph, J., 50
Rampton, A., 292
Rashid, H., 266, 274
Rashidi, R., 37
Ratteray-Davis, J., 54, 55
Raudenbush, S. W., 108
Reay, D., 294
Reddix, J. L., 235, 236
Resnick, L. B., 216
Resnick, M., 70, 93
Ricciuti, A., 81
Richardson, L., 320
Riesbeck, C. K., 92
Rist, R., 60
Ristock, J., 326
Rivers, A., 63, 67, 87, 96, 97, 100
Rivers, E., 15
Rivers, J., 78
Robelen, E. W., 276
Robinson, R., 4, 28, 45
Rock, D. A., 213
Rodgers, W. M. III, 229, 231, 232
Rodney, W., 119, 120
Roehler, L. R., 83
Rogoff, B., 56, 63, 64, 65, 67, 96
Romero, M., 8
Rosberg, C., 122
Rosebery, A., 102
Rosenbaum, J., 213
Rosenbaum, J. E., 210
Rosenblatt, L., 83
Rosenfeld, E., 63, 67, 87, 96, 97, 100
Rosenzweig, M. R., 233, 234
Ross, E. W., 6, 29
Rottenberg, C. J., 208
Runnymede Trust, 293, 294, 295
Rymes, B., 66

S

Sanders, J. P., 328
Sanders, M. G., 94
Sanders, T. R., 10, 102, 347
Saunders, A., 138, 139, 140

Saxe, G., 63, 76, 88
Scarr, S., 57
Scelfo, J., 9
Schank, R. C., 92
Scheurich, J., xiv
Schickedanz, J. A., 100
Schiele, J. H., 330
Schliemann, A. D., 76
Schoenfeld, A., 83
Schofield, J. W., 202
Schorr, J., 208
Schultz, D., 137, 138, 139, 140
Schultz, T. W., 147, 148
Scott, D., 3, 5
Scrase, T. J., 132
Scribner, S., 63, 77, 88
Searle, C., 143, 144
Secada, W., 80
Seixas, P., 65
Selfe, C., 326
Serpell, R., 63, 130
Sewell, T., 291, 293, 294
Shade, B., 67
Shapiro, T., 233
Shaw, A., 92
Sherk, J., 202, 215, 216
Shields, P. M., 204
Shillington, K., 161
Shipp, S. C., 235
Shuey, A., 57
Shujaa, M., 7, 54, 55, 61
Shweder, R. A., 56, 63
Siddle-Walker, E. V., 51, 54, 112, 144
Silva, C. M., 78
Silver, E., 79, 80, 83, 104, 105
Silver, E. A., 80
Simuyu, V., 122
Sinclair, R. L., 215
Singer, J. D., 211
Sizemore, B., 101
Sklar, R. L., 122, 128
Slaughter, D. T., 55
Slaughter-Defoe, D., 52, 53, 54, 94
Slavin, R., 109
Slavin, R. E., 66, 109, 145, 146, 213, 219
Smagorinsky, P., 82
Smith, D., 294
Smith, G. H., 26
Smith, L. T., 10, 21, 326
Smith, M., 82
Smith, M. S., 79, 80, 104, 105

Smith, S., 104
Smitherman, G., 47, 60, 61, 83, 87, 92
Snow, C., 81, 82, 100, 107, 108
Snyder, J., 210
Spencer, M. B., 70, 85, 89, 94, 97
Spencer, S. J., 30
Spring, J., 21
Stahl, S., 100
Staples, B., 13, 33
Steele, C. M., 30, 152, 154, 185
Stevenson, H. W., 112
Stewart, J. B., 232
Stigler, J. W., 56, 63, 77, 112
Stoltzfus, J., 97
Strickland, D., 209
Stringfield, S., 81, 100
Stromquist, N. P., 185, 190, 191
Strutchens, M. E., 80
Stuckey, S., 64, 95
Sulzby, E., 63
Sunderman, G., 40
Swafford, S. O., 214
Swanson, D. P., 94, 97
Swap, S. M., 52, 78
Swartz, E., 28, 40

T

Tabors, P., 86
Talbert, J. E., 213
Tate, W., 79, 328
Tatum, B. D., 185
Taylor, W. L., 205, 206
Teddlie, C., 100
Tedla, E., 8, 33, 34, 54, 330, 340
Teeter, D., 222
Tejeda, C., 70, 87
Thompson, W., 81
Thurow, L. C., 148
Tillman, L., 314, 320
Tillman, L. C., xiv, 314, 315, 317, 320
Toll, R., 331
Tom, D., 60
Tomlinson, S., 294
Toms, F. D., 95
Torres, G., xxv
Traub, J., 110, 111
Travers, K. J., 214
Trimble, K., 215
Tsai, S., 107
Turner, R. R., 47, 60

Twombly, S., 222
Tynes, B., 63, 67, 87, 96, 97, 100
Tyson, L. D., 234

U

Uchitelle, L., 229, 231
Useem, E. L., 214
Usiskin, Z., 214

V

Vaden-Kiernan, M., 81
Van Sertiman, I., 37
Vass, W., 64
Vegas, J., 320
Verba, S., 123, 124
Vignoles, A., 293
Villegas, A. M., 215
Vinson, K. D., 6, 29
Vygotsky, L. S., 56, 107

W

Walberg, H. J., 107
Walker, D., 9
Walker, S., 37
Wallace, L., 320
Wallace, R., 31
Warfield-Coppock, N., 54
Warren, B., 102
Washington, M. H., 39
Wa Thiong'o, N., 162, 164, 172
Watkins, W., 121, 131
Weekes, D., 293
Weinfeld, F. D., 110, 206
Weiss, C., 235
Wenger, E., 56, 63
Wertsch, J., 56, 63, 64
Wesley, C., 309
Westwood, S., 293
Wheelock, A., 145, 214
White, B. J., 65, 103

White, K. R., 107, 108
Whitehead, A. N., 84
Wilder, C., 4
Wilensky, U., 70
Wilkins, R., 273
Willett, J. B., 211
Williams, R., 226, 227, 228, 229
Wilson, A., 47
Wilson, E. O., 266
Wilson, J. J., 31
Wilson, R., 220
Wilson, S., 184
Wilson, W., 187
Wilson, W. J., 192
Wineburg, S., 56, 65, 108
Wise, A. E., 211
Wittke, C. F., 331
Wolf, D., 75
Wolff, E. N., 233
Woods, C., 16, 25, 31
Woods, R., 189
Woodside-Jiron, H., 106
Woodson, C. G., 4, 9, 54, 61, 80, 264, 270, 273, 365
Wright, C., 293, 294
Wright, E. O., 228, 229
Wynter, S., 3, 4, 5, 22, 24, 266, 324, 341

Y

Yankah, K., 8
Yeskel, F., 227, 231, 233
York, D. E., 67
York, R. L., 110, 206
Young, A., 327
Young, M. D., xiv
Young, V. M., 204

Z

Zavlasky, C., 76, 80
Zawojewski, J. S., 80
Zlotnick, M., 208

Subject Index

A

AAVE. *See* African American Vernacular English
Ability, changes in, 75
Academic disciplines, fragmentation of, 266–267
Academy, Black experience in, Readers Theatre on, 329–340
Access
  to education, 21
    and inequality, 147
  to good teaching, 209–210
  to high-quality curriculum, 212–216
Adaptation
  definition of, 20
  research on, 97, 98t
Advocacy Center for Children's Educational Success with Standards, 41
Africa
  and civilization, xxii–xxiii
  colonial education in, 117–134
  conflict in, 126–128
  conservatism and, 124–125
  education in, xxi–xxii, 285–289
    crisis in, 165–167
    future of, 131–133
    recommendations for, 133–134, 177–178
    results of, 160–161
    theory on, 123–124

importance of, 348–349
universities in
  challenges in, 186–190
  transformations of realities in, 183–194
Watkins on, 351
Wynter on, 364–365
African American. *See also* Black
  term, 47
African American Vernacular English (AAVE)
  and domains of literacy, 83
  and literacy experiences, 61
  and mathematics, 77
African-centered research, tenets of, 330–331
African-centered schools, and educational dilemma, 52–55
African-descended people, legacy of, 10
African ethnic family, 20
  and cultural consciousness, 24–29
  and human understanding, 22–23
  and liberatory cultural orientation, 33–37
African Holocaust, term, 50
Africanist principles, 16
  and evaluation, 313–321
African language study, 179
  in Africa, 167
  need for, 12
  Web-based, 172–177, 180–181
African tradition, as research priority, 20

Afrikanus, Shakur, 19
Afro-cultural ethos, 64–65
Aisha Shule, 55, 253–254
Algebra Project, 52, 76–80
Alienation
    of Black intellectuals, 15
    cultural, 140–144
Alvord, John W., 51
American Association of University
        Women, 327
American Educational Research
        Association (AERA), xiii, xxii,
        xxvi. *See also* Commission on
        Research in Black Education
    epistemological crisis in, 6–7, 314
American Society of Muslims, school
        system, 264
Anayme nti, 323–328
    definition of, 323
Apartheid, and education, 186–190
Apprenticeship, 64–65, 313–321
    evaluation of, 315, 317–319, 318*t*,
        319–320
Appropriation, 90–91
    participatory, 67
Armstrong, Samuel, 120
Arts, and Black education, 39
Aspiration, educational underutilization
        and, 153–154
Assessment, reform and, 219–221
Assimilation, 140–144
At-risk students
    concept of, 7, 30, 107
    tracking and, 210
Attendance rates, in Mali, 171, 172*t*
Australia, 141, 148
Authoritarian government, in Africa,
        122–123
Authoritarian schools, in Africa, 129–130,
        162

B

Baker, Ella Jo, 235
Baldwin, James, xxi
Bantu Education Act, 186
Barakat, Yusif, 249–250
Barquet, Norma, 250, 256–257, 259
Bell Curve hypothesis, xxii, 57–58
Beneficial practice, as research priority, 21
Berlin Conference, 119, 161–162

Betty Shabazz International Charter
        School, 55
Biocentric belief system, xxv, 345,
        361–366
Black
    as liminal category, 363–364
    term, 47, 291
Black child
    books and reading of, 48–49, 49*f*
    and educational reform, 252
    test scores of, 47, 48*f*
    views of, 47–50
Black community, diversity of, 68
Black culture, xxiii–xxiv
    themes in, 95
Black education
    in Africa
        colonial, 117–134
        future of, 131–133
        recommendations for, 133–134,
            177–178
        structural adjustment policies and,
            127–128
        theory on, 123–124
    agenda for
        principles for, 20–21
        status of, 6–10
    in Brazil, 297–300
        research agenda on, 303–307
    in Britain, 291–295
    conspiracy against, 285–289
    crisis in, xxi–xxii, xxv, 3–4, 11–12
        Price on, 244–245
        in West Africa, 165–167
    as focus, xiv–xv
    historical experiences in, 137–140
    historical issues in, 50–52
    in Islamic schools, 261–279
    knowledgebase in, global expansion of,
        115–156
    language and policy nexus in,
        157–194
    learning theory and, 43–114
    research on, need for, 155
    school reform and, 197–223
    state of knowledge on, 45–71
    struggle for
        globalizing, 281–308
        research and, 10–15, 19–41
    study of, deficiencies in, xxiv
    term, 304

transformative vision of, 3–17
underutilization of, costs of,
135–156
Wynter on, 357–359
Black intellectuals
alienation of, 15
crisis of, 8–10
independence of, 19–41
silencing of, 62
Black socialization, agenda for
principles for, 20–21
status of, 6–10
Black students
educational achievement of,
201–202
ESL, science learning for, 102–104
school reform and, 197–223
Blair, Tony, 151–152
Blues tradition, and education, 31
Boggs, Grace Lee, 243, 245–248, 255,
257–259
Boilat, Abbé, 287
Bottom-up educational reforms, 198
Leaf on, 252
Thorton on, 249
Brazil, education in, 297–300
research agenda on, 303–307
Britain
Blacks in, 137, 139, 141
education in, 143–145, 291–295
Brown, Charlotte Hawkins, 274
Brown v. Board of Education, xiii, xxvi
Bunch, Ralph J., 183–184, 193–194
Burroughs, Nannie H., 235

C

California Commission on Teaching, 211
California State Department of Education,
213
Cape Town, University of, 188
Capitalism
and Africa, 125
and Black education, xxv
and education, 13–14
and imperialism, 119–120
and prisons, 13
Carlos Chagas Foundation, 305
Catherine Ferguson Academy, 246–248
Catholic schools, and Black education,
38

CD-ROM resources, xxx
Center for Applied Cultural Studies and
Educational Achievement, 95
Center for Applied Research, Social Justice
Report Card, 41
Center for Community Partnerships, 238
Charge to keep, 6, 36, 309–345
definition of, 309
A Charge to Keep, xxix, 341–345
Charter schools, African-centered, 55, 254
Chautauqua Institute, 347
Chèche Konnen, 102–104
Children's Defense Fund, 145
Children's literature, in Brazil, 299–300
Children's Math World, 104–105
China, pedagogy in, 111–112
Circle of Learning Orators, 344–345
Civilization
in Africa, 117
critique of, xxii–xxiii, 289
and education, 120–121
Islamic education and, 264, 271
Clara Muhammad Schools, 262, 264,
274–276
Class size
and educational achievement, 206–207
in Mali, 169, 169*t*
Cognition
culture and, 75–87
assumptions about, 106–109
technology and, 88–93
theory on, and intervention research,
73–114
Cognition & Technology Group at
Vanderbilt, 93
Coleman Report, 206
College choice theory, 151
Colleges, in colonial America, 163
Colonial education
in Africa, 117–134
versus America, 162–165
history of, 119–120
politics of, 117–134
effects of, 286–287, 289
results of, 160–161
Color Line Project, 39
Comer Project, 52, 78–79, 253
Commission on Research in Black
Education (CORIBE), xxvi–xxvii.
See also Transformative Research
and Action Agenda

and Detroit Conversation, 243–244
documentary video, xxix, 341–345
establishment of, xiv, xxii, 6, 10–11
logo of, xxi
methodology of, 15–16
premises of, xxiii–xxiv
principles of, 20–21, 342–343
Working Colloquium, evaluation of,
315
Communalism, in Black culture, 95
Community
and Algebra Project, 78–79
and education, Young on, 256
Islamic education and, 277–278
Online Institute and, 326–327
paradox of, 325–326
teachers and, 52
Compradors, 120, 128
Consciousness. *See also* Cultural
consciousness
changing, in Brazil, 298–300
and cultural identity, 26–27
Conservatism, and Africa,
124–125
Constructionism, 90–92
Content analysis, 324
Coolongatta Statement, 25
Cooperative economic development,
235–237
definition of, 367
Coping mechanisms, and learning,
94–100
CORIBE Evaluation Report, 319, 320
Council of Independent Black Institutions
(CIBI), 54
Counterstorytelling, 38
Credentials, issue of, 230–233
Crime
educational underutilization and,
151–152
lack of education and, 200
Critical Race Theory, 38
Cultural annihilation, 140–144
definition of, 367
Cultural consciousness
in indigenous community knowledge,
27–29
nurturing, 24–29
Cultural ecology, research on, 97–100, 99*f*
Culturally nurturing research, definition
of, 367

Culturally responsive pedagogy, need for,
109–114
Culturally sensitive research and
evaluation, 313–321
Cultural Modeling Project, 81–87, 86*f*
Cultural resistance, 29–33
Cultural rights, 25–26
Culture, 43–114. *See also* Black culture
and Black education, 45–71
in Africa, 128
and cognition, 75–87
assumptions about, 106–109
implications of, 87–88
of exclusion, 144–146
Islamic education and, 267–268
language of, versus education,
159–181
and learning support, 94–97
and literacy, 81–87
mainstream research on, 102–106
and mathematics, 76–80
technology and, 88–93
and transformation, xxii
Culture-systemic analysis, xxv–xxvi, 4–6,
345, 361–366
definition of, 367
Curriculum
in Africa, 166–167
in Brazil, 305–306
content of, problems with,
287–288
and cultural alienation, 143–144
culturally responsive, need for,
109–114
for democratic economic
transformation, models of,
236–238
high-quality, access to, 212–216
reform and, 219–221
Cushing, Benjamin, xiii

D

Daily Telegraph, 148
Dame schools, 162
Daniels, Heidi Lovett, 325
Debt bondage, and Africa, 125–126
Deficit thinking, 7, 59–60
Delpit, Lisa, 344
Democracy
in Africa, 122–123

and economic participation, 225–239
    models of curriculum development
        for, 236–238
    racial, in Brazil, reality of, 297–300, 303
    and resistance, 30–32
    in workplace, 233–235
Dennis, David, 79
Department for Education and
        Employment (DFEE), 295
Department for Education and Skills
        (DFES), 294, 295
A Detroit Conversation, xxx, 243–260
    discussion questions for, 259–260
Detroiters Uniting, 246
Detroit Summer, 246, 250
Development
    in Africa, 123–124
        future of, 132–133
    current paradigms of, contextualizing,
        184–185
Digital divide, 14, 35, 37, 147, 327
    definition of, 367–368
Diop, Cheikh Anta, 287
Direct instruction, 100–102
Discourse
    hybrid, 87–88
    and learning, 65–67
    in Online Institute, 326
Dispossession
    cultural, global, 32–33
    resistance to, 29–33
Domination
    education as, xxiv
    modes of response to, 20
    resistance to, 29–33
Dove, Nah, 318t
Dropouts
    economic viability of, 200
    rates
        decline in, 201
        in Mali, 170–171, 171t
Du Bois, W. E. B., 235, 273

E

Ebonics debate, 60
Economic illiteracy, 32–33
Economics
    and African education, 166
    and Black education, 31–32
    of education, 148

and educational inequities, 206–207
    Wynter on, 362–363
The Economist, 136, 151
Economy
    current state of, 199–201
    participation in, democratic, 225–239
        curriculum models for, 236–238
Education. *See also* Black education;
        Transformation in education
    Blacks in, research on, need for, 155
    as civilizing mission, 120–121
    and cultural alienation, 142–144
    definitions of
        Islam and, 262–264
        Moore on, 251
        Pointer on, 250–251
    as dominance, xxiv
    and economic challenges, 199–201
    humanizing, 241–279
    language of, versus culture, 159–181
    privatization of, 13–14
    as right, xxiii, 21, 25–26
    theory of, Western, critique of,
        265–267
    underutilization of Blacks in, costs of,
        135–156
Educational achievement
    closing gap in, 201–202
    inequality and, 202–206
Educational opportunity, equalization of,
        recommendations for, 216–223
Educational Testing Service, 205, 213
Education for Black Self-Reliance Model,
        53t
Eisenhower, Dwight D., 369
Emotional vitality, in Black culture, 95
Encyclopedia of American Education, 262
Engagement, and learning, 94–100
English-as-a-second-language (ESL)
        students, Black, 102–104
Epistemology
    Africanist, 20, 33–34
    definition of, 6
    of language versus culture, 159–181
Equity
    policy for, recommendations for,
        216–223
    in political economic context, 195–239
    as research priority, 21
Ethnocentric research paradigms,
        definition of, 368

Ethno-class Man, xxv, 7
  biocentric belief system and, 345, 358,
      362–363
  definition of, 368
Euro-Classical Liberal Curriculum, 53t
European societies, Blacks in, 137–138
Evaluation
  culturally sensitive, 313–321
  generative methodology for, 314–316
Excellence, and Black education, xv, xxi,
      xxiv
Exclusion
  in Brazil, 299–300
  in Britain, 293
  culture of, 144–146
Expulsions
  as exclusion, 144–145, 293
  in Mali, 170, 171t
Extension of University Act, 187

F

Federation of Southern Cooperatives, 237
Fitra, 263
Ford Foundation, 305
Fordism, and Africa, 132–133
Fort Hare, University of, 187, 190
Frazier, E. Franklin, 235
Freedman's Bureau, 50–51
Freedom Schools, 258
Fruit of Islam (FOI), 270–272
The Fugees, 84–85

G

Gao School Museum, 133–134, 178
Garimara, Nugi, 141
Garvey, Marcus, 235, 271
Gary Indiana Consumers' Cooperative
      Trading Company, 236–237
Gender, and technology,
      327–328
General Certificate of Secondary
      Education, 292
General Social Survey, 58
Germany, Blacks in, 137–139
Ghetto fabulous, 348
  definition of, 368
Globalization
  and Africa, 124–125
  definition of, 368

and education, 190–193
of struggle for Black education,
      281–308
Gordon, Edmund W., xiv, 344
Governance, in Africa, 122–123
Great Society, 123
Guided participation, 65–67
Gullah culture/language, 19, 27
Guy, M. C., 164

H

Halaqas, 269
Ham, curse of, 265
Hampton Normal School, 120–121
Hampton/Tuskegee Educational Model,
      53t
Head Start, 110–111
Healing, CORIBE and, 15–16
Hegemony, 5
  definition of, 368
  modes of response to, 20
  as research priority, 20–21
  resistance to, 29–33
  transformative research and action
      agenda and, 343–345
Henry, Annette, 318t
Heterosexism, biocentric belief system
      and, 363–364
High Performance Learning Community
      Project, 101–102
Hilliard, Asa G., 343–344
Hispanics, and Blacks, 10, 250
Homo-economicus, 362–363
Hooper, Paula, 344
Hope, xvi
  and schooling transitions, 153
House, Gloria, 253–255, 257
"How the Studios Used Children to
      Test-Market Violent Films,"
      32
Human competence, Gao School Museum
      and, 178
Human freedom, 307–308
  Black intellectuals and, 9
  concept of, 4
  declaration of intellectual
      independence for, 19–41,
      342–343
  liberatory cultural orientation and,
      34–35

Humanism, 5, 359
  in Black culture, 95
  and Black education, 241–279
  Boggs and, 245–246
Humanities, and Black education, 39
Humanity, biocentric belief system and,
    xxv, 22, 345, 358, 362–363
Human potential, underutilization of,
    135–156
  definition of, 147
  nonmonetary costs of, 146–149–154
Human understanding, expanding, 22–24
Hwehwemudua, xxi

I

Ibo Landing, xvii
Icarus Films, 13
ILEA Research and Statistics Group, 292
Imperialism, xxi, 119–120, 351
Improvisation
  and Africanist pedagogy, 16
  definition of, 20
  as metaphor for education, 69–70
Indigenous education
  African, 15–16
  conference on, 25, 37
  definition of, 368
Individual costs, of underutilization of
    Blacks in education, 152–154,
    153*f*
Industrial Education Hampton/Tuskegee
    Model, 53*t*
Inequality
  and achievement, 202–206
  of educational opportunity, factors
    affecting, 147
  postindustrial economy and,
    227–230
  in teacher distribution, 210–212
Institute of Islamic Thought, 277
Integration, Du Bois on, 273
Intellectual independence, 307–308
  declaration of, 342-343, 19–41
Intelligence quotient (IQ)
  versus effort beliefs, 111–112
  traditional conceptions of, versus
    dynamic learning, 57–59
  versus zone of proximal development,
    107
Intergenerational effect, 149–151

International Monetary Fund, 126,
    288–289
Intervention research
  based on current views of cognition
    and learning, 73–114
  in Britain, 294–295
IPN-DNAFLA, 168
Isbey, JoAnne, 255–256, 259
Ishangi, Baba Kwame, 6
Islamic education
  definition of, 262–264
  history of, 268–276
  and immigrants, 276
  in Muslim world, 276–277
  tradition of, 264
Islamic schools, 261–279

J

Jackson, Jacqueline, 253
Jacobs, Harriet, 332
Jasper Series, 90
Jazz
  and Africanist pedagogy, 16
  as metaphor for education, 69–70
Jegna/jegnoch, 313–314, 318*t*
Johns, Vernon, 235
Johnson, Lyndon B., 123

K

Kaupa Maori Theory, 26
King, Joyce E., xvii
King, Martin Luther, Jr., 247
Knowledge
  on Black education, state of, 45–71
  inert, problem of, 83–84
  learning theory on, 56
  prior, and learning, 59–63, 74
  as problem, xxv–xxvi
  racism as, 5
Knowledgebase, in Black education and
    research, global expansion of,
    115–156
Kwanzaa, principles of, 91–92, 237

L

Land Assistance Fund, 237
Language
  codes in, xv

and cultural identity, 26–27
of education, versus culture, 159–181,
        287–288
mainstream research on, 104–106
and policy, 157–194
and politics of repression, 187–188
Latin grammar schools, 163
Lawsuits, on inequalities in school
        facilities, 204–205, 218
Leaf, James G. (Gil), 252, 259
Learning
    by doing, in apprenticeships, 319–320
    as dynamic, 57–59
    engagement and coping mechanisms
        and, 94–100
    metaphors for, 67–70
    prior knowledge and, 59–63
    schooling and, 233–234
    social contexts of, 63–67
Learning theory, 55–67
    and Black education, 43–114
    and intervention research, 73–114
    principles of, 74–75
Left Business Observer, 227
Lest We Forget, 325
Liberatory cultural orientation, 34–37
    as analytical/pedagogical tool, 33–34
Life, as continuum, xiii
Lifelong learning, educational
        underutilization and, 152
Literacy
    culture and, 81–87
        implications of, 87–88
    domains of, 82–83
Locus of control, 100
Logo Writer, 90–91
Lumumba, Patrice, 121, 123
Lyric Reader, 93

M

Mali
    education in, 159–181
    Gao School Museum, 133–134, 178
    Inter-Diaspora Conference, 36–37
Marcus Garvey School, 55
Marx, Karl, 363
Mathematics
    culture and, 76–80
        implications of, 87–88
    gender and, 327–328

opportunities in, distribution of, 212
teacher knowledge of, 111
Media, and education, 191–192
Mentoring. See Jegna/jegnoch
Middle class, 9–10
    biocentric belief system and, xxv
Miseducation, xxiv, 4, 270
    in Mali and Black Belt, 36–37
Modernization, in Africa, 123–124
Mohammed, W. Deen, 264, 274–275, 279
Moore, Ernestine, 251
Motivation, educational underutilization
        and, 153–154
Muhammad, Clara, 272
Muhammad, Elijah, 264, 270–273
Muhammad, Fard, 264, 270
Muhammad the Prophet, 263
Musicality, in Black culture, 95
Music of the Heart, 113
Muslim Girls Training and General
        Civilization Class, 270–271

N

Namibia, universities in, challenges in,
        186–190
National Assessment of Educational
        Progress, reading results for
        17-year-olds, 81–82, 81 f,209
National Association of Black School
        Educators (NABSE), 12
National Center for Education Statistics,
        50, 81, 83, 200, 201, 202, 207, 211,
        213
National Commission on Teaching and
        America's Future (NCTAF),
        211, 213
National Cooperative Business
        Association Web, 235
National Council of Teachers of
        Mathematics, 83
National Council on Education Standards
        and Testing, 218
National Experimental Schools
        Administration, 39–40
National Household Education Survey, 48
National Indian Telecommunications
        Initiative, 25–26
National Institute of Child Health and
        Human Development, 106
National Research Council, 7

National Science Foundation, 328
National State of Black Education
        Movement, 347
Nation of Islam, 270–271, 274
Natural language instruction, in Mali,
        168–172, 169t–172t
New Internationalist, 347
New York Study Group on Outcome
        Equity, 205
Nguzo Saba, 91–92, 237
Nietzsche, Friedrich, 365
Nigeria, Universal Primary Education in,
        121
Nkrumah, Kwame, 121
Nobles, Wade, 95
No Child Left Behind Act, xv, xxii, 13, 40,
        258
non-governmental organizations, and
        education, 192
Nutrition, 237–238, 272
Nyerere, Julius, 121

O

Office of Educational Research and
        Improvement, 7
Online Graduate Research Training
        Institute, 323–328
    conceptual framework of, 324–325
    evaluation of, 315, 317–319
    processes and findings in, 325
Opportunity-to-learn standards, 218–219
Orality, in Black culture, 95
Ore Ire, 309–345
    definition of, 309
Organization of Africans in the Americas
        (OAA), 10
Other, biocentric belief system and,
        363–364
Outcome, and inequality, 147
Output, and inequality, 147

P

Paige Academy, 91–92
Palmer Memorial Institute, 274
Parents, Comer Project and, 253
Paris Club, 125–126
Participation, guided, 65–67
Participatory appropriation, 67
Pass rates, in Mali, 169–170, 170t

Peachtree Urban Writing Project, 344
Pedagogy
    African indigenous, 15–16
    culturally-responsive, need for,
        109–114
    liberatory cultural orientation and,
        33–34
    models of, 52, 53t
    in political economic context, 195–239
Personal style, in Black culture, 95
Phenomenological Variant of Ecological
        Systems Theory (PVEST),
        97–100, 99f
Plessy v. Ferguson, 187
Pointer, Julia, 250–251
Policy
    in Africa, 166–167
    for equality, recommendations for,
        216–223
    language and, 157–194
    in political economic context, 195–239
Politics
    of education, in Africa, 118–119
    of repression, language and, 187–188
Polycentrism, overlapping, 16, 313
Population Registration Act, 186
Portugal, Blacks in, 138, 145
Postindustrial economy
    characteristics of, 227–230
    educating African American youth for,
        225–239
    innovations and flexibility in, 233–235
Price, Glenda, 243–245
Prior knowledge, and learning, 59–63, 74
Prison-industrial complex, 13
    definition of, 368–369
    lack of education and, 200
Privatization, of education, 13–14
Process-building methodology, definition
        of, 369
Professionalization, of teaching,
        recommendations for, 221
Prohibition of Mixed Marriages Act, 186
Project MAPS, 275
PVEST. *See* Phenomenological Variant of
        Ecological Systems Theory

Q

QUASAR Project, 105–106
Qur'an, 263–264, 269, 274, 279

R

Race, biocentric belief system and, xxv, 22, 345, 361–366
Racial democracy, in Brazil, reality of, 297–300, 303
Racism
  biocentric belief system and, xxv–xxvi
  and education, 189
  environmental, 249
  as form of knowledge, 5
Rap music, and domains of literacy, 83–84
Rappin Reader, 92
Readers Theatre, xvi, 329–340
  themes in, 339t
Reading
  Black children and, 48–49, 49f
  NAEP results for 17-year-olds, 81–82, 81f
  teacher preparation and, 209
Realness, in Black culture, 95
Reasoning capacity, as inborn, 56–57
Reddix, Jacob, 235–237
Repression, politics of, language and, 187–188
Research. See also Transformative Research and Action Agenda
  African-centered paradigm for, tenets of, 330–331
  Black, transformative
    definition of, 1
    and struggle for Black education, 19–41
  context in, 21
  CORIBE agenda for, xxvi–xxvii, 301–308
  culturally sensitive, 313–321
  dissemination of, Readers Theatre and, 329–340
  established regime of, 6–7
  ethnocentric paradigms of, definition of, 368
  generative model of, 68–69
  innovations/innovators in, 37–39
  intervention, based on current views of cognition and learning, 73–114
  Islamic education and, 277–278
  knowledgebase in, global expansion of, 115–156

Online Graduate Research Training Institute and, 323
  priorities of, Detroit Conversation on, 248–258
  professional training in, 7–8
  as struggle, xxiv–xxv, 10–15, 19–41
Reservation of Separate Amenities Act, 186
Resilience
  in Black culture, 95
  in Readers Theatre, 339t
Resistance, 29–33
  definition of, 20
Resource equalization, recommendations for, 216–218
Rhythm, in Black culture, 95
Richards, Judy, 344
Rites of passage programs, 54
Rodriguez et al. v. Los Angeles Unified School District, 204
Role strain, research on, 97
Rural education, in Africa, 166

S

Sabbath schools, 51
Sanford, Adelaide L., xvii
Sankofa Shule, 55
Say Say Oh Playmate, 92–93
Scheurich, James, xiv
Schoenfeld, Alan, xiv
Scholarly alienation, definition of, 369
Scholarship, approaches to, xiv, xvi
School Achievement Structure, 101
School reform, and Black education, 197–223
School repeaters, in Malie, 170, 170t
Schools
  influence of, Coleman Report on, 206
  possibilities of, 110–112
Schuyler, George, 235
Science
  Black ESL students and, research on, 102–104
  gender and, 327–328
  opportunities in, distribution of, 212
  Weertz on, 248
Secret, Carrie, 344
Segregation, de facto, 61–62
Self-Reliance Education Model, 53t
Sénégal, 164, 287–288

Sharing time, 62–63
Shujaa, Mwalimu, 318*t*
Signifying, 83–84
Skills gap debate, 230–233
Skin color
    effects of, 9–10
    and religion, 265–266
Slavery
    and Black education, 50
    and Islamic education, 268–269
    Songhoy-Senni language on, 24
Slave trade, 138–139, 285
Smith, Adam, 363
Social-constructionism, 92
Social contexts, of learning, 63–67
Social costs, of underutilization of
        Blacks in education, 149–152,
        150*f*
Social development, in Africa, 128
Socialization, Black, agenda for
    principles for, 20–21
    status of, 6–10
Social Justice Report Card, 41
Social problems, versus school
        possibilities, 110–112
Social totality, definition of, 369
Social transformation, post-apartheid, and
        education, 188–190
Society, current state of, 199–201
Sociocultural theory, 56
Sociogenyence, 365
Soft skills, 225–226
Songhoy-Senni language, xxiii, 27–28, 179
    education in, 159–181
    on slavery, 24
    Web-based learning project on, 27,
        172–177, 180–181
    evaluation of, 315, 319–320
South Africa, universities in
    challenges in, 186–190
    current state of, 185
Southern African Development
        Community, 183
South Korea, 184
Spirituality
    in Black culture, 95
    Islamic education and, 267–268
Standards
    and educational reform, and African
        American students, 197–223

    on opportunity to learn, 218–219
Stereotype threat, 152–154
Structural adjustment policies
    and Africa, 125–126
    impact of, 288–289
    and schooling, 127–128
Student Non-Violent Coordinating
        Committee, 258
Success for All, 109–110
Survival, and inequality, 147

T

Ta'aleem, 264
Talent Development Model, 96
Tauheed, 263
Teachers
    quality of, and educational
        achievement, 207, 209–210
    relation to community, 52
    support for, 255–256
    unequal distribution of, 210–212
Teach for America, experiences with,
        208–209
Teaching
    emancipatory dimension of,
        112–114
    essentials of, 207–216
    good, access to, 209–210
    investment in, recommendations for,
        221–223
Technical Education Research Center,
        102–104
Technology. *See also* Web-based learning
    and Africa, 124–125
    Black education projects in, 35–36
    and culture and cognition, 88–93
    educational underutilization and,
        152
    gender and, 327–328
    opportunities provided by, 89
Technophobia, 325–326
Testing, reform and, 220–221
Textbooks
    in Africa, 130–131, 288–289
    in Brazil, 304
    controversy on, and human
        understanding, 23–24
The Education Trust, 75
The Urban League, 13

Third space, 66
Thornton, Marie L., 248–249, 259
Tillman, Linda C., xiv, 318t
Timbuktu, manuscripts of, xxiii
Timbuktu Academy, 253–255
Town schools, 163
Toyota Families for Learning program, 256
Tracking
  and educational achievement, 202–203, 213–216
  and exclusion, 145–146
Transformation in education, xxi–xxx, 309–345, 347–350
  culture and, xxii, xxiv
  theorizing, 1–41
  in universities, 183–194
  vision of, 3–17
Transformative Black education
  definition of, 1, 369
  goal of, 5
  vision of, 3–17
Transformative Black research
  definition of, 1
  and struggle for Black education, 19–41
Transformative Research and Action
      Agenda, xxvi–xxvii, 39–41, 353–355
  framing, 357–359
  premises of, xxiii–xxiv
  video on, 343–345
  Wynter on, 365–366
transnational corporations, and education, 191–192

U

Ujamaa, 237
Underdevelopment, 120
Uniqueness, in Black culture, 95
United for a Fair Economy, 227, 231, 233
United States
  colonial education in, 162–165
  slavery in, 138–139
United States Bureau of Labor Statistics, 229, 230
United States Census Bureau, 227, 229
United States Department of Commerce, 200

United States Department of Education, 109, 148, 151, 152
United States education
  and Black children, 50
  curriculum in, 144
  exclusion in, 145
Universal Primary Education, Nigeria, 121
Universities
  in Africa, challenges in, 186–190
  transformations of realities in, 183–194
University of Islam, 264, 270–274
Urban Nutrition Initiative, 237–238

V

Validity
  of Online Institute, 326
  as priority, 20
Verbal expressiveness, in Black culture, 95
Vicco, Giambattista, 365
Video resources, xxix–xxx

W

Wealth inequality, 233
W. E. B. Du Bois Academy, 253–254
Web-based learning
  African language study, 172–177, 180–181
  evaluation of, 315, 319–320
  Online Graduate Research Training Institute, 323–328
  evaluation of, 315, 317–319
Weertz, Paul, 248
Wells, Ida B., 324
West Africa, educational crisis in, 165–167
Western Cape, University of, 188
Western educational theory, critique of, 265–267
West-Olatunji, Cirecie A., 318t
Whiteness, privileges of, 10
Whiteward mobility, definition of, 369
Williams et al. v. State of California, 204, 205
Workplace democracy, 233–235
World Bank, 121, 126, 131, 288–289
World's Indigenous People's Education Conference (WIPEC), 25, 37
W. T. Grant Foundation, 200
Wynter, Sylvia, 345, 357–359, 361–366

Y

Yelougnta, 33–34
Yoruba counting system, 76
Young, Alma Harrington, 243, 256,
        259
Young, Coleman, 246

Youth Warriors Environmental Justice
        After School Program, 237

Z

Zone of proximal development,
        107